New Mexico Baptisms
Catholic Parishes and Missions in Taos

Volume I
19 June 1701 ~ 8 October 1826

Extracted by
Amelia Garcia, Donald Dreeson
and Lila Armijo Pfeufer

Compiled by
Margaret Leonard Windham
and
Evelyn Lujan Baca

Published by
New Mexio Genealogical Society

Library of Congress Control Number
2004107937

ISBN: 978-1-942626-04-6

New Mexico Genealogical Society
P O Box 27559
Albuquerque, New Mexico 87125-7559

and

Archdiocese of Santa Fe
4000 St. Joseph's Place NW
Albuquerque, New Mexico 87120

TABLE of CONTENTS

THE TAOS VALLEY

The Taos basin is located in north central New Mexico, just south of the Colorado border. It resides on the eastern edge of an altiplano at an altitude of approximately 7,000 feet, just before where the land rises precipitously into the southern tip of the Rockies. Its three defining geological features are the Sangre de Cristo mountain range, the Río Grande, and the far northern Chihuahuan desert. The mountains run north-south, curling around the eastern perimeter of the valley, roughly parallel to the river. The Río Grande cuts the length of Taos County much as it bisects the state. West of the river, the desert stretches for hundreds miles into Arizona. On the east, eight tributaries drain out of the mountains into the Río Grande across the fertile plain of Taos Valley. Each of these perennial streams originates in a spring or lake high in the mountains, descends an alpine canyon, flows through a valley, and drops down an arroyo. North to south these rivers are: San Cristóbal Creek, the Río Hondo, the Arroyo Seco Creek, the Río Lucero, the Río Pueblo, the Río Fernando, and the Río Grande del Rancho, which has two upper branches, the Río Chiquito and the Rito de la Olla or Pot Creek. The largest and most central of these rivers is the Río Pueblo, of which all the others except San Cristíbal Creek and the Río Hondo are tributaries. The San Cristíbal watershed lies several miles north of Taos Basin; between them, the Río Hondo joins the Río Grande north of the Río Lucero. Lush meadows fill the delta where the other tributaries come together, at the hydrological "vortex" of the valley. The Río Pueblo drains into the Río Grande gorge a few miles below that, at Pilar.

Greater or metropolitan Taos is a collectivity or "multicommunity" of villages, consisting of an aboriginal Tiwa pueblo and approximately sixteen Hispanic settlements that crystallized around it during the eighteenth and early nineteenth centuries. Founded on the banks of the upper Río Pueblo, Taos Pueblo occupies the best farming, hunting, and defensible vantage point in the valley. Its location at the base of Taos Mountain gives easy access to rich mountain resources, including the river itself, as well as to fertile meadows lying immediately to the west and south. The Pueblo was nearly 200 years old when Coronado's lieutenant Pedro Alvarado first saw it in 1540, and reported it to be the largest and most populous of the Indian villages he visited. After 1598 Oñate assigned a priest to the Taos Mission, which was later named for San Gerónimo.

By the middle of the seventeenth century, Hispanic settlers were moving into the valley and occupying lands on at least two royal grants made to the south (on the Río Grande del Rancho) and immediately west (on the Río Lucero) of Taos Pueblo. Some seventy settlers and two priests were killed in the area during the Pueblo Revolt in 1680, which was planned from a kiva at Taos Pueblo because of its strategic remoteness from Spanish headquarters in Santa Fe, roughly sixty-five miles to the south. Settlers reentered the valley with De Vargas's "bloodless Reconquest," which the Taos Indians actively resisted until 1696.

During the early to middle 1700s Hispanic settlers began to establish a permanent foothold in the Taos valley. From three to five royal grants were made to individuals, although only two of them were continuously occupied. They included the Cristobal de la Serna, made in 1710 and revalidated in 1715, which lies several miles south of the Pueblo and encompasses the upper and middle Río Grande del Rancho watershed and evidently corresponded to the pre-Revolt Duran y Chavez grant. The other was the Francisca Antonia de Gijosa grant, made in 1715, which lies west of La Serna and encompasses much of the lower Río Grande del Rancho watershed. A third, on the site of the old Lucero de Godoy grant west of the Pueblo along the Río Lucero, was issued in 1716 to Antonio Martínez of Sonora, who evidently never occupied it. Yet another, the Antoine Leroux grant, made in 1742, overlapped onto the Martínez grant, as well as onto the Pueblo league. Population growth was held in check during much of the eighteenth century by generally harsh conditions, including devastating Comanche raids into the area. During the 1770's *vecinos* moved inside the walls of Taos Pueblo for mutual protection. Domínguez reported 306 non-Indian settlers living inside the heavily fortified Pueblo in 1776, when a plaza was under construction in Las Trampas or Ranchos. The first stable settlements seem to have been in the Ranchos area along the middle Río Grande del Rancho watershed. By the 1790's the Comanche threat had subsided and other parts of the valley were being resettled.

The earliest enumeration of distinct plazas for the Taos area was from 1796, the same year the town, or Don Fernando, grant was made to sixty families. The 1796 census reported a non-Indian population of 774, and listed a total of six placitas besides San Gerónimo or Taos Pueblo, each named for its patron saint, in the Taos Valley: San Francisco (present day Ranchos de Taos), Santa Gertrudis, Nuestra Señora de Guadalupe (Don Fernando), La Purísima Concepción (Upper Ranchitos), San Francisco de Paula (Lower Ranchitos), and Nuestra Señora de Dolores (Cañon). All but Santa

Gertrudis are easily identifiable communities that still exist today. All of these communities cluster along the banks of the Río Pueblo, the Río Lucero, the Río Fernando, and the Río Grande del Rancho. The town of Don Fernando shared its name with the river it first depended on but never enjoyed exclusive rights to, since upstream sits the placita of Nuestra Señora de Dolores or modern Cañon. On the Río Pueblo, Don Fernando sits downstream from Taos Pueblo. As early as 1797 the citizens of the Don Fernando grant petitioned the governor for *sobrante* or surplus rights to waters from both the Río Pueblo and Río Lucero, since one river alone could not sustain their expanding needs. All villages in the Taos constellation exist in some kind of upstream-downstream relationship to one another. Each community sits in an upper, middle, or lower watershed--and this location dictates its relationship to the neighbors with whom it must share irrigation water.

By the early nineteenth century the Upper Río Lucero near the mouth of the Arroyo Seco, and the Río Hondo watershed a few miles to the northwest, were occupied by population overflow from the town. San Cristóbal was established several miles farther north in its own separate watershed. So in addition to the original six, nearly another dozen placitas came into being, some nucleated, others dispersed. They included Talpa, Llano Quemado, Cordillera, and Los Cordovas (assuming it wasn't once Santa Gertrudis) in the Río Grande del Rancho watershed; Valdez, Arroyo Hondo, and Des Montes in the Río Hondo watershed. Des Montes and Arroyo Seco, plus Las Colonias to their southwest, draw mainly on the Río Lucero.

San Gerónimo was the first parish in the Taos Valley, based at Taos Pueblo until 1826, when Padre José Antonio Martínez became priest of the new Nuestra Señora de Guadalupe parish seated in Don Fernando. By then Don Fernando de Taos was the multicommunity hub, destined ultimately to become known as a tourist town. The Ranchos church, completed by 1815, also belonged originally to the San Gerónimo parish, then to Guadalupe, but finally became a separate parish in 1937. Today the Guadalupe parish extends across the Río Pueblo, Río Fernando, and lower Río Lucero watersheds; the Holy Trinity parish embraces the Arroyo Seco, upper Río Lucero, Río Hondo, and San Cristóbal valleys or watersheds. The Río Grande del Rancho watershed is more or less coextensive with the San Francisco de Assisi parish, whose famous, much-photographed mission church defines the Ranchos plaza. Each parish contains a mother church and several chapels, usually located near *camposantos* (cemeteries) and occasional *moradas* (lay chapter houses of the *Penitente* Brotherhood) that serve the constituent communities. Each community or placita identifies itself as a bounded territorial entity, defined in terms of its chapel and patron saint, *morada(s)* and *camposanto(s)*, households and families, farmland and *acequias* (community irrigation ditches).

Sylvia Rodríguez
March 2004

Sylvia Rodriguez was born and raised in Taos. She attended Barnard College, received her Ph.D. from Stanford University, and is an Associate Professor of Anthropology at the University of New Mexico in Alburquerque. Her interest in anthropology developed out of a need to understand the diverse and complex society of Taos and northern New Mexico. She has published a book on the Matachines Dance and has another forthcoming on the *acequia* system of the Taos Valley.

ACKNOWLEDGEMENTS

The New Mexico Genealogical Society is pleased to present NEW MEXICO BAPTISMS, CATHOLIC PARISHES and MISSIONS in TAOS, VOLUME I. This volume has the dates of 1701 to 1826, and is the first of several volumes that we plan to publish. Our goal is to give those who are interested in this area for various reasons publications which are accurate. The extractions are as near to the original documents as we are able to read them, including using abbreviations of names and places if they are found there. We also make use of abbreviations for bap, m., dec., etc. If errors are found when checking our publications with the original records, please let us know about them. After further checking, errors will be published in NEW MEXICO GENEALOGIST.

A large number of people assist in getting a book ready for publication. The extractors of this volume were Amelia Garcia, Donald Dreeson, and Lila Armijo Pfeufer. Those who converted our steno notebooks to computer documents were Evelyn Lujan Baca, Ralph Hayes, Marguerite Kawamoto, and James-Dearden Wilder. Evelyn Lujan Baca did the proofreading of the document against the microfilm. Those who entered index codes in the document were Nancy Anderson, James-Dearden Wilder, and Bill Zamora. Margaret Leonard Windham compiled the indexes. Rose Holte coordinated the index checkers who were Billye Archunde, MaeAllen Forn, Rose Holte, Christina Lloyd, Dorothy Miller, Marjorie Shea, Lenore Stober, and Clara Taylor. Andrés Segura prepared the cover. Ernie Jaskolski did the map and had the manuscript printed. The Society thanks each of these dedicated individuals for their contribution.

We appreciate the introduction to these volumes which was written by Sylvia Rodriguez. She is a Taos native and an Associate Professor of Anthropology at the University of New Mexico in Albuquerque. Her knowledge will be very valuable to our readers.

Also we are thankful for the assistance that we always receive from Marina Ochoa and the staff at the Archives of the Archdiocese of Santa Fe.

ABBREVIATIONS

advoca^{on}	advocacin
alc^{e}	alcalde
Ant.	Antonio
Ant$^{a/o}$	Antonia/o
a^{o}	año, aora/ahora
ARM^{O}	ARMIJO
Asc^{n}	Ascencion
Barb^{a}	Barbara
Baut^{a}	Bautista
Bern$^{da/o}$	Bernarda/o
Cand$^{a/o}$	Candelaria/o
Concep^{n}	Concepcion
d^{ho}	dicho
dif^{tos}, dftos.	difuntos
Dolor^{s}	Dolores
Domin.	Domingo
Encarn^{n}	Encarnacion
esp^{a}	España
Españ^{s}, Esp^{s}	Españoles
Esteb^{n}, Estv^{n}	Esteban, Estevan
felig$^{a/s}$	feligresa, feligreses
FERN^{Z}	FERNANDEZ
Fran$^{a/ca/co}$	Francisca/co
GONZ^{Z}	GONZALEZ
Greg$^{a/o}$	Gregoria/o
herm^{a}, erm^{a}	hermana
J^{a}	Juana
J^{n}	Juan
J^{e}	Jose
J^{s}	Jesus
Jurisd$^{n/on}$	Jurisdicion
Laz^{o}	Lazaro
lexitim^{te}	lexitimente
LUC^{O}	LUCERO
LUS^{O}	LUSERO
M^{a}	Maria
Magdal^{a}	Magdalena/Madalegna
Man$^{l/la}$	Manuel/Manuela
mañ^{a}	mañana
Marg^{ta}	Margarita
Mar$^{na/no}$	Mariana/no
MARQ^{Z}	MARQUEZ
mayor	greater, larger, older
Mig^{l}	Miguel
M^{IN}	MARTIN
MONDRAG^{N}	MONDRAGON

MR^{TN}	MARTIN
mug., mug^{r}	muger
parroq^{a}	parroquia
parroquian^{s}	parroquians
Pasq^{l}	Pasqual
P^{o}	Pedro
Pobla^{on}	poblacion
pp^{río}	proprio
proxime pasado	immediate past
Raf$^{l/la}$	Rafael/a
R^{cho}	Rancho
Resurr^{n}	resurrección
ROM^{O}	ROMERO
sacrist^{n}	sacristan
Salv^{or}	Salvador
SAND^{L}	SANDOVAL
secret^{o}	secretary
S^{N}	SAN
S^{n}Tiago	Santiago
sobre d^{ho}	sobre dicho
solt$^{a/o/s}$	soltera/soltero/solteros
Sta.	Santa
S^{tos}	Santos
tam^{n}	tambien
tes^{gos}	testigos
t$^{o/os}$	testiga/testigos
tod^{s}	todos
Tom^{s}	Tomas
VEG^{L}	VEGIL
VELASQ^{Z}	VELASQUEZ
Vic^{te}	Vicente
Xav^{r}	Xavier
Xtov^{l}	Cristoval
Yg$^{a/o}$	Ygnacia/o
Ynd^{s}	Indians
9re	November

TERMS and PHRASES

á nombre de	in the name of <u>or</u> the name of
abuelos/a/o	grandparents, grandmother, grandfather
adoptada	adopted
agregados	people gathered in
ahora, aora	now
Aiudante (variation of <u>ayudante</u>)	aide or keeper
alcalde	mayor
alzado	raised
ambos	both, both together
año	year
antepasado	ancestor
anterior	yesterday, former
antes	before (this day)
aora (variation of <u>ahora</u>)	now
arriba	upward, above
asi mismo los padrinos	the godparents from the same
assimismo (should be two words)	the same
avitan (variation of <u>habitan</u>)	live here
barrio, varrio	neighborhood
bastarda	bastard female child
becinos	neighbor, citizen
bisabuelos	great grandparents
bocon	big mouth
cantor	singer
casada/os	married
castisos	mixed blood
catequise, exorsise, y baptise	catechized, exorcized, and baptized
Cavecita	Little Head
(the child) y su m^e son vez^s mestiz^s	(the child) and his mother are vecinos mestizos
cojos	lame ones
collote, coyote, coiote	mixed blood
como â las seis dela mañ^a	at about 6 in the a.m.
comprada/o	bought
coniuges	(alternative modern spelling is (<u>conyuges</u>) living together, not married
cuñada	sister-in-law
deel (de el)	of the
del mismo	of the same
del antepasado	of the ancestor or the past
denasion	of the nation
desta/e	of this
dicho	same
difuntos	deceased
doctrina	dictrine, teachings
donde	where
donzella	young, unmarried girl

el qual viven y avitan al presente . . . .
. . . . . . who live and are inhabitants of the present
ella . . . . she
en rescate . . . . redeemed
Enero . . . . January
equibocado . . . . was in error
esposa . . . . wife
espuria/o . . . . spurious, bastard
este . . . . this
estos . . . . these
feligres/a . . . . parishioner
feligresia . . . . parish, church
fiscal . . . . administrative
. . . . officer who acts for the government
foja . . . . page
Fr. . . . . Father
franceces . . . . French
habitan . . . . live here
hermana . . . . sister
hijo/a . . . . child, son, daughter
higlesia . . . . (misspelled) church
hoy . . . . today
huerfano que parece mestiso . . . .
. . . . orphan who appears to be of mixed blood
id . . . . idem
interíno . . . . temporary, interim
interprete . . . . interpreter
item . . . . same day, month & year
Jentil . . . . gentile, here usually
. . . . belonging to the Plains Indians
jurisdicion . . . . jurisdiction
ladinos . . . . mixed blood
latas . . (not in Velasquez but maybe like latillas)
lexitimate . . . . legitimate
llamado antes . . . . called before
madre . . . . mother
mallor . . . . older
marido . . . . husband
mañana . . . . tomorrow
mas o menos . . . . more or less
mayor, maior . . . . older or oldest
mez . . . . month
misma/o . . . . same
muger, mujer . . . . woman, wife
murio . . . . died
nacio . . . . was born
nacion . . . . tribe, nacion
nuera . . . . daughter-in-law

ó . . . . or
originarios . . . . native, descendent, originally from
oriundos . . . . originated, derived from
parroquia . . . . parish
parroquianos . . . . parishioners
parvula/o . . . . small child
pasado . . . . past time
pastor . . . . pastor, shepherd
poblacion . . . . population, citisenry, village, town
poco mas o menos . . . . more or less
propío . . . . proper
Puesto . . . . place, post, assigned post,
. . . . barrack for soldiers
redimida . . . . . redeemed, saved, or paid debt with
referido . . . . the referred or aforementioned
residentes . . . . residents
Rreino (usually not Rr) . . . . kingdom
siendo . . . . being
Siguen las partidas . . . . the entries for
. . . . 1799 follow in the new book
sirviente . . . . servant
sobre . . . . over
sobredicho . . . . above mentioned
sobredichos dia . . . . above mentioned day
sobrina/o . . . . niece/nephew
soltera/o/os . . . . single, unmarried
son . . . . are
tambien . . . . also
termino . . . . The end of anything; boundary;
. . . . district of a town or city
testigos . . . . witnesses
tierra . . . . earth, ground, land
todos/as . . . . all
utsupra (two words in Latin) . . . . as above
varrio, barrio . . . . neighborhood
vezina/o . . . . resident
vicitador . . . . . . the official visitor or inspector
visita . . . . visit or inspection
viuda/o . . . . widow, widower
viven y avitan . . . . live & inhabit
Xtiano . . . . Christian
Yglesia, yglessia . . . . left at door of church
ynterprete . . . . interpreter

RPF--R=reverend, P=presbyter, Fr.=Friar or Father

Origins . . . . "Origins of New Mexico Families,
. . . . . . A Genealogy of the Spanish Colonial Period,
. . . . Revised Edition, 1992," by Fray Angélico Chávez

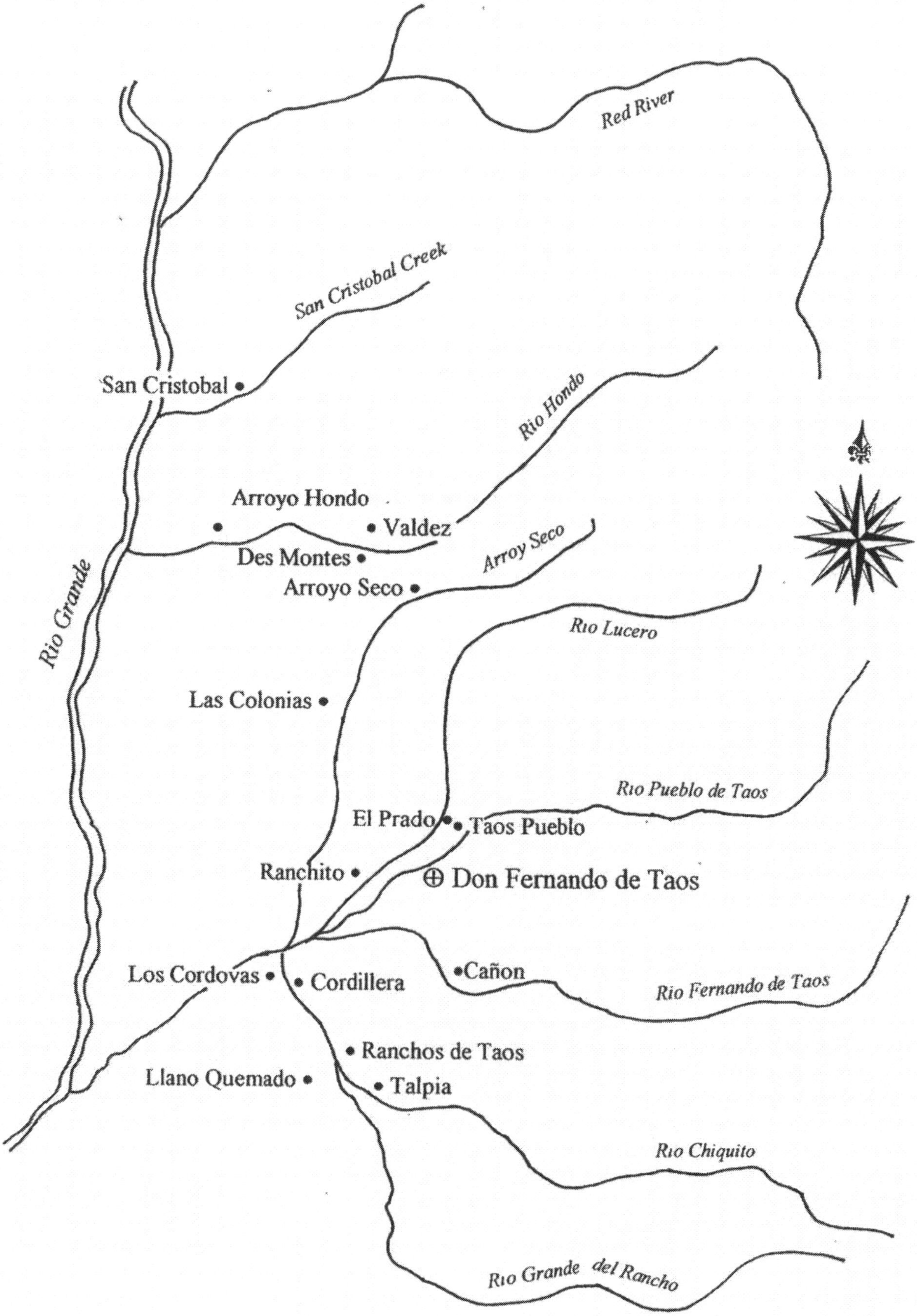
Red River
San Cristobal Creek
San Cristobal
Rio Hondo
Arroyo Hondo
Valdez
Des Montes
Arroy Seco
Arroyo Seco
Rio Grande
Rio Lucero
Las Colonias
Rio Pueblo de Taos
El Prado
Taos Pueblo
Ranchito
⊕ Don Fernando de Taos
Los Cordovas
Cordillera
Cañon
Rio Fernando de Taos
Ranchos de Taos
Llano Quemado
Talpia
Rio Chiquito
Rio Grande del Rancho

Taos Area Map

NEW MEXICO BAPTISMS
CATHOLIC PARISHES and MISSIONS in TAOS
VOLUME I
19 June 1701 - 31 December 1826

Archives of the Archdiocese of Santa Fe Film
Reel #18
19 Jne 1701-15 Oct 1725

Frame 996 (Fr. Pedro de MATHA signing entries)
QUAO, Domingo
bap 19 Jne 1701; s/ Antt^{o} QUAO & Geronima CAQUE; gm/ Maria PAPAC.

MAQUER, Juana
bap *en dho dia*; d/ Ju^{n} Chrr. MAQUER & Ana OAQUER; gf/ Ju^{n} CASBELLANOS.

GUABLAPA (gp), Yssavel
bap *en dho dia*; d/ *Yglessia*; gm/ Cathalina GUABLAPA.

GUENA, Ju^{n}
bap 26 Nov (1701); s/ Antt^{o} GUENA & Maria CANNABE; gf/ Ju^{n} dela CRUZ.

GAVILAN, Ju^{n}
bap *en dho dia*; s/ Pablo GAVILAN & Maria EBALOLA; gf/ Ju^{n} dela MORA.

APONA, Domingo
bap *en dho dia*; s/ Ju^{n} APONA & Rexina PAMAJELA; gm/ Lucia SIANE.

PECHOANA (gp), Margarita
bap *en dho dia*; d/ *de la iglesia*; gm/ Maria PECHOANA.

GUALAPABA (gp), Michaela
bap *en dho dia*; d/ *dela iglesia*; gm/ Catalina GUALAPABA.

QUIAPORA, Geronimo An
bap 28 Dec 1701; s/ Antt^{o} QUIAPORA & Ana CHEACHA; gm/ Geronima OLACA. (Frames 996-997)

Frame 997
UTSULA, Ju^{n}
bap *en dho dia*; s/ Nicolas UTSULA & Maria QUINAMAGUE; gm/ Maria QUABELA.

CHIRMAQUEL, Rossa
bap *en dho dia*; d/ Ju^{n} CHIRMAQUEL & Ana OCQUEZ; gm/ Elena ACHERPA.

Año de 1702

PAQUEMO, Lucia
bap 7 Jan 1702; d/ Ju^{n} PAQUEMO & Maria TOICHAL; gf/ Miguel THENORIO de ALVA.

LLACA, Diego
bap 29 Jan 1702; s/ Geronimo LLACA & Juana ACUNCHE; gm/ Maria PECHAQUE.

GAVAN, Caietano
bap *en dho dia, mes y año*; s/ Felipe GAVAN & Angelina HARRECHONE; gm/ Ana PAHE.

Frame 998
JUETANQUA, Joseph
bap 19 Mch 1702; s/ Ju^{n} JUETANQUA & Maria POICHOLE; gf/ Pedro de ABILA.

PASPICETA, Luis
bap *en dho dia*; s/ Diego PASFOICER & Maria PIANCHORI; gf/ Miguel CARRILLO.

LURTE (gp), Magdalena
bap *en dho dia*; d/ *de la Yglessia*; gm/ Lucia LURTE.

PAQUAAGUACHEN, Juan Antt°
bap *en dho dia*; s/ Diego PAQUAAGUACHEN & Maria QUAPIARO; gf/ Diego ROMERO.

PUSE, Bicente
bap *en dho dia*; s/ Ju^{n} PUSE & Magdalena GUALASSE; gf/ Ju^{n} (n.s.), *Mayor*.

QUENELI, Antt°
bap *en dho dia*; s/ Antt° QUENELI & Lucia LURTE; gm/ Maria PECHAQUE.

NORICHO, Lucia
bap *en dho dia*; d/ Ju^{n} NORICHO & Maria PAPAH; gm/ Maria QUEALA.

CANNATE (gp), Joachin
bap *en dho dia*; s/ *dela hilesia*; gm/ Maria CANNATE.

Frame 999
PUPAH THANO, Nicolas
bap 5 May (1702); s/ Hernando PUPAH THANO & Maria PANNACHAN; gm/ Maria CANNATE.

POTUENTANO, Diego
bap *en dho dia, mes y año*; s/ Fran^{co} POTUENTANO & Magdalena HUIPATE; gm/ Fran^{ca} CATUN.

PATAH, Xpttobal
bap *en dho dia*; s/ Salbador PATAH & Maria EQUEI; gm/ Ju^{a} NORACHEI.

JURE (gp), Sebastian
bap *en dho dia*; s/ *de la yglessia*; gm/ Maria JURE.

TENORIO de ALBA (gp), Miguel
bap *en dho dia*; s/ *de la yglessia*; gp/ Miguel TENORIO de ALBA.

ECHENPARTORQUEAN (gp), Maria
bap *en dho dia*; d/ *de la yglesia*; gm/ Maria ECHENPARTORQUEAN.

QUENMAQUUR, Antt°
bap *en dho dia*; s/ Sebastian QUENMAQUUR & Hissabel TUNNA; gm/ Cathalina GUATAPLA.

Frame 1000
27 May 1702 - Church visit - (signed) Antt° GUERRA, *Custos y Jues Celes°*; *Secrett° y nott°* Fr. Miguel MUÑIZ.

HIELO, Xptobal
bap 8 Jne 1702; s/ Geronimo HIELO & Maria PECHAGUE; gm/ Angelina HUCHAR.

NASBEQUEAN (gp), Juana
bap *en dho dia*; d/ *dela Yglessia*; gm/ Ana HASBEQUEAN.

Frame 1001
JUANAIO, Antt^{o}
bap 24 Jly 1702; s/ Ju^{n} JUANAIO & Maria HUAPAPA; gm/ Ju^{a} NARACHE.

QUINTTA, Maria
bap 15 Aug 1702; d/ Pasqual QUINTTA & Fran^{ca} TARPAUEQUE; gf/ Thoribio SANCHEZ.

QUEAPUARA, Domingo
bap (blank) Sep 1702; s/ Antt^{o} QUIAPUARA & Ana Maria CHIACHA; gm/ Maria TINCHAU.

QUIAU, Margarita
bap *en dho dia*; d/ Antt^{o} QUIAU & Juana PAQUATE; gm/ Chatalina PITORPAP.

PERNAUTE, Magdalena
bap 10 Sep 1702; d/ Andres PERNAUTE & Maria JUIMOGUE; gm/ Cathalina GUALAPA.

Frame 1002
TAGUA, Lazaro
bap 29 Sep 1702; s/ Geronimo TAGUA & Lucia CHIANDA; gm/ Catalina GUATAPLA.

CHANDAGO, Maria (male)
bap *en dho dia, mes y año*; s/ Antt^{o} CHANDAGO & Maria PAUCAL; gf/ Ju^{n} (n.s.), *Mayor*.

TOLIA, Ju^{a}
bap *en dho dia*; d/ Diego TOLIA & Hissabel PIA JUILE; gm/ Maria TURUJUE.

OCTOLA, Rossa
bap *en dho dia, mes y año*; d/ Nicolas OCTOLA & Maria TEQUENA MAGUE; gm/ Ju^{a} OCONCHE.

CHINNAPO, Catalina
bap *en dho dia, mes y año*; d/ Salvador CHINNAPO & Lucia TUNGUANA; gf/ Fran^{co} dela CRUZ.

PAGUE, Lucia
bap 28 Oct 1702; d/ Geronimo PAGUE & Juana PAQUIR; gm/ Catalina GUATLAPA. (Frames 1002-1003)

Frame 1003
CHIERCHAGU, Juana
bap *en dho dia, mes y año*; d/ Ju^{n} CHIERCHAGU & Maria YACHORE PACHORQUEAN; gf/ Juan PACA.

PEAIPUERA, Bicente
bap 18 Nov 1702; s/ Diego PEAIPUERA & Maria ELPIANCHORE; gf/ Diego TOLIA.

GARAPUNDIA, Maria
bap *en dho dia, mes y ano*; d/ Esteban GARAPUNDIA & Angelina UCHUR; gm/ Maria QUAUTLA.

ECHOAHA (gp), Maria
bap *en dho dia*; d/ *de la higlessia*; gm/ Angelina ECHOAHA.

PAQUIMUTLUI, Agustina
bap *en dho dia*; d/ Diego PAQUIMUTLUI & Lucia (n.s.); gm/ Catalina GUARLAPA.

Frame 1004

(1703)

CHIULO, Joseph
bap 14 Apr 1703; s/ Geronimo CHIULO & Juana PATORQUEAN; gm/ Fran[ca] TULBAQUE.

PENLA, Pedro
bap *en dho dia*; s/ Diego PENLA & Maria BESSACHORE; gf/ Pedro MADRID.

TOASQUISSAN (gp), Ju[n]
bap *en dho dia; s/ de la Yglessia*; gf/ Ju[n] TOASQUISSAN.

(Fr. Fran[co] XIMENEZ signing entries)
QUAPUALA, Diego
bap 27 May 1703; s/ Antt[o] QUAPUALA & Maria CHEACHO; gf/ Juan Antt[o] LERCA.

PAAQUEMO, Juana (Maria in margin)
bap *asi mismo*; d/ Juan PAAQUEMO & Maria JOICHEL; gm/ Angelina ECHOL.

VACA, Ana Taos
bap 10 Jne 1703; d/ Diego el VACA & Maria ACHI *de nacion Taas*; gm/ Catarina FIATLOZPAP.

NASTOE, Maria
bap 20 Jne 1703; d/ Juan NASTOE & Juana QUENCA *de nasion Pecuries*; gm/ Maria PECHOGUE.

Frame 1005
GUIUJE, Ildelfonso (Maria in margin)
bap 15 Jly 1703; s/ Estevan GUIUJE & Ma[a] JUNLE *de nasion Taos*; gf/ Diego PAQUEMOTTE.

27 Jly 1703 - church visit - (signed) Fr. Miguel MUÑIZ, *noto* Fr. Antt[o] CAMARGO.

CATHOTLE, Thomas Pecuris
bap 25 Sep 1703; s/ Antt[o] CATHOTLE & Fran[ca] LOAPAP; gf/ Baltasar dela CRUZ.

MORA (gp), Juana Pecuris
bap *asi mismo*; d/ *dela ygl[a]*; gf/ Juan de la MORA.

PUAEJE, Maria Pecuris
bap *asi mismo*; d/ Juan PUAEJE & Maria PAPSEI; gf/ Diego TEREGUIADO. (Frames 1005-1006)

Frame 1006
QUATUI, Pedro Taos
bap 3 Nov 1703; s/ Juan QUATUI & Juana TOMAQUEL; gm/ Juana NARACHES.

MAQUERO, Fran[co] Taos
bap 3 Nov 1703; s/ Ana MAQUERO, single, *todos de nasion Taos*; gm/ Maria PACHA.

CHIUTLO, Diego Taos
bap 3 Nov 1703; s/ Antt[o] CHIUTLO & Juana PATHELQUGAM; gm/ Juana PATTEAQUZ, *todos de nasion Taos*.

CHILMAGEL, Angelina
bap 30 Nov 1703; d/ Juan CHILMAGEL & Ana OQUELI *de nasion Taos*; gm/ Maria CHINQUEPIENCHI.

JIGUACHAPO, Lusia
bap 27 Dec 1703; d/ Antt° JIGUACHAPO & Ysabel PAPACHA *de nasion Taos*; gm/ Ana Maria ARTEQUEM.

CAPTESO, Antt°
27 Dec 1703; s/ Juan CAPTESO & Maria PEYEN *de nasion Taos*; gm/ Maria CAPCHOLE.

VARRIGON, Juana
bap 31 Dec 1703; d/ Diego VARRIGON & Ysabel PEAJUITLI *de nasion Taos*; gm/ Lusia NANTORSE.

Frame 1007
QUENTLAGUE, Catalina
bap 11 Jan 1704; d/ Lusia QUENTLAGUE, single; gm/ Teresa PAQUEM, *todos de nasion Tiguas*.

PISSI, Antt°
bap 28 Jan 1704; d/ Diego PISSI & Magdalena GUALAX *de nasion Taos*; gf/ Antonio CALA.

ATTA, Micaela
*bap 3 Jan 1704; d/ Salbador ATTA & Mariana ECOI *de nasion Taos*; gm/ Juana CHALQUIARA.

LOPEZ PAPPONE, Maria
bap 28 Mch 1704; d/ Diego LOPEZ PAPPONE & Lusia PAMAJEL; gf/ Antt° NAPO.

TAO, Sebastian
bap *en dho dia*; s/ Diego TAO & Ana PAAC; gm/ Juana PATLEACOI.

TLEQUE, Ana
bap *en dho dia*; d/ Geron° TLEQUE & Juana QUGEACHOGUE; gm/ Tomasa JUIPALUIA.

PAPTOO, Phelipe
bap *en dho dia*; s/ Fran[co] PAPTOO & Magdalena JUIPATEE; gm/ Catarina CATUNE.

Frame 1008
CHIOO, Lusia
bap 28 Mch 1704; d/ Pablo CHIOO & Maria EPATLOL; gm/ Ma[a] CAPCHOLE.

QUENTLA, Ysabel
bap *en dho dia*; d/ Pasqual QUENTLA & Fran[ca] TOLVAQUEN; gm/ Juana MASACO.

PUALNACACHEL, Magdalena
bap *en dho dia*; d/ Lorenso PUALNACACHEL & Angelina CAPCHO; gm/ Angelina UHULI.

ONA, Christina
bap *en dho dia*; d/ Antt° ONA & Micaela CHALO; gf/ Diego NATOE.

PIALOQUEGAN, Lusia
bap *en dho dia*; d/ Maria PIALOQUEGAN, single; gm/ Maria PAQUENIO.

CHENDA, Christina
bap 4 May 1704; d/ Diego CHENDA & Maria PAEQUE *de nasion Thaos*; gm/ Catharina CALO.

COAGUAQUEN, Margarita *Tiguas*
bap 11 Jne 1704; d/ Lusia COAGUAQUEN, single; gm/ Maria PEECHOO.

Frame 1009
NORI, Juana
bap 9 Jly 1704; d/ Fernando NORI *de nasion Tiguas* & Maria PAPAB *de nasion Thaos*; gf/ Alonso de AGUILAR, *español*.

PEAXCLI, Geronima
bap 24 Jly 1704; d/ Maria PEAXCLI *de nasion Pecuries* and had been a captive among the Apaches; gf/ el Sr Then^{te} G^{l} Juan PAES HURTADO.

TAQUEO, Xtobal
bap 10 Aug 1704; s/ Diego TAQUEO of Thaos & Ma^{a} QUEUNCHA; gm/ Juana MANACHE.

CAIAJE, Alonso (Yldefonso in margin)
bap 10 Aug 1704; s/ Estevan CAIAJE & Ma^{a} TUULE *de nasion Thaos*; gm/ Catalina GUATLAPI.

NATURE, Pedro
bap 10 Aug 1704; s/ Maria NATURE, single, *de nasion Thaos*; gm/ Catalina CANATA *de nasion Taana*.

YAQUE, Micaela
bap 10 Aug 1704; d/ Sebastian YAQUE & Angelina PATLOTPAN *de nasion Thaos*; gm/ Ma^{a} JIMCHAR *de nasion Tiguas*.

Frame 1010
PASOAGUAQUEAN, Angelina
bap 11 Sep 1704; d/ Maria PASOAGUAQUEAN, single; gm/ Teresa TLEORAQUE, *todos de nasion Thaos*.

OTOLA, Juana
bap 11 Sep 1704; d/ Nicolas OTOLA & Lusia QUIPARPO; gm/ J^{a} CHALQUEAM, all Thaos.

POAO, Manuel
bap 28 Sep 1704; s/ Antt^{o} POAO & Geronima CAQUI; gm/ Ma^{a} TUNCHAE.

PACOAGUACHOL, Ana Maria (Juana Maria in margin)
bap 28 Sep 1704; d/ Diego PACOAGUACHOL & Maria COAPARO *de nasion Tiguas*; gf/ *el Cap*^{n} Joseph DOMINGUEZ.

JUIPCHALE, Xh(r)istobal
bap 9 Nov 1704; s/ Maria JUIPCHALE, single; gm/ Elena PACHIRPAP.

TOCHOLA, Maria
bap 9 Nov 1704; d/ Diego TOCHOLA & Ant^{a} GUALPA; gm/ Juana MASEACOI.

ATOMA, Juana
bap 9 Nov 1704; d/ Lasaro ATOMA & Ana QUELMAJOL; gm/ Catalina QUATLAPAO.

NAPOO, Juana
bap 9 Nov 1704; d/ Ant^{o} NAPOO & Maria TURJUI; gm/ Ant^{a} GUALPAP.

SALA, Juana
bap 19 Dec 1704; d/ Estevan SALA & Angelina OCHOLA; gm/ Ma^{a} CHUIQUEPUENCHOLE.

PUETMALOY, Micaela
bap 19 Dec 1704; d/ Andres PUETMALOY & Ma^{a} CHIUMAYA; gm/ Catarina GUATTAPAP.

Frame 1011

(1705)

EME, Ant°
bap 10 Jan 1705; s/ Juna EME, interpreter, & Ma^a QUANTLA, *entrantos de nasion Tiguas*; gm/ Maria JOIPAP.

CHIUTLO, Antt°
bap 10 Jan 1705; s/ Domingo CHIUTLO & Ant^a PATLOLQUGAM *de nasion Thaos*; gm/ Fran^{ca} JORVAOCUI.

ALOO, Fran^{ca}
bap 10 Jan 1705; d/ Geronimo ALOO *de nasion Thaos* & Maria PEACHAGUE *de nasion Taana*; gm/ Juana NAROCHE.

COAGUACHORE, Antt°
bap 17 Jan 1705; s/ Maria COAGUACHORE, *soltera, de nasion Tiguas*; gm/ Matia TURGUI.

TAYA, Diego
bap 29 Jan 1705; s/ Antt° TAYA & Maria TUI *de nasion Thaos*; gf/ Juan Ray CORDERO.

QUEEDA, Juana
bap 4 Mch 1705; d/ Ant° QUEEDA & Maria CANNATE *de nasion Thaos*; gm/ Juana TOOPA.

PILPAE, Angelina
bap *en dho dia*; d/ Fran^{ca} PILPAE, *soltera, de nasion Thaos*; gm/ Fran^{ca} PIACHELA.

Frame 1012

PEIPORA, Catharina
bap 7 Apr 1705; d/ Diego PEIPORA *de nasion Tiguas* & Lusia PIENCHORE *de nasion Thaos*; gm/ Maria COAGUACHORE.

PAQUERO, Lusia (Catal^a in margin)
bap 6 May 1705; d/ Juan PAQUERO & Maria TOICHALA *de nasion Thaos*; gf/ Fran^{co} JATE.

QUANPAP, Magdalena Maria
bap 6 May 1705; d/ Ysabel QUANPAP, *soltera, de nas(i)on Thaos*; gf/ *el Cap^n* Nicolas ORTIS.

PETA, Ma^a
bap 29 May 1705; d/ Diego PETA & Maria VESECHOLE *denasion Thaos*; gm/ Maria MAGILIOS.

QUIGAACHAPO, Juana
bap 29 May 1705; d/ Ant° QUIGAACHAPO & Ysabel PAPACHA *de nasion Thaos*; gm/ Lusia QUIPTOI.

VESECUI (gp), Miguel
bap 2 Jne 1705; s/ Apaches, *que ubo en rescate*; gm/ Juana VESECUI.

JABE (gp), Vernardo
bap 2 Jne 1705; s/ Apaches, *que ubo en rescate*; gf/ Fran^{co} JABE.

EME (gp), Joseph
bap 2 Jne 1705; s/ Apaches, *que ubo en rescate*; gf/ Juan EME.

YAONA (gp), Margarita
bap 2 Jne 1705; d/ Apaches, *que ubo en rescate;* gm/ Martina YAONA.

Frame 1013
CALA, Fran^co^
bap 18 Jne 1705; s/ Antt° CALA *de nasion Tiguas* & Lusia PAMAGUA *de nasion Thaos;* gm/ Ana PACOAGAACHORE.

QUENAPOO, Fran^co^
bap 27 Jne 1705; s/ Salbador QUENAPOO & Lusia TONQUAM; gm/ Catal^a^ MAQUEAM.

YAPATE, Lusia
bap 27 Jne 1705; d/ Juana YAPATE, single; gm/ Fran^ca^ PIACHOLE.

POYBO, Pedro
*bap 6 Jne 1705; s/ Diego POYBO & Lucia OPELEMOHUE; gf/ Pedro de PERALTA.

TZAAPO, Antonia
bap 6 Jne 1705; d/ Catarina TZAAPO & unknown father; gm/ Martina LUCERO.

CHIU (patron), Antonia
bap *en dho dia;* d/ (unknown), catechized, exorcized & baptized, adult of at least 15 yr; d/ *nacion Panana;* gp/ Pablo CHIU & Martina LUCERO.

Frame 1014
PUENPATE, Diego
bap 21 Jly 1705; s/ Juan PUENPATE & Ma^a^ VEAQUEQUE *de nasion Thaos;* gp/ Marcos (n.s.), fiscal, & Maria CHUEQUEPIERCHOL.

JUENAYO, Maria
bap 21 Sep 1705; d/ Aug^n^ JUENAYO & Maria TLUAPAP *de nasion Thaos;* gm/ Magdalena QUIPATLOLEOI.

LURENI, Domingo
bap 11 Oct 1705; s/ Diego LURENI & Maria PAQUEMO *de nasion Thaos;* gm/ Juana MEASECUI.

PATOO, Fran^co^
bap 11 Oct 1705; s/ Fran^co^ PATOO *de nasion Tano* & Magdalena JUIPATE *de nasion Thaos;* gp/ Fran^co^ NACAYA.

COATOI, Juan
bap 11 Oct 1705; s/ Juan COATOI & Juana THOMAQUET *de nasion Thaos;* gm/ Maria COAGUACHORE.

CAPOALA, Micaela
bap 11 Oct 1705; d/ Ant° CAPOALA & Maria CHOACHA *de nasion Thaos;* gm/ Catharina GUATLAPAP.

Frame 1015
IQUI, Joseph *Thaos*
bap 1 May 1706; s/ Maria IQUI; gm/ Ant^a^ GUALPAB.

PUCHEQUI, Ant° *Thaos*
bap 1 May 1706; s/ Juan PUCHEQUI & Fran^ca^ PIACHOLE; gm/ Ysabel PIAJUITLI.

TLEQUE, Jeronimo *Thaos*
bap 1 May 1706; s/ Geron° TLEQUE & Juana QUECHOGUE; gm/ Maria PAINACHEL.

NATURI, Ant° *Thaos*
bap 1 May 1706; s/ Lusia NATURI, single; gf/ Antt° TAFOYA.

ONEA, Juan *Thaos*
bap 1 May 1706; s/ Antt° ONEA & Micaela CHATO; gf/ Juan LUJAN.

JAEPATO, Lusia *Thaos*
bap 1 May 1706; d/ Ant° JAEPATO & Maria OLA; gm/ Juana PATLEACOI.

INACO, Fabiana *Thaos*
bap 1 May 1706; d/ Pasqual INACO, *Tigua*, dec., & Franca TOLVACOI, Taos; gf/ Juan EME.

PATAA, Getrudis
bap 28 May 1706; d/ Salvador PATAA & Mariana OÇOI *denasion Thaos*; gm/ Maria Rosa JIRON, Spanish.

Frame 1016
LOPES APON, Antta
bap 12 Jne 1706; d/ Diego LOPES APON & Lusia PAMOJET *denason Thaos*; gp/ Ant° VERNAL & Maria Rossa de PEDRASA, *Españoles*.

POAO, Juana
bap 12 Jne 1706; d/ Antt° POAO & Gerona CAGUI; gp/ Alonso RAEL de AGUILAR, Spanish, & Catarina TLAQUA *denasion Tiguas*.

GUALASI, Juan
bap 27 Jne 1706; s/ Magdalena GUALASI, single; gm/ Maria Rosa de PEDRASA, Spanish.

CHIRMAGER, Antt°
bap 27 Jne 1706; s/ Juan CHIRMAGER & Ana OQUIR; gm/ Magdalena JUIPATTOLCOI.

POCA, Magdalena
bap 19 Jly 1706; d/ Diego POCA & Maria UCHI *denasion Thaos*; gm/ Ma CAPCHOLE.

TAQUE, Matias
bap 10 Oct 1706; s/ Diego TAQUE & Maria PIUCHO *denasion Thaos*; gm/ Juana VESEQUE.

NURI, Angelina
bap *en dho dia*; d/ Fernando NURI & Maria PAPALO *denason Thaos*; gm/ Maria CAPCHOLE.

Frame 1017
VESEPOYO, Geronima
bap 31 Oct 1706; d/ Franco VESEPOYO & Maria COAGUACHOLE *denasion Tiguas*; gm/ Lusia COAGUAQUEAM.

COCLA, Lusia
bap 25 Nov 1706; d/ Antt° COCLA & Lusia PAMAGUIA; gp/ (not given).

TAÂ, Roque
bap 19 Dec 1706; s/ Josepha TAÂ, single; gm/ Lusia COAGUAEQUEAM.

ATOQUE, Juana
bap 19 Dec 1706; d/ Lasaro ATOQUE & Maria CUIELMAGUEL *de nasion Thaos*; gm/ Maria CAPCHOLE.

CHIECHO, Diego
bap 27 Dec 1706; s/ Diego CHIECHO & Maria PIECHONE; gm/ Maria COAGUALHOLE.

Frame 1018

(1707)

JUIPALLOTEOI, Luisa
bap 6 Jan 1707; d/ Magdalena JUIPALLOTEOI, *soltera, de nasion Thaos*; gm/ Maria QUAULLTA.

19 Jan 1707 - Church Visit - (signed) Fr. Antt° VICTORINO, *Notario* Fr. Antt° de MIRANDA.

Frame 1019
ALMASAN, Fabiana
bap 29 Jan 1707; d/ Lorenso ALMASAN & Lusia COAGUACHORE *denasion Tiguas*; gm/ Catharina EPAEQUSE.

PUERNACHE, Joseph
bap 10 Feb 1707; s/ Lorenso PUERNACHE & Maria CAPCHO; gm/ Lusia QUIPAYO.

GUECHAVA, Lusia
bap 10 Feb 1707; d/ Stevan GUECHAVA & Maria JULOI; gm/ Fran[ca] CATOÔ.

NAPCO, Lusia
bap 21 Feb 1707; d/ Ant° NAPCO & Maria TURJUI *denas[n] Tiguas*; gm/ Elena PACHAR.

PIEN, Domingo
bap 20 Mch 1707; s/ Gero° PIEN & Juana PATLOLQUEAM; gm/ Juana VESEQUI.

TAOÔ, Miguel
bap 20 Mch 1707; s/ Diego TAOÔ & Ana PAÊ; gf/ Fran[co] PENPE.

MAQUERO, Juana
bap 20 Mch 1707; d/ Ana MAQUERO, single; gm/ Maria CAPCHOLE.

Frame 1020
CAPCHOLE, Micaela
bap 6 Apr 1707; d/ Maria CAPCHOLE, single; gf/ Fran[co] JABE, *Sacristan Maior*.

QUENAPATE, Jeronimo
bap 7 May 1707; s/ Domingo QUENAPATE & Maria CAMNATE *denasion Thaos*; gm/ Lusia CHIENE.

PAQUEMOTLE, Nicolas
bap 7 May 1707; s/ Diego PAQUEMOTLE & Lusia OPELEMOGUE *de nasion Thaos*; gm/ Catarina TLEACIRAQUI.

PANCOS, Juan
bap 7 May 1707; s/ Maria PANCOS, single; gm/ Ana MAQUERO.

MO, Stephania
bap 7 May 1707; d/ Geron° MO & Maria PACHOGUE *denasion Thaos*; gm/ Catarina GUACQUA.

QUIGUACHAPO, Micaela
bap 7 May 1707; d/ Pedro QUIGUACHAPO & Maria APUCHA *denasion Thaos*; gm/ Ana OQUIR.

CUINTLAQUGAN, Fran^co^
bap 26 May 1707; d/ Lusia CUINTLAQUGAN, single; gm/ Teresa (n.s.), *la Panana*.

CHIUU (gp), Rossa Maria
bap 26 May 1707; d/ *Nasion Panana, redimida*; gf/ Pablo CHIUU.

Frame 1021
CHEQUE, Lusia
bap 23 Jly 1707; d/ Miguel CHEQUE *denasion Taano* & Lusia COICHOLE *denasion Thaos*; gm/ Juana VEASECUI.

TACOLI, Ynes
bap 23 Jly 1707; d/ Domingo TACOLI & M[a] PEUSILI *denasion Thaos*; gm/ Antt[a] GUALPALO.

PUERPANA, Esteban
bap 7 Sep 1707; s/ Diego PUERPANA & Maria PONCHORE *denasion Thaos*; gm/ Catarina QUALQUA.

(Fr. Ju[n] de MINGUES signing entries)
QUEMES, Fransisco
bap 9 Oct 1707; s/ Pablo QUEMES & Maria (n.s.), his wife; gf/ Juan PAES URTADO.

MUGUICUY, Lusia
bap *en el mismo dia*; d/ Ju[n] de Dios (n.s.) & Maria MUGUICUY; gm/ Maria TIPAYO.

Frame 1022
TORJUIRI, Lusia
bap *en el mismo dia*; d/ Joseph TORJUIRI & Lusia (n.s.), his wife; gf/ D[n] Felix MARTINES.

GUIONA, Diego
bap 31 Oct 1707; s/ Ju[n] de Dios (n.s.) & Lusia GUIONA; gm/ Maria PIUCA.

PATO, Lusia
bap *en el mismo dia*; s/ Fran[co] PATO & Madalena (n.s.); gm/ Fransisca CAVATU.

SUCUE, Juana
bap *en el mismo dia*; d/ Diego SUCUE & Maria (n.s.), his wife; gm/ Tomasa GOPAEPEE.

(1708)

CABPUELA, Diego
bap 1 Jan 1708; s/ Att[o] CABPUELA & Maria (n.s.), his wife; gm/ Att[a] GUALPO.

UNIA, Lusia
bap *yten en dicho dia*; d/ Att[o] UNIA & Micaela (n.s.), his wife; gm/ Lusia CUCHULI.

Frame 1023
JUENAPU, Eusebio
bap *yten en dicho dia*; s/ Salvador JUENAPU & Lusia (n.s.), *su muger*; gm/ Maria QUIUNCHAL.

CATUNE (gp), Felipe
bap *yten en dicho dia*; s/ Juan Diego (n.s.) & Maria (n.s.), his wife; gm/ Fransisca CATUNE.

PELA, Lusia
bap *yten en dicho dia*; d/ Diego PELA & Juana (n.s.), his wife; gf/ Ju[n] (n.s.), *el interprete*.

CAPULI, Joseph
bap *yten en dicho dia*; s/ unknown; gm/ Maria CAPULI.

(Fr. Fran[co] BROTONS signing entries)
TUCHULA, Lucia
bap 21 Mar 1708; d/ Diego TUCHULA & Maria GUARPA, *coniuges*; gm/ Juana AJACLUI.

JUALACACHE, Maria Zapabepa
bap 11 Apr 1708; d/ Lorenzo JUALACACHE & Angelina CAPSA, *coniuges*; gm/ Maria QUAFIERO.

CRUTATA, Angelina
bap *en dho dia, mes y año*; d/ Juana (n.s.), *viuda de* Antonio CRUTATA, *coniuges*; gm/ Maria CAPULI.

Frame 1024
GUIMAGEL, Pasquala
*bap 7 Apr 1708 baptized in necessity; d/ Margarita GUIMAGEL; gp/ D. Pablo GAVILAN. And on 3 May of said year, administered the holy oils...

NACHO, Lucia Juipte
bap 17 May 1708; d/ Lucia GENACHULE (sic) & Diego NACHO; gf/ Christoval dela SERNA, Spanish.

AZÁ, Antonio
bap *en dho dia, mes y año*; s/ Maria TOI (sic) & Juan AZÁ, *coniuges*; gm/ Lucia TIRCHONE.

HAQUERMO, Lucia
bap *en dho dia, mes y año*; d/ Maria TUICHANS (sic) & Juan HAQUERMO, *coniuges*; gm/ Juana CAJIOVE.

MAQUI, Antonio
bap 28 Jne 1708; s/ Diego MAQUI & Catharina CHAGIO; gp/ Antonio de CHAVES, Spanish.

TOPE, Juana
bap *en el mismo dia, mes y año*; d/ Juana ULOI (sic) & Diego TOPE, *coniuges*; gf/ Pedro de CHAVES, Spanish.

GUARPAIS, Juana
bap 3 Jly 1708; d/ Antonia GUARPAIS; gf/ Andres de ARCHULETA, Spanish.

CHIDE, Christoval
bap 7 Jly 1708; s/ Andres de CHIDE & Lucia HUIMOE, *coniuges*; gf/ Christoval dela CERNA, Spanish.

TUZI, Santiago
bap 29 Jly 1708; s/ Antonio TUZI & Lucia CAMAGER, *coniuges*; gp/ Baltasar ROMERO, *vecino de la villa de Alburquerque*. (Frames 1024-1025)

Frame 1025
QUATUI, Christoval
bap 9 Sep 1708; s/ Juan QUATUI & Juana TUMAC, *coniuges*; gf/ Christoval CHRESPIN, soldier.

PIACHOLMO, Maria
bap *en dho dia, mes y año*; d/ Fran[co] PIACHOLMO & Juana PIACHELPO, *coniuges*; gf/ Diego GONZALES, soldier.

PAMPAM, Juana
bap 8 Oct 1708; d/ Magdalena (n.s.) (sic) & Fran[co] PAMPAM, *coniuges*; gm/ Lucia QUIRCHONE.

NOCHEE, Juan Gome
bap 14 Oct 1708; s/ Pablo NOCHEE & Josepha TAHA, *coniuges*; gm/ Lucia CHIUMAGUS.

CALO, Juan
bap 4 Nov 1708, newly born; s/ Ant[o] CALO & Lucia (n.s.), *coniuges*; gf/ Juan LUJAN.

Frame 1026
(Two entries without surnames)

(1709)

JUANPONE, Raphael
bap 4 Jan 1709 because of necessity by Juan HERRSE, *ynterprete de este pueblo*; s/ Christoval JUANPONE & Maria GELLA, *coniuges*; gp/ (not given). Signed 16 said mo (by priest).

ARMARAN, Maria
bap 8 Jan (1709); d/ Juan ARMARAN & Maria GUAGUACHORA, *coniuges*; gf/ Fran[co] AHÍ. I signed 16 *dicho mes y año*.

BEEPAI, Maria
bap 24 Jan 1709 because of necessity; d/ Maria GUAGUACHENE (sic) & Diego BEEPAI, *coniuges*; gm/ Ana TURUQUI.

AZA, Theresa
bap 4 May 1709; d/ Diego AZA & Maria OLA, *coniuges*; gm/ Theresa MADRID.

LOPE, Maria
PAMAC, Maria
bap *en dho dia, mes y año*; d/ Lucia PAMAC, *viuda*, & Diego LOPE; gm/ Maria de LEDEZMA.

11 Jly 1709 - church visit - (signed) Fr. Juan de la PEÑA, Nott[o] Fr. Miguel MUÑIZ. (Frames 1026-1027)

Frame 1027
NARACHE (gp), Lucia
bap 12 Jly 1709; d/ Jeronimo (n.s.) & Juana (n.s.), *coniuges*; gm/ Juana NARACHE.

PACHECO, Maria Fran[ca] del Rosario *Apacha*
bap 6 Oct 1709; d/ *Apache*; gf/ D. Juan PACHECO.

(1710)

TACOLINA, Maria Rossa
bap 9 Jan 1710; d/ Francisco TACOLINA & Maria PECUSILI, *coniuges*; gf/ Pedro de la CRUZ.

Frame 1028
(Upper part of frame blank because part of this entry is cut) s/ Fran[co] PRACHALMO & Juana GEAQUILPA, *coniuges*; gf/ Martin de VALENZUELA.

JIAUPATLA, Ramon
bap *en dho dia, mes y año*; s/ Juan JIAUPATLA & Lucia VEHAL, *coniuges*; gf/ Ramon GARCIA JURADO, Spanish.

MUQUELE, Barbara
bap *en subre dho dia, mes y año* d/ Juan MUQUELE & Fran[ca] PIACHAL, *coniuges*; gf/ Don Feliz MARTINEZ.

(Fr. Miguel de SOUSA signing entries)
SERNA (gp), Maria
bap 3 May 1710; d/ Antt[o] (n.s.) & Lusia (n.s.); gp/ *el Sargento* Christobal de la SERNA, Spanish, & Juana (n.s.), Indian, *todos Indios deste pueblo de S. Xeronimo de los Thaos*.

Frame 1029
(Reverse side of previous frame where page is cut)

NACHOLA, Christobal
bap 12 Jly 1710; s/ Juan NACHOLA & Maria XINNACHULA, *Indios deste pueblo*; gf/ *el Sarxento* Christobal de la SERNA, Spanish.

YABATIT, Gregoria
bap 3 Aug 1710; d/ Juana YABATIT & unknown father; gf/ Juan de Dios MARTIN, soldier *deste Rreino*.

TLACAT, Maria Rosa
bap 31 Aug 1710; *India* d/ Xeronimo TLACAT & Juana CUNTCHE, *Indios deste pueblo*; gm/ Juana TOSPA, *India deste pueblo*.

Frame 1030
HANCHA (gp), Juana
bap *en dho dia, mes y año*; *India* d/ Maria (n.s.), *India*, & unknown father; gm/ Fran[ca] HANCHA, *Indios deste pueblo*.

(Fr. Fran[co] BROTONS signing entries again)
PUPA, Francisca
bap 14 Oct of this present year; d/ Lucia PUPA, single; gp/ *el Aiudante* Christoval dela SERNA & Juana NARACHE.

JUENAPO, Juan
bap *en dho dia*; s/ Salvador JUENAPO & Lucia TUMQUAM; gm/ Maria TAHA.

SUISPCHAL, Maria
bap *en dho dia*; d/ Maria SUISPCHAL, single; gf/ Estevan QUIOJE.

1711

CABIAM (gp), Mariana de los Reyes
bap 6 Jan 1711; d/ *Nacion Apacha*; gf/ Estevan CABIAM, *fiscal*.

AJEINO, Michaela (Machaela in margin)
bap 21 Jan 1711; d/ Juan AJEINO & Juana CHICELI; gm/ Juana CUNCHEY.

ATÃ, Juan
bap 26 Feb 1711; s/ Salvador ATÃ & Maria EQUE, *coniuges*; gf/ Juan LUXAN, soldier.

Frame 1031
POAJE, Maria

bap *en sobre dho dia, mes y año*; d/ Antonio POAJE & Geronima CAQUI; gm/ Maria XATLA.

MAQUERO, Juana
bap 4 May *de este pres^e año*; d/ Maria MAQUERO, *soltera*; gm/ Juana CUNCHEY.

GLUPE, Maria
bap 19 Jne 1711; d/ Maria TULPACCO (sic) & Diego GLUPE, *coniuges*; gf/ Juan de TORRES & gm/ Juana GEAQUERPA.

GIGUACHAPO, Lusia
bap 28 Jne 1711; d/ Antonio GIGUACHAPO & Ysabel (n.s.), Apacha, *coniuges*; gm/ Maria PEACHONE.

22 Aug 1711 - church visit - (signed) Fr. Miguel MUÑIZ, Nott° Fr. Joseph Antt° de TORRES.

Frame 1032
(In script)

Libro segundo de Baptismos deste Pueblo
de S. Geronimo de los Thaos hecho
por el R. P^r Fr. Lucas de ARE(-)
BALO Ministro Presi(-)
dente dha mission
hecho el Año
de 1714

Frame 1033 (Only the one entry)
20 Feb 1716 - church visit - (signed) Fr. Joseph LOPEZ TELLO, *Notario* Fr. Domingo de ARAOS.

(Note: No entries for rest of 1711, all 1712, 1713 & first part of 1714).

Frame 1034 (Fr. Lucas de AREBALO signing the entries)

Año de 1714

(Entry without surnames)

CHUPUNE (gp), Lucia Monica
bap 4 May 1714; d/ *Nacion Panana*; gf/ Felipe CHUPUNE.

(Entry without surnames)

TEGUA, Maria Rosa
bap *en dho dia mes y a°* (26 Jly 1714); d/ Antonio TEGUA & Maria (n.s.); gp/ Juan del Alamo (n.s.) & Maria (n.s).

MOYA (gp), Michaela
bap 23 Sep *de d^ho a°*; d/ Salvador (n.s.) & Lucia (n.s.); gp/ Pedro Antt° de MOYA & Ana Maria (n.s.), *Españoles*.

LUXANA (gp), Lucia Catharina
bap 24 Nov *de d^ho a°*; d/ Salvador (n.s.) & M^a (n.s.); gm/ Juana LUXANA.

Frame 1035
(Entry without surnames)

Año de 1715

(Entry without surnames)

LUXAN, Maria
bap 7 Feb 1715; d/ Juan LUXAN & Teresa de HERRERA; gm/ Magdalena PIANAL.

DURAN, Juan Lucas
bap 7 *de dho mes y a°*; s/ Nicolas (n.s.) & Maria DURAN; gm/ Juana (n.s.).

NACHULE, Juan
bap 26 Apr *de d^{ho} a°* by Juan del Alamo (n.s.), *Ynterprete*, because of necessity; s/ Juan NACHULE & Lucia ZAPATA; gp/ (not given). The child subsequently died.

(Two entries without surnames)

Frame 1036
PERALTA, Aug^{tin} dela Trinidad
bap 16 Jne *de d^{ho} a°*; s/ Joseph (n.s.) & Cathalina PERALTA; gp/ Diego Antt° (n.s.) & Juana (n.s.).

PINEDA, Clara
bap 18 Jly *de dho a°*; d/ Nicolas (n.s.) & Lucia (n.s.); gf/ Juan de PINEDA.

ASPECTIA (gp), Maria Geronima
bap 30 Sep *de d^{ho} a°*; d/ unknown; gm/ Ynes de ASPECTIA, Spanish.

ASPECTIA (gp), Gertrudis Rosalia
bap 4 Oct *de d^{ho} a°*; d/ *padres infieles*; gm/ Ynes de ASPECTIA, Spanish.

PIASLU, F^{co} Xabier
bap 20 Nov *de dho a°*; s/ Juan PIASLU & Juana (n.s.); gm/ Maria F^{ca} de MOYA, Spanish.

Año de 1716

NACHALE, Pablo dela Cruz
bap 25 Jan 1716; s/ Geronimo NACHALE & Juana (n.s.); gp/ Pedro de Leon (n.s.) & Antt^{e} (n.s.).

Frame 1037
GUTIERREZ (gp), Getrudes
bap *en dho dia mes y año*; d/ *Ynfieles denacion Apacha*; gp/ Felipe GUTIERREZ *de nacion TANO*.

(Entry without surnames)

ALMOSSA, Ana Maria
bap 4 Feb 1716; d/ Fran^{co} ALMOSSA & Maria TIAPA; gp/ Pedro Antt° de MOYA, Spanish.

MOYA (gp), Miguel Fr^{co}, Pedro Antt°, & Maria Antt^{a}
bap 5 Feb *de d^{ho} a°*; 2 boys and an adult woman *de Nacion Apacha*; gf of all three/ Pedro Antt° de MOYA, Spanish.

CRUZ (gp), Juan Antt°
bap 18 Feb *de d^{ho} a°*; s/ Andres (n.s.) & Josepha (n.s.); gf/ Esteban dela CRUZ.

Frame 1038
22 Feb 1716 - church visit - (signed) Fr. Joseph LOPEZ TELLO, *Notario* Fr. Domingo de ARAOS.

(Entry without surnames) 23 April 1716

Frame 1039
CRUZ (gp), Estevan
bap *en dho dia mes y año*; s/ unknown; gf/ Estevan dela CRUZ.

(Three entries without surnames)

PACHECO, Joan (sic) Antt°
bap *asi mismo*; s/ Juan PACHECO & Maria (n.s.); gf/ Pedro Ant° de MOYA, Spanish.

(Three entries without surnames)

LLUGE, Maria Juana
bap 24 *Jne de este pr^te año*; d/ Juan LLUGE & Maria (n.s.) *denacion Pichuries*; gp/ *el Theniente* Xptobal TAFOYA Spanish. (Frames 1039-1040)

Frame 1040
CHELE, Augustina dela Cruz
bap *en dho dia, mes*; d/ Antt° CHELE & Cathalina (n.s.); gm/ Elena (n.s.).

(Two entries without surnames)

Frame 1041
GUALNACHA, Maria Michaela
bap 9 Sep 1716; d/ Francisco (n.s.) & Margarita GUALNACHA; gm/ Maria CHIUPA.

CHUPUNE, Joan
bap en dho dia mes y a°; s/ Felipe CHUPUNE & Rosa MACULUM; gm/ Maria (n.s.).

CRUZ (gp), Fran^co Xabier
bap 13 Oct 1716; s/ unknown; gp/ Estevan dela CRUZ.

11 Nov 1716 - Church visit - (signed) Fr. Antt° CAMARGO, Nott° Fr. Joseph Antt° GUERRERO. (Frames 1041-1042)

Frame 1042
(Two entries without surnames)

DURAN (gp), Juana
bap 7 Dec 1716 because of necessity; d/ *Nacion Yuta*; gf/ D^n Pablo DURAN.

Frame 1043

Año de 1717

FANFAN, Maria Juana
bap 24 Apr 1717; d/ Fran^co FANFAN & Magdalena (n.s.); gm/ Juana (n.s.).

(The next two entries were marked thru; also see similar entries on next frame).
NACHULA, Diego Lujan
bap 5 May 1717; s/ Juan NACHULA & Zecilia GUENACHULY; gf/ Juan LUJAN, Spanish.

PERALTA, Ana Maria
bap *en dho dia mes y año*; d/ Joseph de PERALTA & Rosa PERALTA; gf/ Manuel TENORIO del ALVA, Spanish. (No mention of twins).

Frame 1044
PERALTA, Diego Lujan

bap *6 May 1717*; s/ Joseph de PERALTA & Rosa PERALTA; gf/ Juan LUJAN, *Español*. (No mention of twins).

NACHULA, Ana Maria
bap *en dho dia mes y año*; d/ D^{n} Juan NACHULA & Zecilia QUENACHALE; gf/ Manuel THENORIO de ALVA, Spanish.

ALAMO (gp), Juan Ubaldo
bap 28 May 1717; s/ unknown; gf/ Juan del ALAMO.

Frame 1045
QUENQUENA, Anttonia
bap 19 Sep 1717; d/ Diego QUENQUENA & Maria DURAN; gf/ Joseph XAVIER.

ROMERO, Miguel
bap en dho *dia mes y año*; s/ Andres ROMERO & Josepha HERRERA; gf/ *el Cap^{n}* Miguel THENORIO.

(Two entries without surnames)

Frame 1046
CHOLESE, Maria Josepha
bap *en dho dia utsupra* (19 May 1717); d/ Diego CHOLESE & Lucia (n.s.); gm/ Maria (n.s.).

PIALUCHONE, Geronima
bap 30 Sep 1717; d/ Salbador PIALUCHONE & Lucia PAMMU; gf/ Hernando MARTIN.

(Entry without surnames)

Frame 1047
TUYENCLIA, Barbara
bap 4 Dec 1717; d/ Nicolas Luiz TUYENCLIA & Maria DURAN; gf/ *el Cap^{n}* Miguel THENORIO de ALVA.

THENORIO de ALVA (gp), Marcial Tadeo
bap 8 Dec 1717; s/ *Nacion Apacha*; gf/ Manuel TH^{o} de ALVA, Spanish.

Año de 1718

(Fr. Manuel de SOPEÑA signing entries)
TOIPA, Domingo
bap 23 Jan 1718; s/ Diego (n.s.), *el sacristan*, & Maria TOIPA; gm/ Geronima PAPAJUIA.

Frame 1048
EELUCLI, Xptobal
bap 23 Jan 1718; s/ Diego EELUCLI & Maria SUCHIAPAKA; gp/ Diego ROMERO & Maria (n.s.).

CHEABEA (gp), Maria
bap 23 Jan 1718; d/ Antonio (n.s.), *el cojos*, & Ysabel (n.s.); gp/ Esteban CHEABEA & Maria ZAPATA.

PHUONOTA, Lucia
bap 23 Jan 1718; d/ Antonio PHUONOTA & Maria PEAQUANQUE; gp/ Antonio Luis (n.s.) & Lucia PAILA.

28 Feb 1718 - church visit - Fr. Joan de TAGLE, *Notario* Fr. Manuel de SOPEÑA (Frames 1048-1049)

Frame 1049
(Fr. Lucas de AREBALO signing entries)
HILO (gp), Maria Andrea
bap 4 Apr 1718; adult d/ *Nacion Apacha*; gp/ D^{n} Geronimo HILO & Maria FEACHUA.

CAFLALA, Maria Antt^{a}
bap 9 Apr 1718; d/ Antt^{o} CAFLALA & Ynes (n.s.); gf/ *el Th^{te}* Joseph Xavier (n.s.). (Frames 1049-1050)

Frame 1050
PAQUIME, Maria Antt^{a}
bap 6 May 1718; d/ Joan PAQUIME & Juana CHICHULE; gf/ *el Th^{te}* Joseph Xavier (n.s.).

ARMOSA, Antt^{a}
bap 19 May 1718; d/ Fran^{co} ARMOSA & Maria TEAPU; gm/ Lucia (n.s.).

Frame 1051
DURAN (gp), Franzisca de la Ascencion
bap 2 Jne 1718; adult d/ *Nacion Apacha*; gp/ D^{n} Pablo DURAN & Joseph(a) ZAPATA.

HILO (gp), Geronima
bap 4 Jne 1718; d/ (unknown); gf/ D^{n} Geronimo HILO.

MORA (gp), Marg^{ta} Rosalia
bap 7 Aug 1718; d/ *Infieles*; gf/ Joan de la MORA.

Frame 1052
(Entry without surnames)

GIJOSA, Francisa Antt^{a}
bap 12 Sep 1718; d/ unknown; gm/ Fran^{ca} Antt^{a} de GIJOSA, Spanish.

MOYA (gp), Francisca Maria
bap 25 Sep 1718; d/ Nicolas (n.s.) & Juana (n.s.); gf/ Cayetano Joseph de MOYA, Spanish.

Frame 1053
HILO (gp), Geronimo Domingo
bap *en dho dia,mes y año*; s/ Joan (n.s.) & Cezilia (n.s.); gf/ D^{n} Geron^{o} HILO.

LUXAN, Juana
bap 5 Oct 1718; d/ Joan LUXAN & Teresa de HERRERA; gm/ Magdalena JUEPATU.

MOYA (gp), Cayetano Joseph
bap 22 Nov 1718; s/ Aug^{tin} (n.s.) & Margarita (n.s.); gf/ Cayetano de MOYA, Spanish.

JUESPLA (gp), Maria Michaela
bap *en d^{ho} dia*; d/ Geronimo (n.s.) & Joana (n.s.); gm/ Teresa JUESPLA.

Frame 1054
QUEALTALME, Antt^{o} Basilio
bap 28 Nov 1718; s/ Fran^{co} QUEALTALME & Cathalina GUALNECHU; gf/ Miguel CULUTHABA.

ZAPATA (gp), Domingo
bap 18 Dec 1718; d/ Fr^{ca} de la Ascension (n.s.-sic) & Martin (n.s.); gm/ Josepha ZAPATA.

MOIGE, Juana Magdalena
bap *en d^{ho} dia;* d/ Joan MOIGE & Juana CHOIGUA; gm/ Juana GUALPO.

Frame 1055

(1719)

(Fr. Juan SANCHEZ dela CRUZ signing entries)
PACTEE, Joseph
bap 25 Feb 1719; s/ Geronimo PACTEE & Isabel PAPAP, *hijos deeste pueblo de Thaos;* gm/ Juana (n.s.).

GOMEZ, Nicolasa
bap 26 Apr 1719; d/ Andres GOMEZ & Josepha (n.s.), *hijos deeste pueblo de S Geronimo delos Thaos;* gp/ Nicolas MARTIN, *vecino deel Rio Arriba* & Theresa (n.s.), *vecina de d^{ho} pueblo.*

Frame 1056
BUSTOS (gp), Josepha
bap 9 May 1719; d/ Maria (n.s.-sic) & Diego (n.s.), *vezinos todos deeste pueblo de S. Geronimo delos Thaos;* gp/ Josepha de BUSTOS & Fran^{co} de BUSTOS, *naturales de Mexico.*

BUSTOS (gp), Juan
bap 9 May 1719; s/ Rossa (n.s.-sic) & Joseph (n.s.), *vezinos todos deeste pueblo de S. Geronimo delos Thaos;* gp/ Josepha BUSTOS (sic) & Fran^{co} BUSTOS, *naturales de Mexico.*

PACHILPA, Juan
bap 25 Jne 1719; s/ Antonio PACHILPA & Isabel (n.s.), Apacha, *vezinos de este pueblo de S. Geronimo delos Thaos;* gp/ Fran^{co} CHELMO & Juana SUAIT, *todos vezinos de d^{ho} pueblo.*

Frame 1057
29 Jne 1719 - church visit - (signed) Fr. Gonsalo de SOBENES BARREDA, *Notario* Fr. Domingo de ARAOS.

THENORIO (gp), Isabel
bap 9 Jly 1719; d/ *Nacion Apacha;* gp/ Manuel THENORIO & Diego ROMERO.

Frame 1058
ALAMO (gp), Nicolas
bap 9 Jly 1719; s/ Lorenzo (n.s.) & Angelina (n.s.), *vezinos de d^{ho} pueblo;* gp/ Juan deel ALAMO & Josepha BUSTOS.

GABILAN (gp), Maria
bap 15 Jly 1719; d/ Martin (n.s.) & Fran^{ca} (n.s.); gp/ Theresa (n.s.-sic) & Pablo GABILAN, *todos vezinos de d^{ho} pueblo.*

Frame 1059
San Geronimo de los Thaos
BUSTOS, Maria
bap 30 Jly 1719; d/ Ant^{o} (n.s.) & Maria (n.s.), *vezinos deeste pueblo de S. Geronimo delos Thaos;* gp/ Juan de BUSTOS & Josepha de BUSTOS, *vezinos de Mexico.*

DURAN, Paulo
bap 13 Aug 1719; s/ Joseph DURAN & Theresa (n.s.); gp/ Fran^{co} de BUSTOS & Josepha de BUSTOS, *vezinos deel pueblo de S. Geronimo del Thaos.*

Frame 1060
(Entry without surnames)

BUSTOS (gp), Fran^{co}
bap 18 Oct 1719; s/ Nicolas (n.s.) & Maria (n.s.), *todos vezinos deeste pueblo de S. Geronimo delos Thaos;* gp/ Josepha BUSTOS (sic) & Manuel (n.s.).

BUSTOS (gp), Raphael
bap 18 Oct 1719; d/ Phelipe (n.s.) & Isabel (n.s.), *todos vezinos deeste pueblo de S. Geronimo delos Thaos;* gp/ Josepha de BUSTOS & Manuel (n.s.).

Frame 1061
BUSTOS (gp), Maria
bap 2 Dec 1719; d/ Fran^{co} (n.s.) & Angelina (n.s.), *vezinos de dho pueblo;* gp/ Josepha BUSTOS & Manuel (n.s.).

1720

(No surnames in remainder of this frame)

Frame 1062
(Entry with no surnames)

4 Apr 1720 - church visit - (signed) Fr. Gonsalo de SOBENES BARREDA, (notary) Fr. Domingo ARAOS. (Frames 1062-1063)

Frame 1063
ZERNA (gp), Maria
bap 20 Apr 1720; d/ Margarita (n.s.-sic) & Don Juan (n.s.), legitimately married, *todos vezinos de d^{ho} pueblo;* gp/ Xptoval ZERNA & Josepha de ONTIBEROS.

ZERNA (gp), Maria
bap 20 Apr 1720; d/ Fran^{co} (n.s.) & Antonia (n.s.), *todos vezinos de d^{ho} pueblo;* gp/ Xptoval ZERNA & Josepha ONTIBEROS.

Frame 1064
BUSTOS (gp), Juan
bap 7 Jne 1720; s/ Rossa (n.s.-sic) & Joseph (n.s.), legitimately married, *vezinos de d^{ho} pueblo;* gp/ Josepha de BUSTOS & Manuel (n.s.).

BUSTOS (gp), Juan
bap 7 Jne 1720; s/ Josepha (n.s.-sic) & Antonio (n.s.), legitimately married, *vezinos de d^{ho} pueblo;* gp/ Josepha BUSTOS & Manuel (n.s.).

ONTIBEROS (gp), Petrolina
bap 25 Jne 1720; d/ Domingo (n.s.) & Maria (n.s.), legitimately married, *vezinos de d^{ho} pueblo;* gp/ Josepha de ONTIBEROS & Manuel (n.s.).

Frame 1065
LUJAN (gp), Cayetana
bap 8 Aug 1720; d/ Isabel (n.s.) & unknown father, *vezinos todos de d^{ho} pueblo;* gp/ Antonio LUJAN & the wife (n.n) of Geronimo (n.s.).

LUJAN (gp), Cayetana
bap 8 Aug 1720; d/ Nicolas (n.s.) & Theresa (n.s.), legitimately married,

vezinos todos de dbo pueblo; gp/ Antonio LUJAN & the wife (n.n.) of Geronimo (n.s.).

(Entry without surnames)

Frame 1066
LUJAN (gp), Maria
bap 24 Aug 1720; adult d/ *Nacion Apacha;* gp/ Antonio LUJAN & Maria LUJANA.

LUJAN, Juan
bap 24 Aug 1720; s/ (of the *Apacha* woman above); gp/ Antonio LUJAN & Maria LUJANA.

(No Sep entries)

Frame 1067
(No surnames for 1 Oct)

(Fr. Jun Ant° de CELIS signing entries)
(Entry without surnames)

(1721)

(Entry without surnames)

Frame 1068
(Two entries without surnames, 11 Jan 1721)

DURAN, Francisca
bap *en el mismo dia mes y año;* d/ Nicholas (n.s.) & Francisca DURAN; gf/ *el Alcalde mayor de esta Jurisdiccion* Jun de PINEDA.

SAPATA, Antonia
bap 18 Feb 1721; d/ Pablo (n.s.), the sacristan, & Maria la SAPATA; gf/ Antonio de REYNA.

Frame 1069
QUANTLATEC, Franco
bap 4 Mch 1721; s/ Geronimo QUANTLATEC & Lucia CHALPABAC; gm/ Lucia Maria (n.s.).

UPA (gp), Franco
bap 4 Mch 1721; s/ Magdalena (n.s.) & unknown father; gm/ Tomaza UPA.

JUPLATLA, Ysabel
bap 4 Mch 1721; s/ Nicolas JUPLATLA & Juana MEISLAC; gf/ Diego JUSLI.

Frame 1070
LUSLI, Miguel
bap 23 Mch 1721; s/ Diego LUSLI & Maria TUCHAPAM; gm/ Maria de HURTADO.

TACHIVE, Magdalena
bap 23 Mch 1721; d/ Gregorio TACHIVE & Chatarina JUZOPAPAZ; gm/ Maria TACHOLE.

PERALTA, Juana
bap 23 Mch 1721; d/ Joseph PERALTA & Maria (n.s.); gf/ Miguel MARTIN.

Frame 1071
*20 Apr 1720 - church visit - (signed) Fr. Joan dela CRUZ, *Nott°* Fr. Domingo de ARAOZ

(Fr. Ju[n] SANCHEZ signing entries)
NAPO, Pasquala
bap 23 May 1721; d/ Maria TULUQUE (sic) & Antonio NAPO; gp/ (none given). (Marked thru, see next entry).

Frame 1072
NAPO, Pasquala
bap 23 May 1721; d/ Maria TULUQUE (sic) & Antonio NAPO; gm/ Maria HURTADO.

CALFIALU, Gregoria
bap 24 May 1721; d/ Antonio CALFIALU & Fransisca PUANCHO; gm/ Juana LUGAN.

CEQUE, Juan
bap 24 May 1721; s/ Geronimo CEQUE & Juana Maria (n.s.); gm/ Maria HURTADO.

Frame 1073
(Fr. Carlos DELGADO signing entries)
DOMINGUES, Juan de Píneda
bap 10 Aug 1721; s/ Joseph DOMINGUES & Rosa (n.s.); gf/ *el Capitan* Juan de PÍNEDA.

COCA (gp), Barbara Antonia
bap 23 Aug 1721; d/ *Nacion Apacha*; gf/ *el Capitan* Miguel de COCA.

(Two entries without surnames)

Frame 1074
(Entry without surnames)

ROMERO (gp), Magdalena
bap 4 Nov 1721; d/ *Nacion Apacha*; gf/ Diego ROMERO.

ROMERO (gp), Margarita
bap 4 Nov 1721; d/ *Nacion Apacha*; gf/ Diego ROMERO.

Frame 1075

Año de 1722

ROMERO, Clara Rosa
bap 8 Mch 1722; d/ Andres ROMERO & Jusepa de HERRERA; gf/ *el Capitan* Juan del PINEDA (only).

(Six entries without surnames)

Frame 1076
16 May 1722 in Mission S[n] Lorenzo de los Picuries - church visit - (signed) Fr. Jose de la CRUZ, *Nott°* Fr. Carlos DELGADO

(Entry without surnames)

Frame 1077
(Entry without surnames)

ARCHIBEQUE (gp), Antonio
bap 22 Sep 1723; s/ Fran^{co} (n.s.) & Angelina (n.s.); gf/ Augustin de ARCHIBEQUE.

(Two entries without surnames)

Frame 1078
(Fr. Ju^{n} Joseph MIRABAL signing entries)
(Four without surnames) 23 Oct 1722

Frame 1079
(Two without surnames)

(1723)

DOMINGUEZ, Lorenso
bap 18 Feb 1723; s/ Diego DOMINGUEZ & Rossa (n.s.); gf/ Lorenso GRIEGO.

(Two entries without surnames)

DURAN, Maria Juana
bap 18 Feb 1723; d/ Nicolas (n.s.) & Fransisca DURAN; gm/ Teresa (n.s.). (Frames 1079-1080)

Frame 1080
(Entry without surnames)

LUJAN (gp), Joseph
bap 9 Mch 1723; s/ Antonio (n.s.) & (not given); gf/ Joseph LUJAN.

(Two entries without surnames)

Frame 1081
TRUXILLO, Fran^{co}
bap 9 Jne 1723; s/ Maria Magdalena (n.s.-sic) & Ju^{n} TRUXILLO; gm/ Magdalena (n.s.).

17 Jne 1723 - church visit - (signed) Fr. Joseph GUERRERO, *Nott^{o}* Fr. Domingo de AROS

Frame 1082
(Entry without surnames)

DURAN (gp), Fran^{ca}
bap 8 Oct 1723; d/ Nicolas (n.s.) & Juana (n.s.); gf/ Pablo DURAN.

(Two entries without surnames)

Frame 1083
(Five entries without surnames)

Frame 1084
(Two entries without surnames)

(1724)

DURAN (gp), Miguel
bap 3 Feb 1724; s/ Nicolas (n.s.) & Maria DURAN; gm/ Geronima (n.s.).

(Two entries without surnames)

CORDERO (gp), Maria Antt[a]
bap 3 Feb 1724; d/ unknown; gf/ Joseph CORDERO.

Frame 1085
(Five entries without surnames)

Frame 1086
(Entry entries without surnames)

(This one signed by Fr. Antt[o] GABALDON)
PINEDA (gp), Ju[n] Joseph
bap 6 Mch 1724; s/ unknown; gf/ Ju[n] de PINEDA.

DURAN (gp), Pedro
bap 10 Mch 1724; s/ unknown; gf/ Pablo DURAN.

(Entry without surnames)

Frame 1087
18 May 1724 - church visit - (signed) Fr. Fran[co] de LEPIANE, *Nott[o]*
Fr. Joseph Antt[o] GUERRERO

(Bleed thru, rest of page blank)

Frame 1088
DURAN, Ju[n] Antt[o]
*bap 3 May 1724; s/ Maria DURAN (sic) & Diego (n.s.); gp/ (not given).

(Four entries without surnames)

Frame 1089
(Entry without surnames)

JIRON (gp), Miguel Fran[co]
bap 13 Dec 1724; s/ Diego (n.s.) & Maria (n.s.); gf/ D[n] Miguel Enrriques JIRON.

Frame 1090
(Entry without surnames)

(1725)

LOPEZ GALLARDO (gf), Francisca
bap 18 Apr 1725; s/ Nacion Panana; gf/ Pedro LOPEZ GALLARDO.

(One entry without surnames)

LOPEZ GALLARDO (gp), Joseph, Domingo, & Getrudis
bap 18 Apr 1725; ch/ *Nacion Panana; Joseph, s/ J[n] (n.s.) & Maria (n.s.)*; Domingo, s/ Joseph (n.s.) & Josepha (n.s.); Getrudis, s/ unknown; gp/ Pedro LOPEZ GALLARDO & Cristina Catalina de VILLALPANDO. (Frames 1090-1091)

Frame 1091
(Three entries without surnames)

29 Apr 1725 - church visit - (signed) Fr. Joseph Antt[o] GUERRERO, *Nott[o]* Fr. Fran[co] ROMERO.

Frame 1092
DURAN (gp), Cosme
bap 9 May 1725; s/ *Nasion Panana*; gf/ Lazaro DURAN.

GABILAN (gp), Alberta
bap *en dicho día*; d/ *Nasion Apache*; gf/ Pablo GABILAN.

(Two entries without surnames)

Frame 1093
TRUXILLO, Christobal
bap 22 Jly 1725; s/ Diego TRUXILLO & Gregoria YDALGO, *Españoles*; gp/ Josefa DURAN (sic) & Baltasar TRUXILLO.

FERNANDES (gp), Ana Maria
bap 25 Aug 1725; d/ unknown; gf/ Domingo FERNANDES.

Frame 1094
ROMERO, Barbara
bap 15 Oct 1725; d/ Fran[co] ROMERO & Lusia (n.s.); gf/ Domingo FERNANDES.

6 Jan 1726 - church visit - (signed) Fr. Antt° CAMARGO, *Nott°* Fr. Fernando de CASTRO (Frames 1094-1095)

(Bleed thru -- rest of page blank)

NEW MEXICO BAPTISMS
CATHOLIC PARISHES and MISSIONS in TAOS
VOLUME I
19 June 1701 - 31 December 1826

Archives of the Archdiocese of Santa Fe Film
AASF Reel #18
6 Jan 1777-25 Nov 1798

Frame 1197 Presentation page 14 Jly 1776 with 80 *fojas*

Frame 1198
(Fr. Jose de OLAETA signing entries)

Año de 1777

ROMERO, Manuela Reyes *Vezina*
bap 6 Jan *del sobredicho*; d/ Julian ROMERO, *collote*, & Barbara MARTIN, Spanish, *vezinos de este pueblo*; gp/ D^{n} Pedro Ygnacio SANCHEZ, *Alcalde interino* & his wife, Dª Manuela VEGIL.

LEAL, Sebastían Antonio *Pueblo*
bap 20 Jan *del referido*; s/ Alonzo LEAL & Maria Barbara (n.s.); gm/ Luzia DON JUAN, *todos del pueblo*.

GONZALEZ (gp), Gaspar de Jesus *Vezino*
bap *en este día*; s/ unknown *Yndio*; gp/ Ysidro GONZALEZ & his wife, Feliziana MONTAÑO, *Españoles y vezinos de este pueblo*.

MARTIN, Sebastíana Guadalupe *Vezina*
bap *este pp^{río} día*; d/ Antonio MARTIN, Indian *vezino*, & Maria Margarita CORDOBA, *Española*; gp/ Juana RODRIGUEZ & her son, Jose de la Encarnacion SEGURA, *vezinos de este pueblo*.

NARANJO, Maria Candelaria *Pueblo*
bap 3 Feb *del mismo*; d/ Fran^{co} NARANJO & Micaela ROMERO; gm/ Josefa DEL RIO, wife of Juan GOMEZ, *todos hijos del pueblo*.

LUJAN, Juan de Mata *Del pueblo*
bap 8 Feb *del pp^{rio} a^{o}*; s/ Juan LUJAN & Maria Antonia ORTIZ; gp/ Juan Antonio NARANJO & Lorenza GONZALEZ, *todos de este pueblo*. (Frames 1198-1199)

Frame 1199
GOMEZ, Valentín Fransísco *Del pueblo*
bap 13 Feb 1777; s/ Tomaz GOMEZ & Josefa LUJAN; gp/ *el fiscal Mallor* Pablo CARLOS & his wife, Rosalia RIBERA, *todos del pueblo*.

REDONDO, Mateo *De el pueblo*
bap 25 Feb *del mismo* a^{o} by Augustin CHAVEZ because of necessity; s/ Fransisco REDONDO & Maria Antonia MIRABAL; gm/ Rosa ARIAS, *vezina, los arriba d^{hos} del pueblo*.

ROMERO, Gregorio Fransísco *Vezino*
bap 13 Mch *del sobre d^{ho}*; s/ Jose ROMERO & Fransisca GARSIA, *Yndios vezinos de este pueblo*; gp/ Bartolome MARTIN & his wife, Maria Gertrudis GOMEZ.

MARQUEZ, Maria Fransísca *Del pueblo*
bap *en este día;* d/ Juan Domingo MARQUEZ & Luzia SUAZO; gm/ Fransisca RUIBAL, *todos del pueblo.*

CATUJE, Juan de Díos Jose *Del pueblo*
bap *en este propío día;* s/ Domingo CATUJE & Maria ROMERO; gm/ Monica ROMERO, *todos estos, hijos de esta misión y pueblo de S^n Geron(i)mo de Taos.* (Frames 1199-1200)

Frame 1200
SANDOBAL, Manuela Balvína *Vezina*
*bap 31 Jan *del referido año,* b. 20 *de d^ho mez y año;* d/ Jose Migel SANDOBAL & Maria Paula LEIBA, *Españoles, feligreses, y naturales de este pueblo en el qual viven y avitan al presente* and legitimately married; gp/ Juan Xptobal TRUGILLO, Spanish parishioner of *las Trampas de Pecuries,* & Maria GOMEZ, Spanish parishioner of Taos.

LUJAN, Manuel Fransísco *Del pueblo*
bap 2 Apr *del referido año,* b. 25 Mch; s/ Miguel LUJAN & Angela ROMERO, *naturales de este pueblo;* gp/ Toribio TRUGILLO, & *su muger,* Juana Maria Gertrudis MARTIN, *collotes, vezinos y feligreses aora de esta misíon.*

GONZALEZ, Fransísca Paula *Del pueblo*
bap *en esta día,* b. 29 Mch; d/ Juan Domingo GONZALEZ & Maria LUZERO; gm/ Ma^a LUZERO, *todos naturales de este pueblo.*

LUJAN, Jose Fransísco *Del pueblo*
bap *en este proprío día,* b. 27 Mch; s/ Juan Antonio LUJAN & Juliana MIRABAL; gm/ Micaela DEL RIO, *todos estos hijos y oriundos de este pueblo y misíon de S.S. Geronimo de Taos.*

Frame 1201
GONZALEZ, Xptoval Norberto *Vezino*
bap 12 Jne 1777, b. 9 *del mismo mez;* s/ Bernardo GONZALEZ & Ysabel MADRID, *castisos, oriundos de la villa de S. Fee, vezinos y feligreses de esta mission en donde viven y avitan al presente,* legitimately married; gp/ Juan Aug^n LEAL, married, & Joachina BENAVIDEZ, *donzella, vezinos de esta mission.*

ROMERO, Bacilio Antonio *Del pueblo*
bap 14 Jne 1777, b. 9 *de d^ho mez y a°; Yndio* s/ Juan Domingo ROMERO & Juana Maria LUJAN; gp/ Juan Antt° MARTIN & Juana ROMERO, *todos son hijos de este pueblo en donde viven y avitan* and legitimately married.

(Fr. Andres CLARAMONTE signing entries)
Frame 1202
DOMINGO, Maria Ant^a
bap *item* (7 Jly 1777), ae 3 da; d/ Juan DOM^GO & Juana Maria (n.s.); gp/ Maria ACACHANA.

LUJAN, Maria Paula
bap *item,* ae 8 da; d/ Julian LUJAN & Maria Antonia ROMERO; gp/ Antonio FRESQUIS & his daughter, Manuela FRESQUIS.

(The above entry & the one below are on folded *foja* with the possibility of a missing *foja*).

ROMERO, Jose Santiago
bap 25 Jly 1778, ae 10 da; s/ Miguel ROMERO, *coyote vecino,* & Juana (n.s.), Indian; gp/ Manuel BARELA & Gertrudis RODRIGUES, *todos son vecinos.*

MARTIN, Jose Ygnacio
bap *item*, ae 8 da; *coyote vecino* s/ Antonio MARTIN & Margarita CORDOVA; gp/ Jose Miguel SANDOVAL & his wife, Paula LEYBA, *todos son vecinos*.

ROMERO, Maria
bap 8 Aug 1778, ae 10 da; d/ Balthasar ROMERO, *coyote vecino*, & Josefa (n.s.), Indian; gp/ Ant^{o} Dom^{go} ROMERO & his niece, Maria ROMERO, *todos son vecinos*. (Frames 1202-1203)

Frame 1203
DOMINGO, Juana
bap 4 Oct 1778, ae 3 da; d/ Juan D^{MGO} & Josefa (n.s.); gm/ Maria Ant^{a} (n.s.), *todos son hijos de la mission*.

DOMINGO, Gertrudis
bap *item* (4 Oct 1778), ae 8 da; d/ Juan D^{MGO} & Maria Rosa (n.s.); gm/ Barbara (n.s.), *todos son del pueblo*.

TRUGILLO, Micaela
bap *item* (4 Oct 1778), ae 7 da, *Yndia vecina*; d/ Ylario TRUGILLO & Encarnacion MARTIN; gp/ Domingo ROMERO & Maria Antonia COCA, *vecinos*.

MANSANARES, Jose Gregorio
bap 28 Oct 1778; *huerfano que parece mestiso* s/ parents unknown, *de* Quiteria MANSANARES, *vecina de Taos* who was the *madrina*.

LUJAN, Manuel Ant^{o}
bap 25 Nov 1778, ae 11 da; Spanish s/ Vicente LUJAN & Manuela Manuela (sic) GOMES; gp/ Jose MIRAVAL & *su esposa*, Barbara ROMERO.

Frame 1204
DOMINGO, Martina Antonia
bap 29 Nov 1778, ae 8 da, *Yndia*; d/ Juan DOMINGO & Man^{a} (n.s.), *hijos de la mission*; gp/ Antonio D^{mgo} ROMERO & his sister-in-law, Manuela (n.s.), *Yndia vecinos*.

MIRAVAL, Maria Josefa
bap 12 Dec 1778, ae 10 da, *mestisa vecina*; d/ Baltasar MIRAVAL & Maria MARTIN; gp/ Mariano Concep^{n} ROMERO & his sister, Barbara ROMERO, *todos son vecinos de Taos*.

1778

ROMERO, Maria Geronima *Pueblo*
bap *item* (12 Dec 1778), ae 5 da; d/ Juan Antonio (n.s.) & Juana ROMERO; gp/ Juan Antonio (n.s.) & Rosa (n.s.), *todos son hijos de la mission*.

Ano de 1779

(Fr. Diego MUÑOS JURADO signing entries)
BENAVIDES (gp), Manuela *Pueblo*
bap 17 Jan 1779, b. 5 *de d^{ho} mes y año*; d/ Domingo (n.s.) & Micaela (n.s.), *Yndios de pueblo*; gp/ Fran^{co} BENAVIDES *y su mug^{r}*, Manuela TRUXILLO, *vecinos de d^{ho} pueblo*.

Frame 1205
BARELA, Barbara Antonia *Vezina*
bap 25 Jan 1779, b. 23 *de d^{ho} mes coma a las 4 dela mañana*; d/ Manuel BARELA & Getrudes RODRIGUEZ, legitimately married, *vecinos de este pueblo*; gp/ Juan Ant^{o} BARGAS, *vecino de las Trampas*, & Rosalia MARTINA *de este pueblo*; *testig^{a}*/ Martin (n.s.) & Josef Ant^{o} (n.s.), *Yndios de este pueblo*.

MARTIN, Maria Andrea *Vezina*
bap 4 Feb 1779, b. 1st *de d^{ho} mes y año como â las seis dela mañ^{a}*; d/ Agustin MARTIN & Margarita MANZANARES, legitimately married *y vezinos de este pueblo*; gp/ Juan Miguel MARTIN & his mother, Maria Ynes de CORDOVA, *tambien vez^{s} de d^{ho} pueblo; testigos*/ Josef MARTIN & Juan DOMINGO, *Yndios de este pueblo*.

GONZALES, Josef Miguel *Vez^{o}*
bap 22 Feb 1779, b. 17 Feb; s/ Jose Ant^{o} GONZALES & Maria ROMERO, legitimately married *vez^{os}*; gp/ Ant^{o} FER^{DZ} & Margarita ROMERO, *todos vez^{s} de esta mission*.

ROMERO, Josef Mariano
bap 22 Feb 1779, b. 19 *de d^{ho} mes*; s/ Julian ROMERO & Barbara MARTIN, his legitimately married wife, *vezinos*; gp/ Miguel COCA & his mother, Micaela RUIBALA, *todos vez^{s} de esta mission; testigos*/ Josef MARTIN & Juan DOMINGO, *Yndios de este pueblo*.

SANDOVAL (gp), Andres *Del pueblo*
bap 22 Feb 1779, b. 18 *de d^{ho} mes*; s/ Josef Miguel (n.s.) & Rosalia (n.s.), *Yndio del pueblo*; gp/ J^{ph} SANDOVAL, *vezino*, & Juana Maria (n.s.) *del pueblo*.

CHINA, Maria Rosa *Del pueblo*
bap 22 Feb 1779, b. 14 *de d^{ho} mes*; d/ Michaela CHINA & father unknown; gp/ Agustin CHAVES, *vez.*, & Manuela (n.s.), *Yndia del pueblo*.

CLAVES, Getrudes *Del pueblo*
bap 22 Feb 1779, b. 15 *de d^{ho} mes*; d/ Pablo (n.s.) & Maria (n.s.) *de este pueblo*; gp/ Josef CLAVES, *vezino*, & Lucia (n.s.), *Yndia del pueblo*.

Frame 1206
REYES, Maria Josefa
bap 2 Mch 1779, b. 20 Feb; d/ Gaspar de los REYES & Maria Lugarda SANDOVAL, *vezinos*; gp/ Geronimo RIVERA & Maria Josefa RIVERA, *su hija, vez^{s} de Sta Feé*.

ROMERO, Maria Magdalena
bap 15 Mch 1779, b. 12 *de d^{ho} mes*; d/ Josef ROMERO & Fran^{ca} GARZIA, *vezinos*; gp/ Josef JUILO & Rosa ROMERO, *todos vez^{s} de este pueblo*.

ROMERO, Domingo
bap 18 Apr 1779, b. 23 *de(l) mes anterior*; s/ Salvador ROMERO & Manuela PAEZ, *su legitima mug., vezinos*; gp/ Josef el CHINO & Manuela MIRABAL, *su mug., Yndios de este pueblo; testig^{s}*/ Juan DOMINGO & Juan Ant^{o} (n.s.), *Yndios del pueblo*.

FRESQUES, Juana Rafaela
bap 18 Apr 1779 because of illness sprinkled water on her 26 of said previous (month), b. 22 *del mes anterior*; d/ Juan Manuel (n.s.) & Barbara FRESQUES, *Yndios del pueblo*; gp/ Barth^{e} MARTIN and his daughter, Graziana Beatriz MARTIN, *vez^{s} de este pueblo; testig^{s}*/ Juan DOMINGO & Juan Ant^{o} (n.s.), *Yndios del pueblo*.

LUXAN, Maria Rafaela *Pueblo*
bap 18 Apr 1779, b. 28 *del mes anterior de d^{ho} año*; d/ Josef LUXAN & Maria Antonia ORTIZ, *Yndios de este pueblo*; gp/ Ambrosio de VILLALPANDO & Micaela ROMERO, *su mujer; testigos*/ Juan DOMINGO & Juan Antonio (n.s.), *Yndios del pueblo*.

ROMERO, Thomasa Rafaela *Pueblo*
bap 18 Apr 1779, b. 2 *de d^{ho} mes y año*; d/ Domingo ROMERO & Maria ROMERO,

Yndios de este pueblo; gp/ Fran^{co} REDONDO & Maria Ant^{a} MIRABAL, *su mug.; testigos/* Juan DOMINGO & Juan Antonio (n.s.), *Yndios del pueblo todos.*

Frame 1207

LUXAN (gp), Josef Ant^{o} Rafael *Pueblo*
bap 18 Apr 1779, b. 8 *de d^{ho} mes y año;* nat. s/ Maria Rosa (n.s.), *viuda Yndia de esta mission;* gp/ Miguel LUXAN & Josefa MARQUEZ, *Yndios de esta mision; testigos/* Juan DOMINGO & Juan Ant^{o} (n.s.).

MARTIN (gp), Maria Rafaela *Pueblo*
bap 18 Apr 1779, b. 15 *dho mes y año;* d/ Manuela Juliana (n.s.), *viuda Yndia de este pueblo,* & unknown father; gp/ Barth^{e} MARTIN & Maria GOMEZ, *vecinos de este pueblo; testig^{s}/* Juan DOMINGO & Juan Ant^{o} (n.s.), *Yndios del pueblo.*

MIRABAL, Josef Rafael *Vezino*
bap 25 Apr 1779, b. 16 *de dho mes y año;* nat. s/ Rosa MIRABAL, single, *vezina de este pueblo,* & unknown father; gp/ Jag<u>or</u> Ant^{o} LEIBA & Nicolasa VILLALPANDO, *vesinos de este pueblo; testigos/* Josef MARTIN & Juan Ant^{o} (n.s.), *Yndios de esta mission.*

ROMERO, Juana Rafaela *Pueblo*
bap 27 Apr 1779, b. 23 *de d^{ho} mes y año;* nat. d/ Josef Jacinto (n.s.) & Maria Antonia ROMERO, *Yndios de este pueblo;* gp/ Baltasar ROMERO & Josefa ROMERO, *vezinos de d^{ho} pueblo; testigos/* Josef MARTIN & Domingo ROMERO, *Yndios de dha mision.*

ROMERO, Maria Rafaela *Vezina*
bap 8 May 1779, b. 30 Apr *de d^{ho} año;* nat. d/ Rosa ROMERO, *soltera, vezina de este pueblo,* & unknown father; gp/ Salvador Raymundo MARTIN & Maria Ygnacia CANO, *su mug^{r}, vezinos de este d^{ho} pueblo; testig^{s}/* Josef MARTIN & Fran^{co} (n.s.), *Yndios de esta mision.*

JUILULMA, Juan Rafael *Pueblo*
bap 10 May 1779, b. 6 *de d^{ho} mes y año;* s/ Juan Domingo JUILULMA & Maria Josefa FRANFAEN, *Yndios de esta mision;* gm/ Juana ZAMORA, *viuda Yndia de la d^{ha} mision; testigos/* Domingo ROMERO & Josef MARTIN, *Yndios de d^{ho} pueblo.*

BLEA, Maria Rafaela *Vezin<u>os</u>*
bap 15 May 1779, b. 6 *de d^{ho} mes y año;* d/ Josef Jua<u>qu</u>in BLEA & Maria Ygnacia CHAVES, *vezinos;* gp/ Mariano Concepcion ROMERO & his niece, Rosalia MARTINA, *todos vez^{s} de este pueblo; tes^{gos}/* Josef MARTIN & Juan Ant^{o} (n.s.), *Yndios de esta missi^{n}.*

NARANJO, Maria Rafaela *Pueblo*
bap 21 May 1779, b. 13 *de d^{ho} mes y año;* d/ Juan NARANJO & Maria Fran^{ca} (n.s.), *su mug^{r};* gm/ Juana ZAMORA, *viuda; testigos/* Domingo ROMERO & Josef MARTIN, *todos Yndios de esta mission.*

Frame 1208

ROMERO (gp), Josefa Rafaela *Pueblo*
bap 21 May 1779, b. 14 *de d^{ho} mes y año;* nat. d/ Josefa (n.s.), *que su marido esta alzado,* & unknown father; gp/ Santiago ROMERO & Antonia FAQUAPABA, *su mug.; testigos/* Domingo ROMERO & Josef MARTIN, *todos Yndios de esta mission.*

MARTIN (gp), Juan Josef Rafael *Vezin<u>a</u>* (sic)
bap 23 May 1779, b. 15 *de d^{ho} mes y año;* s/ Maria (n.s.), *Yndia criada de la nacion Panana,* vezina, & unknown father; gp/ Juan Bap^{ta} MARTIN, *vezino del Rio Arriba,* & Ana Maria ROMERO *de este pueblo; testigos/* Josef MARTIN & Santiago (n.s.), *Yndios de este pueblo.*

ROMERO, Rafaela *Pueblo*
bap 26 May 1779, b. 20 *de* d^{ho} *mes y año*; d/ Diego ROMERO & Magdalena ROMERO; gp/ Pablo FER^{NZ} & Rosalia RIVERA, *su* mug^{r}; *testigos*/ Domingo ROMERO & Josef MARTIN, *todos Yndios de esta mision*.

CHULETA, Josef $Fran^{co}$ Rafael *Pueblo*
bap 26 May 1779, b. 23 *de* d^{ho} *mes y año*; s/ Juan Antonio CHULETA & Luisa ORTIZ; gm/ Ysabel POBE; *testigos*/ Domingo ROMERO & Josef MARTIN, *todos Yndios de esta mission*.

COCA, Pasquala Rafaela *Vezina*
bap 26 May 1779, b. 24 *de* d^{ho}, *es u año*; d/ Miguel COCA & Maria ROMERO, *su mug.*; gp/ Andres SENA & Maria de la Luz MARTIN, *su mug.*, *todos* vez^{s} *de este pueblo*; *testigos*/ Josef DOMINGO & Agustin (n.s.), *Yndios de esta mission*.

FLORA CHACHULE, Maria Gerbasia *Pueblo*
bap 4 Jly 1779, b. 9 *de mes anterior*; (note) was kept hidden for 10 days and on 19 *de* d^{ho} *was baptized*; nat. d/ Ana FLORA CHACHULE, single, *Yndia de esta mission*; gm/ Maria Josefa RIVERA, *Yndia genizara*, nat^{l} *de* Sta *Fe*; *testigos*/ Domingo ROMERO & Juan DOMINGO, *Yndios de esta mission*.

Church visit - (signed) Fr. $Fran^{co}$ ZARTE, $Secret^{o}$

Frame 1209
MASSA, Rufina Rafaela *Pueblo*
bap 13 Jly 1779, b. 10 *de* d^{ho} *mes y año*; nat. d/ Manuela MASSA, single, *Yndia de esta mission*, & father unknown; gm/ Maria Barbara ROMERO, *vezina de* d^{ho} *pueblo*; *testigos*/ Domingo ROMERO & Josef (n.s.), *Yndios de esta mission*.

LUXAN, Anacleta Rafaela *Pueblo*
bap 17 Jly 1779, b. 14 *de* d^{ho} *mes y año*; d/ Juan Ant^{o} LUXAN & Maria Juliana MIRABAL, *Yndios de* d^{ho} *pueblo*; gm/ Maria Barbara (n.s.), *vezina de* d^{ho} *pueblo*; *testigos*/ Domingo ROMERO & Josef MARTIN, *Yndios de esta mission*.

ROMERO, Pedro Rafael *Pueblo*
bap 8 Aug 1779, b. 1 *de* d^{ho} *mes y año*; s/ Josef ROMERO & Barbara (n.s.), his legitimate wife; gm/ Cayetana ARCHULETA; *testigos*/ Domingo ROMERO & Josef MARTIN, *todos Yndios de esta* d^{ha} *mission*.

ROMERO, Josefa Rafaela *Pueblo*
bap 27 Sep 1779, b. 18 *de* d^{ho} *mes y año*; d/ Diego ROMERO & Maria DURAN, *Yndios de esta mission*; gm/ Manuela $Fran^{ca}$ (n.s.); *testigos*/ Domingo ROMERO & Josef MARTIN, *todos Yndios del pueblo*.

VILLAPANDO, Ana Maria Rafaela *Vezina*
bap 27 Sep 1779, b. 20 *de* d^{ho} *mes y año*; d/ Ant^{o} Severino VILLAPANDO & Graciana Beatriz MARTIN, *su legitima mug.*; gm/ Maria Getrude(s) GOMEZ, *todos vezinos de este pueblo*; $testig^{s}$/ Domingo ROMERO & Josef MARTIN, *Yndios del pueblo*.

LAZARO, Eustaquia Rafaela *Pueblo*
bap 27 Sep 1779, b. 20 *de* d^{ho} *mes y año*; d/ Josef Ant^{o} LAZARO & Ana Maria Rosa (n.s.), *Yndios de esta mission*; gm/ Nicolasa MARTIN, *vezina de* d^{ho} *pueblo*; *testigos*/ Domingo ROMERO & Josef MARTIN, *Yndios del pueblo*.

Frame 1210
SANDOVAL, Diego Antonio
bap 4 Oct 1779, b. 16 *del mes anterior*; s/ Josef Miguel SANDOVAL & Juana Paula de LEIBA, *vezinos de este pueblo*; gp/ Josef Maximo OROSCO & Barbara MARTIN; $testig^{s}$/ Josef MARTIN & Juan DOMINGO, *Yndios de (sic) este mission*.

DURAN, Diego Rafael *Pueblo*
bap 9 Oct 1779, b. 2 *de* d^{ho} *mes y año*; s/ Juan Ant^{o} DURAN & Maria Josefa (n.s.); gm/ Barbara GABILAN; *testig*^{s}/ Domingo ROMERO & Josef MARTIN, *todos Yndios de esta miss*^{n}.

RAMOS, Maria Rafaela *Pueblo*
bap 9 Oct 1779, b. 7 *de* d^{ho} *mes y ano*; d/ Miguel RAMOS & Josefa MARQUEZ; gm/ Rosalia RIVERA; *testig*^{s}/ Domingo ROMERO & Josef MARTIN, *todos Yndios de esta mission*.

GONZALEZ, Maria $Fran^{ca}$ Rafaela *Vezina*
bap 11 Oct 1779, b. 5 *de* d^{ho} *mes y año*; d/ Manuela GONZALEZ, *viuda*, & unknown father; gp/ Ambrosio VILLALPANDO & Micaela ROMERO, *Yndios del pueblo*, (the child) *y su* m^{e} *son vez*^{s} *mestiz*^{s}; *testigo*/ Josef MARTIN, *Yndio del pueblo*.

GOMEZ, Maria Rosa *Pueblo*
bap 24 Oct 1779, b. 15 *de* d^{ho} *mes y año*; d/ Juan GOMEZ & Magdalena (n.s.), *Yndios de esta mission*; gm/ Nicolasa ROMERO, *vezina de* d^{ho} *pueblo*; *testigos*/ Domingo ROMERO & Josef MARTIN, *Yndios del pueblo*.

ROMERO, Pedro Rafael
bap 24 Oct 1779, b. 17 *de* d^{ho} *mes y año*; s/ Josef ROMERO & $Fran^{ca}$ (n.s.), *Yndios del pueblo*; gm/ Barbara ROMERO, *vezina*; *testig*^{s}/ Domingo ROMERO & Josef MARTIN, *Yndios de esta mission*.

Frame 1211
CISNEROS, Juan Domingo
bap 3 Nov 1779, b. 23 *del mes anterior*; s/ Josefa CISNEROS, single, & unknown father; gm/ Maria Antonia (n.s.).

ROMERO, Juan Rafael
bap 6 Nov 1779, b. 27 Oct; s/ Josef ROMERO & Juana Maria GOMEZ, *Yndios del pueblo*; gp/ Juan Josef de ARGUELLO & Juaquina RODRIGUEZ, *vezinos delas Trampas de Picuries*; *testig*^{s}/ Domingo ROMERO & Josef MARTIN, *Ynd*^{s} *de este pueblo*.

GOMEZ, Juan Antonio Rafael
bap 6 Nov 1779, b. 3 *de* d^{ho} *me y año*; s/ Pablo GOMEZ & Rosalia RIVERA, *Yndios del pueblo*; gm/ Manuela (n.s.); *testigos*/ Domingo ROMERO & Josef MARTIN, *todos Yndios de esta* d^{ha} *mission*.

LUCA, Ana Rafaela
bap 6 Nov 1779, b. 3 *de* d^{ho} *mes y año*; d/ Josef LUCA & Lucia (n.s.), *Yndios de este pueblo*; gp/ $Barth^{e}$ MARTIN & Juana Cathalina MARTIN, *su hija, vez*^{s} *de este pueblo*; *testig*^{s}/ Domingo ROMERO & Josef MARTIN, *Yndios de* d^{ha} *mission*.

RIVERA, Manuel Rafael *Genizaro*
bap 20 Nov 1779, b. 11 *de* d^{ho} *mes y año*; s/ Diego (n.s.), dec., *natural de S. Yldefonso*, & Josefa RIVERA *de la villa de Sta Fe*; gm/ Maria Ant^{a} MIRABAL, single, *vezina de este pueblo*; *testig*^{s}/ Juaquin ARAGON & Juan DOMINGO.

ARMIJO, Josef Ygnacio *Vezino*
bap 20 Nov 1779, b. 15 *de* d^{ho} *mes y año*; s/ Juan Miguel ARMIJO & Maria Josefa LEIBA, *vezinos de este pueblo*; gp/ Juaquin ARAGON, *vezino delas Trampas*, & Maria Getrudes COCA, *vez*^{a} *de este pueblo*; *testigo*/ Juan DOMINGO. (Frames 1211-1212)

Frame 1212
ROMERO (gp), Juan Ant^{o} Rafael *Pueblo*
bap 21 Nov 1779, b. 8 *de* d^{ho} *mes y año*; s/ Josef $Fran^{co}$ (n.s.) & Maria Ant^{a}

(n.s.); gm/ Ana ROMERO; *testig*^{s}/ Pablo GOMEZ & Josef MARTIN, *todos Yndios de esta mission.*

ROMERO, Manuel Rafael
bap 7 Dec 1779, b. 26 *del mes anterior de d*^{ho} *año;* s/ Josef ROMERO & Cayetana REYNA, *Yndios de esta mission;* gm/ Ant^{a} Getrudes ROMERO, single, *vezina de este pueblo; testig*^{s}/ Josef MARTIN & Juan Christobal (n.s.), *Yndios de d*^{ha} *mission.*

ROMERO, Josef Rafael
bap 16 Dec 1779, b. 12 *de d*^{ho} *mes y año;* s/ Juan Christobal ROMERO & Ana ROMERO, *su legit*^{a} *muger, Yndios de esta mission;* gm/ Maria Ant^{a} BEYTA, *Española y vezina del Rio Arriba, Termino de S. Juan; testig*^{s}/ Josef MARTIN & Juan DOMINGO, *Yndios de d*^{ho} *pueblo.*

DOMINGO, Juan Ant^{o} Rafael
bap 19 Dec 1779, b. 15 *de d*^{ho} *mes y año,* "on 17th poured water on account of danger of death"; s/ Juan DOMINGO & Mª LUCERO, *Yndios del pueblo;* gm/ Lucia LUZERO (sic) on the 17th, & at the ceremony, Manuela CHINA, single; *testigos*/ Juan DOMINGO & Fran^{co} (n.s.), *todos los quales Ynd*^{s} *de esta d*^{ha} *mission.*

MARTIN, Josef Fran^{co} Rafael
bap 19 Dec 1779, b. 17 *de d*^{ho} *mes y año;* s/ Josef MARTIN & Lucia (n.s.), his legitimate wife, *Yndios de este pueblo;* gm/ Manuela FRESQUIS, single, *vezina; testig*^{s}/ Juan DOMINGO & Fran^{co} (n.s.), *Ynd*^{s} *de d*^{ha} *mission.*

Frame 1213

Año de 1780

MARTIN, Maria Josefa Rafaela *Pueblo*
bap 3 Jan 1780, b. 28 Dec '79; d/ Domingo MARTIN & Cayetana ROMERO *del pueblo;* gm/ Ysabel POBE; *testigo*/ Josef MARTIN, *son todos Yndios de d*^{ha} *mission.*

DOMINGO, Manuel Rafael *Pueblo*
bap 9 Jan 1780, b. 1 *de d*^{ho} *mes y año;* s/ Juan DOMINGO & Maria ROMERO, *su legit*^{a} *muger, Yndios de d*^{ha} *mission;* gm/ Manuela FRESQUIS, single, *Yndia, vezina de d*^{ho} *pueblo; testigo*/ Josef MARTIN, *Yndio del pueblo.*

MARTIN, Josef dela Cruz *Vezino*
bap 10 Jan 1780, b. 9 *de d*^{ho} *mes año;* s/ Salvador MARTIN, Spanish, & Ygnacia CANO, *mestiza su legitima mug*^{r}*, vezinos de este pueblo;* gp/ Josef Fran^{co} URIOSTE & his sister, Barbara URIOSTE, *solteros, tambien vezinos de d*^{ho} *y nat*^{s} *de S*^{ta} *Fe; testigo*/ Josef MARTIN, *Yndio del pueblo.*

MIRABAL, Barbara *Pueblo*
bap 25 Feb 1780, b. 12 *de d*^{ho} *mes y año;* d/ Fran^{co} (n.s.) & Maria Ant^{a} MIRABAL, *su lexit*^{a} *muger;* gm/ Rosa (n.s.), *son todos hijos de este pueblo.*

ROMERO, Maria Manuela *Vezina*
bap 25 Feb 1780, b. 3 *de d*^{ho} *mes y año;* d/ Ant^{o} Domingo ROMERO & Maria COCA, *vez*^{s} *de este pueblo;* gp/ Ant^{o} FRESQUIS & his daughter, Manuela FRESQUIS.

ROMERO, Josef *Vezino*
bap 25 Feb 1780, b. 9 *de d*^{ho} *mes y año; coyote* s/ Baltasar ROMERO & Maria Josefa (n.s.), *vez*^{s} *de este pueblo;* gf/ Santiago ZISNEROS, *fiscal ma*^{or} *del pueblo.*

Frame 1214
AZUELA (gp), Manuel Maria Rafael
bap 28 Feb 1780, ae about 2-3 yr; s/ *Gentiles dela Nacion Nataxe;* gf/ D.

Manuel dela AZUELA, *Capitan Grad° y teniente del Presidio de S Sta Fe; testigo/* Don Salvador GARZIA.

GARZIA (gp), Maria del Rosario
bap 28 Feb 1780, ae 4-5 yr; d/ *Gentiles dela Nacion Nataxe*; gf/ D. Salvador GARZIA; *testigo/* D. Manuel AZUELA.

(Fr. Tomas Salv^{or} FR^{NDZ}, who is the priest at S^{n} Lorenzo de Picuries, signing entries)
ZAMORA (gp), Juan Domingo *Yndio del pueblo*
bap 9 Mch 1780, b. 5 *del ref° mes*; s/ Juana ZAMORA, *viuda*, & unknown father; gp/ Juan Ant° LUCERO & Antonia ROMO, *Yndios del pueblo*.

PACHECO, Maria Catarina *Yndia del pueblo*
bap 9 Mch 1780, b. 6 *del ref° mes*; d/ Juan PACHECO & Maria Rosa ROMERO, *Yndios del pueblo*; gm/ Josefa (n.s.), *Yndia assimismo del pueblo*. (Frames 1214-1215)

Frame 1215
URIOSTE, Antonio Felipe *Espan^{l} vezino*
bap 11 Mch 1780, b. 10 *del ref° mes*; s/ Feliz URIOSTE & Josefa ROMERO, *Españoles y vez^{s} del pueblo*; gp/ Jose MIRABAL, *vez° del pueblo*, & Manuela ROMERO, *Yndia nativa y del pueblo*.

(Fr. Diego MUÑOZ JURADO signing entries again)
HURTADO, Maria Guadalupe *Esp^{a} y vezina*
bap 27 Mch 1780, b. 15 *de d^{ho} mes y año*; d/ Josef Ant° HURTADO & Maria PINEDA, *Esp^{s} vez^{s} de este pueblo*; gp/ Josef MARTIN, *Españ^{l} solt°, nat^{l} y vez° del Embudo*, & Rosalia MARTIN, *solt^{a} Española, nat^{l} y vez^{s} de d^{ho} pueblo*.

CISNEROS (gp), Josef Rafael
bap 14 Apr 1780, b. 6 *de d^{ho} mes y año*; nat. s/ Maria (n.s.), *soltera del pueblo*; gm/ Josefa CISNEROS, *soltera; testig^{s}/* Santiago CISNEROS & Josef Ant° (n.s.), *todos Yndios de esta d^{ha} mission*. (Frames 1215-1216)

Frame 1216
REYES (gp), Maria Rafaela
bap 14 Apr 1780, b. 8 *de d^{ho} mes y año*; d/ Salvador (n.s.) & Ana (n.s.), *su legitima mug^{r} del pueblo*; gm/ Damasia REYES; *testig^{s}/* Santiago CISNEROS & Josef Ant° (n.s.), *todos Yndios hijos de esta d^{ha} miss^{n}*.

GOMEZ, Maria Micaela
bap 17 Apr 1780, b. 13 *de d^{ho} mes y año*; d/ Pablo GOMEZ & Maria Guadalupe GONZALEZ, *vezinos de este pueblo*; gp/ Juan Miguel ATENCIO & Juan(a) Maria MARQUEZ, *su mug^{r}, tambien vez^{s} de d^{ho} pueblo; testigo/* Josef MARTIN, *Yndio del pueblo*.

DELGADO, Maria de los Dolores
bap 18 Apr 1780, b. 15 *de d^{ho} mes y año*; d/ Luis DELGADO & Micaela RUIBALA, *su legitima mug^{r}, Yndios de esta mission*; gp/ Pasqual Ant° ARAGON & Mª Getrudes COCA, *su mug^{r}, vezinos de este d^{ho} pueblo; testigos/* Josef MARTIN & Juan DOMINGO, *Yndios de d^{ha} mission*.

DOMINGO, Ana Maria
bap 2 May 1780, b. 21 *del mes anterior y d^{ho} año*; d/ Juan DOMINGO & Maria (n.s.), *Yndios del pueblo*; gm/ Ana Maria ROMERO, single, *vezina de este pueblo d^{ho}; testigo/* Josef MARTIN, *Yndio de d^{ha} mission*. (Frames 1216-1217)

Frame 1217
DOMINGO (gp), Maria Rafaela

bap 4 May 1780, b. 20 *de d^{ho} mes y año*; d/ Juan DOMINGO & Maria (n.s.), *su mug^{r}, Yndios de este d^{ho} pueblo*; gm/ Maria ROMERO, *Yndia tambien del pueblo*; *testigo*/ Josef MARTIN, *hijo de d^{ha} miss^{n}*.

TRUXILLO, Maria de la Luz *Vezina*
bap 1 Jne 1780, b. 27 *del mes anterior y d^{ho} año*; d/ Hilario TRUXILLO & Maria Encarnacion MARTIN, *Yndios vezinos de d^{ho} pueblo*; gp/ Juan Miguel MARTIN & his sister, Mª Simona MARTINA, *solt^{s} vez^{s} de d^{ho} pueblo*; *testigo*/ Josef MARTIN, *hijo de d^{ha} miss^{n}*.

(Fr. Tomas Salv^{r} FR^{NZ} signing entries)
LUJAN, Manuel Ciriaco *Yndio del pueblo*
bap 8 Aug 1780, b. 6 *del ref^{o} mes*; s/ Santiago LUJAN & Angelina (n.s.), *Yndios legitimam^{te} cassados nativos y del pueblo*; gm/ Juana Maria ROIBAL, *Yndia assi mismo nativa y del pueblo*.

CORDOVA (gp), Jose Antonio Ute Indian
bap 15 Aug 1780, about 15 yr; s/ *padres gentiles dela nacion Yuta*; gp/ Sevastian CORDOVA & his wife, Josefa DOMING^{Z}, *nativos y vezinos delas Trampas de Picuries*.

Frame 1218
FRESQUIS, Lorenza Jacinta *Yndia vez^{a}*
bap 16 Aug 1780, b. 10 *del ref^{o} mes*; d/ Maria Manuela FRESQUIS, *Yndia solt^{a} vez^{a} deeste pueblo*, & unknown father; gp/ Jose MIRABAL & his wife, Barbara ROMERO, *vezinos de este pueblo*.

SERNA, Joachin *Yndio del pueblo*
bap 20 Aug 1780, b. 16 *del ref^{o} mes*; s/ Juan Ant^{o} SERNA & Juana ROMERO, *Yndios legitimam^{te} cassados, nativos y del pueblo*; gm/ Maria VEJIL, *Yndia nativa y del pueblo*.

ACACHANA, Jose Antonio *Yndio del pueblo*
bap 7 Sep 1780, b. 4 *del ref^{o} mes*; s/ Andres ACACHANA, dec., & Fran^{ca} CHAVES, *Yndios legitimam^{te} cassados, nativos y del pueblo*; gm/ Ysabel LUJAN, *Yndia assi mismo nativa y del pueblo*.

VIATI, Fran^{co} *Yndio del pueblo*
*bap 9 Aug 1780, b. 7 *del ref^{o} mes*; s/ Lorenzo VIATI & Lucia GOMEZ, *Yndios legitimam^{te} cassados, nativos y del pueblo*; gm/ Josefa CISNEROS, *assimo Yndia, nativos y del pueblo*.

Frame 1219
PAQUEELINO, Fran^{ca} dela Cruz *Yndia del pueblo*
bap 14 Sep 1780, b. 12 *del ref^{o} mes*; d/ Juan PAQUEELINO & Maria CUENPAER, *Yndios legitamam^{te} cassados, nativos y del pueblo*; gm/ Barbara GAVILAN, *assmismo nativa y del pueblo*.

LUCERO, Juan Antonio *Yndio del pueblo*
bap 25 Sep 1780, b. 22 *del ref^{o} mes*; s/ Juan Ant^{o} LUCERO & Antonia ROMO, *Yndios legitamam^{te} cassados, nativos y del pueblo*; gm/ Juana Maria MIRABAL, *Yndia assimisma nativa y del pueblo*.

(Fr. José PALACIO signing entries)
MIRAVAL, Ygnacio Mariano *Y^{o} veci^{o}*
bap 28 Oct 1780, ae 6 da; nat. s/ Josefa MIRAVAL, *Yndia, vecina de este pueblo*; gm/ Manuela MARAVAL, *Yndia tambien de este pueblo*.

Frame 1220
LUJAN (gp), Maria delos Dolores *Y^{o} del pueblo*
bap 31 Oct 1780, ae 3 da; d/ Juan Xtoval (n.s.) & Barbara (n.s.), legitimately married *Yndios, naturales de d^{ho} pueblo*; gp/ José Ant^{o} (n.s.) & Maria LUJAN, *Yndios del pueblo y legitimam^{te} casados.*

NARANJO, José Ant^{o} *Y^{o} del pueblo*
bap 2 Nov 1780, ae 3 da; s/ Juan NARANJO & Maria JUILO, legitimately married *Yndios, naturales del pueblo*; gp/ José MIRAVAL & his niece, Rosalia MARTIN, *mestizos y vecinos del sobred^{ho} pueblo.*

LAZARO, Maria Josefa *Del pueblo*
bap 13 Nov 1780, ae 4 da; d/ Santiago LAZARO & Maria REYNA, legitimately married *y naturales del pueblo*; gm/ Maria Josefa (n.s.), *Yndia tambien del pueblo.*

Frame 1221
SAN JUAN (gp), Catarina delos Dolores *Del pueblo*
bap 20 Nov 1780, ae 3 da; d/ Juan Andres (n.s.) & Maria (n.s.), legitimately married *y nat^{s} del pueblo*; gm/ & Lucia de S^{N} JUAN, *casada con Martin José (n.s.), natur^{s} tambien del pueblo.*

TORRES (gp), Micaela delos Dolores *Criada*
bap 24 Nov 1780; d/ *Nacion Cumanche*; gf/ Antonio TORRES, single, Spanish *y vecino tambien de este pueblo.*

Frame 1222
ORTIZ (gp), José Fran^{co} *Yndio del P^{o}*
bap 25 Nov 1780, ae 3 da; nat. s/ Maria Joachina (n.s.), *Yndia viuda de este pueblo*; gm/ Rosalia ORTIZ, *casada con* José Mig^{l} (n.s.), *Yndios, naturales de este pueblo.*

SAN JUAN (gp), Juan Domingo *Yndio del P^{o}*
bap 30 Nov 1780, ae 3 da; s/ Juan Tomas (n.s.) & Juana Maria (n.s.), legitimately married *Yndios, naturales del pueblo*; gm/ Lucia de S^{N} JUAN, *casada con* Martin José (n.s.), *nat^{s} del pueblo.*

ARMENTA (gp), Nicolas Ant^{o} *Yndio del P^{o}*
bap 10 Dec 1780, b. newly born; s/ Juan Ant^{o} (n.s.) & Juana Maria (n.s.), legitimately married *Yndios del pueblo*; gp/ Miguel ARMENTA & Mª Josefa ARMENTA, *Españoles solteros y vecinos dela villa de Sta Fe.*

Frame 1223

Año de 1781

Nota: Falta una partida que hallaras al Num. 23 es de una niña vesina <u>sas hiote</u> dia 6 de Enero de 1781 a! (Entry has no name. Entries are rarely numbered and page 23 has May, June & July records. On Frame 1232 the 25 July entry at the end of the July record is the word *Nota* where the child was baptized but born 5 Jan-Maria de los Reyes).

ROMERO, Mª Rosa *Del P^{o}*
bap 12 Jan 1781, ae 3 da; d/ Diego ROM^{o} & Lucia (n.s.), legitimately married *é Yndios, nat^{s} de d^{ho} pueblo*; gp/ Juan CERNA & Mª Cecilia (n.s.), legitimately married *y nat^{s} del p^{o}.*

ROMERO, Juana *Del P^{o}*
bap 27 Feb 1781, ae 2 da; d/ Domingo ROMERO & Mª LUCERO, legitimately married *Yndios, nat^{s} del sobre d^{ho} pueblo*; gm/ M^{a} ROM^{o}, *Yndia casada del d^{ho} pueblo.*

ROMERO, Mª Josefa *Del P^{o}*
bap 12 Mch 1781, ae 4 da; d/ José ROMERO & Juana GOMEZ, legitimately married *Yndios del p^{o}*; gm/ Manuela (n.s.), *Yndia, viuda del d^{ho} pueblo.*

Frame 1224
MARTIN, M^{a} delos Dolores Yuta
bap 20 Mch 1781, ae 4 yr; d/ *Nacion Yuta*; gm/ Rosalia MARTIN, Spanish, single *y vecina de d^{ho} pueblo.*

LUJAN, Maria *Del P^{o}*
bap 6 Apr 1781, ae 3 da; d/ José LUJAN & Mª DURAN, legitimately married e *Yndios de d^{ho} p^{o}*; gm/ Josefa CISNEROS, single *y tambien Yndia del pueblo.*

(Note: There is a break in the dates.)
(Fr. Ambrosio GUERRA signing entries)
GARCIA, Rafaela *Yndia del pueblo*
bap 22 Sep (17)81; d/ Jose Antonio (n.s.) & Mª Antonia GARCIA; gm/ Ysabel GONZALEZ, *tambien Yndia del pueblo.*

Church visit - (signed) Fr. Santiago F^{RNZ} de SIERRA, *secret^{o}*

Frame 1225 (reverse side of frame 1224)
(Fr. Fran^{co} M^{RN} BUENO signing entries)
TUSA, Jose Fran^{co} *Pueblo*
bap 14 Apr 1782, b. (no da) Dec *del antepasado* (1781); s/ Juan Domingo TUSA & Maria Rosa ROMERO, *Yndios de este pueblo*; gm/ Rosalia CORTES.

SERRNA, Josef Antonio *Pueblo*
bap 14 Apr 1782, b. Dec *del antepasado*; s/ Juan Antonio SERRNA & Zecilia LUJAN *del pueblo*; gp/ Ambrosio VILLALPANDO & Micaela DEL RIO.

DEL RIO, Josef Fran^{co} *Pueblo*
bap 14 Apr 1782, b. Dec *del antepasado*; s/ Juan Domingo DEL RIO & Fran^{ca} ROMERO *del pueblo*; gm/ Manuela D^{N} JUAN.

LUJAN, Juan Domingo *Pueblo*
bap 14 Apr 1782, b. Dec *del antepasado*; s/ Lucas LUJAN & Luisa LUSERO *del pueblo*; gm/ Antonia Damasia TELLES.

CHAVES (gp), Maria de la Luz *Españo(la)*
bap *en d^{ho} dia mes y año* (14 Apr 1782), b. *en el mes de Enero en este presente año* (Jan 1782); d/ Maria Manuela (n.s.) single, Spanish; gp/ Agustin CHAVES & Rosa Getrudis de ARIAS.

LUJAN, Josefa *Pueblo*
bap *en d^{ho} dia mes y año*, b. *en el mes de Enero en este presente año*; d/ Josef Fran^{co} LUJAN & Lucia DEL RIO [*del pueblo*]; gm/ Josefa ROMERO.

ROMERO, Maria Antonia *Pueb.*
bap *en d^{ho} dia mes y año*, b. *en el mes de Enero en este presente año*; d/ Josef ROMERO & Maria GOMES; gp/ Mariano ROMERO & Fran^{ca} ARMENTA.

DURAN, Maria Fran^{ca}
bap *en d^{ho} dia mes y año*, b. *en el mes de Enero en este presente año*; d/ Fran^{co} DURAN & Micaela ROMERO; gm/ Juana ZAMORA.

GONSALES (gp), Maria de la Lus
bap *en d^{ho} dia mes y año*, b. *en el mes de Enero en este presente año*; nat. Josefa (n.s.), *soltera del puebla*; gm/ Manuela GONSALES.

ROMERO, Maria Magdalena *Pueblo*
bap *en* d^{ho} *dia mes y año*, b. *en el mes de Enero en este presente año*; d/ Juan Antonio ROMERO & Antonia ROMO; gm/ Maria REYNA.

ROMERO, Juan Domingo *Español*
bap *en* d^{ho} *dia mes y año*, b. 25 Dec *del año pasado*; s/ Salvador ROMERO & Manuela PAIS, *Españoles*; gp/ $Fran^{co}$ BENAVIDES & Ysabel PANDO.

COCA, Jose Rafael *Español*
bap 16 Apr 1782, b. 28 Mch *del referido año*; s/ Miguel COCA & Maria ROMERO, *Españoles*; gp/ Juan Antonio BARGAS (only).

MARTIN, Maria Josefa de Jesus *Española*
bap *en* d^{ho} *dia mes y año*; b. 12th *del referido mes y año*; d/ Agustin MARTIN & Margarita MANSANARES, *Españoles*; gp/ Luis Antonio BELTRAN & Juana Catalina M^{RN}.

ARAGON, Maria Manuela Española
bap 20 Apr 1782, b. 13 Apr *del referido año*; d/ Pasqual ARAGON & Ygnacia COCA, *Españoles*; gf/ Juan Lorenzo MARQUES.

Frame 1226
ROMERO, Jose Maria *Pueblo*
bap 6 May 1782, b. 7 *del pasado mes*; s/ Jose ROMERO & $Fran^{ca}$ (n.s.); gm/ Micaela DEL RIO.

LASO, Jose Antonio *Pueblo*
bap 6 May 1782, b. 1 May *de este año*; s/ Jose Antonio LASO & Ana TUSA; gm/ Manuela GAVILAN, *todos Yndios de este pueblo*.

DEL RIO, Maria Rosa *Pueblo*
bap 6 May 1782, b. 30 Apr *de este presente año*; d/ Alonso DEL RIO & Rosa Juachina (n.s.)1; gm/ Manuela Antonia (n.s.).

ROMERO, Maria Encarnacion *Pueb(lo)*
bap 6 May 1782, b. 30 Apr *del referido año*; d/ Josef $Fran^{co}$ (n.s.) & Maria Antonia ROMERO; gp/ Luis DELGADO & Josefa ZISNEROS.

GOMES, Maria de la Ascension *Vesina*
bap 20 May 1782, b. 12 *de* d^{ho} *mes y año*; d/ Pablo GOMES & Maria Guadalupe GONSALES, *vesinos de este pueblo*; gf/ Antonio FRESQUIS.

ROMERO, Juan Agustin *Vesino*
bap 30 May 1782, b. 22 *de* d^{ho} *mes y año*; s/ Ventura ROMERO & Maria Antonia MORENO, *Yndios, vesinos de este pueblo*; gf/ Hermeregildo ZISNEROS, *Españoles, vesinos de* S^{n} *Juan*.

MARTIN, Juana Rafaela (Juan Rafael in margin) *Pueblo*
bap 4 Jne 1782, b. 1 *de* d^{ho} *mes y año*; d/ Santiago M^{RN} & Maria LUJAN, *Yndios de este pueblo*; gm/ Juana ZAMORA.

ROMO, Pablo
bap 14 Jne 1782, b. 2 *de* d^{ho} *mes y año*; s/ Jose ROMO & Lucia SERRNA, *Yndios del pueblo*; gm/ Lucia D^{N} JUAN.

PUSLAPAC, Juan Antonio *Pueblo*
bap 14 Jne 1782, b. 2 *de* d^{ho} *mes y año*; s/ Josefa PUSLAPAC, *Yndia del pueblo*; gm/ Micaela DEL RIO.

Frame 1227
COCA, Antonio del Espiritu Sant(o) *Vecino*
bap 19 Jne *de(l) referido año*, b. 13 Jne 1782; s/ Maria Antonia COCA, *vesina de este pueblo*, & unknown father; gp/ Bartolome TAFOYA & Maria GOMES.

GONSALES, Salvador Raymundo *Vesino*
bap 28 *del referido mes y año*, b. 21 Jne 1782; s/ Josef Antonio GONSALES & Maria GUILCHA, *vesinos de este pueblo*; gp/ Bartolome TAFOYA & Maria GOMES.

ROMERO, Juan Manuel *Vesino*
bap 29 Jne (17)82, b. 22 *de* d^{ho} *mes y año*; s/ Julian ROMERO & Barbara M^{RN}, *vesinos de este pueb(lo)*; gf/ Adauto FRESQUIS.

MARTIN, Maria Josefa *Pueblo*
bap *de dhos dia mes y año*, b. 22 *del referido mes y año*; s/ Domingo MRN & Josefa TUSA, *Yndios del pueblo*; gm/ Cayetana REINA.

LUJAN, Rafael *Pueblo*
bap *sobre* d^{ho} *dia mes y año*, b. 23 *del referido mes y año*; s/ Juan Antonio LUJAN & Lucia LUSERO, *Yndios del pueblo*; gm/ Maria ROMERO.

ROMERO, Juan *Pueblo*
bap 22 Jly (17)82, b. 13 *de* d^{ho} *mes y año*; s/ Juan ROMERO & Mariquita (n.s.), *Yndios de este pueblo*; gm/ Lucia NARANJO.

ROMERO, Ysabel *Vesina*
bap *en* d^{ho} *dia mes y año*, b. 15 *del referido mes y año*; d/ Antonio Domingo ROMERO & Maria COCA, *vesinos*; gf/ Mariano ROMERO.

Frame 1228
ROMERO, Jose Antonio de Jesus *Vesino*
bap *en el* d^{ho} *dia mes y año*, b. 10 *del referido mes y año*;, s/ Mariano ROMERO & $Fran^{ca}$ ARMENTA; gp/ Josef MIRAVAL & Barbara ROMERO, *vesinos*.

BENAVIDES, Jose Pablo & Juan de Jesus *Vesinos*
bap *en* d^{hos} *dia mes y año*, b. 12 *del referido mes y año*; sons/ Juan BENAVIDES & Getrudis ROMERO, *vesinos de esta* mis^{n}; gp of Jose Pablo/ $Fran^{co}$ BENAVIDES & Ysabel PANDO & gp of Juan de Jesus/ Bartolome TAFOYA & Maria GOMES. (Twins not mentioned)

VACA (gp), Maria Juana *Cumancha*
bap 10 Aug 1782, ca 1 yr; d/ *Padres Ynfieles de la nacion Cumancha*; gm/ Agustina VACA.

ROMERO, Josef Mariano *Pueblo*
bap 18 Aug 1782, b. 14 *de* d^{ho} *mes y año*; s/ Domingo ROMERO & Josefa (n.s.), *Yndios del pueblo*; gp/ Antonio $FERNAND^{S}$ & Margarita ROMERO.

DEL RIO, Micaela *Pueblo*
bap 5 Sep (17)82, b. 1 *del referido mes y año*; d/ Juan Antonio DEL RIO & Anica REINA, *Yndios del pueblo*; gm/ Manuela DEL RIO.

GOMES, Maria *Pueblo*
bap 5 Sep '82, b. 1 *del referido mes y año*; d/ Lucia GOMES, single, & unknown father; gm/ Maria Antonia (n.s.).

ROMERO, Maria Antonia *Pueblo*
bap 7 *del referido mes y año*;, b. 4 *del referido mes y año*; d/ Santiago ROMERO

(written over) & Manuela (n.s.), *Yndios de este pueblo*; gp/ Josef Antonio DELGADO & Teodora (n.s.).

Frame 1229
VILLALPANDO, Salvador *Pueblo*
bap 13 Sep '82, b. 7 *de dho mes y año*; s/ Ambrosio VILLALPANDO & Micaela DEL RIO, *Yndios de este pueblo*; gp/ Julian ROMERO & Teresa GONSALES.

GOMES, Micaela *Pueblo*
bap 15 Sep '82, b. 13 *del referido mes y año*; d/ Juan Antonio Juan (sic) GOMES & Maria ROMERO, *Yndios de este pueblo*; gm/ Josefa (n.s.).

CHONGO, Josef Manuel *Pueblo*
bap 15 Sep '82, b. *el mismo dia*; s/ Juan Domingo CHONGO & Lucia (n.s.); gm/ Maria SANCHES.

LUJAN, Maria Franca *Pueblo*
bap 27 Sep '82, b. 14 *de dho, es y año*; d/ Josef LUJAN & Maria Antonia ORTIS, *Yndios de esta mision*; gm/ Manuela MIRAVAL.

JATUSE, Rosa *Pueblo*
bap 14 Oct 1782, b. 10 *de dha mes y año*; d/ Domingo JATUSE & Maria ROMERO, *Yndios de esta misn*; gm/ Manuela DEL RIO.

(Fr. Jose dela PRADA signing entries)
MIRABAL, Maria Santos *Vecina*
bap 3 Nov 1782, ae 4 da; nat. d/ Maria Rosa (MIRABAL), *soltera*, (who is) d/ Domingo MIRABAL, *Yndio vecino*; gf/ Clemente MESTAS, Spanish, *soltero, residente en este pueblo*.

Frame 1230
FULQUATTI, Maria Ysabel *Pueblo*
bap 20 Nov 1782, ae 5 da; d/ Jose Antonio FULQUATTI & Ana Maria CHULTÉ; gm/ Maria Martin PAYCHULE, *viuda, todos son Yndios del pueblo*.

FULBASENIO, Juan Thomas *Pueblo*
bap 30 Nov 1782, ae 8 da; s/ Juan Ant° FULBASENIO & Maria PAGMAJETA; gm/ Rosalia PILNÁS, wife of Juan Thomas SISTÉ, *todos son Yndios del pueblo*.

Año de 1783

SULE, Maria Margarita *Pueblo*
bap 4 Jan 1783, ae 11 da; d/ Juan Thomas SULE & Rosalia PILNAS; gm/ Josefa EBAPA, wife of Jose Franco ASLUNA, *todos Yndios del pueblo*.

PADILLA, Francisco *Vecino*
bap 18 Jan 1783, ae 12 da; s/ Jose Antonio PADILLA & Francisca Ynez BENAVIDEZ, *coyotes, vecinos de esta mision*; gp/ Franco CHINAGO & his wife, Maria Concepcion AGUYUCHE, *Yndios del pueblo de Sn Juan*.

MIRABAL, Jose Manuel *Apache adulto*
bap 6 Feb 1783 after being taught the faith, ae 26 yr old, *poco mas ó menos*; *s/ Gentiles*; gf/ Jose MIRABAL, *vecino de este pueblo*, husband of Barbara ROMERO. *Case y vele* (a) Jose Manuel was married the next day, (doesn't say to whom). (Frames 1230-1231)

Frame 1231
BOCON, Maria Anica (Maria Ana in margin) *Pueblo*
bap 28 Feb 1783, ae 7 da; d/ Santiago el BOCON & Maria PIANQUIPA; gm/ Maria PAPPAÉ, wife of Franco DURAN, *todos Yndios del pueblo*.

CHIFAYO, Esteban *Pueblo*
bap 28 Feb 1783, ae 10 da; s/ Jose Duran CHIFAYO & Manuela PASUIAO; gm/ Michaela COYO, single, daughter of Jose PACUÁ, *todos Yndios del pueblo*.

(Fr. Fran^{co} M^{RN} BUENO signing entries)
MIRAVAL, Miguel *Pueblo*
bap 10 Apr 1783, b. 24 Mch *del d^{ho} año*; s/ Fran^{co} (n.s.) & Maria Antonia MIRAVAL; gp/ Julian TALACHE & Barbara MARTIN.

ZAMORA, Anica *Pueblo*
bap *en el referido dia mes y año*, b. 20 Mch *de d^{ho} año*; d/ Jose Fran^{co} ZAMORA & Jusepa YPAPA; gm/ Lucia (n.s.).

GOMES, Juan Domingo *Pueblo*
bap 3 May 1783, b. 1 *de d^{ho} mes y año*; s/ Juan GOMES, dec., & Ysabel (n.s.), *su legitima muger, Yndios de este pueblo*; gm/ Ana Maria (n.s.).

Frame 1232
MARTIN, Catalina *Vesina*
bap 8 May 1783, b. 30 Apr *del d^{ho} año*; d/ Ynacio M^{RN} & Maria Manuela GONSALES, *vesinos de esta mis^{n}*; gm/ Juana Josefa M^{RN}.

LUCERO, Maria de la Ascencion *Pueblo*
bap 6 Jne 1783, b. 4 *de d^{ho} mes y año*; d/ Antonio LUCERO & Manuela SERRNA; gm/ Anica (n.s.) *Yndia del pueblo*.

DELGADO, Miguel *Pueblo*
bap 27 Jne, b. 24 *de d^{ho} mes y año*; s/ Luis DELGADO & Josefa ZISNEROS, *Yndios de este pueblo*; gp/ Bartolome TAFOYA & Maria GOMES.

MADRID, Juan Bartolome *Vesino*
bap *en el referido dia, mes y año*, b. 25 *del referido mes y año*; s/ Ysabel MADRID, *viuda*, & unknown father; gf/ Christoval Clemente MESTAS, Spanish.

SERRNA, Lugarda *Pueblo*
bap 25 Jly 1783, b. 21 Jly; d/ Juan Antonio SERRNA & Juana (n.s.); gp/ Bartolome TAFOYA & Maria GOMES.

PINO, Maria de los Reyes *Vesina*
Nota (See also *Nota* on Frame 1223) On 25 Jly 1783 a birth certificate was requested by Antonio Fernand^{z} PINO and Margarita ROMERO for their child, Maria de los Reyes (PINO), who they claim was born 5 Jan 1781. No such record was found registered but the parents and godfather, Jose ROMERO, *Yndio del pueblo*, and other witnesses affirmed this to be true and that she had been baptized by Fr. Jose PALACIOS and they swore by God and the Sign of the Cross.

Frame 1233
TAYALA, Josefa *Pueblo*
bap 4 Aug 1783, b. 1 Aug; d/ Juan Domingo TAYALA & Josefa (n.s.), *Yndios de este pueblo*; gm/ Lucia ORTIS.

FRESQUIS, Maria Veronica *Vesina*
bap 5 Aug 1783, b. 1 *de d^{ho} mes y año*; d/ Antonio FRESQUIS, genisaro, & Maria Ygnacia CANO, Spanish, *vesinos de esta mis^{n}*; gp/ Juan BENAVIDES & Getrudis ROMERO.

PAIS, Angelina *Pueblo*
bap 5 Aug 1783, b. 2 *de d^{ho} mes y año*; d/ Juan Domingo Juan (sic) PAIS & Micaela CUYUSULI, *Yndios del pueblo*; gm/ Angelina ROMERO, *Yndia del pueblo*.

MARQUES, Juan Miguel *Vesino*
bap 1 Oct 1783, b. 28 Sep *del año* d^{ho}; s/ Lorenso MARQUES & Maria Simona LEAL, *vesinos de este pueblo*; gp/ Juan Baptista ROMERO & Maria Clara FERNAND(E)S.

Church visit - (signed) Fr. Diego MUÑOS JURADO, *secret°*

TANE, Juan Jose *Pueblo*
bap 6 Nov 1783, b. 2 *de* d^{ho} *mes y año*; s/ Jose Manuel TANE & Maria Guadalupe QUIÚ, *Yndios del pueblo*; gf/ Juan MIRAVAL.

Frame 1234
CHAVES, Luis Manuel Narsiso *Vesino*
bap 7 Nov 1783, b. 29 Oct *del referido año*; s/ Luis Manuel CHAVES & Juana Catalina TAFOYA, *Españoles, vesinos de esta* mis^{n}; gp/ Miguel MARTIN & Lorensa BENAVIDES, *vesinos del Potrero, Jurisdicion de la villa* Sta *Crus de la Cañada*.

MARTIN, Manuel *Vesino*
bap 27 Nov 1783, b. 20 *de* d^{ho} *mes y año*; s/ Jose Miguel MARTIN & Maria Antonia ROMERO, *vesinos de esta* mis^{n}; gp/ Mariano ROMERO & $Fran^{ca}$ ARMENTA.

Año 1784

NARANJO, Juan Andres *Pueblo*
bap 7 Jan 1784, b. 3 *de* d^{ho} *mes y año*; s/ Manuela NARANJO, single, *natural del pueblo*, & unknown father; gm/ Maria Antonia ROMERO, *Yndia de este pueblo*.

SASANTIA, Maria Rosa *Pueblo*
bap 15 Jan 1784, b. 10 *de* d^{ho} *mes y año*; d/ Juan Andres SASANTIA & $Fran^{ca}$ (n.s.), *Yndios de este pueblo*; gm/ Josefa ROMERO.

ROMERO, Santiago *Pueblo*
bap 25 Feb 1784, b. 20 *de* d^{ho} *mes y año*; s/ Domingo ROMERO & Josefa ROMERO, *Yndios de este pueblo*; gm/ Maria ROMERO.

Frame 1235
ROMERO, Maria Ygnacia *Vesina*
bap 22 Mch 1784, b. 15 *del referido mes y año*; d/ Antonio Domingo ROMERO & Maria COCA, *vesinos*; gp/ $Fran^{co}$ BENAVIDES & Ysabel PACHECO.

ROMERO, Antonio Josef *Pueblo*
bap *en* d^{ho} *dia mes y año*, b. 20 *del referido mes y año*; s/ Juan Domingo ROMERO & Juana LUJAN; gp/ Antonio FERNANDES & Margarita ROMERO.

FAGILACELMEC, Ysidro *Pueblo*
bap *en el referido dia, mes y año*, ae 3 da; s/ Geronimo FAGILACELMEC & Josefa TECOA, *Yndios del pueblo*; gf/ Ysidro MONTOYA.

TUNGAYO, Santiago *Pueblo*
bap 12 Apr 1784, b. 7 *de* d^{ho} *mes y año*; s/ Juan Antonio TUNGAYO & Ana Maria CACHANA; gm/ Juana Maria MACUCHI, *todos Yndios, naturales de la referida* mis^{n}.

ROMERO, Lorenso *Pueblo*
bap 17 May 1784, b. 10 *de* d^{ho} *mes y año*; s/ Juan Antonio ROMERO & Antonia ROMA, *Yndios de este pueblo*; gm/ Maria ROMERO.

ROMERO (gp), Jose Miguel *Pueblo*
bap 17 May 1784, b. 10 *de* d^{ho} *mes y año*; s/ Jose Antonio (n.s.) & Juana Maria (n.s.), *Yndios de este pueblo*; gm/ Maria Antonia ROMERO, *muger del (illegible)*.

LUJAN, Jose Fran^{co} *Pueblo*
bap 1 Jne 1784, b. 26 May *del referido año*; s/ Jose LUJAN & Maria Antonia ORTIS; gp/ Juan Domingo LEAL & Maria Veronica CORTES. (Frames 1235-1236)

Frame 1236
TECOA, Lucia *Pueblo*
bap 1 Jne 1784, b. 26 May *del referido año*; d/ Miguel TECOA & Maria MARTIN, *Yndios de este pueblo*; gm/ Lucia NARANJO.

CHININI, Lucia Geronima *Pueblo*
bap 9 Jne 1784, b. 5 *de d^{ho} mes y año*; d/ Juan Manuel CHININI & Josefa REYNA, *Yndios de este pueblo*; gm/ Maria GUÀNÀNA.

LOMA, Fran^{ca}/Fran^{co} *Pueblo*
bap 24 Jly 1784, b. 10 *de d^{ho} mes y año*; child/ Jose LOMA & Lucia (n.s.), *Yndios de este pueblo*; gm/ Lucia GOMES. (*Una niña* then *hijo legitimo* and later *d^{ha} niña Fran^{ca}*).

ROMERO, Pedro *Pueblo*
bap 25 Jly 1784, b. 20 *de d^{hos} mes y año*; s/ Jose ROMERO & Maria GOMES, *Yndios de este pueblo*; gp/ Antonio Jose LUJAN & Juana GOMES.

NARANJO, Juan Andres *Pueblo*
bap 3 Aug 1784, b. 1 *de d^{hs} mes y año*; s/ Juan Antonio NARANJO & Manuela FRESQUIS, *Yndios del pueblo*; gm/ Maria CUIBALTEPA.

DOMINGO, Juan de Jesus *Pueblo*
bap 3 Aug 1784, b. 1 *de d^{hs} mes y año*; s/ Juan DOMINGO & Maria Rosa (n.s.), *Yndios del pueblo*; gm/ Maria GOMES.

Frame 1237
ROMERO, Maria Dolores *Vesina*
bap 29 Aug 1784, b. 25 *de d^{ho} mes y año*; d/ Mariano ROMERO & Fran^{ca} ARMENTA, *vesinos de este pueblo*; gp/ Pascual ARAGON & Maria Getrudis COCA.

LUJAN, Jose Bernardo *Pueblo*
bap 14 Sep 1784, b. 8 *de d^{ho} mes y año*; s/ Juan Antonio LUJAN & Juana Maria MIRAVAL, *Yndios del pueblo*; gm/ Maria GOMES.

DELGADO, Juana Maria *Pueblo*
bap 14 Sep 1784, b. 10 *de d^{ho} mes y año*; d/ Jose Antonio DELGADO & Ana Maria (n.s.), *Yndios de este pueblo*; gm/ Antonia Damasia (n.s.).

TAFOYA (gp), Francisca *Yndia Caygua*
bap 4 Oct 1784, ae ca 6 yr; d/ *Nacion Caygua*; gp/ Bartolome TAFOYA & Maria GOMES.

CUIALA (gp), Diego de la Consepcion *Pueblo*
bap 14 Oct 1784, b. 10 *de d^{ho} mes y año*; s/ Bernarda la Princesa (n.s.), *Yndia, viuda de este pueblo*; gm/ Fran^{ca} CUIALA, *Yndia del pueblo*.

VEGIL, Jose Fran^{co} *Vesino*
bap *en d^{hs} dia, mes y año*, b. 12 *de d^{hs} mes y año*; s/ Carlos VEJIL & Juana SANCH^{S}, *Españoles, vesinos de este pueblo y naturales de Chimayo*; gp/ Juan Felipe MARTIN & Maria Ygnacia VEJIL.

VEJIL, Juan Christoval *Pueblo*
bap 26 Nov 1784, b. 17 *de d^{hs} mes y año*; s/ Fran^{co} (n.s.), el cantor, & Manuela VEJIL, *Yndios de este pueblo*; gm/ Barbara FIAGUARPA. (Frames 1237-1238)

Frame 1238
MARTIN, Pablo Antonio *Pueblo*
bap *en d^{hs} dia, mes y año*, b. 21 *del referido mes y año*; s/ Jose M^{RN} & Lucia D^{N} JUAN, *Yndios de este pueblo*; gm/ Maria Josefa ORTIS.

PINO, Pedro Nolasco *Vesino*
bap 27 Nov 1784, b. 23 *de d^{hs} mes y año*; s/ Antonio Fern^{z} PINO & Margarita ROMERO, *vesinos de esta mis^{n}*; gp/ Bartolome TAFOYA & Maria GOMES.

GOMES, Salvador *Pueblo*
bap 30 Nov 1784, b. 23 *de d^{hs} mes y año*; s/ Juan GOMES & Maria Antonia FIASAY, *Yndios de este pueblo*; gm/ Catalina ROMERO.

ROMERO, Tomasa *Vesina*
bap 18 Dec 1784, b. 15 *de d^{hs} mes y año*; d/ Antonio ROMERO & Teresa RUIVAL, *coyotes, vesinos de esta mision*; gm/ Maria GOMES, *Yndia del pueblo*.

DOMINGO, Maria Ygnacia *Pueblo*
bap 18 Dec 1784, b. 14 *de d^{hs} mes y año*; d/ Juan DOMINGO & Mariquita QUANERA, *Yndios del pueblo*; gm/ Catalina M^{RN}.

PILNÃO, Juan Antonio *Pueblo*
bap *en los sobredichos dia, mes y año*, b. 16 *del referido mes*; s/ Juan Tomas (n.s.) & Rosalia PILNÃO, *Yndios del pueblo*; gm/ Maria Rosa YGUALPA.

ROMERO, Tomasa
bap *en dhs dia, mes y año*, b. 13 *de d^{hs} mes y año*; d/ Santiago ROMERO & Josefa (n.s.), *Yndios del pueblo*; gm/ Maria PAPAV.

Frame 1239
GAVILAN, Juan de Jesus *Pueblo*
bap 28 Dec 1784, b. 25 *del referido mes y año*; s/ Juan Andres GAVILAN & Juana Maria MACUCHI, *Yndios del pueblo*; gm/ Manuela BAJEMO.

GIELNUACHA, Micaela *Pueblo*
bap *en d^{hs} dia, mes y año*, b. 24 *de d^{hs} mes y año*; d/ Fran^{co} GIELNUACHA & Micaela (n.s.), *Yndios de este pueblo*; gf/ Fran^{co} Xaviel MESTAS.

Año 1785

JIAGUIL, Santiago *Pueblo*
bap 2 Jan 1785, b. 26 Dec *del año proxime pasado*; s/ Lucas (n.s.) & Lucia JIAGUIL, *Yndios de este pueblo*; gm/ Josefa COMPAÉ.

ROMERO, Fran^{co} *Pueblo*
bap 7 Jan 1785, b. 2 *del referido mes y año*; s/ Jose Fran^{co} (n.s.) & Maria Antonia ROMERO, *Yndios de este pueblo*; gm/ Maria PÃPÂ.

CHAGUA, Juan de Jesus *Pueblo*
bap 9 Jan 1785, b. 7 *del referido mes y año*; s/ Jose Antonio CHAGUA & Maria JUIPA, *Yndios de este pueblo*; gp/ Agustin M^{RN} & Margarita MANSANARES.

GOMES, Maria Juliana *Vesina*
bap 1 Feb 1785, b. 26 Jan *del d^{ho} año*; d/ Pablo GOMES & Maria Guadalupe GONSALES, *Yndios de esta mis^{n} y vesinos*; gp/ Miguel de S^{n} Juan MARTIN & Maria Felipa ARCHULETA, *vesinos de S^{o} Domingo de Cundiyo*.

Frame 1240
GONSALES, Juan Jose *Vesino*

bap 6 Feb 1785, b. 1 *de* d^{hs} *mes y año;* s/ Jose GONSALES & Maria JUILCHULI, *coyotes, vesinos de esta mis*^{n}; gp/ Antonio FRESQUIS & Maria Ygnacia CANO.

LEAL, Maria de Monsarrate *Vesina*
bap 20 Feb 1785, b. 10 *de* d^{hs} *mes y año;* d/ Juan Domingo LEAL & Maria Veronica CORTES, *vesinos de esta mis*^{n}; gp/ Luis Antonio BELTRAN y CHAVES & Juana Catalina TAFOYA.

MIRAVAL, Jose Antonio *Yndio de S*^{n} *Juan*
bap 6 Mch 1785, b. 2 *de* d^{hs} *mes y año;* s/ Jose (n.s.) & Maria Tomasa MIRAVAL, *Yndios de S*^{n} *Juan;* gm/ Maria Matiana ROMERO.

LEIVA, Juana Dominga *Pueblo*
bap 10 Mch 1785, b. 6 *del referido mes y año;* d/ Jose LEIVA & Rosa MIRAVAL, *Yndios de esta mis*^{n}; gm/ Anica (n.s.).

DURAN, Lucia *Pueblo*
bap 10 Mch 1785, b. 6 *del referido mes y año;* d/ Jose DURAN & Manuela (n.s.), *Yndios de este pueblo;* gm/ Getrudis ROMERO.

PACHECO, Jose Santos *Pueblo*
bap 9 Apr 1785, b. 6 *de* d^{hs} *mes y año;* s/ Juan PACHECO & Lucia (n.s.), *Yndios del pueblo;* gp/ Antonio FERNAND(E)S & Maria Clara $FERNAND^{S}$.

ACACHANA, Maria Rosa *Pueblo*
bap 11 Apr 1785, b. 7 *de* d^{hs} *mes y año;* d/ Juan Antonio (n.s.) & Maria ACACHANA, *Yndios del pueblo;* gm/ Maria Barbara ROMERO.

DOMINGO, Lucia *Pueblo*
bap 11 Apr 1785, b. 7 *de* d^{hs} *mes y año;* d/ Juan DOMINGO & Maria Getrudis TUSA; gf/ Juan MIRAVAL. (Frames 1240-1241)

Frame 1241
QUAFUENTIELME, Juana *Pueblo*
bap 20 Apr 1785, b. 15 *del referido mes y año;* d/ Santiago QUAFUENTIELME & Maria (n.s.), *Yndios de este pueblo;* gm/ Josefa CAMPAU.

PAŸS, Juan Antonio *Pueblo*
bap 5 May 1785, b. 2 *del referido mes y año;* s/ Jose PAŸS & Micaela CUYUCHULI, *Yndios del pueblo;* gm/ Juana ROMERO.

CHOLUÁ, Maria de la Ascension *Pueblo*
bap *en dho dia, mes y año;* b. *el di(c)ho dia del referido mes y año;* d/ Tomas CHOLUÁ & Josefa ACHIMUA; gm/ Micaela TUACHULPA.

PARLUNA, Ygnacia *Pueblo*
bap 7 May 1785, b. 3 *de* d^{hs} *mes y año;* d/ Jose $Fran^{co}$ (n.s.) & Maria Josefa PARLUNA, *Yndios de este pueblo;* gm/ Josefa TAGUEBAJUE.

CUYÚ, Juan Pablo *Pueblo*
bap 13 Jne, b. 8 *de* d^{hs} *mes y año;* s/ Santiago CUYÚ & $Mariq^{ta}$ (n.s.); gm/ Juana ROMERO.

DELRIO, Juana *Pueblo*
bap 13 Jne 1785, b. 9th; d/ Jose $Fran^{co}$ DELRIO & Lucia (n.s.); gm/ Maria Rosa (n.s.).

MALINCHE, Maria Ygnacia *Pueblo*
bap 25 Oct 1785, b. 20 Sep *del referido año*; d/ Jul(sic) Domingo el MALINCHE & Maria Fran^{ca} (n.s.), *Yndios del pueblo*; gp/ Felipe M^{RN} & Maria Ygnacia VEJIL.

Frame 1242
ROMERO, Maria Ygnacia Pueblo de Tesuq^{e}
bap *en d^{ho} dia, mes y año*; d/ Juan Manuel (n.s.) & Ana Maria ROMERO, *Yndios del pueblo de Tesuque*; gp/ Juan Felipe M^{RN} & Maria Ygnacia VEJIL.

PONSAY (gp), Jose Anton^{o} *Pueblo*
bap 28 Oct 1785, b. 30 Sep *del referido año*; s/ Alonso (n.s.) & Rosa (n.s.), *Yndios de este pueblo*; gm/ Lucia PONSAY.

CANBAY, Juan Anton^{o} *Pueblo*
bap *en d^{ho} dia mes y año*, b. 15 Oct *del referido año*; s/ Domingo (n.s.) & Josefa CANBAY, *Yndios del pueblo*; gm/ Manuela PAJEMAC.

TANE, Geronima *Pueblo*
bap *en el referido dia, mes y año*, b. 30 Sep *del referido año*; d/ Jose Ant. el TANE, dec., & Maria Guadalupe QUIŨ, *Yndios del pueblo*; gm/ Juana ROMERO.

COCA, Tomas *Vesino*
bap 28 Dec 1785, b. 21 *de d^{ho} mes y año*; s/ Miguel COCA & Maria ROMERO, *vecinos de esta mis^{n}*; gp/ Jose Bernardo SALASAR & Maria Gregoria SANCHES.

ACAHANA, Antonio Jose *Pueblo*
bap 29 Dec *del referido año*, b. 30 Nov *del d^{ho} año*; s/ Juan Antonio (n.s.) & Ana Maria ACAHANA, *Yndios del pueblo*; gm/ Getrudis ROMERO.

Frame 1243

Año 1786

FUILMAGIL, Maria Ygnacia Indian
bap 2 Jan 1786, b. 2 Dec *del año proximo pasado*; d/ Juan Andres FUILMAGIL & Fran^{ca} PIARLAPAPA, *Yndios del pueblo*; gm/ Barbara COCA.

FIALUCHALMA, Jose Fran^{ca} *Pueblo*
bap 7 Jan 1786, b. 4 *del referido mes y año*; s/ Juan Domingo FIALUCHALMA & Josefa (n.s.), *Yndios del pueblo*; gp/ Juan Felipe M^{RN} & Maria Ygnacia VEJIL.

FRESQUIS, Regina *Vesina*
bap 8 Jan 1786, b. 4 *del referido mes y año*; d/ Antonio FRESQUIS & Maria Ygnacia CANO, *vesinos de esta mis^{n}*; gp/ Antonio BUENO & Graciana Beatris TAFOYA.

MARTIN, Juana *Vesina*
bap 7 Feb 1786, b. 18 *del referido año*; d/ Geronimo Fran^{co} MRN & Maria Barbara COCA, *vesinos de esta mis^{n}*; gp/ Manuel COCA & Juana Calista GOMES.

CHAVES, Maria Apolonia *Vesina*
bap *en dhs dia, mes y año*, b. 15 Jan *del dho año*; d/ Manuel Antonio CHAVES & Maria Simona LEAL; gp/ Jose Maria COCA & Juana BENAVIDES.

QUITE, Maria del Carmen *Pueblo*
bap 25 Apr 1786, b. 15 Feb *del referido año*; d/ Jose QUITE & Maria Rosa LUISGUANPA, *Yndios del pueblo*; gp/ Nicolas LEAL & Ambrosia M^{RN}. (Frames 1243-1244)

ROMERO, Maria Angela *Pueblo*
bap 25 Apr 1786, b. 15 *del referido año*; d/ Juan Antonio (n.s.) & Antonia ROMERO; gm/ Ysabel VILLALPANDO. (Frames 1243-1244, 3 entries in one & faded)

ROMERO, Maria Concepcion *Pueblo*
bap 25 Apr 1786, b. 15 *del referido año*; d/ Jose Antonio ROMERO & Manuela YARQUICHULE, *Yndios del pueblo*; gm/ Maria Antonia ROMERO. (Frames 1243-1244)

Frame 1244
ROMERO, Juan de Jesus *Vesino*
bap *en dhos dia, mes y año*, b. 9 Mch *del referido año*; s/ Antonio Domingo ROMERO & Maria COCA, *Españoles de la tierra (sic)*; gp/ Miguel COCA & Maria ROMERO.

QUICHO, Antonio Jose *Pueblo*
bap *en dhos dia, mes y año*; s/ Ysabel QUICHO, wid; gm/ Rosa MIRAVAL, *Yndios del pueblo*.

COCA, Juan Antonio *Vesino*
bap 5 May 1786, b. 2 *de d^{hs} mes y año*; s/ Maria Antonia COCA, *soltera*, & unknown father; gm/ Juana ROMERO, *Yndia del pueblo*.

TUJUANA, Maria de Loreto Indian
bap 19 May 1786, b. 15 *del referido mes y año*; d/ Maria TUJUANA, *Yndia, viuda del d^{ho} pueblo*; gm/ Getrudis ROMERO.

PACHECO, Juan Pablo *Pueblo*
bap 31 Jly (17)86, b. 16 *del dho mes y año*; s/ Jose PACHECO & Lucia (n.s.); gm/ Catalina ROMERO.

MARTIN, Juan Agustin *Vesino*
bap 24 Sep 1786, b. 29 Aug *del d^{ho} año*; s/ Juan Felipe M^{RN} & Maria Ygnacia VEJIL; gp/ Juan Ygnacio VEJIL & Maria Jacinta ARAGON, *todos vesinos de esta mis^{n}*.

Frame 1245
BOYO, Paulin *Pueblo*
bap 25 Sep 1786, b. 26 Aug; s/ Domingo BOYO & Lucia (n.s.), *Yndios del pueblo*; gm/ Maria Antonia ORTIS.

DOMINGO, Jose *Pueblo*
bap 25 Sep 1786, 15 Sep *del referido año*; s/ Juan DOMINGO & Maria Rosa (n.s.), *Yndios del pueblo*; gm/ Manuela (n.s.).

CHIFAYO, Maria *Pueblo*
bap 25 Sep 1786, b. 15 Sep *del referido año*; d/ Jose CHIFAYO & Manuela (n.s.) *legitimam^{te} casados*; gm/ Lucia (n.s.).

Año de 1787

(Fr. Sant^{o} FERN^{Z} de SIERRA signing entries)
There was no priest in this church for 3½ months. (The next 9 baptisms were all in one entry, no ae given)
ZAMORA (gp), Santiago *Pueblo*
bap 11 Feb 1787; s/ Ant^{o} (n.s.) & Mª Rosa (n.s.); gm/ Juana ZAMORA.

LUJAN, Manuela *Pueblo*
bap 11 Feb 1787; d/ Ant^{o} LUJAN & Mª GAVILAN; gm/ Juana ZAMORA.

DOMINGO, Mª Ant^{a} *Pueblo*
bap 11 Feb 1787; d/ Juan DOMINGO & Maria (n.s.); gm/ J^{pha} (n.s.).

FRESQUIS, J^{ph} de la Crus *Pueblo*
bap 11 Feb 1787; s/ Manuela FRESQUIS, wid., & unknown father; gm/ Maria (n.s.).

GOMES (gp), Mª Soledad *Pueblo*
bap 11 Feb 1787; d/ Agustin (n.s.) & Mª Gertrud^{s} (n.s.); gm/ Juana GOMES.

LOMAS, Ana Mª *Pueblo*
bap 11 Feb 1787; d/ Miguel LOMAS & J^{pha} (n.s.); gf/ Simon ARMENTA.

DELGADO, Mª Victoria *Pueblo*
bap 11 Feb 1787; d/ Luis DELGADO & J^{pha} de LUMBRE; gp/ Mariano SANCHES & Mª Paula LOBATO.
The *testigos* for the above (9) baptisms were *el Govr del pueblo* (n.n.) *y el interprete* (n.n.).

(Entry with no surnames)

MIRABAL (gp), Mª Rosa *Rancho India Caigua*
bap 11 Feb 1787; d/ *Nacion Caigua*; gp/ J^{ph} MIRABAL & Mª Barb^{a} ROM^{o}; *testigo*/ J^{ph} MARTIN, *el interprete de d^{ho} pueblo*.

COCA, J^{ph} Fran^{co} *Rancho*
bap 11 Feb 1787; s/ J^{ph} Mª COCA & Juana BENAVIDES, *vecin^{s} desta jurisd^{on}*; gf/ Mariano Concepc^{n} ROMERO; *testig^{s}*/ Vicente LUJAN & Estevan MARQ^{z}.

CORTES, Ant^{o} Concepc^{on} *Rancho vecina*
bap 12 Feb 1787; s/ Man^{l} CORTES & Mª Ant^{a} MR^{TN}, *vecin^{s} desta jurisdicion*; gp/ Man^{l} COCA & Juana GOMES; *testig^{s}*/ Vicente LUJAN & Estv^{n} MARQ^{z}.

Frame 1246
DURAN, Juan Domingo *Pueblo*
bap 1 Mch 1787, ae 8 da; s/ Fran^{co} DURAN & Micaela ROM^{o}, *Yndios de d^{ho} pueblo*; gm/ Rosa (n.s.); *testig^{s}*/ *el interprete* Juan MIRABAL *y el sacristan* J^{ph} M^{RTIN}.

(Fr. Fran^{co} M^{RN} BUENO signing entries)
LASO, Jose Antonio (Juan Antonio in margin but see father) *Pueblo*
bap 22 Apr 1787, b 20 *del referido mes y año*; s/ Juan Antonio LASO & Maria Antonia CACHÊ, *Yndios del pueblo*; gm/ Juana ROMERO.

LEYVA, Ana Maria *Pueblo*
bap 22 Apr 1787; d/ Jose LEYVA & Rosa MIRAVAL, *Yndios del pueblo*; gm/ Maria ROMERO.

MARTIN, Juan Christoval *Vesino*
bap *en d^{ha} dia, mes y año*; s/ Geronimo M^{RN} & Barbara COCA; gf/ Juan Jose LOVATO, *todos vesinos del Rancho de las Trampas*.

ROMERO, Juan Pablo *Pueblo*
bap 28 May 1787, b. 27 Apr *del dho año*; s/ Jose ROMERO & Maria GOMES, *Yndios del pueblo*; gp/ Jose JUILO & Maria Rosa (n.s.).

VEJIL, Juana Teresa *Vesina*
bap *en d*^{hs} *dia, mes y año*, b. 10 May *del referido año*; d/ Carlos VEJIL & Juana de HERRERA, *vesinos de esta Jurisd*^{n}; gp/ Pasqual ARAGON & Maria Getrudis COCA.

PACHECO, Juana Manuela *Vecina*
bap 29 May 1787, b. 1 May *del referido año*; d/ Juana PACHECO & unknown father, *natural del Bosque y vesina de esta Jurisdic*^{n}; gm/ Rosa ARIAS.

Frame 1247
MARTIN, Maria Rosa *Pueblo*
bap 9 Jly 1787, b. 23 Jne *del referido año*; d/ Jose M^{RN} & Lucia (n.s.), *Yndios del pueblo*; gp/ Jose MIRAVAL & Maria Barbara ROMERO.

SUASO, Santiago *Pueblo*
bap 9 Jly 1787; s/ Jose Antonio SUASO & Maria (n.s.), *Yndios del pueblo*; gm/ Josefa (n.s.), *Yndia del pueblo*.

TECOA, Juan Pablo *Pueblo*
bap 9 Jly 1787; s/ Miguel TECOA & Maria (n.s.), *Yndios del pueblo*; gm/ Maria VEJIL.

TAU, Maria Josefa *Pueblo*
bap 25 Sep 1787, b. 20 Jly del d^{ho} año; d/ Juan Christoval TAU & Micaela (n.s.); gm/ Manuela MIRAVAL.

GONSALES, Jose Viterbo *Vec*^{o}
bap 25 Sep 1787, b. 15 Sep *del d*^{ho} *ano*; s/ Jose Antonio GONSALES & Maria JUILCHULI, *vesinos de esta jurisdicion*; gm/ Maria ROMERO.

BRITO, Rosa Mistica *Vec*^{a}
bap 25 Sep 1787, b. 18 Sep *del referido año*; d/ Fran^{co} BRITO & Margarita GONSALES; gp/ J^{n} Domingo LEAL & Josefa Veronica CORTES.

PAIS, Juan *Pueblo*
bap 25 Sep 1787, b. 20 *del referido mes y año*; s/ Ju^{n} Domingo PAIS & Micaela CUYULCHULI, *Yndios del pueblo*; gm/ Micaela GUEQUE.

Church visit - (signed) Fr. Sant^{o} FERNZ de SIERRA, secret^{o}

(Fr. Gabriel de LAGO signing entries)
VENAVIDES, Jose Fran^{co} de los Dolores *Ves*^{o}
bap 24 Oct 1787, ae 14 da; s/ Ju^{n} VENAVIDES & Mª Getrudis ROMERO, *v*^{os} *de S Fran*^{co} *delas Trampas, felig*^{s} *de esta parroq*^{a}; gp/ Domingo ROMERO & *su esp*^{a}, Josefa ROMERO, *Yndios de este pueblo*.

GONSALES, Jose Andres delos Dolores *Pueblo*
bap 30 Nov 1787, b. 29 *de d*^{ho} *mes*; s/ Sant^{o} GONS^{S} & Josefa ROMERO; gm/ Maria ROMERO, *todos hijos de este pueblo*.

Frame 1248
GOMEZ, Ju^{n} Fran^{co} delos Dolores *Yndios*
bap 2 Dec 1787, b. 4 *de 9*^{re} *en el Rancho*; s/ Pablo GOM^{Z} & Mª Guadalupe GONSALES; gp/ Jose Mar^{o} MONDRAGON & *su esp*^{a}, Mª Encarna^{on} ESPINOSA, *v*^{os}, *todos de d*^{ho} *Rancho*; *testig*^{s}/ Jose MARTIN & Fran^{co} SUASO.

ROMERO, Fran^{ca} delos Dolores *Pueblo*
bap 4 Dec 1787, b. 20 *de 9*^{re}; d/ Dom^{o} ROM^{O} & Josefa ROM^{O}, *hijos de este pueblo*; gp/ Jose ROM^{O} TALACHE & his daughter, Catalina ROMERO, *v*^{os} *del Rancho*; *t*^{os}/ Jose MARTIN & Ju^{a} MIRABAL, *ynterprete*.

CORDOVA, Jose Mig^{l} delos Dolores *Ves^{ns}*
bap 9 Dec 1787, b. 29 *de 9re en el Rancho;* s/ Margarita CORDOVA, wid., & father unknown; gp/ Jose Ant^{o} PADILLA, *hijo de este d^{ho} pueblo,* & Mª Getrudis CASAOS, *vesina de d^{ho} Rancho;* t^{os}/ Ju^{n} MIRABAL, *ynterprete,* & Jose MARTIN.

LUJAN, Mª Concep^{on} delas Dolores *Pueblo*
bap 24 Dec 1787, b. 8 *de d^{ho} mes;* d/ Ju^{n} Dom^{o} LUJAN & Mª Ant^{a} REYNA; gm/ Mª Ant^{a} ROMERO, *todos hijos del pueblo;* t^{o}/ Jose MARTIN.

MARTIN, Ant^{o} Dolores dela Concep^{on} *Rancho*
bap 26 Dec 1787, b. 8 *de d^{ho} mes;* s/ Pablo MARTIN & Mª MONDRAGON, *Esp^{s}, vesinos del Rancho;* gp/ Manuel COCA & his wife, Juana GOM^{z}, *vesin^{s} de d^{ha} Pobla^{on};* t^{os}/ Ju^{n} Felipe MARTIN & Jose MARTIN.

Año de 1788

MARTIN, M^{a} delos Dolores *Rancho*
bap 6 Jan 1788, ae (torn); d/ Gervacio MARTIN & Ana Mª CHAV^{S}; gp/ Felipe MARTIN & his wife, Mª Ygnacia VEGIL, *vesinos, todos de d^{ha} pobla(cion*-torn); *testig^{s}*/ Ju^{n} MIRABAL & Jose MARTIN. (Frames 1248-1249)

Frame 1249
LUCERO, Pablo Baltasar delos Dolores *Pueblo*
bap 9 Jan 1788, b. 6 *de d^{ho} mes;* s/ Ju^{n} Fran^{co} LUCERO & Mª Ant^{a} DEL RIO; gm/ M^{a} de S^{N} JU^{N}, *todos hijos de este pueblo;* t^{os}/ Ju^{n} MIRABAL & Jose MART^{N}.

CHAVES, Mª Candelaria delos Dolores *Rancho*
bap 10 Feb 1788, b. 1 de d^{ho} *mes en el Rancho de S^{n} Fran^{co} delas Trampas;* d/ Luys CHAV^{S} & Catalina MARTIN^{Z}, v^{os} de d^{ho} puesto; gp/ Asencio ZAMORA & his wife, Mª Teresa HURTADO, *v^{os} delas Trampas de Pecuries;* t^{o}/ Jose MARTIN, *sacrist^{n} mayor.*

PADILLA, Mª Viviana Candelaria delos Dolores *Pueblo*
bap 14 Feb 1788, b. 2 *de d^{ho} mes;* d/ Sant^{o} PADILLA & Josefa LUJAN, *hijos de este pueblo;* gp/ Ju^{n} Nepomuceno DURAN y CHAVES & his sister, Dª Mª Rosa DURAN y CHAVES, *Españoles, residentes en este pueblo;* t^{o}/ Jose MARTIN, *sacrist^{n} mayor.*

FERNANDEZ, Mª Luz delos Dolores *Rancho*
bap 17 Feb 1788, b. 15 *de d^{ho} mes en el Rancho de N. P. S^{n} Fran^{co} delas Trampas de esta Jurisd^{on};* d/ Ant^{o} FERN^{Z} & Margarita ROMERO, *Esp^{s} v^{os} d^{ho} puesto;* gp/ Ju^{n} Ant^{o} BARGAS & his wife, Mª Natividad LUJAN, *v^{os} y Esp^{s} delas Trampas de Pecuries;* t^{o}/ Jose MARTIN, *sacrist^{n} mayor.*

ROMERO, Ju^{n} Dom^{o} delos Dolores *Rancho*
bap 28 Feb 1788, *en el Rancho de N. en el Rancho de N. P. S Fran^{co} delas Trampas de esta Jurisd^{on};* s/ Ant^{o} Dom^{o} ROM^{O} & Mª COCA; gp/ Ju^{n} TORRES & his wife, Maria Getrudis BEITIA, *Españoles y vesinos, todos de d^{ho} puesto;* t^{o}/ D^{n} Ju^{n} Nepomuseno DURAN y CHAV^{S}. (Frames 1249-1250)

Frame 1250
MARTIN, Mª Dolores *Rancho*
bap 7 Mch 1788, *en el Rancho de N. en el Rancho de N. P. S^{n} Fran^{co} delas Tramp^{s};* d/ Yg^{o} MARTIN & Manuela GON^{Z}; gp/ Man^{l} CORTES & his wife, Mª Ant^{a} MARTIN, *v^{os}, todos de d^{ho} puesto; t^{s}*/ Mariano MONDRAGON y Jose MARTIN, *sacrist^{n} m^{or}.*

SUAZO, Ju^{n} Jose delos Dolores *Pueblo*
bap 26 Apr 1788, b. 3 *de d^{ho} mes;* s/ Fran^{co} SUAZO & Mª VIJIL; gm/ Josefa SUAZO,

todos Yndios de este d^{ho} pueblo; t^{os}/ Jose Ant^{o} ARCHULETA, *Yndio de S^{n} Ju^{n}*, & Jose MARTIN, *sacrist^{n} ma^{or}*.

ALONSO, Jose Rafael delos Dolores *Pueblo*
bap 26 Apr (17)88, b. 18 *de d^{ho} mes;* s/ Ju^{n} Man^{l} de ALONSO & Josefa ROMERO; gm/ Getrudis REYNA, *todos hijos de este pueblo.*

DURAN, Pablo delos Dolores *Pueblo*
bap 26 Apr '88, b. 12 *de d^{ho} mes;* s/ Fran^{co} DURAN & Micaela ROM^{O}; gm/ Ju^{a} Mª MIRABAL, *todos hijos de este pueblo.*

ROMERO, Juan Jose de los Dolores *Pueblo*
bap 26 Apr 1788, b. 8 *de este d^{ho} mes;* s/ Ant^{o} ROMERO & Teresa RUYBAL, *hijos de este d^{ho} pueblo;* gp/ Ju^{n} Jose LOBATO & his sister, Rafaela Barvara LOBATO, *v^{os} de esta Jurisd^{on} y resident^{s} eneste d^{ho} pueblo; testi^{os}*/ Jose Ant^{o} ARCHULETA & Jose MART^{N}, *sacrist^{n} maior.*

ARCHULETA, Fran^{co} Esteban delos Dolor^{s} *Pueblo*
bap 26 Apr 1788, b. 23 *de este d^{ho} mes en el Rancho dela advoca^{on} de N. P. S Fran^{co} delas Trampas;* s/ Jose Ant^{o} ARCHULETA & Tomasa MIRABAL, *hijos del pueblo;* gf/ Ju^{n} Jose CASTILLO *del mismo pueblo; test^{os}*/ Ju^{n} Jose LOBATO & Jose MART^{N}.

No May baptisms. Frame 1251 is the reverse side of 1250.

Frame 1251
LEAL, M^{a} delos Dolores *Vesina*
bap 5 Jne 1788, b. 1 *de d^{ho} mes en el Rancho;* d/ Ju^{n} Dom^{o} LEAL & Mª CORTES; gp/ Salv^{or} Man^{l} MARTIN *y su sobrina,* Mª Manuela delos Reyes DELGADO, *vesinos de d^{ho} pueblo.*

ROMERO, Mª Manuela delos Dolores *V^{a}*
bap 13 Jne 1788, b. 7 *de d^{ho} mes en el Rancho;* d/ Mariano ROM^{O} & Fran^{ca} ARMENTA, *v^{os} de d^{ho} puesto;* gp/ Ju^{n} Ant^{o} SANDOBAL, *ves^{o} del Quemado,* & Ju^{a} Nepomucen$\underline{o}$ DURAN y CHAV^{S}.

ROMERO, Mig^{l} delos Dolor^{s} *Pueblo*
bap 26 Jne 1788, ae 6 da; s/ Ju^{n} Andres ROM^{O} & Mª Concep^{n} (n.s.); gm/ Lucia LUCERO, *todos Yndios de este pueblo.*

LISTON, Juana M^{a} delos Dolor^{s} *Pueblo*
bap 26 Jne 1788, ae 6 da; d/ Ju^{n} D^{o} LISTON & Josefa PAIS; gm/ Rosa MIRABAL, *Yndios de este pueblo.*

ROMERO, Fran^{co} delos Dolores *Pueblo*
bap 28 Jne (17)88, b. 10 *d^{ho} mes;* s/ Ju^{n} Ant^{o} ROM^{O} & Ant^{a} GOMA, *Yndios de este pueblo;* gm/ Mª Matiana ROM^{O}, *vesina del Rancho.*

ROMERO, Ju^{n} Martin delos Dolor^{s} *Pueblo*
bap 30 Jne '88, ae 21 da; s/ Geronimo ROM^{O} & Josefa TECOA; gm/ Angela ROM^{O}, *todos Yndios de este pueblo.*

DELGADO, Mª Paula delos Dolores *Pueblo*
bap 13 Jly 1788, ae 12 da; d/ Jose Ant^{o} DELGADO & Ana Mª ORTIS, *Yndios de este pueblo;* gp/ Ramon MESTAS & Rosalia MARTIN, *Españoles.*

Frame 1252
VEJIL (patron), M^{a} delos Dolores *Yndia Caigua - Rancho*
bap 13 Aug 1788, ca 11 yr; d/ *Caiguas,* under the patronage of D^{n} Christov^{l}

VEJIL, *vezino del Rancho*; gp/ D^{n} Ju^{n} Viz^{te} MONTAÑO & *su esposa*, Dª Mª Rosa DURAN y CHAVES, *que al presente residen en esta Jurisd^{on}*. "Instructed in the faith... and found ready to receive the sacraments."

LASO, Mª Fran^{ca} dlos (sic) Dolores *Pueblo*
bap 3 Aug '88, ae 10 da; d/ Mathias LASO & Guadalupe MART^{N}; gm/ Fran^{ca} DURAN, *todos Yndios del pueblo*.

LUCERO, Jose Bernardo delos Dolores *Pueblo*
bap 4 Aug '88, b. 21 Jly; s/ Ant^{o} LUCERO & Angela ROM^{o}, *Yndios del pueblo*; gp/ Mig^{1} Mar^{o} SANCH^{z} & his wife, Paula LOBATO, *Esp^{s} que reciden en este pueblo*.

ROMERO, Ana M^{a} delos Dolores *Pueblo*
bap 4 Aug '88, ae 10 da; d/ Viz^{te} ROMERO & Michaela SUAZO, *Yndios del pueblo*; gp/ Mig^{1} Man^{1} SANCHEZ & his wife, Paula LOBATO, *Españ^{s}*.

DEL RIO, Jose Pablo delos Dolores *Pueblo*
bap 24 Sep 1788, ae 13 da; s/ Sant^{o} DEL RIO & Rosa ROMERO, *Yndios de este pueblo*; gp/ Simon ARMENTA & Margarita MARTIN, *vesinos de este pueblo, Españ^{s}*.

FRESQUIS, Ju^{n} Nepomuzeno (Ju^{n} Nepomuzeno delos Dolores in margin) *Vezino*
bap en d^{ho} dia 4 Sep (17)88, ae 15 da; s/ Ant^{o} FRESQUIS & Ygn^{a} GONS^{s}; gm/ Mariana LISTON, *v^{os}, todos del Rancho*. (Frames 1252-1253)

Frame 1253
LEAL, Mª Guadalupe delos Dolores *Vezina*
bap 24 Sep (17)88, ae 4 da; d/ Man^{1} LEAL & Mª QUINTANA; gp/ Jose Man^{1} MONDRAGON & his wife, Encarna^{on} ESPINOSA, todos v^{os} del Rancho.

GUIPAT, Ju^{a} Catalina delos Dolores *Pueblo*
bap 24 Sep '88, ae 8 da; d/ Sant^{o} GUIPAT & Maria (n.s.); gm/ Lucia ORTIS, *todos Yndios del pueblo*.

RIGUANA, Angela delos Dolores *Pueblo*
bap 24 Sep '88, b. *en el pueblo* 18 *de d^{ho} mes*; d/ Ju^{n} Dom^{o} RIGUANA & Maria (n.s.); gm/ Getrudis ROMERO, *todos del d^{ho} pueblo*.

JUILU, Mª Ant^{a} delos Dolores *Pueblo*
bap 24 Sep '88, b. 22 *del pasado*; d/ Jose JUILU & Rosa (n.s.); gm/ Mª Ant^{a} (n.s.), *todos del mismo pueblo*.

MARTIN, Mª Manuela delos Dolores *Rancho*
bap 12 Oct 1788, b. 10 *de d^{ho} mes en el Rancho, de este Jurisd^{on}*; d/ Jose Ant^{o} MARTIN & Mª Getrudis GALVES; gp/ Jose Mª CHAVES & Rosa ARIAS, *todos del mismo puesto*.

SANCHEZ, Mª Concep^{on} delos Dolores *Pueblo, Esp^{a}*
bap 12 Oct 1788, b. 4 *de d^{ho} mes en este pueblo*; d/ Mig^{1} SANCHEZ & Paula LOBATO; gp/ D^{n} Ant^{o} LOBATO, *alcalde de esta Jurisdicion de Taos, y su esp^{a}*, Margarita MARTIN, *vesinos, todos de esta Jurisd^{on}*.

Frame 1254
MARTIN, Diego Ant^{o} delos Dolores *Rancho*
bap 27 Nov 1788, b. 12 *de d^{ho} mes en el Rancho de N. P. S. Fran^{co} delas Trampas de Taos*; s/ Ju^{n} Phelipe MARTIN & Maria Ygnacia VEGIL; gp/ Ju^{n} Nepomuzeno DURAN y CHAVES & *su esp^{a}, D^{a} M^{a}* Clara SANCHEZ, *ves^{s} de d^{ho} puesto, Españoles*.

MARTIN, Fran^{co} Santos delos Dolores *Rancho Ves^{o}*
bap 30 Dec '88, 1 *de d^{ho} mes en el Rancho de esta Jurisd^{on}*; s/ Geronimo MARTIN & Barvara COCA, *v^{os} de d^{ho} puesto*; gp/ Mig^{l} SANCH^{Z} & *su esp^{a}*, Paula LOVATO, *v^{os} de este pueblo, Esp^{s}*.

MARTIN, Mig^{l} Ang^{l} delos Dolores *Rancho ves^{o}*
bap 30 (sic) Nov '88, b. 24 *de d^{ho} mes en el puesto del Rancho*; s/ Pablo MARTIN & Catalina MONDRAGON, *Esp^{s}*; gp/ Ant^{o} FRESQ^{S}, *v^{o} de d^{ho} puesto*, & his daughter, Manuela FRESQ^{S}, *hija de este pueblo*.

LOMA, Barv^{a} Rosalia delos Dolor^{s} *Pueblo*
*bap 29 Dec 1788, b. 3 *de d^{ho} mes en este pueblo*; d/ Martin LOMA & Micaela DEL RIO; gm/ Rosalia LOMA, *hijos del pueblo*.

VEGIL, Mª Manuela delos Dolores *Rancho*
bap 29 Dec '88, b. 24 *de d^{ho} mes en el Rancho de esta Jurisd^{on}*; d/ Ju^{n} dela Cruz VEGIL & Mª Clara FERN^{Z}, *ves^{s} de d^{ho} Rancho*; gf/ Asencio ZAMORA, *ves^{o} delas Trampas de Pecuries*.

(Note: No Jan or Feb entries).

Año de 1789

MONDRAGON, Man^{l} Ant^{o} delos Dolores *Rancho*
bap 8 Mch 1789, b. 28 Feb *en el Rancho de d^{ha} Jurisd^{on}*; s/ Mariano MONDRAGON & Mª Encarna^{on} ESPINOSA; gp/ Ant^{o} Dom^{o} ROMERO *y su esp^{a}*, Mª COCA, *todos ve^{os} de d^{ho} puesto*.

Frame 1255

ROMERO, Mª Juliana delos Dolores *Rancho*
bap 8 Mch 1789, b. 15 Jan *en la Pobla^{on} del Rancho de esta Jurisd^{on}*; d/ Ju^{n} ROMERO & Juana Agustina MARTIN; gp/ Jose VEGIL & his wife, Petra de Jesus ROJO, *todos ves^{s} de d^{ha} Pobla^{on}*.

ROMERO, Ju^{n} Andres delos Dolores *Pueblo*
bap 8 Mch 1789, b. 11 Feb *en este pueblo*; s/ Jose ROM^{O} & M^{a} GOM^{Z}; gp/ Andres GAVILAN & his wife, Maria ROM^{O}, *todos hijos de este d^{ho} pueblo*.

ROMERO, Mª Manuela delos Dolores *R^{cho}*
bap 8 Mch 1789, b. 27 Feb *en la Pobla^{on} del Rancho de esta Jurisd^{on}*; d/ Concep^{on} ROM^{O} & Mª Rosa QUINTANA; gp/ Ju^{n} Phelipe MART^{N} & his wife, Mª Ygn(a)cia (blot) VEGIL, *ves^{s}, todos de d^{ha} Pobla^{on}*.

FRESQUIS, M^{a} dela Luz delos Dolores *Rcho*
bap 8 Mch 1789, b. 14 Feb *en la Pobla^{on} del Rancho de esta Jurisid^{on}*; d/ Ju^{n} Lor^{o} FRESQUIS & Mª Ant^{a} GONZ^{S}; gf/ Domingo MIRABAL, *ves^{s}, todos de d^{ha} Pobla^{on}*.

SANCHES (gp), Mª Ju^{a} Guadalupe delos Dolores *Pueblo*
bap 8 Mch 1789, b. 8 Feb *en este d^{ho} pueblo en casa del Alc^{e} mayor de esta d^{ha} Jurisd^{on}*; d/ *Nacion A*; gp/ Mig^{l} SANCHES & his wife, Mª Paula LOVATO, *vesinos en d^{ho} pueblo*.

DEL RIO, Ju^{n} Ant^{o} delos Dolores *Pueblo*
bap 8 Mch 1789, b. 26 Jan *en este pueblo*; s/ Ju^{n} Dom^{o} DEL RIO & Fran^{ca} LUCERO; gm/ Mª Rosa LUCERO, *todos hijos de este d^{ho} pueblo*.

LUCA, Jose Antonio delos Dolores *Pueblo*
bap 8 Mch 1789, b. 3 *de este mes en este pueblo*; s/ Ju^{n} Andres LUCA & Ju^{a} Maria PECURINA; gm/ Josefa LUCERO, *todos hijos de este d^{ho} pueblo*.

Frame 1256 (Top of this entry is torn)
DURAN, Gregorio delos Dolores *Esp^{l}*
bap (torn); s/ Yg^{o} DURAN & Mª Ant^{a} SANC(HES-torn); gp/ Ju^{n} Nepomuceno (n.s.-torn) & *su esp^{a}*, Mª Clara SANCHES, *ves^{s} de d^{ho} puesto*.

CORTES, Ju^{n} Pedro delos Dolores *Rancho*
bap 26 Apr 1789, b. 15 *de d^{ho} mes enla pobla^{on} del Rancho*; nat. s/ Mª Fran^{ca} CORTES & unknown father; gp/ Ju^{n} Cristov^{l} CORTES & his stepmother, Mª Ant^{a} ROM^{o}, *vesinos de d^{ha} Pobla^{on}*.

LOMA, Ygnacia delos Dolores Indian
bap 27 Apr 1789, b. 9 Mch *en este pueblo*; d/ Mig^{l} LOMA & Lucia GOM^{z}; gm/ Josefa LUCERO, *todos de deste pueblo*.

MARTIN, Ju^{n} Dom^{o} delos Dolores *Pueblo*
bap 27 Apr 1789, b. 18 Apr; s/ Jose Ant^{o} MART^{N} & Ju^{a} Mª MIRABAL, *naturales de d^{ho} pueblo*; gm/ Ju^{a} M^{a} ROM^{o}, wid., *vesina del Rancho*.

CAÀN, Fran^{ca} delos Dolores *Pueblo*
bap 27 Apr 1789, b. 18 *de este d^{ho} mes en este pueblo*; nat. d/ Bernarda CAÀN alias Princesa, wid; gm/ Angelina CHUÌPAFUÈ, *todos naturales de este d^{ho} pueblo*.

LUJAN, Jose Ant^{o} delos Dolores *Pueblo*
bap 27 Apr 1789, b. 12 Mch *en este pueblo*; nat. s/ Ant^{o} Jose LUJAN alias Malinche, *Yndio de este pueblo*, married, & (the mother is) Tomasa (n.s.), *Yndia Jentil de nacion A*, who has been *criada* of his father, Julian LUJAN, for a year and 3 mo; gm/ Teresa RUYBAL, *Yndia de este d^{ho} pueblo*.

(Entry with no surnames because the top of the next frame is torn). (Frames 1256-1257)

Frame 1257
BUENO PANDO, Feliz de los Dolores *V^{o}*
bap 27 Apr 1789, b. 24 *de d^{ho} mes en el Rancho*; s/ Ant^{o} BUENO PANDO & Graciana MARTIN, *vezinos de Condillo Jurisd^{on} dela villa dela Cañada*; gp/ Jacinto PINEDA & his grandmother, Nicolasa ROMERO, *vezinos de d^{ho} Rancho*.

CORTES, Salvador Man^{l} delos Dolores *Rancho V^{o}*
bap 9 May 1789, b. 18 Apr *en el Rancho*; s/ Juan Cruz CORTES & Ju^{a} MONTOYA, *vesinos de d^{ho} puesto*; gp/ Ju^{n} Ant^{o} SANDOBAL & *su esp^{a}*, Mª Josefa ROM^{o}, *v^{os} del pueblo de Quemado*.

CORTES, Jose Fran^{co} delos Dolores *R^{cho} V^{o}*
bap 27 May 1789, b. 25 Apr *en el Rancho*; s/ Man^{l} CORTES & Mª Ant^{a} MART^{N}; gp/ Ant^{o} FERN^{Z} & his daughter, Mª Nicomedes (FERNANDEZ), *v^{os}, todos de d^{ha} Pobla^{on}*.

LUJAN, Sant^{o} delos Dolores *Pueblo*
bap 27 May '89, b. *d^{ho} dia*; s/ Ant^{o} Jose LUJAN & Ju^{a} GOM^{z}; gp/ Fran^{co} ROM^{o} & his mother, Ju^{a} ZAMORA, *todos naturales de este pueblo*.

SANCHEZ (gp), Felipe Sant^{o} delos Dolores *Pueblo*
bap 28 May 1789, ae ca 4 yr more or less; s/ *Nacion Aa*; gp/ Mig^{l} SANCHEZ & his wife, Mª Paula LOVATO, *v^{os} de este pueblo*.

CAIGUA, Diego delos Dolores *Pueblo*
bap 30 May 1789, b. 18 *de este mes en este pueblo*; s/ Jose Man^{l} CAIGUA & Mª Getrudis ROM^{o}; gp/ Fran^{co} SUASO & *su mug^{r}*, Mª VEGIL, *todos de este puesto*.

Frame 1258

CHIMAYO, Ju^{a} M^{a} delos Dolores *Pueblo*
bap 30 May 1789, b. 28 *de d^{ho} mes en este pueblo*; d/ Pedro CHIMAYO & Mª Guadalupe (n.s.); gm/ Micaela LUCERO, *todos de d^{ho} pueblo*.

GONSALES, Mª Manuela delos Dolores *Rcho*
bap 9 Jne 1789, b. 22 May *en el Rancho*; d/ Jose Mig^{l} GONS^{S} & Victoria MARTIN, *v^{os} de d^{ho} puesto*; gp/ Jose Baltasar LOBATO & Marg^{ta} OLGUIN.

MARTINEZ, Man^{l} Dolores de Jesus *Pueblo v^{a}*
bap 18 Jne 1789, b. 14 May *en el Rancho*; d/ Jose Mig^{l} MARTIN^{Z} & Mª Ant^{a} VENAVIDES, *v^{os} del pueblo Quemado*; gp/ Pedro CORTES & Mª Ant^{a} ROM^{O}, *ve$\underline{c}^{s}$ del Rancho*.

LEYBA, Dom^{o} Ant^{o} delos Dolores *Pueblo*
bap 20 Jne 1789, b. 31 May *en el pueblo*; s/ Jose LEYBA & Rosa MIRABAL; gm/ Mª Ant^{a} LUJAN, *todos de este pueblo*.

LUCERO, Fran^{co} delos Dolores *Pueblo*
bap 7 Jly 1789, b. 4 *de d^{ho} mes en este pueblo*; s/ Jose Ant^{o} LUCERO (written over) & Manuela ZERNA; gm/ Ju^{a} PAN^{O}, *todos de este pueblo*.

LUJAN, Ju^{a} M^{a} delos Dolores *Pueb^{o}*
bap 9 Aug 1789, b. 26 Jly *en el pueblo*; d/ Sant^{o} LUJAN & Mª GAVILAN, *hijos de este d^{ho} pueblo*; gp/ Lorenso LOBATO & his wife, Mª ARMIJO, *ves^{s} de d^{ho} pueblo*.

DURAN, Sant^{o} delos Dolores *Pueblo*
bap 9 Aug 1789, b. 29 Jly *en el pueblo*; s/ Fran^{co} DURAN & Micaela ROM^{O}; gm/ Mª Rosa ROM^{O}, *todos de d^{ho} pueblo*.

GONZALES, Ju^{n} Ant^{o} delos Dolor^{s} *Pueblo*
bap 9 Aug 1789, b. 5 *de d^{ho} mes en este pueblo*; s/ Sant^{o} GONZ^{S} & Josefa ROM^{O}; gm/ Josefa ROM^{O}, *todos del pueblo*.

Frame 1259

FULGUIS, M^{a} delos Dolores *Pueblo*
bap 9 Aug 1789, b. 8 *de d^{ho} mes* in the pueblo; d/ Viz^{te} FULGUIS & Micaela SUASO; gm/ Mariquita ROM^{O}, *todos del pueblo*.

CHAVES, Man^{l} delos Dolores *Rcho*
bap 11 Sep 1789, b. 28 Aug in the Rancho; s/ Man^{l} CHAVES & Simona LEAL; gp/ Ant^{o} FRESQUIS, *v^{o} de d^{ho} puesto*, & his daughter, Manuela (FRESQUIS), of this pueblo.

ROMERO, Ju$\underline{^{n}}$ Bue$\underline{n}$aventura delos Dolores *Pueblo Yndio*
bap 11 Sep 1789, b. 26 Aug in this pueblo; s/ Ju$\underline{^{n}}$ Ant^{o} ROM^{O} & Catalina CHULA, *todos del pueblo*; gp/ Ju^{n} Bap^{ta} MARTIN & his wife, Nicolasa TRUJILLO, *v^{os} de d^{ho} pueblo*.

GONZALES, Fran^{co} Ant^{o} delos Dolores *Rcho*
bap 1 Oct 1789, b. 19 Sep in *el Rancho*; s/ Jose Ant^{o} GONZ^{S} & M^{a} ROM^{O}; gp/ Pedro CORTES & his wife, Mª Ant^{a} ROMERO, *v^{os} de d^{ho} puesto*.

VEGIL, Mª Micaela delos Dolores *Rcho*
bap 1 Oct 1789, b. 29 Sep in *el Rancho*; d/ Jose VEGIL & Petrona ROJO; gp/ Ju^{n} Yg^{o} VEGIL & his wife, Mª Jacinta ARAGON, *v^{os}, todos de d^{ho} puesto*.

PAIS, Yg^{o} Ant^{o} delos Dolores *Pueblo*
bap 1 Oct 1789 in this pueblo; s/ Ju^{n} Ant^{o} PAIS & Ana SANCHES; gm/ Mª Ant^{a} ZAMORA, *todos naturales de este pueblo.*

BRITO, Fran^{co} delos Dolores *Pueb^{o}*
bap 2 Nov 1789, b. 4 Oct in this pueblo; s/ Fran^{co} BRITO & Marg^{ta} GONZ^{S}, *v^{os} de d^{ho} pueblo;* gp/ Jose Ant^{o} MARTIN & his wife, Mª Ygnes LEAL, *v^{os} del Rancho.*

VEGIL, Mª Josefa delos Dolores *Rcho vesina*
bap 2 Nov 1789, b. 30 Oct in *el Rancho;* d/ Marcelino VEGIL & Mª Micaela MART^{N}; gp/ Ju^{n} BENAVIDES & his wife, Mª Getrudis ROMERO, *v^{os}, todos de d^{ha} Pobla^{on}.* (Frames 1259-1260)

Frame 1260
JUILU, Ju^{n} Andres delos Dolores *Pueblo Yndio*
bap 2 Nov 1789, b. 19 Oct in this pueblo; s/ Ju^{n} Cristov^{l} JUILU & Ju^{a} LUJAN; gm/ Ju^{a} ROM^{O}, *todos naturales de este pueblo.*

LUJAN, Esteban delos Dolores *Pueblo*
bap 2 Nov 1789, ae 8 da; s/ Juan Ant^{o} LUJAN & Ju^{a} Maria ROMERO; gm/ Ant^{a} ROMERO, *todos de d^{ho} pueblo.*

Año de 1790

VEGIL (gp), Jose Ermenegildo delos Dolores
bap 25 Jan 1790, b. 5 Dec in *el Rancho;* s/ unknown; gp/ Carlos VEGIL & his wife, Ju^{a} Mª SANCH^{Z}, *v^{os}, todos de d^{ha} Pobla^{on}.*

LUCERO, Jose Pablo delos Dolores *Pueblo Yndio*
bap 25 Jan 1790, b. 29 Dec in this pueblo; s/ Ju^{n} Dom^{o} LUCERO & Mª Jetrudis ROMERO, Indians of said pueblo; gp/ Ant^{o} FERN^{Z} & his wife, Marg^{ta} ROM^{O}, *v^{os} de(l) Rancho.*

GONZALEZ, Jose Santos delos Dolores *Pueblo Yndios*
bap 25 Jan 1790, b. 18 Dec in this pueblo; s/ Dom^{o} GONZ^{Z} & Josefa ROM^{O}; gp/ Jose ROM^{O} & Mª GONZ^{Z}, Indians of said pueblo.

CAÓ, Paulin delos Dolores *Pueblo*
bap 25 Jan 1790, b. 21 Dec; s/ Jose Ant^{o} CAÓ & Mª Josefa LUCERO; gp/ Mª Ant^{a} RYO, all Indians of the pueblo.

Frame 1261
COCA, Mª Rosa delos Dolores *Rcho ves^{a}*
bap 25 Jan 1790, b. 10 *de este mes* in el Rancho; d/ Man^{l} COCA & M^{a} Ju^{a} GOM^{Z}; gp/ Jose Ant^{o} MART^{N} & his wife, Ygnes LEAL, *ves^{s} del R^{cho}.*

GONZALEZ, Mª Reyes delos Dolores *Rcho ves^{a}*
bap 25 Jan 1790, b. 6 *de este mes en el Rancho;* d/ Jose Santos GON^{Z} & Mª LISTON, *ves^{s} de d^{ha} Pobla^{on};* gp/ Ju^{n} Dom^{o} ROM^{O} & his mother, Manuela DEL RYO, Indians of this pueblo.

ROMERO, Ant^{a} Rosa delos Dolores *Pueblo Ynd^{a}*
bap 25 Jan 1790, b. 28 Dec; d/ Ju^{n} Dom^{o} ROM^{O} & Mª NARANJO; gp/ Fran^{ca} LUCERO, all of said pueblo.

ROMERO, Mª Rosa delos Dolores *Rcho vez^{a}*
bap 10 Feb 1790, b. 7 *de este mes* in *el Rancho;* d/ Mariano ROM^{O} & Fran^{ca} ARM^{TA}; gp/ D^{n} Ju^{n} Ygnacio SANCH^{S} & his wife, Pascuala VEGIL, residents of this settlement.

LOVATO (gp), Jose Fran^{co} delos Dolores *Pueblo Na^{on} Aa - vez^{s}*
bap 11 Feb 1790, ae 7 yr *mas ó menos*; s/ *Nacion Aa*; gp/ Ant^{o} Jose LOVATO & *su (h)erm^{a}*, Mª Paula LOVATO, *resid^{s} en este pueblo*.

ROMERO (gp), Mª Dolores *Rcho - vez^{a}, Na^{on} Aa*
bap 11 Feb 1790, ae 7 yr & a few mo; d/ *Nacion Aa*; gf/ Ant^{o} Concep^{on} ROM^{o}, *ves^{o} del Rancho*.

LOMA, Ju^{o} delos Dolores *Pueblo*
bap 11 Feb 1790, b. 29 Jan in this pueblo; s/ Ju^{n} Cristov^{l} LOMA & Mª Ant^{a} GOM^{z}; gp/ Mª Rosa MARQ^{z}, all of the pueblo.

CONCHA, Mª Encarna^{n} delos Dolores *Pueblo*
bap 11 Feb 1790, b. 28 Jan in this pueblo; d/ Ju^{n} Dom^{o} CONCHA & Mª Rosa LUJAN; gp/ Fran^{ca} LUCERO, all of this pueblo.

(Note: No Mch or Apr baptisms).

Frame 1262
CORTES, Ju^{n} Nepomuceno Encarna^{on} delos Dolores *Rancho*
bap 9 May 1790, b. 25 Mch in *el Rancho*; s/ Ju^{n} Cruz CORTES & Mª Luz MONTOYA; gp/ D^{n} Ju^{n} Nepomuceno DURAN y CHAVES & *su esposa*, Mª Clara SANCH^{z}, *todos vez^{s} de d^{ho} Rancho*.

COCA, M^{a} del Rossario delos Dolores *Rcho vez^{s}*
bap 9 May 1790, b. 13 Apr *en la Poblacion del Rancho*; d/ Jose Mª COCA & Ju^{a} VENAVIDES; gp/ Tomas HURIOSTE & his sister, Mª Concep^{on} (HURIOSTE), all of the said settlement.

DURAN, Ju^{a} M^{a} delos Dolores *Pueblo Yndia*
bap 9 May 1790, b. 4 Apr in this pueblo; d/ Ju^{n} DURAN & Barvara MARTIN, *naturales del pueblo*; gp/ Pablo GOM^{z} & his wife, Mª Guadalupe GON^{z}, *vez^{s} del Rancho*.

DEL RYO, Man^{l} Gregorio delos Dolores *Pueblo Yndio*
bap 10 May 1790, b. 2 Apr in this pueblo; s/ Sant^{o} DEL RYO & Mª Rosa ROM^{o}, *Yndios del pueblo*; gp/ Carlos VEGIL & his wife, Ju^{a} SANCH^{z}, *vez^{s} del Rancho*.

ROMERO, Buenaventura delos Dolores *Pueblo Yndia*
bap 10 May 1790, b. 14 Apr in this pueblo; s/ Ju^{n} Ant^{o} ROM^{o} & Antonica LOMA, Indians of this pueblo; gp/ Ju^{n} Dom^{o} LOVATO & Rosalia ESQUIBEL, *vez^{s} agregados en este pueblo*.

LAZO, Sant^{o} delos Dolores *Pueblo Yndia*
bap 10 May 1790, b. 14 Apr in this pueblo; s/ Mathias LAZO & Guadalupe MARTIN, Indians of this pueblo; gp/ Lorenzo LOVATO & his wife, Mª ARMIJO, *vez^{s} agregados en este pueblo*.

CORDOBA, M^{a} delos Dolores *Pueblo Yndia*
bap 10 May 1790, b. 2 *de este mes* in this pueblo; d/ Jose CORDOBA & Manuela GAVILAN, Indians of this pueblo; gm/ Lucia ORTIZ, *natur^{l} de este pueblo*.

LOVATO (patron), Mª Concep^{on} delos Dolores *Aa India, vezina*
bap 19 Jne 1790, ae adult; d/ *Na^{on} Aa*, instructed on and accepted the faith; ward/ D^{n} Jose Ant^{o} LOVATO, *Alca^{e} mayor de este pueblo y Jurisd^{on}*; gp/ Ju^{n} Jph LOVATO & M^{a} dela Luz MESTAS, *v^{os} de esta d^{ha} Jurisd^{on}*. (Frames 1262-1263)

Frame 1263
DEL RIO, Fran^{ca} delos Dolores *Pueblo*

bap 19 Jne 1790, ae 20 da; d/ Ant^{o} DEL RIO & Ju^{a} MOYA; gm/ Mª Fran^{ca} LUJAN, all Indians of this pueblo.

VEGIL, Mª Trinidad delos Dolores *Rcho v^{os}*
bap 20 Jne 1790, b. 30 May; d/ Ju^{o} Cruz VEGIL & Mª Clara FERN^{Z}; gm/ Barbara ROMERO, *vez^{s} del Rancho*.

ROMERO [alias] CHAYO, Ju^{n} Ant^{o} delos Dolores *Rcho vez^{s}*
bap 20 Jne 1790, b. 3 *de d^{ho} mes en el Rancho*; s/ Mariano ROM^{O} [alias] CHAYO & Teodora DEL RYO; gp/ Ju^{n} Pablo MART^{N} & his wife, Josefa MONDRAGON, *todos v^{os} de esta Jurisd^{on}*.

MARTIN, Maria Manuela de los Dolores *Vez^{a} del Rancho*
bap 8 Sep 1790, b. 29 *del mes pasado* in *el Rancho*; d/ Ant^{o} Jose MARTIN & Mª Norberta TRUJILLO, *vez^{s} de d^{ba} Pobla^{on}*; gp/ D^{n} Ant^{o} Jose LOBATO, *Alcalde mayor de esta Jurisd^{on}*, & his wife, Margarita MARTIN.

PACHECO, Mª Guadalupe delos Dolores Pueblo Yndia
bap 8 Sep 1790, b. 1 *de este mes*; d/ Ju^{n} PACHECO & Lucia GOM^{Z}, Indian of said pueblo; gp/ Sant^{o} SILBA & his wife, Ju^{a} Encarna^{on} VELASQ^{Z}, *vez^{s} de esta Jurisd^{on}*.

SILBA, Mª Nieves delos Dolores *Pueblo vezina*
bap 8 Sep 1790, b. 5 *del mes pasado* in this pueblo; d/ Sant^{o} SILBA & Ju^{a} VELASQ^{Z}, *vezinos*; gp/ Ant^{o} Jose GUERRERO & his wife, Ju^{a} GOM^{Z}, *hijos de este pueblo*.

Frame 1264
GOMEZ, Ana Maria delos Dolores *Rcho vez^{a}*
bap 8 Sep 1790, b. 26 Jly in *el Rancho*; d/ Pablo GOM^{Z} & Guadalupe GON^{Z}, *vez^{s} del Rancho*; gp/ Jose MART^{N} & his wife, Lucia (n.s.), *de* D^{n} Juan (n.s.), *Yndios de este pueblo*.

ROMERO, Ju^{n} Andres delos Dolores *Pueblo Ynd^{a}*
bap 8 Sep 1790, b. 2 *de este mes* in this pueblo; s/ Jose Ant^{o} ROM^{O} & Mª Teodora ORTIZ; gp/ Mª Ant^{a} ROMERO, *Yndios de este d^{ho} pueblo*.

LUJAN, Mª Catalina delos Dolores *Pueblo Yndio*
bap 8 Sep 1790, b. 29 Jly (sic) in this pueblo; d/ Santiago LUJAN & Mª Josefa ROM^{O}; gp/ Ju^{n} Man^{l} ROM^{O} & Mª Josefa REYNA, *todos hijos de este pueblo*.

LUCERO, Mª Micaela delos Dolores *Pueblo Yndia*
bap 8 Sep 1790, b. 1 *de este mes* in this pueblo; d/ Ju^{n} Ant^{o} LUCERO & Manuela ROM^{O}; gm/ Angelina ROMERO, *todos hijos de este pueblo*.

MARTIN, Mª Josefa delos Dolores *Rcho Esp^{la}*
bap 12 Sep 1790, b. 23 *del mes pasado en el Rancho*; d/ Ju^{n} Felipe M^{IN} & Mª Ygn^{a} VEGIL, *v^{os} de d^{ba} Pobla^{on}*; gp/ Mig^{l} de LUNA & his wife, Mª Catalina BALDES, *v^{os} dela Jurisd^{on} de Abiquiú*.

(Fr. Andres VILLANUEBA signing entries)
SUESO, Jose Martin *Pueblo Yndio*
bap 19 Sep '90, b. 12 *del mismo mes en d^{ho} pueblo*; s/ Fran^{co} SUESO & Maria RIYO; gm/ Josefa ROMERO.

Frame 1265
BEJIL, Jose Ramon *Rcho Esp^{l}*
bap 22 Sep '90, b. 16 *de d^{ho} mes en el Rancho delas Trampas*; s/ Carlos BEJIL

& Juana SANCHES; gp/ Jose Ramon MESTAS & Maria Rosalia MARTINEZ, *vezinos de d^{ho} pueblo.*

MARTIN, Maria Matilde *Pueblo Esp^{l}*
bap 26 Sep '90, b. 20 *de d^{ho} mes en el Rancho delas Trampas*; d/ Gervasio MARTIN & Anne Maria CHAVES, *Españoles y vecinos de el Rancho*; gp/ Marcos MONTOYA & Rosalia VACA, *Españoles y vecinos de el pueblo de Aviquiú.*

DOMINGO, Xeronimo *Pueblo Yndio*
bap 21 Oct '90, b. 30 Sep *de el mismo año en el mismo pueblo de Taos*; s/ Juan DOMINGO & Michaela (n.s.); gm/ Lucia ROMERO, *todos hijos de el pueblo.*

PADILLA, Maria Lucia *Pueblo India*
bap 6 Nov '90, b. 2nd *de d^{ho} mes y año en el mismo pueblo de Taos*; d/ Santhiago PADILLA & Josefa LUXAN; gm/ Antto^{a} LOMA, [*todos Yndios de este pueblo*].

DELGADO, Fran^{ca} Antto^{a} *Pueblo Yndios*
bap 23 Nov '90, b. 10 *de d^{ho} mes*, ae 6 da; d/ Jose Antto^{o} DELGADO & Anna Maria ORTIZ, *hijos de este pueblo*; gm/ Fran^{ca} ALDERETE, *Española y vecina de este pueblo.*

Frame 1266
TRUXILLO, Juan Andres *Rancho Esp^{l}*
bap 24 Nov '90, b. 20th *en el Rancho delas Trampas*; s/ Andres TRUXILLO & Antto^{a} LOPEZ; gp/ Fran^{co} Esteban ROMERO & Maria Dolores LUCERO, *vecinos de el Rancho.*

LOVATO (gp), Maria Fran^{ca} *Yndia Comanche*
bap 30 Nov '90, near death and asking for the water of holy baptism, ca 20 yr; d/ Gentiles; gp/ D^{n} Juan Domingo LOVATO & D^{a} Margarita (n.s.-blank space).

TECOA, Jose Antto^{o} *Pueblo Yndio*
bap 9 Dec '90, b. 6th *en este pueblo*; s/ Mig^{l} TECOA & Maria MARTIN; gp/ Mathio LAZO & Guadalupe MARTIN, *todos Yndios de este pueblo.*

LUSERO, Maria Concep^{n} Pueblo
bap 28 Dec '90, ae 5 da; d/ Antto^{o} LUSERO & Angela ROMERO; gm/ Josefa LUCERO, *todos naturales de el sobre d^{ho} pueblo.*

Año de 1791

MES, Maria Bibiana *Rancho Esp^{s}*
bap 6 Jan '91, ae 4 da, *en el pro^{o} pueblo*; d/ Antto^{o} MES & Maria Concep^{n} URTADO, *Espa^{s} y vesi^{s} de el Embudo*; gp/ Jose Mig^{l} LOBATO & Maria Barbara URTADO, *tambien Esp^{s} y vesi^{s} de el Rancho de las Trampas, Juris^{n} de este pueblo.*

COCA, Maria Manuela *Rancho Esp^{s}*
bap 16 Jan 1791, ae 6 da, *en el Rancho de esta Jurisd^{n}*; d/ Mig^{l} COCA & Maria ROMERO; gp/ Manuel CORTES & Maria Antto^{a} MARTINES, *todos Españoles y vesinos de el Rancho.*

Frame 1267
LEAL, Juana Manuela *Pueblo Esp^{a}*
bap 16 Jan '91, b. 12 Jan, *en en el Rancho Jurisd^{n} de este pueblo*; d/ Juan Domingo LEAL & Veronica CORTES, *Esp^{s} y ves^{s} de d^{ho} Rancho*; gf/ Juan Antto^{o} MONTES BEJIL, *Espa^{l} y vesi^{o} de la Cañada.*

CORTES, Maria Manuela *Rancho*
bap 18 Jan '91, b. 14th, *en el Rancho Juris^{n} de este pueblo*; d/ Jose CORTES & Juana MONTOYA; gm/ Marga^{a} ROMERO, *todos Esp^{s} y vesinos de d^{ho} Rancho*.

MARTIN, Maria delos Reyes *Rancho Esp^{a}*
bap 19 Jan '91, b. 16th, *en el Rancho Juris^{n} de este pueblo*; d/ Geronimo MARTIN & Barbara COCA, *Esp^{s} y ves^{s} de este de Taos*; gp/ D^{n} Rafael SERRANO & his wife, Ysabel LUSERO, *Esp^{s} y ves^{s} de este de Taos*.

GOMES, Migel *Pueblo Yndio*
bap 22 Jan '91, ae 5 da, *que nacio en el mismo pueblo*; s/ Juan Antto^{o} GOMES & Maria ROMERO; gm/ Lucia RUIBAL, *todos Yndios de d^{ho} pueblo*.

DELGADO, Maria Ygnasia *Pueblo Yndia*
bap 24 Jan '91, b. 19 Jan in this pueblo; d/ Juan Luiz DELGADO & Josefa JUILO; gm/ Rossa MIRA^{L}, *todos Yndios de d^{ho} pueblo*.

SERRANO (gp), Marcelo *Pueblo Yndio Cumanche*
bap 27 Jan '91, b. 17 *de d^{ho} mes en este pueblo*; s/ unknown father & Maria (n.s.), a baptised Commanche Indian; gp/ D^{n} Rafael SERRANO & D^{a} Ysabel LUSERO.

LUXAN, Juana *Pueblo Yndia*
bap 27 Jan '91, b. 22 *de d^{ho} mes en el mismo pueblo*; d/ Santhi(a)go LUXAN & Maria Rossa (n.s.); gm/ Anna LUXAN.

This entry forgotten (so squeezed in here)
CHAVES, Ma^{a} Soledad *Vecina*
bap 7 Feb, b. 26 Jan '91; d/ Luis Man^{l} CHAVES & Catalina TAFOLLA; gm/ Fran^{ca} ALDERETE.

Frame 1268
MARTIN, Jose Pablo *Pueblo/ coyote*
bap 13 Feb '91, b. 11 *de d^{ho} el Rancho, jurisd^{n} de este pueblo*; s/ Juan Ygnasio MARTIN & Manuela GONZALES; gp/ Antto^{o} LUSERO & Angela ROMERO, *todos coyotes y vesinos de el Rancho*.

CORTES, Salbador Manuel *Rancho Esp^{l}*
bap 21 Feb '91, b. 17 *de d^{ho} mes en el Rancho*; s/ Man^{l} CORTES & Maria Antto^{a} MARTIN; gp/ Cruz BEJIL & Maria Clara FERNANDEZ, *todos Esp^{s} y vesinos de el Rancho jurisd^{n} de este pueblo*.

MONDRAGON, Antto^{o} José *Rancho Esp^{l}*
bap 22 Feb '91, b. 15 de d^{ho} *mes en el Rancho, jurisd^{n} de este pueblo*; s/ Mariano MONDRAGON & Encarnacion ESPINOZA, *Esp^{s} y vecinos de el Rancho*; gp/ Juan Anttonio ESPINOZA, *Esp^{l} y vecino de el pueblo de Chimayó*, & Maria Antto^{a} MARTIN, *Esp^{a} y vecina de este pueblo*.

VENAVIDES (gp), Jose Manuel *Rancho Cumanche*
bap 27 Feb '91, b. 22nd *en el Rancho Jurisd^{n} de este pueblo*; s/ Maria Antto^{a} (n.s.), of the Commanche nation who was baptised, & unknown father; gp/ Juan VENAVIDES & Maria Gertrudis ROMERA, *Esp^{s} y vecinos de d^{ho} Rancho*.

DURÀN, Juan Antto^{o} *Rancho Esp^{l}*
bap 6 Mch '91, b. 1st *de dho mes en el Rancho de esta jurisd^{n}*; s/ Ygnacio DURÀN & Antto^{a} SANCHES; gp/ Concep^{n} ROMERO & Maria Rosa QUINTANA, *todos vec^{s} y Esp^{s} vecinos de el mismo Rancho*.

SUASO, Maria Rossa *Pueblo coyotes*
bap 7 Mch '91, b. 4 *de d^{ho} mes;* d/ Juan José SUASO & Maria de la Luz LOBATO, *coyotes;* gp/ Antto^{o} Jose (n.s.) & Juana GOMEZ, *todos*...(end of page torn).

Frame 1269
COCA, Maria Manuela *Rancho*
bap 7 Mch '91, b. 3 *de d^{ho} mes;* d/ Matheo COCA & Guadalupe TAFOYA; gp/ Antto^{o} BUENO & Maria Ygnasia BUENO, *todos Espa^{s} y vesi^{s} de el Rancho, jursid^{n} de este pueblo.*

GONZALES, José Fran^{co} *Rancho*
bap 8 Mch '91, b. 4 *de d^{ho} mes;* s/ Jose Mig^{l} GONZALES & Victoria MARTINA; gp/ Jose Maria COCA & Juana BENABIDES, *todos Espa^{s} y vesi^{s} de el Rancho, jursid^{n} de este pueblo.*

ROMERO, José Victor *Pueblo, coyote*
bap 10 Mch '91, b. 6 *de d^{ho} mes;* s/ Antto^{o} ROMERO & Tereza RUIBAL, *coyotes* of this pueblo; gp/ Rafael SERRANO & Ysabel LUCERO, *Espa^{s} y ve^{s} de el pueblo.*

ESPINOSA, Jose Lucio *Pueblo*
bap 12 Mch '91, b. 7 *de d^{ho} mes;* s/ Jose Antto^{o} ESPINOSA & Catharina ROMERO, *Ynd^{s} de el pueblo;* gp/ D^{n} Rafael SERRANO & Ysabel LUCERO, *Espa^{s} y vesi^{s} de el pueblo.*

MONTOYA, Maria Antto^{a} *Rancho*
bap 13 Mch '91, b. 11 *de d^{ho} mes;* d/ Thomas MONTOYA & Maria Ageda ROMERO; gp/ Antto^{o} Domingo ROMERO & Maria Antto^{a} COCA, *Espa^{s} y vesi^{s} de el Rancho, jursid^{n} de este pueblo.*

LEAL, Maria Manuela *Pueblo*
bap 21 May '91, b. 25 Apr *en el Rancho;* d/ Man^{l} José LEÀL & Mariana QUINTANA; gp/ Juan Chris^{l} SILVA & María Guertrudis SILVA, all Indians of this pueblo.

JUEL, (n.n.-torn)
bap *en d^{ho} dia, mes y ano de* 91, b. 30 Apr; s/ José JUEL & Maria Rossa MARQUEZ; gp/ (torn-reverse of Frame 1268).

Frame 1270
MARTIN, Juan de Jesus *Rancho*
bap 5 May '91, b. 1 *de d^{ho} mes en el Rancho, juris^{n} de el mismo pueblo;* s/ Juan Pablo MARTIN & Josefa ESPINOSSA, *Esp^{s} y ve^{s} de el Rancho;* gp/ Juan Andres ESPINOSA (sic) & Maria Andrea ESPINOSSA, *Españo^{s} y ves^{s} de el pueblo de Chimayo.*

ROMERO, Juan *Rancho*
bap en el mismo dia, mes y año de '91, b. 2 *de d^{ho} mes en el Rancho, jurisd^{n} de este pueblo;* s/ Juan ROMERO & Juana Augustina (n.s.); gp/ Jose Antto^{o} MARTIN & Maria Ynes LEAL, *todos Esp^{s} y ves^{s} de el d^{ho} Rancho.*

FRESQUIZ, Antto^{o} Mathias *Rancho*
bap 18 May '91, b. 15th *en el Rancho, jurisd^{n} de este pueblo;* s/ Antto^{o} FRESQUIZ & Ignasia de CANA, *Espa^{s} y ves^{s} de d^{ho} Rancho;* gp/ Chris^{l} MONDRAGON & Maria Josefa QUINTANA, *Espa^{s} y ves^{s} de el pueblo de Cundiyo.*

DURAN, Blas Jose Ysidro delos Dolores *Rancho*
bap 21 May '91, b. 15 *de d^{ho} mes;* s/ Juan Nepomuseno DURAN y CHAVES & Maria Clara SANCHES, *vesinos del Rancho;* gp/ Jose Graviel MONTAÑO & Anna Quitera DURAN.

SANCHEZ, Maria Guertrudis Phelipa *Pueblo*
bap 29 May '91, b. 26 *de d^{ho} mes en este pueblo*; d/ Migel SANCHEZ & Paula LOBATO; gp/ Antto^{o} LOBATO & Maria Barbara LOBATO, *todos Espa^{s} y ve^{s} de este pueblo*.

BEJIL, Antto^{o} Josè *Rancho*
bap 23 Jne '91, b. 19th; *s*/ Juan Ygn^{o} BEJIL & Jacinta ARAGON; gp/ Antto^{o} PINO & Marg^{a} ROMERO, *todos Esp^{s} y ve^{s} de el Rancho de este pueblo*.

Frame 1271
SANCHEZ, Jose Antto^{o} *Rancho*
bap 24 Jne '91, b. 17 *de d^{ho}*; s/ Juan Ygnasio SANCHEZ & Pasquala BEJIL; gp/ Juan Nep^{o} DURAN & Clara SANCHES, *todos Espa^{s} y ves^{s} de el Rancho, jurisd^{n} de este pueblo*.

(Entries signed by Fr. Diego MARTINEZ)
DOMINGO, Maria Manuela *Hija del pueblo*
bap 3 Jly '91, b. 23 Jne; d/ Juan DOMINGO & Juana Maria (n.s.), *hijos del pueblo*; gp/ Juan ROMERO & his wife, Augustina MARTIN, *vesinos*.

ROMERO, Pedro Cirilo *Hijo del pueblo y tambien, todos*
bap 13 Jly '91, b. 10 *(de)* d^{ho}; s/ Vicente ROMERO & Micaela SUASO; gp/ Jose An^{o} ESPINOSA & Catalina ROMERO.

LOMA, Juan Antonio Mariano *Pueblo*
bap 5 Aug '91, b. 27 Jly; s/ Cristobal LOMA & Maria Anto^{a} ROMERO, *hijos del pueblo*; gm/ Maria Rosa (n.s.), la princessa, *hija del pueblo*.

GARCIA, Jose Pedro Vecino
bap 8 Aug '91, b. 1st *de d^{ho} mes*; s/ Jose GARCIA & Antonia MARTINES, *vecinos deste pueblo*; gp/ Antonio TORRES, *vecino del Emvudo*, & Barbara COCA, *vesina del Rancho*.

SISNEROS, Maria Micaela Ypolita *Vecina*
bap (blot) 16 Aug '91; d/ Polonio SISNEROS & Fran^{ca} CORTES, *vecinos deste pueblo*; gp/ Manu^{l} VEGIL & Andrea ESPINOZA, *vecinos del Rancho*.

ROMERO, Jose Yanuario *Hijo del pueblo*
bap 25 Sep '91; s/ Jose ROMERO & Maria Rita (n.s.), *hijos del pueblo*; gp/ Antoñico LUSERO & A(n)gela ROMERO, *hijos del pueblo*.

BLEA, Maria Casilda *Vecina*
bap 25 Sep '91; d/ Jose Juaquin BLEA & Ygnacia CHAVES, *vecinos*; gp/ B(a)rtolo Bartolo (sic) TAFOLLA & Maria GOMES. (Frames 1271-1272)

Frame 1272
ORTEGA, Jose Mateo *Vecino*
bap 25 Sep '91; s/ Manuel ORTEGA & Rita COCA, *vecinos*; gp/ Carlos VEGIL & his wife, Maria Antonia ROMERO.

MARTIN, Maria Marusia *Pueblo*
bap 25 Sep '91; d/ Jose MARTIN & Maria Juana (n.s.), *hijos del pueblo*; gp/ Julian MALINCHE & Maria Antonia ROMERO.

MARTIN, Cosme y Damian *Pueblo*
bap 30 Sep '91; *s*/ Manu^{l} MARTIN & Gertrudis ROMERO, *hijos del pueblo*; gp/ Antonio (n.s.) & Maria de la Luz (n.s.).

ROMERO, Maria Justina *Pueblo*
bap 30 Sep '91; d/ Domingo ROMERO & Fran^{ca} LUJAN, *hijos del pueblo*; gp/ Maria Av^{a} (n.s.), (only).

ROMERO, Maria Teodora *Pueblo*
bap 17 Oct '91, b. 2 dias *antes*; d/ Pedro ROMERO & Guadalupe DURAN, *hijos del pueblo*; gp/ Julian GUERERO & *su nuera*, Juana GOMES.

LUJAN, Maria Martina *Pueblo*
bap 19 Nov '91, b. 13 *de d^{ho}*; d/ Juan A^{to} LUJAN & B$^{ar(a)}$ ROMERO; gp/ Barbara LERNA (only).

GONZALES, Maria Cecilia *Pueblo*
bap 24 Nov '91, b. 22 *(del) d^{ho}*; d/ Domi(n)go GONZALES & Josefa ROMERO; gm/ Juana Maria MATA DORMIDA.

LUSERO, Maria Cecilia *Pueblo*
bap 25 Nov '91, b. 22 *de d^{ho}*; d/ Juan (written over) Ato LUSERO & Gert^{s} (written over) ROMERO; gm/ Juana ROMERO.

VEGIL, Maria Bibiana Rosa *Vesina*
bap 4 Dec '91, b. 2 *de d^{ho}*; d/ Carlos VEGIL & Juana SANCHES; gp/ Jose VEGIL & *su esposa*, Petra de Jesus ROJO.

Frame 1273
ROMERO, Ma^{a} Esperidiona *Vecina*
bap 22 Dec '91, b. 14 *d^{ho}*; d/ Concepcion ROMERO & Rosa QUINTANA; gp/ Antonio PINO & Margarita ROMERO.

SANBO, Jose Tomas *Pueblo*
bap 24 Dec '91, b. 21 d^{ho}; s/ Juan Cristoval SANBO & Juana Maria (n.s.), *hijos del pueblo*; gp/ Juan Diego GARCIA & Ma^{a} MARTI^{z}.

MASCAREÑAS, Maria Servula *Vecina*
bap 26 Dec 1791, b. 23 d^{ho}; d/ Nicolas MASCAREÑAS & Dolores MARTIN, *vesinos de Chimayo*; gp/ Jose Toribio MASCAREÑAS (only).

Año de 1792

MARTIN, Jose Inosencio Ermeregildo *Vesino*
bap 6 Jan 1792, b. 28 Dec; s/ Juan Felipe MARTIN & Ygnacia VEGIL; gp/ Bartolo TAFOLLA & Maria GOMES.

ROMERO, Julian Aquilino *Pueblo*
bap 9 Jan '92, b. 4 *de d^{ho}*; s/ Andres Juan ROM^{RO} & Fra^{ca} (n.s.), *hijos del pueblo*; gp/ Juan Mig^{l} BARELA & his cousin, Maria Fr^{ca} Xaviera VEGIL.

DURAN, Agaton Reyes *Pueblo*
bap 9 Jan '92, b. 6 *de d^{ho}*; s/ Juan Antonio DURAN & Ma^{a} Barbara MARTIN; gp/ Juan Domingo ROMERO & his step-daughter, Ma^{a} Soledad (n.s.), *todos hijos del pueblo*.

LUJAN, Tiofilo Eginio *Pueblo*
bap 22 Jan '92, b. 8 *de d^{ho}*; s/ Juan Antonio LUJAN & Ma^{a} (n.s.), *todos hijos del pueblo*; gm/ Lucia COMES (sic).

ROMERO, Teodora Higinia *Pueblo*
bap 11 Jan '92, b. 2 *de d^{ho}*; d/ Juan Domingo ROMERO & Ysavel MARQUES; gp/ Mariano LOMA & Ma^{a} Ygn^{a} MARTINES, *todos hijos del pueblo*.

Frame 1274

ROMERO, Higinia Reyes *Pueblo*
bap 17 Jan '92, b. 6 *de d^{ho}*; d/ Juan Dom(in)go ROMERO & Ma^{a} NARANJO; gp/ Juana TRIGO & Fran^{co} ROMERO (in this order).

LEYVA, Crispin Pablo *Pueblo*
bap 19 Jan '92, b. 7 *de d^{ho}*; s/ Jose LEYVA & Ma^{a} Rosa MIRAVAL, *hijos del pueblo*; gp/ Jose Rafael LOVATO & his sister, Josefa Ma^{a} LOVATO.

DURAN, Hilario Fulgencio *Pueblo*
bap 16 Jan '92, b. 14 d^{ho}; s/ Jose DURAN & Miguela LUCERO, *hijos del pueblo*; gp/ Catalina ROMERO (only).

LOMA, Anastacio *Pueblo*
bap 24 Jan '92, b. 22 d^{ho}; s/ Pablo LOMA & Lucia ESPINOSA; gp/ Julian GUERERRO & Ma^{a} Antonia ROMERO.

GONZALEZ, Paubla Fr^{ca} *Vecina*
bap 29 Jan '92, b. 25 *de d^{ho}*; d/ Jose Anton GONZA^{z} & Maria ESQUIÑE; gp/ Tomas ORIOSTE *y su madre*, Josefa ROMERO.

LOMA, Hilario Fran^{co} *Pueblo*
bap 29 Jan '92, b. 24 *de d^{ho}*; s/ Jose Fran^{co} LOMA & Ma^{a} Josefa EUQEDVEL, *hijos del pueblo*; gm/ Catarina TAFOLLA.

LUCERO, Fran^{ca} Petra *Pueblo*
bap 31 Jan '92, b. 23 *de d^{ho}*; d/ Jose Fran^{co} LUCERO & Ma^{a} Antonia RIO; gp/ Manuela MIRABAL (only).

ROMERO, Felipe de Jesus *Pueblo*
bap 5 Feb '92, b. 31st; s/ Geronimo ROMERO & Josefa (n.s.), *hijos del pueblo*; gp/ Mig^{l} TECOA & Lucia MARTINA.

BAPAONA, Venigno Julian *Pueblo*
bap 16 Feb '92, ae (illegible); s/ Santiago BAPAONA & Barbara (n.s.-illegible) of the pueblo; gp/ Jose MANZANARES (this entry & the one above almost illegible with bad ink, written over and bleed thru).

ROMERO, Benigna Juliana *Pueblo*
bap 16 Feb '92; d/ Juan Domg^{o} ROMERO & Encarnacion LUJANA, *hijos del pueblo*; gm/ Ma^{a} Josefa ROMERO.

Frame 1275

CHAVES, Eusevia Casimira *Vecina*
bap 5 Mch '92, b. 4 d^{ho}; d/ Jose Maria CHAVES & Maria de la Luz ORTEGA; gp/ Santiago SILVA & Juana Encarnacion VELASQUES.

SAMORA, Graviel dela Encarnacion *Pueblo*
bap 25 Mch '92, b. 18 *de d^{ho}*; s/ Santiago SAMORA & Ma^{a} ESQUIÑE, *hijos del pueblo*; gm/ Catarina TAFOLLA.

BRITO, Jose Dionicio *Vecino*
bap 9 Apr 1792, b. 8 *del d^{ho}*; s/ Juan Fran^{co} BRITO & Maria Antonia GONSALEZ; gp/ Manuel LOVATO & *su hermana*, Margarita LOVATO.

VEGIL, Ermenegilda Sotera *Vecina*
bap 22 Apr '92, b. 12 *de d^{ho}*; d/ Marcelino VEGIL & Micaela MARTIN; gp/ Juan ROMERO & Agustina MARTIN.

VEGIL, Juan Ramon de la Cruz *Vecino*
bap 6 May '92, b. 3 *d^{ho}*; s/ Juan de la Crus VEGIL & Clara FERNANDES; gp/ Juan Felipe MARTIN & Maria Yg^{a} VEGIL.

Church visit - (signed) Fr. Severo PATERO, *secra^{o}*
MEDINA, Petra Ysidora (Maa Petra Ysidora in margin) *Vecina*
bap 15 May '92, b. 13 d^{ho}; d/ Ygnacio MEDINA & Ma(r)garita CORDOVA; gp/ Mig^{l} COCA & Maria ROMERO.

BRUNO, Maria Fernanda Isaac *Vecina*
bap 3 Jne '92, b. 30 May; d/ Antonio BRUNO & Graciana Beatris TAFOLLA; gp/ Concepcion ROMERO & Ma^{a} Rosa QUINTANA.

LASO, Norverta Margarita *Pueblo*
bap 10 Jne '92, b. 6 d^{ho}; d/ Jose Antonio LASO & Josefa MARTIN *del pueblo*; gp/ Guadalupe LUCERO (only) *del pueblo*.

ROMERO, Manuel Onofre *Vecino*
bap 17 Jne '92, b. 12 *de d^{ho}*; s/ Mariano ROMERO & Maria Fran^{ca} ARMENTA; gp/ Antonio MARTIN & Maria TAFOYA.

ROMERO, Jose Maa Tranquilino *Pueb(lo)*
bap 7 Jly '92, b. 2 *d^{ho}*; s/ Jose Antonio ROMERO & Maa Lucia ORTIS; gm/ Josefa LUJANA.

Frame 1276
ROMERO, Pedro Pablo Fermin *Pueblo*
bap 8 Jly '92, b. 29 Jne; s/ Jose Ant^{o} ROMERO & Ma^{a} ORTIZ, *hijos del pueblo*; gp/ Antonio LOVATO & Margarita MARTIN.

GONSALES, Jose Fran^{co} Maximo *Vecino*
bap 10 Jly '92, b. 25 Jne; s/ Jose Ynes GONSALES & Ma^{a} LISTONA; gm/ Gertrudis COCA.

ROMERO, Ma^{a} Manuela Magdalena *Vecina*
bap 22 Jly 1792, b. 15 *de d^{ho}*; d/ Mariano ROMERO & Teodora RIOS; gf/ Esmeregildo SISNEROS.

SUASO, Fran^{co} Enrriq^{s} *Pueblo*
bap 24 Jly '92, b. 15 *de d^{ho}*; s/ Jose Antoni(o) SUASO & Maria ROMERO; gm/ Guadalupe MARTIN.

SANCHES, Jose Magdaleno *Vecino*
bap 29 Jly '92, b. 22 *de d^{ho}*; s/ Diego SANCHES & Ma^{a} Magdalena MARTIN; gp/ Mig^{l} SANCHES & Paubla MARTIN LOVATO.

LUJAN, Domingo Lorenzo *Pueblo*
bap 10 Aug (1792), b. 4 *de d^{ho}*; s/ Jose Antonio LUJAN & Juana MIRAVAL, *hijos del pueblo*; gm/ Micaela GONZALES.

ROMERO, Teodora Eustaq^{a} *Vecina*
bap 20 Sep '92, b. 15 *de d^{ho}*; d/ Juan ROMERO & Agustina MARTIN; gp/ Di(e)go SANCHES & Maria Magdalena MARTIN.

TAFOLLA, Mig^{l} Mateo *Vecino*
bap 29 Sep '92, b. 21 d^{ho}; s/ Juan Domingo TAFOLLA & Maria Dolores MA(ESE---see Frame 1286); gf/ Juan S^{N} GIL.

ATENCIO, Jose Fran^{co} Maria *Vecino*
bap 10 Oct '92, b. 24 Sep; s/ Bicente ATENCIO & Juana MONTOLLA; gm/ Josefa LOBATO.

ROMERO, Lino Eduardo *Pueblo*
bap 13 Oct '92, b. 23 Sep; s/ Juan Antonio (n.s.) & Antonica ROMERO, *hijos del pueblo*; gm/ Josefa LUJAN.

ROMERO, Simona delos Santos
bap 29 Oct '92, b. 28 d^{ho}; d/ Josesito (sic) ROMERO & Maria GOMES; gp/ Jose MARTIN & Lucia S JUAN.

TECOA, Evaristo delos Santos *Pueblo*
bap 1 Nov '92, b. 28 Oct; s/ Toribio TECOA & Mari(a) Rosa (n.s.); gm/ Felipa CASAQ^{E}.

SILVA, Maria Ursula *Vecina*
bap 2 Nov '92, b. 24 Oct; d/ Santiago SILVA & Juana PELONA, *Yndios*; gp/ A(n)ton(i)o FRESQU(I)S & Ma^{a} Ygn^{a} CANO.

Frame 1277

DOMINGO, Martina Salome *Pueblo*
bap 17 Nov '92, b. 13 *de* d^{ho}; d/ Juan DOMINGO & Josefa LUCERO; gm/ Maria ROMERO, *todos hijos del pueblo*.

BARGAS, Juana Diega *Vesina*
bap 18 Nov '92, b. 12 d^{ho}; d/ Mar(c)elo BARG^{S} & Nicomeda FRERNANDES; gp/ Jose Antonio MARTIN & Ma^{a} Ygnes (n.s.).

CORTES, Maa Ysavel Josefa *Vecina*
bap 21 Nov '92, b. 19 d^{ho}; d/ Christoval CORTES & Maa SANDOVAL; gp/ Jose Antonio CORTES & Juana Gertrudis MONTOLLA.

LUJAN, Maria Narcisa *Pueblo*
bap 21 Nov '92, b. 29 Oct; d/ Juan Domingo LUJAN & Josefa ROMERO, *hijos del pueblo*; gm/ Catalina ROMERO.

TRUGILLO, Ma^{a} dela Cruz Antonia *Vecina*
bap 27 Nov '92, b. 24 Nov; d/ Andres TRUGILLO & Antonia LOPES; gp/ Mariano ROMERO & Teodora RIOS.

LASARO, Albina Melchiadis *Pueblo*
bap 16 Dec '92, b. 10 *de* d^{ho}; d/ Juan Jose LASARO & Anna Maria ROMERO *del pueblo*; gp/ Juan Nepomuseno CHAVES & Clara SANCHES.

MARTINEZ, Dario Tomasa *Vesino*
bap 21 Dec '92, b. 19 *de* d^{ho}; s/ Jose Antonio MART(INE)Z & Alverta BENAVIDES; gp/ Jose Antonio MARTIN & Gertrudis MONTOLLA.

MONDRAGON, Servulo Albino *Vecino*
bap 23 Dec '92, b. 16 d^{ho}; s/ Mariano MONDRAGON & Maria Encarnacion (n.s.); gp/ Jose Antonio MARTIN & Maria Gertrudis MONTOLLA.

Frame 1278

Año de (17)93

RIOS, Pedro Tomas *Pueblo*
bap 17 Jan '93, b. 29 Dec '92; s/ Antonio RIOS & Juana MARQ^{S}, *hijos del pueblo*; gp/ Luiz DELGADO & Josefa JUILO.

GAVILAN, Anna Maria *Pueblo*
bap 18 Jan '93, b. 24 Dec; d/ Jose Antonio GAVILAN & Josefa Maria (n.s.), *hijos del pueblo*; gm/ Maria Rosa MIRAVAL.

COCA, Jose delos Reyes *Vecino*
bap 21 Jan '93, b. 6 d^{ho}; s/ Jose Maria COCA & Juana VENAVIDES; gp/ Jose Mig^{l} URTADO & Antonia MARTI(N).

DURAN, Jose Domingo de los Reyes *Vecino*
bap 21 Jan '93, b. 6 d^{ho}; s/ Juan Yg^{o} DURAN & Antonia SANCHES; gp/ Juan de la Cruz CORTES & Lus MONTOYA.

VEGIL, Antonio Jose Sevastian *Vecino*
bap 22 Jan '93, b. 20 d^{ho}; s/ Juan Yg^{o} VEGIL & Jasinta ARAGON; gp/ Salvador Jesus VEGIL & Maria Barba(ra) VACA.

DURAN, Pablo Juan de Jesus *Vecino*
bap 25 Jan '93, b. 15 d^{ho}; s/ Pablo de Jesus DURAN & Margarita SANCHES; gp/ Felipe de Jesus MART(INE)Z & Maria Nicomeda FERNANDES.

(Fr. Ramon Ant^{o} GONZ^{z} signing entries)
GUERRERO, Jose dela Candelaria *Pueblo*
bap 12 Feb 1793. b. 2 *de d^{ho} mes*; s/ Jose GUERRERO & Juana GOMES, *Yndios de este pueblo*; gf/ Jose Man^{l} SANCHES, *vesino dela mis^{on} de S^{n} Juan*.

Frame 1279
LUSERO, Man^{l} *Vezino*
bap 13 Feb 1793, b. 11 *de d^{ho} mes*; s/ Bernardo LUSERO & J^{pha} MARTIN, *ves^{s} del Rancho*; gp/ Miguel SANCHES & Paula LOBATO, *ves^{s} de esta Jurisd^{on}*.

CORTES, Juan Miguel *Vezino*
bap 17 Feb '93, b. 8 *de d^{ho} mes*; s/ Man^{l} CORTES & Maria Ant^{a} MARTIN; gp/ Juan Ygn^{o} SANCHES & Pascuala VEJIL, *ves^{s}, todos del Rancho*.

CHAVES, Juan Cristoval *Vezino*
bap 17 Feb '93, b. 13 *de d^{ho}*; s/ Juan Nepomuceno CHAVES & Maria Clara SANCHES; gp/ Juan dela Cruz VEJIL & Maria Clara FERN^{z}, *v^{s}. todos del Rancho*.

COCA, Juan de Jesus *Vezino*
bap 26 Feb '93, b. 24th; s/ Mig^{l} COCA & Maria ROM^{o}, dec.; gp/ Salv^{r} DURAN & Maria Ygn^{a} MARTIN, *vez^{s} de esta Jurisd^{on}*.

RUIBAL, Pablo *Pueblo*
bap 2 Mch 1793, b. 28 Feb; s/ Ant^{o} RUIBAL & Man^{la} DURAN; gm/ Phelipa ROM^{o}, all of the pueblo.

BLEA, Juan Pablo *Vecino*
bap 7 Mch 1793, b. 3rd; s/ Jose Juaquin BLEA & Maria Ygnacia CHAVES; gp/ Jose Ant^{o} MARTIN & Maria Yg(n)es LEAL, *todos v^{s} del Rancho*.

Frame 1280
LEAL, Ant^{o} Jose *Vez^{o}*
bap 7 Apr (1793), b. 4th; s/ Domingo LEAL & Veronica CORTES; gp/ Jose Man^{l} VENABIDES & Maria Getrudes ROMERO, *v^{s} del Rancho*.

GONZALEZ, Maria dela Encarn^{on} *Vez^{a}*
bap 7 Apr (1793), b. 24 Mch; d/ Jose Ant^{o} GONZ^{z} & Josefa VARELA; gp/ Juan Phelipe MARTIN & Maria Ygn^{a} VEJIL, *v^{s} del Rancho*.

MATEO, Antonio *Pueblo*
bap 7 Apr (1793), b. 26 Mch; s/ Juan Domingo MATEO & Ysabel PAEZ, *Yndios del pueblo*; gp/ Miguel SANCHES (only), *vez^{o} del Rancho delos Lobatos*.

BLEA, Maria Encarnacion *V^{na}*
bap 9 Apr (17)93, b. 25 Mch; d/ Ant^{o} BLEA & Barbara MONTOYA; gp/ Pascual ARAGON & Getrudis COCA, *v^{s} del Rancho*.

LOBATO, Maria Concep^{on} *Ves^{a}*
bap 14 Apr 1793, b. 11th; d/ Salv^{or} LOBATO & Maria CORDOVA; gp/ Antonio LOBATO & Marg^{ta} MARTIN, *v^{s} de esta Jurisd^{or}*.

GOMES, Juana *Pueblo*
bap 29 Apr 1793, b. 26 *de d^{ho}*; d/ Pedro GOMES & Maria Ant^{a} MARTIN; gp/ Luis DELGADO & Maria Josefa JUILO.

Frame 1281

ROMERO, Santiago *Vesino*
bap 3 May 1793, b. 30 Apr; s/ Ant^{o} ROM^{RO} & Maria Ant^{a} VEJIL; gp/ Viz^{te} MARTIN & Maria VEJIL, *ves^{s} del Rancho*.

MARTIN, Jose Fran^{co} *Ves^{o}*
bap 5 May 1793, b. 1st; s/ Juan Pablo MARTIN & Jp^{ha} MONDRAGON; gp/ Tomas URIOSTE & Concep^{on} URIOSTE, *v^{s} del Rancho*.

MARTIN, Maria Ysidora *Ves^{a}*
bap 20 May 1793, b. 16th; d/ Geronimo MARTIN & Barbara RUIBAL; gp/ Mariano MONDRAGON & Encarn^{on} ESPINOSA, *ves^{s}*.

SANDOVAL, Mª Serafina *Vesina*
bap 26 May '93, b. 18th; d/ Nicolas SANDOVAL & Getrudes SUAZO; gp/ Man^{l} CORTES & Maria Ant^{a} MARTIN, *v^{s}*.

MARTIN, Maria Man^{la} *Ves^{a}*
bap 2 Jne '93, b. 29 May; d/ Ramon MARTIN & Paula MARTIN; gp/ Diego SANCHES & Magdalena M^{TIN}.

MONTOYA, Maria dela Trinidad *Ves^{a}*
bap 2 Jne '93, b. 26 May; d/ Bernardo MONTOYA & Encarn^{on} MARTIN; gp/ Miguel SANCHES & Paula LOBATO, *v^{s} de esta Jurisd^{on}*.

Frame 1282

MARTIN, Maria Manuela *Vezina*
bap 15 Jne '93, b. 8th; d/ Gervasio MARTIN & Juana CORTES; gp/ Juan Cristoval MARTIN & Juana CERDA, *ves^{s} de Abiquiu*.

TRUJILLO, Juan Estevan *Vez^{o}*
bap 24 Jne '93, b. 20th; s/ Ygn^{a} TRUJILLO & unknown father; gp/ Santiago SILVA & Juana VELASQUES, *v^{s} del Rancho*.

LUSERO, Soledad
bap 24 Jne '93, b. 20th; d/ Ant^{o} LUS^{o} & Angela ROM^{o}; gm/ Antonia LOMA, *todos del p^{o}*.

GUERRERO, Margarita *Pueblo*
bap 2 Jly '93, b. 20 Jne; d/ Juan Domingo GUERRERO & Fran^{ca} LUS^{o} *del p^{o}*; gp/ Jose Man^{l} LOBATO & Rosalia MARTIN, *ves^{s}*.

LOMA, Paula *Pueblo*
bap 6 Jly '93, b. 28 Jne; d/ Mariano LOMA & Ygn^{a} MARTIN, *del pueblo*; gm/ Maria Ant^{a} GUERRERO, *tambien del pueblo*.

TUSA, Paula *Pueblo*
bap 6 Jly '93, b. 28 Jne; d/ Jose Ant^{o} TUSA & Dominga TECOA; gm/ Juana MATADORMIDO *del pueblo*.

ROMERO, Manuel Ant^{o} *Pueblo*
bap 24 Jly '93, b. 22nd; s/ Juan Domingo ROM^{o} & Fran^{ca} LUJAN *del pueblo*; gp/ Jose Ant^{o} MARTIN & Maria Ynes LEAL, *ves^{s}*. (Frames 1282-1283)

Frame 1283
CORTES, Salv^{or} Man^{l} *Vez^{o}*
bap 25 Jly '93, b. 18th; s/ Jose CORTES & Juana MONTOYA; gp/ Jose Maria ROM^{o} & Maria ROMERO, *ves^{s} del Rancho*.

ROMERO, Juana Maria *Pueblo*
bap 28 Jly '93, b. 25th; d/ Fran^{co} ROMERO & Phelipa ROM^{o}; gm/ Maria Phelipa ROM^{o} *del pueblo*.

GONZALEZ, Juan Andres *Pueblo*
bap 10 Aug '93, b. 6th; s/ Domingo GONZ^{z} & J^{pha} ROM^{o}; gm/ Juana ROM^{o}, *todos del pueblo*.

MONTOYA, Juan Antonio *Vezino*
bap 10 Aug '93, b. 4th; s/ Jose Rafael MONTOYA & Maria Luisa Seferin<u>o</u> (n.s.); gp/ Jose Dionisio VEJIL & Ana Maria VEJIL, *ves^{s}*.

CATUFE, Maria Polonia *Pueblo*
bap 10 Aug '93, b. 4 *de d^{ho}* mes; <u>s</u> (sic)/ Juan Domingo CATUFE & Maria ROM^{o}; gm/ Manuela FRESQUIS *del pueblo*.

Frame 1284
ORTIS (gp), Fran^{co} de Paula P.
bap 26 Aug '93, b. 18th; s/ Juana Maria (n.s.) *del pueblo* & unknown father; gp/ Jose Fran^{co} ORTIS & Candelaria PAEZ, *ves^{s}*.

LOMA, Maria Rosa P.
bap 10 Sep '93, b. 4th; d/ Mariano (n.s.) & Maria LOMA *del p^{o}*; gp/ Ant^{o} BUENO & Graciana TAFOYA, *ves^{s}*.

ROMERO, Maria Barbara P.
bap 18 Sep '93, b. 12 *de d^{ho}*; d/ Vis^{te} ROM^{o} & Micaela SUAZO; gm/ Maria Rosa (n.s.), *todos del pueblo*.

MIRABAL, Maria Micaela V.
bap 24 Sep '93, b. 23 *anterior*; d/ Tomasa MIRABAL & unknown father; gp/ Hilario TRUJILLO & Barbara LUJAN, *ves^{s} de esta Jurisd^{on}*.

SANCHES, Maria Getrudes V.
bap 1 Oct 1793, b. 30 Sep; d/ Jose SANCHES & Maria Ant^{a} XARAMILLO *desta*; gp/ Lorenzo LOBATO & Maria Greg^{a} ARMIJO, *v^{s}*.

Frame 1285
MARTIN, Magdalena
bap 6 Oct '93, b. 3 *de d^{ho} mes*; d/ Ant^{o} MARTIN & Josefa RIO; gm/ Ana LUJAN *del p^{o}*.

TAFOYA, Jose Miguel *Vesino*
bap 7 Oct '93, b. 29 Sep; s/ Man^{l} TAFOYA & Maria Ant^{a} MONTOYA, *v^{s}*; gf/ Pascual FERNANDES, *ves^{no} de la Cañada*.

LUJAN, Maria Antonia *Pueblo*
bap 18 Oct '93, b. 14th; d/ Jose Ant^{o} LUJAN & Maria Rosa MIRABAL; gp/ Ant^{o} LOBATO & Marg^{ta} MARTIN.

GONZALES, Juan Domingo *Vezino*
bap 25 Oct '93, b. 20th; s/ Juan Domingo GONZ^{z} & Rosalia TRUJILLO; gp/ Mariano ROM^{o} & Fran^{ca} ARMENTA, v^{s}.

REYNA, Jose Ant^{o} *Pueblo*
bap 27 Oct '93, b. 20th; s/ Jose REYNA & Getrudes ROM^{o}; gm/ Maria ROM^{o} *del pueblo*.

CHININI, Jose Santos *Pueblo*
bap 1 Nov '93, b. 24 Oct; s/ Man^{l} CHININI & Micaela (n.s.) *del pueblo*; gp/ Juan Jose LOBATO & Rosalia MARTIN, *v^{s}*.

Frame 1286

GONSALEZ, Maria Jpha *V.*
bap 3 Nov '93, b. 28 Oct; d/ Diego GONSALEZ & Juana MARTIN; gp/ Juan Domingo TAFOYA & Maria Dolores MAESE, *ves^{s} del Rancho*.

LUSERO, Santiago *P.*
bap 9 Nov '93, b. 5th; s/ Juan Domingo LUS^{o} & Maria Getrudes (n.s.); gm/ Getrudes REYNA, *todos del p^{o}*.

ROMERO, Maria Manuela *Pueblo*
bap 8 Dec '93, b. 5th; d/ Salv^{or} ROM^{o} & Man^{la} PAES *del p^{o}*; gp/ Salv^{or} VEJIL & Jacinta ARAGON, *vezinos*.

GONZALEZ, Pedro *Pueblo*
bap 8 Dec '93, b. 4th; s/ Santiago GONZ^{z} & Josefa LUS^{o}; gm/ Antonia LOMA, *todos del pueblo*.

LOMA, Jose Ramon *P.*
bap 20 Dec '93, b. 18th; s/ Mig^{l} LOMA & Lucia GOMEZ *del pueblo*; gp/ Viz^{te} LOBATO & Rosalia MARTIN, *ves^{s}*.

ROMERO, Jose Antonio *V*
bap 26 Dec '93, b. 20th; s/ Fran^{co} ROM^{o} & Dolores SALAZAR; gp/ Jose VEJIL & Petrona PACHECO, *v^{s} del Rancho*.

Frame 1287

Año de 1794

SANCHES, Jose Estevan *Vec.*
bap 3 Jan 1794, b. 26 Dec *anterior*; s/ Miguel SANCHES & Paula LOBATO; gp/ Ant^{o} LOBATO & Maria CHAVES, *v^{s}*.

ROMERO, Manuel Salvador *Pueb^{o}*
bap 12 Jan '94, b. 6th; s/ Jose Ant^{o} ROM^{o} & Man^{la} LUS^{o} *del p^{o}*; gp/ Carlos VEJIL & Juana SANCHES, *ves^{s}*.

MARTIN, Maria Rosa *P.*
bap 24 Jan '94, b. 16th; d/ Ant^{o} MARTIN & Guadalupe ROM^{o} *del p^{o}*; gp/ Jose VEJIL & Maria Fran^{ca} VEJIL, *vez^{s}*.

RIO, Fran^{co} *P.*
bap 26 Jan '94, b. 19 *de d^{ho}*; s/ Santiago RIO & Maria Rosa ROM^{o}; gm/ Maria NARANJO *del p^{o}*.

ROMERO, Victoria *P.*
bap 26 Jan '94, b. 25 Jan; d/ Geronimo ROM^{o} & Maria Jpha TECOA; gm/ Rosalia MARTIN *del p^{o}*.

PADILLA, Fran^{ca} *Pueblo*
bap 11 Feb '94, b. 4th; d/ Santiago PADILLA & Josefa LUJAN; gm/ Rafaela MIRABAL *del p^{o}*.

Frame 1288
ARMIJO, Ant^{o} Jose de Jesus Vec^{o}
bap 13 Feb '94, b. 8th; s/ Jose ARMIJO & J^{pha} CENTENO; gp/ Ant^{o} LOBATO & Maria J^{pha} CHAVES, *v^{s}*.

ROMERO, Miguel de S^{n} Juan *P.*
bap 20 Feb 1794, b. 12th; s/ Pedro ROM^{o} & Guadalupe (n.s.) *del p^{o}*; gp/ Luis DELGADO & Josefa JUILO *del p^{o}*.

LOBATO, Antonio Matias *Ve^{o}*
bap 1 Mch '94, b. 24 Feb; s/ Maria LOBATO, *Yndia Cumanche*, & unknown father; gp/ Santiago ARMIJO & Maria Luz MARTIN, *vez^{s}, todos del Ranchito*.

BARGAS, Maria Getrudis *Ve^{o}*
bap 11 Mch '94, b. 8th; d/ Estevan BARGAS & Andrea TAFOYA; gp/ Juan Cristoval CORTES & Fran^{co} SANDOVAL, *v^{s}*.

GONZALEZ, Jose Eulogio *Ve^{o}*
bap 14 Mch '94, b. 11th; s/ Juan GONZ^{z} & Maria Ant^{a} MARTIN; gp/ Ant^{o} Jose TAFOYA & Maria Encarn^{on} LUJAN, *ves^{s}*.

ARGUELLO, Jose Man^{l} *V^{o}*
bap 14 Mch 1794, b. 8th; s/ Ysidro ARGUELLO & Guadalupe ZAMORA, *ves^{s} delas Trampas de Picuries*; gp/ Jose Mariano FERNANDEZ & Reyes FERN^{z}, *v^{s} de esta Jurisd^{on}*.

Frame 1289
MARTIN, Maria dela Encarn^{on} *Pueblo*
bap 19 Mch '94, b. 11th; d/ Juan Andres (n.s.) & Maria Barbara MARTIN; gm/ Ant^{a} LOMA *del p^{o}*.

ROMERO, Maria Encarn^{on} *Ve*
bap 25 Mch '94, b. 21st; d/ Concep^{on} ROM^{o} & Rosa QUINTANA; gp/ Juan Ygn^{o} VEJIL & Jacinta ARAGON, *v^{s} de Taos*.

CHIQUITO, Juan de Jesus *P^{o}*
bap 25 Mch '94, b. 20th; s/ Ant^{o} CHIQUITO & Teresa (n.s.), *del p^{o}*; gp/ Jose GONS^{z} & Candelaria PAES, *ves^{s}*.

LUJAN, Juana Maria *P.*
bap 27 Mch '94, b. 21st; d/ Juan Ant^{o} LUJAN & Juana ROM^{o}; gm/ Barbara MATADORMIDO *del p^{o}*.

BUENO, Juana Josefa Serafina *V^{e}*
bap 27 Mch '94, b. 22nd; d/ Ant^{o} BUENO & Graciana TAFOYA; gp/ Juan Cruz CORTES & Maria Luz MONTOYA, *ves^{s}*.

GAVILAN, Maria Manuela *P.*
bap 30 Mch '94, b. 24 Mch; d/ Jose Ant^{o} GAVILAN & Maria ROM^{o} *del pueblo*; gp/ Ant^{o} LOBATO & Rosalia MARTIN, *ves^{s}*.

GONSALEZ, Jose Ant^{o} *V.*
bap 30 Mch '94, b. 22nd; s/ Jose Santos GONSALEZ & Maria LISTON; gp/ Jose VEJIL & Maria Man^{la} VEJIL, *ves^{s}, todos del Rancho*.

ORTEGA, Maria Concep^{on} *V.*
bap 30 Mch '94, b. 29th; d/ Man^{l} ORTEGA & Maria Rita COCA; gp/ Juan Pablo MARTIN & Ant^{a} Josefa MONDRAGON, *ves^{s}, todos del Rancho*.

BRITO, Jose dela Encarnacion *V.*
bap 1 Apr '94, b. 25 Mch; s/ Juan Fran^{co} BRITO & Margarita GONZ^{z}; gp/ Manuel TRUJILLO & Maria Concep^{on} URIOSTE, *ves^{s}*. (Frames 1289-1290)

CHINO, Santiago *P.*
bap 5 Apr '94, b. 30 Mch; s/ Santiago CHINO & Rosa ROM^{o}; gm/ Rosalia LOMA *del pueblo*.

VARGAS, Maria Getrudes *V.*
bap 5 Apr '94, b. 4th; d/ Mauricio VARGAS & Maria FERN^{z}; gp/ Ygn^{o} DURAN & Ant^{a} SANCHES, *v^{s} del Rancho*.

DURAN, Jose dela Trinidad *V.*
bap 13 Apr '94, b. 6th; s/ Fran^{co} DURAN & Juana SANDOVAL; gp/ Miguel COCA & Getrudes COCA, *v^{s} del Rancho*.

MIRABAL, Maria Man^{la} *V.*
bap 13 Apr '94, b. 11th; d/ Domingo MIRABAL & Maria MIRABAL; gp/ Juan Rafael LEAL & Maria Veronica CORTES, *ves^{s} del Rancho*.

LUJAN, Juan Mig^{l} *P.*
bap 13 Apr '94, b. 4th; s/ Jose Ant^{o} LUJAN & Maria Rosa (n.s.); gp/ Luis DELGADO & Josefa JUILO, *todos del pueblo*.

LUJAN, Jose Bernardo *P.*
bap 13 Apr '94, b. 8th; s/ Juan Domingo LUJAN & Jpha ROM^{o}; gm/ Angela ROM^{o}, *todos del pueblo*.

LEAL, Man^{l} de Jesus *V.*
bap 20 Apr '94, b. 18th; s/ Man^{l} LEAL & Matiana QUINTANA; gp/ Salv^{or} Man^{l} MARTIN & Maria MONTOYA, *ves^{s}*.

PAES, Juan Ramos *P.*
bap 20 Apr '94, b. 14th; s/ Domingo PAES & Micaela CHINA; gm/ Antonia GARCIA, *todos del pueblo*.

Frame 1291
MARTIN, Maria Catalina *Vez^{a}*
bap 5 May '94, b. 1st; d/ Juan Phelipe MARTIN & Maria Ygn^{a} VEJIL; gp/ Mig^{l} VEJIL & Ana Maria VALLEJOS, *v^{s} del Rancho*.

VARELA, Juan Cristoval dela Cruz *Vesino*
bap 5 May '94, b. 3rd; s/ Cristoval VARELA & Teresa MARTIN; gp/ Jose Ant^{o} MONDRAGON & Maria Encarn^{on} ESPINOSA, *v^{s} del Rancho*.

GARCIA, Maria Concep^{on} *Vesina*
bap 13 May 1794, b. 6th; d/ Jose GARCIA & Maria MARTIN, *v^{s} del Ranchito*; gp/ Jose Ant^{o} MARTIN & Maria Ynes LEAL, *ves^{s} del Rancho*.

FRESQUIZ, Juan Ysidro *Vesino*
bap 18 May '94, 14th; s/ Antonio FRESQUIZ & Ygn^{a} CANO *del Rancho*; gp/ Pasqual MONTOYA, *ves^{o} el Quemado*, & Ant^{a} MONTOYA, *ves^{a} del Rancho*.

DURAN, Maria Ant^{a} *Vesina*
bap 22 May '94, b. 19th; d/ Pablo DURAN & Margarita SANCHEZ; gp/ Diego SANCHEZ & Magdalena MARTIN, *vez^{s}*.

Frame 1292
PACHECO, Salvador *Vezino*
bap 24 May '94, b. 19th; s/ Ant^{o} PACHECO & Maria Ygn^{a} SANDOVAL; gp/ Juan Ant^{o} SANDOVAL & Ant^{a} Teresa LOPEZ, *v^{s} del Rancho*.

GALLEGO, Jose Ant^{o} *Vez^{no}*
bap 25 May '94, b. 20th; s/ Pascual GALLEGO & Matiana SILVA; gp/ Juan de CHAMA & Maria Jpha MARTIN, *ves^{s}*.

ROMERO, Maria Man^{la} *Pueblo*
*bap 30 May (sic) '9<u>3</u>, b. 18th; s/ Juan Domingo ROM^{o} & Encarn^{on} GAVILAN; gf/ Luis DELGADO *del pueblo*.

ROMERO, Jose Fran^{co} *V*
bap 4 Jne '94, b. 4th; s/ Mariano ROM^{o} & Teodora RIO, *v^{s} del Rancho*; gm/ Maria Ant^{a} RIO *del pueblo*.

LUSERO, Juana *Pueblo*
bap 27 Jne '94, b. 20th; d/ Jose Fran^{co} LUS^{o} & Maria Ant^{a} RIO; gp/ Jose JUILO & Maria Carmen JUILO.

LUJAN, Ant^{o} *Pueblo*
bap 27 Jne '94, b. 12th; s/ Santiago LUJAN & Maria GAVILAN; gm/ Lucia RUIBAL, *todos del pueblo*.

Frame 1293
CONCHA, Ysabel *Pueblo*
bap 4 Jly '94, b. 1st; d/ Jose Ant^{o} CONCHA & Ysabel CUALÒ; gm/ Tomasa MIRABAL, *todos del p^{o}*.

ROMERO, Fran^{co} Ant^{o} *Pueblo*
bap 10 Jly '94, b. 9 *de d^{ho}*; s/ Jose Ant^{o} ROM^{o} & Juana GOMES *del p^{o}*; gp/ Fran^{co} Ant^{o} LUJAN & Barbara LUJAN, *ves^{s} del Rio Arriva*.

ROMERO, Juan Jose *Pueblo*
bap 10 Jne 1794, b. 4th; s/ Juan Domingo ROM^{o} & Barbara LUJAN *del pueblo*; gp/ Ant^{o} LOBATO & Marg^{ta} MARTIN, *v^{s} del Ranchito*.

LASSO, Pablo *Pueblo*
bap 10 Jne 1794, b. 8th; s/ Jose Ant^{o} LASSO & Ana TUSA; gm/ Micaela CERNA, *todos del pueblo*.

ROMERO, Santiago *Pueblo*
bap 11 Jly '94, b. 8th; s/ Fran^{co} ROM^{o} & Concep^{on} ROM^{o}; gm/ Antonia LOMA *del pueblo*.

LOMA, Jose Francisco *Pueblo*
bap 11 Jly '94, b. 6th; s/ Jose Fran^{co} LOMA & Jpha ROM^{o} *del pueblo*; gp/ Juan DURAN & Maria Ygn^{a} GONZ^{z}, *vez^{s} del Rancho*.

VEJIL, Maria Soledad *Vesina*
bap 24 Jly '94, b. 18 *de d^{ho}*; d/ Juan Mig^{l} VEJIL & Ana Maria BALLEJOS, *v^{s} del Rancho*; gp/ Juan Ygn^{o} VEJIL & Jacinta ARAGON, *ves^{s}*.

Frame 1294
ATENSIO, Maria Ursula *Ves^{a}*
bap 6 Aug '94, b. 1st; d/ Vis^{te} ATENSIO & Juana MONTOYA; gp/ Jose GONZALEZ & Candelaria PAEZ, *todos vez^{s}*.

ROMERO, Maria Bibiana *Pueblo*
bap 13 Aug '94, b. 10th; d/ Fran^{co} ROM^{o} & Phelipa CATAJE *del pueblo*; gp/ Ant^{o} LOBATO & Maria Jpha CHAVES, *v^{s} del Ranchito*.

SANDOVAL, Maria Lorenza *Vesina*
bap 13 Aug '94, b. 10th; d/ Matias SANDOVAL & Maria Ygn^{a} BUENO; gp/ Fran^{co} Estevan ROM^{o} & Maria Dolores SALAZAR, *v^{s} del Rancho*.

JUILO, Maria Man^{la} *Pueblo*
bap 15 Aug '94, b. 8th; d/ Juan Cristoval JUILO & Juana (n.s.) *del pueblo*; *gp/* D^{a} Micaela BACA (sic) & *su hijo*, Fran^{co} ORTIS, *vez^{s} de esta Jurisd^{on}*.

MONTOYA, Jose Ant^{o} *Vezino*
bap 8 Sep '94, b. 7th; s/ Jose Rafael MONTOYA & Maria Luisa ROM^{o}, ves^{s}; gp/ Juan Domingo TAFOYA & Maria Dolores MAESSE.

PACHECO, Jose Maria *Pueblo*
bap 8 Sep '94, b. 1st; s/ Juan PACHECO & Lucia GOMES *del pueblo*; gp/ Ant^{o} LOBATO & Marg^{ta} MARTIN, *vez^{s} del Ranchito*.

LUJAN, Jose Ant^{o} *Pueblo*
bap 8 Sep '94, b. 2nd; s/ Juan Ant^{o} LUJAN & Maria ROM^{o} *del p^{o}*; gp/ Mig^{l} SANCHEZ & Paula LOBATO, *vez^{s} del Ranchito*.

TUSA, Lorensa *Pueblo*
bap 8 Sep '94, b. 5th; d/ Jose Ant^{o} TUSA & Maria Dominga TECOA; gm/ Josefa LUZ^{o} *del pueblo*.

Frame 1295
LUJAN, Barbara *Pueblo*
bap 10 Sep '94, b. 4th; d/ Juan Ant^{o} (n.s.) & Maria Rosa LUJAN; gm/ Juana MATADORMIDO *del p^{o}*.

SILVA, Jacinta Vezina
bap 14 Sep '94, b. 9th; d/ Juan Cristoval SILVA & Maria URIOSTE; gp/ Juan BENAVIDES & Maria Getrudes ROM^{o}, *v^{s} del Rancho*.

(Fr. Jose de VERA signing entries)
VEJIL, Maria Gertrudis *Vec^{a}*
bap 26 Sep '94, ae 6 da; d/ Jose VEJIL & Petrona MARTINES, *vesinos*; gp/ Mig^{l} VEJIL & his wife, Anna Mª VALLEJO, *vecinos de la Jurisd^{n}*.

GOMEZ, Maria del Rosario *Yndia de(l) pueb^{o}*
bap 12 Oct '94, ae 8 da; d/ J^{n} GOMEZ & Manuela NARANJO, *Ynd^{s} del pueblo dho*; gp/ J^{n} Ant^{o} ROMERO & his wife, Ant^{a} ROMERO.

ROMERO, Pedro Ant^{o} *Vec^{o}*
bap 21 Oct '94, ae 4 da; s/ Jose ROMERO & Juana TAFOYA, *vec^{s} del Rancho*; gp/ J^{n} Jose dela CRUZ, *vec^{o} de* Chimayo, & Mª Fran^{ca} CORT^{S}, *ve^{a} de esta Jurisd^{te}*. (Frames 1295-1296)

Frame 1296
DELGADO, Maria Rosa *Pueblo*
bap 21 Oct '94, ae 15 da; d/ Luis DELGADO & Josefa (n.s.), *Ynd^{s} de este pueblo*; gp/ Juan de la Crus VEJIL & Mª Clara FERNDZ, *vecinos del Rancho*.

BLEA, Jose Teodosio *Vec^{o}*
bap 4 Nov '94, ae 3 da; s/ Ant^{o} BLEA & Mª Barbara MONTOYA, *vecinos*; gp/ Ant^{o} Jose ROMERO & Mariana BENAVIDES, *vesin^{s}*.

HURTADO, Mª Concepcion *Vec^{a}*
bap 8 Nov (1)794, b. yesterday; s/ Juan HURTADO & Matiana ROMERO, *lexitim^{te} casados*, parishioners & *vec^{s} de esta*; gp/ Jose Mauricio VASQ^{S} & his wife, (n.n.), *parroquian^{s} de la dha*.

DELGADO (gp), Jose Manuel *Pueblo*
bap 8 Nov '94, ae 9 da; s/ Juan Cristoval (n.s.) & Josefa (n.s.), *Ynd^{s} y parroquianos de esta, lexitim^{te} casados*; gf/ Luis DELGADO, *Ynd^{o}* parishioner *de esta Yg^{a}*.

MIERA (gp), Jose Clemente Bernardo *Yn^{o} de(l) pueb^{o}*
bap 23 Nov (1)794, ae 8 da; s/ Jose Ant^{o} (n.s.) & Teresa (n.s.), *Ynd^{s}*, parishionors *de dha Yg^{a}, lexitim^{te} casados*; gp/ Jose MIERA & his sister, Anna M^{a} (MIERA), *felig^{s} de la dha*. (Frames 1296-1297)

Frame 1297
PINEDA, Maria Guadalupe *Vec^{a}*
LEAL, Maria Guadalupe
bap 1 Dec (1)794, ae 4 da; *espuria* d/ Jacinto PINEDA [who was punished by the law] & his cuñada, Lorenza LEAL, *soltera y felig^{s} de esta dha Yg^{a}*; gp/ Jose Mª ROMERO & his sister, Juana (ROMERO), *parroq^{s} de esta*.

ROMERO, Pedro *Pueblo*
bap 11 Dec (1)794, ae 4 da; s/ J^{n} Ant^{o} ROMERO & Ant^{o} LOMA, *lexitim^{te} casados, Ynd^{s} del pueblo*; gp/ Jose MONTOYA & his wife, Mariana CORDOVA, *felig^{s} de dha Yg^{a}*.

DURAN, Mª Ant^{a} Pueb^{o}
bap 11 Dec '94, ae 7 da; d/ Fran^{co} DURAN & Micaela ROMERO, *lexitim^{te} casad^{s}, Ynd^{s} felig^{s} en esta*; gp/ Ant^{o} LUS^{O} & his wife, Angela ROMERO, *Ynd^{s} felig^{s} en esta*.

MEDINA, Antonio de Jesus *Vec^{o}*
bap 19 Dec '94, ae 6 da; s/ Ygnacio MEDINA & Magarita CORDOVA, *vec^{s} felig^{s} en esta*; gp/ Pablo TRUXILLO for Felipe MARTIN & his wife, Maria Concep^{n} TRUXILLO, *vec^{s} de dha parroquia*. (Frames 1297-1298)

Frame 1298
ARMIJO, Jose Cipriano *Vec^{o}*
bap 19 Dec '94, ae 7 da; s/ Ynes ARMIJO, single, parishioner *de esta Yg^{a}, vec^{a}*; gp/ Lorenzo LOBATO & his wife, Mª DURAN ARMIJO, *vec^{s} felig^{s} de la misma*.

Año de 1795

ROMERO, Maria Manuela *Vec^{a}*

bap 8 Jan '95, ae 1 da; d/ Jose ROMERO & Dolores SANDOVAL, *parroquianos en esta*; gp/ Jose Diego CASILLAS & Ysidora MADRID, *felig^{s} tam^{n} de dha*.

ROMERO, Mª Bibiana *Vec^{a}*
bap 25 Jan '95, ae 9 da; d/ J^{n} ROMERO & Augustina MARTIN, *vec^{s} felig^{s} en esta*; gp/ Pablo DURA(N) & his wife, Margarita SANCHES, *ves^{s} del Rancho*.

BLEA, Ramon Ant^{o} *Vec^{o}*
bap 1 Feb 1795, ae 8 da; s/ Jose Joaquin BLEA & Ygnacia CHAVES, *vec^{s} felig^{s} en esta*; gp/ Pasqual ARAGON & his wife, Gertrudis COCA *de esta d^{ha} felig^{a}*.

ZAMORA (gp), Margarita *Yn^{a} del pueblo*
bap 7 Feb '95, ae 7 da; d/ Jose Ant^{o} (n.s.) & Teodora (n.s.), *Ynd^{s} felig^{s} en este pueblo*; gm/ Juana ZAMORA, *Yndia tambien del pueblo*. (Frames 1298-1299)

Frame 1299
TAFOYA, Maria Josefa *Vec^{a}*
bap 8 Feb '95, ae 6 da; d/ Manuel TAFOYA & Antonia MONTOYA, *vecinos de esta feligresia*; gp/ Jose Antonio MARTIN & his wife, Ynes LEAL.

VEJIL, Maria Antonia delos Dolores *Vec^{a}*
bap 18 Feb '95, ae 8 da; d/ Carlos VEJIL & Juana SANCHEZ, *vecinos de esta Felig^{a}*; gp/ Salv^{r} Ant^{o} LEIBA & his wife, Mª Ant^{a} MARTINES, *vecinos delas Trampas de Pecuries*.

ROMERO, Micaela *Ynd^{a} del pueb^{o}*
bap 28 Feb '95, ae 9 da; d/ Domingo ROM^{o} & Ysab^{l} PAES, *Ynd^{s} felig^{s} en esta*; gm/ Mª Rosa GUERR^{o}, *Ynd^{a} de esta d^{ha}*.

LUZERO, Matiana Rita Pueb^{o}
bap *en dho dia, mes y año*; d/ J^{n} Ant^{o} LUZ^{o} & Josefa (n.s.), *Ynd^{s} de esta dha felig^{s}*; gm/ Josefa ROMERO, *Ynd^{a}*.

GONSALES, Juan Man^{l} Matias *Vec^{o}*
bap 1 Mch '95, ae 7 da; s/ Juan Jose GONSALES & Maria REYNA, *felig^{s} del Rancho*; gp/ Jose Mª CORTES & Mª Ant^{a} ROMERO *dela dha Jurisd^{n}*.

MARTIN, Juana Matiana *Ve^{a}*
bap 1 Mch 1795, ae 7 da; d/ Salv^{r} MARTIN & Balvaneda MONTOYA, *felig^{s} de esta*; gp/ Juan Yg^{o} BEITIA & his sister, Teodora (BEITIA). (Frames 1299-1300)

Frame 1300
BRITO, Maria Micaela *Ve^{a}*
bap 15 Mch '95, ae 3 da; d/ Fran^{co} BRITO & Margarita ROMERO, *ve(c)inos en dha felig^{a}*; gp/ Juan Ant^{o} LOBATO & his sister, Mª Ant^{a} (LOBATO) *de dha*.

MARTIN, Mª Josefa dela Encarn^{n} *Ve^{a}*
bap 25 Mch '95, ae 9 da; s/ Gervasio MARTIN & Juana CORTES, *vecinos de esta Jurisdiccion*; gp/ Tomas URIOSTE & his mother, Josefa ROM^{o}, *de dha felig^{a}*.

COCA, Maria Dolores *Vec^{a}*
bap 27 Mch '95, ae 7 da; d/ Manuel COCA & Rafaela MARTIN, *vecinos felig^{s} de esta Jurisdiccion*; gp/ Juan Jose TAFOYA, *ves^{o} delas Truchas*, & his *sobrina*, Rosalia MARTIN, *de esta felig^{a}*.

GOMEZ, Mª Josefa *Ynd^a*
*bap 7 (sic) Mch '95, ae 5 da; d/ Jose Ant^a GOMEZ & Mª Ant^a ROMERO, *Yndios del pueblo*; gp/ D^n Ant^o LOBATO & Margarita MARTIN, *vec^s de esta Jurisd^n*.

VEGIL, Maria Bentura *Ynd^a comprada*
bap 5 Apr '95, ae 5 yr; s/ (unknown), *Yndia comprada y adoptada por* J^n Yg^o VEJIL & his wife, Jacinta ARAGON, *vecin^s de esta Jurisd^n* who were the gp.

ROMERO, Mª Concepcion *Vecina*
bap 5 Apr '95, ae 9 da; d/ Ant^o ROM^o & Mª Ant^a VEJIL, *vecinos dela Jurisd^n*; gp/ Felipe MARTIN & Concep^n (n.s.) *dela misma*. (Frames 1300-1301)

Frame 1301
SANCHEZ, Maria Ysabel *Vec^a*
bap 12 Apr '95, ae 4 da; d/ Ant^o SANCHEZ & Magdalena MARTIN, *vec^s de esta Jurisdiccion*; gp/ Jose Ant^o BEITIA *del Rio Arriba* & Mª Augustina MARTIN *de esta Jurisd^n*.

CHAVES, Maria Ygnacia *Vec^a*
bap *item*, ae 8 da; d/ Jose Mª CHAVES & Mª Carmen CORTES *de la Jurisd^n*; gp/ Tomas MONTOYA & Agueda ROM^o *de la dha*.

MADRID, Maria Rosalia *Vec^a*
bap 19 Apr '95, ae 5 da; d/ Salv^r Orta MADRID & Mª Lus BLEA; gp/ Ant^o BUENO & Graciana TAFOYA *y todos son vecinos de esta Jurisd^n*.

ROMERO, Miguel *Pueblo*
bap 26 Apr '95, ae 4 da; d/ Jose ROMERO & Mª LOMA, *Ynd^s del pueblo*; gp/ Julian GUERRERO & Mª Paula (n.s.) *del pueblo*.

ROMERO, Micaela *Pueblo*
bap *item*, ae 8 da; d/ Andres ROMERO, dec., & Maria ROMERO, widow; gm/ Rosalia MARTIN *del pueblo*.

SILVA, Juan Ant^o *Vecino*
bap *en d^{ho} dia*, ae 9 da; s/ Santiago SILVA & Juana ORTEGA; gp/ Felipe MARTIN & Concep^n (n.s.), *todos ves^s de esta Jurisdiccion*.

Frame 1302
MARTIN, Antonia Marg^{ta} *Pueblo*
bap 15 May '95, ae 8 da; d/ Jose MARTIN & Paula MARTIN, *Ynd^s del pueblo*; gp/ Jose Ant^o LOBATO & Rosalia MARTIN, *vec^s dela feligresia*.

ROMERO, Jose Pablo *Pueblo*
bap *item*, ae 6 da; s/ Juan ROM^o & Rafaela MIRABAL; gm/ Mª Rafaela (n.s.), *Ynd^s de este pueblo*.

ROMERO, Juan Antonio *Pueblo*
bap 17 May '95, ae 9 da; s/ J^n Domingo ROM^o & Juana (n.s.), *Ynd^s del pueblo*; gp/ J^n Cruz VEJIL & his sister-in-law, Nicomeda FERN^z, *vecinos desta Jurisd^n*.

VEJIL, Feliciana *Vec^a*
bap 25 May '95, ae 8 da; d/ J^n Cruz VEJIL & Clara FERNANDEZ, *vecinos dela Jurisdiccion*; gp/ Ant^o LUZ^o *de Rio Arriba* & Mª Dolores ORTEGA *de esta Jurisd^n*.

LAZO, Mª Guadalupe *Pueblo*
bap *item*, ae 5 da; d/ Matias LAZO & Guadalupe (n.s.); gm/ Guadalupe (n.s.), all of the pueblo.

ROMERO, Mª Encarnacion *Pueblo*
bap *item*, ae 3 da; d/ J^{n} Domingo ROMERO & Fran^{ca} LUXAN; gm/ Mª Encarnacion (n.s.), *Yndios del pueblo*.

MONTOYA, Mª Juana
bap 7 Jne '95, ae 9 da; d/ Bernardo MONTOYA & Encarnacion MARTIN; gp/ Juan Jose LOBATO & Barbara (LOBATO), his sister, all of this jurisdiction.

RIO, Fran^{ca} *Pueblo*
bap 14 Jne '95, ae 7 da; d/ Ant^{o} RIO & Juana (n.s.); gm/ Mª MARTINA, *Yndios del pueblo*.

CHAVES, Mª Teodora *Vec^{a}*
*bap 9 Jne (sic) '95, ae 12 da; d/ Juan Nepomu^{o} CHAVES & Clara SANCHEZ; gp/ Jose ARAGON & Mª Ant^{a} *idem* (ARAGON), *tod^{s} dela Jurisd^{n}*.

Frame 1303
PINEDA, Jacinto *Vec^{o}*
bap 21 Jne '95, ae 6 da; s/ Jacinto PINEDA & Josefa LEAL; gp/ J^{n} Jose LOBATO & Margarita MARTIN, *vecinos de la jurisd^{n}*.

GOMEZ, Mariano *Pueblo*
bap *item*, ae 10 da; s/ J^{n} GOM^{z} & Mª Ant^{a} (n.s.); gm/ Mª Ygnacia (n.s.), *Yndios del pueblo*.

LUCERO, Domingo *Pueblo*
bap 25 Jne '95, ae 20 da; s/ Ant^{o} LUCERO & Angela ROM^{o}; gm/ Juana ROMERO, all Indians of this pueblo.

LOBATO, Juan Domingo *Vec^{o}*
bap 28 Jne '95, ae 10 da; s/ Domingo LOBATO & Clara TAFOYA; gp/ J^{n} Ant^{o} (n.s.) & Elena LOBATO, *vec^{s} dela Jurisd^{n}*.

AUIRE (gp), Pablo *Pueb^{o}*
bap 6 Jly '95, ae 5 da; s/ Jose Ant^{o} (n.s.) & Catarina (n.s.), *Yndios del pueblo*; gp/ Jose AUIRE & Ana M^{a} (AUIRE), his sister.

PUNTE, Jose *Pueb^{o}*
bap 12 Jly '95, ae 3 da; s/ Jose Ant^{o} de PUNTE & Josefa (n.s.); gm/ Mª Josefa (n.s.), *Ynd^{s} del pueb^{o}*.

MARTIN, Mª Ysidora delos Dolores *Vec^{a}*
bap *dho dia*, ae 9 da; d/ Geronimo MARTIN, dec., & Barb^{a} COCA; gp/ J^{n} Felipe MARTIN & Mª Ygnacia BEJIL, *vec^{s} dela Jurisdiccion tod^{s}*.

(Entry with no surnames)

LUCERO, Maria Margarita *Ve^{a}*
bap 21 Jly '95, ae 2 da; d/ Bernardo LUC^{o} & Tomasa MARTIN; gp/ Julian LUZ^{o} of Rio Arriba & Candelaria PAES *de esta Jurisd^{n}*.

GARCIA, Antonio
bap *item*, ae 4 da; s/ Jose GARCIA & Ant^{a} MARTIN; gp/ Cruz CORTES & Mª Lus MONTOYA, *vecinos tod^{s} de esta Jurisd^{n}.*

DURAN, Maria Ant^{a} del Carmen *Vec^{a}*
bap 2 Aug '95, ae 4 da; d/ Pablo DURAN & Margarita SANCHEZ; gp/ Manuel CORTES & Mª Ant^{a} MARTIN, *todos son vecinos de la Jurisdicion.* (Frames 1303-1304)

Frame 1304
(Entry with no surnames)

CHINO, Juan *Pueb^{o}*
bap 16 Aug '95, ae 8 da; s/ Jose Ant^{o} CHINO & Juana Maria (n.s.); gm/ Mª Ant^{a} (n.s.), *todos Ynd^{s} de este pueblo.*

CORTES, Luis *Vec^{o}*
bap 27 Aug '95, ae 3 da; s/ Jose Ant^{o} CORT^{S} & Juana Gertrudis GONZALEZ; gp/ J^{n} Fran^{co} BRITO & Marg^{ta} GO(N)Z^{z}, *todos vecinos dela Jurisd^{n}.* (See entry at top of Frame 1305)

VEJIL, José Mariano *Vec^{o}*
bap 21 Sep '95, ae 3 da; s/ Juan Yg^{o} VEJIL & Jacinto ARAGON, *vecinos de la Jurisd^{n}*; gp/ *el Alc^{e} D^{n}* Jose ORTIS & his wife, D^{a} Micaela BACA.

DURAN, Maria Gertrudis *Ve^{a}*
bap 27 Sep '95, ae 4 da; d/ Ygnacio DURAN & Ant^{a} SANCHEZ; gp/ Bern^{do} LUZ^{O} & Tomasa MARTINEZ *y todos son vecinos de la Jurisd^{n}.*

CISNEROS, Juana Bautista *Ve^{a}*
bap 27 Sep '95, ae 7 da; d/ Polonio CISNEROS & Fran^{ca} CORTES; gp/ J^{n} Bautista VEJIL & his sister, Josefa (VEJIL), *vecinos todos dela Jurisd^{n}.*

ROMERO, Jose Ygnacio *Ve^{o}*
bap 27 Sep '95, ae 9 da; s/ Man^{l} Jose ROM^{O} & Juana VARELA; gp/ Salv^{or} MARTINEZ & Balvaneda MONTOYA, *todos vecinos dela Jurisdiccion.*

Frame 1305
(Following item is crossed out--see Frame 1304)
CORTES, Luis *Vec^{o}*
bap (cut from reverse side, missing), ae 3 da; s/ Ant^{o} CORT^{S} & Juana Gertrud^{s} GONZALEZ; gp/ Fran^{co} BRITO & Marg^{ta} GONZ^{z}, *todos son vecinos de la Jurisd^{n}.*

MONDRAGON, Jose Ubaldo *Vec^{o}*
bap 14 Oct '95, ae 7 da; s/ Mariano MONDRAGON & Encarn^{n} ESPINOSA; gp/ Cristov^{l} ESPINOSA *de Chimayo* & Fran^{ca} CORT^{S} *de esta Jurisd^{n}.*

MONTOYA, Juan Cristoval *Vec^{o} murio*
bap 18 Oct '95, ae 6 da; s/ Rafel (sic) MONTOYA & Mª Luiza ROM^{O}; gp/ Bartolome MONDRAGON & his sister, Ynes (MONDRAGON).

LOBATO, Mª Ursula *Vec^{a}*
bap 21 Oct '95, ae 11 da; d/ Salv^{or} LOBATO & Candelaria CORDOVA; gp/ Jose Fran^{co} URIOSTE & his sister, Co(n)cep^{n} (URIOSTE), *vecinos dela Jurisd^{n}.*

PADILLA, Mª Catarina *Pueblo*
bap 2 Dec '95, ae 8 da; s/ Santiago PADILLA & Josefa LUXAN, *Ynd^s del pueblo*; gp/ Jose Mª GARCIA & Ana Mª MIERA *de la Jurisd^n*.

(Entry with no surnames)

ROMERO, Santiago *Pueb^o*
bap 20 Dec '95, ae 7 da; s/ Jose ROM^o & Man^{la} SERNA; gp/ Josefa RIO, *Ynd^s (d)el pueb^o*.

FERNANDES, Mª Ysabel *Vec^a*
bap 20 Dec '95, ae 4 da; d/ Jose Mariano FERNANDES & Ascencion LUS^o, *vec^s dela Jurisd^n y asi mismo los padrinos*; gp/ J^n ROMERO & Aug(us)tina MARTIN.

Frame 1306
MIRAVAL, Juan del Carmen *Vec^o*
bap 26 Dec '95, ae 4 da; s/ Luis MIRAVAL & Damasia GONZALEZ; gp/ Jose PACHECO & Xaviera GARCIA, *todos ves^s dela Jurisd^n*.

Año de 1796

TAFOYA, Maria de Jesus *Ve^a*
bap 1 Jan 1796, ae 9 da; d/ Mig^l TAFOYA & J^a ROM^o; gp/ Jose ARMIJO & Lorenza ORTIZ, *vec^s todos dela Jurisd^n*.

CORTEZ, Maria Pasquala *Vecina*
bap 1 Jan '96, ae 6 da; d/ Cruz CORTEZ & M^a dela Luz MONTOYA; gp/ Miguel VEJIL & Juana CHAVES, *vecinos todos dela Jurisd^n*.

ORTEGA, Maria Paula *Vec^a*
bap 20 Jan '96, ae 7 da; d/ Manuel ORTEGA & Rita COCA; gp/ Jose Ant^o CORTES & J^a Gertrudis MONTOYA, *todos vecinos de mi Jurisd^n*.

GONZALEZ, Maria de Jesus *Ve^a*
bap 24 Jan '96, ae 9 da; d/ J^n Domingo GONZALEZ & Rosalia TRUXILLO, *vecinos*; gp/ Salvador MARTIN & Balvaneda MONTOYA, *vec^s todos dela Jurisd^n*.

VARGAS, Jose Pablo *Vec^o*
*bap 31 Jan (sic) '95, ae 7 da; s/ Jose Pablo VARG^S & Nicomeda FERN^Z, vec^s; gp/ Jose MIRAV^L & Barbara ROM^o, *vec^s*.

DURAN, Pedro Nolasco *Pueb^o*
bap *item en dho dia, mes y año*, ae 9 da; s/ J^n Ant^o DURAN & Barbara MARTIN *del pueb^o*; gp/ Felipe MARTIN & Concep^n TRUXILLO, *vec^s*.

GONZALEZ, Jose Ant^o *Vec^o*
bap *item*, ae 9 da; s/ Jose Sant^s GONZALEZ & Mª LISTON, vec^s; gf/ Jose Fran^{co} LOBATO, *ve^o*.

ROMERO, Jose Vicente *Vecino*
bap 3 Feb '96, ae 5 da; s/ Fran^{co} Estevan ROM^o & Mª Dolores SALAZAR, *vecinos dela Jurisd^n*; gp/ J^n Ant^o DURAN *de(l) Rio Arriba* & Lugarda TORRES *de esta Jurisd^n*.

Frame 1307
LOMA, Mª Veronica *Pueb^o*
bap 7 Feb '96, ae 8 da; d/ Santiago LOMA & M^a ROM^o; gm/ Rosalia (n.s.), *Ynd^s de este pueb^o*.

ROMERO, Juana *Pueb^{o}*
bap 14 Feb '96, ae 12 da; d/ J^{n} Domingo ROM^{o} & Ana M^{a} (n.s.); gm/ Mª Rosa (n.s.), *Yndios todos de este pueb^{o}.*

TECOA, Mª Manuela *Pueb^{o}*
bap 14 Feb '96, ae 6 da; d/ Toribio TECOA & Mª Rosa (n.s.), *Ynd^{s} del pueb^{o};* gp/ Man^{l} BACA & Ana Mª MIERA, *vec^{s} dela Jurisd^{n}.*

PACHECO, Maria Fran^{ca} Micaela *Vecina*
bap 14 Feb '96, ae 7 da; d/ Ant^{o} PACHECO & Mª Yg^{a} SANDOV^{L}, *vec^{s} de la Jurisd^{n};* gp/ Fran^{co} Ant^{o} DURAN & Juana SANDOVAL, *vec^{s} del Pueblo Quemado.*

GUERRERO, Salvador *Pueblo*
bap 14 Feb '96, ae 9 da; s/ Ant^{o} Jose GUERRERO & Juana GOMEZ, *Ynd^{s} del pueb^{o};* gp/ Concep^{n} ROM^{o} & Maria Rosa QUINTANA, *vec^{s} dela Jurisd^{n}.*

ARMENTA, Mª Ygnasia *Vec^{a} Esp^{a}*
bap 21 Feb '96, ae 4 da; d/ Simon ARMENTA & Marta MARTIN, *Españoles, vec^{s} de esta Jurisd^{n};* gp/ D^{n} J^{n} Yg^{o} SANCHEZ & Pasquala VEJIL.

MARTIN, Juan Ygnacio *Vec^{o}*
bap 21 Feb '96, ae 5 da; s/ J^{n} Pablo MARTIN & Josefa MONDRAGON, *vec^{s} de la Jurisd^{n};* gp/ Felipe MARTIN & Concep^{n} TRUXILLO, *vec^{s} de la Jurisd^{n}.*

CONCHA, Juan Manuel *Pueblo*
bap 21 Feb '96, ae 9 da; s/ J^{n} Domingo CONCHA & Josefa (n.s.); gm/ Fran^{ca} (n.s.), *todos Ynd^{s} de este pueb^{o}.*

ROMERO, Ana Mª *Pueblo*
bap 28 Feb '96, ae 8 da; d/ Juan ROM^{o} & Micaela GONZ^{z}; gm/ Fran^{ca} LUXAN, *todos Ynd^{s} de este pueb^{o}.*

ROMERO, Mª Beatriz *Pueblo*
bap 3 Mch '96, ae 7 da; d/ Ant^{o} ROM^{o} & Teresa RUIB^{L}, *Ynd^{s} del pueblo;* gp/ Manuel COCA & Rafaela MARTIN, *vec^{s}.*

COCA, Mª Dolores *Vec^{a}*
bap 4 Mch '96, ae 8 da; d/ Jose Mª COCA & Juana BENAVIDES, *vec^{s} dela Jurisd^{n};* gp/ D^{n} Xtov^{l} SANCHEZ *dela Cieneguilla* & Encarnacion MUÑIZ. (Frames 1307-1308)

Frame 1308
CHININI, Juan Aug^{n} *Pueblo*
bap 6 Mch '96, ae 7 da; s/ J^{n} Man^{l} CHININI & Josefa ROM^{o}; gp/ Luis DELG^{DO} & Josefa JUILO, *todos Ynd^{s} de este pueb^{o}.*

BUENO, J^{a} Paula *V^{a}*
bap 10 Mch '96, ae 2 da; d/ Ant^{o} BUENO & Graciana TAFOYA, *vec^{s} dela Jurisd^{n};* gp/ J^{n} Domingo TAFOYA & Dolores MAESE, *v^{s}.*

LEAL, Mª Tomasa *Vec^{a}*
bap 13 Mch '96, ae 8 da; d/ J^{n} Domingo LEAL & Veronica CORTES, *vec^{s} dela Jurisd^{n};* gp/ Pasq^{l} ARAG^{N} & Gertrudis COCA, *vec^{s} dela d^{ha}.*

ROMERO, Juana Maria *Pueb^{o}*
bap 13 Mar '96, ae 7 da; d/ Vicente ROM^{o} & Micaela SUASO; gm/ J^{a} Maria ROM^{o}, *Ynd^{s} de este pueblo.*

ROMERO, Maria Gertrudis *Vecina*
bap 20 Mar '96, ae 10 da; d/ Mariano ROM^{o} & Teodora RIO; gp/ Felipe MARTIN & Concep^{n} TRUXILLO, *todos vecin^{s} dela Jurisd^{n}.*

ARMIJO, Mª Josefa *Vecina*
bap 23 Mar '96, ae 6 da; nat. d/ Ynes ARMIJO, *vec^{a} de esta Jurisd^{n}*; gp/ Jose Ant^{o} LOBATO & Rosalia MARTIN, *dela d^{ha} Jurisd^{n}.*

ARMIJO, Mª Antonia *Vecina*
bap 27 Mar '96, ae 20 da; d/ Jose ARMIJO & Josefa CENTENO; gp/ (torn) MIERA & Rafaela BACA, *todos vecinos dela Jurisd^{n}.*

VERA (patron), Andres Jose *Apache*
bap 10 Apr (1)796, ae 4-5 yr; s/ *Nacion Apache Gicarilla*, captive in war with Commanche and taken out of captivity by Juan Jose LOBATO, single, *vec^{o} de esta Jurisd^{n}* who presented him to the priest (Fr. Jose de VERA) as a servant and to educate him; gp/ Bernardo MONTOYA, *mi sirviente, vec^{o}*, & my cook, Rosa ARIAS, *v^{a} ambos de esta Jurisd^{n}.*

LUXAN, Maria Guadalupe *Pu^{o}*
bap 17 Apr '96, ae 7 da; d/ J^{n} Domingo LUXAN & Josefa (n.s.), *Yndios de este pueblo*; gp/ Polonio CISNEROS & Fran^{ca} CORTES, *vec^{s} dela Jurisd^{n}.*

LUSERO, Mª Catarina *Pueb^{o}*
bap *item*, ae 8 da; d/ J^{n} Domingo LUS^{o} & Gertrudis ROM^{o}; gm/ Fran^{ca} (n.s.), *d^{ho} pueblo.*

RODRIGUEZ, Mª Guadalupe *Vecina*
bap 24 Apr '96, ae 5 da; d/ Jose RODRIGUEZ & Ana ARGUELLO; gp/ Man^{l} CHAVES & Simona LEAL, *vecin^{s}.*

Frame 1309
ROMERO, Maria (Mª de Monserrate in margin) *Vec^{a}*
bap 1 May 1796, ae 7 da; d/ Mariano ROM^{o} & Fran^{ca} ARMENTA; gp/ Jose VEJIL & Petrona ROXO, *todos vec^{s} dela Jurisd^{n}.*

VEJIL, Jose Atanasio *Vec^{o}*
bap 1 May '96, ae 5 da; s/ Cruz VEJIL & Clara FERN^{z}; gp/ Cruz CORTEZ & Luz MONTOYA, *todos son vecinos dela Jurisd^{n}.*

PINO, Mª Man^{la} *Pueblo*
bap 1 May '96, ae 7 da; d/ Santiago PINO & Rosa (n.s.); gm/ Magdalena (n.s.), *Ynd^{s} todos del pueblo.*

MARTIN, Ant^{o} Jose *Vec^{o} criado*
bap 1 May '96, ae 5 yr; s/ *Nacion Apache Gicarilla*, taken from the captivity of the Commanches & adopted/ J^{n} Bautista MARTIN, *ves^{o} dela Jurisd^{n}*; gp/ Bernardo MONTOYA & his wife, Mª MARTIN, *vec^{s} dela d^{ha}.*

ROMERO, Jose dela Ascencion *Vec^{o}*
bap 8 May '96, ae 3 da; s/ Concep^{n} ROM^{o} & Rosa QUINTANA; gp/ Mig^{l} VEJIL & Ana Mª VALLEJOS, *todos vec^{s} dela Jurisd^{n}.*

SANDOVAL, Mª Antonia *Vecina*
TRUXILLO, Mª Antonia
bap 8 May '96, ae 9 da; d/ Manuel SANDOVAL & Ygnacia TRUXILLO, *solteros de la Jurisd^{n}*; gp/ Ant^{o} Domingo ROMERO & Mª Antonia COCA, *vec^{s} dela d^{ha}.*

CHACON (gp), Fernando *(Cuma)nche (adu)lto* (torn)
bap 11 May '96 *en la villa de Sta Fe* by Fr. Fran^{co} de HOCIO, ae adult; s/ *Nacion Cumanche;* gf/ D^{n} Fernando CHACON, *Gov^{or} de la Provincia;* entered in the book of baptisms in Taos, 14th May.

CASILLAS (gp), J^{n} Augustin *Pueb^{o}*
bap 15 May '96, ae 8 da; s/ Tom^{s} (n.s.) & Micaela (n.s.); gp/ Bern^{do} CASILLAS & Maria Rosa (n.s.), *todos Ynd^{s} del pueblo.*

JUILO, Mª Ant^{a} *Pueb^{o}*
bap 6 Jne '96, ae 5 da; d/ Juan Cristoval JUILO & J^{a} Maria (n.s.), *Ynd^{s} de(l) pueblo;* gp/ Jose PACHECO & his daughter, Mª Ant^{a} (PACHECO), *vec^{s} ^{de} esta Jurisd^{n}.*

VARGAS, Jose Ramon *Vec^{o}*
bap 5 Jne '96, ae 5 da; s/ Estevan VARGAS & Andrea TAFOYA, *ves^{s} de esta Jurisd^{n};* gp/ Juan Domingo GONZALEZ & his daughter, Mª Gertrudis (GONZALEZ), *de* Cundiyo. (Frames 1309-1310)

Frame 1310
GAVILAN, Mª Manuela *Pueb^{o}*
bap 12 Jne '96, ae 8 da; d/ José GAVILAN & Micaela MARTIN, *Ynd^{s} de este pueblo;* gp/ Jose GONZ^{z} & Candelaria PAEZ, *vec^{s}.*

ARMIJO, Ana Maria *Vec^{a}*
bap 13 Jne '96, ae 4 da; d/ Mª Josefa (ARMIJO), step-daughter/ Lorenzo LOBATO & daughter/ Mª ARMIJO, *vec^{s} de esta Jurisd^{n};* gp/ D^{n} Ant^{o} LOBATO & Marg^{ta} MARTIN.

MARTIN, Tomas José *Pueb^{o}*
bap 3 Jul '96, ae 7 da; s/ Ant^{o} MARTIN & Guadalupe ROMERO; gp/ Tomas MARTIN & Micaela LOMA, *Yndios todos del pueblo.*

GARCIA, José Justo *Españ Vec^{o}*
bap 21 Jul '96, ae 3 da; s/ Jose Maria GARCIA & Ana Mª MIERA, *Españoles y vec^{s} de esta Jurisd^{n};* gp/ *el Alc^{e} D^{n}* Ant^{o} Jose ORTIZ & his wife, Dª Micaela BACA.

ORTIZ, Maria Magdalena dela Asuncion *Vec^{a} Esp*
bap 20 Aug '96 by the lector and administrator of *S^{n} Lorenzo de Picuries,* (signed) Fr. Jayme CANALS, ae 6 da; d/ D^{n} Ant^{o} Jose ORTIZ & Dª Micaela BACA, *Españoles y vecinos de esta Jurisd^{n};* gp/ D^{n} Miguel ORTIZ & his wife, Dª Maria Ysabel BACA, *vecinos dela villa de Sta Fe.*

CORDOVA, Ant^{o} *Vec^{o}*
FRESQUIZ, Ant^{o}
bap 20 Aug '96, ae 6 da; nat. s/ Jose Mig^{l} CORDOVA, single, & Ana Mª FRESQUIZ, single, *vecinos de esta Jurisd^{n};* gp/ Jose MONTOYA & Maria CORDOVA, *v^{s} dela d^{ha}.*

DURAN (gp), Mª Rita *Pueb^{o}*
bap 21 Aug '96, ae 5 da; d/ Jose Anton(io-torn) (n.s.) & J^{a} Maria (n.s.) *del pueb^{o};* gp/ J^{n} DURAN & Lugurda TORRES, *vecinos de la Jurisd^{n}.* (Frames 1310-1311)

Frame 1311
CRUZ, Mª Lorenza *Vec^{a}*
bap 22 Aug '96, ae 9 da; d/ Alexo CRUZ & Guadalupe DURA(N); gp/ Man^{l} Anast^{o} VEJIL & Fran^{ca} VERNAL *de esta Jurisd^{n}.*

CASILLAS, Luis Maria *Vec^{a}*
bap 28 Aug '96, ae 4 da; s/ Bern^{do} CASILLAS & Dolores MADRID; gp/ Mariano ROMERO & Fran^{ca} ARMENTA, *vecinos todos de esta Jurisd^{n}.*

TRUXILLO, Maria del Carmen *Vec^{a}*
bap 7 Sep '96, ae 2 da; d/ Andres TRUXILLO & Maria LOPEZ, *vecinos*; gf/ Miguel SANCHEZ, *vecino, todos de esta Jurisd^{n}.*

ARCHULETA, José Eugenio *Vec^{o}*
LOBATO, José Eugenio
bap 8 Sep '96, ae 3 da; nat. s/ Pablo ARCHULETA & Barbara LOBATO, *solteros, vecinos de esta Jurisd^{n}* and legitimized by their marriage 10 Jan 1797 with dispensation of 4th degree of consanguinity; gp/ Jose LOBATO & Rosalia MARTIN, *vec^{s} dela Jurisd^{n}.*

MARTIN, Jose Manuel *Vec^{o}*
bap 11 Sep '96, ae 4 da; s/ Jose Pablo MARTIN & Carmen SONDOV^{L}, *vecinos*; gp/ Jose Matias VEJIL & his sister, Fran^{ca} Xaviera (VEJIL), *vecinos, todos de esta Jurisd^{n}.* (Frames 1311-1312)

Frame 1312
ORTIZ (gp), Maria Nicolasa *Ynd^{a} Apacha de Ga^{s}*
bap 11 Sep '96, ae 6 yr; d/ *Nacion Apache*, captive redeemed from Comanches during war; gp/ *el Alc^{e} D^{n}* Jose ORTIZ & his wife, D^{a} Micaela BACA.

ROMERO, Micaela *Pueblo*
bap 21 Sep '96, ae 4 da; d/ Fran^{co} ROMERO & Felipa (n.s.), *Ynd^{s} del pueb^{o}*; gm/ Fran^{ca} (n.s.).

ROMERO, Mª Josefa (Mª Micaela in margin) *Pueb^{o}*
bap 25 Sep '96, ae 7 da; d/ J^{n} Domingo ROM^{o} & Encarnacion (n.s.), *Ynd^{s} deeste pueb^{o}*; gm/ Yg^{a} MARTIN.

MARTIN, Jose Mariano *Vec^{o}*
bap 2 Oct '96, ae 7 da; s/ Juan Felipe MARTIN & Mª Yg^{a} VEJIL, *vec^{s} de esta Jurisd^{n}*; gp/ Pablo TRUXILLO & Teresa HURTADO.

ZALAZAR, Jose Mariano *Vec^{o}*
bap 2 Oct '96, ae 9 da; s/ Fran^{co} ZALAZAR & Mª S^{tos} CORDOVA, *vec^{s} de esta Jurisd^{n}*; gp/ Paulin CORTES & Mª Ant^{a} MARTIN.

LUXAN, Juana Mª *Pueb^{o}*
bap 16 Oct '96, ae 7 da; d/ Juan Ant^{o} LUXAN & Manuela DURAN, *Ynd^{s} del pueb^{o}*; gm/ Guadalupe (n.s.).

MONTOYA, Jose Ant^{o} *Vec^{o}*
*bap 9 Oct '96, ae 6 da; s/ Jose Rafael MONTOYA & Luisa ROMERO, *vec^{s} dela Jurisd^{n}*; gp/ José Domingo LOBATO & Mª Clara TAFOYA, *vec^{s}.*

PACHECO, Rosa *Pueb^{o}*
bap 16 Oct '96, ae 10 da; d/ J^{n} PACHECO & Lucia GOMEZ; gm/ Fran^{ca} ROM^{o}, *Indios, todos del pueb^{o}.* (Frames 1312-1313)

Frame 1313
ROMERO, Josefa *Pueb^{o}*
bap 13 Nov '96, ae 4 da; s/ Geronimo ROM^{o} & Paula GUERRERO; gm/ Josefa ROM^{o}, *Yndios, todos del pueb^{o}.*

LUCAS, Francisca *Pueblo*
bap 13 Nov '96, ae 4 da; d/ J^{n} Ant^{o} LUCAS & Micaela ROM^{o}; gm/ Juana ROM^{o}, *Ind^{s} del pueblo.*

LOMA, Juan Antonio *Pueb^{o}*
bap 27 Nov '96, ae 7 da; s/ Mig^{l} LOMA & Lucia GOM^{z}; gm/ Micaela RIO, *Ynd^{s} del pueb^{o}.*

SANCHEZ, Mª Greg^{a} *Vec^{a}*
bap 27 Nov '96, ae 9 da; d/ Diego SANCHEZ & Magdalena MARTIN; gp/ Nepomuceno CHAVES & Clara SANCHEZ, *todos vec^{s} de esta Jurisd^{n}.*

ZAMORA, Tomasa *Vec^{o}*
bap 23 Dec '96, ae 8 da; d/ Eusevio ZAMORA & Rafaela (n.s.), *Ynd^{s} del pueb^{o};* gf/ Concep^{n} ROMERO, *vecino de esta Jurisd^{n}.*

MARTIN, Manuel *Vec^{o}*
bap 30 Dec '96, ae 7 da; s/ Gervasio MARTIN & Juana CORTES, *ves^{s} de esta jurisd^{n};* gp/ Gregorio CISNEROS & his wife, Mª Yg^{a} GOMEZ, *vec^{s} de Abiquiu.*

Año de 1797

BORIDA, Mª Manuela *Pueblo*
bap 13 Jan '97, ae 8 da; d/ Jose Ant^{o} BORIDA & Teresa (n.s.), *Ynd^{s} de este pueblo;* gp/ Simon ARMENTA & Marta MARTIN, *ves^{s} dela felig^{a}.*

RAEL, Domingo Salvador *Vec^{o}*
bap 17 Jan '97, ae 3 da; s/ Laz^{o} RAEL & Concep^{n} PAEZ, *vec^{s};* gp/ Ant^{o} ESPINOSA & Catarina ROM^{o}, *Ynd^{s} ladinos del pueb^{o}.* (Frames 1313-1314)

Frame 1314

MEDINA, Fran^{co} Antonio *Vec^{o}*
bap 29 Jan '97, ae 7 da; s/ Yg^{o} MEDINA & Marg^{ta} CORDOVA; gp/ Silvestre LOPEZ & Rosalia GONZ^{z}, *tod^{s} vecinos de la Jurisd^{n}.*

MALINCHE, Fran^{co} *Pueb^{o}*
bap 29 Jan '97, ae 8 da; s/ Juan Domingo MALINCHE & Fran^{ca} LUC^{o}; gm/ Ana Mª ORTIZ, *todos Ynd^{s} de este pueb^{o}.*

XARAMILLO, Juan Felipe *Vec^{o}*
bap 8 Feb '97, ae 4 da; s/ Patricio XARAMILLO & Josefa de la CRUZ, *ves^{s};* gp/ Jose Mig^{l} LOP^{z} & Clara BERN^{L}, *vec^{s} dela Jurisdiccion.*

ROMERO, Mª Man^{la} *Vec^{a}*
bap 12 Feb '97, ae 6 da; d/ Juan ROM^{o} & Aug^{na} MARTIN; gp/ Bern^{do} LUS^{o} & Tomasa MARTIN, *vecinos tod(o)s dela Jurisd^{n}.*

ATENSIO, Mª Candelaria *Vec^{a}*
bap 12 Feb '97, ae 8 da; d/ Vic^{te} ATENSIO & Juana MONTOYA; gp/ Jose Mª CHAVES & his sister, Juana (CHAVES), *vecinos dela Jurisd^{n}.*

VIJIL, Teresa de Jesus *Vec^{a}*
bap 5 Mar '97, ae 2 da; d/ Dionisio VIJIL & Man^{la} DELGADO; gp/ Pablo TRUXILLO & Teresa HURTADO, *todos vecinos dela Jurisd^{n}.*

NARANJO, Jacinto *Pueb^{o}*
bap 5 Mar '97, ae 6 da; s/ Santiago NARANJO & Juliana (n.s.); gm/ Josefa ROM^{o}, *todos Ynd^{s} del pueb^{o}.*

GOMEZ, Jose *Pueb^{o}*
bap 19 Mar '97, ae 8 da; s/ Jose GOMEZ & Man^{la} NARANJO, *Ynd^{s} del pueb^{o}*; gp/ Jose GON^{z} & Candelaria PAEZ, *vec^{s} dela Jurisd^{n}*.

RIOS, Juan Jose *Pueb^{o}*
bap 19 Mar '97, ae 8 da; s/ Jose Fran^{co} RIOS & Josefa (n.s.); gm/ Anna LUXAN, *tod^{s} Ynd^{s} del pueb^{o}*. (Frames 1314-1315)

Frame 1315
SANDOVAL, Nicolas dela Ascencion (Nicholas in margin) *Vec^{o}*
bap 21 Mar '97, ae 5 da; s/ Matias SANDOVAL & Ygnacia BUENO; gp/ Santiago FRESQ^{z} *delas Truchas* & Marg^{ta} CORDOVA, *vecinos dela Jurisd^{n}*.

LOBATO (patron), Jose Man^{l} *Vec^{o}*
bap 26 Mar '97, ae 5 da; s/ Maria (n.s.), *Ynd^{a} [criada de* Ant^{o} LOBATO] & unknown father; gp/ Jose GARCIA & Mª Ant^{a} MARTIN, *vec^{s} dela Jurisd^{n}*.

(Entry with no surnames)
LUXAN, Mª Dominga *Pueb^{o}*
bap 15 Apr '97, ae 7 da; d/ J^{n} Ant^{o} LUXAN & Mª Ant^{a} LOMA, *Ynd^{s} del pueb^{o}*; gp/ Juan GONZ^{z} & Mª Ant^{a} MARTIN, *vec^{s} dela Jurisd^{n}*.

CHACON, Jose Martin *Pueb^{o}*
bap 25 May '97, ae 10 da; s/ Fern^{do} CHACON, *Ynd^{o} Cumanche Xtiano*, & Mª Rosa (n.s.), *Ynd^{a}*; gm/ Ana M^{a} ROM^{o}.

SUASO, Mª Concep^{n} *Pueb^{o}*
bap 28 May '97, ae 8 da; d/ Fran^{co} SUASO & M^{a} RIO; gm/ Josefa ROM^{o}, *tod^{s} Indios del pueb^{o}*.

BEITIA, Mª Gertrudis *Vec^{a}*
bap 28 May '97, ae 7 da; d/ J^{n} Ant^{o} BEITIA & Andrea LUZ^{o}, *ves^{s} dela Jurisd^{n}*; gp/ Felipe MARTIN & Mª Teodora MONTOYA *del Rio Arriba*.

CAIGUA, Gertrudes *Pueb^{o}*
bap 11 Jne '97, ae 8 da; d/ Jose CAIGUA & Gertrudis REYNA; gm/ Catarina ROM^{o}, *todos Indios de este pueb^{o}*.

MARTIN, Mª Martina *Pueb^{o}*
bap 11 Jne '97, ae 5 da; d/ Tomas MARTIN & Micaela (n.s.); gm/ Josefa LUX^{N}.

Frame 1316
BLEA, Ant^{o} Jose *Vec^{o}*
bap 15 Jne '97, ae 3 da; s/ Ant^{o} BLEA & Barb^{a} MONTOYA; gp/ Ant^{o} MARTIN & Marg^{ta} ROM^{o}, *vec^{s} dela Jurisd^{n}*.

LOMA, Antonio *Pueb^{o}*
bap 20 Jne '97, ae 5 da; s/ Jose LOMA & Ana Mª ORTIZ; gm/ Mª Yg^{a} MARTIN *del pueb^{o}*.

ROMERO, Micaela *Pueb^{o}*
bap 9 Jly '97, ae 3 da; d/ Santiago ROM^{o} & Josefa (n.s.); gm/ Micaela (n.s.) *del pueb^{o} tod^{s}*.

GONZALEZ, Ant^{o} Jose *Pueb^{o}*
bap 9 Jly '97, ae 5 da; s/ Domingo GONZ^{z} & Josefa ROM^{o} *del pueblo*; gp/ Jose Mariano FERN^{z} & Ascension LUZ^{o}, *vec^{s} dela Jurisd^{n}*.

MARTIN, Mª Dolores *Vec^{a}*
bap 12 Jly '97, ae 6 da; s/ Salv^{r} Man^{l} MARTIN & Mª MONTOYA; gp/ Ant^{o} MONDRAGON & Catarina MARTIN, *vec^{s} dela Jurisd^{n}*.

MARQUEZ, J^{n} Domingo *Pueb^{o}*
bap 23 Jly '97, ae 8 da; s/ Juan Ant^{o} (n.s.) & Guadalupe MARQ^{z}; gm/ J^{a} Raf^{la} (n.s.) *del pueb^{o}*.

SILVA, Geronimo *Ve^{o}*
bap 23 Jly '97, ae 4 da; s/ Santiago SILVA & Juana MESTAS; gp/ Mig^{l} SANCHES & Paula LOBATO, *vec^{s} dela Jurisd^{n}*.

ARCHULETA, Camilo *Vec^{o}*
bap 30 Jly '97, ae 8 da; s/ Ant^{o} ARCHULETA & J^{a} Rosa MARTIN; gp/ Jose MIRAB^{L} & Barb^{a} ROM^{O}, *vecinos dela Jurisdiccion*.

MONTOYA, Mª Elena *Vec^{a}*
bap 6 Aug '97, ae 4 da; d/ Ber^{do} MONTOYA & Mª Encarn^{n} MARTIN; gp/ Lorenzo LOBATO & Mª ARMIJO, *tod^{s} vec^{s} dela Jurisd^{n}*.

LOPEZ, Sixto *Ve^{o}*
bap 6 Aug '97, ae 8 da; s/ Silvestre LOPEZ & Rosalia GON^{z}; gp/ Miguel SANCHEZ & Paula LOBATO, *tod^{s} vec^{s} dela Jurisd^{n}*.

Frame 1317
ARMENTA, Juan Yg^{o} *Vec^{o}*
bap 10 Aug '97, ae 2 da; s/ Simon ARM^{TA} & Marta MARTIN; gp/ *el S. Ten^{te}* Ant^{o} Jose ROM^{O} & Mª BACA, *tod^{s} feligreses de esta p^{o}*.

CHINO, J^{a} Dominga *Pueb^{o}*
bap 13 Aug '97, ae 8 da; d/ Jose Ant^{o} CHINO & Juana M^{a} (n.s.); gm/ Josefa JUILO of the pueblo.

LUXAN, Mª Hipolita *Pueb^{o}*
bap 13 Aug '97, ae 5 da; d/ J^{n} Ant^{o} LUX^{N} & J^{a} M^{a} ROM^{O} *del pueb^{o}*; gp/ Jose MONTOYA & Mariana CORDOVA, *ves^{s} dela Jurisd^{n}*.

ROMERO, Mª Barbara *Vec^{a}*
bap 13 Aug '97, ae 3 da; d/ Ant^{o} ROM^{O} & Mª Ant^{a} BEJIL; gp/ J^{n} Luis MIRABAL & Damasia GONZ^{z}, *tod^{s} vec^{s}*.

MARTIN, Juana Paula *Vec^{a}*
bap 15 Aug '97, ae 3 da; d/ J^{n} Pablo MARTIN & Josefa ESPINOSA, *ves^{s} dela Jurisd^{n}*; gp/ Jose Ant^{o} ARCHULETA & Mª Ant^{a} PADILLA, *ves^{s} del Rio Arriba*.

GONZALEZ, Jose Justo *Vec^{o}*
bap 15 Aug '97, ae 2 da; s/ Juan GONZ^{Z} & Mª Ant^{a} MARTIN, *ves^{s} dela Jurisd^{n}*; gp/ Rafael de LUNA & Ana Mª TAFOLLA, *vecinos de Sta Fee*.

SUASO, Maria Gertrudis *Ve^{a}*
bap 18 Aug '97, ae 3 da; d/ Mig^{l} SUASO & Josefa PANDO; gp/ Bernardo ORTIZ & Marg^{ta} TRUXILLO, *todos vec^{s} dela Jurisd^{n}*.

LEAL, Mª Serafina *Vec^{a}*
bap 27 Aug '97, ae 8 da; d/ Man^{l} Jose LEAL & Mª QUINTANA; gp/ Felipe MARTIN & Ynes LEAL, *tod^{s} vec^{s} dela Jurisd^{n}*.

CHAVEZ, Ant° Nerio *Vec°*
bap 28 Aug '97, ae 4 da; s/ J^{n} Nepum° CHAVEZ & Clara FERNAND^{z}; gp/ Juan DURAN & Candelaria PAEZ, *tod^{s} ves^{s}.* (Frames 1317-1318)

Frame 1318
CORTES, Maria Rosa *Vec^{a}*
bap 13 Sep '97, ae 5 da; d/ Jose CORTES & Juana MONTOYA; gp/ Joaq^{n} BLEA & his daughter, Nasarena (BLEA), *vec^{s} de esta Jurisd^{n}.*

CHINO, Juana Dominga (Entry has lines drawn through it) *Pueb°*
bap 13 Sep '97, ae 8 da; d/ Jose Ant° CHINO & J^{a} Maria (n.s.); gm/ Josefa JUILO *del pueb°.*

LUXAN, Maria Hipolita (Entry has lines drawn through it) *Pueb°*
bap 13 Sep '97, ae 5 da; d/ J^{n} Ant° LUXAN & Juana M^{a} (n.s.) *del pueb°*; gp/ Jose MONTOYA & Mariana CORDOVA, *vec^{s}.*

DELGADO, Jose Victoriano *Pueb°*
bap 17 Sep '97, ae 6 da; s/ Luis DELG^{O} & Josefa JUILO *del pueb°*; gp/ Jose MIERA & Man^{la} ROMERO, *vec^{s}.*

VARELA, Ramona de Jesus *Vec^{a}*
bap 1 Oct '97, ae 10 da; d/ Man^{l} VARELA & Mª MONTOYA, *vecs^{s} desta Jurisd^{n}*; gp/ Ant° MONDRAG^{N} & Silveria (MONDRAGON), his sister, *vec^{s} dela Cañada.*

PADILLA, Mª Fran^{ca} *Pueb°*
bap 15 Oct '97, ae 7 da; d/ Jose Ant° PADILLA *[Ynd^{s} del pueb°]*; & Rosalia MARTIN; gp/ *el Ten^{te}* Ant° Jose ROM° & Mª BACA.

GOMEZ, Juana *Pueb°*
bap 15 Oct '97, ae 8 da; d/ Pedro GOM^{z} & Mª Ant^{a} MARTIN; gm/ Juana ROMERO, *Ynd^{s} de(l) pueb°.*

LAZO, Juan Ant° *Pueb°*
bap 22 Oct '97, ae 9 da; s/ Marcos LAZO & Guadalupe MARTIN; gm/ Mª Encarna^{n} (n.s.), *tod^{s} Ynd^{s} de(l) pueb°.*

CORTES, Juan Ant° de Jesusi(t)o *Vec°*
bap 15 Nov '97, ae 10 da; s/ Mariano CORTES & Dolores VEJIL; gp/ Paulin de HERRERA & M^{a} del Carmen MADRID, *vecinos tod^{s} dela Jurisd^{n}.*

PACHECO (gp), Maria Rosa *Pueb°*
bap 19 Nov '97, ae 8 da; d/ Juan Pedro (n.s.) & Guadalupe (n.s.), *Ynd^{s} del pueb°*; gp/ Juan Jose PACHECO & Mª Ant^{a} (PACHECO), his daughter, *vec^{s} dela Jurisdiccion.* (Frames 1318-1319)

Frame 1319
CHULA, Leonarda *Pueb°*
bap 19 Nov '97, ae 8 da; d/ Jose Ant° (n.s.) & Catarina CHULA, *Ynd^{s} del pueb°*; gm/ Micaela BACA, *vec^{a}.*

LUZERO, Lorenzo *Pueb°*
bap 26 Nov '97, ae 5 da; s/ Ant° LUZ° & Angela ROMERO; gm/ Mª Raf^{la} (sic) LUX^{N}, *Ynd^{s} del pueb°.*

ROMERO, Mª Ant^{a} *Pueb°*
bap 26 Nov '97, ae 8 da; d/ Geronimo ROM° & Josefa TECOA; gm/ Mª Ant^{a} ROM°, *Ynd^{s} del pueb°.*

DEL RIO, Antonio *Pueb^{o}*
bap 10 Dec '97, ae 7 da; s/ Jose Ant^{o} (n.s.) & M^{a} DEL RIO, *Ynd^{s} del pueb^{o}*; gm/ Josefa TECOA.

RIO, Mª Bibiana *Pueb^{o}*
bap 31 Dec '97, ae 4 da; d/ Ant^{o} RIO & Juana (n.s.); gm/ Anica (n.s.), *tod^{s} del pueb^{o}*.

Año de 1798

GONZALEZ, Ygnacio Albino *Vec^{o}*
bap 7 Jan '98, ae 6 da; s/ Jose GONZ^{z} & Dorotea BACA; gp/ Ant^{o} Jose ROM^{o} & Mª BACA, *tod^{s} vecinos de esta Jurisd^{n}*.

PACHECO, Mª Guadalupe *Pueb^{o} murio*
bap 7 Jan '98, ae 4 da; s/ Mig^{l} PACHECO & Brijida ROM^{o}; gp/ And^{s} GAVILAN & Man^{la} FRESQ^{z}, *tod^{s} Indios de este pueb^{o}*.

Frame 1320
FLORES, Andres de Jesus *Vec^{o}*
bap 14 Jan '98, ae 8 da; s/ Martin FLORES & Gertrudis GARCIA; gp/ Lorenzo LOBATO & Mª Greg^{a} ARMIJO, *tod^{s} vecinos*.

ARCHULETA, Jose de Jesus *Ve^{o}*
bap 17 Jan '98, ae 3 da; s/ Pablo ARCHULETA & Barb^{a} LOBATO; gp/ Ant^{o} LOBATO & Marg^{ta} MARTINEZ, *tod^{s} vec^{s} dela Jurisdicion*.

LUXAN, Mª Magdalena *Pueb^{o}*
bap 21 Jan '98, ae 7 da; d/ J^{n} Domingo LUXAN & Josefa ROM^{o}; gp/ Jose Ant^{o} LEIBA & Micaela ROM^{o}.

CORTES, Mª Rafaela *Vec^{a}*
bap 22 Jan '98, ae 4 da; d/ Cristov^{l} CORT^{s} & Fran^{ca} MONTOYA; gp/ Bartolome TAFOYA & Mª GOMEZ, *tod^{s} vec^{s} dela Jurisdicion*.

MONTOYA, Juana Pasq^{la} (Juana in margin) *Vec^{a}*
bap 2 Feb '98, ae 6 da; d/ J^{n} Cand^{o} MONTOYA & Mª Barbara MARTIN; gp/ José Mª CHAVES & Maria ORTEGA, *tod^{s} vecinos de la Jurisd^{n}*.

BLEA, Mariano Cand^{o} de Jesus *Vec^{o}*
bap 4 Feb '98, ae 4 da; s/ José Joaq^{n} BLEA & Soledad SANCHEZ; gp/ Man^{l} RAMOS & Manuela SANDOVAL, *vecinos todos dela Jurisd^{n}*.

COCA, Mª Manuela *Vec^{a}*
bap 4 Feb '98, ae 5 da; d/ Manuel COCA, dec., & Rafaela MARTIN, wid.; gp/ J^{n} Yg^{o} SANCHEZ & Pasquala VEJIL.

GONZALEZ, Fran^{co} *Vec^{o}*
bap 11 Feb '98, ae 6 da; s/ Jose S^{tos} GONZ^{z} & Mª REYNA, *vecinos dela Jurisd^{n}*; gm/ Juana ROMERO *del pueblo*.

Frame 1321
SILVA, Juan Ant^{o} *Vec^{o}*
bap 18 Feb '98, ae 7 da; s/ Juan Xtoval SILVA & Concepcion URIOSTE; gp/ Cruz VEJIL & Clara FERNANDEZ *dela Jurisd^{n}*.

MIRABAL, Juana Dominga *Vec^{a}*
bap 23 Feb '98, ae 6 da; d/ Juan Luis MIRABAL & Damasia GONZ^{z}; gp/ Rafael MIRABAL *de esta Jurisd^{n}* & Barbara RODRIGUES *de Rio Arriba*.

GOMEZ, Jose Ant^{o} *Pueb^{o}*
bap 26 Feb '98, ae 9 yr; s/ Jose GOMEZ & Teodora (n.s.); gp/ Jose Ant^{o} LEIBA & Micaela ROM^{O}, *tod^{s} Yndios deste pueb^{o}*.

MARTIN, Mª Marta *Vec^{a}*
bap 26 Feb '98, ae 5 da; d/ Ramon MARTIN & Paula GONZ^{Z}; gp/ Joaquin MARTIN & Candelaria CHAVEZ, *tod^{s} vec^{s} dela Jurisd^{n}*.

MEDINA (gp), Antonio de Jesus *Vec^{o}*
bap 1 Mch '98, ae 2 da; s/ unknown; gp/ Pedro Yg^{o} MEDINA & Margarita CORDOVA, *vecinos de la Jurisd^{n}*.

DURAN, Juan Miguel *Vec^{o}*
bap 4 Mch '98; s/ unknown, placed in the house of Salvador DURAN who was gp with his wife, Ynacia MARTIN; legitimized by Marcos DURAN & Mª Yg^{a} TRUXILLO on 7 May *del año*.

VARGAS, Jose Ant^{o} *Vec^{o}*
bap 18 Mch '98, ae 7 da; s/ Mauricio VARGAS & Nicomeda FERNANDES, *vecinos dela Jurisd^{n}*; gp/ Juan Ant^{o} VARGAS & Mª Natividad LUXAN, *delas Trampas (d)e Picuries*.

FERNANDEZ, Jose Fran^{co} *Vec^{o}*
bap *item*, ae 7 da; s/ Jose Mariano FERNANDEZ & Asencion LUS^{O}, *ves^{s} (d)ela Jurisd^{n}*; gp/ Juan Policarpio (n.s.) & Juliana ROM^{O} *(d)elas Tramp^{s} de Picuries*.

LUXAN, Maria Soledad *Pueb^{o}*
bap *item*, ae 6 da; d/ Jose Fran^{co} LUXAN & M^{a} RIO *del pueblo*; gm/ Ana Maria TUZA.

DURAN, Mª Ant^{a} delos Dolores Vec^{a}
bap *item*, ae 3 da; d/ Yg^{o} DURAN & Ant^{a} SANCHEZ; gp/ Pablo DURAN & Margarita SANCHEZ, *vecinos dela Jurisd^{n}*.

ZAMORA, Juana Mª *Pueb^{o}*
bap *item*, ae 8 da; d/ Santiago ZAMORA & Rosa ROM^{O} *del pueb^{o}*; gp/ J^{n} Ant^{o} DURAN & Mª Ygnacia GONZ^{Z}, *vec^{s} (d)ela Jurisd^{n}*.

ARGUELLO, Jose de la Cruz *Vec^{o}*
bap *item*, ae 8 da; s/ Ysidro ARGUELLO & Guadalupe GONZ^{Z}, *vecinos dela Jurisd^{n}*; gp/ Anastacio ARGUELLO & Mª MARTIN *delas Tramp^{s} de Picuries*.

Frame 1322
MIERA, Mª Gabriela *Vec^{a}*
bap 18 Mch '98 because of necessity, ae hours, on the next day was annointed with holy oils; d/ Jose MIERA & Manuela ROM^{O}; gp/ the grandparents, Ant^{o} Jose ROM^{O} & Mª BACA, *vecinos de Taos*.

GAVILAN, Fran^{ca} *Pueb^{o}*
bap 19 Mch '98, ae 5 da; d/ Juan And^{s} GAVILAN & Manuela FRESQUIS; gm/ Fran^{ca} LUXAN, *Ynd^{s} del pueb^{o}*.

LUXAN, Mª Soledad *Pueb^{o}*
bap 15 Apr '98, ae 10 da; s/ Jose Ant^{o} LUXAN & Mª Rosa REYNA; gp/ Luis DELGADO & Josefa JUILO of the pueblo.

CASILLAS, Maria Fran^{ca} *Vec^{a}*
bap 16 Apr '98, ae 7 da; d/ Bernardo CASILLAS & Dolores MADRID; gm/ Maria Lus BLEA, *vecinos de esta Jurisd^{n}*.

PADILLA, Ana Maria *Pueb^{o}*
bap 22 Apr '98, ae 8 da; d/ Santiago PADILLA & Josefa LUXAN, *Ynd^{s} del pueb^{o}*; gp/ Josefa LOBATO, *vec^{a}*.

VARELA, Mª Dolores *Vec^{a}*
bap 6 May '98, ae 10 da; d/ Mig^{l} VARELA & Juana ROM^{o}; gp/ Man^{l} TAFOYA & Ant^{a} MONTOYA, *vecinos*.

DURAN, Augustin *Pueb^{o}*
bap 6 May '98, ae 8 da; s/ Juan Ant^{o} DURAN & Barbara MARTIN; gm/ Concep^{a} (n.s.), *Ynd^{s} del pueb^{o}*.

ROMERO, Ant^{o} Domingo *Pueb^{o}*
bap 6 May '98, ae 8 da; s/ Ant^{o} ROM^{o} & Micaela (n.s.); gm/ Micaela SERNA, *tod^{s} del pueb^{o}*.

MARTIN, Maria dela Cruz *Vec^{a}*
bap 6 May '98, ae 5 da; d/ Bernardo MARTIN & Mª Gertrudis ARCHULETA; gp/ Juan Ant^{o} DURAN & Ascencion LUS^{o}, *tod^{s} vecinos dela Jurisd^{n}*. (Frames 1322-1323)

Frame 1323
MARTINES, Mª Bibiana *Vec^{a}*
*bap 6 May (sic) '96, ae 5 da; d/ Pedro MARTINES & Mª Reyes FERNANDES; gp/ Juan Ant^{o} DURAN & Ascencion LUS^{o}, *vecinos dela Jurisdiccion*.

ROMERO, Jose *Pueblo*
bap 13 May '98, ae 3 da; s/ Jose Ant^{o} ROM^{o} & Manuela SERNA; gm/ Rafaela MIRABAL.

MARTIN, Fran^{co} *Pueb^{o}*
bap 13 May '98, ae 7 da; s/ Ant^{o} MARTIN & Guadalupe ROM^{o}; gm/ Encarnacion LUZ^{o}, *Ynd^{s} del pueb^{o}*.

CASILLAS, Micaela *Pueb^{o}*
bap 13 May '98, 7 da; d/ Jose CASILLAS & Rosa RIOS; gm/ Rosalia LOMA, *Ynd^{s} del pueb^{o}*.

LUZERO, Juan Man^{l} *Vec^{o}*
bap 1 Jne '98, ae 8 da; s/ Bernardo LUZ^{o} & Tomasa MARTIN, *vecinos dela Jurisd^{n}*; gp/ Ant^{o} LUZ^{o} of Rio Arriba & Rosa QUINTANA *de esta*.

ROMERO, Pablo *Pueb^{o}*
bap 1 Jne '98, ae 8 da; s/ J^{n} Miguel ROM^{o} & Fran^{ca} (n.s.); gm/ Lugarda SERNA *del pueb^{o}*.

REYNA, Dominga *Pueb^{o}*
bap 1 Jne '98, ae 8 da; d/ Geronimo REYNA, dec., & Paula GUERRERO; gp/ Juana Mª SUASO *del pueb^{o}*.

VARGAS, Mª Rita *Vec^{a}*
bap 1 Jne '98, ae 7 da; d/ Estevan VARGAS & Andrea TAFOYA; gp/ Bartolome MONDRAGON & Mª Ynes (MONDRAGON), his sister, *vecinos, tod^{s} dela Jurisd^{n}*.

Frame 1324
ROMERO, Juan Domingo (This entry has lines drawn through) *Pueb^{o}*
bap 10 Jne '98, ae 8 da; s/ Man^{l} ROM^{o} & Juana TAFOYA; gm/ Mª Regina (n.s.), *Ynd^{s} del pueb^{o}.*

ROMERO, Juan Domingo *Vec^{o}*
bap 10 Jne '98, ae 8 da; s/ Man^{l} Jose ROMERO & Juana TAFOYA; gp/ Jose Fran^{co} TAFOYA & his sister, Mª Regina FRESQUIS, *todos vecinos.*

MIRABAL (patron), Maria Manuela *Vec^{a}*
bap 13 Jne '98, ae 7 da; d/ Marian Antonia (n.s.), *criada de* (n.n.) MIRABAL, & unknown father; gp/ Jose Mig^{l} RODRIGUEZ & Ana Mª ARGUELLO.

ROMERO, Maria del Carmen *Vec^{a}*
bap 13 Jne '98, ae 3 da; d/ Mariano ROM^{o} & Mª Fran^{ca} ARMENTA, *vecinos dela Jurisd^{n}*; gp/ Jose Fran^{co} MARTINEZ *dela Jurisd^{n} (d)el Embudo* & Luz MONTOYA *de esta.*

LOBATO, Jose Victor *Vec^{o}*
bap 17 Jne '98, ae 3 da; s/ Domingo LOBATO & Clara MARTINEZ; gp/ Anamaria VEJIL & Mª Fran^{ca} BERNAL, *vecinos, tod^{s} de la Jurisdiccion.*

Frame 1325
MARTINEZ, Juan Antonio *Vec^{o}*
bap 24 Jne '98, ae 3 da; s/ Felipe MARTINEZ & Concepcíon TRUXILLO; gp/ Bentura ROMERO & Maria Ant^{a} REYNA, *vecinos de la Jurisd^{n}.*

ROMERO, Juana *Pueb^{o}*
bap 24 Jne '98, ae 1 hr; d/ Fran^{ca} ROMERO, wid., who died in birthing, *Ynd^{a} del pueb^{o}*; gp/ J^{a} Mª PICURIES.

LUXAN, Andres *Pueblo*
bap 29 Jne '98, ae 6 da; d/ Juan Domingo LUXAN & Josefa LUZERO, *Ynd^{s} del pueb^{o}*; gm/ Maria MARTINA *de idem.*

LUXAN, Juana Man^{la} *Vec^{a}*
bap 12 Aug '98, ae 7 da; d/ Mª Josefa (LUXAN), single, *vecina de esta Jurisd^{n}* who is daughter of Pablo LUX^{N} & Mª GARCIA; gp/ J^{n} Yg^{o} GONZ^{z} & Marg^{ta} BARELA, *vecinos de esta misma.*

MADRID, Juan de Jesus *Vec^{o}*
bap 19 Aug 1798, ae 3 da; s/ Salv^{or} Horta MADRID & Maria Luz BLEA; gp/ Jose Miguel LOPEZ & Barbara LOPEZ, *todos vecinos de esta Jurisdiccion.*

LUNA, Mª Lorenza *Vec^{a}*
bap 19 Aug 1798, ae 8 da; d/ Juan del Carmen (n.s.) & Nazarena LUNA; gp/ Juan Cruz CORTES & Maria Luz MONTOYA, *todos vecinos de esta Jurisdiccon.* (Frames 1325-1326)

Frame 1326
LEAL, Juan del Carmen *Vec^{o}*
bap 3 Sep (1)798, ae 3 da; s/ Juan Domingo LEAL & Veronica CORTES; gp/ Rafael VEJIL & his sister, Ant^{a} Nicolasa (VEJIL), *vecinos, todos dela Jurisdiccion.*

30 Sep 1798 - Church visit - (signed) (Fr.) Jose Bivian de ORTEGA, *vicitador,* & Fr. Diego MUÑOS JURADO, *secret^{o} de visita*

MARTIN, Mª Antonia *Vec^{a}*
bap 30 Sep '98, ae 7 da; d/ Jose MARTIN & Gertrudis MONTOYA; gp/ Jose VEJIL & Petra ROXO, *tod^{s} vecinos dela Jurisd^{n}*.

PINIDA, Juana M^{a} *Ve^{a}*
bap 1 Oct '98, ae 8 da; d/ Jacinto PINIDA & Josefa LEAL; gp/ Dionisio VEJIL & Man^{la} DELGADO.

LUXAN, Josè *Pueb^{o}*
bap 1 Oct '98, ae 7 da; s/ Jose Ant^{o} LUX^{N} & Gertrudis LASO; gm/ Mª Ascencion LUZ^{o}, *todos Indios de este pueb^{o}*.

Frame 1327
CAMARGO, Jose Miguel *Ve^{o}*
bap 7 Oct '98, ae 8 da; s/ Jose Mª CAMARGO & Ana Maria MIERA; gp/ Juan Yg^{o} VEJIL & Jacinta ARAGON, *todos vecinos*.

ROMERO, Jose Ant^{o} *Pueb^{o}*
bap 14 Oct '98, ae 7 da; s/ Mariano ROM^{O} & Mª Luz GAVILAN; gm/ Ysabel (n.s.), *todos Yndios del pueb^{o}*.

GOMEZ, Alfonso *Pueb^{o}*
bap 14 Oct '98, ae 7 da; s/ Juan GOMEZ & Mª Ant^{a} (n.s.); gp/ Magdalena MARTIN, *tod^{s} del pueb^{o}*.

DURAN, Ant^{o} *Vec^{o}*
bap 18 Oct '98, ae 10 da; s/ Nicolas DURAN & M^{a} ROM^{O}; gp/ Jose MONTOYA & Mariana CORDOVA, *vecinos*.

TENORIO, Mª Teresa *Vec^{a}*
bap 21 Oct '98, ae 7 da; d/ Felipe TENORIO & Ant^{a} Rosa (n.s.); gp/ Jose MIERA & Manuela ROM^{O}, *vecinos*.

CHINO, Fran^{co} *Pueb^{o}*
bap 21 Oct '98, ae 10 da; s/ Santiago CHINO & Fran^{ca} DURAN; gm/ Rafaela MIRABAL, *Ynd^{s} del pueb^{o}*.

MONDRAGON, Juana *Vec^{a}*
bap 14 Nov '98, ae 12 da; d/ Ant^{o} MONDRAGON & Catarina MARTIN; gp/ Jose Yg^{o} BEITIA & his sister, Teodora (BEITIA).

CHAVES, Maria Micaela *Vec^{a}*
bap 17 Nov '98, ae 10 da; s/ Juan Nepomuceno CHAVES & Clara SANCHEZ; gp/ Silvestre LOPEZ & Rosalia GONZ^{Z}, *tod^{s} vecinos de desta Jurisd^{n}*. (Frames 1327-1328)

Frame 1328
ROMERO, Jose Vicente Cleto *Vec^{o}*
bap 18 Nov '98, ae 5 da; s/ Ant^{o} ROM^{O} & Mª Ant^{a} VEJIL; gp/ Bartolome MONDRAGON & Mª Ynes (MONDRAGON), his sister, *todos vecinos de esta Jurisd^{n}*.

LUXAN, Geronimo *Pueb^{o}*
bap 25 Nov '98, ae 6 da; s/ J^{n} Ant^{o} LUX^{N} & Micaela SERNA; gm/ Josefa MARTIN, Indians of the pueblo.

ROMERO, Juana Maria
bap 25 Nov '98, ae 6 da; d/ Fran^{co} ROMERO & Felipa (n.s.); gm/ Mª Rosa ROM^{O}, *Yndios del pueb^{o}*.

ROMERO, Mª Soledad *Pueb^{o}*
bap 12 Dec '98, ae 4 da; d/ Juan Domingo ROM^{o} & Encarnacion LUX^{N}; gp/ Jose PACHECO & his daughter, Mª Ant^{a} (PACHECO), *vecinos de esta Jurisd^{n}*.

VEJIL, Juan Xtoval *Vec^{o}*
bap 12 Dec '98, ae 12 da; s/ Juan Yg^{o} VEJIL & Mª Ant^{a} ARAGON; gp/ Juan Ygnacio VIJIL & Jacinta ARAGON, *todos vecinos desta Jurisd^{n}*.

GAVILAN, Mª Man^{la} *Pueb^{o}*
bap 16 Dec '98, ae 5 da; d/ Jose GAVILAN & Luz MARTIN, *Ynd^{s} deste pueb^{o}*; gp/ Ant^{o} Jose ROM^{o} & Mª BACA, *vecinos de esta Jurisd^{n}*.

LUXAN, Mª Josefa *Ynd^{s} Pueb^{o}*
bap 17 Dec '98 in a case of extreme necessity, later anointed, ae 5 da; d/ Juan Domingo LUXAN & M^{a} ROM^{o}, *Ynd^{s} del pueb^{o}*; gp/ Cand^{a} PAEZ (sic), *vecina de esta Jurisd^{n}*, & her son, Jose GONZ^{z}. (Frames 1328-1329)

Frame 1329
BORICA, Mª Tomasa de Jesus *Pueb^{o}*
bap 23 Dec '98, ae 7 da; d/ Jose Ant^{o} BORICA & Teresa MELENIA, *Ynd^{s} de este pueb^{o}*; gp/ Jose Tom^{s} ROM^{o} & Mª Manuela ROM^{o}, *vecinos de esta Jurisd^{n}*.

ROMERO, Jose Miguel *Pueb^{o}*
bap 26 Dec 1798, ae 5 da; s/ Jose Francisco ROM^{o} & Concep^{n} REYNA, *Yndios del pueb^{o}*; gp/ Jose Joaquin MARTIN & Juana Mª Cand^{a} CHAVES, *vecinos*.

CORTES, Juan Pasqual *Vecino*
bap 30 Dec 1798, ae 5 da; s/ Jose Maria CORTES & Rafaela ROM^{o}; gp/ Cruz CORTES & Mª Concepcion PAEZ, *todos vecinos de esta Jurisd^{n}*.

"Siguen las partidas, año de 1799 enel Libro nuevo. (Signed) Fr. Jose de VERA. (The entries for 1799 are in the new book.)

(End of reel, end of book).

NEW MEXICO BAPTISMS
CATHOLIC PARISHES and MISSIONS in TAOS
VOLUME I
19 June 1701 - 31 December 1826

Archives of the Archdiocese of Santa Fe Film
AASF Reel #19
13 Jan 1799 - 8 Oct 1826

Frame 1 Presentation page

Frame 2
ROMERO, Francisco *Pueb^o*
bap 13 Jan 1799, ae 8 da; s/ Juan ROMERO & Rafaela MIRABALL, *Yndios de este pueb^o*; gm/ Rafaela XAN.

LOBATO, Maria Soledad *Vec^a*
bap 13 Jan (1)799, ae 3 da; d/ Salvador LOBATO & Candelaria (worn-COR)DOVA; gp/ Juan Yg^o SANCHEZ & Pasquala VEJIL, *todos vecinos de esta Jur(isd^n-worn)*.

GONZALEZ, Maria Dolores *Vec^a*
bap 13 Jan '99, ae 7 da; d/ Juan Domingo GONZALEZ & Rosalia TRUXILLO; gp/ Ant^o MONDRAGON & his daughter, Gertrudis (MONDRAGON), *todos vecinos de la Jurisd^n*.

MONTOYA, Jose Rafael *Vec^o*
bap 20 Jan '99, ae 5 da; d/ Antonio MO(NTOYA-worn) & Rosa SANDOVAL; gp/ Juan Domingo TAFOYA & Dolores MAESE, *todos son vec^s desta Jurisdiccion*.

CHAVES, Jose Pablo *Vec^o*
bap 27 Jan '99, ae 4 da; s/ (torn-n.n.) CHAVES & Maria ORTEGA; gp/ Ygnacio DURAN & Antonia SANCHEZ, *todos (des)ta (torn) Jurisdiccion*.

M(torn)TIA, Juan Rafael *Vec^a*
ARELLANO, Juan Rafael
bap 29 Jan '99, ae 10 da; s/ José M(torn)TIA, *vecino del Rio Arriba*, & Rafaela ARELLANO, *vecina, ambos solteros*; gp/ Cruz MARTINEZ & Mª Luz *id* (MARTINEZ), *vecinos de esta Jurisd^n*.

(torn)MA, Paula
ESPINOSA, Paula *Pueb^o*
bap 3 Feb '99, ae 3 da; d/ Migue(l) (torn)MA & Lucia ESPINOSA; gp/ Jualian MALINCHE & Lucia DURAN, *tod(os) del pueb^o*.

MARTINEZ, Mª Candelaria *Vec^a*
bap 6 Feb '99, ae 5 da; d/ (torn-Ger)vacio MARTINEZ & Juana CORTES; gp/ Juan Yg^o SANCHEZ & Tomasa (n.s.), *todos vecinos dela Jurisd^n*.

Frame 3
ARMENTA, Maria Augustina *Vec^a Esp^a*
bap 11 Feb '99, ae 1 da; d/ Simon ARMENTA & Marta MARTIN; gm/ Mª Tomasa MARTIN, vecinos todos de la Jurisd^n.

GARCIA, Miguel Ant^o Vec^o
bap 17 Feb '99, ae 5 da; s/ Juan Angel GARCIA & Manuela MARTIN; gp/ Juan Rafael (n.s.) & Josefa LEAL, *todos vecinos de esta Jurisdiccion*.

TIO, Manuel *Pueb^{o}*
bap 17 Feb '99, ae 7 da; s/ Jose Ant^{o} TIO & Maria TUSA, *Ynd^{s} deste pueb^{o}*; gm/ Marta MARTIN, *v^{a} dela Jurisd^{n}*.

ROMERO, Mª Rosa *Pueb^{o}*
bap 3 Mch '99, ae 4 da; d/ Juan Domingo ROMERO & Fran^{ca} LUXAN; gm/ Ana M^{a} ROM^{o}, *Ynd^{a} de este pueb^{o}*.

DURAN, M^{a} Yg^{a} *(torn-Vec)^{a}*
bap 14 Mch '99, ae 3 da; d/ Pablo DURAN & Margarita SANCHEZ; gp/ Jose Mariano FERNAND^{z} & Mª Ascencion LUZ^{o}, *todos vecinos dela Jurisdiccion*.

LUXAN, Juan Ant^{o} (torn-*Pueb)^{o}*
bap 15 Mch '99, ae 4 da; s/ Juan Antonio LUXAN & Josefa MARTIN; gm/ Juana GOMEZ, *Ynd^{s} deste pueb^{o}*.

MOYA, Mª Dolores (torn)
bap 15 Mch '99, ae 5 da; d/ Eusevio MOYA & Rafaela ROM^{o}; gp/ Jose GONZ^{z} & Candelaria PAEZ, *vecinos*.

ORTIZ, Jose Pablo (torn)
bap 30 Mch '99, ae 9 da; s/ *el Alc^{e}* Ant^{o} Jose ORTIZ & Micaela BACA; gp/ Fran^{ca} ORTIZ & Maria GARCIA, *todos vecinos*.

MARTIN, Manuel Greg^{o} (torn)
bap 31 Mch '99, ae 10 da; s/ Juan Felipe MARTIN & Yg^{a} VEJIL, *vec^{s} de esta Jurisd^{n}*; gp/ Juan de Jesus MARTIN & Magdalena MARTIN *del Rio Arriba*.

MEDINA, Mª Paula (torn)
bap 31 Mch '99, ae 8 da; d/ Yg^{o} MEDINA & Marg^{ta} CORDOBA; gp/ Bernardo LUZ^{o} & Tomasa MARTIN, *(torn-vec)inos dela Jurisdiccion*.

Frame 4
ROMERO, Jose Man^{l} *Vec^{o}*
bap 31 Mch '99, ae 9 da; s/ Concepcio(n-worn) ROM^{o} & Rosa QUINTANA; gp/ Silvestre LOPEZ & Rosalia GONZ^{z}, *todos vec^{s} dela Jurisd^{n}*.

MARTIN, Jose Santos *Vec^{o}*
bap 31 Mch '99, ae 12 da; s/ Juan Pablo MARTIN & Guadalupe CHACON, *ves^{s} de Chimayo*; gp/ Juan Ant^{o} DURAN & Candelaria PAEZ *de esta Jurisd^{n}*.

CHACON, Mª Encarnacion *Pueb^{o}*
bap 7 Apr '99, ae 7 da; d/ Fer(nan-torn)do CHACON, *alias* Jose Ant^{o} (n.s.), *Ynd^{o} Cumanche Xtiano deste pueblo*, & Mª Luz GA(torn), *nat^{l} de este mismo*; gm/ Ana M^{a} ROM^{o}, *tamb^{n} del pueb^{o}*.

MONTOYA, Jose Victoriano *Vec^{o}*
bap 7 Apr '99, ae 10 da; s/ Bernardo MONTOYA & Mª MARTIN; gp/ Jose LOBATO & Rosalia MARTIN, *todos v(^{s} de-torn) Taos*.

LASO, Jose Pablo *Pueb^{o}*
bap 14 Apr '99, ae 5 da; s/ Matias LASO & Gu(adalupe-torn, see Frame 76) MARTIN; gm/ Juana ZAMORA, *Yndios del pueb^{o}*.

LUZERO, Jose Rafael *Vec^{o}*
bap 14 Apr '99, ae 5 da; s/ Juan de Jesus LUZ^{o} & Mª Yg^{a} ARAGON *del Rio Arriba*; gp/ Jose VEJIL & Petrona PAC(HECO-torn), *vec^{s} de Taos*.

GONZALEZ, Jose Angel *Vec^{o}*
bap 23 Apr '99, ae 7 da; s/ Jose Santos GONZ^{z} & Mª Dominga MARTIN LISTON; gp/ Ant^{o} ARCHULETA & Jua(na) MARTINEZ, *todos vecinos dela Jurisd^{n}.*

MARTIN, Jose de la Cruz *Vec^{o}*
bap 5 May '99, ae 3 da; s/ (torn-n.n.) MARTIN & Mª Reyes FERNANDEZ; gp/ Bern^{do} LUZ^{O} & Tomasa (n.s.-torn), *todos vec^{s} desta.*

ORTIZ (gp), Maria Juliana *Ynd^{a} Vec^{a}*
bap 12 May '99 after being instructed in the faith, ae *adulte*; d/ *Apache Xicarilla*; gp/ D^{n} Jose ORTIZ & D^{a} Micaela BACA, *amos de ella*. (Frames 4-5)

Frame 5
BRITO, Mª Manuela *Vec^{a}*
bap 23 May '99, ae 3 da; d/ Fran^{co} BRITO & Margarita GONZ^{z}; gp/ Felipe TENORIO & Ant^{a} Rosa GABALDON, *vecinos.*

ROMERO, Juan Salvador *Vec^{o}*
bap 30 May '99, ae 6 da; s/ Lazaro ROMERO & Barbara GONZ^{z}; gp/ Salvador Orta MADRID & Mª Luz BLEA, *todos vecinos de esta.*

RAEL, Antonio Maximino *Vec^{o}*
bap 13 Jne '99, ae 5 da; s/ Lazaro RAEL & Concepcion PAEZ; gp/ J^{n} Yg^{o} GONZALEZ & Margarita BERNAL, *todos vec^{s} de Taos.*

RIO, Juan Domingo *Pueb^{o}*
bap 24 Jne '99, ae 10 da; s/ Fran^{co} RIO & Josefa LUZ^{O}; gm/ Lugarda SERNA, *siendo tod^{s} Yndios de este pueb^{o}.*

HERRERA, Pedro Ant^{o} *Vec^{o}*
bap 3 Jly '99, ae 5 da; s/ Jose Simon HERRERA, *llamado antes* Vic^{te} ATENSIO, & Juana MONTOYA; gp/ Miguel (n.s.) & Gertrudis COCA, *todos vecinos.*

MIRABALL, Mª Clara *Vec^{a}*
bap 15 Aug '99, ae 4 da; d/ Domingo MIRABALL (sic) & Mª MIRAB^{L}; gp/ Rafael VEJIL & Nicolasa id (VEJIL), *todos vecinos de Taos.*

TUZA, Petra
*bap 7 (sic) Jly '99, ae 9 da; d/ Domingo TUZA & Dominga DURAN, *Ynd^{s}*; gp/ Ant^{o} ARAG^{N} & Petrona PA(CHE-torn)CO, *vec^{s}.*

Frame 6
MONTOYA, Mª Juana Vec^{s}
bap 16 Jly '99, ae 5 da; d/ Jose Raf^{l} MONTOYA & Luiza ROMERO; gp/ Ant^{o} BLEA & Barbara MONTOYA, *tod^{s} vecinos de Taos.*

RAMOS, Enrique Desiderio *Vec^{o}*
bap 21 Jly '99; s/ Man^{l} RAMOS & Mª SANDOV^{L}; gp/ Cruz VEJIL & Mª Clara FERN^{Z}, *tod^{s} vec^{s} de Taos.*

GOMEZ, Jose Fran^{co} *Pueblo*
bap 18 Aug '99, ae 9 da; s/ Jose GOMEZ & Manuela NARANJO; gm/ Yg^{o} RIOS, *Ynd^{s} de Taos.*

GOMEZ (gm), Mª Soledad *Pueb^{o}*
bap 25 Aug '99, ae 3 da; d/ Jose (torn-n.s.) & Mª Rosa (n.s.); gm/ Juana GOMEZ, *Ynd^{s} Taoses.*

LUZERO, Juan Man^{l} *Pueb^{o}*
bap 25 Aug '99, ae 4 da; s/ Juan Domingo LUZ^{o} & Gertrudis ROMERO; gm/ Josefa ROM^{o}, *Yn(d^{s} Ta)oses.*

SANDOVAL, Jose Miguel *Vec^{o}*
bap 8 Sep '99, ae 4 da; s/ Matias SANDOVAL & Yg(^{a}) BUENO; gp/ Gervasio MARTIN & Juana CORT^{S}, *tod^{s} vec^{s} de Taos.*

COCA, Mª Dominga *Vec^{a}*
bap 8 Sep '99, ae 8 da; d/ Jose M^{a} C(OCA-torn) (see Frame 45) & Juana BENAVIDES; gp/ Jose Mar^{no} FERNANDEZ & Ascencion LUZERO, *vec^{s} de Taos.*

MARTIN, Mª Manuela *Vec^{a}*
bap 8 Sep '99, ae 10 da; d/ Roque MARTIN & Mª Greg(o-torn)ria ARMIJO; gp/ Jose MIERA & Manuela ROMERO, *vecinos de Taos.*

ORTEGA, Manuel Vicente Vec^{o}
bap 15 Sep '99, ae 7 da; s/ (Ma)nuel ORTEGA & Rita COCA; gp/ Jose Ant^{o} ROM^{o} & Mª Ant^{a} CORTES, *(ve)cinos de Taos.*

BLEA, Miguel Cipriano *Ve^{o}*
bap 29 Sep '(9)9, ae 5 da; s/ Ant^{o} BLEA & Barbara MONTOYA; gp/ Estevan BACA & Luz MARTINEZ, *vecinos de Taos.* (Frames 6-7)

Frame 7
LOBATO, Maria Micaela *Vec^{a}*
bap 29 Sep '99, ae 2 da; s/ Ant^{o} LOBATO & Mª CHAVES; gp/ Bernardo LUZERO & Tomasa MARTIN, *vecinos de Taos.*

RIOS, Pablo *Pueb^{o}*
bap 6 Oct '99, ae 7 da; s/ Juan Ant^{o} RIOS & Magdalena ROM^{o}; gm/ Paula GUERRERO, *Yndios Taoses.*

CRUZ, Fran^{co} Ant^{o} *Vec^{o}*
bap 20 Oct '99, ae 16 da; s/ Mariano Ant^{o} CRUZ & Mª Dolores VEJIL; gp/ Salv^{or} Ant^{o} MEDINA & Mª Josefa MARTIN *de Chimayo.*

MEDINA, Mª Rosa Bibiana
bap 20 Oct '99, ae 9 da; d/ J^{n} Xtoval MEDINA & Josefa CORDOVA; gp/ Jose Pablo BACA & Josefa VEGIL, *vec^{s}.*

VEJIL, Jose Rafael
bap 27 Oct '99, ae 8 da; s/ Juan Yg^{o} VEJIL & Jacinta ARAGON, *vec^{s} de Taos;* gf/ D^{n} Juan Rafael ORTIZ, *casado con D^{a}* M^{a} del Rosario TRONCOSO, *vecinos dela villa de Sta Fee.*

ARCHULETA, Jose Vic^{te} *Vec^{o}*
bap 31 Oct '99, ae 6 da; s/ Pablo ARCHULETA & Barbara LOBATO; gf/ Juan DURAN, *vecinos de Taos.*

RIO, Barbara *(Pue)b^{o}*
bap 17 Nov '99, ae 4 da; d/ Ant^{o} RIO & Juana OJAS AMARRADAS; gm/ Maria Ant^{a} ORTIZ, *tod^{s} del pueb^{o}.*

ROMERO, Mª Josefa (torn)
bap 17 Nov 1799, ae 6 da; d/ Antonio (torn-ROM)ERO & Mª MONTOYA; gp/ Lorenzo XARAMILLO & Mª Luz ROM^{o}.

Frame 8
MONDRAGON, Maria Teodora Alvina *Vec^{a}*
bap 23 Nov '99, ae 8 da; d/ Mariano MONDRAGON & Encarn^{n} ESPINOSA; gp/ Juan Xtov^{l} CORT^{S} & Mª Fran^{ca} SANDOVAL, *vecinos de Taos.*

ARCHULETA, Mª Soledad *Pueb^{o}*
bap 1 Dec '99, ae 10 da; d/ Juan Domingo ARCHULETA & Mª Rosa CATUJE; gm/ Maria Tomasa ROMERO, *Ynd^{s} Taoses.*

CHAYA, Ysidro *Pueb^{o}*
bap 8 Dec '99, ae 8 da; s/ Ju(an) Antonio (n.s.) & Ant^{a} CHAYA, *Ynd^{s} Taoses;* gp/ Jose GONZALE(S) & his daughter, Sebastiana (GONZALES) *dela Cieneguilla* .

An entry very definitely crossed out
DURAN, M(aria-torn) Guadalupe *Vecino*
bap 17 Dec '99 because of necessity, ae 6 da; d/ Nicolas DURAN & Juana BARELA; gp/ Jose MARTIN & his sister, (torn) *vecinos dela Jurisd^{n}.* (Frames 8-9)

Frame 9
GONZALEZ, Maria Rosa *Pueblo*
bap 22 Dec '99, ae 7 da; d/ Domingo GONZALEZ & Josefa ROM^{O}; gm/ Juana M^{a} ROM^{O}.

Año de 1800

SANCHEZ, Maria Reyes *V^{a}*
bap 12 Jan 1800, ae 7 da; d/ Diego SANCHEZ & Magdalena MARTIN, *vecinos del Rio Arriba;* gp/ Miguel VEJIL & Ana Mª VALLEJOS, *vecinos de esta.*

ROMERO, Rafael *Pueb^{o}*
bap 12 Jan 1800, ae 8 da; d/ Juan Domingo ROM^{O} & Fran^{ca} (n.s.); gm/ Rafaela GONZ^{Z}, *Yndios Taoses.*

GOMEZ, Ant^{o} (torn)
bap 12 Jan 1800, ae 6 da; s/ Fran^{co} GOM^{Z} & Lucia TECOA; gm/ Encarn^{n} LUJAN, *Ynd^{s} Taoses.*

ROMERO, Juana Josefa *V^{a}*
bap 15 Jan 1800, ae 4 da; d/ Fran^{co} Estevan ROM^{O} & Mª Dolores SALAZAR, *vecinos de esta;* gf/ Juan Ysidro LOBATO, *v^{o} de Chama.*

BUENO, Jose Rafael *V^{o}*
bap 19 Jan 1800, ae 6 da; s/ Pedro BUENO & Mª ROMERO; gp/ Jose ARAGON & Rafaela BUENO, *todos vecinos de Taos.*

ARCHULETA, Mª Man^{la} *V^{a}*
bap 19 Jan 1800, ae 9 da; d/ Ant^{o} ARCHULETA & Juana MARTIN; gp/ Silvestre LOPEZ & Rosalia GONZALEZ, *vecinos todos de esta.* (Frames 9-10)

Frame 10
LEAL, Jose de la Cruz *V^{o}*
bap 19 Jan 1800, ae 2 da; s/ Juan Domingo LEAL & Mª Veronica CORTE^{S}; gm/ Josefa LEAL.

CHULA (patron), Maria *Ynd^{a} C^{a} pueb^{o}*
bap 19 Jan 1800, ae about 20 yr; d/ *Ynd^{a} Cumamcha, criada de* Catarina CHULA, Taos Indian; gp/ Simon ARMENTA & Marta MARTIN, *vecin^{s}.*

SILVA, Juana Paula V^{a}
bap 26 Jan 1800, ae 6 da; d/ Jose Roque SILVA & Rafaela PINEDA; gp/ Juan Pedro BUENA & Man^{la} ROM^{o}, *vecinos*.

TRUXILLO, Man^{l} Ant^{o} V^{o}
bap 2 Feb 1800, ae 8 da; s/ Andres TRUXILLO & M(^{a}) Ant^{a} LOPEZ; gp/ Ant^{o} Domingo ROM^{o} & Mª COCA, *vecinos*.

CAIGUA, Juan Domingo P^{o}
bap 2 Feb 1800, ae 8 da; s/ Juan Domingo CAIGUA & Fran^{ca} REYNA; gm/ Juana ROM^{o}, *Ynd^{s} Taoses*.

LUXAN, Juana P^{o}
bap 2 Feb 1800, ae 7 da; d/ Fran^{co} LUXAN & Mª Anton(ia) GONZ^{z}; gm/ Fran^{ca} LUCERO, *Ynd^{s} Taoses*.

GONZALEZ, Mª Ant^{a} P^{o}
bap 2 Feb 1800, ae 10 da; d/ J^{n} Domingo GONZ^{z} & Mª Ant^{a} MARTIN; gm/ Ant^{a} GONZ^{z}, *Ynd^{s} Taoses*.

MARQUEZ, Mª Rosa V^{o}
bap 2 Feb 1800, ae 9 da; d/ Domingo MARQUEZ & Mª Ascencion LOMA; gm/ Rosa COLORADO *de Taos*.

CONTRERAS, Mª Ysabel Indian
bap 16 Feb 1800, ae 8 da; d/ Juan Cruz CON(TRERAS--see Frame 56) & Mª MONTOYA; gp/ Pablo DURAN & M^{a} dela Luz SANCHES, *vecino desta*. (Frames 10-11)

Frame 11
MARTIN, Maria Man^{la} V^{a}
bap 16 Feb 1800, ae 6 da; d/ Jose Pablo MARTIN & Mª Gertrudis BALLEJOS; gf/ Juan Bautista BALLEJOS, *tod^{s} ves^{s}*.

ARAGON, Jose Ant^{o} V^{o}
bap 16 Feb 1800, ae 3 da; s/ Ant^{o} ARAGON & Xaviera VEJIL; gp/ Ant^{o} Jose VEJIL & Jacinta ARAG^{N}, *tod^{s} vecinos*.

LAZO, Maria Soledad P^{o}
bap 16 Feb 1800, ae 2 da; d/ Jose Ant^{o} LAZO & Ana TUZA; gp/ Gulian GUERRERO & Lucia DURAN, *tod^{s} Ynd^{s} Taoses*.

LUXAN, Catarina P^{o}
bap 16 Feb 1800, ae 3 da; d/ Juan Ant^{o} LUXAN & Barb^{a} ROM^{o}; gm/ Micaela ROMERO, *todos del pueb^{o}*.

DURAN, Fran^{co} P^{o}
bap 1 Mch 1800, ae 8 da; s/ Juan Domingo DURAN & Barbara MARTIN; gm/ Micaela GONSALEZ, *todos Ynd^{s} Taoses*.

GONZALEZ, Juana
bap 1 Mch 1800 because of extreme necessity by Ana Mª MEDINA, midwife; d/ Juan GONZALEZ & Ant^{a} MARTIN; gf/ Hermenegildo CISNEROS, *vec^{o} del Rio Arriba*. (Frames 11-12)

Frame 12
MARTIN, Maria Ygnacia V^{a}
bap 9 Mch 1800, ae 8 da; d/ Ramon MARTIN & Paula MARTIN, *alias* CHAVACANO; gp/ Juan (n.s.) & Fran^{ca} LOPEZ, *todos vecinos de esta*.

GONZALEZ, Mª Magdalena *V^{a}*
bap 30 Mch 1800, ae 11 da; d/ Jose GONZ^{z} & Dorotea BACA; gp/ Rafael LUNA & Manuela ROM^{o}, *vecinos dela Jurisd^{n}*.

CORTES, Jose Fran^{co} *V^{o}*
bap 3 Apr 1800, ae 2 da; s/ Jose CORTES & Juana MONTOYA; gp/ Paulin de HERRERA & M^{a} del Carmen MADRID.

DURAN, Jose Fran^{co} *V^{o}*
bap 3 Apr 1800, ae 3 da; s/ Pedro Yg^{o} DURAN & Mª Ant^{a} SANCHEZ; gp/ Pedro MA(R)TIN & Mª Reyes FERNANDEZ.

CASADO, Francisco *P^{o}*
bap 20 Apr 1800, ae 8 da; *espurio* s/ Fran^{co} CASADO & Juana M^{a} (n.s.), *la Picuries*; gm/ Man^{la} DURAN.

LUXAN, Mariano *P^{o}*
bap 27 Apr (18)00, ae 10 da; s/ J^{n} Ant^{o} LUXAN & Micaela SERNA; gm/ Mª Yg^{a} MARTIN, *Ynd^{s} Taoses*. (Frames 12-13)

Frame 13
LOPEZ, Mª Micaela *V^{a}*
bap 27 Apr 1800, ae 3 da; d/ Silvestre LOPEZ & Rosalia GONZ^{z}; gp/ Pablo DURAN & Marg^{ta} SANCHEZ, *vecinos*.

CRUS, Jose Ant^{o} *V^{o}*
bap 27 Apr 1800, ae 4 da; s/ Ant^{o} Casimiro CRUS & Ynes ARMIJO; gp/ Juan Yg^{o} VEJIL & Mª Ant^{a} ARAGON, *todos vec^{s}*.

FRESQUIZ, Domingo *V^{o}*
bap 27 Apr 1800, ae 8 da; s/ father unknown & Ana FRESQUIZ; gp/ Juan Yg^{o} GONZ^{z} & Marg^{ta} BARELA, *vec^{s}*.

VARELA (patron), Maria dela Cruz *V^{a}*
bap 3 May 1800, ae 3 da; d/ father unknown & Mª Fran^{ca} (n.s.), *coyota de* Felipe VARELA; gp/ Joaq^{n} MARTIN & Cand^{a} CHAVES.

TAFOYA, Juana Catarina *V^{a}*
bap 4 May 1800, ae 6 da; d/ Miguel TAFOYA & Juana ROM^{o}; gp/ Pedro Yg^{o} ESPINOSA & his daughter, Maria de la Luz (ESPINOSA), *de Chimayo, vec^{s}*.

RAMOS (gp), Joseph
bap 11 May 1800 in extreme nesessity, ae about 8 da; s/ unknown; gp/ Manuel RAMOS & Manuela SANDOBAL, *becinos de esta*.

Frame 14
ROMERO, Andres *P^{o}*
bap 11 May 1800, ae 8 da; s/ Antonio ROMERO, dec., & Teresa ROYBAL; gm/ Lucia ROYBAL, *Yndios Taoses*.

ROMERO, Toribio *P^{o}*
bap 11 May 1800, ae 9 da; s/ Ju(an) Antonio ROMERO & Micaela NARANJO; gp/ Maria Rosa COLORADO, *Yndios Tauses*.

SUASO, Juan *Pu(e)b^{o}*
bap 18 May 1800, ae 8 da; s/ Jose Ant^{o} SUASO & Rafaela GONZ^{z}; gm/ Man^{la} LUXAN, all Indians.

LOBATO (patron), Felipe *V^o*
bap 28 May 1800, ae 6 da; s/ father unknown & M^a (n.s.), *Ynd^a criada de* Ant^o LOBATO; gf/ Antoñito LOBATO.

SILVA, Maria Rosalia *V^a*
bap *V^o* (illegible) Jne 1800, ae 8 da; d/ Santiago SILVA & Encarnacion ESPINOSA VELASQUEZ; gf/ Juan DURAN, *el pastor, vec^s de esta.*

CHAFALOTE, Jose Pablo P^o
*bap 1 Jne 1800, ae 9 da; s/ Jose Ant^o CHAFALOTE & Soledad SUAZO; gm/ Juana RIO, *Ynd^s Taoses.*

LUXAN, Lucia *P^o*
bap 5 Jne 1800, ae 4 da; d/ J^n Do(mingo) LUXAN & Fran^{ca} ROM^O; gm/ Rafaela ROM^O, *Ynd^s Taoses.*

GOMEZ, Jose Martin *P^o*
bap 8 Jne 1800, ae 4 da; s/ father unknown & Juana GOMEZ, *Ynd^a Taos;* gf/ Jose GARCIA, *v^o.* (Frames 14-15)

Frame 15
GARCIA, Mª Dolores *P^a*
bap 8 Jne 1800, ae 5 da; d/ Jose GARCIA & Mª Ant^a MARTIN; gm/ Juana de LUNA, *vec^s de este.*

ROMERO, Mª Cecilia *P^o*
bap 8 Jne 1800, ae 9 da; d/ Jose Ant^o ROMERO & Man^{la} LUCERO, *Indios Taoses;* gm/ Rosa ARIAS, *vec^a.*

TIO, Juana *P^o*
bap 22 Jne 1800, ae 10 da; d/ Jose Anton^o TIO & Mª TUZA; gm/ Juana PAEZ, *Ynd^s Taoses.*

ROMERO, Jose Ant^o *P^o*
bap 22 Jne 1800, ae 10 da; s/ Juan Domingo ROM^O & Mª LUCERO; gm/ Man^{la} FRESQUIZ, *Ynd^s Taoses.*

PADILLA, Juan de Jesus *P^o*
bap 24 Jne 1800, ae 8 da; s/ Santiago PADILLA & Josefa LUXAN; gm/ Fran^{ca} ZAPATA, *Ynd^s Taoses.*

VARGAS, Jose *V^o*
bap 20 Jly 1800, ae 6 da; s/ Maurilo VARGAS & Nicomeda FERN^Z; gp/ Juan DURAN, *vecinos de este Jurisd^n.*

ROMERO, Juan del Carmen
bap 20 Jly 1800, ae 5 da; s/ Ant^o ROM^O & Josefa LUXAN; gp/ Ant^o BLEA & Barbara MONTOYA, *vecinos dela Jurisd^n.*

Frame 16
LOBATO (patron), Maria Ant^a *V^a Yn*
bap 27 Jly 1800, ae 6 mo; d/ *Apacha de D^n* Ant^o LOBATO; gp/ Bern^{do} MONTOYA & Mª MARTIN, *ves^s.*

FERNANDEZ, Juan Lorenzo *V^o*
bap 10 Aug 1800, ae 2 da; s/ Jose Mar^{no} FERN^Z & Mª Ascencion (n.s.); gp/ J^n Nepom^{no} MARES & Clara SANCHEZ.

ARGUELLO, Juan de Jesus *V*^{o}
bap 19 Aug 1800, ae 9 da; s/ Fran^{co} ARGUELLO & Clara SANDOVAL; gp/ Ant^{o} Jose ROM^{o} & Mª Ant^{a} CORTES, *todos vecinos*.

LUXAN, Jose Vicente *P*^{o}
bap 24 Aug 1800, ae 8 da; s/ Juan Domingo LUXAN & Josefa ROM^{o}; gm/ Teresa ROIBAL *del pueb*^{o}.

MADRID, Mª Lorenza *V*$^{\underline{o}}$
bap 3 Sep 1800, ae 18 da; d/ Juan MADRID & Prudencia XARAMILLO; gp/ Salv^{or} MADRID & Filena MARTIN *de la* Cieneguilla.

BUENO, Jose Vicente *V*^{o}
bap 7 Sep 1800, ae 6 da; s/ Antonio BUENO & Mª Rosalia VALDES; gp/ Jose Ant^{o} (n.s.) & Mª Ynes LEAL, *v*(^{s}*-torn*).

LOBATO, M^{a} Ma(torn) *V*^{a}
bap 7 Sep 1800, ae 8 da; d/ Domingo LOBATO & Clara MARTIN; gp/ Jose (torn-see Frames 45 & 62--CO)CA & J^{a} BENAVIDES, *vec*^{s}.

Frame 17
HOLGUIN, Jose Ant^{o} *V*^{o}
bap 7 Sep 1800, ae 4 da; s/ father unknown & Mª Gertrudis HOLGUIN, single; gp/ Feliz MARTIN & Yg^{a} GONZ^{z}, *vecinos*.

ROMERO, Geronimo *P*^{o}
bap 14 Sep 1800, ae 8 da; s/ Jose Ant^{o} ROM^{o} & Micaela RASO; gm/ Micaela SERNA *del pueb*^{o}.

PASQUA, Fran^{co} *P*^{o}
bap 5 Oct 1800, ae 7 da; s/ Jose Ant^{o} PASQUA & J^{a} M^{a} ROM^{o}; gm/ Mª Raf^{la} MIRABAL *del pueb*^{o}.

ROMERO, Ant^{o} *P*^{o}
bap 12 Oct 1800, ae 9 da; s/ Juan Mig^{l} ROM^{o} & Fran^{ca} (n.s.); gm/ Magdalena MARTIN *del pueb*^{o}.

MARTIN, Fran^{ca} *P*^{o}
bap 2 Nov 1800, ae 8 da; d/ Ant^{o} MARTIN & Guadalupe (n.s.); gm/ Teresa (n.s.) *del pueb*^{o}.

ZAMORA, Jose Pablo *P*^{o}
bap 6 Nov 1800, ae 3 da; s/ Ant^{o} ZAMORA & Josefa (n.s.); gm/ Catarina CHULA *del pueb*^{o}.

BACA, Mª de Jesus *P*$^{\underline{o}}$
bap 6 Nov 1800, ae 2 da; d/ Jose Pablo BACA & Josefa VEJIL; gp/ Bautista VEJIL & Rosalia MARTIN, *vec*^{s}.

Frame 18
MARTIN, Juan Yg^{o} de Jesus *V*^{o}
bap 22 Nov 1800, ae 11 da; s/ Jose Joaquin MARTIN & Candelaria CHAVES; gp/ Juan GONZ^{z} & Mª Ant^{a} MARTIN, *vecinos*.

BUENO, Andres de Jesus *V*^{o}
bap 30 Nov 1800, ae 8 da; s/ Pedro BUENO & Man^{la} ROM^{o}; gp/ Man^{l} Ant^{o} SANDOVAL & Mª Antonia LOBATO, *vecin*^{s}.

GARCIA, Mª Micaela *V^{a}*
bap 30 Nov 1800, ae 10 da; d/ Juan Ang^{l} GARCIA & Mª Man^{la} MARTIN; gp/ Yg^{o} MEDINA & Margarita CORDOVA, *vec^{s}*.

AÑOQUEVIENE, Ana M^{a} *P^{o}*
bap 12 Dec 1800, ae 9 da; d/ J^{n} Domingo AÑOQ^{E}VIENE & Josefa LUC^{O}; gm/ Ana LUXAN, *Ynd^{s} Taoses*.

BRITO, Mª Concepcion *V^{a}*
bap 14 Dec 1800, ae 7 da; d/ Jose BRITO & Dolores SANCHEZ; gp/ Jose Ant^{o} SUASO & Mª Josefa VILLALPANDO, *vecinos*.

DURAN, Mª Dolores *V^{a}*
bap 21 Dec 1800, ae 4 da; d/ Pablo DURAN & Marg^{ta} SANCHEZ; gp/ Fran^{co} MARTINEZ & Tomasa SANCHEZ, *vec^{s}*.

Año 1801

VEJIL, Juana M^{a} *V^{a}*
bap 1 Jan 1801, ae 7 da; d/ J^{n} Yg^{o} VEJIL & Mª Ant$^{\underline{o}}$ ARAGON; gp/ Mig^{l} VEJIL & Ana Mª VALLEJOS, *vec^{s}*.

MARTIN, Manuel Jose *V^{o}*
bap 4 Jan 1801, ae 8 da; s/ Felipe MARTIN & Concep^{n} TRUXILLO; gp/ Jose Yg^{o} MART(IN-torn) & (torn-Ma)ria Josefa TRUXILLO, *vecinos*. (Frames 18-19)

Frame 19
LUXAN, Juan Gaspar *P^{o}*
bap 6 Jan 1801, ae 4 da; s/ Jose Fran^{co} LUXAN & Mª Ant^{a} ROM^{O}, dec; gm/ Maria LUX^{N}, *todos Ynd^{s} Taoses*.

ROMERO, Juan delos Reyes *V^{o}*
bap 9 Jan 1801, ae 5 da; s/ Jose ROM^{O} & Juana TAFOYA; gp/ Pedro MARTIN & Mª Reyes FERNAN^{Z}, *vecinos*.

REYNA, Juan Ant^{o} *P^{o}*
bap 11 Jan 1801, ae 3 da; s/ Jose REYNA & Rosa LOMA; gm/ M^{a} ROM^{O}, *Ynd^{s} Taoses*.

SERNA, Manuela *P^{o}*
bap 11 Jan 1801, ae 7 da; d/ Juan Domingo SERNA & Mª Luisa ROM^{O}; gm/ J^{a} M^{a} ROM^{O}, Taoses.

PINEDA, M^{a} Yg^{a} *V^{a}*
bap 18 Jan 1801, ae 8 da; d/ Jacinto PINEDA & Josefa LEAL; gp/ Salv^{or} GONZ^{Z} & M^{a} *ids* (GONZ^{Z}), *vecinos*.

TUZA, J^{a} Maria Pueb^{o}
bap 18 Jan 1801, ae 3 da; d/ Domingo TUZA & Dominga TECOA; gm/ Juana ROM^{O}, Taoses.

MARQUEZ, Fran^{co} *P^{o}*
bap 18 Jan 1801, ae 7 da; s/ Eusevio MARQ^{Z} & Rafaela ROM^{O}; gm/ Mª Rosa MARTIN.

LOBATO, Juan de Jesus *V^{o}*
bap 19 Jan 1801, ae 5 da; s/ father unknown & Josefa LOBATO, single; gp/ J^{n} Jose LOBATO & Mª Ant^{a} SANCHEZ, *vecinos*.

LOBATO, Marcelo *V^{o}*
bap 19 Jan 1801, ae 4 da; s/ Antonio LOBATO & Mª CHAVES; gp/ Rafael LUNA & Ana Mª TAFOYA, *vecinos*.

ARMENTA, Mariano (torn)
bap 21 Jan 1801, ae 14 da; s/ Simon ARMENTA & Marta MARTIN; gp/ *el Ten^{te} de Pecuries* Tomas LOPEZ & Juana TENORIO, *todos vecinos*. (Frames 19-20)

Frame 20
ARGUELLO, Jose Pablo *V^{o}*
bap 1 Feb 1801, ae 9 da; s/ Ysidro ARGUELLO & Guadalupe GONZALEZ; gp/ Concep^{n} ROM^{o} & Ascencion LUC^{o}, *todos vecinos*.

BARGAS, Juan Nepomuceno *V^{o}*
bap 2 Feb 1801, ae 4 da; s/ Estevan BARGAS & Mª Ant^{a} TAFOYA; gp/ Jose Ant^{o} MARTIN & Mª Ynes LEAL, *vec^{s}*.

MARTIN, Maria Olaya *V^{a}*
bap 12 Feb 1801 because of extreme necessity, ae 6 da; d/ J^{n} del Carmen MARTIN & Mª Nazarena (n.s.), *vecinos*; gp/ (not given).

ROMERO, Rosalia *P^{o}*
bap 15 Feb 1801, ae 8 da; d/ J^{n} Ant^{o} ROM^{o} & Ant^{a} LOMA; gm/ Josefa ROMERO, *Ynd^{s} Taoses*.

ROMERO, Mª Juana *P^{o}*
bap 15 Feb 1801, ae 3 da; d/ Fran^{co} ROM^{o} & Concep^{n} GUERRERO *del pueb^{o}*; gp/ Maurito VARG^{S} & Nicomeda FERNANDEZ, *vecinos*.

ROMERO, Mª Antonia *V^{a}*
bap 17 Feb 1801, ae 4 da; d/ Concep^{n} ROM^{o} & Rosa QUINTANA; gp/ Jose MIRABAL<u>L</u> (sic) & Barb^{a} ROM^{o}, *vecinos*.

LUXAN, Jose Man^{l} *P^{o}*
bap 1 Mch 1801, ae 5 da; s/ Santiago LUXAN & Mª Rosa CHINO; gm/ Maria CHAYO *del p^{o}*.

MONDRAGON, Mig^{l} Vicente *V^{o}*
bap 5 Mch 1801, ae 13 da; s/ Xtoval MONDRAG^{N} & Rafaela GONZ^{Z}; gp/ Jose Mª CORT^{S} & Raf^{la} ROM^{o}, *vecinos*.

MARTIN, Jose Mig^{l} *P^{o}*
bap 5 Mch 1801, ae 3 da; s/ Jose Ant^{o} MARTIN & Asc^{n} LOMA *del p^{o}*; gp/ Felipe MARTIN & Concep^{n} TRUXILLO, *ves^{s}*.

MARTIN, Mª Silveria *V^{a}*
bap 8 Mch 1801, ae <u>7</u> da; d/ Gero^{o} MARTIN & J^{a} CORTES; gp/ J^{n} Ant^{o} BEITIA & A(torn) LUCERO, *vecinos*.

MARTIN, Man^{l} *V^{a}*
bap 8 Mch 1801, ae 5 da; s/ Salv^{r} MARTIN & M. Balvaneda MONTOYA; gp/ Dionisio VEJIL & Manuela REYES, *vecinos*. (Frames 20-21)

Frame 21
TAFOYA, Miguel Ant^{o} *V^{o}*
bap 8 Mch 1801, ae 5 da; s/ Jose Fran^{co} TAFOYA & Micaela RIOS; gp/ Dionisio VEJIL & Manuela REYES, *tod^{s} vecinos*.

NARANJO, Micaela P^{o}
bap 8 Mch 1801, ae 8 da; d/ Santiago NARANJO & J^{a} Maria MARTIN; gm/ Fran^{ca} GOMEZ *del pueb*^{o}.

CASADOS, Juana Gertrudis V^{a}
bap 10 Mch 1801, ae 3 da; d/ J^{n} Ant^{o} CASADOS & Catarina BACA; gp/ Rafael LUNA & Ana Mª TAFOYA, *vecinos*.

MIRAVALL, Santiago V^{o}
bap 15 Mch 1801, ae 4 da; s/ Juan Luis MIRAVALL (sic) & Mª Damasia GONZ^{z}; gp/ J^{n} Dom. GONZ^{z} & Mª Rosalia TRUXILLO, *vecinos*.

ROMERO, Juan Ant^{o} P^{o}
bap 22 Mch 1801, ae 7 da; s/ Ant^{o} ROM^{O} & J^{a} DURAN; gm/ Guadalupe ROMERO *del puebl*^{o}.

BLEA, Jos^{a} Patricia (sic--but has parvulo, hijo, leg^{o}) V^{a}
bap 22 Mch 1801, ae 6 da; child/ Ant^{o} BLEA & Barb^{q} MONTOYA; gp/ Jos. Mª CORTES & Rafaela ROMERO.

MONTOYA, Jose de la Encarn^{n} V^{o}
bap 29 Mch 1801, ae 5 da; s/ Bern^{do} MONTOYA & Maria MARTIN; gp/ J^{n} Nicolas MONTOYA & J^{a} Acasia SANDOV^{L}, *vecinos*.

LOBATO, Mª Man^{la} V^{a}
bap 4 Apr 1801, ae 3 da; d/ Fran^{co} LOBATO & Andrea SANDOVAL; gp/ Juan del Carmen MARTIN & Mª Nazarena LUC^{O}, *todos vec*^{s}.

MARTIN, Mª Dolores P^{o}
bap 5 Apr 1801, ae 10 da; d/ Mª Magdalena MARTIN, single, *del pueblo*; gp/ Simon ARM^{TA} & Marta MARTIN, *vec*^{s}.

MADRID, Josefa (torn)
bap 22 Apr 1801, ae 13 da; d/ Diego Ant^{o} MADRID & Mª Ant^{a} MARTIN, dec., *vec*^{s}; gp/ Simon ARMENTA & Marta MARTIN, *vec*^{s}. (Frames 21-22)

Frame 22

LUCERO, Mª Josefa V^{a}
bap 22 Apr 1801, ae 11 da; d/ Bernardo LUCERO & Tomasa MARTIN; gp/ Dionisio VEJIL & Manuela DELGADO, *todos vecinos*.

CHAVES, Mª Rafaela V^{a}
bap 23 Apr 1801, ae 8 da; d/ Juan CHAVES & Clara SANCHEZ; gp/ Juan Yg^{o} VEJIL & Jacinta ARAGON, *tod*^{s} *vec*^{s}.

ROMERO, Juan Miguel V^{o}
bap 26 Apr 1801, ae 13 da; s/ Santiago ROM^{O} & Mª Ant^{a} LOBATO; gp/ Juan Augustin ROM^{O} (only).

DURAN, Yg^{o} P^{o}
bap 26 Apr 1801, ae 14 da; s/ Juan Andres DURAN & Lugarda SERNA *del pueb*^{o}; gp/ Jose GONZ^{z} & Dorotea BACA, *vec*^{s}.

ROMERO, Mª Pasquala V^{a}
bap 26 Apr 1801, ae 12 da; d/ Ant^{o} ROM^{O} & Mª Ant^{a} VEJIL; gp/ Ant^{o} TAFOYA and his sister, Mª Resurr^{n} (TAFOYA), *vecinos*.

MARTIN, Mª Fran^{ca} *V^{a}*
bap 26 Apr 1801, ae 8 da; d/ J^{n} Cand^{o} MARTIN & Mª Juliana VALLEJOS; gp/ Xtoval VARELA & Raf^{la} MARTIN, *vec^{s}*.

ROMERO, Rosalia *P^{o}*
bap 26 Apr 1801, ae 9 da; d/ J^{n} ROM^{o} & Rafaela LOCCA; gm/ J^{a} Mª LUXAN *del pueb^{o}*.

MARTIN, Mª Soledad *V^{a}*
bap 3 May 1801, ae 10 da; d/ Jose Roque MARTIN & Greg^{a} ARMIJO; gp/ Domingo CHAVES & Juliana (torn, see Frames 39, 47 & others--VALE)RIO.

ROMERO, Ant^{o} Rafael *V^{o}*
bap 14 May 1801, ae 4 da; s/ Mariano ROM^{o} & Fran^{ca} ARMENTA; gp/ Pedro MARTIN & Mª Reyes FERNANDEZ, *vecinos de esta Jurisd^{n}*. (Frames 22-23)

Frame 23
ROMERO, Ygnacia *P^{o}*
bap 14 May 1801, ae 7 da; d/ Pedro ROM^{o} & M. Guadalupe NARANJO; gm/ Ygnacia DURAN *del pueblo*.

MARTIN, Mª Micaela *P^{a}*
bap 17 May 1801, ae 10 da; d/ Tomas MARTIN & Juana (n.s.); gm/ Mª LUXAN, *tod^{s} Taoses*.

TAFOYA, Jose Concep^{n} *V^{o}*
bap 17 May 1801, ae 9 da; s/ Juan Domingo TAFOYA & Dolores MAESE; gp/ Jose TAFOYA & Mª Yg^{a} CANO, *vesinos*.

DURAN, Maria Ysidora *V^{a}*
bap 17 May 1801, ae 10 da; d/ J^{n} Nicolas DURAN & Juana ROMERO; gp/ Jose Mig^{l} TAFOYA & Juana ROMERO, *vecinos*.

VEJIL, Maria Rafaela *V^{a}*
bap 12 Jne 1801, ae 5 da; d/ Juan Yg^{o} VEJIL & Jacinta ARAGON; gf/ Diego MONTOYA, *v^{o} de Sta Fee*.

CHAVES, Juan Ant^{o} *V^{o}*
bap 21 Jne 1801, ae 10 da; s/ Domingo CHAVES & Candelaria DURAN; gp/ Jose MARTIN & Gertrudis MONTOYA, *vec^{s}*.

RODARTE, Juan Bautista *V^{o}*
bap 28 Jne 1801, ae 3 da; s/ Juan Gabriel RODARTE & Juana Tomasa GARCIA; gp/ Felipe VARELA & his daughter, Rafaela (VARELA), *vecinos*.

Frame 24
CASILLAS, Juana de Jesus *V^{a}*
bap 28 Jne 1801, ae 3 da; d/ Jose Lino CASILLAS & Serafina CORTES; gp/ J^{n} Domingo TAFOYA & Yg^{a} CANO, *vecinos de esta*.

ORTIZ, Paula *P^{a}*
bap 12 Jly 1801, ae 14 da; d/ Fran^{co} ORTIZ & Rosa CHIMINI; gm/ Gertrudis ROM^{o}, *Ynd^{s} Taoses*.

GONZALEZ, Ana M^{a} *P^{a}*
bap 12 Jly 1801, ae 7 da; d/ Santiago GONZ^{z} & Josefa ROM^{o}; gm/ Mª Yg^{a} MARTIN, *Taoses*.

DURAN, Ventura dela Encarn^{n} *V^{o}*
bap 12 Jly 1801, ae 8 da; s/ Man^{l} DURAN & Gerarda MASCAREÑAS, *vec^{s} de esta*; gp/ Rafael VARELA & Mª Magdalena LOPEZ of Chimayo.

TAFOYA, Juan de Jesus *V^{o}*
bap 19 Jly 1801, ae 5 da; s/ Miguel TAFOYA & Juana ROM^{o}; gp/ Jos(e) Rafael VEJIL & Elena LOBATO.

TENORIO, Fran^{co} *V^{o}*
bap 25 Jly 1801, ae 2 da; s/ Julian TENORIO & Lorenza LOPEZ; gp/ Rafael LUNA & Ana Mª TAFOYA.

MADRID, Santiago Ant^{o} & Santiago Jose *V^{o}*
bap 27 Jly 1801, b. 25th; twin sons/ Salvador Horta MADRID & Mª Luz BLEA, *vecinos*; gp 1st/ Dionisio (n.s.) & Magdalena BRITO, *vec^{s}*; gp 2nd/ Jose MONTOYA & Mariana CORDOVA.

TENORIO, Jose Santiago *V^{o}*
bap 29 Jly 1801, ae 7 da; s/ Felipe TENORIO & Ant^{a} Ros. GAVALDON; gp/ Antonio LOBATO & Marg^{ta} MARTIN, *vec^{s}*.

CHAVES, Santiago *V^{o}*
bap 2 Aug 1801, ae 9 da; s/ Jose Mª CHAVES & (torn-n.n.) ORTEGA; gm/ Ana Mª MIERA, *vec^{s}*.

SERNA, Maria Paula *P^{o}*
bap 2 Aug 1801, ae 14 da; d/ Juan Ant^{o} SERNA, *alias Cavecita de Cumanche*, married, & Juana Mª NARANJO, single, *doctrina*; gm/ Lucia DURAN *del pueb^{o}*. (Frames 24-25)

Frame 25
RIO, Juan Ant^{o} *P^{o}*
bap 9 Aug 1801, ae 6 da; s/ Ant^{o} RIO & Josefa TIO; gm/ Juana ZAMORA *del pueb^{o}*.

BEITIA, Juana Gertrudis *V^{a}*
bap 16 Aug 1801, ae 8 da; d/ Jose Yg^{o} BEITIA & Rafaela MARTIN; gp/ Jose TAFOYA & Yg^{a} CANO, *vecin^{s}*.

SILVA, Jose de Jesus *V^{o}*
bap 22 Aug 1801, ae 7 da; s/ unknown father & M^{a} As<u>c</u>encion SILVA, single; gp/ Ant^{o} BLEA & Barbara MONTOYA, *vecinos*.

DURAN, Mª Felipa *P^{a}*
GONZALEZ, Mª Felipa
bap 23 Aug 1801, ae 10 da; d/ Jose Ant^{o} DURAN, married, & Ysabel GONZ^{z}, wid.; gm/ Paula GUERR^{o} *del pueb^{o}*.

LUCERO, Jose Pablo *P^{o}*
ROMERO, Jose Pablo
bap 23 Aug 1801, ae 10 da; s/ Jose Ant^{o} LUC^{o} & Man^{la} ROM^{o}, *solteros*; gm/ Lucia DURAN *del pueb^{o}*.

MEDINA, Ramon *V^{o}*
bap 23 Aug 1801, ae 7 da; s/ Yg^{o} MEDINA & Margarita CORDOVA; gp/ Jose GONZ^{z} & Cand^{a} PAEZ, *vecin^{s}*.

GONZALEZ, Fran^{ca} *V^{a}*
bap 28 Aug 1801, ae 3 da; d/ Jose S^{tos} GONZ^{Z} & Mª LISTON; gp/ Jacinto PINEDA & Fran^{ca} SANDOVAL, *vecinos*.

CORTES, Mª Ysabel *V^{a}*
bap 6 Sep 1801, ae 7 da; d/ Jose Mª CORTES & Rafaela ROM^{o}; gp/ Jose Jose (sic) CORTES & Juana Gertrudis MONTOYA, *vecinos*.

LEAL, Fran^{co} Ant^{o} *V^{o}*
bap 13 Sep 1801, ae 7 da; s/ J^{n} Domingo LEAL & Veronica CORTES; gp/ Juan Cruz MARTIN & Dolores TORRES, *vecinos*.

ROMERO, Pedro Ant^{o} torn
bap 15 Sep 1801, ae 10 da; s/ Mariano ROM^{o} & Josefa LOMA, *vecinos*; gf/ Man^{l} SANDOVAL from Rio Arriba.

Frame 26
AGUILAR, Jose Ramon *V^{o}*
bap 19 Sep 1801, ae 9 da; s/ Laz^{o} AGUILAR & Concep^{n} PAEZ; gp/ Jos(e) Baut^{a} VEJIL & Rosalia MARTIN, *vec^{s}*.

ALIRI, Mª Josefa
LOBATO, Mª Josefa *Va*
bap 19 Sep 1801, ae 3 da; d/ Paula LOBATO, wid., & (father) thought to be *de* Juan Lorenzo ALIRI, *alias* LIRA, single, *vecinos de esta Jurisd^{n}*; gp/ Ant^{o} LOBATO & Mª CHAVES.

ESPINOSA, Jose Rafael *P^{o}*
bap 20 Sep 1801, ae 8 da; s/ Jose Ant^{o} ESPINOSA & Catarina CHULA *del pueb^{o}*; gm/ Ana Mª TAFOYA, *vec^{a}*.

LUXAN, Mª Rosa *P^{a}*
bap 20 Sep 1801, ae 9 da; d/ Salv^{or} LUXAN & Margarita MARTIN; gm/ Mª Rosa LUXAN *del pueb^{o}*.

GOMEZ, Mª Dominga *P^{a}*
bap 27 Sep 1801, ae 4 da; d/ Josef GOMEZ & Man^{la} NARANJO *del pueb^{o}*; gp/ *el Alc^{e} D^{n}* Ant^{o} Jose ROMERO & Mª BACA.

PADILLA, Jose Ramon *V^{o} murio*
VEJIL, Jose Ramon Died in infancy
LOBATO, Jose Ramon
bap 27 Sep 1801, ae 7 da; s/ Rafael VEJIL & Elena LOBATO (one line drawn thru above names and in a note at end of entry) *espurio* s/ Julian PADILLA, married, & Nicolasa VEJIL, single; gp/ Bartolome MONDRAG^{N} & Yg^{a} CANO, *todos vecinos*.

PADILLA, Geronimo (blank)
LUXAN, Geronimo
bap 12 Oct 1801, ae 13 da; s/ Santiago PADILLA, wid., & Fran^{ca} (LUXAN), single, d/ S^{n}Tiago LUXAN & Mª GABILAN *del pueb^{o}*; gm/ Marta MARTIN, *vec^{a}*.

MONDRAGON, Juan Manuel *V^{o}*
bap 18 Oct 1801, ae 9 da; s/ unknown father & Gertrudis (MONDRAGON), d/ Mariano MONDRAGON & Encarn^{n} ESPINOSA; gp/ J^{n} Xtov^{l} MONDRAGON & Juana GONZ^{Z}.

BACA, M^{a} dela Luz *V^{a}*
bap 25 Oct 1801, ae 9 da; d/ Man^{l} BACA & Manuela CASADOS; gp/ Jose MIERA & Man^{la} ROM^{o}, *vecin^{s}*.

ROMERO, Mariana *P°*
bap 25 Oct 1801, ae 7 da; d/ Mari(ano-torn) ROMERO & Ascencion DURAN; gm/ Lucia ORTIZ *del pueb°*.

LOPEZ, Tomas Ant° *V°*
bap 28 Oct 1801, ae 8 da; s/ (torn-n.n.) LOPEZ & Teresa TRUXILLO; gp/ Tom^{s} LOBATO & Cand^{a} GONZ^{z}, *todos vecinos*.

Frame 27
ORTEGA, Mª Manuela *V^{a}*
bap 1 Nov 1801, ae 9 da; d/ Man^{l} ORTEGA & Rita COCA; gp/ J^{n} Yg° GONZ^{z} & Margarita BARELA, vecinos.

RAMOS, Mª Fran^{ca} *V^{a}*
bap 17 Nov 1801 because of necessity, ae 9 da; d/ Man^{l} RAMOS & Man^{la} SANDOVAL; gp/ J^{n} Domingo MAESE & Juana Mª HERRERA, *vecinos*.

BUENO, Mª Fran^{ca} *V^{a}*
bap 22 Nov 1801, ae 8 da; d/ Pedro BUENO & Teodora BEITIA; gp/ Jose Lino CASILLAS & Serafina CORT^{S}, *vecinos*.

GOMEZ, Jose Ant° *P°*
bap 22 Nov 1801, ae 4 da; s/ Fran^{co} GOMEZ & Lucia DURAN; gm/ Lucia ORTIZ *del pueb°*.

LUXAN, Mª Martina *P°*
bap 22 Nov 1801, ae 9 da; d/ Ant° LUXAN & Josefa MARTIN; gm/ Teresa MELENUDO *del pueb°*.

TRUXILLO, Jose Fran^{co} *V°*
bap 22 Nov 1801, ae 8 da; s/ Vic^{te} TRUXILLO & Mª Dolores MADRID; gp/ J^{n} Ant° CASADOS & Catarina BACA, *vecinos*.

RIO, Vicente *P°*
bap 6 Dec 1801, ae 7 da; s/ Santiago RIO & Mª Rosa ROMERO; gm/ Maria ROM^{O} *del pueb°*.

MIERA (patron), Mª Guadalupe *Yndia Yuta*
bap 6 Dec 1801, ae about 8 yr; d/ (*Nacion Yuta*), *criada de* Jose MIERA; gp/ Rafael LUNA & Ana Mª TAFOYA, *vecinos*.

ROMERO (gp), Francisco *Adulto Cum*
bap 8 Dec 1801 sufficiently catechized, ae about 23 yr; s/ *Nacion Cumanche*; gf/ *el Alc^{e} m^{or} de esta Jurisd^{n}, D^{n}* Ant° Jose ROMERO.

ROMERO (patron), Maria Concep^{n} *(A)pacha*
bap 8 Dec 1801, ae about 1½ yr; d/ (*Nacion*) *Apacha*, orphan; gf/ Salvador ROM°, *Ynd° de* <u>*este*</u> *pueb°*, to whom the mother left her child upon her death.

ROMERO (patron), Eusebio (torn)
bap 13 Dec 1801, ae about 4 yr; s/ (*Nacion*) *Apache*; gp/ Salvador ROMERO *del pueb°* to whom the mother left her child upon her death.

Frame 28
MARTIN, Mª Yg^{a} Concep^{n} *V°*
bap 13 Dec 1801, ae 6 da; d/ Feliz MARTIN & Yg^{a} GONZ^{z}; gp/ Jose LOBATO & Rosalia MARTIN, *vecinos*.

CORTES, Jose Manuel V^{o}
bap 26 Dec 1801, ae 8 da; s/ Paulin CORTES & Mª Concep^{n} MARTIN; gp/ Man^{l} SANCHEZ & Nicolasa SANDOVAL, *vecinos*.

Año de 1802

CRUZ, Manuel Anastacio V^{o}
bap 3 Jan 1802, ae 3 da; s/ Mariano CRUZ & Dolor^{s} VEJIL; gp/ Ant^{o} LOBATO & Mª CHAVES, *tod^{s} vecinos*.

LAZO, Maria P^{o}
bap 3 Jan '802, ae 10 da; d/ Fran^{co} LAZO & Juana LISTON; gm/ Juana ROM^{o} *del pueb^{o}*.

GAVILAN, J^{n} Reyes P^{o}
bap 3 Jan '802, ae 10 da; s/ Juan Andres GAVILAN & Manuela FRESQUIS *del pueb^{o}*; gp/ Pablo RAMO & Mª Angela OJALA *dela Ysleta*.

LUXAN, Fran^{ca} P^{a}
bap 3 Jan '802, ae 8 da; d/ Raf^{l} LUXAN & Fran^{ca} GONZ^{z}; gm/ Maria ROM^{o} *del pueb^{o}*.

MARTIN, Juan Yg^{o} V^{o}
bap 3 Jan '802, ae 3 da; s/ Fran^{co} MARTIN & Tomasa SANCHEZ; gp/ Miguel VEJIL & Ana Mª VALLEJOS, *vecinos*.

SILVA, Mª Man^{la} V^{a}
bap 6 Jan '802, ae 6 da; d/ J^{n} Xtoval SILVA & Maria URIOSTE; gp/ Juan Julian QUINTANA & Mª Felipa MAESE, *vecin^{s}*.

TORRES, Mariano Reyes V^{o}
bap 10 Jan '802, ae 5 da; s/ Diego TORRES & Concep^{n} TRUXILLO; gp/ Felipe TENORIO & Barbara BERNAL, *vecinos*.

LASO, Micaela P^{a}
bap 10 Jan '802, ae 8 da; d/ Matias LASO & Guadalupe MARTIN; gm/ Micaela GONZ^{z} *del pueb^{o}*.

SANCHEZ, Mª Luz V^{a}
bap 17 Jan '802, ae 5 da; d/ Felipe SANCHEZ & J^{a} Dolor^{s} MARTIN; gp/ Bernardo LUC^{o} & Tomasa MARTIN, *vec^{s}*.

VARELA, Pedro Ant^{o} V^{o}
bap 17 Jan '802 because of necessity, ae 1 mo; s/ Juan Ysidro VARELA & Juana MARTIN; gp/ Mª Ascension LUCERO (only), *vecinos*.

GONZALEZ, Ant^{o} V^{o}
bap 17 Jan '802, ae 8 da; s/ Jose Mig^{l} GONZ^{z} & Mª Ysabel VEJIL; gp/ Augustin (n.s.) & Matiana ROMERO, *vecinos*.

PACHECO, Juan Jose P^{o}
bap 17 Jan '802, ae 6 da; s/ Miguel PACHECO & Brigida ROMERO *del pueb^{o}*; gp/ Antonio ARCHULETA & J^{a} MARTIN, *vecinos*.

MONTE, Hilario V^{o}
bap 17 Jan '802, ae 5 da; s/ Ant^{o} del MONTE & Ynes MARTIN; gp/ Manuel ATENSIO & Ana Mª MIERA, *vecinos*.

DURAN, Mª Josefa *P^a*
bap 18 Jan 1802, ae 11 da; d/ Juan Ant^o DURAN & Maria MARTIN; gm/ Juana Mª GAVILAN *del pueb^o*. (Frames 28-29)

Frame 29
ESPINOSA, Mª de Jesus *V^a*
bap 19 Jan '802, ae 10 da; d/ Mª Josefa ESPINOSA, wid, *vec^a*, & unknown father; gp/ Juan Angel GARCIA & Man^{la} MARTIN, *vec^s*.

LUNA, Mª Josefa de Jesus *V^a*
bap 22 Jan '802, ae 4 da; d/ Rafael de LUNA & Ana Mª TAFOYA; gp/ *el Alc^e D^n* Ant^o Josef ROMERO & Maria BACA.

VERA (patron), Maria Paula *Yn. Criada Yuta*
bap 25 Jan '802, ae about 5 mo; d/ (*Nacion Yuta*), whose mother and her husband gave the child up to the priest (Fr. Joseph de VERA) and he redeemed her (no names given); gp/ Simon ARMENTA & Marta MARTIN, *vec^s*.

ROMERO, Mª Fran^{ca} de Jesus *V^a*
bap 25 Jan '802, ae 7 da; d/ Jose ROM^o & Mª Dolores QUINTANA; gp/ Miguel VARELA, *alias* TAFOYA, & J^a ROM^o.

SANCHEZ, Jose Victor *V^o*
bap 2 Feb '802, ae 11 da; s/ Diego SANCHEZ & Magdalena MARTIN; gp/ Juan Crus MARTIN & Mª Dolores TORRES, *vecinos*.

SANDOVAL, Jose Mariano de Jesus *V^o*
bap 2 Feb '802, ae 4 da; s/ Matias SANDOVAL & Mª Yg^a BUENO; gp/ Pedro FERNANDEZ & Mª REYES, *vecinos*.

MONTOYA, Mª Rosa *V^a*
bap 7 Feb '802, ae 7 da; d/ Rafael MONTOYA & Mª Luisa ROMERO; gp/ Bernardo CASILLAS & Dolores MONTOYA, *vecinos*.

LUXAN, Domingo *P^o*
bap 21 Feb 1802, ae 8 da; s/ Juan Ant^o LUXAN & Rafaela GONZALEZ; gm/ Mª Yg^a MARTIN *del pueb^o*.

MARTIN, Mª Paula dela Luz *V^a*
bap 7 Mch 1802, ae 14 da; d/ Juan Jose MARTIN & Mª Ant^a CENTENO; gp/ Ant^o MARTIN & Ana Mª ARMENTA, *vecinos*.

BRITO, Jose Matias *V^o*
bap 7 Mch 1802, ae 12 da; s/ Fran^{co} BRITO & Margarita GONZ^z; gp/ Juan Cruz CORTES & Mª Luz MONTOYA, *vecinos*.

DURAN, Mª Pasquala (torn)
bap 15 Mch '802, ae 7 da; d/ Pedro Yg^o DURAN & Ant^a SANCHEZ; gp/ Juan Bautista VEJIL (only), *todos vec^s*.

LOBATO, Maria Josefa *V^a*
bap 19 Mch '802, ae 7 da; d/ Juan Antonio LOBATO & Mª Yg^a SANCHEZ; gp/ Man^l SANCHEZ & Nicolasa SANDOVAL, *vec^s*. (Frames 29-30)

Frame 30
MARTIN, Mª Luz *V^a*
bap 19 Mch '802, ae 7 da; d/ Ant^o Jose MARTIN & Alberta BENAVIDES; gp/ Roque MARTIN & Greg^a ARMIJO.

MARTIN, Juan Ant^{o} *P^{o}*
bap 4 Apr '802, ae 12 da; s/ Jose Ant^{o} MARTIN & Mª Asc^{n} LOMA; gm/ Micaela ROM^{o} *del pueb^{o}*.

ARAGON, Mª Barb^{a} *V^{a}*
bap 4 Apr '802, ae 5 da; d/ Ant^{o} ARAGON & Xaviera VEJIL; gp/ Jose Vic^{te} ARAGON & Juana de LUNA, *vec^{s}*.

MIRABALL (patron), Juan Domingo *V^{o}*
bap 4 Apr '802, ae 8 da; s/ Maria Ant^{a} (n.s.), *Ynd^{a} solt^{a} criada de* (n.n.) MIRABAL<u>L</u> (sic), *vec^{o}*, & father unknown; gp/ Pasqual ARAGON & Gertrudis COCA, *vec^{s}*.

VEJIL, Miguel Ant^{o} *V^{o}*
bap 11 Apr '802, ae 3 da; s/ J^{n} Yg^{o} VEJIL & Soledad DURAN; gp/ Bernardo LUC^{o} & Tomasa MARTIN, *vec^{s}*.

ROMERO, Jose Fran^{co} *P^{o}*
bap 11 Apr '802, ae 9 da; s/ Juan Domingo ROM^{o} & Fran^{ca} LUXAN; gm/ Josefa LUC^{o} *del pueblo*.

FRESQUIS, Fran^{co} *P^{o}*
bap 11 Apr 1802, ae 9 da; s/ Blas FRESQUIS, dec., & Dolores MARTIN; gm/ Mª Rosa LUXAN *del pueb^{o}*.

CASILLAS, Maria Rezurr^{n} *V^{a}*
bap 25 Apr '802, ae 8 da; d/ Jose Lino CASILLAS & Mª Serafina CORTES; gp/ Jose Ant^{o} MARTIN & Ynes LEAL, *vecinos*.

FLORES, Juan Bautista *V^{o}*
bap 25 Apr '802, ae 7 da; s/ Martin FLORES & Gertrudis GARCIA; gp/ Jose MARTIN & Gertrudis MONTOYA, *vec^{s}*.

FERNANDEZ (patron), Fran^{co} *Apache*
bap 25 Apr '802, ae about 9 yr; s/ (*Nacion Apache*); gf/ Ant^{o} FERNANDEZ who took him away from Commanche captivity.

Frame 31

MAESE, Pedro *V^{o}*
bap 29 Apr '802, ae 4 da; s/ Juan MAESE & Manuela ROM^{o}; gp/ Jose Miguel MARTIN & Josefa MARTIN, *v^{s}*.

ZUASO, Rosa *P^{a}*
bap 2 May '802, ae 9 da; d/ Simon ZUASO & Yg^{a} RIO; gm/ Juana RIO *del pueb^{o}*.

DURAN, Jose Rafael *V^{o}*
bap 2 May '802, ae 5 da; s/ Pablo DURAN & Margarita SANCHEZ; gp/ Ant^{o} LOBATO & Mª CHAVES, *vec^{s}*.

CRUZ, Felipe Santiago *V^{o}*
bap 3 May '802, ae 4 da; s/ Alexo CRUZ & Guadalupe DURAN; gp/ Manuel CHAVES & Simona LEAL.

MIERA, Yg^{a} Atanasia *V^{a}*
bap 6 May '802, ae 5 da; d/ Jose MIERA & Manuela ROMERO; gf/ Juan de Jesus MARTIN.

VARELA, Mª Josefa *V^{a}*
bap 9 May '802, ae 2 da; d/ Xtoval VARELA & Rafaela MARTIN; gp/ Pablo LUZ^{O} & Paula LARRAÑAGA, *vec^{s}*.

GARCIA (gp), Joseph *V^{o}*
bap 9 May 1802; s/ (unknown), child who appears to be Spanish & *vecino*, found among some <u>chamios</u> (not in Velazquez Dictionary) on this side dela Zequia de Pando next to the *plaza del Rio de D^{n}* Fernando by Juan Angel GARCIA, who was on his way to cut *latas* (not in Velazquez) at dawn; gp/ Juan Angel GARCIA & his wife, Mª Manuela MARTIN, *vec^{s}*.

GONZALEZ, Fran^{co} *V^{o}*
bap 23 May '802, ae 14 da; s/ Juan GONZ^{z} & Ant^{a} MARTIN; gp/ Simon ARMENTA & Marta MARTIN, *vecinos*.

LOBATO, Pedro Jose *V^{o}*
bap 23 May 1802, ae 13 da; s/ J^{n} Jose LOBATO & Rosa MESTAS; gp/ Juaquin MESTAS & Margarita MARTIN, *abuelos*.

GONZALEZ, Fran^{co} (torn)
bap 23 May '802, ae 3 da; s/ Jose GONZ^{z} & Dorotea VACA; gp/ Pedro MARTIN & Mª Reyes FERNANDEZ, *todos vec^{s}*.

Frame 32
ARCHULETA, Juana Maria *V^{a}*
bap 27 May 1802, ae 3 da; d/ Julian ARCHULETA & Manuela VARELA; gp/ Juan de Jesus LUC^{O} & Mª Yg^{a} ARAGON, vec^{s}.

CASILLAS, Jose dela Ascencion *V^{o}*
bap 30 May '802, ae 4 da; s/ Bernardo CASILLAS & Dolores MADRID; gp/ J^{n} Luis MIRABAL<u>L</u> (sic) & Mª Damasia GONZ^{z}, *vecinos*.

MUÑIZ (ó CHAMA), Mª Ascencion *V^{a}*
bap 30 May '802, ae 4 da; d/ unknown father & Gertrudis (MUÑIZ ó CHAMA), single, d/ Juan MUÑIZ *ó CHAMA* & Josefa PANDO; gf/ J^{n} Jose MARTIN, *vecinos de Picuries*.

VEJIL, Mª Josefa *V^{a}*
bap 17 Jne '802, ae 8 da; d/ Rafael VEJIL & Elena LOBATO; gp/ Dionisio VEJIL & Manuela DELGADO.

HERRERA, Pedro Pablo *V^{o} murio*
bap 4 Jly '802, ae 3 da; s/ Jose Simon de HERRERA & Juana MONTOYA; gp/ Gervacio MARTIN & Juana CORTES.

TECOA, Alfonso *P^{o}*
bap 18 Jly '802, ae 8 da; s/ Joaquin TECOA & Mª MARTIN; gm/ Lucia DURAN.

TRUXILLO, Mª Dolores *V^{a}*
bap 18 Jly '802, ae 8 da; d/ Andres TRUXILLO & Mª Ant^{a} LOPEZ; gp/ Juan Ant^{o} LOBATO & Mª Ygnacia SANCHEZ, *vecinos*.

MARTIN, M^{a} Yg^{a} *P^{a}*
bap 25 Jly '802, ae 9 da; d/ Jose MARTIN & Gertrudis ROM^{O}; gm/ Mª Yg^{a} MARTIN *del pueblo*.

ARMENTA, Anna Josefa Jacoba *V^{a}*
bap 26 Jly 1802, ae 1 da; d/ Simon ARMENTA & Marta MARTIN; gm/ Manuela VALLEJOS, *vecinos de Taos*.

SANCHEZ, Mª Rita V^{a}
bap 1 Aug '802, ae 3 da; d/ Manuel SANCHEZ & Nicolasa SAND^{L}; gp/ Santiago SANDOVAL & Mª Candelaria VALDES *del Rio Arriba*.

VILLALPANDO, Maria Concep^{n} V^{a}
bap 15 Aug 1802, ae 7 da; d/ Rafael VILLALPANDO & Manuelita DOMINGUES; gp/ Ant^{o} MARTIN & Mª Reyes FERNANDEZ, *vecinos de esta Jurisd^{n}*.

ROMERO, Juan Ant^{o} P^{o}
bap 22 Aug 1802, ae 9 da; s/ (Do)mingo ROM^{o} & Micaela GONZ^{z}; gm/ Barbara ROM^{o} *del pueblo*. (Frames 32-33)

Frame 33
LOBATO, Juan Bautista V^{o}
bap 30 Aug '802, ae 4 da; s/ Maria LOBATO, *Ynd^{a} criada, soltera*, & unknown father; gp/ Manuel Anast^{o} VEJIL & Fran^{ca} BERNAL.

SANDOVAL, Maria Margarita V^{a}
bap 29 Sep '802, ae 4 da; d/ Man^{l} SANDOVAL & Mª Ant^{a} LOBATO; gp/ Felipe MARTIN & Concep^{n} TRUXILLO, *vecinos*.

MARTIN, Barbara P^{a}
bap 10 Oct 1802; ae 3 da; d/ Jose Ant^{o} MARTIN & Mª Geronima (n.s.); gm/ Juana Mª GAVILAN, *Yndios Taoses*.

VEJIL, Jose Fran^{co} V^{o}
bap 10 Oct '802, ae 6 da; s/ Juan Yg^{o} VEJIL & Mª Ant^{a} ARAGON; gp/ Pablo GONZ^{z} & Josefa SANCHEZ, *vecinos de esta Jurisd^{n}*.

BORICA, Micaela P^{a}
bap 13 Oct '802, ae 10 da; d/ Jose Ant^{o} BORICA & Teresa MELENUDO, *Ynd^{s} Taoses*; gp/ Ant^{o} LOBATO & Margarita MARTIN, *vecinos*.

ARMIJO, Jose Tomas V^{o}
bap 7 Nov '802, ae 12 da; s/ Santiago ARMIJO & Juana ROMERO; gm/ Ana Maria MIERA, *todos vecinos de Taos*.

ORTIZ, Mª Ascencion P^{a}
bap 7 Nov '802, ae 10 da; d/ J^{n} Andres ORTIZ & Micaela LUXAN; gm/ Rafaela RIO.

VALLEJOS (patrona), Jose Rafael V^{o}
bap 7 Nov 1802, ae 10 da; s/ Catarina (n.s.), *Ynd^{a} criada de Man^{la}* VALLEJOS, & unknown father; gp/ Pablo LUC^{o} & Mª MARTIN, *vecinos de esta*.

GONZALEZ, Juan Fran^{co} (torn)
bap 7 Nov 1802, ae 13 da; s/ Juan Domingo GONZ^{z} & Rosalia TRUXILLO; gp/ Juan Domingo TAFOYA & Dolores MAESE, *vecin^{s}*. (Frames 33-34)

Frame 34
LOMA, Juan Ant^{o} & Pablo P^{o}
bap 7 Nov 1802; twin sons/ Juan Domingo LOMA & Juana RIO, who died at birth (of twins); gm/ Lucia DURAN (only).

MONDRAGON, Mª Fran^{ca} V^{a}
bap 8 Nov 1802, ae 15 da; d/ Bartolome MONDRAGON & Regina FRESQUIS; gp/ Luis CHAVES & Candelaria idem (CHAVES), *vecinos*.

MARTIN, Juan Yg^{o} *V*^{o}
bap 14 Nov 1802, ae 7 da; s/ Man^{l} Gregorio MARTIN & Rafaela MEDINA; gp/ Jose Ant^{o} CORTES & J^{a} Gertrudis MONTOYA, *todos vecinos deesta*.

CORTES, Mª Fran^{ca} *V*^{a}
bap 23 Nov 1802, ae 7 da; d/ Cruz CORTES & Luz MONTOYA; gp/ Tomas LOBATO & Candelaria GONZ^{z}.

BLEA, Mª Guadalupe *V*^{a}
bap 28 Nov 1802, ae 4 da; d/ Jose Joaquin BLEA & Mª Soledad SANCHEZ; gp/ Jose Ant^{o} CORTES & Fra(n)cisca SANDOVAL.

SANCHEZ, Jose Fran^{co} *P*^{o}
bap 28 Nov 1802, ae 9 da; s/ Diego SANCHEZ & Ysabel ROM^{o}; gm/ Fran^{ca} LUXAN *del pueb*^{o}.

MARTIN, Jose Pablo *P*^{o}
bap 5 Dec 1802, ae 4 da; s/ Fran$^{c(o)}$ MARTIN & Josefa RIO; gm/ Teresa ROIBAL, *Yndios de este pueb*^{o}.

CHAVES, Maria Soledad *V*^{a}
bap 5 Dec 1802, ae 8 da; d/ Ant^{o} (torn-see Frame 50---Domin)go CHAVES & Cand^{a} DURAN; gf/ Juan DURAN, *todos vecin*^{s} *de esta parroq*^{a}.

Frame 35
ROMERO, Francisco *P*^{o}
bap 12 Dec 1802, ae 8 da; s/ Juan Miguel ROMERO & Fran^{ca} LUC^{o}; gm/ Fran^{ca} ROMERO.

ROMERO, Santiago *P*^{o}
bap 19 Dec 1802, ae 7 da; s/ Juan Domingo ROMERO & Manuela LUXAN; gm/ Felipa CATUGE.

DURAN, Mª Guadalupe *V*^{a}
bap 21 Dec 1802, ae 11 da; d/ Juan Nicolas DURAN & J^{a} Mª ROMERO; gp/ *el Alc*^{e} *D*^{n} Ant^{o} ROM^{o} & Rafaela LUNA, *todos vecinos de esta*.

BUENO, Mª Luz *V*^{a}
bap 21 Dec 1802, ae 4 da; d/ Ant^{o} BUENO & Rosalia VALDES; gp/ Juan Yg^{o} VEJIL & Soledad DURAN, *vecinos*.

MARTIN, Josefa *P*^{a}
bap 26 Dec 1802, ae 4 da; d/ Juan Jose MARTIN & Manuela ROM^{o}; gm/ Felipa ROMERO *del pueblo*.

Año de 1803

ROMERO, Jose Ant^{o} *P*^{o}
bap 2 Jan '803, ae 8 da; s/ Jose ROM^{o} & Manuela SERNA *del pueblo*; gp/ Jose GONZ^{z} & Candelaria PAEZ, *vecinos*.

MIRABALL, Maria de Jesus *V*^{a} *murio*
bap 9 Jan 1803, ae 3 da; d/ Juan Luis MIRABAL<u>L</u> (sic) & Damasia GONZ^{z}; gp/ J^{n} Yg^{o} BEITIA & Rafaela MARTIN.

ARCHULETA, Mª Tomasa *V*^{a}
bap 15 Jan 1803 in extreme necessity, ae 4 da; d/ Ant^{o} Casimiro ARCHULETA & Mª Monserrate LEAL, *vecinos deesta Jurisd*^{n}; (gm)/ Manuela ROM^{o}.

DURAN, M[a] Manuela *(P)*[a]
bap 16 Jan 1803, ae 9 da; d/ J[n] Andres DURAN & Lugarda SERNA *del pueb°*; gp/ Miguel LOPEZ & Barb[a] BERNAL, *vecinos*. (Frames 35-36)

Frame 36
VEJIL, Jose Manuel *V°*
bap 16 Jan 1803, ae 5 da; s/ Jose Santiago VEJIL & Juana MESTAS of Abiquiu; gp/ Fran[co] Esteb[n] ROM[o] & M[a] Resurr[n] TAFOYA, *vecinos de esta*.

PADILLA, Ant° Domingo *V°*
bap 16 Jan 1803, ae 8 da; s/ Julian PADILLA & Juana MAESE; gp/ Ant° MONDRAGON & Catarina MARTIN, *vecinos*.

MARTIN, Jose Santiago *V°*
bap 23 Jan '803, ae 9 da; s/ Gervacio MARTIN & Juana CORTES; gf/ Juan DURAN, *todos vecinos de esta parroq[a]*.

DURAN, Juan Xtov[1] *P°*
bap 29 Jan 1803, ae 6 da; s/ Juan Antonio DURAN & Barbara MARTIN; gm/ Fran[ca] DURAN *del pueblo*.

LEAL, Pedro Nolasco *V°*
bap 2 Feb 1803, ae 3 da; s/ M[a] Lorenza LEAL, single, *vecina deesta Jurisd[n]* who died at birth of child, & unknown father; gf/ Jose Julian MARTINEZ.

ARCHULETA, M[a] dela Luz *V[a]*
bap 9 Feb 1803, ae 7 da; d/ Antonio ARCHULETA & Juana MARTIN; gf/ Ant° FERN[z].

ROMERO, M[a] dela Luz
GUERRERO, M[a] dela Luz *P[a]*
bap 12 Feb 1803, ae 9 da; d/ Paula GUERRERO, wid. *de este pueb°*, & "it is said" Salvador ROM[o], single, *del pueb°*; gp/ M[a] Ant[a] MARTIN (sic) & J[n] GARCIA, *vecin[s]*.

MARTIN, Juana *P°*
bap 12 Feb 1803, ae 7 da; d/ Ant° MARTIN & G(uada)lupe ROM[o] *del pueb°*; gm/ M[a] Yg[a] ARAG[n], *vec[a]*.

Frame 37
GUERRERO, Maria Trinidad *P[a]*
MARTIN, Maria Trinidad
bap 13 Feb 1803, ae 8 da; d/ Fran[co] GUERRERO, dec., & Juana MARTIN, *viudos de este pueblo*; gp/ Miguel LOPEZ & Barb[a] BERNAL, *vecinos*.

ROMERO, Geronimo *P°*
bap 14 Feb 1803, ae 12 da; s/ Jose Ant° ROM[o] & Teodora GONZ[z] ROM[o], *dif[tos]*; gm/ M[a] Geronima LAZO *del pueb°*.

ROMERO, M[a] Josefa *V[a]*
bap 20 Feb 1803, ae 7 da; d/ M[a] Dolores ROM[o], single, & unknown father, *vec[a] de esta Jurisd[n]*; (Manuel Greg° ARCHULETA was entered and then crossed out. Evidently an error, as this is the father of the following child); gp/ Jose Mar[no] FERNANDEZ & Asc[n] LUS[o].

ARCHULETA, M[a] Juliana *V[a]*
bap 20 Feb 1803, ae 4 da; d/ Man[l] Gregorio ARCHULETA & Catarina GARCIA; gm/ Andrea LUZERO *deesta Jurisd[n]*.

BEITIA, Juan de Jesus *Vº*
bap 22 Feb 1803, ae 7 da; s/ Jose Ygº BEITIA & Rafaela MARTIN *de esta Feligª*; gp/ Jose Andres TRUXILLO & Josefa ARGUELLO *de Pecuries*.

TUZA, Julian *Puebº*
bap 26 Feb 1803, baptized because of necessity the 15th, ae 8 da; s/ Jose Antº TUZA & Dominga TECOA; gp/ (not given).

ZAMORA, Maria Rosa *Puebº*
bap 26 Feb 1803 baptized 16th, ae 3 da; d/ Eusebio ZAMORA & Raf^{la} ROMº, *todos Indios de este puebº*; gp/ (not given).

LUSERO, Mª Paula delos Dolores (torn)
bap 6 Mch 1803, ae 5 da; d/ Pablo LUSº & Paula LARRAÑAGA; gm/ Jacinta ARAGON.

Frame 38
TENORIO, Mª de Jesus *Vª*
bap 6 Mch 1803, ae 6 da; d/ Julian TENORIO & Lorenza LOPEZ; gp/ Cruz CORTES & Mª Luz MONTOYA.

LOBATO, Juan Xto^{val} *Vº*
bap 6 Mch 1803, ae 6 da; s/ Fran^{co} LOBATO & Andrea TAFOYA; gp/ Antº LOBATO & Mª CHASES.

MARTIN, Juan Tomas *Vo*
bap 9 Mch 1803 because of extreme necessity by *el Alc^{e} D^{n}* Antº ROMERO, ae 3 da; s/ Ventª MARTIN & Rafaela MAESE, *vecin^{s}*; gp/ (not given).

BRITO, Teodora *Vª*
bap 13 Mch '803, ae 6 da; d/ Jose BRITO & Dolores SANCHES; gp/ Fran^{co} LOBATO & Gertrudis MONDRAGON.

LUNA, Jose Fran^{co}
MIERA, Jose Fran^{co} *Vº*
bap 19 Mch 1803, ae 10 da; *espurio* s/ Ana Mª MIERA, married (to another) & Rafael LUNA, married (to another) according to the mother; gp/ D^{n} Antº Jose ROMº, Alc^{e}, & Maria VACA.

ROMERO, Jose Antº *Vº*
bap 19 Mch '803, ae 8 da; s/ Concepcion ROMº & Rosa QUINTANA; gp/ Bernardo LUCERO & Tomasa MARTIN.

ROMERO, Juana *Pº*
bap 19 Mch 1803, ae 8 da; d/ J^{n} Domingo ROMERO & Encarnacion LUXAN; gm/ Mª RIO *del pueblo*.

SILVA, Juana Martina *Vª*
bap 20 Mch 1803 because of extreme necessity by Paula ROMERO, certified midwife, *vecina dela Cañada*; d/ Santiago SILVA & Juana VELASQUES; gp/ (not given).

MONDRAGON, Juan Xav(crossed out) (Juan Gabriel in margin) *Vº*
bap 16 Apr 1803, ae 19 da; s/ Xtoval MONDRAGON & Rafaela GONZ^{z}; gp/ Fran^{co} (n.s.-torn) & Margarita VERELA *delas Truchas*. (Frames 38-39)

Frame 39
MARTIN, Antº Dionisio *Vº*

bap 17 Apr '803, b. 8th *de d^{ho}*; s/ Juan Candelario MARTIN & Juliana VALLEJOS; gp/ Bautista MARTIN & Nicolasa TRUXILLO.

CORTES, Juan Yg^{o} *V^{o}*
bap 17 Apr '803, b. 6th; s/ Jose CORTES & J^{a} Josefa MONTOYA; gp/ Man^{l} Anast^{o} VEJIL & Fran^{ca} BERNAL.

VARGAS, Julian *V^{o}*
bap 17 Apr '803, b. 12th; s/ Esteban VARGAS & Andrea TAFOYA; gp/ J^{n} Ant^{o} VALDES & Bibiana BACA.

MAESE (patron), Fran^{co} *V^{o} mur^{o}*
bap 17 Apr 1803; s/ unknown, no identification, left on the 12th at the door of Juan Domingo MAESE; gp/ Paulin (n.s.) & Soledad MAESE.

ROMERO, Lucia *P^{o}*
bap 17 Apr '803, ae 20 da; d/ Pedro ROM^{o} & Mª Guadalupe NARANJO *del p^{o}*; gm/ Mª Ant^{a} LUXAN.

MADRID, M^{a} Yg^{a} *V^{a}*
bap 17 Apr '803, b. 8th; d/ Diego MADRID & Juliana VALERIO; gp/ Ant^{o} LOBATO & Marg^{ta} MARTIN.

CHAVES, Mª Encarn^{n} *V^{a}*
bap 17 Apr '803, b. 6th; d/ Jose Mª CHAVES & Mª ORTEGA; gp/ Tomas LOBATO & Candelaria GONZ^{z}. (Frames 39-40)

Frame 40
MONTOYA, Mª Fran^{ca} *V^{a}*
bap 17 Apr '803 by the licensed midwife Paula ROM^{o}, b. 10th; d/ Juan Nicolas MONTOYA & Ygnacia SANDOV^{L}; gp/ (not given).

TAFOYA, Salv^{or} Raymundo *V^{o}*
bap 17 Apr '803, b. 5th; s/ Jose TAFOYA & Micaela ROMERO; gp/ J^{n} Yg^{o} VEJIL & Soledad DURAN.

MARTIN, Ant^{a} Rosa *V^{a}*
bap 17 Apr '803, b. 8th; d/ Yg^{o} MARTIN & Paula SALAZAR; gp/ Manuel SANCHEZ & Nicolasa SANDOVAL.

CASADOS, Maria Concep^{n} *V^{a}*
bap 24 Apr 1803, ae 7 da; d/ Juan Ant^{o} CASADOS & Catarina BACA; gp/ Jose MIERA & Manuela ROM^{o}.

MONDRAGON, Juan Ant^{o} *V^{o}*
bap 1 May '803, ae 7 da; s/ Mariano MONDRAGON & Encarnacion ESPINOSA; gp/ Jose Ant^{o} CORTES & J^{a} MONTOYA.

GONZALEZ, Jose Mariano *V^{o}*
bap 8 May '803, ae 3 da; s/ Jose Miguel GONZ^{z} & Ysabel VEJIL; gp/ Juan Xtoval CORTES & Fran^{ca} MONTOYA.

DURAN, Juan dela Cruz *V^{o}*
bap 8 May 1803, ae 6 da; s/ Salvador DURAN & Fabiana FRESQUIZ; gp/ Pedro MA(RTIN-torn--see Frame 42) & Mª Reyes FERNANDEZ.

Frame 41
BUENO, Mª Josefa *V^{a}*

bap 15 May 1803, ae 5 da; d/ Pedro BUENO & Man^{la} ARM^{o}; gp/ Dionisio VEJIL & Manuela DELGADO, *todos v(e)cin^{s}*.

GOMEZ, Mª Gertrudis *P^{o}*
bap 15 May '803, ae 6 da; d/ Juan GOMEZ & M^{a} ROM^{o}, *Ynd^{s} Taoses*; gp/ Mig^{l} LOPEZ & Barb^{a} VERNAL, *vecin^{s}*.

LOBATO, Ant^{a} Margarita *V^{a}*
bap 15 May '803, ae 7 da; d/ Rafael LOBATO & Mª Luz ESPINOSA; gf/ Juan Ant^{o} DURAN, *todos vecinos*.

CRUZ, Maria del Carmen *V^{a}*
bap 15 May 1803, ae 3 da; d/ Jose dela CRUZ & Luisa ARCHULETA; gp/ Antonio ARCHULETA & Mª Monserrate LEAL, *todos vecinos*.

TAFOYA, Juan(a) Paula *V^{a}*
bap 5 Jne 1803, ae 7 da; d/ Juan Domingo TAFOYA & Mª Dolores MAESE; gp/ Bartolome MONDRAGON & Mª Regina FRESQUIS, *todos vec^{s}*.

LUCERO, J^{n} Bautista *V^{o}*
bap 29 Jne 1803, ae 6 da; s/ Bern^{do} LUCERO & Tomasa MARTIN; gp/ J^{n} Yg^{o} VEJIL & Jacinta ARAGON.

VARGAS, Jose Vicente *V^{o}*
bap 29 Jne 1803, ae 10 da; s/ Maurilo VARGAS & Nicomeda FERNANDEZ; gp/ J^{n} Cruz VEJIL & Clara FERNANDEZ.

Frame 42
MONTOYA, Jose Rafael *V^{o}*
bap 29 Jne 1803, ae 12 da; s/ Juan MONTOYA & M^{a} dela CRUZ; gf/ Ant^{o} Jos. SANDOVAL, *vec^{s}*.

MARTIN, Mª Man^{la} *V^{a}*
bap 25 Jly 1803, ae 5 da; d/ J^{n} del Carmen MARTIN & Mª Nazarena LUZ^{o}; gp/ Felipe AVILA, *vecino del Ojo Caliente*, & Rafaela MAESE *de esta Jurisd^{n}*.

ROMERO, Mª Encarnacion *P^{o}*
bap 14 Aug '803, ae 7 da; d/ Jose Fran^{co} ROMERO & Juana Mª ZUASO; gm/ Mª Ascencion GOMEZ, *todos del pu(e)b^{o}*.

MARTIN, Mª Ascencion *V^{a}*
bap 8 Sep 1803, ae 5 da; d/ Pedro MARTIN & Mª Reyes FERN^{z}; gp/ Felipe MARTIN & Concep^{n} TRUXILLO, *vecinos*.

LUXAN, Geronimo *P^{o}*
bap 18 Sep 1803, ae 10 da; s/ Jose Ant^{o} LUXAN & Lucia LOMA; gm/ Fran^{ca} LUC^{o} *del pueb^{o}*.

MARTIN, Felipe de Jesus *V^{o}*
bap 18 Sep '803, ae 6 da; s/ Yg^{o} MARTIN & Mª Josefa TRUXILLO, *alias* MARQ^{z}; gp/ Pablo TRUXILLO & Teresa HURTADO, *vecinos*.

TAFOYA, Cipriano *V^{o}*
bap 30 Sep '803, ae 5 da; s/ Nicolas TAFOYA & Barbara COCA; gp/ Juan Ant^{o} PAEZ & Barbara MONTOYA, *vecinos*.

MONDRAGON, Juan *V^{o}*
bap 30 Sep '803, ae 8 da; d/ Ant^{o} MONDRAG^{N} & Catarina GONZ^{z}; gm/ Rafaela BUENO, *vecin^{s}*.

LUCERO, Geronimo P^{o}
bap 9 Oct '803, ae 10 da; s/ Juan Ant^{o} LUC^{o} & Ant^{a} LOMA; gm/ Fran^{ca} LUCERO *del pueblo*.

ORTIZ, Juan Ant^{o} P^{o}
bap 1 Nov '803, ae 8 da; s/ Fran^{co} ORTIZ & (torn-n.n.) CHININI; gm/ Ana ORTIZ *del pueb^{o}*. (Frames 42-43)

Frame 43
PANDO, Juan Ant^{o} P^{o}
bap 20 Nov '803, ae 8 da; s/ Salvador PANDO & Ana Mª LOMA; gm/ Ant^{a} LOMA [*del pueb^{o}*].

MARTINEZ, Mª Rosa V^{a}
bap 27 Nov '803, ae 4 da; d/ Fran^{co} MARTINEZ & Mª Tomasa SANCHEZ; gp/ Bernardo LUC^{O} & Tomasa MARTIN.

SANCHEZ, Juana Catarina V^{o}
bap 10 Dec 1803, b. *ayer*; d/ Manuel SANCHEZ & Nicolasa SANDOVAL; gp/ Jose MIRABAL & Barbara ROMERO, *todos vecinos de esta*.

PACHECO, Jose M^{a} V^{o}
bap 11 Dec '803, b. 5th; s/ Juan Pedro PACHECO & Luz MARTIN; gp/ Mateo COCA & Guadalupe VARELA *de esta Jurisd^{n}*.

BLEA, Maria de Jesus P^{o}
bap 11 Dec 1803, b. 6th; d/ Ant^{o} BLEA & Barbara MONTOYA; gp/ Fran^{co} CHAVES & Ant^{a} BACA *de esta*.

LEIBA, Ventura
GAVILAN, Ventura P^{o}
bap 11 Dec '803, b. 5th; *espurio* s/ Jose Ant^{o} LEIBA, casado, & Mª Ant^{a} GAVILAN, single; gm/ M^{a} ROM^{O}, *Ynd^{a} [del pueb^{o}]*.

VARELA, Mª Faustina V^{a}
bap 20 Dec 1803, b. 16th; d/ Juan Ysidro VARELA & Juana MARTIN; gp/ Ju(a)n Cruz VEJIL & Clara FERNAND^{Z} *de esta*.

1804

DURAN, Mª Rafaela V^{a}
bap 4 Jan 1804, b. 30 Dec; d/ Pablo DURAN & Marg^{ta} SANCHEZ; gp/ Juan Yg^{o} VEGIL & Jacinta ARAGON, *vecinos*.

CHAVES, Jose Gabriel (torn)
bap 6 Jan '804, b. *ayer*; s/ Juan CHAVES & Clara SANCHEZ; gp/ Pablo LUC^{O} & Man^{la} VALLEJOS, *vecinos todos de esta*.

Frame 44
LUCERO, Jose Man^{l} P^{o}
ROMERO, Jose Man^{l}
bap 8 Jan 1804, b. 1st *del mes*; *espurio* s/ Juan Domingo LUS^{o}, *casado*, & Teresa ROM^{O}, wid., *Ynd^{s} de este pueb^{o}*; gm/ Patricia MARTIN, *vecina*.

BUENO, Juan Antonio V^{o}
bap 8 Jan 1804, b. 4th; s/ Juan Eugenio BUENO & Teodora BEITIA; gp/ Jose ARAGON & Rafaela BUENO.

ESPINOSA, Jose Pablo *P^{o}*
bap 15 Jan 1804, b. 11th; s/ Jose Ant^{o} ESPINOSA & Catarina ROMERO *del pueblo*; gm/ Ana Mª ARMENTA, *vecina*.

GONZALEZ, Juan Ant^{o} *P^{o}*
bap 15 Jan 1804, b. 7th; s/ Santiago GONZALEZ & Josefa ROM^{o}; gm/ Mª Ant^{a} ROMERO, *tod^{s} del pueb^{o}*.

ROMERO, Mª Micaela *V^{a}*
bap 26 Jan '804, b. 22nd; d/ Santiago ROM^{O} & Mª Ant^{a} LOVATO; gp/ Cipriano ROM^{O} & Magdalena ROM^{O}.

CONCHA, Fran^{ca} *P^{a}*
bap 26 Jan '804, 22nd; d/ Juan Domingo CONCHA & Josefa GONZ^{Z}, *Taoses*; gf/ Pablo SANDOVAL, *vec^{o}*.

ROMERO, Juan Ant^{o} *V^{o}*
bap 29 Jan 1804, b. 21st; s/ Francisco Esteban ROMERO & Mª Resurr^{n} TAFOYA; gp/ J^{n} Domingo TAFOYA & Dolores MAESE, *sus abuelos*.

LUXAN, Ana M^{a} *P^{o}*
bap 4 Feb '804, b. 29 Jan; d/ Juan Ant^{o} LUXAN & Micaela ROMERO; gm/ Rafaela ROM^{O} *del pueb^{o}*.

ARMENTA, Mª Josefa Rita Atanasia *V^{a}*
bap 4 Feb 1804, b. 28 Jan; d/ Simon ARMENTA & Marta MARTIN; gp/ Julian LUCERO & Manuela VALLEGOS (and she was named by) *á nombre de* Hermenejildo CI(S)NEROS & Mª Rita LUC^{O}, *vecinos (d)el Rio Arriba*.

ROMERO, M^{a} del Carmen *V^{a}*
bap 5 Feb 1804, b. 3 *de este mes*; d/ Juan ROMERO & Bibiana TORRES; gp/ J^{n} Ant^{o} LOBATO & Mª Yg^{a} SANCHEZ.

BACA, Rosalia *V^{a}*
bap 12 Feb 1804, b. 10th; d/ Esteban BACA & Mª Luz MARTIN; gp/ Aug^{n} (n.s.) & (torn-Ma)tiana ROMERO.

Frame 45

MEDINA, Jose M^{a} *V^{o}*
bap 12 Feb 1804, b. 8th; s/ Jose Yg^{o} MEDINA & Damiana MARTIN; gp/ Jose Mª COCA & J^{a} BENAVIDES.

RIO, Juan Andres *P^{o}*
bap 25 Feb 1804, b. 18th; s/ Ant^{o} RIO & Magdalena LUCERO, *Ynd^{s} del pueb^{o}*; gm/ Ana Maria TAFOYA, *vec^{a}*.

SANDOVAL, Marcos *V^{o}*
bap 26 Feb 1804, b. 18th; s/ Manuel SANDOV^{L} & Mª Ant^{a} LOBATO; gp/ Jose Mariano FERNANDEZ & Ascencion LUCERO.

SALAZAR, Mª Manuela *V^{a}*
bap 26 Feb 1804, b. 23rd; d/ Fran^{co} SALAZAR & Mª S^{tos} CORDOVA; gm/ Mª REYNA, *vecinos*.

FLORES, Matias *V^{o}*
VARELA, Matias
bap 2 Mch 1804, b. 24 Feb; s/ Francisca VARELA, *Ynd^{a} criada, solt^{a}*, & Martin FLORES, married, according to the mother; gp/ J^{n} Yg^{o} VEJIL & Mª Ant^{a} ARAGON.

MARTIN, Mª de Jesus *V*^{a}
bap 4 Mch 1804, ae 7 da, b. 26 Feb; d/ Juan Cruz MARTIN & Mª Dolores TORRES; gp/ Manuel SANCHEZ & Nicolasa SANDOVAL.

QUINTANA, Mª de la Luz *V*^{a}
bap 7 Mch 1804, b. 2nd; d/ Juan QUINTANA & Mª Balvanada ROMERO; gp/ Felipe S.tiago MARTIN & his daughter, Mª Rosa (MARTIN), [*vecinos*].

GONZALEZ, Juan Domingo *P*^{o}
bap 7 Mch 1804, b. 2nd; s/ Santiago GONZ^Z & Micaela ROMERO *del pueb*^{o}; gm/ Manuela MARTIN, *vec*^{a}.

MARTIN, Fran^{co} *P*^{o}
bap 10 Mch '804, b. 27 Feb; s/ Jose Fran^{co} MARTIN & Juana LUXAN; gm/ Yg^a RIO [*del pueb*^{o}].

ORTEGA, Juan Domingo *V*^{o}
bap 11 Mch 1804, b. 4th; s/ Manuel ORTEGA & Rita COCA; gp/ Alexandro TRUXILLO & Manuela ARCHULETA.

AGUILAR, Mª Victoria (torn)
bap 11 Mch '804, b. 5th; d/ Laz^o AGUILAR & Concep^n PAEZ; gp/ Juan Miguel (n.s.) & Juana PAEZ. (Frames 45-46)

Frame 46
CRUZ, Mª Eusevia *V*^{a}
bap 11 Mch '804, b. 4th; d/ Mariano CRUZ & Dolores VEJIL; gp/ Mig^l COCA & Catarina MARTIN.

FLORES, Mª Dolores *V*^{a}
bap 25 Mch 1804, b. 20th; d/ Martin FLORES & Gertrudis GARCIA; gp/ Pablo LUZ^o & Paula LARRAÑAGA.

MARTIN, Mª Resurr^n (blank)
bap 1 Apr '804, b. 26 Mch; d/ Felipe MARTIN & Mª Concep^n TRUXILLO; gp/ Pedro (FERNANDEZ) & his sister, Luz FERNAND^Z, *todos vec*^{s}.

LUXAN, Mª Encarnacion *P*^{o}
bap 1 Apr '804, b. 24 *del pasado*; d/ Jose Ant^o LUXAN & Gertrudis LAZO; gf/ Juan Luis MIRABALL (sic).

ROMERO, Santiago *P*^{o}
bap *en d*^{ho} *dia & a*$^{(ño)}$, b. 26 *pasado*; s/ Juan ROMERO & Rafaela MIRABAL; gm/ Rosalia LUX^N, *todos Ynd*^{s} *Taoses*.

CHAFALOTE, Juana *P*^{o}
bap 8 Apr '804, b. 2nd; d/ Domingo CHAFALOTE & Mª Victoria DELGADO; gm/ Mª Rosa LUXAN [*del pueblo*].

BACA, Maria Juliana *V*^{a}
bap 15 Apr '804, b. 12th; d/ Man^l BACA & Manuela CASADOS; gp/ Juan GONZ^Z & Mª Ant^a MARTIN [*vesinos*].

MONTOYA, Ramon *V*^{o}
bap 15 Apr '804, b. 9th; s/ Bernardo MONTOYA & Mª MARTIN; gp/ Ant^o LOBATO & Margarita MARTIN [*vecinos*].

RENDON, Juan Rafael *Vº*
bap 21 Apr '804, b. 15th; s/ Jose Gabriel RENDON & Mª dela Luz ALARÍ; gp/ Jose MIERA & Man^{la} ROMERO, [*vecinos*].

DURAN, Mª Candelaria *Pº*
bap 21 Apr '804, b. 16th; d/ Jose Antº DURAN & Mª NARANJO; gm/ Josefa JUILO [*del puebº*].

TORRES, Antº Jose *Pº*
bap 29 Apr '804, b. 22nd; s/ Pedro TORRES & Mª Luz SANCHEZ; gp/ J^{n} Cruz MARTIN & Dolores TORRES, [*vecinos*].

CORDOVA, Mª dela Cruz *Vª*
bap 3 May '804, b. 1st; d/ Antº Jose CORDOVA & Casilda AGUILAR; gp/ Manuela (sic) ROMº & J^{n} Esteb^{n} MAESE. (Frames 46-47)

Frame 47
GONZALEZ, Jose dela Cruz *Vº*
bap 7 May '804, b. 3rd; s/ Jose GONZ^{z} & Dorotea BACA; gp/ Jose Bautista VEJIL & Rosalia MARTIN^{z}.

ARCHULETA, Mariano *Vº*
bap 10 May '804, ae 3 da; s/ Pablo ARCHULETA & Barbara LOBATO; gp/ J^{n} Man^{l} ARCHULETA & Gertrudis TRUXILLO, [*vecinos*].

VARELA, Jose Antº *Vº*
bap 20 May '804, ae 8 da; s/ Xtoval VARELA & Rafaela MARTIN; gp/ Manuel CORTES & Mª Antª MARTIN.

MADRID, Mª Soledad *Vª*
bap 27 May '804, ae 5 da; d/ Xtoval MADRID & Dolores MAR(T)IN; gp/ Diego MADRID & Juliana VALERIO.

LUXAN, Lorenzo *Pº*
bap 3 Jne '804, ae 9 da; s/ J^{n} Domingo LUXAN & Josefa ROMERO; gm/ Micaela GONZ^{z} [*del puebº*].

TENORIO, Venancio *Vº*
bap 5 Jne '804, ae 15 da; s/ Felipe TENORIO & Antª Rosa GAVALDON; gp/ Raf^{l} LUNA & Ana Mª TAFOYA.

CRUZ, Mª Soledad *Vª*
bap 10 Jne '804, ae 8 da; d/ Pedro dela CRUZ & Mª Encarn^{n} CORDOVA; gp/ Bern^{do} MONTOYA & Mª MARTIN.

VEJIL, Antº Jose *Vº*
bap 10 Jne '804, ae 6 da; s/ J^{n} Ygº VEJIL & Soledad DURAN; gp/ Ygº VEJIL & Mª Antª ARAGON.

TRUXILLO, Antº Cleto *Pº*
bap 10 Jne '804, ae 8 da; s/ Juan Antº TRUXILLO & Antª BUENO; gp/ Pedro BUENO & Mª Manuela ROMº.

ZUASO, Mariano (torn)
bap 17 Jne '804, ae 5 da; s/ Juan ZUASO & Mª Ygª MARTIN; gm/ Mª Antª ROMº [*del puebº*].

ROMERO, Geronimo (torn)
bap 17 Jne '804; s/ Fran^{co} ROM^{o} & Felipa ROM^{o}; gm/ Mª GOMEZ [*del pueb^{o}*]. (Frames 47-48)

Frame 48
SANDOVAL, Mª Rita *V^{a}*
bap 29 Jne '804, ae 6 da; d/ Matias SANDOVAL & Mª Yg^{a} BUENO; gp/ Jose de Jesus TAFOYA & Mª Yg^{a} CANO, [*vecinos*].

AÑOQUEVIENE, Mª Juana *P^{a}*
bap 1 Jly '804, ae 8 da; d/ Juan Domingo AÑOQ^{E}VIENE & Josefa LUC^{O}; gm/ Yg^{a} ESPINOSA [*del pueb^{o}*].

LUXAN, Juan Andres *P^{o}*
bap 1 Jly '804, ae 9 da; s/ J^{n} Ant^{o} LUXAN & J^{a} ROMERO; gm/ Mª Rosa LUXAN [*del pueb^{o}*].

DURAN, Pedro Mauricio *V^{o}*
bap 2 Jly '804, ae 4 da; s/ Man^{l} DURAN & Gerarda MASCAREÑAS; gp/ Luis CHAVES & Candelaria CHAVES, [*vecin^{s}*].

MARTIN, Jose Gabriel *V^{o}*
bap 8 Jly '804, ae 8 da; s/ Guadalupe MARTIN, single, & father unknown, *criada de* Juan Ysidro VARELA; gf/ Juan Antonio DURAN.

MONTOYA, Vicente *V^{o}*
bap 15 Jly '804, ae 9 da; s/ Rafael MONTOYA & Luisa ROM^{O}; gp/ Manuel Gregorio MARTIN & Rafaela MEDINA.

TAFOYA, Josefa Enrique *V^{a}*
QUINTANA, Josefa Enrique
bap 15 Jly '804, ae 8 da; nat. d/ Jose de Jesus TAFOYA & Lorenza QUINTANA, *solteros*; gp/ Jose ARAGON & Raf^{la} BUENO.

LEAL, Esteban *V^{o}*
bap 22 Jly '804, baptized 20th, ae 7 da; s/ Man^{l} Jose LEAL & Mar^{na} QUINTANA; gp/ Raf^{l} ROM^{O} & J^{a} Prudencia (n.s.).

PACHECO, Juana Magdalena *P^{o}*
bap 22 Jly '804, ae 8 da; d/ J^{n} Ant^{o} PACHECO & Magdalena MARTIN; gm/ Mª Ysab^{l} PAEZ.

MARTIN, Jose Santiago *V^{o}*
MARTINEZ (in margin), Jose Santiago
bap 29 Jly '804, ae 5 da; s/ Severino (torn-MAR)TIN & Mª SANTIESTEB^{N}; gp/ Pablo LUC^{O} & Paula LARRAÑAGA. Ojo forward.

ZUASO, Paula Indian
bap 5 Aug '804, ae 8 da; d/ Simon ZUASO & Yg^{a} RIO; gm/ Felipa ROMERO [*del pueb^{o}*]. (Frames 48-49)

Frame 49
MEDINA, Maria del Carmen *V^{a}*
*bap 30 Jly '804, ae 15 da; d/ Yg^{o} MEDINA & Margarita CORDOVA; gp/ Anast^{o} VEJIL & Fran^{ca} BERNAL.

CORTES, Juan Domingo V^{o}
bap 12 Aug '804, ae 8 da; s/ Jose Mª CORTES & Raf^{la} CORDOVA; gp/ Jose Bautista VEJIL & Rosalia MARTIN.

TRUXILLO, Mª Tiburcia V^{a}
bap 12 Aug 1804, ae 2 da; d/ Vicente TRUXILLO & Mª MADRID; gp/ *los abuelos* Pablo TRUXILLO & Ant^{a} Teresa HURTADO.

ORTIS, Eusebio P^{o}
bap 15 Aug '804, ae 5 da; s/ Jose Ant^{o} (n.s.) & Lucia ORTIZ *del pueb^{o}*; gm/ Lucia DURAN.

GONZALEZ, Tomas V^{o}
bap 19 Aug '804, ae 6 da; s/ Jose S^{to} GONZ^{z} & Mª LISTON, *vec^{s}*; gf/ Domingo MIRABALL (sic).

GONZALEZ, Mª Juana V^{o}
bap 19 Aug '804, ae 6 da; d/ Jose Miguel GONZ^{z} & Mª Ysabel VEJIL; gp/ Juan Ant^{o} ARCHULETA & Felipa RAMIRES, [*vec^{s}*].

MEDINA, Maria *(V)^{a}*
bap 26 Aug '804, ae 6 da; d/ Greg^{o} MEDINA & Ysabel ROMERO; gp/ Jose Ant^{o} MARTIN & Ynes LEAL.

VARELA, Gregorio de Jesus V^{o}
bap 30 Aug '804, ae 6 da; s/ Mig^{l} VARELA & J^{a} ROM^{o}; gp/ J^{n} Ysidro VARELA & Juana MARTIN, vec^{s}. (Frames 49-50)

Frame 50
CORTES, Hipolito V^{o}
bap 5 Sep '804, ae 8 da; s/ Paulin CORTES & Concep^{n} MARTIN; gp/ Felis (n.s.) & Concep^{n} URIOSTE.

ROMERO, Mª Manuela V^{a}
bap 9 Sep '804, ae 3 da; d/ Jose M^{a} ROM^{o} & Rafaela PINEDA; gp/ Pedro FERNANDEZ & Marg^{ta} ROM^{o}.

COCA, Cornelio V^{o}
bap 16 Sep '804, ae 9 da; s/ Miguel COCA & Catarina MARTIN; gp/ Pasq^{l} (n.s.) & Manuela ARAGON.

CHAVES, Maria Antonia V^{a}
bap 16 Sep '804; d/ Domingo CHAVES & Candelaria DURAN; gp/ Pedro Yg^{o} DURAN & Mª Ant^{a} SANCHEZ.

MALINCHE, Jose Fra^{co} P^{o}
bap 21 Sep '804, ae 4 da; s/ Juan Andres MALINCHE & Manuela ORTIZ; gp/ Francisco Ant^{o} TRUXILLO & Gertrudis MARTIN, *vec^{s}*.

LUXAN, Maria P^{o}
bap 23 Sep 1804, ae 8 da; d/ Valentin LUXAN & Josefa MARTIN; gm/ Fran^{ca} LUXAN *del pueb^{o}*.

SANDOVAL, J^{a} Gertrudis V^{a}
bap 23 Sep 1804, ae 5 da; d/ Fran^{co} SANDOVAL & Mª Yg^{a} CHAVES; gf/ Juan Ant^{o} DURA(N).

MARTIN, Angela P^{o}
bap 29 Sep '804, ae 7 da; d/ Jose Ant^{o} MARTIN & Ascencion LOMA; gm/ Fran^{ca} LUC^{o} *del pueb^{o}*.

LU(torn), Cayetana
ROMERO, Cayetana P^{a}
bap 29 Sep '804, ae 9; d/ Fran^{co} LU(torn), married, & Brigida ROMERO, wid.; gm/ Margarita TISLÉ *del pueb^{o}*.

Frame 51
ESPINOSA, Juana M^{a} P^{a}
bap 29 Sep '804, ae 8 da; d/ J^{n} Ant^{o} ESPINOSA & Rafaela GONZ^{z}; gm/ Rosa CATUJE.

LOBATO, Ant^{o} Mateo V^{o}
bap 29 Sep 1804, ae 9 da; d/ Rafael LOBATO & Mª Luz ESPINOSA; gp/ Cruz VEJIL & Clara FERN^{z}, *vecin^{s}*.

MONDRAGON, Geronimo V^{o}
bap 30 Sep '804, ae 8 da; s/ Cristov^{l} MONDRAGON & Juana GONZ^{z}; gp/ Paulin de HERRERA & Mª Carmen MADRID, *vec^{s}*.

GONZALEZ, J^{n} Jose P^{o}
bap 30 Sep '804, ae 8 da; s/ Juan GONZ^{z} & Mª Soledad PULULU *del pueb^{o}*; gm/ J^{a} GARCIA.

DURAN, Mª Fran^{ca} V^{a}
bap 7 Oct '804, ae 7 da; d/ J^{n} Nicolas DURAN & J^{a} ROMERO; gm/ Juana VELASQ^{z}, [*vecinos*].

ROMERO, Fran^{ca} P^{a}
bap 7 Oct '804, ae 4 da; d/ Fran^{co} ROM^{o} & Mª Carmen ROM^{o} *del pueb^{o}*; gp/ Julian TENORIO & Lorenza LOPEZ, *vec^{s}*.

RIO, Mª Rosa P^{a}
bap 7 Oct '804, ae 7 da; d/ Juan Ant^{o} RIO & J^{a} MARQUES; gm/ Lucia DURAN [*del pueb^{o}*].

GAVILAN, Mariano P^{o}
bap 14 Oct '804, ae 10 da; s/ Jose Ant^{o} GAVILAN & Geronima MARTIN; gm/ Fran^{ca} LUC^{o}.

RIO, Mª Encarn^{n} P^{a}
bap 4 Nov '804, ae 15 da; d/ Santiago RIO & Mª Rosa CHAFALOTE; gm/ Rosa CATUGE *del pueb^{o}*.

PICURIES, Mª Rosa P^{a}
bap 4 Nov '804; d/ Juan Cayetano PICURIES & Mª Loreta (n.s.); gm/ M^{a} Yg^{a} ROM^{o} [*del pueb^{o}*]. (Frames 51-52)

Frame 52
ZUASO, Fran^{ca} V^{a}
bap 4 Nov '804, ae 11 da; d/ Jose ZUASO & Josefa CASADOS; gp/ Dionisio QUINTANA & Petrona VARELA, *vec^{s}*.

GONZALEZ, Alonso P^{o}
bap 11 Nov 1804, ae 11 da; s/ Fran^{co} GONZ^{z} & Lucia TECOA; gm/ Manuela LUXAN.

ROMERO, Juan Ant^{o} P^{o}
bap 11 Nov '804, ae 9 da; s/ Jose ROMERO & Ana Mª ORTIZ; gm/ Mª Concepcion CONEJO.

LUCERO, Man^{l} Greg^{o} P^{o}
bap 18 Nov 1804, ae 15 da; s/ Juan Domingo LUC^{O} & Juliana GOMEZ; gm/ Mª Ant^{a} ZAMORA.

MONTOYA, Jose Rafael V^{o}
bap 2 Dec '804, ae 8 da; s/ Juan MONTOYA & M^{a} (d)ela CRUZ; gp/ Jose Mª CORTES & Mª Magdalena BRITO, *vec^{s}*.

FERNANDEZ, Mª Manuela V^{a}
bap 6 Dec '804, ae 6 da; d/ Domingo FERNANDEZ & Fran^{ca} GARCIA; gp/ Manuel SANCHEZ & Dolores TORRES.

LUXAN, Antonia P^{a}
bap 9Dec '804, ae 8 da; d/ Jose Ant^{o} LUXAN & Manuela GONZ^{z}; gm/ Josefa MARTIN *del pueb^{o}*.

CRUZ, Mª Concepcion V^{a}
bap 9 Dec '804, ae 3 da; d/ Jose CRUZ & Mª Luisa ARCHULETA; gp/ Dionisio VARELA & Mª TRUXILLO, [*vec^{s}*].

LASO, Gertrudis P^{a}
bap 16 Dec 1804, ae 7 da; d/ Matias LASO & G(ua)dalupe MARTIN; gm/ Gertrudis LASO *del pueb^{o}*.

TORRES, Jose Manuel (blank)
bap 27 Dec '804, ae 4 da; s/ Diego TORRES & Mª Concep^{n} TRUXILLO; gp/ Jose RAMOS & Mª Ant^{a} MARTÍN, *vec^{s}*. (Frames 52-53)

Frame 53
GARCÍA, Juana M^{a} V^{a}
bap 30 Dec '804, ae 4 da; d/ J^{n} de Jesus GARCÍA & Simona BEITIA *de Chama*; gp/ Jose ARAGON & Raf^{la} BUENO.

Año de 1805

CASILLAS, Mª Manuela V^{a}
bap 6 Jan '805, ae 6 da; d/ Bernardo CASILLAS & Dolores MADRID; gp/ Paulin de HERRERA & Mª Carmen MADRID.

CASILLAS, Mª Josefa V^{a}
bap 6 Jan '805, ae 3 da; d/ Jose Lino CASILLAS & Sarafina CORTES; gp/ Juan de Jesus MARTIN & Juana CORTES.

MARTÍN, Man^{l} de los Reyes V^{o}
bap 6 Jan '805, ae 7 da; s/ Bentura MARTÍN & Rafaela MAESE; gp/ J^{n} Yg^{o} VEJÍL & Mª Ant^{a} ARAGON.

MIERA, Vicente Higino V^{o}
bap 17 Jan '805, ae 7 da; s/ Jose MIERA & Man^{la} ROM^{O}; gp/ *sus abuelos*, D^{n} Ant^{o} Jose ROMERO, *Alc^{e} m^{or}*, & Mª BACA.

SANCHEZ, Juan Pablo V^{o}
bap 27 Jan '805, ae 3 da; s/ Diego SANCHEZ & Magdalena MARTIN; gp/ Juan Ant^{o} LOBATO & Mª Yg^{a} SANCHEZ.

MONTES, Mª Juliana *V*^{a}
bap 2 Feb '805, ae 6 da; d/ Ant^o MONTES & Ynes MARTÍN; gp/ Severino MARTÍN & Mª Carmen SANTISTEBAN.

VALDES, Jose Julian *V*^{o}
*bap 30 Jan '805, ae 3 da; s/ Juan VALDES & Bibiana BACA; gp/ Julian LUC^o & Paula LARRAÑAGA.

MARQUEZ, Mª Ant^a *P*^{a}
bap 3 Feb '805, ae 4 da; d/ Manuel MARQUEZ & Paula DELGADO *del pueb*^{o}; gf/ Jose GARCIA, *vecino*. (Frames 53-54)

Frame 54
MARTÍN, Francisco *P*^{o}
bap 10 Feb '805, ae 8 da; s/ Ant^o MARTÍN & Guadalupe ROM^o; gm/ Felipa CATUGE.

CHINO, Agustin *P*^{o}
bap 17 Feb '805, ae 8 da; s/ Jose Ant^o CHINO & J^a M^a ROM^o; gm/ Magdalena MARTÍN *del pueb*^{o}.

DURAN, Juan de Jesus *V*^{o}
bap 17 Feb 1805, ae 8 da; s/ Pablo DURAN & Mª VALDES; gp/ Ygnacio DURAN & Mª Reyes FERNAND^z.

LOBATO, Mª Manuela *V*^{a}
MESTAS, Mª Manuela
bap 17 Feb '805, ae 3 da; d/ Jose Man^l LOBATO, *Ynd*^{o} *criado, soltero*, & Josefa MESTAS, *solt*^{a}, *Española*; gp/ Jose LOBATO & Ana Mª VALLEJOS.

VALLEJOS (patron), Leonarda *V*^{a}
bap 20 Feb '805, ae 3 da; d/ Catarina (n.s.), *Ynd*^{a} *criada de* Manuela VALLEJOS, & father unknown; gp/ Cri(s)tovl (written over) LUC^o & his daughter, Dolores (LUCERO).

MADRID, Maria Angela *V*^{a}
VALERIO, Maria Angela
bap 21 Feb '805, b. 19 Feb; d/ Diego MADRID, dec., & Juliana VALERIO, wid.; gp/ Jose GONZ^z & Dorotea BACA.

LOBATO, Jose Ant^o *V*^{o}
bap 24 Feb '805, ae 6 da; s/ Fran^{co} LOBATO & Gertrudis MONDRAGON; gp/ Jose Mª CHAVES & Mª HORTEGA.

GONZALEZ, Mª Rafaela *V*^{a}
bap 24 Feb 1805, ae 3 da; d/ Juan GONZ^z & Mª Ant^a MARTÍN; gp/ Cristoval LUC^o & Paula LARRAÑAGA.

MARTIN, Mª Ramona *V*^{a}
bap 10 Mch '805, ae 10 da; d/ Salv^{or} Man^l MARTÍN & Mª Ant^a MONTOYA; gp/ Jose Mar^{no} FERN^z & Maria Ant^a MONTOYA (sic).

ARCHULETA, Miguel Ant^o *V*^{o}
bap 17 Mch '805, ae 5 da; s/ Ant^o ARCHULETA & Maria Monserrate LEAL, *vec*^{s}; gp/ J^n Yg^o VEGIL & Mª Ant^a ARAGON.

MIRABALL, Mª Luz *V*^{a}
bap 17 Mch '805, ae 6 da; d/ Juan Luís MIRABAL<u>L</u> (sic) & Mª GONZ^z; gp/ Ant^o RODRIGUEZ & Mª BEITIA.

MARTIN, Pablo *Pº*
bap 17 Mch '805, ae 8 da; s/ Jose MARTÍN & Gertrudis ROMº; gm/ Juana Lucia ROMERO *del puebº*. (Frames 54-55)

Frame 55
CASILLAS, Juana Paula *Vª*
bap 24 Mch '805, ae 4 da; d/ Cristobal CASILLAS & Mª Luisa TAFOYA; gp/ Felis (n.s.) & Mª URIOSTE.

MADRID, Jose Antº *Vº*
bap 24 Mch '805, ae 4 da; s/ Tomas MADRID & Victoria GARCIA; gp/ Jose Antº CORTES & Juana MONTOYA.

CRUZ, Jose *Vº*
bap 24 Mch '805, ae 6 da; s/ Alexo CRUZ & Guadalupe DURAN; gp/ Andres TRUXILLO & Mª Antª LOPEZ.

FLORES, Mª Josefa *Vª*
bap 24 Mch '805, ae 6 da; d/ Martín FLORES & Gertrudis GARCIA; gp/ Alexandro TRUXILLO & Manuela GARCIA, *vecª*.

ARAGON (patron), Mª Antª *Yuta*
bap 24 Mch '805, ae about 5 yr; d/ *(Yutas)*, *criada de* Jacinta ARAGON & redeemed from the *Nacion*; gf/ Jose Vicente ARAGON.

ARAGON (patron), Mª Barbara *Yuta*
bap 24 Mch '805, ae about 3 yr; d/ (*Yutas*), *criada de* Jacinta ARAGON redeemed from the *Nacion*; gf/ Jose Vicente ARAGON.

MARTINEZ (patron), Juana *Yuta*
bap 25 Mch '805, ae 3 yr; d/ (*Yutas*) *criada de* Julian MARTINEZ; gf/ Fran^{co} MARTINES.

VEGIL, Maria *Vª*
bap 31 Mch '805, b. 26th; d/ Juan de Jesus VEGIL & Rosa DURAN; gp/ J^{n} Ysidro VARELA & Jª MARTÍN.

MARTIN, Gregorio *Vº*
bap 23 Apr '805, ae 8 da; s/ Juan MARTÍN & Juliana VALLEJOS; gp/ Cristoval LUCº & Manuela SANDOVAL.

TAFOYA, Juan *Pº*
bap 28 Apr '805, b. 13th; s/ Antonio TAFOYA & Rosalia DURAN; gp/ Xtoval CASILLAS & Luisa TAFOYA. (Frames 55-56)

Frame 56
BUENO, Antonio *Vº*
bap 28 Apr '805, ae 5 da; s/ Antº BUENO & Rosalia VALDES; gp/ Pedro MARTÍN & Clara FERNANDEZ.

MARTIN, Ana Mª *Vª*
bap 28 Apr '805, ae 7 da; d/ Ygº MARTIN & Mª Paula SALAZAR; gp/ Maurilo VARGAS & Nicomeda PORTI^{Z}.

DURAN, Mª Rafaela *Vª*
bap 28 Apr (1805), b. 8th; d/ Pablo DURAN & Margarita SANCHEZ; gp/ Juan CHAVES & Clara SANCHEZ.

ARCHULETA, Hermeregildo V^o
bap 28 Apr '805, ae 13 da; s/ Julian ARCHULETA & Manuela VARELA; gp/ Alfonso GARCIA & Tomasa GARCIA.

MARTIN, Juan V^o
bap 28 Apr '805, ae 6 da; s/ Manuel Gregorio MARTIN & Rafaela MEDINA; gp/ Jose GARCIA & Ant^a MARTIN.

VEGIL, Maria dela Luz V^a
bap 28 Apr '805, b. 8 *del mes;* d/ J^n Yg^o VEGIL & Soledad DURAN; gf/ Felipe RAEL.

BLEA, M^a dela Luz V^a
bap 3 May '805, ae 9 da; d/ Mª Nasarena BLEA, single, father unknown; gp/ Juan Cruz CONT^S & Mª Luz MONTOYA.

CRUZ, Maria Polonia V^a
bap 3 May '805, ae 16 da; d/ Mariano CRUZ & Dolores VEGIL; gp/ Mateo COCA & Greg^a ARMIJO.

MARTIN, Jose
RIO, Jose P^o
bap 5 May '805, ae 5 da; *espurio* s/ Fran^{co} MARTIN, *casado*, & Josefa RIO, wid., *[del pueb^o]*; gm/ Lucia NARANJO.

BEITIA, Mª Josefa V^a
bap 7 May '805, b. *ayer;* d/ Jose Yg^o BEITIA & Mª Rafaela MARTIN; gp/ Tor(ibio-torn) LOBATO & Candelaria GONZ^Z.

BLEA, Felipa Cayetana V^a
bap 12 May '805 because of extreme necessity on the 8th, b. 1st; d/ Ant^o BLEA & Barb^a MONTOYA; gp/ Vicente TRUXILLO & Mª Dolores MADRID. (Frames 56-57)

Frame 57
LUCERO, Mª Josefa V^a
bap 25 May '805, ae 8 da; d/ J^n de Jesus LUC^O & Mª Yg^a ARAGON; gp/ Severino MARTÍN & M^a del Carmen SANTISTEB^N.

CORDOVA, Mª Josefa V^a
bap 26 May '805, ae 9 da; d/ Manuel CORDOVA & Ana Mª GUILLEN; gp/ Pedro LUCERO & Mª Luz FERNANDEZ.

TENORIO, Felipe V^o
bap 5 Jne '805, b. *hoy;* s/ Julian TENORIO & Lorenza LOPEZ; gm/ Manuela ROMERO.

CAYGUA, J^n Ant^o P^o
bap 9 Jne '805, ae 8 da; s/ Domingo CAYGUA & Victoria DELGADO; gm/ Mª Yg^a MARTIN *del pueb^o*.

MARTIN, Jose Ant^o V^o
bap 9 Jne '805, ae 8 da; s/ Mª Concepcion MARTIN, single, & father unknown; gp/ Felipe SANCHEZ & J^a Mª MARTINEZ, *vec^s*.

DURAN, Ant^a Margarita V^a
bap 13 Jne '805, b. *ayer;* d/ Salv^{or} DURAN & Candelaria CORDOVA; gp/ Bernardo LUC^O & Tomasa MARTIN.

SANCHEZ, Juan Ygº *Vº*
bap 16 Jne '805, ae 7 da; s/ Manuel SANCHEZ & Nicolasa SANDOVAL; gp/ Cruz VEGIL & Clara FERNAND^{z}.

NARANJO, Mª Antª *Pª*
bap 16 Jne '805, ae 4 da; d/ Santiago NARANJO, dec., & Micaela CHINO; gm/ Mª ROMº *del pueblo*.

ROMERO, Maria Josefa *Vª*
bap 23 Jne '805, ae 9 da; d/ Concepcion ROMº & Rosa QUINTANA; gp/ Jose Mariano FERNAND^{z} & Mª Reyes FERN^{z}. (Frames 57-58)

Frame 58
LUXAN, Santiago *Pº*
bap 7 Jly '805, ae 7 da; s/ Jose Antº LUXAN & Gertrudis LASO; gm/ Mª Antª ROMERO [*del pueblo*].

MARTIN, Juan Antº *Vº*
bap 7 Jly '805, ae 6 da; s/ Antº Jos. MARTIN & Alberta ROMº; gp/ Jos. Bautista VEGIL & Rosalia MARTIN, *vec^{s}*.

SANDOVAL, Juan *Vº*
bap 21 Jly '805, ae 3 da; s/ Jose Ramon SANDOVAL & Dolores MARTIN; gp/ Jose (n.s.) & Ascencion SILVA, *vec^{s}*.

ARCHULETA, Ana Mª *Vª*
bap 21 Jly '805, ae 7 da; d/ Antº ARCHULETA & Jª MARTÍN; gp/ Juan de Jesus LUCº & Mª Ygª ARAGON, [*vec^{s}*].

DURAN, Mª Lorenza *Vª*
bap 15 Aug '805, ae 6 da; d/ Ygº DURAN & Antª SANCHEZ; gp/ Pablo DURAN & Mª VALDES.

BACA, Luisa *Vª*
bap 25 Aug '805, ae 7 da; d/ Manuel BACA & Manuela CASADOS; gp/ Jose GONZ^{z} & Dorotea BACA.

ROMERO, Jose Antonio *Vº*
bap 5 Sep '805, ae 6 da; s/ Francisco Esteban ROMERO & Mª Resurreccion TAFOYA; gp/ Gregorio SANDOVAL & Gregoria CORDOVA, *vecin^{s} de las Truchus*.

ZUASO, Miguel *Vº*
bap 29 Sep '805, ae 6 da; s/ Miguel ZUASO & Mariana MONTOYA; gp/ Lazaro ROMERO & Barbara GONZ^{z}.

ARAGON, Jose Fran^{co} *Vº*
*bap 29 Sep '805, ae 16 da; s/ Antº ARAGON & Xaviera VEGIL; gp/ Pedro MARTIN & Rita LUCº.

LEAL, Mª Rosa *Vª*
bap 29 Sep '805, ae 14 da; d/ Manuel Jose LEAL & Mariana QUINTANA; gp/ Jose Mig^{l} GONZ^{z} & Mª Ysabel VEGIL. (Frames 58-59)

Frame 59
ROMERO, Geronimo *Pº*
bap 30 Sep '805, ae 8 da; s/ Juan ROMERO & Mª Rafaela MIRABALL (sic); gp/ Juan Antº DURAN & Juliana LUXAN.

TUILQUILLO, Josefa P^{a}
bap 6 Oct '805, ae 7 da; d/ Vicente TUILQUILLO, dec., & Mª Encarnacion LUXAN, *viuda*; gm/ Josefa ROMERO *del pueblo*.

CORTES, Mariano *V^{o}*
bap 13 Oct '805, ae 8 da; s/ Paulin CORTES & Serafina MARTIN; gp/ Jose MARTIN & Gertrudis MONTOYA.

LUCERO, Juana M^{a} *V^{a}*
bap 20 Oct '805, ae 9 da; d/ Pedro LUC^{o} & Mª FERNANDEZ; gp/ Pedro (n.s.) & Mª Reyes FERNANDEZ.

CORTES, Maria Andrea *V^{a}*
bap 10 Nov 1805, ae 8 da; d/ Jose CORTES & Magdalena BRITO; gp/ Xtoval LOPEZ & Teresa TRUXILLO.

MIER, Ysabel *V^{a}*
bap 10 Nov '805, ae 9 da; d/ Juan MIER (sic) & Micaela GONZ^{z} gm/ Ysabel ROM^{o} *del pueblo*.

MADRID, Juan Ant^{o} *V^{o}*
bap 10 Nov '805, ae 10 da; s/ Xtoval MADRID & Dolores MARTIN; gp/ Anastasio ARGUELLO & Mª Luz MARTIN.

MARTIN, Ana Teresa *V^{a}*
bap 10 Nov '805, ae 8 da; d/ Juan Pablo MARTIN & Mª Sta Ana (n.s.); gp/ Mateo PAEZ & Beronica MONTOYA.

VARGAS, Mª Fran^{ca} *V^{a}*
bap 21 Nov '805, ae 3 da; d/ Esteban VARGAS & Andrea TAFOYA; gp/ Pedro MARTIN & Cayetana VEGIL *del Embudo*.

LUXAN, Mª Dolores *P^{a}*
bap 24 Nov '805, ae 5 da; d/ Fran^{co} LUXAN & Yg^{a} ESPINOSA *del pueb^{o}*; gp/ Aug^{n} (n.s.) & Matiana ROM^{o}. (Frames 59-60)

Frame 60
MARTÍN, Matias *P^{o}*
bap 8 Dec '805, ae 9 da; s/ Jose MARTÍN & Micaela DURAN; gm/ Rosa CATUGE.

GONZALEZ, Mª Ant^{a} *V^{a}*
bap 17 Dec '805, ae 3 da; d/ Ant^{o} GONZALEZ & Manuela ROM^{o}; gp/ Juan de Jesus LUC^{o} & Yg^{a} ARAGON.

1806

LUCERO, Felipe *V^{o}*
bap 9 Feb '806, ae 5 da; s/ Bern^{do} LUCERO & Tomasa MARTIN; gp/ Miguel VEGIL & Ana Mª VALLEJOS.

ZUASO, Jose M^{a} *V^{o}*
bap 9 Feb '806, ae 4 da; d/ Jose ZUASO & Mª Josefa CASADOS; gp/ Mateo COCA & Manuela (COCA), his daughter.

MARTIN, Jose Fran^{co} *V^{o}*
bap 9 Feb '806, ae 6 da; s/ Xtoval MARTIN & Teodora FRESQUIS; gp/ Juan Ant^{o} DURAN & Ascencion LUC^{o}.

LUCERO, Tomas *P^{o}*
bap 9 Mch 1806, ae 12 da; s/ Juan Ant^{o} LUC^{o} & Ant^{a} ROMERO *del pueblo*; gp/ Manuel SANCHES & Mª Rosa MARTIN.

MIRABALL, Mª Dolores *V^{a}*
bap 9 Mch '806, ae 11 da; d/ J^{n} Luis MIRABALL (sic) & Damasia GONZ^{z}; gp/ Jose M^{a} ROM^{o} & Rafaela PINEDA.

LOBATO, Juan Domingo *V^{a}*
bap 11 Mch '806, ae 12 da; s/ Fran^{co} LOBATO & Andrea SANDOV^{L}; gp/ J^{n} Jose ZUASO & Mª Luz LOBATO.

TAFOYA, Jose Greg^{o} *V^{o}*
bap 12 Mch '806, ae 3 da; s/ Jose TAFOYA & Micaela RIO; gp/ Juan Mig^{l} MARQ^{z} & Gertrudis MONTOYA.

DURAN, Fran^{co} *V^{o}*
bap 15 Mch '806, ae 7 da; s/ Pablo DURAN & M(^{a}) de Jesus VALDES; gf/ Pablo LUCERO.

MONTOYA, Mª Manuela
bap 16 Mch '806, ae 8 da; d/ J^{n} MONTOYA & Mª CRUZ; gp/ Fran^{co} LOBATO & Gertrudis MONDRAGON. (Frames 60-61)

Frame 61
LUCERO, Tomas *V^{o}*
bap 16 Mch '806, ae 3 da; s/ Pablo LUC^{o} & Paula LARRAÑAGA; gp/ *el Alc^{e} D^{n}* Tomas ORTIS & his wife, Mª Rosa MARTIN.

ORTEGA, Juan Ant^{o} *V^{o}*
bap 16 Mch '806, ae 12 da; s/ Man^{l} ORTEGA & Rita COCA; gp/ Bernardino MARTÍN & Manuela ARAGON.

VEGIL, Ant^{a} Teresa *V^{a}*
bap 16 Mch '806, ae 12 da; d/ Juan VEGIL & Josefa LOBATO; gp/ Matias VEGIL & Mª Dolores PACHECO.

ROMERO, Mª Soledad *V^{a}*
bap 19 Mch 1806, ae 7 da; d/ Santiago ROM^{o} & Mª Ant^{a} LOBATO; gp/ Domingo CHAVES & Mª Candelaria DURAN.

ROMERO, Josefa *P^{a}*
bap 23 Mch '806, ae 9 da; d/ Juan Domingo ROMERO & Fran^{ca} PRINCESA; gm/ Josefa ROM^{o} *del pueblo*.

MARTIN, Mª Micaela *V^{a}*
bap 23 Mch 1806, ae 5 da; d/ Bentura MARTÍN & Rafaela MAESE; gp/ Domingo CHAVES & Candelaria DURAN.

LEAL, Mª Guadalupe *V^{a}*
bap 23 Mch '806, ae 3 da; d/ Josefa LEAL & father unknown; gp/ Pedro Yg^{o} ZAMORA & Mª Rafaela CASILLAS.

DURAN, Jose Pablo *V^{o}*
bap 25 Mch '806, ae 5 da; s/ Juan DURAN & Fran^{ca} SANTISTEVAN; gp/ J^{n} LUC^{o} & Yg^{a} ARAGON.

AÑOQUEVIENE, M^{a} Yg^{a} *P*^{a}
bap 25 Mch 1806, ae 6 da; d/ Domingo AÑOQUEVIENE & Josefa LUCERO; gm/ Mª Ascencion GOMEZ [*del pueblo*]. (Frames 61-62)

Frame 62
BUENO, Jose Vicente *V*^{o}
bap 27 Mch 1806, ae 7 da; s/ J^{n} Eugenio BUENO & Teodora BEITIA; gp/ Bartolome MONDRAGON & Gertrudis (MONDRAGON), his sister.

MONTOYA, Jose *V*^{o}
bap 30 Mch '806, ae 3 da; s/ Jose Rafael MONTOYA & Luisa ROM^{o}; gp/ Paulin de HERRERA & Mª Carmen MADRID.

VARGAS, Jose Fran^{co} *V*^{o}
bap 30 Mch '806, ae 3 da; s/ Maurilo VARGAS & Nicomeda FERNAND^{z}; gp/ Fran^{co} MARTIN & Tomasa SANCHEZ.

COCA, Mª Dolores *V*^{a}
bap 30 Mch 1806, ae 3 da; d/ Jose Mª COCA & Juana BENAVIDES; gp/ Juan GONZ^{z} & Mª Ant^{a} MARTIN.

VEGIL, M^{a} dela Luz *V*^{a}
bap 6 Apr '806, ae 5 da; d/ J^{n} Yg^{o} VEGIL & Soledad DURAN; gp/ J^{n} CHAVES & Clara SANCHEZ.

TORRES, Vicente *V*^{o}
bap 13 Apr '806, ae 9 da; s/ Diego TORRES & Concep^{n} TRUXILLO; gp/ Fran^{co} LOBATO & Gertrudes MONDRAGON.

TAFOYA, Mª Resurr^{n} *V*^{a}
bap 13 Apr '806, ae 8 da; d/ Nicolas TAFOYA & Barbara COCA; gp/ Jose ARGUELLO & Yg^{a} ROM^{o}.

MONTOYA, Jose *V*^{o}
MARTIN, Jose
bap 30 Apr '806, ae 20 da; nat. s/ Manuel MONTOYA & Patricia MARTIN, *solteros*; gp/ Jose Ramon SANDOV^{L} & Mª Ascencion SILVA.

AGUILAR, Juliana *V*^{a}
bap 13 Apr '806, ae 2 da; d/ Lazaro AGUILAR & Mª Concepcion PAEZ; gp/ Xtoval LUC^{o} & Mª Man^{la} SANDOVAL. (Frames 62-63)

Frame 63
ARCHULETA, Mª Josefa *V*^{a}
bap 26 Apr '806, ae 4 da; d/ Julian ARCHULETA & Manuela VARELA; gp/ Juan Gabriel VALVERDE & Mª Encarn^{n} ARCHULETA.

MONDRAGON, Jose *V*^{o}
bap 26 Apr '806, ae 3 da; s/ Bartolome MONDRAGON & Mª Regina FRESQUIS; gp/ Santiago LUC^{o} & Rosa AGUILAR.

LOBATO, Juana Maria *V*^{a}
bap 26 Apr '806, ae 5 da; d/ Juan Ant^{o} LOBATO & Mª Yg^{a} SANCHEZ; gp/ Fran^{co} MARTIN & Tomasa SANCHEZ.

ZUASO, Josefa *P*^{o}
bap 26 Apr'1806, ae 10 da; d/ Jose Ant^{o} ZUASO & Rafaela ROM^{o} *del pueblo*; gm/ Mariana CORDOVA, *vecina*.

PADILLA, Fran^{co} V^{o}
bap 26 Apr '806, ae 4 da; s/ Pedro PADILLA & Lucia CHAV^{S}; gp/ Matias VEGIL & Mª Dolores PACHECO.

TAFOYA, Maria V^{a}
bap 1 May '806, ae 4 da; d/ Juan de Jesus TAFOYA & Lorenza QUINTANA; gp/ Dionisio VEGIL & Manuela DELGADO.

PAEZ, Jose Miguel P^{o}
bap 4 May '806, ae 6 da; s/ Juan PAEZ & Lugarda SERNA; gp/ Jose Mig^{l} GONZ^{z} & Mª REYNA. (Frames 63-64)

Frame 64
SANCHEZ, Yg^{o} P^{o}
bap 4 May '806, ae 4 da; s/ Diego SANCHEZ & Ysabel ROM^{o}; gm/ Mª Ant^{a} RIO.

VALVERDE, Pedro Ant^{o} V^{o}
bap 4 May (1806), ae 8 da; s/ Juan Gabriel VALVERDE & Tomasa GARCIA; gf/ Fran^{co} VEGIL.

GONZALEZ, Mª de la Cruz V^{a}
bap 8 May '806, ae 6 da; d/ Jose Mig^{l} GONZ^{z} & Ysabel TRUXILLO; gp/ Jose Gab^{l} TRUXILLO & Mª Manuela MARTIN.

ZUASO, Fran^{co} V^{o}
bap 11 May '806, ae 9 da; s/ Fran^{co} ZUASO & Ygnasia RIO; gm/ Rosalia RIO.

TRUXILLO, Jose Mig^{l} V^{o}
bap 11 May '806, ae 3 da; s/ Pedro TRUXILLO & Mª Ant^{a} SANCHES; gp/ Ant^{o} LOBATO & Margarita MARTÍN, *sus bisabuelos.*

CHAVES, Juan Xtov^{l} V^{o}
bap 11 May '806, ae 5 da; s/ Jose Mª CHAVES & Mª ORTEGA; gp/ Xtov^{l} LUCERO & his daughter, Polonia (LUCERO).

MARTIN, Juan Pasq^{l} V^{o}
bap 22 May '806, ae 6 da; s/ Severino MARTÍN & Mª Carmen SANTIST^{N}; gp/ J^{n} Domingo VALDES & Mª Luz MARTÍN.

CRUZ, Mª Man^{la} P^{a}
bap 25 May '806, ae 3 da; d/ Alexo CRUZ & Mª DURAN; gp/ J^{n} Domingo TAFOYA & Dolores MAESE.

PADILLA, Pedro V^{o}
bap 25 May '806, ae 5 da; s/ Salvador PADILLA & Josefa MARTIN; gp/ Pedro FERN^{z} & Mª Yg^{a} MARTÍN.

LOBATO, Juan Xtoval V^{o}
bap 25 May 1806, ae 8 da; s/ Jose Domingo LOBATO & Clara TAFOYA; gp/ Fran^{co} LOBATO & Andrea SANDOV^{L}.

Frame 65
MARTIN, Mª Ant^{a} P^{a}
bap 25 May '806, ae 9 da; d/ Jose Ant^{o} MARTIN & J^{u} Fran^{ca} (n.s.); gm/ Paula REDONDO.

VARELA, Manuel Antº *Vº*
bap 26 May '806, ae 3 da; s/ Miguel VARELA & Mª Juana ROMERO; gm/ *su abuela*, Mª Antª TAFOYA.

GONZALEZ, Mª de la Luz *Vª*
bap 1 Jne '806, ae 5 da; d/ Salvador GONZ^{z} & Ana Mª VEGIL; gp/ Jose Mig^{l} GONZ^{z} & Mª Ysabel VEGIL.

PANDO, Juan Andres *Pº*
bap 1 Jne '806, ae 8 da; s/ Salvador PANDO & Ana Mª LOMA; gm/ Mª Ygª MARTIN.

CAOS, Marcelina *Vª*
bap 5 Jne '806, ae 4 da; d/ Juan Antº CAOS & Catarina BACA; gp/ Tomas ROMº & Ysidora MARTIN.

MARTIN, Juan Domingo *Vº*
bap 5 Jne '806, ae 5 da; s/ Jose MARTIN & Gertrudis GALVES; gp/ Antº FERN^{z} & Margarita ROMERO.

ALIRI, Manuel *Pº*
bap 8 Jne '806, ae 5 da; s/ Marcos ALIRI & Catarina PANDO; gf/ Juan Lorenzo ALIRI.

GONZALEZ, Jose Manuel *Pº*
bap 8 Jne '806, ae 4 da; s/ Santiago GONZ^{z} & Jª LISTON; gm/ Josefa ROMº.

MIERA, Fran^{co} *Vº*
bap 8 Jne '806, ae 3 da; s/ Jose MIERA & Manuela ROMERO; gp/ Pedro MARTIN & Jacinta ARAGON.

MONTE, Felipe *Vº*
bap 8 Jne '806, ae 10 da; s/ Antº del MONTE & Ynes MARTÍN; gp/ Clemente MARTÍN & Josefa MARTIN.

FERNANDEZ, Mª dela Luz *Vª*
bap 22 Jne '806, ae 6 da; d/ J^{n} de Jesus FERN^{z} & Rosa ROMERO; gp/ Cruz MARTIN & Mª Dolores TORRES. (Frames 65-66)

Frame 66
MARQUEZ, Mª dela Luz *Vª*
bap 22 Jne '806, ae 8 da; d/ Miguel MARQUEZ & Gertrudis MONTOYA; gf/ Feliz URIOSTE.

ZAMORA, Mª Ygª *Vª*
bap 22 Jne '806, ae 11 da; d/ Pedro ZAMORA & Mª Rafaela CASILLAS; gp/ Juan Luis MIRABALL (sic) & Damasia GONZ^{z}.

ROMERO, Jose Antº *Vº*
bap 22 Jne '806, ae 11 da; s/ Jose Antº ROMERO & Mª Antonia VEGIL; gp/ Felipe AVILA & Ramona VEGIL.

MARTIN, Jose Victor *Vº*
bap 22 Jne '806, ae 5 da; s/ Felipe MARTÍN & Concep^{n} TRUXILLO; gf/ Juan Antº DURAN.

SANDOVAL, Juan Antº *Vº*
bap 22 Jne '806, ae 3 da; s/ Fran^{co} SANDOVAL & Mª Ygª CHAVES; gp/ Jose Norberto MARTIN & Gertrudis (blot) BEITIA.

DURAN, Mª Ygnacia *V^{a}*
bap 29 Jne '806, ae 3 da; d/ Juan Nicolas DURAN & Juana ROMERO; gp/ Paulin (n.s.) & Mª Soledad MAESE.

ROMERO, Juan Andres *P^{o}*
bap 20 Jly '806, ae 3 da; s/ J^{n} Domingo ROMERO & Mª Ysabel PAEZ; gm/ Magdalena LUC^{o}.

ARMENTA, Mª Guadalupe Ventura
bap 21 Jly 1806, ae 8 da; d/ Simon ARMENTA & Marta MARTINEZ; gp/ D^{n} Tomas ORTIZ & Mª Rosa MARTINEZ.

VEGIL, J^{n} Carlos *V^{o}*
bap 25 Jly (1806), ae 2 da; s/ Rafael VEGIL & Elena LOBATO; gf/ Manuel SANCHEZ.

ARAGON, M^{a} del Rosario *V^{a}*
bap 25 Jly '806, ae 5 da; d/ Jose ARAGON & Luisa ARCHULETA; gp/ Jose CAND^{o} & Fran^{ca} MARTÍN.

MARTIN, Ana M^{a} *V^{a}*
bap 26 Jly '806, ae 3 da; d/ J^{n} Cand^{o} MARTIN & Juliana VALLEJOS; gp/ Esteban (n.s.) & Gertrudis SANCHEZ.

GONZALEZ, Jose Santiago *V^{o}*
bap 27 Jly '806, ae 9 da; s/ Jose S^{tos} GONZ^{z} & Mª LISTON; gp/ Santiago LUC^{o} & Mª Rosa AGUILAR.

Frame 67
MUÑOS, Mª Soledad *V^{a}*
bap 3 Aug '806, ae 5 da; d/ Ant^{o} MUÑOS & Maria ARCHULETA; gp/ Vent^{a} (n.s.) & Mª Ant^{a} VALDES.

BACA, Lorenzo *V^{o}*
bap 15 Aug '806, ae 7 da; s/ Est^{n} BACA & Luz MARTÍN; gp/ Tomas ROM^{o} & Mª Ysidora MARTIN.

TRUXILLO, Mª Bartola *V^{a}*
bap 15 Aug 1806, ae 4 da; d/ Esteban TRUXILLO & Dolores MALDONADO; gp/ Jose GARCIA & Mª Ant^{a} MARTIN.

MARTIN, Mª Encarnacion *V^{a}*
bap 15 Aug '806, ae 3 da; d/ Man^{l} Greg^{o} MARTÍN & Rafaela MEDINA; gp/ Bautista VEGIL & Rosalia MARTÍN.

ORTIZ, Jose M^{a} *P^{a}*
bap 23 Aug '806, ae 3 da; s/ Fran^{co} ORTIZ & Rosa CHININI *del pueblo*; gp/ Gaspar GALLEGO & his daughter, Mª de la Luz (GALLEGO).

LUXAN, Jose *P^{o}*
bap 24 Aug 1806, ae 8 da; s/ Jose Ant^{o} LUXAN & Lucia RIO; gm/ Rosa RIO.

LUXAN, Juan Man^{l} *P^{o}*
bap 24 Aug '806, ae 7 da; s/ Juan LUXAN & Mª ROMERO; gm/ Rosalia TECOA.

GONZALEZ, M^{a} Yg^{a} *V^{a}*
bap 30 Aug '806, ae 12 da; d/ Juan GONZALEZ & Dorotea BACA; gp/ Diego CISNEROS & Mª Rosa GARCIA.

LASO, Luisa *Pª*
bap 30 Aug '806, ae 6 da; d/ Jose Antº LASO & Rosa MIRABAL<u>L</u> (sic); gm/ Josefa ROMERO.

GARCIA, Mª Rosa *Vª*
bap 31 Aug 1806, ae 3 da; d/ Alfonso GARCIA & Mª Encarnacion ARCHULETA; gp/ Antº LOBATO & Margarita MARTIN.

(Although Fr. Diego MARTINEZ is performing the baptisms on this one frame, the pastor, Fr. Jph de VERA, is signing them.)

LUXAN, Juan Antº *Pº*
bap 27 Sep '806, ae 8 da; s/ Juan Antº LUXAN & Mª Soledad (n.s.) *del pueblo*; gm/ Mª Rosa MARTIN. (Frames 67-68)

Frame 68

TIA, Jª Catarina *Pª*
bap 27 Sep '806, ae 8 da; d/ Antº (n.s.) & Juana TIA; gm/ Lucia ORTIZ.

MEDINA, Juan *Vº*
bap 28 Sep '806, ae 10 da; s/ Juan Pasqual MEDINA & Jª Teresa ESPINOSA; gp/ Matias SANDOVAL & Mª Rafaela BUENO.

BLEA (gp), Jose Dionisio *Vº*
bap 28 Sep '806, ae 10 da; s/ unknown; gp/ Jose BLEA & Nasarena BLEA.

SANCHEZ, Mª Manuela *Vª*
bap 28 Sep '806, ae 8 da; d/ Felipe SANCHEZ & Jª Mª MARTINEZ; gp/ J^{n} Ysidro VARELA & Margarita SANCHEZ.

BUENO, Mª Ygª *Vº*
bap 28 Sep '806, ae 8 da; d/ Antº BUENO & Rosalia VALDES; gp/ Jose Antº MARTÍN & Gertrudis MESTAS.

GUERRERO (gp), Juana Mª *Pª*
bap 28 Sep '806, ae 10 da; d/ Pedro (n.s.) & Juana (n.s.); gp/ Julian GUERRERO & Lucia (n.s.).

LOBATO, Mª Ygª *Vª*
bap 5 Oct '806, ae 12 da; d/ Fran^{co} LOBATO & Gertrudis MONDRAGON; gp/ Jose Mª (n.s.) & Ursula SILVA. (Frames 68-69)

Frame 69

MONDRAGON, Mª Dolores *Vª*
bap 12 Oct '806, ae 7 da; d/ Antº MONDRAGON & Guadalupe MARTIN; gp/ Antº Jose VARELA & Mª Dolores (VARELA), his daughter.

LUXAN, Jose Rafael *Pº*
bap 12 Oct '806, ae 3 da; s/ Jose Antonio LUXAN & Gertrudis LASO *del puebº*; gp/ J^{n} Esteb^{n} MAESE & Manuela ROMERO.

NARANJO, Jose Antº *Pº*
bap 19 Oct '806, ae 7 da; s/ Fran^{co} NARANJO & Jª Mª ZUASO *del puebº*; gm/ Soledad ZUASO.

MEDINA, Mª Manuela *Vª*
bap 26 Oct '806, ae 8 da; d/ Gregorio MEDINA & Ysabel ROMERO; gp/ Pedro FERNANDEZ & Ascencion LUCº.

LOBATO, Manuela *Vª*
bap 26 Oct '806, ae 7 da; d/ Jose LOBATO & Ana Mª VALLEJO; gm/ Manuela VALLEJO.

LUCERO, Mª Rosa *Vª*
bap 2 Nov '806, ae 4 da; d/ Pedro LUCº & Mª FERNANDEZ; gp/ Juan LUCº & Mª Ygª ARAGON.

VARELA, Jose Gabriel *Vº*
bap 16 Nov '806, ae 12 da; s/ J^{n} Ysidro VARELA & Jª MARTIN; gp/ Dionisio QUINTANA & Petrona VARELA.

TRUXILLO, Jose Mª *Vº*
bap 23 Nov '806, ae 7 da; s/ Vicente TRUXILLO & Dolores MADRID; gf/ Policarpio TRUXILLO.

CASILLAS, Pedro Antº *Vº*
bap 7 Dec '806, ae 5 da; s/ Bartolome CASILLAS & Elena VEGIL; gp/ Pedro TORRES & Mª Luz SANCHEZ.

BALDES, Fran^{co} *Vº*
bap 10 Dec '806, ae 8 da; s/ J^{n} BALDES & Bibiana BACA; gp/ Pedro VALDES & Magdalena MARTIN. (As written)

Frame 70
ROMERO, Jose Man^{l} *Pº*
bap 11 Dec '806, ae 10 da; s/ Juan Domingo ROMº & Ascencion LOMA; gp/ J^{n} ROMº & Mª Barbara CORDOVA.

MARTIN, Tomas *Vº*
bap 20 Dec '806, ae 5 da; s/ Salv^{or} MARTIN & Mª MONTOYA; gf/ Diego SANCHEZ.

GONZALEZ, Juana *Vª*
bap 20 Dec '806, ae 6 da; d/ Jose Mª GONZ^{z} & Dolores LEIBA; gp/ Andres (n.s.) & Ynes ARMIJO.

RIO, Geronimo *Pº*
bap 28 Dec '806, ae 4 da; s/ Santiago RIO & Mª Luisa ROMº; gm/ Mª Rosa S^{N} JUAN.

GONZALEZ, Andres *Pº*
bap 28 Dec '806, ae 7 da; s/ Domingo GONZ^{z} & Dolores ROMº *del pu(e)bº*; gm/ Mª MUNIS.

GARCIA, Mª Tomasa *Vª*
bap 28 Dec '806, ae 7 da; d/ J^{n} GARCIA & Simona MARTÍN; gp/ Antº Domingo ROMº & Josefa QUINTANA.

FERNANDEZ, Mª de Jesus *Vª*
bap 28 Dec '806, ae 5 da; d/ Pedro FERN^{DEZ} & Mª Ygª MARTIN; gp/ J^{n} Domingo FERNANDEZ & Mª Fran^{ca} GARCIA.

1807

MARTIN, Jose Man^{l} *Vº*
bap 4 Jan '807, ae 4 da; s/ J^{n} Jose MARTIN & Mª Antª CENTENO; gm/ Patricia MARTIN.

TRUXILLO, Manuel *V^o*
bap 4 Jan '807, ae 4 da; s/ J^n Ant^o TRUXILLO & Ant^a BUENO; gp/ Xtoval LOPEZ & Mª Antonio TRUXILLO.

DURAN, Mª Reyes *V^a*
bap 6 Jan '807, ae 3 da; d/ Pablo DURAN & Marg^{ta} SANCHEZ; gp/ Bernardo LUC^o & Tomasa MARTIN.

VEGIL, M^a J^a *V^a*
bap 11 Jan 1807, ae 8 da; d/ Matias VEGIL & Dolores PACHECO; gp/ Ramon (n.s.) & Mª Trinidad VEGIL.

MARTIN, Juan Ant^o *V^o*
bap 15 Jan '807, ae 5 da; s/ Roque MARTIN & Greg^a ARMIJO; gp/ Pedro (n.s.) & Rosa SALAZAR.

LOBATO, Mª Dolores *V^a*
bap 18 Jan '807, ae 6 da; d/ Rafael LOBATO & Mª Luz ESPINOSA; gp/ Juan Cruz MARTIN & Mª Dolores TORRES.

MONDRAGON, M^a Yg^a *V^a*
bap 25 Jan '807, ae 6 da; d/ Ant^o MONDRAGON & Rosalia SANDOV^L; gp/ Pedro MADRID & Mª Luz MOYA.

VEGIL, Jose Rafael *V^o*
bap 25 Jan '807, ae 4 da; s/ Ant^o VEGIL & Mª MESTAS; gp/ Jose Rafael GARCIA & Beatris SANDOVAL. (Frames 70-71)

Frame 71
MARTIN, Jose Miguel *V^o*
bap 1 Feb '807, ae 8 da; s/ Fran^{co} MARTIN & Tomasa SANCHEZ; gp/ Xtoval LUC^o & Manuela SANDOVAL.

LUNA, Ant^o Martin *V^o*
bap 4 Feb '807, ae 6 da; s/ Rafael LUNA & Ana Mª TAFOYA; gp/ *D^n* Tomas ORTIZ & Mª Rosa MARTIN.

MARTIN, Mª Polonia *P^a*
bap 10 Feb '807, ae 2 da; d/ Tomas MARTIN & Micaela MARTIN; gm/ Josefa MARTIN.

BERNAL, Salvador *V^o*
*bap 4 Feb '807, ae 12 da; s/ Jose BERNAL & Mª VALVERDE; gm/ Teodora FRESQUIS.

SANDOVAL, Ant^o *V^o*
bap 15 Feb '807; s/ Matias SANDOVAL & Mª Yg^a BUENO; gm/ Matiana ROMERO.

MARTIN, Santiago *P^o*
bap 15 Feb '807, ae 4 da; s/ Jose MARTÍN & Ana Mª CORDOVA; gm/ Felipa ROMERO *del pueb^o*.

ROMERO, Bibiana *P^a*
bap 15 Feb '807, ae 7 da; d/ Guadalupe ROM^o & Jose(fa) MARTÍN; gm/ Rosa CATUGA.

GARCIA, J^n Lorenzo *V^o*
bap 15 Feb '807, ae 6 da; s/ Jose Cand^o GARCIA & Rita ARCHULETA; gp/ Martin FLORES & Gertrudis GARCIA.

CHAVES, Mª Gertrudis *V^{a}*
bap 22 Feb 1807, ae 8 da; d/ Domingo CHAVES & Candelaria DURAN; gp/ Esteban MAESE & Manuela ROM^{o}.

MARTIN, Mª Encarnacion *V^{a}*
bap 1 Mch '807, ae 10 da; d/ Bautista MARTIN & Lorenza SALAZAR; gp/ J^{n} Ant^{o} LOBATO & Mª Yg^{a} SANCHEZ.

MADRID, Jose Ant^{o} *V^{o}*
bap 1 Mch '807, ae 4 da; s/ Yg^{o} MADRID & Damiana MARTIN; gp/ Xtoval MADRID & Dolores RAMOS.

MEDINA, Mª de Jesus *V^{a}*
bap 1 Mch '807, ae 5 da; d/ Yg^{o} MEDINA & Marg^{ta} CORDOVA; gp/ Jose Ant^{o} GONZ^{z} & Mª Concep^{n} URIOSTE.

GOMEZ, Santiago *P^{o}*
bap 1 Mch '807, ae 7 da; s/ Fran^{co} (n.s.) & Mª Rosa GOMEZ; gm/ Micaela SERNA *del pueblo*.

DURAN, Yg^{a} *P^{a}*
bap 1 Mch '807, ae 7 da; d/ J^{N} Ant^{o} DURAN & Barb^{a} MARTIN; gm Fran^{ca} LUXAN *del pueb^{o}*.

CISNEROS, Mª Guadalupe *V^{a}*
bap 5 Mch '807, ae 7 da; d/ Nerio CISNEROS & Teodora MARTIN; gp/ Pablo LUC^{O} & Paula LARRAÑAGA.

Frame 72
FERNANDEZ, Jose Pablo *V^{o}*
bap 8 Mch '807, ae 3 da; s/ Domingo FERNANDEZ & Fran^{ca} GARCIA; gp/ Jos. Ant^{o} MARTIN & Ynes LEAL.

TRUXILLO, Pedro Ant^{o} *V^{o}*
bap 15 Mch '807, ae 6 da; s/ Fran^{co} TRUXILLO & Gertrudis MARTIN; gp/ Jose LOBATO & Ana Mª VALLEJOS.

LOMA, Josefa *P^{a}*
bap 25 Mch '807, ae 3 da; d/ Juan Domin. LOMA & Mauricia MARTIN; gm/ Micaela LUXAN *del pueb^{o}*.

LUNA, Mª Casimira *V^{a}*
bap 19 Apr '807, ae 8 da; d/ Miguel LUNA & Juana BACA; gp/ Xtoval LUC^{O} & his daughter, Polonia (LUCERO).

LUCERO (patron), Maria Antonia *Yn^{a} Yuta*
bap 19 Apr '807, ae about 6 yr; d/ (Nacion Yuta), purchased by Pablo LUC^{O} & with the Governor's (n.n.) permission, also baptized; gp/ Ber^{do} LUC^{O} & Tomasa MARTIN.

BUENO, Jose Dionisio
bap 19 Apr '807, ae 7 da; s/ J^{n} BUENO & Teodora BEYTIA; gp/ Juan Ysidro VARELA & Josefa MARTIN.

MARTIN, Jose Fran^{co} *V^{o}*
VARELA, Jose Fran^{co}
bap 26 Apr '807, ae 10 da; nat. s/ Pedro MARTIN & Fran^{ca} VARELA, *solteros*; gp/ Julian ARCHULETA & Man^{la} VARELA.

BACA, Maria Rafaela *V^a*
bap 2 May '807, ae 4 da; d/ Man^l BACA & Man^la CASADOS; gp/ Bautista VEGIL & Rosalia MARTIN.

VEGIL, J^n de la Cruz *V^o*
bap 7 May '807, ae 7 da; s/ J^n Yg^o VEGIL & Soledad DURAN; gp/ Yg^o DURAN & Ant^a SANCHEZ.

GONZALEZ, J^n dela Cruz *V^o*
bap 10 May '807, ae 9 da; s/ J^n Jos. GONZ^z & Mª Guadalupe LEAL; gp/ J^n Ant^o ARCHULETA & Felipa RAMIRES.

MARTINEZ, Mª Ascencion *V^a*
bap 10 May '807, ae 4 da; d/ J^n Cruz MARTINEZ & Mª Dolor^s TORRES; gp/ J^n Cruz VEGIL & Clara FERNANDEZ.

COCA, M^a *V^a*
bap 17 May '807, ae 12 da; d/ Miguel COCA & Catarina MARTÍN; gp/ Tomas LOBATO & Cand^a GONZ^z.

VALLEJOS, Ant^o Jose *V^o*
bap 17 May '807, ae 4 da; s/ Juan VALLEJOS & Gertrudis MARTIN; gp/ Jos(e) Miguel LUC^o & Dolores LUCERO.

VARGAS, Jose *V^o*
bap 24 May '807, ae 8 da; s/ Maurilo VARGAS & Mª Nicomedes FERN^z; gp/ Yg^o DURAN & Mª Reyes FERN^z.

LUNA (patron), Jose Miguel Ute Indian
bap 31 May '807, ae about 5 yr; s/ (Nacion) Yuta; gp/ Rafael LUNA & Ana Mª TAFOYA, *sus amos*, who had permission from the Governor, (n.n.). (Frames 72-73) (Repeat of the next entry).

LUNA (patron), Mª de la Luz Ute Indian
bap 31 May 1807, ae about 6 yr; d/ *(Nacion) Yuta*; gp/ Rafael LUNA & Ana Mª TAFOYA, *sus amos*, who had permission from the Governor, (n.n.). (Repeat of the previous entry). (Frames 72-73)

Frame 73 *V^o*
ABILA, Jose Urbano
bap 2 Jne '807, ae 7 da; s/ Santiago ABILA & Juana Ramona VEGIL; gf/ Domingo ORTEGA.

ROMERO, Maria Antonia *P^a*
bap 13 Jne '807, ae 8 da; d/ J^n Domingo ROM^o & Mª MIRABALL (sic); gm/ M^a ROM^o *del pueb^o*.

ROMERO, Mª Luisa *V^a*
bap 21 Jne '807, ae 3 da; d/ Tomas ROM^o & Ysidora MARTIN; gm/ Mª Rafaela LUNA.

MASCAREÑAS, Man^l Ant^o *V^o*
bap 21 Jne '807, ae 12 da; s/ Bautista MASCAREÑAS & Lusia MARTIN; gp/ Xtov^l LUC^o & Polonia LUC^o.

VALLEJOS (patron), J^a Gertrudis *Yuta*
bap 24 Jne '807 because of extreme necessity, ae about 4 mo; d/ *Yutas*, redeemed by Man^la VALLEJOS; gp/ Greg^o LUC^o & Mª Man^la MARTIN.

GONZALEZ, Juana *V^{a}*
bap 28 Jne '807, ae 5 da; s/ Juan GONZ^{z} & Mª Ant^{a} MARTIN; gp/ Bernardo LUC^{o} & Toma(sa) (see Frame 22 among others) MARTIN.

GONZALEZ, Juan *V^{o}*
bap 28 Jne '807, ae 5 da; s/ J^{n} Domingo GONZ^{z} & Mª Ant^{a} VEGIL; gp/ Ant^{o} MARTIN & Mª TAFOYA.

SANCHEZ, Mª Manuela *V^{a}*
bap 29 Jne '807, ae 2 da; d/ Manuel SANCHEZ & Nicolasa SANDOVAL; gp/ Fran^{co} MARTIN & Mª Tomasa SANCHEZ.

ROMERO, Paula *Ynd^{a}*
bap 5 Jly '807, ae 5 da; d/ Fran^{co} ROM^{o} & Mª ROMERO; gm/ Mª Yg^{a} MARTIN *del pueblo*.

CASILLAS, Luis *V^{o}*
bap 5 Jly '807, ae 12 da; s/ Bernardo CASILLAS & Dolores MADRID; gp/ Ant^{o} ABILA & Catarina MARTIN.

ROMERO, Ana M^{a} Yn^{a}
bap 15 Jne '807, ae 8 da; d/ J^{n} Domingo ROM^{o} & Mª Ysabel PAEZ; gm/ Mª Soledad ZUASO.

ZUASO, Juan del Carmen *V^{o}*
bap 19 Jly '807, ae 7 da; s/ Jose ZUASO & Mª Josefa CASADOS; gp/ Gabriel RENDON & Mª Dolores MARTIN. (Frames 73-74)

Frame 74

AVILA, Mª Josefa *V^{a}*
bap 26 Jly '807, ae 7 da; d/ Rafael AVILA & Mª Ant^{a} GALLEGO; gp/ Domingo LOBATO & Mª Clara TAFOYA.

MARTIN, Maria Rosa *P^{a}*
bap 2 Aug '807, ae 8 da; d/ Juan Domingo MARTIN & Gertrudis ROM^{o} *del pueb^{o}*; gm/ Ana Mª ARMENTA.

TORRES, Mariana *V^{a}*
bap 2 Aug 1807, ae 11 da; d/ Diego TORRES & Concep^{n} TRUXILLO; gm/ Juana PAEZ.

LUXAN, J^{n} Lorenzo *P^{o}*
bap 10 Aug '807, ae 4 da; s/ J^{n} Domingo LUXAN & Josefa SERNA; gm/ Felipa ROMERO *del pueb^{o}*.

ORTIZ, Fran^{co} *P^{o}*
bap 10 Aug '807, ae 6 da; s/ Juan And^{s} ORTIZ & Micaela GONZ^{z}; gm/ Felipa ROM^{o} *del pueb^{o}*.

ROMERO, Juan Jose *V^{o}*
bap 23 Aug '807, ae 10 da; s/ Jos. Man^{l} ROM^{o} & Pasquala AGUILAR; gf/ Jose Ramon ARCHULETA.

GOMEZ, Mª Bartola *V^{a}*
bap 28 Aug '807, ae 2 da; d/ Ant^{o} GOMEZ & Man^{la} ROM^{o}; gp/ Pedro MARTIN & Mª FERN^{z}.

AGUILAR, Jos(e) Yg^{o} *V^{o}*
bap 28 Aug '807, ae 8 da; s/ Lazaro AGUILAR & Concep^{n} PAEZ; gp/ Pedro BUENO & Man^{la} ROMERO.

BERNAL, Bibiana *P^{a}*
bap 13 Sep '807, ae 6 da; d/ Jose BERNAL & Micaela LUXAN; gm/ Ant^{a} LOMA *del pueblo*.

ZUASO, Domingo *P^{o}*
bap 13 Sep '807, ae 8 da; s/ J^{n} Ant^{o} ZUASO & Mª CONCHA; gm/ Mª Rosa GONZ^{z}.

ARCHULETA, Juan Bautista *V^{o}*
bap 13 Sep '807, ae 4 da; s/ Ant^{o} Jose ARCHULETA & Margarita MEDINA; gf/ Juan Nicolas MONTOYA.

TAFOYA, Jose Rafael *V^{o}*
bap 20 Sep '807, ae 4 da; s/ Ant^{o} Roman TAFOYA & Rosalia DURAN; gp/ Rafael (n.s.) & Yg^{a} QUINTANA.

MONDRAGON, Mª Man^{la} *V^{a}*
bap 27 Sep '807, ae 7 da; d/ Jose MONDRAGON & Dolores CASADOS; gm/ Josefa MONDRAGON.

SANDOVAL, Teodora *V^{a}*
bap 27 Sep '807, ae 3 da; d/ Man^{l} SANDOVAL & Mª Ant^{a} LOBATO; gp/ Paulin CORTES & Concep^{n} MARTIN.

CRUZ, Jose Lino *V^{o}*
bap 27 Sep '807, ae 10 da; s/ Mariano CRUZ & Dolores VEGIL; gp/ Diego SANCHEZ & Magdalena MARTIN. (Frames 74-75)

Frame 75
LUXAN, Geronimo *P^{o}*
bap 27 Sep '807, ae 3 da; s/ Ant^{o} LUXAN & Fran^{co} ROM^{o}; gm/ Soledad ZUASO *del pueb^{o}*.

ARMIJO, Mig^{l} Ant^{o} *V^{o}*
bap 28 Sep '807, ae 5 da; s/ Ant^{o} Eustaquio ARMIJO & Josefa GARCIA; gp/ Man^{l} (n.s.) & Mª Ynes ARMIJO.

ORTEGA, Mª Geronima *V^{o}*
PADILLA, Mª Geronima
bap 30 Sep '807, ae 4 da; d/ Yg^{o} ORTEGA, married, & Marta PADILLA, single; gp/ Jose Fran^{co} ORTEGA & Mª Encarnacion PADILLA.

LUXAN, Fran^{co} *P^{o}*
bap 4 Oct '807, ae 6 da; s/ J^{n} Ant^{o} LUXAN & Guadalupe PADILLA; gm/ Mª Soledad ZUASO.

FRESQUIS, Mª Guadalupe
bap 4 Oct '807, ae 4 da; *espuria* d/ Juan Xtov^{l} (n.s.), *casado*, & Mª FRESQUIS, single; gp/ Felipe SANCHEZ & J^{a} Mª MARTIN.

MARTIN, Jose Yg^{o} *V^{o}*
bap 12 Oct '807, ae 7 da; s/ J^{n} MARTIN & Mª Luz GONZ^{z}, *vecinos*; gp/ Fran^{co} SANDOVAL & Concepcion SANCHEZ.

RENDON, Maria Soledad V^{a}
bap 12 Oct '807, ae 5 da; d/ Gabriel RENDON & Dolores MARTIN, *vec^{s}*; gp/ Salv^{or} LUC^{o} & Polonia LUC^{o}.

LUXAN, Lorenzo P^{o}
bap 18 Oct '807, ae 12 da; s/ Juan Ant^{o} LUXAN & Micaela GONZ^{z} *del pueb^{o}*; gm/ Micaela DURAN.

TENORIO, J^{n} Cristoval V^{o}
bap 18 Oct '807, ae 6 da; s/ Fran^{co} TENORIO & Rosa GABALDON, *vec^{s}*; gp/ Jose ZUASO & Gertrudis COCA.

ARCHULETA, Mª Luisa V^{a}
bap 18 Oct '807, ae 8 da; d/ Ant^{o} ARCHULETA & Catarina ARROYO, *vec^{s}*; gp/ Diego Ant^{o} MARTIN & Rafaela LUNA.

LUXAN, Mariano P^{o}
bap 1 Nov '807, ae 5 da; s/ Fran^{co} LUXAN & Yg^{a} ESPINOSA *del pueb^{o}*; gp/ *D^{n}* Tomas ORTIZ & Mª Rosa MARTIN.

LUCERO, Mª Soledad V^{a}
bap 3 Nov '807, ae 3 da; d/ Bernardo LUC^{o} & Tomasa MARTIN; gf/ Greg^{o} LUC^{o}.

CORTES, Jose Carmen V^{o}
bap 15 Nov '807, ae 9 da; s/ Jose Mª CORTES & Magdalena BRITO; gp/ Jose HERRERA & Mª Carmen MADRID.

VALLEGOS, Mª Dolores V^{a}
bap 15 Nov '807 by Fr. Diego MARTINEZ, ae 8 da; d/ Miguel VALLEGOS & Mª Ramona GONZ^{z}; gp/ Jose Pablo CORTES & Manuela (n.s.). Signed by the pastor. (Frames 75-76)

Frame 76
ROMERO, Jose V^{o}
bap 22 Nov '807, b. 3 Nov; s/ Jose M^{a} ROM^{o} & Rafaela PINEDA; gp/ Felis URIOSTE & Polonia GUTIERRES.

PADILLA, Jose Ant^{o} V^{o}
bap 22 Nov '807, ae 4 da; s/ Salvador PADILLA & Josefa MARTIN; gp/ Felipe MARTIN & Mª Dolores SANDOVAL.

LUCERO, Jose Man^{l} V^{o}
bap 25 Nov '807, ae 5 da; s/ Cristov^{l} LUC^{o} & Man^{la} SANDOVAL; gp/ J^{n} Ant^{o} GARCIA & Gertrudis ORTIZ.

LASO, Maria P^{a}
bap 29 Nov '807, ae 7 da; d/ Matias LASO & Mª Guadalupe MARTIN; gm/ Paula LOMA.

ROMERO, Jose Rafael V^{o}
bap 8 Dec '807, ae 4 da; s/ Concepcion ROM^{o} & Rosa QUINTANA; gp/ Cruz VEGIL & Mª Clara FERN^{z}.

ARMENTIA (gp), Mª Guadalupe V^{a} *Ind^{a}*
bap 12 Dec '807, ae about 7 yr; d/ *Gentiles Apaches*; gp/ *sus amos* Simon ARMENTIA & Marta MARTIN.

ARCHULETA, Jª Guadalupe *Vª*
bap 13 Dec '807, ae 3 da; d/ Antº ARCHULETA & Mª Monserrate LEAL; gp/ Jose MIERA & Manª ROMERO.

1808

MARTIN, Julian *Pº*
bap 10 Jan '808, ae 8 da; s/ Jose Man^{l} MARTIN & Mª ROMº; gm/ Manuela LUXAN *del puebº*.

DURAN, Antonio *Vº*
bap 17 Jan '808, ae 6 da; s/ Pablo DURAN & Mª de Jesus VALDES; gp/ Rafael LUNA & Ana Mª TAFOYA, *vecinos*.

ROMERO, Mª Rosa *Vª*
bap 17 Jan '808, ae 8 da; gp/ Jose ROMº & Teresa VEGIL; gp/ Pedro Antº LUCº & Mª FERNANDEZ, *vecinos*.

MONTOYA, Mª Hilaria *Vª*
bap 17 Jan '808, ae 4 da; d/ Bernardo MONTOYA & Mª MARTIN; gp/ J^{n} del Carmen ROMERO & Rosa MARTIN, *vecinos*.

CHAVES, Jose Antº *Vº*
bap 17 Jan '808, ae 11 da; s/ Polonia CHAVES, single, & unknown father; gp/ Man^{l} Jose CHAVES & Mariana QUINTANA, *vecinos*.

ROYBAL (patron), Juan Nepomuseno *Pº*
bap 24 Jan '808, ae 4 da; s/ unknown; gm/ Teresa ROYBAL, *Yndª de este pueblo*, at whose home the child was left.

MADRID, Maria Paula *Vª*
bap 25 Jan '808, ae 2 da; d/ Xtoval MADRID & Dolores RAMOS; gp/ Xtoval LUCº & his daughter, Polonia (LUCERO), *vecinos*.

LUCERO, Mª Soledad *Vª*
bap 31 Jan '808, ae 7 da; d/ J^{n} de Jesus LUCº & Mª Ygª ARAGON; gp/ Felipe MARTIN & Mª Concep^{n} TRUXILLO, *vecinos*.

SALAZAR, Mª Candelaria *Vª*
bap 31 Jan '808, ae 6 da; d/ Gervasio SALAZAR & Rosario COCA; gp/ Jose GONZ^{z} & Dorotea BACA, *vecinos*.

MONTE, Mª Fran^{ca} *Vª*
bap 2 Feb '808, ae 5 da; d/ Antº del MONTE & Ynes MARTIN; gp/ Juan Lorenzo ALIRI & Josefa BEITIA, *vec^{s}*. (Frames 76-77)

Frame 77
LEIBA, Juan Antº *Pº*
bap 7 Feb '808, ae 7 da; s/ Jose LEIBA & Lucia TECOA; gm/ Juliana ROMERO, *Yndª del pueblo*.

SALAZAR, Mª Candelaria *Vª*
bap 10 Feb '808, ae 9 da; d/ Manuel SALAZAR & Jª Josefa VALDES; gp/ Bautista LALANDA & Rita BEITIA, *vec^{s}*.

CORTES, Jª Catarina *Vª*
bap 14 Feb '808, ae 9 da; d/ Pablo CORTES & Mª Nasarena BLEA; gp/ Felipe de HERRERA & Mª Dolores VARELA, *vecinos*.

LUSERO, Jose Rafael V^{o}
bap 21 Feb '808, ae 4 da; s/ Pablo LUSERO & Paula LARRAÑAGA; gp/ Salv^{or} LUS^{o} & Manuela VALLEJOS.

DURAN, Jose Ramon V^{o}
bap 21 Feb '808, ae 4 da; s/ Miguel DURAN & Dolores BENAVIDES; gp/ Miguel ARAGON & J^{a} Mª ROYBAL.

BENAVIDES, J^{n} Nepomuceno V^{o}
bap 21 Feb '808, ae 5 da; s/ unknown father & Josefa BENAVIDES, single; gp/ Vent^{a} DURAN & Mª Man^{la} QUINTANA.

MIRABALL, Mª Alvina V^{a}
bap 21 Feb '808, ae 4 da; d/ J^{n} Luis MIRABALL (sic) & Mª Damasia (n.s.); gp/ J^{n} Jose GONZ^{z} & Guadalupe LEAL, *vecinos*.

QUINTANA (gp), Jose Gabriel *Yuta*
bap 6 Mch '808, ae 4 yr; s/ *Ynd$^{o(s)}$ Yuta*; gp/ Dionisio QUINTANA, su amo, & Rosa QUINTANA.

ORTIZ (patron), Maria Rosa V^{a}
bap 6 Mch '808, ae 1 1/2 yr; d/ *(Nacion)* Yuta, *criada de* D^{n} Tomas ORTIZ, *Alc^{e}*; gp/ Ant^{o} (n.s.) & Ana Mª ARMENTIA.

GONZALEZ (patron), Maria Dolores V^{a}
bap 6 Mch '808, ae 8 yr; d/ *Yndio(s) Caigua, criada de* Jose GONZ^{z}; gf/ Jose MARTIN, *alias* QUERON.

LUCERO, Mª Gertrudis V^{a}
bap 6 Mch '808, ae 5 da; d/ Vic^{te} LUC^{o} & Marta ATENSIO; gp/ Ventura DURAN & Man^{la} ARAGON.

DURAN, Jose Rafael V^{o}
bap 19 Mch '808, ae 7 da; s/ Juan Nicolas DURAN & J^{a} ROMERO; gp/ Yg^{o} DURAN & Ant^{a} SANCHEZ.

MARTIN, Mª Josefa V^{a}
bap 19 Mch '808, ae 7 da; d/ Jose MARTIN & Rita LUC^{o}; gp/ Blas TRUXILLO & Paula LARRAÑAGA.

GONZALEZ, Mª Encarn^{n} V^{a}
bap 3 Apr '808, ae 4 da; d/ J^{n} GONZ^{z} & Josefa MESTAS; gp/ Vic^{te} LUC^{o} & Marta ATENSIO.

ALCON, Jose dela Cruz
VALLEJOS, Jose dela Cruz V^{a}
bap 3 Apr '808, ae 3 da; s/ Juan Ant^{o} ALCON, wid., & Catarina VALLEJOS, single; gp/ Jose Mig^{l} VALLEJOS & Ramona GONZ^{z}.

MARTIN, M^{a} Yg^{a} V^{a}
bap 3 Apr '808, ae 2 da; d/ Pedro MARTIN & Mª REYES; gp/ Blas TRUXILLO & Mª Man^{la} SANCHEZ. (Frames 77-78)

Frame 78
MARTIN, Mª Dolores V^{a}
bap 13 Apr '808, ae 6 da; d/ Vent^{a} MARTIN & Rafaela MAESE; gf/ Jose Mª MAESE.

VEGIL, Ant° V°
bap 17 Apr '808, ae 11 da; s/ Raf[l] VEGIL & Elena LOBATO; gp/ Feliz URIOSTE & Polonia GUTIERREZ.

PAEZ, Anastasio V°
bap 18 Apr '808, ae 4 da; s/ Nicolas PAEZ & Tomasa LOPEZ; gp/ Severino MARTIN & M[a] Carmen SANTISTEB[N].

MARTÍN, Maria V[a]
bap 19 Apr '808, ae 8 da; d/ Diego MARTÍN & Rosa MADRID; gp/ Xtoval LOPEZ & Teresa TRUXILLO.

BACA, M[a] Ygnacia V[a]
bap 24 Apr '808, ae 4 da; d/ Esteban BACA & M[a] Luz MARTÍN; gp/ Simon QUINTANA & M[a] Paula VALDES.

ROMERO, Geronimo P°
bap 24 Apr 1808, ae 9 da; s/ Fran[co] ROM[O] & Felipa REYNA; gm/ Micaela LOPEZ.

TAFOYA, M[a] Veronica V[a]
bap 1 May '808, ae 7 da; d/ Jose TAFOYA & M[a] Lorenza QUINTANA; gp/ Jose Ant° GONZ[z] & M[a] URIOSTE.

SANCHEZ, Marcos V°
bap 3 May '808, ae 8 da; s/ Diego SANCHEZ & Magdalena MARTIN; gp/ Fran[co] TRUXILLO & Gertrudis MARTIN.

LOBATO, Ant[a] Marg[ta] V[a]
bap 8 May '808, ae 4 da; d/ Ant° LOBATO & M[a] Yg[a] SANCHEZ; gp/ Jose Bautista VEGIL & Rosalia MARTIN.

ALIRI, J[n] Ygn° V°
bap 8 May '808, ae 4 da; s/ J[n] Lorenzo ALIRI & Josefa BEITIA; gp/ J[n] GONZ[z] & M[a] Ant[a] MARTIN.

MARTIN, Jose Ygn° V°
bap 8 May '808, ae 7 da; s/ Jose Ant° MARTIN & M[a] MARTIN; gp/ Pedro ZAMORA & Serafina CORTES.

GUERRERO, Jose Bernardo V°
bap 5 Jne '808, ae 8 da; s/ Jose Ant° GUERR[O] & J[a] PAEZ; gp/ Jose Fran[co] SANDOVAL & Lugarda QUINTANA.

GONZALEZ, Jose Ant° V°
bap 12 Jne '808, ae 9 da; s/ Jose S[tos] GONZ[z] & M[a] MARTIN; gp/ Jose GARCIA & his wife, (n.n.).

BACA, M[a] Encarnacion V[a]
bap 12 Jne '808, ae 4 da; d/ Salv[or] BACA & Tomasa SILVA; gp/ Julian TENORIO & Lorenza LOPEZ.

VEGIL (gp), J[n] Lorenzo V° Yuta
bap 26 Jne '808, ae 3 yr; s/ *(Nacion) Yuta*; gp/ Jose Bautista VEGIL & Rosalia MARTIN. (Frames 78-79)

Frame 79
MOYA, M[a] Soledad
MARQUEZ, M[a] Soledad
CATUGA, M[a] Soledad P[a]

bap 26 Jne '808, ae 8 da; d/ Eusebio MOYA, *alias* MARQUEZ, wid., & Mª Rosa CATUGA, wid., *Ynd^{s} del pueblo*; gp/ Ant^{o} GONZ^{z} & Mª Ant^{a} SENA.

MARTIN, Tomas *P^{o}*
bap 26 Jne '808, ae 7 da; s/ Ant^{o} MARTIN & Guadalupe ROM^{o} *del pueb^{o}*; gp/ Tomas LOBATO & Candelaria GONZ^{z}.

MARTIN, Mª Paula *V^{o}*
bap 9 Jly '808, ae 9 da; d/ Diego Ant^{o} MARTIN & Rafaela LUNA; gp/ J^{n} Xtoval QUINTANA & Ant^{a} Rosa LUNA.

CONDE, Juana M^{a} *V^{a}*
bap 11 Jly '808, ae 8 da; d/ Santiago CONDE & Mª Ant^{a} LOBATO; gm/ Petrona PACHECO.

MONDRAGON, Santiago *V^{o}*
bap 26 Jly '808, ae 4 da; s/ Xtoval MONDRAGON & J^{a} GONZ^{z}; gp/ Fran^{co} FRESQUIS & Encarnacion MARTIN.

QUINTANA, Mª Rosa *V^{a}*
bap 26 Jly '808, ae 10 da; d/ Candelario QUINTANA & Barbara MARTIN; gp/ Ant^{o} SANDOVAL & Lugarda QUINTANA.

MADRID, Tomas *V^{o}*
bap 31 Jly '808, ae 3 da; s/ Pedro MADRID & Mª Luz MOYA y ORTIZ; gf/ Jose Man^{l} VALENZUELA, soldier from Coaguila.

MARTIN, Jose Rafael *V^{o}*
bap 4 Aug '808, ae 8 da; s/ Francisco MARTIN & Tomasa SANCHEZ; gp/ J^{n} Ysidro VARELA & J^{a} Josefa MARTIN.

GONZALEZ, Bernardo *P^{o}*
bap 7 Aug '808, ae 7 da; s/ Jose Ant^{o} GONZ^{z} & Josefa MARTIN *del pueblo*; gm/ Dolor^{s} MADRID.

SANCHEZ, M^{a} dela Luz *V^{a}*
bap 7 Aug '808, ae 7 da; d/ Pablo SANCHEZ & Mª MARTIN; gf/ Jose Dionisio TREBINO, soldier from Coaguila.

ARAGON, Jose Mar^{no} *V^{o}*
bap 10 Aug '808, ae 5 da; s/ Ant^{o} ARAGON & Xaviera VEGIL; gm/ Matiana ROMERO.

ORTEGA, Mª Ysabel *V^{a}*
bap 14 Aug '808, ae 12 da; d/ Man^{l} ORTEGA & Rita COCA; gp/ Xtoval MEDINA & Josefa CORDOVA. (Frames 79-80)

Frame 80
FERNANDEZ, Mª Clara *V^{a}*
bap 14 Aug '808, ae 3 da; d/ Jose Mar^{no} FERNANDEZ & Asuncion LUC^{o}; gp/ J^{n} Cruz VEGIL & Clara FERNANDEZ.

ROMERO, M^{a} *V^{a}*
bap 15 Aug '808, ae 5 da; d/ Mariano ROM^{o} & Fran^{co} ARMENTA; gp/ Jose Ant^{o} GONZ^{z} & Mª URIOSTE.

MAESE, J^{n} Jose *V^{o}*
bap 19 Aug '808, ae 3 da; s/ J^{n} MAESE & Manuela ROM^{o}; gp/ Jose ROMERO & Mª Luz TRUXILLO.

MARTIN, Atanasia *V^{a}*
bap 24 Aug '808, ae 8 da; d/ Juan MARTIN & Mª SANGÍL; gp/ Luis TRUXILLO & Gertrudis SANCHEZ.

MADRID, (n.n.) *V^{o}*
bap 28 Aug '808, ae 8 da; child/ Horta MADRID & Mª BLEA; gp/ Vic^{te} LUC^{o} & Marta ATENCIO.

ROMERO, Mª Bartola *V^{a}*
bap 28 Aug '808, ae 5 da; d/ Ant^{o} Dom^{o} ROM^{o} & Josefa QUINTANA; gp/ Feliz URIOSTE & Polonia GUTIERREZ.

TAFOYA, Mª Agustina *V^{a}*
bap 30 Aug '808, ae 4 da; d/ Jose TAFOYA & Micaela RIO; gp/ Felipe MARTIN & Mª Concep^{n} TRUXILLO.

BACA, Raf^{l} *V^{o}*
bap 4 Sep 1808, ae 2 da; s/ Man^{l} BACA & Manuela CASADOS; gp/ Tomas LOBATO & Candelaria GONZ^{z}.

REYNA, Juan *P^{o}*
bap 18 Sep '808, ae 3 da; s/ Jose Antonio REYNA & Ascencion GOMEZ; gm/ J^{a} Mª DURAN *del pueblo*.

MARTIN, Jose Ant^{o} *V^{o}*
bap 18 Sep '808, ae 8 da; s/ Cristoval MARTIN & Teodora FRESQUIS; gf/ Jose Ant^{o} GONZ^{z}.

GALLEGO, Pedro Ant^{o} *V^{o}*
bap 30 Sep '808, ae 3 da; s/ Jose Jesus GALLEGO & Mª Micaela VEGIL; gp/ Tomas ROM^{o} & Mª Ysidora MARTIN.

MARTIN, M^{a} *V^{a}*
bap 2 Oct '808, ae 7 da; d/ Ant^{o} Jose MARTIN & Josefa BENAVIDES; gp/ Alexandro TRUXILLO & Mª ARCHULETA, *vec^{s}*.

DURAN, Mª Ygn^{a} *V^{a}*
bap 4 Oct 1808, ae 3 da; d/ Ygn^{o} DURAN & Ant^{a} SANCHEZ; gp/ Fran^{co} MARTINEZ & Tomasa SANCHEZ.

RAMOS, Jose Fran^{co} *V^{o}*
bap 9 Oct '808, ae 8 da; s/ Man^{l} RAMOS & Manuela MARTIN; gp/ Mariano LEON (only), soldier from Coaguila.

Frame 81
TENORIO, Jose Raf^{l} *V^{o}*
bap 9 Oct '808, ae 2 da; s/ Julian TENORIO & Lorenza LOPEZ; gf/ Jose BACA, soldier from Sta. Fe.

VEGIL, Jose Domingo *V^{o}*
bap 11 Oct '808, ae 3 da; s/ Jose Amador VEGIL & Mª Ygn^{a} QUINTANA; gp/ Feliz URIOSTE & Polonia GUTIERREZ.

MARTIN, Mª Serafina *V^{a}*
bap 16 Oct '808, ae 7 da; d/ Agustin MARTIN & Mª Candelaria CHAVES, *vec^{s}*; gp/ D^{n} Vic^{te} ORTIZ & Barbara SILVA.

VARELA, Jose Fran^{o} *V^{o}*
bap 28 Oct '808, ae 9 da; s/ Juan Ysidro VARELA & Juana MARTIN; gp/ J^{n} Ant^{o} CASADOS & Mª Ysabel CASADOS.

TAFOYA, Maria Rafaela *V^{a}*
bap 30 Oct '808, ae 8 da; d/ Man^{l} TAFOYA & Rosa OLONA; gp/ Rafael LUNA & Ana Mª TAFOYA.

MARTIN, Juan Domingo *P^{o}*
bap 30 Oct '808, ae 11 da; s/ Jose Ant^{o} MARTIN & J^{a} (n.s.); gm/ Teresa ROIBAL *del pueb^{o}*.

MUÑIZ, Jose Rafael *V^{o}*
bap 23 Nov '808, ae 8 da; s/ J^{n} Ant^{o} MUÑIZ & Mª DURAN; gp/ Lorenzo CORDOVA & Juliana VALERIO, *vec^{s}*.

GONZALEZ, Juan Santos *V^{o}*
bap 27 Nov '808, ae 12 da; s/ J^{n} Domingo GONZ^{z} & J^{a} CHAVES; gp/ Salv^{or} GONZ^{z} & Ana Mª VEGIL, *vec^{s}*.

LISTON, Lucia *P^{a}*
bap 27 Nov '808, ae 5 da; d/ Jose LISTON & Ana M^{a} RIO; gm/ Ana Mª SANCHEZ *del p^{o}*.

VEGIL, Bernardo *V^{o}*
bap 27 Nov '808, ae 6 da; s/ Juan VEGIL & Josefa LOBATO; gp/ J^{n} Ramon VEGIL & Man^{la} VEGIL.

GARCIA, Mª de Jesus *V^{a}*
bap 27 Nov '808, ae 15 da; d/ Alfonso GARCIA & Mª Encarn^{n} ARCHULETA; gp/ Julian ARCHULETA & Lorenza CR(UZ-blot).

CRUZ, Mª Soledad *V^{a}*
bap 27 Nov '808, ae 12 da; d/ Jose CRUZ & Mª Luisa ARCHULETA; gp/ Miguel Ant^{o} ARAGON & Mª Dolores MARTIN.

MONDRAGON, Mª Man^{la} *V^{a}*
bap 30 Nov '808, ae 5 da; d/ Felipe MONDRAGON & Ant^{a} SANDOVAL; gp/ Rafael VALLEJOS & Manuela ARAGON, *vec^{s}*. (Frames 81-82)

Frame 82
ARELLANO, Mª Ygn^{a} *V^{a}*
bap 4 Dec '808, ae 4 da; d/ Ramon ARELLANO & Ana Mª ARMENTIA; gm/ Paula LARRAÑAGA.

MIERA, Fran^{ca} Xavier *V^{a}*
bap 9 Dec '808, ae 6 da; d/ Jose MIERA & Manuela ROMERO; gp/ Man^{l} TAFOYA & Rosa OLONA.

COCA, Jose dela Concep^{n} *V^{o}*
bap 18 Dec '808, ae 11 da; s/ Miguel COCA & Cat^{a} MARTIN; gp/ Dionisio QUINTANA & Petrona VARELA.

LALANDA, Mª Josefa V^{a}
bap 25 Dec 1808, ae 9 da; d/ Bautista LALANDA & Rita BEYTIA; gp/ Xtov^{l} LUC^{o} & Maria Man^{la} SANDOVAL.

GONZALEZ, Ascencio P^{o}
bap 25 Dec '808; s/ Domingo GONZ^{z} & Dolores ROM^{o}; gm/ Mª Ant^{a} RIO *del pueb*^{o}.

LUNA (patron), Jose Ant^{o} P^{o}
bap 27 Dec '808, ae 7 yr; s/ *(Nacion) Yuta, criado de* Rafael LUNA; gf/ Mariano HOLGUIN, soldier.

1809

TRUXILLO, Mª Dolores V^{a}
bap 6 Jan 1809, ae 4 da; d/ Blas TRUXILLO & Mª SANCHEZ; gp/ Julian LUC^{o} & Paula LARRAÑAGA.

MARTIN, Mª Juliana V^{a}
bap 15 Jan '809, ae 7 da; d/ Man^{l} Greg^{o} MARTIN & Rafaela MEDINA; gp/ Jose (n.s.) & Ascencion MEDINA, *vec*^{s}.

SANDOVAL, Jose Julian V^{o}
bap 15 Jan '809, ae 7 da; s/ Fran^{co} SANDOVAL & Mariana TAFOYA; gp/ J^{n} Lorenzo QUINTANA & Balvanada ROMERO, *vecinos*.

GONZALEZ, Juana Catarina V^{a}
bap 15 Jan '809, ae 5 da; d/ Jose Mig^{l} GONZALEZ & Mª Ysabel MESTAS; gp/ Dionisio VEGIL & Man^{la} DELGADO, *vec*^{s}.

CHAVES, Jose Mig^{l} V^{o}
bap 22 Jan '809, ae 8 da; s/ Domingo CHAVES & Cand^{a} DURAN; gp/ J^{n} de J^{s} LUC^{o} & Mª Ygn^{a} ARAGON, *vec*^{s}.

BARELA, Hilario V^{o}
bap 22 Jan '809, ae 4 da; s/ Miguel BARELA & J^{a} ROMERO; gp/ Jose TAFOYA & Micaela RIO, *vec*^{s}.

MEDINA, Ant^{o} Domingo V^{o}
bap 22 Jan '809, ae 8 da; s/ Greg^{o} MEDINA & Ysabel ROM^{o}; gp/ Patricio MONTOYA & Rafaela BUENO, *vec*^{s}.

ARAGON, Mª Ant^{a} V^{a}
bap 22 Jan '809, ae 6 da; d/ Ant^{o} ARAGON & Mª Dolores MARTIN; gp/ Ant^{o} Jose ARAGON & Barb^{a} RUIBAL, *vec*^{s}. (Frames 82-83)

Frame 83
FERNANDEZ, Mª Rita V^{a}
bap 29 Jan '809, ae 5 da; d/ J^{n} Jose FERN^{z} & Rosa ROM^{o}; gp/ Bernardo LUC^{o} & Tomasa MARTIN, *vec*^{s}.

GOMEZ, Mª Carmen V^{a}
bap 29 Jan '809, ae 3 da; d/ Ant^{o} GOMEZ & Man^{la} ROM^{o}; gp/ Jose ARAGON & Raf^{la} BUENO, *vec*^{s}.

LUXAN, Jose Mariano P^{o}
bap 29 Jan '809, ae 6 da; s/ Jose Ant^{o} LUXAN & Luisa LOMA; gm/ Mª Ascencion LOMA *del pueblo*.

VEGIL, Mª Paula *V^a*
bap 29 Jan '809, ae 5 da; d/ Rafael VEGIL & J^a SANDOVAL; gp/ Juan VEGIL & Josefa LOBATO, *vec^s*.

CHAVES, Mª Candelaria *V^a*
bap 2 Feb '809, ae 3 da; d/ Luis CHAVES & Mª Luz QUINTANA; gp/ Pedro FERN^Z & Mª Ygn^a MARTIN, *vec^s*.

LOBATO, Jose Cand^o *V^o*
bap 2 Feb '809, ae 7 da; s/ Fran^{co} LOBATO & Andrea TAFOYA; gp/ Vent^a DURAN & Manuela ARAGON, *vecinos*.

ROMERO, Jose *V^o*
bap 12 Feb '809, ae 4 da; s/ Jose Man^l ROM^O & Pasquala AGUILAR; gp/ Jose Mª CORTES & Magdalena BRITO, *vec^s*.

MONDRAGON, Mª Ygn^a *V^a*
bap 19 Feb '809, ae 3 da; d/ Bartolome MONDRAGON & Regina FRESQUIS; gp/ Ant^o MARTIN & Mª TAFOYA, *vec^s*.

GONZALEZ, Jose Pablo
MADRID, Jose Pablo *V^o*
bap 26 Feb '809, ae 8 da; s/ Jose Man^l MADRID & J^a GONZALEZ, *solteros*; gp/ Jose Mig^l VALLEJOS & Angela GONZ^Z.

MARTIN, Mª Guadalupe *P^a*
bap 26 Feb '809, ae 3 da; d/ Diego MARTIN & Rosalia GUERRERO *del pueblo*; gp/ Nerio CISNEROS & Teodora MARTIN, *vec^s*.

CASILLAS, Jose Lino *V^o*
bap 5 Mch '809, ae 8 da; s/ Bernardo CASILLAS & Dolores MARTIN; gp/ Man^l Jose LEAL & Mariana QUINTANA, *vec^s*.

GONZALEZ, Mª Ant^a *V^o*
bap 5 Mch '809, ae 7 da; d/ Jose Ant^o GONZ^Z & Concep^n URIOSTE; gp/ J^n Ant^o (n.s.) & Lugarda PADILLA, *vec^s*.

MONTOYA, Eusebio *V^o*
bap 5 Mch '809, ae 8 da; s/ Jose Raf^l MONTOYA & Mª Luisa ROM^O; gp/ J^n MARTIN & Mª Paula MARTIN, *vec^s*. (Frames 83-84)

Frame 84
ARCHULETA, Juana Gert^s *V^a*
bap 12 Mch 1809, ae 5 da; d/ Marcos ARCHULETA & Mª Paula SANCHEZ; gp/ Jose Pablo ARCHULETA & Barb^a LOBATO, *vec^s*.

PANDO, Mª Ant^a *P^o*
bap 12 Mch '809, ae 6 da; d/ Salv^{or} PANDO & Ana Mª LOMA; gm/ Paula REDONDO *del pueb^o*.

GONZALEZ, Mª Paula *V^a*
bap 12 Mch '809, ae 8 da; d/ J^n Jose GONZ^Z & Guadalupe LEAL; gp/ Jose Ant^o GARCIA & Reyes MARTIN, *vec^s*.

MARQUEZ, Jose Tomas *V^o*
bap 12 Mch '809, ae 7 da; s/ Mig^l MARQUEZ & Gertrudis MONTOYA; gp/ Jose Fran^{co} VEGIL & Mª Concep^n HURTADO, *vec^s*.

LOBATO, Jose Fran^{co} *V*^{o}
bap 12 Mch '809, ae 6 da; s/ Jose LOBATO & Ana Mª VALLEJOS; gp/ Jose Vic^{te} ARAGON & Juana LUNA, *vec*^{s}.

BUENO, Ant^{o} Jose *V*^{o}
bap 19 Mch '809, ae 6 da; s/ Ant^{o} BUENO & Rosalia VALDES; gp/ Mig^{l} VEGIL & Ana Mª VALLEJOS, *vec*^{s}.

ARMIJO, Mª Dolores *V*^{a}
bap 19 Mch '809, ae 5 da; d/ Santiago ARMIJO & J^{a} ROM^{o}; gp/ Felipe TENORIO & Mª GABALDON, *vec*^{s}.

ARCHULETA, J^{n} Jose *V*^{o}
bap 19 Mch '809, ae 7 da; s/ Ant^{o} ARCHULETA & Catarina ARROLLO; gp/ Salv^{or} (n.s.) & Dolor^{s} LUC^{o}, *vec*^{s}.

ROMERO, Jose
CHAYO, Jose
LOBATO, Jose *V*^{o}
bap 19 Mch '809, ae 6 da; nat. s/ Xtov^{l} ROMERO, *alias* CHAYO, & Magdalena LOBATO, *solteros*; gp/ Jose VALDES & Marg^{ta} LOBATO.

ROMERO, Mª Josefa (Mª Teodora in margin) *V*^{a}
bap 1 Apr '809, ae 7 da; d/ Jose ROM^{o} & Mª Luz TRUXILLO; gp/ Raf^{l} LUNA & Ana Mª TAFOYA, *vec*^{s}.

SANDOVAL, Jose Fran^{co} *V*^{o}
bap 2 Apr '809, ae 3 da; s/ Matias SANDOV^{L} & Mª Ygn^{a} BUENO; gp/ Pedro MADRID & Mª Luz MOYA, *vec*^{s}.

CORTES, Ana M^{a} *V*^{a}
bap 3 Apr '809, ae 8 da; d/ Paulin CORT^{S} & Mª Concep^{n} MARTIN; gp/ Ygn^{o} DURAN & Ant^{a} SANCHEZ, *vec*^{s}.

NARANJO, Jose Raf^{l} *P*^{o}
bap 4 Apr '809, ae 5 da; s/ Fran^{co} NARANJO & J^{a} Mª ZUASO *del pueb*^{o}; gp/ Salv^{or} (n.s.) & Mª Dolores LUC^{o}, *vec*^{s}.

DURAN, Santiago *P*^{o}
bap 9 Apr '809, ae 3 da; s/ J^{n} Ant^{o} DURAN & Barb^{a} MARTIN; gm/ Felipa ROM^{o} *del pueb*^{o}. (Frames 84-85)

Frame 85
GONZALEZ, Juana *P*^{a}
bap 9 Apr '809, ae 3 da; d/ Juan Ant^{o} GONZ^{Z} & Soledad S^{N} AUG^{N}; gm/ Veronica MONTOYA, *vec*^{a}.

MEDINA, J^{a} de Jesus *V*^{a}
bap 9 Apr '809, ae 6 da; d/ Pasqual MEDINA & J^{a} ESPINOSA; gp/ Guadalupe ESPINOSA (only), *vec*$^{\underline{s}}$.

SANDOVAL, Mª Josefa *V*^{a}
bap 16 Apr '809, ae 8 da; d/ Jose Ramos SANDOVAL & Mª Dolor^{s} MARTIN; gp/ Jose ZUASO & Josefa CASADOS, *vec*^{s}.

TRUXILLO, Mª Encarn^{n} *V*^{a}
bap 16 Apr '809, ae 9 da; d/ Ant^{o} TRUXILLO & J^{a} Ant^{a} BUENO; gp/ Bautista MARTIN & Lorenza SALAZAR, *vec*^{s}.

BUENO, Ant^{o} *V^{o}*
bap 16 Apr '809, ae 4 da; s/ J^{n} Eugenio BUENO & Teodora BEITIA; gf/ J^{n} Ant^{o} DURAN, *vec^{s}*.

MARTIN, Mª Casilda *V^{a}*
bap 16 Apr '809, ae 8 da; d/ Felipe MARTIN & Mª Concep^{n} TRUXILLO; gp/ Agustin MARTIN & Candelaria CHAVES, *vec^{s}*.

LUNA, Jose Raf^{l} *V^{o}*
bap 23 Apr '809, ae 8 da; s/ Raf^{l} LUNA & Ana Mª TAFOYA; gp/ Pedro MARTIN & Jacinta ARAGON.

TAFOYA, Man^{l} Ant^{o} *V^{o}*
bap 30 Apr '809, ae 7 da; s/ Salv^{or} TAFOYA & Josefa TRUXILLO; gp/ J^{n} Yg^{o} VEGIL & Soledad DURAN, *vec^{s}*.

CASILLAS, Mª Ygn^{a} *V^{a}*
bap 30 Apr 1809, ae 3 da; d/ Bartolome CASILLAS & Elena VEGIL; gp/ Jose Ramon PACHECO & Mª Trinidad VIGIL, *vec^{s}*.

ARCE, Maria Josefa *P^{a}*
ROMERO, Maria Josefa
bap 1 May '809, ae 3 da; nat. d/ D^{n} Jose Mª ARCE, *Alferez del Presidio de Sta. Fee*, & Mª Angela ROMERO, *Yndia, viuda de este pueblo*; gm/ Teresa ROIBAL *del pueb^{lo}*.

DURAN, Jose Pablo *V^{o}*
bap 7 May '809, ae 4 da; s/ J^{n} DURAN & Fran^{ca} SANTISTEB^{N}; gp/ Jose Ant^{o} GONZ^{Z} & Mª Ant^{a} ARAGON, *vec^{s}*.

ZAMORA, Jose *V^{o}*
bap 7 May '809, ae 4 da; s/ Pedro Yg^{o} ZAMORA & Rafaela MADRID; gp/ Pedro MARTIN & Mª Reyes FERNAND^{Z}, *vecinos*. (Frames 85-86)

Frame 86
SANDOVAL, Mª Ascencion *V^{a}*
bap 14 May '809, ae 4 da; d/ Fran^{co} SANDOVAL & Concepcion PACHECO; gp/ Roque MARTIN & Greg^{a} ARMIJO, *vec^{s}*.

ROMERO, Mª Guadalupe *P^{a}*
bap 14 May '809, ae 3 da; d/ J^{n} Domingo ROMERO & Mª Ant^{a} DELGADO; gm/ M^{a} ROM^{o} *del pueb^{o}*.

VAZQUES, Mª Dolor^{s} *V^{a}*
bap 14 May '809, ae 3 da; d/ Ant^{o} VAZQUES & Mª ARAGON; gp/ Jose Ant^{o} HOLGUIN & Marg^{ta} GONZ^{Z}.

VEGIL, Ysidora *V^{a}*
bap 21 May '809, ae 6 da; d/ Cruz VEGIL & Clara FERNANDEZ; gp/ Raf^{l} LUNA & Ana Mª TAFOYA.

BENAVIDES, Jose Fran^{co} *V^{o}*
bap 22 May '809, ae 3 da; s/ Man^{l} BENAVIDES & Mª Concep^{n} ARGUELLO, *vec^{s}*; gp/ Jose Fran^{co} VEGIL & Concepcion HURTADO.

ROMERO, Jose de Jesus *P^{o}*
bap 23 May '809, ae 4 da; s/ J^{n} Ant^{o} R(illegible-blot) & Magdalena ROM^{o}; gm/ Mª Ant^{a} SENA, *vecina*.

DURAN, Mª Ramona V^a
bap 1 Jne '809, ae 5 da; d/ Jose Raf^l DURAN & Man^{la} HURTADO; gp/ Feliz URIOSTE & Polonia GUTIERR^S, *vec^s*.

GONZALEZ, Mª Man^{la} V^a
bap 1 Jne '809, ae 6 da; d/ Jose GONZ^Z & Dorotea BACA; gp/ Pablo LUC^O & Paula LARRAÑAGA.

ROMERO, Manuel P^o
bap 4 Jne '809, ae 8 da; s/ J^n Domingo ROM^O & Man^{la} LUXAN; gm/ Ygn^a ESPINOSA *del pueb^o*.

ESPINOSA, Manuela P^a
bap 4 Jne '809, ae 5 da; d/ Jose Ant^o ESPINOSA & Raf^{la} ROM^O; gm/ Mª Reyes ESPINOSA *del pueblo*.

PADILLA, Ant^o Feliz V^o
bap 4 Jne '809, ae 7 da; s/ Pedro PADILLA & Lucia CHAVES; gp/ Jose Ant^o GONZ^Z & Concep^n URIOSTE, *vec^s*.

LOPEZ, Juan Bautista V^o
bap 4 Jne 1809, ae 7 da; s/ J^n Xtobal LOPEZ & Teresa TRUXILLO; gp/ Jose Pablo BACA & Josefa VEGIL, *vec^s*.

LOBATO, Ant^o V^o
bap 13 Jne '809, ae 3 da; s/ Raf^l LOBATO & Marg^{ta} ESPINOSA; gp/ Lorenzo <u>G</u>ORDOVA & Marg^{ta} MARTIN, *vec^s*.

LUCERO, Pedro Antt^o V^o
bap 18 Jne '809, ae 7 da; s/ Pedro LUC^O & Mª Luz FERN^Z; gp/ Pedro MARTIN & Mª Reyes FERNANDEZ, *vec^s*.

Frame 87
FLORES, Mª Man^{la} V^a
bap 24 Jne '809, ae 8 da; d/ Martin FLORES & Gertrudis GARCIA; gp/ Jose Ramon SANCHEZ & Mª Gertrudis *idem* (SANCHEZ), *vec^s*.

VALLEJOS, J^n Bautista V^o
bap 25 Jne '809, ae 2 da; s/ Miguel VALLEJOS & Ramona GONZ^Z; gp/ Pablo LUC^O & Paula LARRAÑAGA.

GALLEGOS, Mª de Jesus V^a
bap 9 Jly '809, ae 9 da; d/ Ant^o de Jesus GALLEGOS & Mª Micaela VIGIL; gp/ Faustin VIGIL & Mª Soledad VEGIL, *vecinos*. (As written)

MARTIN, J^n Carmen V^o
bap 23 Jly '809, ae 8 da; s/ Jose MARTIN & Gertrudis CHAVES; gp/ Andres (n.s.) & Luz MARTIN.

VEGIL, Matias V^o
bap 6 Aug '809, ae 6 da; s/ Matias VEGIL & Mª Dolores PACHECO; gp/ Jose Mig^l HURTADO & Mª SANDOV^L, *vec^s*.

MARTIN, Juan de Jesus V^o
bap 6 Aug 1809, ae 3 da; s/ Cruz MARTIN & Dolores TORRES; gp/ Jose Mar^{no} FERN^Z & Mª Ygn^a MARTIN, *Vec^s*.

VARGAS, Jose Ramon *V^o*
bap 10 Aug '809, ae 4 da; s/ Maurilo VARGAS & Nicomeda FERN^Z; gp/ Jose Miguel HURTADO & Mª SANDOV^L, *vec^s*.

ROMERO, Lorenzo *V^o*
bap 13 Aug '809, ae 4 da; s/ Jose ROM^O & Mª Ant^a VEGIL; gp/ Felipe SANCHEZ & J^a Maria MARTIN, *vec^s*.

BENAVIDES, Ant^o *V^o*
bap 20 Aug '809, ae 7 da; s/ Jose BENAVIDES & Rita BEITIA; gp/ Ant^o LOBATO & Marg^{ta} MARTIN.

RIO, Mª Man^{la} *P^a*
bap 20 Aug 1809, ae 7 da; d/ Ant^o RIO & Juana TECOA *del pueb^o*; gm/ Man^{la} CORTES, *vec^a*.

ZUASO, Mª Dolores *V^a*
bap 27 Aug '809, ae 9 da; d/ Miguel ZUASO & Mar^{na} MONTOYA; gp/ J^n de Jesus MARTIN & Ant^o Jose MONDRAGON, *vec^s*.

MARTIN, Juan Agustin
LEAL, Juan Agustin *V^o*
bap 30 Aug '809, ae 4 da; s/ Xtobal MARTIN & Mª Dolor^s LEAL, *solteros*; gp *sus padres*/ Domingo LEAL & Veronica CORTES, *vec^s*.

LUXAN, Jose Manuel
MARTIN, Jose Manuel *V^o*
bap 17 Sep '809, ae 6 da; s/ Juan LUXAN, soldier of Vizcaya, & Mª Fran^{ca} MARTIN, single; gm/ Mª Dolores MARTIN. (Frames 87-88)

Frame 88
LOBATO, Jose Ant^o *V^o*
bap 17 Sep '809, ae 5 da; s/ Fran^{co} LOBATO & Gertrudis MONDRAGON; gm/ Paula LOBATO, *vec^s*.

BUENO, Pedro Mateo
bap 24 Sep '809, ae 5 da; s/ Pedro BUENO & Man^{la} ROM^O; gp/ Ramon PACHECO & Trinidad VEGIL, *vecinos*.

SALAZAR, Mª Serafina *V^a*
bap 24 Sep '809, ae 7 da; d/ Gervasio SALAZAR & Mª Rosa COCA; gp/ Agustin MARTIN & Candelaria CHAVES, *vec^s*.

CORDOVA (gm), Mª Ant^a *V^a*
bap 29 Sep '809, ae 6 da; d/ unknown; gm/ Mª Ygn^a CORDOVA, *vecina dela Cieneguilla*.

ZUASO, Geronimo P^o
bap 30 Sep '809, ae 3 da; s/ Simon ZUASO & Ygn^a RIO; gm/ Teresa ROIBAL *del pueb^o*.

AVILA, Mª Luz *V^a*
bap 1 Oct '809, ae 5 da; d/ Rafael AVILA & Mª Ant^a GALLEGOS; gp/ J^n Jose ZUASO & Mª Nicolasa LOBATO, *vecinos*.

CHAVES, Mª Rosa *V^a*
bap 1 Oct '809, ae 7 da; d/ Jose Mª CHAVES & Mª ORTEGA; gp/ Nicolas DURAN & Mª Ant^a ROM^O.

SANCHEZ, Mª Barb^{a} *V^{a}*
bap 15 Oct '809, ae 7 da; d/ Felipe SANCHEZ & J^{a} Mª MARTIN; gp/ J^{n} Nepom^{no} CHAVES & Clara SANCHEZ, *vec^{s}*.

COCA, Jose Fran^{co} *V^{o}*
bap 15 Oct '809, ae 3 da; s/ Jose Mª COCA & J^{a} BENAVIDES; gp/ Jose Mª SILVA & J^{a} Encarn^{n} VELASQUEZ, *vec^{s}*.

MARTIN (patron), Maria Rosa *Yuta*
bap 1 Nov '809, ae about 1 yr; d/ *Nacion Yuta*; gp *sus amos*/ Severino MARTIN & Mª Carmen SANTISTEBAN, *vec^{s}*.

ROMERO, Mª Marta *V^{a}*
bap 1 Nov '809, ae 12 da; d/ J^{n} ROM^{O} & (blank space); gp/ Pedro FERNANDEZ & Ygn^{a} MARTIN, *vec^{s}*.

ARCHULETA, Mª Barbara *V^{a}*
bap 1 Nov '809, ae 12 da; d/ Ant^{o} Jose ARCHULETA & Barb^{a} MEDINA; gp/ Salvador GONZ^{Z} & Mª VEGIL, *vec^{s}*.

Frame 89
FERNANDEZ, Jose Fran^{co} *V^{o}*
bap 1 Nov '809, ae 8 da; s/ J^{n} Domingo FERN^{Z} & Fran^{co} GARCIA; gf/ Fran^{co} VALDES, *vec^{s}*.

MARTIN, Mª Guadalupe *V^{a}*
bap 1 Nov '809, ae 5 da; d/ Agustin MARTIN & Cand^{a} CHAVES; gp/ Jose CHARVÈ & Claudia ARAGON.

PAEZ, Man^{l} Ant^{o} *V^{o}*
bap 3 Nov '809, ae 7 da; s/ Miguel PAEZ & Mª Soledad MAESE; gp/ Paulin (n.s.) & Mª Asuncion MEDINA, *vec^{s}*.

CORTES, Pedro Pasqual
LOBATO, Pedro Pasqual *V^{o}*
bap 3 Nov '809, ae 10 da; nat. s/ Bautista CORTES & Juana LOBATO, *solteros*; gp/ Diego Ant^{o} MARTIN & Rafaela LUNA.

GONZALEZ, Jose *V^{o}*
bap 5 Nov '809, ae 6 da; s/ J^{n} GONZ^{Z} & Mª Ant^{a} MARTIN; gp/ J^{n} Gabriel RENDON (only), *vec^{s}*.

GARCIA, Mª de Jesus *V^{a}*
bap 5 Nov '809, ae 7 da; d/ Jose Cand^{o} GARCIA & Rita ARCHULETA; gp/ Julian ARCHULETA & Manuela VARELA.

ROMERO, Barbara *P^{a}*
bap 5 Nov 1809, ae 7 da; d/ J^{n} ROM^{O} & Rafaela MIRABALL; gm/ Dominga LEYBA *del pueblo*.

MADRID, Mª Luisa *V^{a}*
LOBATO, Mª Luisa
bap 19 Nov '809, ae 6 da; d/ Jose Man^{l} MADRID, married, & Juana (LOBATO), *Yndia, soltera, criada de* (n.n.) LOBATO; gf/ Jose Ygn^{o} SANCHEZ, *vec^{s}*.

ARCHULETA, Juan de J^{s} *V^{o}*
bap 19 Nov '809, ae 6 da; s/ Damian ARCHULETA & J^{a} Micaela SALAZAR; gp/ Marcos ARCHULETA & Dolores SANCHEZ, *vecinos*.

MARTIN, Jose *V^{o}*
bap 19 Nov '809, ae 6 da; s/ Juan MARTIN & Mª Man^{la} COCA; gp/ Bernardino MARTIN & Man^{la} ARAGON, *vec^{s}*.

MARTIN, Ygn^{a} *V^{o}*
bap 19 Nov 1809, ae 8 da; d/ Salv^{or} Man^{l} MARTIN & Mª MONTOYA; gp/ Jose Fran^{co} SANDOV^{L} & Lugarda QUINTANA, *vec^{s}*.

LUXAN, Mª Encarn^{n} *P^{a}*
bap 19 Nov '809, ae 7 da; d/ Jose Ant^{o} LUXAN & Fran^{a} ROM^{O}, *Yndios del pueb^{o}*; gm/ Mª BACA, *vecina*.

ZUASO, Mª Dolores *P^{a}*
bap 19 Nov '809, ae 5 da; d/ Juan ZUASO & Mª CONCHA *del pueb^{o}*; gm/ Mariana CORDOVA, *vec^{a}*. (Frames 89-90)

Frame 90
GARCIA, Domingo
CHAMA ó MUÑIS, Domingo
bap 19 Nov '809, ae 6 da; *spurio* s/ Jose Dolores GARCIA, *soldado de Namiquipa casado*, & Gertrudis CHAMA ó MUÑIS, single; gm/ Teresa ABALOS, *Yndia del pueb^{o}*.

VALDES, Juan Feliz & Feliz de Jesus *V^{o}*
bap 22 Nov '809, ae 4 da; twin sons/ Juan VALDES & Biviana BACA; gp 1st/ Jose Vic^{te} ARAGON & Mª Carmen VALDES; 2nd/ Salv^{or} PADILLA & Josefa MARTIN, *vec^{s}*.

TORRES, Mª Encarn^{n} *V^{a}*
bap 26 Nov '809, ae 9 da; d/ Diego TORRES & Mª TRUXILLO; gp/ J^{n} Luis MIRABAL & Damasia GONZ^{Z}, *vec^{s}*.

CRUZ, Fran^{co} Xav^{r} *V^{o}*
bap 3 Dec 1809, ae 7 da; s/ Mariano CRUZ & Dolor^{s} VEGIL; gm/ Paula LOBATO, *vec$^{\underline{s}}$*.

CORTES, Jose Guadalupe *V^{o}*
bap 3 Dec '809, ae 8 da; s/ Jose Mª CORT^{S} & Magdalena BRITO; gp/ Juan de J^{s} MARTIN & J^{a} Paula MARTIN, *vec^{s}*.

GONZALEZ, Mª Barb^{a} *V^{o}*
bap 7 Dec '809, ae 3 da; d/ Jose Ant^{o} GONZ^{Z} & Mª Ant^{a} ARAGON; gm/ Mª Carmen SANTISTEBAN, *vec$^{\underline{s}}$*.

VEGIL, Mª Albina *V^{a}*
bap 18 Dec '809, ae 3 da; d/ Fran^{co} VEGIL & Mª Trinidad SALAZAR; gp/ Ramon SALAZAR & Soledad VEGIL, *vec^{s}*.

FRESQUIS, Tomas *V^{o}*
bap 24 Dec '809, ae 5 da; s/ Juan FRESQUIS & Man^{la} DURAN; gp/ Jose Ramon PACHECO & Trinidad VEGIL, *vec^{s}*.

ROMERO, Mª Rosalia *P^{a}*
bap 24 Dec '809, ae 6 da; d/ Pedro ROMERO & Mª LASO; gm/ Gertrudis ROM^{O} *del pueblo*.

VEGIL, Josefa *V^{a}*
bap 24 Dec '809, ae 6 da; d/ J^{n} Ygn^{o} VEGIL & Soledad DURAN; gp/ Ant^{o} Jose MARTIN & Rita LUC^{O}, *vec^{s}*.

CORTES, Mª Man^{la} *V^{a}*
bap 24 Dec '809, ae 3 da; d/ Cruz CORTES & Juana PADILLA; gf/ Juan Ant^{o} DURAN, *vec^{s}*.

ROMERO (patron), Juan Domingo *Yuta hom*
bap 27 Dec '809, ae 6 yr; s/ (*Nacion Yuta*) *criado de* Ventura ROM^{o}; gp/ Simon ARMENTA & Marta MARTIN.

ROMERO, Man^{l} *V^{o}*
bap 27 Dec '809, ae 3 da; s/ Jose de J^{s} ROM^{o} & J^{a} Teresa VEGIL; gp/ Rafael VEGIL & Elena LOBATO, *vec^{s}*.

MONDRAGON, Juana Pasquala *V^{a}*
bap 31 Dec '809, ae 4 da; d/ Ant^{o} MONDRAGON & Mª VEGIL; gp/ Jose Viterbo GONZ^{z} & Mª VEGIL.

Año de 1810

MEDINA, Mª Manuela *V^{a}*
bap 1 Jan 1810, ae 2 da; d/ Felipe MEDINA & Guadalupe NIETO; gp/ J^{n} VALDES & Bibiana BACA, *vec^{s}*. (Frames 90-91)

Frame 91
ROMERO (patron), Jose Ant^{o} *Yuta H.*
bap 7 Jan '810, ae about 8 yr; s/ (*Nacion*) *Yuta*, *criado de* Barbara ROM^{o} who was the gm.

LEAL, Mª Ynes *V^{a}*
bap 14 Jan '810, ae 4 da; d/ Man^{l} Jose LEAL & Mariana QUINTANA; gp/ Juan Jose GONZ^{z} & Mª Guadalupe LEAL, *vec^{s}*.

GOMEZ, Mª Soledad *V^{a}*
bap 21 Jan '810, ae 4 da; d/ Ant^{o} GOMEZ & Manuela ROM^{o}; gp/ Blas TRUXILLO & Manuela SANCHEZ, *vec^{s}*.

ARMIJO, Mª Paula *V^{a}*
bap 21 Jan '810, ae 3 da; d/ Ant^{o} ARMIJO & J^{a} GARCIA; gm/ Estefana MARTIN, *vec^{s}*.

CRUZ, Paula *V^{a}*
bap 21 Jan '810, ae 4 da; d/ Alexo CRUZ & Guadalupe DURAN; gp/ J^{n} Ygn^{o} (n.s.) & Mª Ant^{a} TRUXILLO, *vec^{s}*.

BERNAL (patron), Juana Mª *Yuta*
bap 21 Jan '810, ae about 6 mo; d/ (*Nacion*) *Yuta*, *criada de* Pedro BERNAL; gp/ Tomas LOBATO & Candelaria GONZ^{z}.

GONZALEZ, Fran^{co} Ant^{o} *V^{o}*
bap 28 Jan '810, ae 6 da; s/ Juan GONZ^{z} & Josefa MESTAS; gp/ Ant^{o} Jose BENAVIDES & Rita RIVERA, *vec^{s}*.

LUXAN, Juan Domingo *P^{o}*
bap 28 Jan '810, ae 8 da; s/ J^{n} LUXAN & Manuela ROM^{o}; gm/ Rafaela MIRABALL *del pueblo*.

ARCHULETA, Jose Pablo *V^{o}*
bap 28 Jan '810, ae 8 da; s/ Fran^{co} ARCHULETA & J^{a} Manuela ROM^{o}; gp/ Ant^{o} ARCHULETA & Margarita MEDINA, *vec^{s}*.

RIO, J^{n} Ant^{o} *P^{o}*
bap 2 Feb '810, ae 6 da; s/ Hilario RIO & Fran^{ca} GUERRERO; gm/ Mª Rosa GOMEZ *del pueblo*.

CORTES (patron), (n.n.) *Ynd^{o} vec^{o}*
bap 2 Feb '810, ae about 1 yr; s/ *Nacion Cuampi, criado de* Xtoval CORTES; gp/ Pedro SALAZAR & Ursula HERRERA, *vecin^{s}*.

ARAGON, Juan Fran^{co} *V^{o}*
bap 4 Feb '810, ae 12 da; s/ Ant^{o} ARAGON & Dolores MARTIN; gp/ Pablo ARCHULETA & Barbara LOBATO.

ORTIZ, Juan Ant^{o} *P^{o}*
bap 4 Feb '810, ae 7 da; s/ Fran^{co} ORTIZ & Rosa ROM^{O}; gm/ Mª Ygn^{a} MARTIN *del pueblo*.

LUCA, Juana *P^{a}*
bap 11 Feb 1810, ae 5 da; d/ Jose Ant^{o} LUCA & Guadalupe PACHECO *del pueb^{o}*; gp/ Ramon ARELLANO & Ana Mª ARMENTIA, *vec^{s}*.

ORTEGA, Mª Polonia *V^{a}*
bap 11 Feb '810, ae 2 da; d/ Manuel ORTEGA & Rita COCA; gp/ J^{n} Bautista CORTES & Rosa MARTIN, *vec^{s}*. (Frames 91-92)

Frame 92
DURAN, M^{a} del Carmen *V^{a}*
bap 11 Feb '810, ae 5 da; d/ Pablo DURAN & Mª VALDES; gp/ Jose CHARVE & Claudia ARAGON, *vec^{s}*.

ARCHULETA, Juan Xtoval *V^{o}*
bap 11 Feb '810, ae 3 da; s/ Julian ARCHULETA & Man^{la} VARELA; gp/ Jose GARCIA & Ant^{a} MARTIN, *vec^{s}*.

GONZALEZ, Jose Silverio *V^{o}*
bap 11 Feb '810, b. *hoy*; s/ Jose Ant^{o} GONZ^{z} & Mª URIOSTE; gm/ Antonia Gertrudis SANCHEZ, *vec^{s}*.

LUCERO, Mª Polonia *V^{a}*
bap 13 Feb '810, ae 2 da; d/ Pablo LUC^{O} & Paula LARRAÑAGA; gp/ Diego Ant^{o} MARTIN & Rafaela LUNA.

CHAVES, Mª Encarn^{n} *V^{a}*
bap 18 Feb '810, ae 7 da; d/ Julian CHAVES & Manuela CORTES; gp/ Jose MIERA & Man^{la} ROM^{O}.

GUERRERO, Jose Ant^{o} *V^{o}*
bap 18 Feb '810, ae 10 da; s/ Jose Ant^{o} GUERRERO & Juana PAEZ; gp/ Fran^{co} LOBATO & Mª MONDRAGON.

ROMERO, Mª Josefa *P^{a}*
bap 24 Feb '810, ae 8 da; d/ Juan Domingo ROM^{O} & Ascencion LOMA *del pueb^{o}*; gp/ Bern^{do} LUC^{O} & Tomasa MARTIN, *vec^{s}*.

BACA, Juan *V^{o}*
bap 24 Feb '810, ae 6 da; s/ Man^{l} BACA & Manuela CASADOS, *ves^{s}*; gp/ Dionisio QUINTANA & Petrona VARELA.

MOYA, Juan *P^{o}*
CATUGE, Juan

bap 24 Feb 1810, ae 6 da; incestiovo (not in Velazquez) s/ Eusebio MOYA, wid., & Rosa CATUGE, single, *del pueb*º; gm/ Margarita LOBATO, *vec*ª.

ARCHULETA, Mª Ygnª *V*ª
bap 4 Mch '810, ae 8 da; d/ Antº ARCHULETA & Mª Monserrate LEAL; gm/ Mª Reyes FERN^{z}, *vec*^{s}.

DURAN, Mª Ygnª *P*ª
ROMERO, Mª Ygnª
bap 7 Mch '810, ae 9 da; *espuria* d/ Jose Antº ROMº, married to Luisa ORTIZ, & Manuela DURAN, *viuda, Ynd*^{s} *del pueblo*; gm/ Mariana CORDOVA, *vecina*.

ROMERO, Jose Casimiro *V*º
bap 11 Mch '810, ae 7 da; s/ Tomas ROMº & Mª Ysidora MARTIN; gp/ Jose MIERA & Man^{la} ROMº, *vec*^{s}.

TAFOYA, Mª Antª *V*ª
bap 11 Mch '810, ae 6 da; d/ Nicolas TAFOYA & Polonia CHAVES; gp/ Jose ARAGON & Rafaela BUENO, *vec*^{s}.

LUCERO, Domingo
LUXAN, Domingo Indian
bap 11 Mch '810, ae 9 da; d/ Juan LUCERO, *Cabo del Presid*º *de Sta. Fe*, & Rafaela LUXAN, *viuda de este pueblo*; gm/ Antª LOMA. (Frames 92-93)

Frame 93
ROMERO, Mª Rosa *V*ª
bap 11 Mch '810, ae 7 da; d/ Concepcion ROMº & Rosa QUINTANA; gp/ Dionisio QUINTANA & Petrona VARELA, *sus abuelos*.

DEL NORTE, Mª Ygnª *V*ª
bap 14 Mch '810, ae 3 da; d/ Antº DEL NORTE & Ynes MARTIN; gm/ Margarita MARTIN, her sister.

MARTIN, Jose Gabriel *V*º
bap 18 Mch '810, ae 6 da; s/ J^{n} MARTIN & Juliana VALLEJOS; gp/ Paulin de HERRERA & Carmen MADRID, *vec*^{s}.

ARAGON, Jose Mig^{l} *V*º
bap 18 Mch '810, ae 4 da; s/ Jose Cruz ARAGON & Luisa ARCHULETA; gp/ Tomas SANDOV^{L} & Concep^{n} CHACON, *vec*^{s}.

MARTIN, Mª Josefa *V*ª
bap 18 Mch '810, ae 4 da; d/ J^{n} MARTIN & Paula SANGIL; gm/ Man^{la} VALLEJOS.

ESPINOSA, Mariano *P*º
bap 18 Mch '810, ae 8 da; s/ Jose Antº ESPINOSA & Catarina ROMº; gm/ Mª Ygnª MARTIN *del pueb*º.

GARCIA, J^{n} Rafael *V*º
VEGIL, J^{n} Rafael
bap 19 Mch '810, ae 4 da; s/ Julian GARCIA & Mª Reyes VEGIL, *solteros*; gp/ Antº de J^{s} GALLEGO & Mª Micaela VEGIL, *vec*^{s}.

PACHECO, Mª Rafaela *V*ª
bap 1 Apr '810, ae 3 da; d/ Jose Ramon PACHECO & Mª Trinidad VEGIL; gp/ Nicolas MONTOYA & Guadalupe MONTOYA, *vec*^{s}.

DURAN, Polonia *V*^{a}
bap 1 Apr '810, ae 5 da; d/ J^{n} Nicolas DURAN & J^{a} Ant^{a} ROM^{o}; gp/ Xtoval LOPEZ & Teresa TRUXILLO, *vec*^{s}.

TAFOYA, Jose Mig^{l} *V*^{o}
bap 1 Apr '810, ae 3 da; s/ Jose TAFOYA & Lorenza QUINTANA; gp/ J^{n} de Jesus ROM^{o} & Candelaria QUINTANA, *vc*^{s}.

MADRID, Jose dela Encarnac^{n} *V*^{o}
bap 1 Apr '810, ae 8 da; s/ Jose Pedro MADRID & Luz MOYA; gp/ Ant^{o} GONZ^{z} & Mª Ant^{a} SENA, *vc*^{s}. (Frames 93-94)

Frame 94
CORTES, Mª Rosa
MEDINA, Mª Rosa *V*^{o}
bap 4 Apr '810, ae 5 da; d/ Fran^{co} Man^{l} CORTES & Mª Greg^{a} MEDINA, *solteros*; gp/ Fran^{co} (n.s.) & Rosa SALAZAR, *vec*^{s}.

ROMERO, Lorenzo
LUCERO, Lorenzo *P*^{o}
bap 4 Apr '810, ae 10 da; s/ *el Cabo del Presid*^{o} Juan LUC^{o} & Josefa ROMERO, *soltera, Ynd*^{a} *de este pueblo*; gp/ Juan XARAMILLO & Mariana CORDOVA, *vec*^{s}.

CHAVES, Jose Miguel *V*^{o}
bap 8 Apr '810, ae 5 da; s/ Juan Nepom^{o} CHAVES & Clara SANCHES; gp/ Jose Miguel BEITIA & Barb^{a} SANCHEZ, *vec*^{s}. (As written)

MARTIN (patron), María *Yuta*
bap 8 Apr '810, ae 8 yr; d/ *Yutas*; gf/ Severino MARTIN who redeemed her.

MONTOYA, J^{n} Xtobal *V*^{o}
bap 8 Apr '810, ae 7 da; s/ Jose MONTOYA & Rosa VEGIL; gp/ Santiago LUC^{o} & Rosa AGUILAR, *vec*^{s}.

MADRID, Mª Fran^{ca} *V*^{a}
bap 8 Apr '810, ae 4 da; d/ Xtoval MADRID & Dolores MARTIN *ó* RAMOS; gp/ Ygn^{o} GONZ^{z} & Guadalupe VARELA, *v*^{s}.

LUXAN, Francisco *P*^{o}
bap 8 Apr '810, ae 4 da; s/ Fran^{co} LUXAN & Ygn^{a} ESPINOSA *del pueb*^{o}; gp/ Lorenzo CORDOVA & Marg^{ta} MARTIN, *vec*^{s}.

BACA, Ant^{o} *V*^{o}
bap 15 Apr '810, ae 5 da; s/ Salv^{or} BACA & Tomasa SILVA; gp/ J^{n} Ant^{o} ALCON & Catarina VALLEJOS, *vec*^{s}.

MAESE, Juliana *V*^{a}
ARMIJO, Juliana
bap 15 Apr '810, ae 5 da; d/ Joachin MAESE, *solt*^{o}, & Mª Ynes ARMIJO, wid.; gp/ Fran^{co} CHAVES & Lorenza CRUZ, *vec*^{s}.

TECOA, Jose Ant^{o} *P*^{o}
RIO, Jose Ant^{o}
bap 22 Apr '810, ae 3 da; s/ Pablo TECOA, wid., & Fran^{ca} RIO, single; gm/ Ant^{a} ARCHULETA *del pueb*^{o}.

CASILLAS, Manuel *V*^{o}
bap 22 Apr '810, ae 4 da; s/ Xtoval CASILLAS & Mª Luisa TAFOYA; gp/ J^{n} Nicolas VARELA & Polonia CHAVES, *vec*^{s}.

AVILA, Juliana V^a^
bap 24 Apr '810, ae 7 da; d/ Santiago AVILA & Ramona VEGIL; gp/ Xtov^l^ LOPEZ & Teresa TRUXILLO, *vec^s^*.

VALLEJOS (patron), Maria Josefa Yuta
bap 3 May '810, ae about 7 yr; d/ *Yutas*; gm/ Man^la^ VALLEJOS who redeemed her.

BUENO, Mª Luz V^a^
bap 3 May '810, ae 7 da; d/ Mateo BUENO & Josefa VEGIL; gp/ J^n^ Raf^l^ MONDRAGON & Fran^ca^ VEGIL, *vec^s^*. (Frames 94-95)

Frame 95
CORTES, M^a^ dela Cruz V^a^
bap 3 May '810, ae 6 da; d/ Pablo CORTES & Nasarena BLEA; gp/ Diego SALAZAR & Josefa DURAN.

MEDINA, Mª Felipa V^a^
BRITO, Mª Felipa
bap 5 May '810, ae 6 da; nat. d/ Jose MEDINA & Micaela BRITO, *solt^s^*; gp/ Candelaria GONZ^z^ & Jose Man^l^ MADRID.

PADILLA, Agustin
CORTES, Agustin V^o^
bap 13 May '810, ae 7 da; nat. s/ Jose Miguel CORTES & Lugarda PADILLA, *solt^s^*; gp/ (not given).

MADRID, Mª Monica V^a^
bap 13 May '810, ae 9 da; d/ Jose Man^l^ MADRID & Ant^a^ Teodora LOBATO; gp/ Jose MIERA & Mª Ygn^a^ MIERA, *vec^s^*.

MARTIN, Juan Ant^o^ V^o^
bap 13 May '810, ae 8 da; s/ J^n^ MARTIN & Concepcion CHAVES; gp/ J^n^ Miguel MARQUES & Gertrudis MONTOYA, *vec^s^*.

LOBATO, Mª Josefa V^a^
bap 13 May '810, ae 7 da; d/ Domingo LOBATO & Clara TAFOYA, *vec^s^*; gp/ Jose LOBATO & Ana Mª VALLEJOS.

ROMERO, Diego P^o^
bap 13 May '810, ae 8 da; s/ Pedro ROM^o^ & J^a^ MARTIN; gm/ Mª Ygn^a^ MARTIN *del pueblo*.

QUINTANA, J^n^ Nepom^no^ V^o^
bap 20 May '810, ae 5 da; s/ J^n^ QUINTANA & Balvaneda ROM^o^; gp/ Simon QUINTANA & Paula VALDES, *vec^s^*.

LOBATO, M^a^ V^a^
bap 20 May '810, ae 8 da; d/ Fran^co^ LOBATO & Andrea VARELA; gp/ Martin FLORES & Gertrudis GARCIA, *vec^s^*.

ZUASO, Domingo P^o^
bap 20 May '810, ae 8 da; s/ Ant^o^ Jose ZUASO & Josefa OÑENGUE; gm/ Victoria DELGADO *del pueb^o^*.

MONTOYA, Mª Guadalupe V^a^
bap 20 May '810, ae 8 da; d/ Rafael MONTOYA & Lucia CHAVES; gp/ Fran^co^ LOBATO & Mª MONDRAGON, *vec^s^*.

PADILLA, Mª Polonia *V^{a}*
bap 27 May '810, ae 3 da; d/ Salvador PADILLA & Josefa MARTIN; gp/ Jose Gabriel (n.s.) & Mª Ant^{a} MARTIN.

MARTIN, J^{n} Ant^{o} *P^{o}*
bap 27 May '810, ae 7 da; s/ Ant^{o} MARTIN & Manuela ROMERO; gm/ Josefa ZAMORA, *Yndios del pueblo.* (Frames 95-96)

Frame 96
ROMERO, Mª Concepcion
LOMA, Mª Concepcion *P^{o}*
bap 31 May '810, ae 5 da; nat. d/ Xtoval ROM^{O}, *alias* CHAYO, *vec^{o}*, *solt^{o}*, & Paula LOMA *del pueb^{o}*; gm/ Matiana ROM^{O}, *vec^{a}*.

BACA, Pedro *V^{o}*
bap 10 Jne '810, ae 5 da; s/ Esteban BACA & Mª Luz MARTIN; gp/ Felipe MARTIN & Concepcion TRUXILLO, *vec^{s}*.

VEGIL, Maria Josefa 0/0 *(ojo?)*
bap 10 Jne '810, a declaration was made that Mª Josefa was baptized 26 Jly 1807, ae 7 da; d/ Rafael VEGIL & J^{a} Acacia SANDOVAL, [then both single & now married], and is not a child of Rafael AVILA & Mª Ant^{a} GALLEGO as it was entered on page 39, second entry, (Frame 74, 1st full entry and partially marked thru) as per the godfather, who has confessed to have given the info with malice and fraud as well as said parents; (from Frame 74; gp/ Domingo LOBATO & Maria Clara TAFOYA).

MARTIN, Agustin *P^{o}*
bap 13 Jne '810, ae 3 da; s/ Pablo MARTIN & Agustina LUXAN; gm/ Manuela ROMERO *del pueb^{o}*.

MEDINA, Mª Man^{la} *V^{a}*
bap 14 Jne '810, ae 9 da; d/ J^{n} MEDINA & Cand^{a} VEGIL; gp/ Mateo BUENO & Josefa VEGIL, *vec^{s}*.

MARTIN, Juan Agustin *V^{o}*
bap 24 Jne 1810, ae 5 da; s/ J^{n} B(a)utista MARTIN & Lorenza SALAZAR; gf/ Juan Ant^{o} MARTIN, *vec^{s}*.

LUCERO, M^{a} dela Luz *V^{a}*
bap 1 Jly '810, ae 2 da; d/ Juan de J^{s} LUC^{O} & Ygn^{a} ARAGON; gp/ Salvador (n.s.) & Dolores LUCERO, *vec^{s}*.

SALAZAR, Juana Gertrudis *V^{a}*
SANDOVAL, Juana Gertrudis
bap 8 Jly '810, ae 6 da; nat. d/ Diego SALAZAR & Mª SANDOVAL, *solteros*; gp/ Jose Joachin BLEA & Rosalia MARTIN, *vec^{s}*.

MARTIN, Pedro Ant^{o} *V^{o}*
bap 15 Jly '810, ae 3 da; s/ Pedro MARTIN & Man^{la} GONZ^{Z}; gp/ Vic^{te} ARAGON & Mª Carmen VALDES, *vec^{s}*.

MARTIN (patron), Norverto (blank)
bap 19 Jly 1810, ae about 6 yr; s/ *(Nacion) Yuta, criado de* Pedro MARTIN; gf/ J^{n} Ant^{o} MARTIN, *vec^{s}*.

(Fr. Josef Benito PEREYRO signing entries)
VEGIL, Maria Dolores

bap 25 Jly (1810), ae 11 da; d/ Juan de Jesus VEGIL & Maria Rosa DURAN; gp/ Bicente ESPINOSA & Maria dela Luz ROMERO. (Frames 96-97)

Frame 97
GONZALES, Juana Maria
bap *el mismo dia y año*, ae 8 da; nat. d/ Josefa GONZALES; gf/ Man^{l} SANCHEZ.

(No August entries)

MARTIN, Maria Dolores
bap 22 Sep (1810), ae 4 da; d/ Pedro MARTIN & Maria FERNANDES; gp/ Jose Bautista BEJIL & Rosalia MARTIN.

LOVATO (gp), Benita (Jose Benito in margin)
bap 24 Sep 1810, ae 4 da; d/ unknown; gp/ Ant^{o} Josef LOVATO & Maria Josefa CHAVEZ.

ARCHULETA, Ant^{o} Maria
bap 26 (Sep 1810); s/ Ant^{o} ARCHULETA & Catarina ARROYO; gp/ Simon QUINTANA & Mª Paula BALDES.

BEJIL, Josef Rafel
bap 27th, ae 3 da; s/ Josef Fran^{co} BEJIL & Mª HURTADO; gp/ Faustin BEJIL & M^{a} dela Luz MARTIN.

Frame 98
MARTIN, Geronimo
bap 30 Sep, ae 5 da; s/ Christoval MARTIN & Theodora FRESQUIZ; gp/ Tomas GALLEGO & Juana Mª GUTI(E)RREZ.

TAFOYA, Bernabel
bap 8 Oct, ae 3 da; s/ Josef TAFOYA & Mª Mequela ROMERO; gf/ Juan Ant^{o} DURAN.

QUINTANA, Josef Mig^{l}
*bap 28 Oct, ae 7 da; s/ Juan Candelario QUINTANA & Varvara MARTIN; gp/ Josef Rafel (sic) MARTIN & Mª Gregoria ARMIJO.

SISNEROS, M^{a} del Carmen
bap 30 Oct, ae 4 da; d/ Nerio SISNEROS & Theodora MARTIN; gp/ Baltasar SANDOVAL & Mª Ant^{a} SENA.

DURAN, Juan Nepomoseno *Equibocado* (error)
*bap 8 Oct, ae 3 da; s/ Rafel (sic) DURAN & Guadalupe MEDINA; gp/ Josef Pablo ARCHULETA & Barvara LOVATO.

Frame 99
CORTEZ, Mª Alvina
bap 14 Oct, ae 5 da; d/ Juan Bautista CORTEZ & Mª Ant^{a} MONTOYA; gp/ Julian CHAVES & Mª CORTES.

MONDRAGON, Maria Rosa
bap 20 Oct, ae 6 da; d/ Juan Ygnacio (n.s.) & Getrudez MONDRAGON; gp/ Rafel (sic) LOVATO & M^{a} dela Luz ESPINOSA.

LUCERO (gp), Maria Guadalupe
bap 23 Oct, ae about 7 yr; d/ *Nacion Lluta*; gp/ D. Pablo LUCERO & D^{a} Paula LARRAÑADA (sic).

SALASAR, Maria de Gracia
bap *el mismo dia*, ae 3 da; d/ Diego SALASAR & Mª Cristerna SANDOBAL; gp/ Josef BLEYA & Mª MEDINA.

MONDRAGON, Carlos Indian
bap 1 Nov, ae 7 da; nat. s/ Felipe (n.s.), *Yndio*, & Josefa MONDRAGON; gp/ Man^{l} Ant° MONDRAGON & Mª Encarnacion (n.s.).

(Page 52 missing, but most probably the numeral was skipped).

Frame 100
LEYBA, Josef Benito
bap 4 Dec, ae 3 da; s/ Bisente LEYBA & Mª Encarnacion ESPINOSA; gp/ Felis URIOSTE & Mª Polonia BUTI(E)RRES.

GARCIA, Ysabel
bap *ydem*, ae 7 da; d/ Mig^{l} GARCIA & Margarita LUCERO; gp/ Man^{l} SANCHEZ & Nicolasa SANDOVAL.

SALASAR, Nicolasa
bap 6 Dec 1810, ae 4 da; d/ Ramon SALASAR & Soledad BEJIL; gp/ Juan de Jesus ROMERO & Nicolasa ROMO.

MARTIN, Maria Claudia
bap *ydem*, ae 3 da; nat. d/ Diego MARTIN, *Yndio*, & Barvara MALINCHE; gp/ D^{n} Josef EXARBE (See Frame 123) & Mª Claudia (n.s.).

MARTIN, Josef Benito
bap 9 Dec, ae 7 da; s/ Pablo MARTIN & Consecion ROMERO; gp/ Fran^{co} CHAVES & Lorensa LEYBA.

SANDOVAL, Juana Teresa
bap *Ydem*, ae 6 da; d/ Gervacio SANDOVAL & Ramona BARELA; gp/ Josef Ant° MIERA & Man^{la} ROMERO.

DURAN (gp), Maria Manuela
bap 30 Dec, ae 7 d; d/ Bernardo (n.s.) & Encarnacion (n.s.); gp/ Pablo DURAN & Mª BALDEZ.

Frame 101
GALLEGO, Jose Ant°
bap 13 Jan, ae 3 da; s/ Jose Ant° (n.s.) & Juana de Jesus GALLEGO; gp/ Maria Rosa BIJIL (only).

SANCHES (patron), Maria Paula
*bap 31 Dec 1810, ae 4 da; d/ (unknown), as declared by Juan SANCHES *de los Lovatos*; gp/ Mariano SALASAR & Mª CORDOVA.

BEJIL, Maria Josefa
bap *ydem*, ae 4 da; d/ Rafel BEJIL & Juana SANDOVAL; gp/ Mariano SALASAR & Mª CORDOVA.

MARTIN, Maria Benita
bap *ydem*, ae 5 da; d/ Alfonso MARTIN & Mª ARCHULETA; gp/ Rafel (sic) ROMERO & Maria SANDOV^{L}.

Año de 1811

ROMERO, Benito

bap 16 Jan, ae 3 da; s/ Santi(a)go ROMERO & Mª CORDOVA; gp/ Maria CORDOVA (only).

BELMONTE, Mª Dolores
bap 17 Jan, ae 6 da; d/ Ant^{o} BELMONTE & Ygnes MARTIN; gp/ Josef Andres MARTIN & Mª Dolores MARTIN.

GARCIA, Mª Dolores
bap *ydem*, ae 3 da; d/ Toribio GARCIA & Mª BALDEZ; gp/ Juan Pablo PACHECO & Maria Fran^{ca} PACHECO.

MARTIN, Josef Benito
bap 18th, ae 5 da; s/ Bentura MARTIN & Mª Rafela MAES; gp/ Felis URIOSTE & Mª Polonia BUTI(E)RREZ.

Frame 102
MAES, Man^{l} Ant^{o}
bap 20 Jan (1811), ae 7 da; s/ Juan MAES & Mª Man^{la} ROMERO; gp/ Rafel (sic) LUCERO & Polonia LUCERO.

FERNANDEZ (gp), M^{a} delos Reyes Ute
bap *ydem*, ae about 1 yr; d/ *Nacion Yuta*; gp/ Juan Domingo FERNANDEZ & Fran^{ca} GARCIA.

FERNANDEZ, Maria del Carmen
bap *ydem*, ae 5 da; d/ Juan de Jesus FERNANDEZ & Rosa ROMERO; gp/ Juan Christoval BEJIL & Ant^{a} Biviana TORREZ.

ROMERO, Juan
bap 31 Jan, ae 3 da; s/ Salvador ROMERO & Mecaela (sic) (n.s.); gm/ Maria Ygnacia (n.s.) (only).

ROMERO, Juana
bap *ydem*, ae 6 da; d/ Man^{l} Josef ROMERO & Juana TAFOYA; gf/ Juan DURAN.

TAFOYA, Maria Juana
bap *ydem*, ae 4 da; d/ Ramon TAFOYA & Ana Mª ARMENTA; gm/ Matiana ROMERO.

ABILA, Mariano
*bap 30 Jan, ae 7 da; s/ Usebi(o) ABILA & Mª PADILLA; gp/ Lasaro RAEL & M^{a} (n.s.).

(See Frame 109 for 2 Feb entries. For last part of March see Frame 107 & 1st part of Apr on Frame 108. Also see Frame 108 for more Jan 1811).

Frame 103
LUCERO, Jose Benito
bap 21 Apr (1811), ae 6 da; s/ Mig^{l} LUCERO & Ramona GONSALEZ; gp/ Josef Pablo SANCHEZ & Mª Julpana SANCHEZ.

MONDRAGON, Juan delos Reyes
bap 28th, ae 3 da; s/ Ant^{o} MONDRAGON & Ana Mª BEJIL; gp/ Josef Amador BEJIL & Mª Yg^{a} QUINTANA.

DURAN, Josef Rafel
bap 28th, ae 5 da; s/ Gregorio DURAN & Rosa URIOSTE; gp/ Pedro FERNANDEZ & Mª Yg^{a} MARTIN.

MARTIN, Juan Jose del Rosario
bap 28th, ae 7 da; s/ Ant^{o} MARTIN & Mª Getrudez BEJIL; gp/ Salvador GONSALEZ & Ana Mª BEJIL.

MARTIN, Josef Benito
bap 21 May, ae 4 da; s/ Geronimo MARTIN & Juana MEDINA; gp/ Josef Man^{l} MEDINA & Mª LOVATO.

BEJIL, Josef Benito
bap *ydem*, ae 6 da; s/ Amador BEJIL & Mª Ygnacia QUINTANA; gp/ Ramon PACHECO (only).

Frame 104 (See Frame 106 for July)
MARTIN, Josef Felipe
bap 23rd (no mo or yr), ae 7 da; s/ Fran^{co} MARTIN & Maria SANCHES; gp/ Pedro MARTIN & Maria Reyes FERNANDES.

BARELA, Maria Asencion
bap *ydem*, ae 7 da; d/ Mig^{l} BARELA & Juana ROMERO; gp/ Tomas SANDOVAL & Mª CHACON.

BEJIL, Salvador de Jesus
bap *ydem*, ae 3 da; s/ Pedro BEJIL & Maria QUINTANA; gp/ Man^{l} SANCHES & Nicolasa SANDOVAL.

MADRIL, Estevan
bap 27th, ae 3 da; s/ Ygnacio MADRIL & Matiana MARTIN; gp/ Josef Fran^{co} SANDOVAL & Teodora ROMERO.

TAFOYA, Maria Soledad
bap 28 Aug 1811, ae 6 da; d/ Salvador TAFOYA & Maria TRUJILLO; gp/ Josef PACHECO & Maria BEJIL.

BEJIL, Maria Dolores
*bap 27 Aug, ae 5 da; *espuria* d/ Jabiela BEJIL; gp/ Ant^{o} BASQUES & Maria ARAGON.

ROMERO, Maria
bap 29th, ae 4 da; d/ Josef Ant^{o} ROMERO & Maria Encarnacion (n.s.); gp/ Jose Mariano FERNANDES & Mª Sencion LUCERO.

Frame 105
MARTIN, Josefa delos Dolores
bap *ydem*, ae 7 da; d/ Felipe MARTIN & Maria TRUJILLO; gp/ Dionisio QUINTANA & Petrona BARELA.

BUENO, Tomas
bap 22 Sep 1811, ae 4 da; s/ Mateo BUENO & Maria Josefa BEJIL; gp/ Juan Yg^{o} BEJIL & Soledad DURAN.

ROMERO, Geronimo
bap *ydem*, ae 3 da; s/ Santiago ROMERO & Maria Ant^{a} LOVATO; gp/ Pablo DERRERA & Ana Bentura DURAN.

MARTIN, Josefa del Rosario
bap 6 Oct 1811, ae 5 da; d/ Santos MARTIN & Man^{la} ROMERO; gp/ Josef Rafel (sic) BEJIL & Maria Elena LOVATO.

CASADOS, Juana Geronima
bap 7 Oct 1811, ae 3 da; d/ Juan Ant° CASADOS & Guadalupe GARCIA; gp/ Jose Ant° SUASO & Maria Josefa CASADOS.

GOMES, Josef Santiago
bap 21 Oct 1811, ae 6 da; s/ Josef Ant° (n.s.) & Maria Consecion GOMES; gp/ Mariano JARAMILLO & Teodora MARTIN.

BARJAS, Jose Domingo
bap *ydem*, ae 3 da; s/ Maurilo BARJAS & (Ni)Comeda FERNANDES; gp/ Ant° MONTOYA & Rita ROMERO.

Frame 106
DURAN, Jose Santiago
bap 25 Jly 1811, ae 1 da; s/ Ju^{n} Nicolas DURAN & Juana Ant^{a} SANDOVAL; gp/ Jose Man^{l} SAIS & Margarita LOVATO.

LOVATO, Bentura
bap 7 Aug 1811, ae 5 da; d/ Juan LOVATO & (Y)g^{a} SANCHES; gp/ Pedro MARTIN & Mª Jasinta ARAGON.

GALLEGO, Mariana
bap *ydem*, ae 3 da; d/ Tomas GALLEGO & Juana Maria BUTIERRES; gp/ Josef Ant° GONSALES & Polonia BUTIERRES.

MARTIN, Policarpio
bap 16 Aug 1811, ae 3 da; s/ Diego MARTIN & Maria Rosa MADRIL; gp/ Man^{l} ORTEGA & Maria Consecion ORTEGA.

LUNA, Maria Dolores
bap *ydem*, ae 4 da; d/ Rafel (sic) LUNA & Ana Maria TAFOYA; gp/ Bisente TRUJILLO & Maria MADRIL.

ARAGON, Maria Ysabel
ARMIJO, Maria Ysabel
bap 20 Aug &, ae 3 da; *espuria* d/ Josefa ARMIJO & Josef ARAGON, married; gp/ Jose Domingo (n.s.) & Maria Ant^{a} (n.s.).

Frame 107 (See Frame 103 for part of Mch)
BLEA, Josef Benito
bap 24 *d^{ho}*, ae 5 da; s/ Joaquin BLEA & Rosalia MEDINA; gp/ Gervacio SALASAR & Maria del R(os)ario COCA.

MARQUES, Josef Benito
bap *ydem*, ae 3 da; s/ Mig^{l} MARQUES & Getrudes MONTOYA; gp/ Juan Bautista MARTIN & Maria Lorensa SALASAR.

BEJIL, Maria Encarnacion
bap 26 Mch, ae 5 da; d/ Juan Cristoval BEJIL & Biviana TORRES; gp/ Jose Mariano FERN^{DES} & Maria LUCERO.

MARTIN, Josef Encarnacion
bap *ydem*, ae 3 da; s/ Salvador MARTIN & Maria MONTOYA; gp/ Josef Fran^{co} MARTIN & Juana MARTIN.

Frame 108 (See before Frame 103 re: notes on dates of entries)
BACA, Juan Mig^{l}
bap 5 Apr 1811, ae 6 da; s/ Estevan BACA & Maria dela Lus MARTIN; gp/ Jose Bautista BEJIL & Maria MARTIN.

SANDOVAL, Maria Soledad
bap *ydem*, ae 4 da; d/ Matias SANDOVAL & Maria BUENO; gp/ Ant^{o} MARTIN & Maria TAFOYA.

HERRERA, Maria Guadalupe
bap 30 Apr 1811, ae 7 da; d/ Felipe de HERRERA & Maria Dolores BARELA; gm/ Lugarda QUINTANA.

(This is in middle of Frame 108. See Frame 102 for rest of Jan 1811).
GARCIA, Josef Benito
*bap 26 Jan 1811, ae 3 da; s/ Toribio GARCIA & Maria BUSTOS; gp/ Tomas ARCHULETA & Juana Getrudes MARTIN.

NARANJO, Maria Dolores
bap *ydem*, ae 4 da; d/ Fran^{co} NARANJO & Juana Maria SOAZA; gp/ Maria Soledad SOAZA (only).

CORTES, Josef Benito
bap 29 *d^{ho}*, ae 3 da; s/ Crus CORTES & Juana PADILLA; gp/ Martin FLORES & Juana Getrudes GARCIA.

Frame 109 (See note on Frame 103).
MARTIN, Josef Benito
*bap 2 Feb 1811, ae 4 da; s/ Pedro MARTIN & Manuela GONSALES; gp/ Juan Grabiel DURAN & Tomasa GARCIA.

FERNANDES, Jose Francisco
bap 4 Feb, ae 4 da; s/ Juan Domingo FERNANDES & Fran^{ca} GARCIA; gp/ Bisente GARCIA & Juliana ROMERO.

ROMERO, Maria dela Lus
*bap 13 Dec 1811, ae 5 da; d/ Tomas ROMERO & Maria Ysidora MARTIN; gp/ Juan LOVATO & Maria Dorotella ROMERO.

ROMERO, Maria dela Lus
bap *ydem*, ae 3 da; d/ Pedro ROMERO & Man^{la} (n.s.), single; gp/ Tomas LOVATO & Candelaria GONSALES.

SANDOVAL, Josef Benito
bap 15 Dec 1811, ae 4 da; s/ Fran^{co} SANDOVAL & Mariana TAFOYA; gp/ Josef Ant^{o} MIERA & Mª Man^{la} ROMERO.

ALCON, Josef Benito
bap *ydem*, ae 7 da; s/ Juan Ant^{o} ALCON & Catarina LUCERO; gp/ Ant^{o} Josef BEJIL & Maria Dolores LUCERO.

Frame 110
MARTIN, Catarina de los Dolores
bap *ydem*, ae 6 da; d/ Juan MARTIN & Paula SONGIL; gp/ Josef Rafel (sic) LUCERO & Polonia LUCERO.

MADRIL, Juan Cristoval
bap *ydem*, ae 7 da; s/ Cristoval MADRIL & Maria Man^{la} PADILLA; gp/ Fran^{co} CHAVES & Maria Polonia MESA.

MUÑES, Josef Antonio
bap 18 Dec 1811, ae 4 da; s/ Juan Ant^{o} MUÑES & Maria Rosalia DURAN; gp/ Juan MUÑES & Biviana REYNA.

ROMERO, Diego
bap *ydem*, ae 7 da; s/ Cristoval ROMERO & Paula LOMA, *Yndios*; gp/ Felipe MARTIN & Maria Consecion TRUJILLO.

ROMERO, Maria Manuela
bap 27 Dec 1811, ae 3 da; d/ Juan de Jesus ROMERO & Maria Candelaria QUINTANA; gp/ Felis URIOSTE & Mª Polonia BUTI(E)RRES.

SALASAR, Miguel
bap 29th, ae 3 da; s/ Diego SALASAR & Cristerna SANDOVAL; gp/ Pedro FERNANDES & Maria Ygnacia MARTIN.

Frame 111

Año de 1812

ROMERO, Josef Benito
bap 11 Jan, ae 6 da; s/ Ant^o Josef ROMERO & Guadalupe PACHECO; gp/ Juan Lorenso QUINTANA & Maria Balvañeda ROMERO.

TENORIO, Juana Josefa
bap *ydem*, ae 3 da; d/ Julian TENORIO & Lorensa LOPES; gp/ Josef Ant^o MIERA & Yg^a MIERA.

SOASO, Maria Dolores
bap *ydem*, ae 5 da; d/ Juan Josef SOASO & Josefa MIRABAL; gp/ Ant^o Josef GONSALES & Mª Ant^a SENA.

DURAN, Sebastian
bap 24 Jan, ae 3 da; s/ Pablo DURAN & Maria de Jesus BALDES; gp/ Gervacio SALASAR & Maria COCA.

GOMES, Maria Paula
bap *ydem*, ae 7 da; d/ Ant^o GOMES & Mª ROMERO; gp/ Josef ROMERO & M^a dela Lus TRUJILLO.

CORTES, Juan Domingo
bap *ydem*, ae 7 da; s/ Bautista CORTES & Maria Ant^a MONTOYA; gp/ Pedro SALASAR & Hursala (sic) HERRERA.

Frame 112

BEJIL, Pablo Jose
bap 25 Jan 1812, ae 6 da; s/ Fran^{co} BEJIL & Maria SALASAR; gp/ Cristoval BEJIL & M^a dela Lus MARTIN.

GONSALES, Mª Guadalupe
bap 26th, ae 3 da; d/ Josef Mig^l GONSALES & Mª BEJIL; gp/ Juan Josef GONSALES & Mª LEAL.

(Entry without surnames) 23 Apr 1812

ROMERO, Josef Benito
bap 26 (Apr 1812), ae 7 da; s/ Cons(e)cion ROMERO & Maria Rosa QUINTANA; gp/ Josef GONSALES & Dorotea BACA.

BACA, Josef Marcelino
bap 27 Apr, ae 3 da; s/ Salvador BACA & Tomasa SILBA; gp/ Jose MIERA & Mª BACA.

MARTIN, Josef Felipe
bap 3 May 1812, ae 4 da; s/ Juan MARTIN & Man$^{1(a)}$ COCA; gp/ Juan del Carmen ROMERO & Mª MARTIN.

Frame 113
BEJIL, Benita
bap 12 May 1812, ae 2 da; d/ Juan BEJIL & Josefa LOVATO; gp/ Rafel (n.s.) & Mª dela Lus ESPINOSA.

LUCERO, Maria dela Luz
bap 15 May 1812, ae 3 da; d/ Pablo LUCERO & Maria Paula LARRAÑAGA; gp/ Juan Antº MARTIN & Maria Cecilia MARTIN.

MARTIN, Josef Benito
bap 17 May 1812, ae 5 da; s/ Antº MARTIN & Maria Alverta BENABIDES; gp/ Santiago SILBA & Juana Encar(na)cion BELASQUES.

ARCHULETA, Juan Ysidro
bap 17 May 1812, ae 2 da; s/ Antº ARCHULETA & Monsorrate LEAL; gp/ Josef Rafel ROMERO & Anamaria ORTIZ. (Frames 113-114)

Frame 114
SALASAR, Maria Guadalupe
bap 17 *de* d^{ho}; d/ Carpio SALASAR & Maria Luisa BEJIL; gp/ Pedro FERN^{DES} & Maria Ygnacia MARTIN.

BEJIL, Josef Benito
bap 7 Jne (1812), ae 3 da; s/ Faustin BEJIL & Maria MARTIN; gp/ Ramon SALASAR & Soledad BEJIL.

URIOSTE, Maria Dolores
bap *en* d^{ho} *dia, mes y año*, ae 2 da; d/ Juan URIOSTE & Maria BEJIL; gp/ Josef Antº TORRES & Maria FERNANDES.

SISNEROS, Maria Josefa
bap 9 Jne; d/ Nerio SISNEROS & Teodora MARTIN; gm/ Matiana ROMERO.

Frame 115
CHAVES, Maria Soledad
bap 10 Jne; d/ Josef Maria CHAVES & Maria ORTEGA; gp/ Juan Domingo MONTOYA & Maria GONSALES.

MARTIN, Josef Benito
bap *en* d^{ho} *dia, mes y año*; s/ Pedro MARTIN & Jacinta ARAGON; gp/ Antº Josef BEJIL & Maria Dolores LUCERO.

ARAGON, Antº Josef
bap 14 Jne; s/ Antº ARAGON & Maria MARTINA; gp/ Roque MARTIN & Gregoria ARMIJO.

RIO, Maria Paula
bap 16 Jne, ae 6 da; d/ Juan Antº RIO & Maria Ma(gda)lena ROMERO; gm/ Viviana RÉYNA.

MONDRAGON, Josef Antonio
bap 17 Jne, ae 4 da; s/ Josef MONDRAGON & Josefa ARCHULETA; gp/ Man^{1} Antº MONDRAGON & Teodora MONDRAGON.

MADRIL, Josef Benito
bap *en d^{ho} dia, mes y año*, ae 2 da; s/ Pedro MADRIL & Maria MOYA; gp/ Ygnacio MEDINA & Maria MEDINA.

BENABIDEZ, Juan Gonsaga
bap *en d^{ho} dia, mes y año*, ae 3 da; d/ Ant^{o} Josef BENABIDEZ & Rita RIVERA; gp/ Juan GONSALES & Maria Ant^{a} MONTOYA.

Frame 116
ROMERO, Maria Dolores
bap 26 Jne, ae 3 da; d/ Bentura ROMERO & Maria Rafela LUJAN; gp/ Fran^{co} BEJIL & Maria HURTADO.

GARCIA, Juan
bap 28 Jne, ae 4 da; s/ Jose Ant^{o} GARCIA & Maria Reyes MARTIN; gp/ Jesus GALLEGO & Maria Mequela (sic) BEJIL.

ARMIJO, Maria Dolores
bap *en d^{ho} dia, mes y año*, ae 1 da; d/ Andres ARMIJO, dec., & Fran^{ca} MARTIN; gp/ Marcos ARCHULETA & Maria SANCHES.

SANDOVAL, Josef Benito
bap 9 Jly, ae 6 da; s/ Felipe SANDOVAL & Polonia MAES; gm/ Maria Manuela SANCHES.

MEDINA, Maria Dolores
bap 12 Jly, ae 7 da; d/ Felipe MEDINA & Guadalupe QUINTANA; gp/ Salvador QUINTANA & Balvaneda ROMERO.

(Entry without surnames) (D^{ho} dia, mes Y año)

Frame 117
SALASAR, Ygnacio
bap *en d^{ho} dia, mes y año*, ae 3 da; s/ Gervacio SALASAR & Maria COCA; gp/ Josef Rafel (sic) LUCERO & Maria Dolores LUCERO.

CHAVES, Mariano
bap 26 Jly, ae 3 da; s/ Julian CHAVES & Maria Man^{la} CORTES; gp/ Josef Ant^{o} CORTES & Juana Getrudes MONTOYA.

ROMERO, Josef Benito
bap *en d^{ho} dia, mes y año*, ae 4 da; s/ Josef Antonio (n.s.) & Bitoria ROMERO; gm/ Luisia ORTIS.

GARCIA, Anamaria de Jesus
bap *en d^{ho} dia, mes y año*, ae 2 da; d/ Mig^{l} GARCIA & Margarita LUCERO; gp/ Josef Rafel (sic) ROMERO & Anamaria ORTIS.

PACHECO, Mariano
bap *en d^{ho} dia, mes y año*, ae 1 da; s/ Gregorio PACHECO & Brigida TRUJILLO; gp/ Juan Ant^{o} LUCERO & Maria Paula LUCER(O-blot).

MARTIN, Maria Dolores
bap 12 Aug 1812, ae 5 da; d/ Josef Ant^{o} MARTIN, dec., & Maria Juana PAIS; gp/ Nicolas ROMERO & Juana ROMERO.

GARCIA, Jacinto
bap 16 Aug 1812, ae 4 da; s/ Julian GARCIA & Anamaria ROMERO; gp/ Juan Christobal VEGIL & Biviana TORRES. (Frames 117-118)

Frame 118
ESPINOSA, Santiago
bap 22 A0ug 1812, ae 11 da; s/ Jose Eulogio ESPINOSA & Anamaria ROMERO; gm/ Anamaria SOAZA.

BARELA, Rosa
bap 30 Aug 1812, ae 8 da; d/ Juan BARELA & Maria Juliana MARQUEZ; gp/ Gregorio DURAN & Rosa URIOSTE.

ORTIZ, Maria Ana
bap *Yd*^{m}; d/ Fran^{co} ORTIZ & Maria Rosa (n.s.); gm/ Maria Ant^{a} (n.s.), *todos del pueblo*.

LUCERO, Jesus Maria
bap 4 Sep 1812, ae 4 da; s/ Juan An^{to} LUCERO & Barbara An^{ta} CORDOBA; gp/ Julian MARTIN & Guadalupe CERDA.

DURAN, Maria Dolores
bap 6 Sep 1812, ae 8 da; d/ An^{to} DURAN & Maria Fran^{ca} SANTISTEBAN; gp/ Lorenzo ROMERO & Maria Jesus SANDOBALA.

Frame 119
FRESQUIS, Maria Soledad
bap *en el mismo dia, mes y año*, ae 2 da; d/ Juan Ysidro FRESQUIS & Maria Rosa MARTIN; gp/ Ramon VEJIL & Maria MARTIN.

CORTES, Josef Felipe
bap 19 Sep 1812, ae 15 da; s/ Josef Maria CORTES & Maria Magdalena BRITA; gp/ Xabier GARCIA & Maria Rosario APODACA.

CHABES, Jesus Maria
bap 20 Sep 1812, ae 5 da; s/ Luis CHABES & Maria dela Luz QUINTANA; gp/ Josef Ramon QUINTANA & Maria Micaela BALDESA.

FRESQUIS, Maria Matiana
bap 1 Oct 1812, ae 5 da; d/ Juan FRESQUIS & Maria Man^{la} DURAN; gp/ Manuel Gregorio DURAN & Maria Geroalda MASCAREÑAS.

MADRIL (gp), Maria Dolores
bap 1 Oct 1812, ae 5 da; s/ Pedro (n.s.) & Juana (n.s.), *hijos del pueblo*; gp/ Josef Yg^{o} MADRIL & Maria Damiana MARTIN.

Frame 120
FERNANDEZ, Maria Soledad
bap *Yd*^{m}, ae 3 da; d/ Pedro FERNANDEZ & Maria Yg^{a} MARTIN; gp/ Pedro VEGIL & Maria VEG^{L}.

MIERA, Maria Micaela
bap 4 Oct 1812, ae 5 da; d/ Josef MIERA & Maria Manuela ROMERO; gp/ Man^{l} Ant^{o} CISNEROS & Rita LUCERO.

GARCIA, Josef Benito
bap 5 Oct 1812, ae 4 da; s/ Bicente GARCIA & Juliana ROMERO; gp/ Ramon PACHECO & Maria VEGILA.

LOMA, Fran^{co}
bap *en el mismo dia*; s/ Juan Domingo LOMA & Maria MARTIN; gm/ Barbara MARTIN.

GONZALES, Maria Dolores
bap 11 Oct 1812, ae 5 da; d/ Juan GONZ^{s} & Maria An^{ta} MARTIN; gp/ Simon QUINTANA & Maria Paula BALDES. (Frames 120-121)

Frame 121
LUCERO, Josef Julian
bap 20 Nov (written over Marzo) 1812, ae 2 da; s/ Josef LUCERO & Maria Paula BARELA; gp/ Josef Rafel (sic) ROMERO & Ana Maria ORTIZ.

BEJIL, Maria Ygnacia
bap 1 Dec 1812, ae 3 da; d/ Ygnacio BEJIL & Juana MARQUES; gp/ Juan dela Cruz BEJIL & Maria Feliciana BEJIL.

ROMERO, Josef Rafel
bap 5 Dec 1812, ae 6 da; s/ Felipe ROMERO & Maria Encarnacion ARCHULETA; gp/ Pedro GARCIA & Ana Maria GARCIA.

ARAGON, Juan Pomuseno
bap 15 Dec 1812, ae 7 da; s/ Visente ARAGON & Maria BALDEZ; gp/ Juana de LUNA (only).

TAFOYA, Maria Dolores
bap 20 Dec 1812, ae 4 da; d/ Juan Domingo TAFOYA & Getrudes CORDOVA; gp/ Man^{l} SANCHES & Nicolasa SANDOVAL.

Año de 1813

MARTIN, Juan Domingo
bap 5 Jan 1813, ae 3 da; s/ Ant^{o} MARTIN & Guadalupe ROMERO; gp/ Juan Domingo MIRABAL & Man^{la} ROMERO. (Frames 121-122)

Frame 122
MADRIL, Maria Dolores
bap 10 Jan 1813, ae 6 da; d/ Josef Man^{l} MADRIL & T(e)odora LOVATO; gp/ Tomas SANDOVAL & Mª Consecion CHACON.

GONSALES, Mª Fran^{ca}
bap 14 Jan 1813, ae 3 da; d/ Josef Mig^{l} GONSALES & Ysavel BEJIL; gp/ Juan Ant^{o} SERNA & Juan(a) ROMERO.

TORRES, Pedro
bap 20 Jan 1813, ae 2 da; s/ Ant^{o} TORRES & M^{a} (Y)Savel FERNANDES; gp/ Man^{l} SANCHES & Nicolasa SANDOVAL.

BEJIL, Juan de Jesus
bap 4 Feb 1813, ae 7 da; s/ Ramon BEJIL & Varvara MARTIN; gp/ Pedro FERNANDES & Ygnacia MARTIN.

Frame 123
DURAN, Jesus Mª de la Trinidad
bap 8 Feb 1813, ae 5 da; s/ Pablo DURAN & Maria de Jesus BALDES; gp/ Man^{l} Ant^{o} SISNEROS & Mª Rita LUCERO.

DURAN, Josef de la Crus
bap 15 Feb 1813, ae 3 da; s/ Pablo DURAN & Maria de Jesus BALDES; gp/ Pablo LUCERO & Paula LARRAÑAGA.

MARTIN, Maria dela Crus
bap 1 Mch 1813, ae 6 da; d/ Josef MARTIN & Ana Maria (n.s.); gp/ Martin FLORES & Juana Getrudes GARCIA.

ARCHULETA, Maria la Crus
bap 4 Mch 1813, ae 5 da; d/ Pablo ARCHULETA & Varvara LOVATO; gp/ Juan LUCERO & Maria Ygnacia ARAGON.

SUASO, Maria Dolores
bap 10 May 1813, ae 6 da; d/ Josef SUASO & Maria CASADOS; gp/ D^n Josef EXARBE (See Frame 100) & Maria CASADOS.

ROMERO, Maria de Jesus
bap 16 May 1813, ae 4 da; d/ Ant^o Domingo ROMERO & Juana DURAN; gp/ Juan Domingo FERNANDES & Maria Dolores FERNANDES. (Frames 123-124)

Frame 124
ROMERO, Maria de Jesus
bap *en el mismo dia, mes y año*, ae 6 da; d/ Ant^o Domingo ROMERO & Josefa QUINTANA; gp/ Pedro GARCIA (only).

ARCHULETA, Maria Dolores
bap 19 May 1813, ae 7 da; d/ Ant^o ARCHULETA & Maria Catalina ALLORRO; gp/ Juan Ant^o LUCERO and Paula LARAÑADA.

CRUS, Gregorio
bap *en el mismo dia, mes y año*, ae 3 da; s/ Josef Mariano dela CRUS & Dolores BEJIL; gp/ Man^l BACA & Manuela CASADOS.

ARGUELLO, Maria Soledad
bap 25 May 1813, ae 7 da; d/ Juan ARGUELLO & Clara SANDOVAL; gp/ Balentin PADILLA & Ysidora MARTIN.

GUERRERO, Juan Antonio
bap *en el mismo dia, mes y año*, ae 7 da; s/ Diego GUERRERO & Margarita (n.s.); gp/ Juan Ant^o LUJAN & Fran^ca ROMERO. (Frames 124-125)

Frame 125
LUCERO, Maria Soledad
bap 22 May 1813, ae 6 da; d/ Ant^o LUCERO & Juliana BALERIO; gp/ (not given).

LUCERO, Josef Miguel
bap 23 May 1813, ae 3 da; s/ Pedro LUCERO & M^a dela Lus FERNANDES; gp/ Fran^co ROMERO & M^a del Carmen LUCERO.

LOPES, Maria Felipa
bap *en el mismo dia, mes y año*, ae 5 da; d/ Cristoval LOPES & Ant^a TRUJILLO; gp/ Mig^l TAFOYA & Juana BACA.

TRUJILLO, Maria Susana
bap 26 May 1813, ae 7 da; d/ Pablo TRUJILLO & Feliciana ORTIS; gp/ Rafel (sic) LUNA & Ana Mª TAFOYA.

TRUJILLO, Pablo Manuel
bap 28 May 1813, ae 4 da; s/ Luis TRUJILLO & Maria Getrudes SANCHES; gm/ Teresa URTADO.

ROMERO, Juan Ysidro
bap *en el mismo dia, mes y año*, ae 5 da; s/ Juan Ant^o ROMERO & Maria Vitoria DELGADO; gp/ Luis DELGADO & Mª Rosa DELGADO.

Frame 126
(Entry without surnames) (6 Jne 1813)

SAMORA, Ylario *Pb^{o}*
bap *en el mismo dia, mes y año*, ae 4 da; s/ Ylario SAMORA & Fran^{ca} (n.s.); gm/ Miquela (n.s.).

LOVATO, Maria de la Luz
bap 15 Jne 1813, ae 5 da; d/ Juan Domingo LOVATO & Maria TAFOYA; gp/ Juan Domingo TAFOYA & Maria M(A)ESE.

COCA, Maria Juliana
bap *en el mismo dia, mes y año*, ae 7 da; d/ Tomas COCA & Lorensa SANDOVAL; gp/ Bisente GARCIA & Juliana ROMERO.

BORREGO, Mª Dorotea
bap 18 Jne 1813, ae 4 da; d/ Cristoval BORREGO & Espiritu S^{to} TAFOYA; gp/ Juan Felipe CORDOVA & Maria Mequela GONSALES.

ROMERO, Francisco
bap 20 Jne 1813, ae 3 da; s/ Josef Ant^{o} ROMERO & Juan(a) PAIS; gp/ Fran^{ca} (n.s.) (only).

Frame 127
MONTOYA, Maria Encarnacion
bap 22 Jne 1813, ae 7 da; d/ Man^{l} MONTOYA & Maria BARELA; gp/ Josef Julian CHAVES & Maria CORTES.

BUENO, Maria Manuela
bap 25 Jne 1813, ae 3 da; d/ Mateo BUENO & Josefa BEJIL; gp/ Miguel MASCAREÑAS & Maria BUENO.

MARTIN, Josef Benito
bap 1 Jly 1813, ae 3 da; s/ Fran^{co} MARTIN & Maria SANCHES; gm/ Maria dela Lus SANCHES.

SALASAR, Ant^{o} de Jesus
bap *en el mismo dia, mes y año*, ae 3 da; s/ Ramon SALASAR & Soledad BEJIL; gp/ Josef Rafel BEJIL & Maria LOBATO.

MARTIN, Manuel Gregorio
bap 12 Jly 1813, ae 4 da; s/ Diego MARTIN & Maria Rafela (sic) LUNA; gp/ Josef ROMERO & Maria dela Lus TRUJILLO.

BRITO, Juan Nepomuseno
bap 15 Jly 1813, ae 7 da; s/ Fran^{co} BRITO & Margarita GONSALES; gp/ Roque MARTIN & Maria Gregoria ARMIJO.

Frame 128
TAFOYA, Maria del Carmen
bap *en el mismo dia, mes y año*, ae 3 da; d/ Vartolo TAFOYA & Maria Ant^{a} GONSALES; gp/ Josef Ant^{o} GONSALES & Ana Maria URIOSTE.

RILLO, Maria Soledad
bap 20 Jly 1813, ae 6 da; d/ Ant^{o} RILLO & Juana BILLA; gp/ Luis DELGADO & Maria Josefa JUILO.

MARTIN, Juan Bautista
bap 25 Jly 1813, ae 4 da; s/ Estevan MARTIN & Maria Encarnacion LUCERO; gp/ Juan Bap^{ta} LALANDA & Polonia LUCERO.

TRUJILLO, Antonio Josef
bap 29 Jly 1813, ae 2 da; s/ Fran^{co} TRUJILLO & Juaquina DURAN; gp/ Felis URIOSTE & Man^{la} BEJIL.

MONDRAGON, Jesus Maria
bap *en el mismo dia, mes y año*, ae 6 da; s/ Bartolo MONDRAGON & Maria FRESQUIZ; gp/ Felis URIOSTE & Man^{la} BEJIL.

SAMORA, Dolores
bap 30 Jly 1813, ae 5 da; d/ Pedro SAMORA & Rafela (sic) CASILLAS; gp/ Jesus GALLEGO & Mequela (sic) BEJIL. (Frames 128-129)

Frame 129
BARELA, Benita
bap 5 Aug 1813, ae 3 da; d/ Jose BARELA & Dolores SANDOVAL; gp/ Salvador BACA & Tomasa SILVA.

CASILLAS, Maria Guadalupe
bap 10 Aug 1813, ae 4 da; d/ Bartolo CASILLAS & Elena BEJIL; gp/ Josef Ant^{o} MARTIN & Maria BEJIL.

PANDO, Juan Antonio
bap *en el mismo dia, mes y año*, ae 5 da; s/ Salvador PANDO & Ana Maria LOMA; gm/ Josefa QUILO.

PAIS, Maria de la Luz
bap 15 Aug 1813, ae 6 da; d/ Mig^{l} PAIS & Maria MAES; gp/ Roque MARTIN & Gregoria ARMIJO.

MEDINA, Marta
bap 27 Aug 1813, ae 5 da; d/ Josef Man^{l} MEDINA & Juan(a) LOVATO; gp/ Juan Ant^{o} ALCON & Juana BALLEJOS.

Frame 130
GONSALES, Maria Soledad
bap 12 Oct 1813, ae 3 da; d/ Juan GONSALES & Maria MESTAS; gp/ Julian ARCHULETA & Maria BARELA.

BLEA (gp), Juan Nepomuseno
bap 12 Dec 1813, ae 2 da; s/ Juan Ant^{o} (n.s.) & Soledad (n.s.); gp/ Ant^{o} BLEA & Catarina MARTIN.

CORTES, Josef Benito
bap 16 Dec 1813, ae 3 da; s/ Josef Maria CORTES & Madalena BRITA; gp/ Juan JARAMILLO & Mariana CORDOVA.

MARTIN, Juan Fran^{co}
bap 19 Dec 1813, ae 4 da; s/ Mig^{l} MARTIN & Andrea CASADOS; gp/ Nicolas MARTIN & Rosa SALASAR.

PADILLA (gp), Jose Benito
bap 20 Dec 1813, ae 5 da; s/ Luisa (n.s.), wid; gp/ Pedro PADILLA & Maria CHAVES.

ROMERO, Maria Manuela
bap 27 Dec 1813, ae 6 da; d/ Salvador ROMERO & Catarina (n.s.); gm/ Manuela ROMERO.

Frame 131
MONTOYA, Maria Manuela dela Natividad
bap 28 Dec 1813, ae 2 da; d/ Rafel (sic) MONTOYA & Lusiana CHAVES; gp/ Diego Ant^{o} LUERAS (written over) & Maria Rita LUCERO.

GABALDON, Maria Ysidora
bap *en el mismo dia, mes y año*, ae 4 da; d/ Jose Man^{l} GABA(L)DON & Susana MARTIN; gp/ Ant^{o} Josef (n.s.) & Margarita MARTIN.

SALASAR, Juan Manuel
bap 30 Dec 1813, ae 3 da; s/ Xervacio SALASAR & Maria COCA; gp/ Luis TRUJILLO & Maria SANCHEZ.

Año de 1814

LALANDA, Tomas Benito
bap 1 Jan 1814, ae 3 da; s/ Baptista LALANDA & Maria Polonia LUCERO; gp/ Ant^{o} Jose BEJIL & Maria Rita LUCERO.

ARCHULETA, Pedro
bap 10 Jan 1814, ae 5 da; s/ Ant^{o} ARCHULETA & Monserrate LEAL; gp/ Juan Rafel (sic) LEAL & Juana LEAL.

Frame 132
ROMERO, Estevan
bap *en el mismo dia, mes y año*, ae 2 da; s/ Juan de Jesus ROMERO & Candelaria QUINTANA; gp/ Juan ARGUELLO & Ygnacia ROMERO.

BEJIL, Maria Trinidad
bap 6 Jan 1814, ae 2 da; d/ Rafel (sic) BEJIL & Elena LOVATO; gp/ Faustin BEJIL & Maria dela Luz MARTIN.

MARTIN, Juan de los Reyes
bap 9 Jan 1814, ae 4 da; s/ Fran^{co} MARTIN & Maria SILVA; gp/ Mig^{l} PAIS & Mª MAES.

LUJAN (gp), Juan Domingo
bap *en el mismo dia, mes y año*, ae 3 da; s/ Jose Maria (n.s.) & Miquela (n.s.); gp/ Juan Domingo LUJAN & Juliana GOMES.

GONSALES, Maria delos Reyes
bap 10 Jan 1814, ae 5 da; d/ Santiago GONSALES & Loreta ARCHULETA; gp/ Jose Man^{l} ROMERO & Teresa RUIBAL.

GARDUÑO, Mª Dolores
bap 12 Jan 1814, ae 1 da; d/ Ant^{o} Jose GARDUÑO & Fernanda BUENO; gp/ Ant^{o} TORRES & Mª Ysavel FERNANDES.

Frame 133
GALLEGO, Jesus
bap 13 Jan 1814, ae 3 da; s/ Tomas GALLEGO & Juan(a) GUTIERRES; gp/ J^{n} Pablo de ERRERA & Ana Bentura DURAN.

GONSALES, Juan
bap 16 Jan 1814, ae 4 da; s/ Salvador GONSALES & Maria BEJIL; gp/ Agustin ROMERO & Maria FERNANDES.

ESPINOSA, Amaria Refugio (Ana M^{a} del Refugio in margin)
bap *en el mismo dia, mes y año*, ae 3 da; d/ Juan Yg^{o} ESPINOSA & Mª GONSALES; gp/ Ramon BEJIL & Maria MARTIN.

PADILLA, Juan Santos
bap 2 (sic) Nov 1814, ae 6 da; s/ Salvador PADILLA & Mª Josefa MARTIN; gp/ Jose Antº ARCHULETA & Mª Salome ARCHULETA.

CORTES, Mª Paula
bap 26 Jan 1814, ae 4 da; d/ Cruz CORTES & Juana PADILLA; gp/ Simon QUINTANA & Maria Paula BALDES.

LUNA, Mª Paula Bentura
bap 28 Jan 1814, ae 6 da; d/ Rafel LUNA & Ana Maria TAFOYA; gp/ Juan Bautista LALANDA & Mª Manuela SANDOVAL.

Frame 134
SOAZO, Martin
bap 30 Jan 1814, ae 6 da; s/ Juan Antº SOAZO & Fran^{ca} SAMORA; gp/ Antº Jose LUCERO & Mª Manuela (n.s.).

MALDONADO (gp), Jose Miguel
bap 1 Feb 1814, ae 7 yr; s/ *Nacion Yuta*; gf/ Dª Jose MALDONADO.

BUENO, Maria de Jesus
bap 2 Feb 1814, ae 5 da; d/ Antº Bueno & Rosalia BALDEZ; gp/ Lorenso CORDOVA & Mª TRUJILLO.

QUINTANA, Mª Concepcion
bap *en el mismo dia, mes y año*, ae 3 da; s/ Jose Rafel QUINTANA & Maria dela Lus MONDRAGON; gp/ Jose PACHECO & Mª (n.s.).

LUCERO, Maria Candelaria
bap 3 Feb 1814, ae 4 da; d/ Juan Antº LUCERO & Barvara CORDOVA; gp/ Ramon SALASAR & Maria BEJIL.

Frame 135
SALASAR, Mª Dolores
bap 6 Feb 1814, ae 7 da; d/ Diego SALASAR & Cristerna SANDOVAL; gp/ Blas TRUJILLO & Mª Man^{la} SANCHES.

MARTIN, Juana Rafela
bap 16 Feb 1814, ae 6 da; d/ Ygº MARTIN & Encarnacion BLEA; gp/ Man^{l} MARTIN & Man^{la} SANDOVAL.

CRUZ, Mª dela Luz
bap 17 Feb 1814, ae 6 da; d/ Man^{l} CRUZ & Ana Maria GARCIA; gp/ Salvador GONSALES & Maria Carmen BEJIL.

FERNANDES, Pedro Antº
bap 24 Feb 1814, ae 7 da; s/ Juan Domingo FERNANDES & Fran^{ca} GARCIA; gp/ Pedro Antº BALDES & Mª Encarnacion BALDES.

LUJAN, Santiago
bap 27 Feb 1814, ae 6 da; s/ Jose LUJAN & Maria ROMERO; gm/ Fran^{ca} (n.s.), *Yndios*.

SANTISTEVAN, Juan de Jesus
bap 1 Mch 1814, ae 6 da; s/ Ysidro SANTISTEVAN & Mª Rosario (n.s.); gp/ Rafel (sic) SISNEROS & Mª Guadalupe SISNEROS.

Frame 136
LUCERO, Pedro Antº

bap 6 Mch 1814, ae 2 da; s/ Mig^{l} LUCERO & Ramona GONSALES; gm/ Maria Rita LUCERO.

ZAMORA, Maria Dolores
bap *en el mismo dia, mes y año*, ae 5 da; d/ Pablo ZAMORA & Maria Alvina (n.s.); gm/ Maria Ygnacia (n.s.).

BEJIL, Mª Rosa
bap 7 Mch 1814, ae 4 da; d/ Juan BEJIL & Mª Consecion LOVATO; gp/ Rafel (sic) BEJIL & Mª Elena LOVATO.

PADILLA, Mª Dolores
bap 8 Mch 1814, ae 3 da; d/ Juan Ant^{o} PADILLA & Trenidad VEJIL; gp/ Andres MARTIN & Margarita CORDOVA.

(Entry without surnames) 13 Mch 1814

Frame 137
DURAN, Mª Dolores
bap *en el mismo dia, mes y año*, ae 8 da; d/ Juan Ant^{o} DURAN & Mª Fran^{ca} (n.s.); gp/ Pablo DURAN & Margarita SANCHEZ.

(Two entries without surnames)

VEJIL, Jesus
bap 22 Mch 1814, ae 6 da; s/ Fran^{co} VEGIL & Mª Trenidad SALASAR; gp/ Juan VEJIL & Luisa SALASAR.

COCA, Diego Ant^{o}
bap 25 Mch 1814, ae 7 da; s/ Juan Ant^{o} COCA & Maria Fran^{ca} (n.s.); gp/ Jose Fran^{co} BARELA & Mª SANDOVAL.

MARTIN, Mª Encarnacion
bap 25 Mch 1814, ae 4 da; d/ Estevan MARTIN & Mª LUCERO; gp/ Jose Consecion ARGUELLO & Ygnacia ROMERO.

Frame 138
GOMEZ, Jose Miguel
bap 27 Mch 1814, ae 5 da; s/ Ant^{o} GOMEZ & Mª ROMERO; gp/ Juan LOVATO & Ygnacia SANCHES.

MONDRAGON, Jose Manuel
bap *en el mismo dia, mes y año*, ae 3 da; s/ Jose Vitor MONDRAGON & Josefa ARCHULETA; gp/ Jose Ant^{o} MONDRAGON & Mª CASADOS.

ROMERO, Santiago
bap 28 Mch 1814, ae 7 da; s/ Bentura ROMERO & Juana (n.s.); gm/ Maria LOMA *del pueb^{o}*.

GOMEZ, Ant^{o}
bap *en el mismo dia, mes y año*, ae 5 da; s/ Pedro GOMEZ & Mª Ant^{a} ARCHULETA; gm/ Madalena (n.s.).

(Partial entry without surnames)

SANDOVAL, Jose Benito
bap 4 Apr 1814, ae 6 da; s/ Matias SANDOVAL & Mª Yg^{a} BUENO; gp/ J^{n} BEJIL & Soledad PEREYRO.

LOVATO, Juan Nepu(mo)seno
bap *en el mismo dia, mes y año*, ae 4 da; s/ Fran^{co} LOVATO & Mª MONDRAGON; gp/ Bernardino MARTIN & Mª Man^{la} ARAGON.

Frame 139
GARCIA, Mª Josefa dela Luz
bap 7 Apr 1814, ae 1 da; d/ Juan Jose GARCIA & Mª Teodora CHAVES; gp/ Tomas Ant^{o} BESERRA & Mª Miguela CHAVES.

MARQUEZ, Epifiano
bap 11 Apr 1814, ae 4 da; s/ Mig^{l} MARQUEZ & Getrudes MONTOYA; gp/ Jose Ant^{o} GONSALES & Mª Ant^{a} ARAGON.

SANCHES, Mª Soledad
bap *en el mismo dia, mes y año*, ae 4 da; d/ Jose Pablo SANCHES & Getrudes MARTIN; gp/ Man^{l} Estevan PACHECO & Mª Biviana PACHECO.

MONTOYA, M^{a} dela Luz
bap 17 Apr 1814, ae 6 da; s/ Man^{l} MONTOYA & Serafina ARCHULETA; gp/ Ant^{o} ARCHULETA & Margarita MEDINA.

MONTOYA, Maria de Jesus
bap *en el mismo dia, mes y año*, ae 3 da; d/ Jose MONTOYA & Mª Rosa VEJIL; gp/ Juan LOVATO & Mª Yg^{a} SANCHES.

CHAVES, Juan Agustin
bap 18 Apr 1814, ae 5 da; s/ Juan Agustin CHAVES & Gregoria MEDINA; gp/ Pedro GARCIA & Ana Maria GARCIA.

ROMERO, Juana Catarina
bap *en el mismo dia, mes y año*, ae 7 da; d/ Ologio ROMERO & Maria (n.s.); gp/ Usebio HAVILA & Catarina MARTIN. (Frames 139-140)

Frame 140
CONCHA, Jose Miguel
bap 23 Apr 1814, ae 7 da; s/ Juan Domingo CONCHA & Maria SOASO; gp/ Gregoria PACHECO & Maria TRUJILLO.

(Entry without surnames)

ROMERO, M^{a}
bap 1 May 1814, ae 4 da; d/ Diego ROMERO & Man^{la} COCA; gp/ Mig^{l} PAIS & Maria Soledad (n.s.).

LUJAN, Mª Josefa
bap *en el mismo dia, mes y año*, ae 5 da; d/ Jose Ant^{o} LUJAN & Mª Rosa (n.s.); gm/ Madalena (n.s.) *del p^{o}*.

GONSALES, Jose dela Cruz
bap 8 May 1814; s/ Juan Domingo GONSALES & Juana LUJAN; gp/ Jose Mariano FERNANDES & Mª LUCERO.

BEJIL, Bentura de Jesus
bap 15 May 1814, ae 6 da; d/ Juan Cristoval BEJIL & Biviana TORREZ; gp/ Man^{l} SANCHEZ & Nicolasa SANDOVAL.

Frame 141
EXARVE, Juana Getrudes

bap *en el mismo dia, mes y año*, ae 5 da; d/ Josef EXARVE & Maria CASADOS; gp/ Juan Cristobal TRUJILLO & Mª SALASAR.

ROMERO, Maria Dolores
bap 16 May 1814, ae 3 da; d/ Jose Rafel ROMERO & Lucia LUJAN; gm/ Rafela LUJAN.

MARTIN, Nicolasa
bap *en el mismo dia, mes y año*, ae 4 da; d/ Jose Ant^o^ MARTIN & Xaviela BEJIL; gp/ Man^l^ DURAN & Geralda MASCAREÑAS.

(Entry without surnames)

ROMERO, Josefa
bap 23 May 1814, ae 7 da; d/ Jose ROMERO & Maria LUCERO; gp/ Andres MARTIN & Teresa (n.s.) *del p^o^*.

GOMES, Ygnacia
bap *en el mismo dia, mes y año*, ae 3 da; d/ Jose Ant^o^ GOMES & Paula de ERRERA; gm/ Madalena ROMERO *del p^o^*.

MESTAS, Maria Pascuala
bap 24 May 1814, ae 6 da; d/ Juan Cristobal MESTAS & Juana Bentura ROMERO; gp/ Marcos TRUJILLO & Man^la^ ROMERO. (Frames 141-142)

Frame 142
SILBA, Mª de Esquipula
bap 29 May 1814, ae 7 da; d/ Siriaco SILBA & Cencion MEDINA; gp/ Fran^co^ VEJIL & Maria Trenidad SALASAR.

MARTIN, Juan Bentura
bap 30 May 1814, ae 4 da; s/ Juan Felipe MARTIN & Mª Man^la^ COCA; gp/ Fran^co^ Xavier GARCIA & M^a^ del Rosario APODACA.

MARTIN, Maria Yg^a^
bap 1 Jne 1814, ae 5 da; d/ Man^l^ Gregorio MARTIN & Mª Rafela MEDINA; gp/ Juan Lorenso CORDOVA & Margarita MARTIN.

ROMERO, Maria Soledad
bap *en el mismo dia, mes y año*, ae 3 da; d/ Salvador ROMERO & Dolores REYNA; gp/ Juan Yg^o^ LUJAN & Maria Clara ROMERO.

ROMERO, Maria Trenidad
bap *ydem*, ae 8 da; d/ Jose ROMERO & Juana BARELA; gp/ Ant^o^ MEDINA & Maria ESPINOSA.

BEJIL, Maria Rafela de Jesus
bap 8 Jne 1814, ae 4 da; d/ Matias BEJIL & Maria SALASAR; gp/ Ant^o^ MEDINA & Maria ESPINOSA. (Frames 142-143)

Frame 143
MEDINA, Juan Ant^o^
bap 13 Jne 1814, ae 5 da; s/ Juan Ysidro MEDINA & Maria TRUJILLO; gp/ Mig^l^ TAFOYA & Maria M(A)ESE.

MARTIN, Dolores
bap *en el mismo dia, mes y año*, ae 4 da; d/ Felipe MARTIN & Mª TRUJILLO; gp/ Ramon BEJIL & Maria MARTIN.

CHAVES, Manuel Ant^{o}
bap 19 Jne 1814, ae 7 da; s/ Julian CHAVES & Maria CORTES; gp/ Pablo LUCERO & Paula LARRAÑAGA.

(Entry without surnames) 20 Jne 1814

GOMEZ, Paula
bap *en el mismo dia, mes y año*, ae 7 da; d/ Juan Ant^{o} GOMEZ & Miquela RIO; gm/ Fran^{ca} LUJAN.

CRUZ, Ant^{a} Nicolasa
bap 1 Jly 1814, ae 6 da; d/ Fran^{co} CRUZ & Mª Josefa MEDINA; gp/ Juan MONTOYA & Mª Guadalupe ESPINOSA.

Frame 144
BALDES, Maria Dolores
bap 12 Jly 1814, ae 5 da; d/ Fran^{co} BALDES & Mª Paula M(A)ESE; gp/ Juan de Dios ARMENTA & his sister, Agustina ARMENTA.

BACA, Jose Benito
bap 17 Jly 1814, ae 4 da; s/ Salvador BACA & Tomasa SILVA; gp/ Marcos TRUJILLO & M^{a} Yg^{a} M(A)ESE.

TRUJILLO, Juana Rafela
bap *en el mismo dia, mes y año*, ae 3 da; d/ Juan Mig^{l} TRUJILLO & Ana Maria BALDES; gp/ Jose Yg^{o} MADRIL & Mª Damiana (n.s.).

CONTRERAS, Man^{l} de Jesus
bap 21 Jly 1814, ae 4 da; s/ Geraldo CONTRERAS & Mª Encarnacion CHAVES; gp/ Man^{l} de Jesus LEAL & Mariana QUINTANA. (No mention of twins)

CONTRERAS, Juan
bap *en el mismo dia, mes y año*, ae 4 da; s/ Geraldo CONTRERAS & Mª Encarnacion CHAVES; gp/ Man^{l} URTADO & Mª Getrudes BEJIL. (No mention of twins)

GARCIA, Mª Encarnacion
bap 24 Jly 1814, ae 5 da; d/ Yldefonso GARCIA & Dolores PADIYA; gp/ Martin FLORES & Getrudes GARCIA.

Frame 145
GONSALES, Maria Josefa
bap *en el mismo dia, mes y año*, ae 5 da; d/ Juan Ant^{o} GONSALES & Catarina LUCERO; gp/ Julian CHAVES & Teodora ROMERO.

BORREGO, Juana Maria
bap 25 Jly 1814, ae 3 da; d/ Cristoval BORREGO & Santos MARTIN; gp/ Felipe GONSALES & Man^{la} SALASAR.

TRUJILLO, Mª Dolores
bap 13 Aug 1814, ae 6 da; d/ Pablo TRUJILLO & Felisiana ORTIZ; gp/ Marcos TRUJILLO & Mª Luisa TRUJILLO.

SANDOVAL, Jose Bicente
bap 14 Aug 1814, ae 3 da; s/ Felipe SANDOVAL & Polonia M(A)ESE; gp/ Bisente TRUJILLO & Mª Dolores MADRIL.

FERNANDO, Fran[co]
bap 21 Aug 1814, ae 5 da; s/ Juan Ant[o] FERNANDO & Josefa GAVILAN; gm/ Rosa FERNANDES.

BALDES, Jose Maria
bap 4 Sep 1814; s/ Bentura BALDES & Juana Catarina (n.s.); gp/ Jose Mig[l] ARAGON & Cisilia MARTIN.

SANCHEZ, Estevan Rafel
bap 9 Aug 1814, ae 4 da; *espurio* s/ Rita SANCHEZ; gp/ Estevan Rafel MARTIN & M[a] LUCERO. (Frames 145-146)

Frame 146
(Entry without surnames)

ROMERO, M[a] Soledad
bap 11 Sep 1814, ae 5 da; d/ Consecion ROMERO & Rosa QUINTANA; gp/ Juan Domingo FERNANDEZ & Fran[ca] GARCIA.

LEAL, Jose Benito
bap 16 Sep 1814, ae 4 da; s/ Rafel LEAL & Maria BEJIL; gp/ Juan delos Reyes SENA & Maria CHAVES.

LUCERO, Vernardo
bap 2 Oct 1814, ae 2 da; s/ Man[l] LUCERO & Andrella LAVADILLA; gp/ J[n] Man[l] LUCERO & M[a] Josefa LUCERO.

MARQUEZ, Santiago
bap 9 Oct 1814, ae 7 da; s/ Usevio MARQUEZ & Maria Rosa (n.s.); gp/ M[a] Dominga LUCERO (only).

REYNA, Geronimo
bap 9 Oct 1814, ae 4 da; s/ Juan Domingo REYNA & Rosalia (n.s.); gp/ Josef Maria M(A)ESE (only). (Frames 146-147)

Frame 147
MARTIN, Juan Nepumuseno
bap 23 Oct 1814, ae 5 da; s/ Roque MARTIN & Gregoria ARMIJO; gp/ (blank space).

BLEA, Maria Serafina
bap *en el mismo dia, mes y año*, ae 4 da; d/ Ant[o] BLEA & Catalina MARTIN; gp/ Nerio SISNEROS & Teodora MARTIN.

CORDOVA, M[a] Encarnacion
bap 24 Oct 1814, ae 8 da; d/ Juan Ant[o] CORDOVA & (mother not given); gp/ Carpio CORDOVA & M[a] Mequela GONSALES.

LION, M[a] Teresa
bap *en el mismo dia, mes y año*, ae 7 da; d/ Jose Ant[o] LION & Man[la] ARAGON; gp/ Ramon ROMERO & M[a] Rafela (sic) BEJIL.

BARELA, Maria Dolores
bap 25 Oct 1814, ae 6 da; d/ Juan BARELA & Juliana TRUJILLO; gp/ Ramon PACHECO & Trenidad BEJIL.

SANCHEZ, Pedro Ygnacio
bap *en el mismo dia, mes y año*, ae 3 da; s/ Jose SANCHEZ & Margarita BUSTOS; gp/ Pedro Ygnacio DURAN & Ant[a] SANCHEZ.

Frame 148
BEJIL, Maria Manuela
bap 27 Oct 1814, ae 4 da; d/ Fran^{co} BEJIL & Candelaria GONSALES; gp/ Jose GARCIA & Margarita LUCERO.

GONSALES, Jose Rafel (sic)
bap 13 Nov 1814, ae 3 da; s/ Juan GONSALES & Josefa MESTAS; gp/ Pablo TRUJILLO & Felisiana ORTIZ.

MONDRAGON, Juan delos Reyes
bap *en el mismo dia, mes y año*, ae 4 da; s/ Ant^{o} MONDRAGON & Mª BEJIL; gp/ Juan URIOSTE & Man^{la} BEJIL.

ROMERO, Jose Joaquin
bap 14 Nov 1814, ae 6 da; s/ Felipe ROMERO & Serafina LEAL; gp/ Juan Ant^{o} ROMERO & Biviana ARCHULETA.

ROMERO, Pablo
bap 25 Dec 1814, ae 4 da; s/ Juan Domingo ROMERO & Juana M^{a} (n.s.); gp/ Juan Bautista LALANDA & Mª Polonia LUCERO.

Año de 1815

CHAVES, Mª Serafina
bap 2 Jan 1815, ae 5 da; d/ Luis CHAVES & M^{a} dela Luz QUINTANA; gp/ Cruz MARTIN & Dolores TORRES.

DOMINGES, Jose Anastacio
bap 3 Jan 1815, ae 7 da; s/ Jose Ant^{o} (n.s.) & Juana DOMINGES; gm/ Rafela (sic-n.s.). (Frames 148-149)

Frame 149
TORRES, Mª Manuela
bap *en el mismo dia, mes y año*, ae 6 da; d/ Diego TORRES & Mª TRUJILLO; gp/ Jose Man^{l} ROMERO & Mª AGUILAR.

MESTAS, Maria Manuela
bap 14 Jan 1815, ae 4 da; d/ Jose Man^{l} MESTAS & Mª Juana MARTIN; gf/ Jose Rafel ROMERO.

VEJIL, Pedro Antonio
bap 26 Jan 1815, ae 3 da; s/ Jose Fran^{co} VEJIL & Mª URTADO; gp/ Ramon SALASAR & Mª BEJIL.

GONSALES, Mª Andrea
bap 29 Jan 1815, ae 6 da; d/ Ant^{o} GONSALES & Fran^{ca} RIO; gp/ Luis DELGADO & Mª Josefa JUILO.

ROMERO, Maria Paula
bap *en el mismo dia, mes y año*, ae 3 da; d/ Juan Andres ROMERO & M^{a} TIO; gm/ Dominga LEIBA.

ARCHULETA, Maria Paula
bap 20 Feb 1815, ae 4 da; d/ Damian ARCHULETA & Miquela SALASAR; gp/ Man^{l} ARCHULETA & Mª Pascuala ROMERO.

Frame 150
BARELA, Maria Manuela
bap 21 Feb 1815, ae 3 da; d/ Jose Man^{l} BARELA & Fran^{ca} MARTIN; gp/ Ant^{o} ARAGON & Maria MESTAS.

RIVERA, Fran^{co}
bap *en el mismo dia, mes y año*, ae 1 da; s/ Luis RIVERA & Juan(a) PADILLA; gp/ Bentura VALDES & Juana Catarina LOVATO.

GARCIA, Felipe de Jesus
*bap 6 Feb 1815, ae 4 da; s/ Mig^{1} GARCIA & Margarita LUCERO; gp/ Pedro Nolasco FERNANDEZ & Mª Yg^{a} MARTIN.

CORTES, Ma dela Luz
bap 9 Feb 1815, ae 5 da; d/ Paulin CORTES & Maria MARTIN; gp/ Jose Ant^{o} MARTIN & Barvara TRUJILLO.

PADILLA, Felipe de Jesus
bap 12 Feb 1815, ae 6 da; s/ Man^{1} PADILLA & Esmeregilda BEJIL; gp/ Man^{1} Ant^{o} BEJIL & M^{a} del Carmen GONSALES.

MOLINA, Maria Dolores
bap *en el mismo dia, mes y año*, ae 5 da; d/ Alegandro MOLINA & Biviana BACA; gp/ Lorenso CORDOVA & Margarita MARTIN.

Frame 151
BARELA, Jose Benito
bap 27 Feb 1815, ae 8 da; s/ Mig^{1} BARELA & Juana ROMERO; gp/ Reymundo TRUJILLO (only).

PAIS, Jose Fran^{co}
bap *en el mismo dia, mes y año*, ae 6 da; s/ Mig^{1} PAIS & Mª Soledad (n.s.); gp/ Juan del Carmen ROMERO & Mª MARTIN.

MONTOYA, Juan Domingo
bap 28 Feb 1815, ae 3 da; s/ Jose Patricio MONTOYA & Juan(a) URTADO; gp/ Jose ARAGON & Ana Mª BUENO.

SANDOVAL, Dolores
bap 29 Feb 1815, ae 4 da; d/ Fran^{co} SANDOVAL & Mariana TAFOYA; gp/ Juan del Carmen ROMERO & Mª MARTIN.

PADILLA, Mª Juliana
bap 1 Mch 1815, ae 4 da; d/ Salvador PADILLA & Josefa MARTIN; gp/ Pedro MARTIN & Jacinta ARAGON.

ARMIJO, Juan Angel
bap 2 Mch 1815, ae 4 da; s/ Santiago ARMIJO & Juana ROMERO; gp/ Marcos TRUJILLO (only).

CHAVES, Jose Benito (Jose Fran^{co} in margin)
bap *en el mismo dia, mes y año*, ae 7 da; s/ Blas CHAVES & Dolores MARTIN; gp/ Juan Felipe MARTIN & Mª Yg^{a} BEJIL.

Frame 152
SANDOBAL, Mª Biviana
bap 3 Mch 1815, ae 5 da; d/ Ant^{o} Jose SANDOBAL & Mª BALDES; gp/ Tomas SANDOVAL & Mª CHACON.

LUCERO, Jose Julian
bap *en el mismo dia, mes y año*, ae 3 da; s/ Pablo LUCERO & Paula LARRAÑAGA; gp/ Tomas SANCHES (only).

RIO, Man^{l}
bap 5 Mch 1815, ae 4 da; s/ Ylario RIO & Fran^{ca} ROMERO; gm/ Soledad LUCERO.

GARCIA, Juan de Jesus
bap *en el mismo dia, mes y año*, ae 2 da; nat. s/ Mª Clara GARCIA; gp/ Juan Jose GARCIA & Teodora CHAVES.

BALDES, Jose Benito
bap 20 Mch 1815, ae 3 da; s/ Juan BALDES & Soledad BEJIL; gp/ Jose Domingo DURAN & Mª Ant^{a} DURAN.

TAFOYA, Jose Ant^{o}
bap 26 Mch 1815, ae 6 da; s/ Romano TAFOYA & Mª Rosalia DURAN; gp/ Bernardo DURAN & Feliciana BEJIL.

Frame 153
BASQUEZ, Mª de Jesus
bap 2 Apr 1815, ae 7 da; d/ Ant^{o} BASQUEZ & Mª Dolores PADILLA; gp/ Ant^{o} Josef ARCHULETA & Margarita MEDINA.

DURAN, Maria Dolores
bap 9 Apr, ae 4 da; d/ Juan Andres DURAN & Polonia (n.s.); gm/ Maria Ant^{a} (n.s.).

ESPINOS(A), Juan de Jesus
bap 9 Apr 1815, ae 4 da; s/ Juan Yg^{o} ESPINOS(A) & Yg^{a} GONZALES; gp/ Mig^{l} ARCHULETA & Maria TRUGILLO.

MAES, Maria Serafina
bap 24 Apr 1815, ae 5 da; d/ Paulin MAES & Ynasia BARELA; gp/ Jose Maria CORTES & Maria Madalena BRITO.

Frame 154
QUINTANA, Jose dela Cruz
bap 20 May 1815, ae 4 da; s/ Ramon QUINTANA & M^{a} dela Cruz MARTIN; gp/ Man^{l} GARCIA & Mª Trenidad QUINTANA.

CASADOS, Maria Dolores
bap 30 May 1815, ae 5 da; *espuria* d/ Mª CASADOS; gp/ Jose Ant^{o} SUAZO & Mª Josefa CASADOS.

TRUJILLO, Mª Dorotea
bap 9 Jne 1815, ae 4 da; d/ Luis TRUJILLO & Maria Getrudes SANCHEZ; gp/ Jose Benito TRUJILLO & Mª Man^{la} TRUJILLO.

LUCERO, Pedro Regalado
bap *en el mismo dia, mes y año*, ae 5 da; s/ Fran^{co} LUCERO & Mª Paula BARELA; gp/ Jose Ant^{o} GONSALEZ & Mª URIOSTE.

BEJIL, Maria de Gracia
bap 11 Jne 1815, ae 6 da; d/ Ant^{o} BEJIL & Simona MONTOYA; gp/ Bisente ESPINOSA & M^{a} dela Luz ROMERO. (Frames 154-155)

Frame 155
COCA (gp), Pedro Ygnacio
bap *en el mismo dia, mes y año*, ae 7 da; s/ nat. s/ Maria Guadalupe (n.s.), Indian; gm/ Getrudes COCA.

ROMERO, Juan de Jesus
bap 13 Jne 1815, ae 7 da; s/ Pedro ROMERO & Manuela ORTIZ; gm/ Teresa (n.s.).

BLEA, Josef
bap *en el mismo dia, mes y año*, ae 1 da; s/ Joaquin BLEA & Rosalia MEDINA; gp/ Juan MARTIN & Mª ROMERO.

(Entry without surnames)

Frame 156
MARTIN (gp), Barvara
bap 24 Jne 1815, ae 5 da; d/ Juan de Dios (n.s.) & Juana Maria (n.s.), *Yndios del pueblo*; gp/ Ant^{o} MARTIN & Barvara TRUJILLO.

LEIBA, Mig^{l} Ant^{o}
bap 29 Jne 1815, ae 5 da; s/ Bisente LEIBA & Encarnacion ESPINOSA; gp/ Juan Angel GARCIA & Man^{la} MARTIN.

RIO, Mª Soledad
bap *en el mismo dia, mes y año*, ae 7 da; d/ Juan Ant^{o} RIO & Madelena LUCERO; gm/ Biviana ROMERO *del pueblo*.

GARCIA (gp), Mª Sencion
bap *en el mismo dia, mes y año*, ae 8 da; d/ unknown; gp/ Tanislado GARCIA & Mª de Gracia (n.s.).

SANDOVAL, Manuel de Esquipulas
bap 30 Jly 1815, ae 4 da; s/ Jesus SANDOVAL & Petrona LOVATO; gp/ Bernardino MARTIN & Mª Man^{la} ARAGON. (Frames 156-157)

Frame 157
ORTIZ, Tomas
bap *en el mismo dia, mes y año*, ae 3 da; s/ Fran^{co} ORTIZ & Mª Rosa ROMERO; gm/ Ana Mª NARANGO.

MARTIN, Bisente
*bap 2 Jly 1815, ae 6 da; s/ Ant^{o} MARTIN & Guadalupe ROMERO; gm/ Mª Ant^{a} ROMERO.

MONTOYA, Maria Soledad
bap *en el mismo dia, mes y año*, ae 4 da; d/ Rafel MONTOYA & Luciana CHAVEZ; gp/ Josef Maria CHAVEZ & Maria Casimira (n.s.).

MONDRAGON, Maria Paula
bap 3 Jly 1815, ae 5 da; d/ Jose MONDRAGON & Maria CASADOS; gp/ Tomas LOVATO & Mª Meregilda CASADOS.

LAVADILLA, Juana Maria
bap 5 Jly 1815, ae 4 da; d/ Pablo LAVADILLA & Mª Rosa SISNEROS; gp/ Jose Yg^{o} BALDES & Mª Josefa BALDES. (Frames 157-158)

Frame 158
ABILA, Mariano
bap 13 Jly 1815, ae 3 da; s/ Usebio ABILA & Mª Consecion PADILLA; gp/ Santiago ABILA & Juana Ramona BEJIL.

CASADOS, Josef Miguel
bap 23 Jly *del precente*, ae 1 da; s/ Juan Ant° CASADOS & Guadalupe GARCIA; gp/ Josef Bauptista VEJIL & Rosalia MA(R)TIN.

CONCHA, Lorenso
bap 20 Aug 1815, ae 3 da; s/ Juan Domingo CONCHA & Miquela (n.s.); gp/ Fran^co^ CORDOVA & Guadalupe CORDOVA.

TRUJILLO, Mª Clara Elena
bap 21 Aug 1815, ae 2 da; d/ Juan Christoval TRUJILLO & Maria Soledad SALASAR; gp/ Josef ROMERO & Mª de la Luz TRUJILLO.

SALASAR, Rafaela
bap 15 Sep 1815, ae 5 da; d/ Ramon SALASAR & Soledad BEJIL; gp/ Ant° MARTIN (only). (Frames 158-159)

Frame 159
BORREGO, Maria de los Reilles
bap 17 Sep 1815, ae 4 da; d/ Juan Christoval BORREGO & Santos TAFOYA; gp/ Santos MARTIN & Man^la^ ROMERO.

CORTEZ, Juan Christobal (Fran^co^ Cristoval in margin)
bap 23 Sep 1815, ae 6 da; s/ Baptista CORTEZ & Maria Ant^a^ MONTOYA; gp/ Juan Christoval BEJIL & Viviana TORREZ.

LOVATO, Geronimo
bap 27 Sep 1815, ae 7 da; s/ Rafael LOVATO & Mª Asencion GOMEZ; gp/ Paula LOMA (only).

GOMES, Manuel
bap *en el mismo dia, mes y año*, ae 6 da; nat. s/ Juana GOMES; gm/ Rafaela MIRAVAL.

MARTIN, Mª Ygnacia
bap 30 Sep 1815, ae 8 da; d/ Diego MARTIN & Mª Rafaela de LUNA; gp/ Juan Pomuseno de LUNA & Mª Josefa de LUNA.

Frame 160
GARCIA (gp), Geronimo
bap 1 Oct 1815, ae 8 da; s/ Pedro (n.s.) & Sicilia (n.s.); gp/ Ramon GARCIA & Maria del Rosario APODACA.

SAMORA, Mª Ant^a^
bap 18 Oct 1815, ae 3 da; d/ Fran^co^ SAMORA & Mª Rosa DELGADO; gf/ Josef Maria M(A)ESE.

MONTOYA, Maria Dolores
bap 22 Oct 1815, ae 8 da; d/ Felipe MONTOYA & Mª Ant^a^ SANDOVAL; gp/ Pablo LUCERO & Mª Paula LARRAÑAGA.

GARCIA, Juana Getrudes
bap 29 Oct 1815, ae 4 da; d/ Pedro GARCIA & Dolores RODARTE; gp/ Juan Bap^ta^ LUJAN & Anamaria GARCIA.

SAIS, Maria Rita
CORTEZ, Maria Rita
bap 1 Nov 1815, ae 7 da; nat. d/ Jose Man^l^ SAIS & Mª Ysavel CORTEZ; gp/ Salvador PADILLA & Mª Josefa MARTIN.

Frame 161
GONSALEZ, Mª Galvina (Alvina in margin)
bap 5 Nov 1815, ae 8 da; d/ Jose Mig^{l} GONSALEZ & Ysabel BEJIL; gp/ Jose Biterbo GONSALEZ & Maria Ygnacia BEJIL.

ARCHULETA, Josef Santos
bap *en el mismo dia, mes y año*, ae 3 da; s/ Julian ARCHULETA & Mª Man^{la} BARELA; gp/ Jose Norato ARCHULETA & Maria Man^{la} ARCHULETA.

ROMERO, M^{a} dela Luz
bap 6 Nov 1815, ae 3 da; s/ Diego ROMERO & Maria COCA; gp/ Juan Ant^{o} MARTIN & Mª MARTINES (sic).

ROMERO, Juan Antonio
bap 8 Nov 1815, ae 2 da; s/ Christoval ROMERO & Paula LOMA; gf/ *el Sacristan*, (n.n.).

TAFOYA, Severino
bap 12 Nov 1815, ae 3 da; s/ Felipe TAFOYA & Maria Luisa TRUJILLO; gp/ Blas TRUJILLO & Mª Man^{la} SANCHEZ.

ROMERO, Fran^{co}
bap *en el mismo dia, mes y año*, ae 7 da; s/ Juan Domingo ROMERO & Mª Rosa (n.s.); gm/ Rosa GOMEZ. (Frames 161-162)

Frame 162
ROMERO, Manuel
bap 23 Nov 1815, ae 2 da; s/ Juan de Jesus ROMERO & Juana (n.s.); gm/ Fran^{ca} (n.s.).

ROMERO, Maria Estefana
bap 27 Nov 1815, ae 3 da; d/ Tomas ROMERO & Ysidora MARTIN; gp/ Jose Gabriel MARTIN & Ygnacia SANCHEZ.

FERNANDEZ, Maria Ysavel
bap 29 Nov 1815, ae 6 da; d/ Jesus FERNANDEZ & Rosa ROMERO; gp/ Mig^{l} MARQUEZ & Maria Getrudes MONTOYA.

TRUJILLO, Maria Soledad
bap *en el mismo dia, mes y año*, ae 3 da; d/ Andres TRUJILLO & Juaquina DURAN; gp/ Fran^{co} DURAN & Man^{la} GONSALES.

TRUJILLO, Bisente
bap *en el mismo dia, mes y año*, ae 8 da; s/ Juan TRUJILLO & Man^{la} ROMERO; gp/ Bisente GARCIA & Juliana ROMERO.

COCA, Andres
bap *en el mismo dia, mes y año*, ae 7 da; s/ Tomas COCA & Lorensa SANDOVAL; gp/ Felis URISOSTE & Maria BUTIERRES. (Frames 162-163)

Frame 163
SALASAR, Josef Fran^{co}
bap 30 Nov 1815, ae 6 da; s/ Gervacio SALASAR & Maria Rosario COCA; gp/ Ylario SANDOVAL & Mª Ant^{a} SANDOVAL.

PACHECO, Maria Soledad
bap *en el mismo dia, mes y año*, ae 3 da; d/ Ramon PACHECO & Trenidad BEJIL; gp/ Dom^{o} CHAVEZ & Matiana ROMERO.

TAFOYA, Josef Casarias (sic)
bap 1 Dec 1815, ae 5 da; s/ Ant° Josef TAFOYA & Nateresa (sic) BORREGO; gp/ Ant° Josef MARTIN & Pascuala MARTIN.

SANCHEZ, Maria Dolores
bap *en el mismo dia, mes y año*, ae 4 da; d/ Felipe SANCHEZ & Juana MARTIN; gp/ Gregorio DURAN & Rosa URIOSTE.

TAFOYA, Mª de la Cencion
bap *en el mismo dia, mes y año*, ae 5 da; d/ Josef TAFOYA & Fran^ca^ BERNAL; gp/ Josef BEJIL & Rosalia MARTIN.

Frame 164
MONTOYA, Jesus Maria
bap 11 Dec 1815, ae 2 da; s/ Man^l^ MONTOYA & Clara TAFOYA; gp/ Josef Ygnacio SANDOVAL & Guadalupe SANTISTEVAN.

LUCERO, Maria Soledad
bap *en el mismo dia, mes y año*, ae 3 da; d/ Ant° LUCERO & Mª Antª CORTES; gp/ Josef Maria CHAVEZ & Maria Casimira CHAVEZ.

Año de 1816

SANCHEZ, Pedro Ant°
bap 9 Jan 1816, ae 8 da; s/ Felipe SANCHEZ & Maria BUTIERREZ; gp/ Juan GONSALEZ & Juana MESTAS.

ROMERO, Juan Domingo
bap *en el mismo dia, mes y año*, ae 3 da; s/ Ant° Domingo ROMERO & Josefa QUINTANA; gp/ Blas CHAVEZ & Maria BARELA.

ARCHULETA, Julian
bap 12 Jan 1816, ae 3 da; s/ Marcos ARCHULETA & Maria SANCHEZ; gp/ Juan GONSALES & Josefa MESTAS.

ORTIZ (gp), Manuela
bap 14 Jan 1816, ae 7 da; d/ Juan Felipe (n.s.) & Quiteria (n.s.); gm/ Anamaria ORTIZ.

Frame 165
SANDOVAL, Jose Guadalupe
bap 23 Jan 1816, ae 3 da; s/ Gervacio SANDOVAL & (mother not given); gp/ Salvador QUINTANA & Maria Soledad LUCERO.

TAFOYA, Maria Soledad
bap 24 Jan 1816, ae 4 da; d/ Jesus TAFOYA & Lorensa QUINTANA; gp/ Ysidro FRESQUIZ & Rosa MARTIN.

TAFOYA, Josef Pablo
bap 25 Jan 1816, ae 3 da; s/ Salvador TAFOYA & Josefa TRUJILLO; gp/ Pedro HERRERA & Anaventura DURAN.

GARCIA (gp), Catalina
bap *en el mismo dia, mes y año*, ae 1 da; d/ Josef (n.s.) & Josefa (n.s.); gp/ Simon GARCIA & Biviana MARTIN.

DURAN, Josef Julian
bap 28 Jan 1816, ae 5 da; s/ Pablo DURAN & Maria BALDEZ; gp/ Ygnacio BEJIL & Paula QUINTANA.

SILVA, Jose Pablo
bap 31 Jan 1816, ae 3 da; s/ Fran^{co} (n.s.) & Mª SILVA; gp/ Juan Man^{l} CHAVEZ & Mª SANCHEZ.

Frame 166
(Entry without surnames)

ROMERO, Josef Tomas
bap *en el mismo dia, mes y año*, ae 6 da; s/ Juan de Jesus ROMERO & Candelaria QUINTANA; gp/ Ygnacio BEJIL & Paula QUINTANA.

BARELA, Maria Paula
bap 4 Feb 1816, ae 3 da; d/ Josef BARELA & Dolores SANDOVAL; gp/ Man^{l} Estevan PACHECO & Maria Viviana PACHECO.

MEDINA, Maria Guadalupe
bap *en el mismo dia, mes y año*, ae 6 da; d/ Ysidro MEDINA & Maria CORDOVA; gp/ Juan Rafael MONDRAGON & Maria BEJIL.

GOMEZ, Juan Manuel
bap 10 Feb 1816, ae 1 da; s/ Ant^{o} GOMEZ & Manuela ROMERO; gp/ Juan Christoval BEJIL & Biviana TORREZ.

(Entry without surnames)

Frame 167
PAIS, Mª Paula
bap 15 Feb 1816, ae 6 da; d/ Juan Ant^{o} PAIS & Juana MESTAS; gp/ Jose ARCHULETA & Man^{la} ARCHULETA.

ESPINOSA, Juana Maria
bap *en el mismo dia, mes y año*, ae 2 da; d/ Felipe ESPINOSA & Candelaria de HERRERA; gp/ Ant^{o} Mariano de la CRUZ & Dolores BEJIL.

BEJIL, Maria del Refugio
bap 16 Feb 1816, ae 6 da; d/ Matias BEJIL & Man^{la} SALASAR; gp/ Faustin BEJIL & M^{a} dela Luz MARTIN.

BRITO, Maria Candelaria
bap 20 Feb 1816, ae 3 da; d/ Miquela BRITO; gf/ *el sacristan*, (n.n.).

GONZALES, Maria Josefa
bap 3 Mch 1816, ae 4 da; d/ Josef GONZALES & Dorotea BACA; gp/ Ant^{o} GOMEZ & Manuela ROMERO.

Frame 168
SILVA, Josef Rafael
bap *en el mismo dia, mes y año*, ae 3 da; s/ Jose Maria SILVA & Mª Ant^{a} MONTOYA; gp/ Ysidro MEDINA & Maria CORDOVA.

ROMERO, Jose Antonio
bap 8 Mch 1816, ae 4 da; s/ Man^{l} ROMERO & Mª DURAN; gp/ (n.n.) MAESE & Maria SANDOVAL.

CORTEZ, Maria Juliana
bap 15 Mch 1816, ae 6 da; d/ Cruz CORTEZ & Juana PADILLA; gp/ Josef Ant^{o} PACHECO & Maria Dolores JAQUEN.

AGUILAR, Josef Ramon
bap *en el mismo dia, mes y año*, ae 4 da; s/ Salvador AG(U)ILAR & Mª Ant^{a} BALDEZ; gp/ Jose Pablo ARCHULETA & Mª Barvara LOVATO.

(Entry without surnames)

ROMERO, Mª Paula
bap *en el mismo dia, mes y año*, ae 4 da; d/ Juan Jose ROMERO & Juana (n.s.); gm/ Maria (n.s.).

Frame 169
CHAVEZ, Maria Serafina
bap 20 Mch 1816; d/ Julian CHAVEZ & Man^{la} CORTES; gp/ Juan LOVATO & Maria Madalena LOVATO.

MARTIN, Maria Dolores
bap *en el mismo dia, mes y año*, ae 4 da; d/ Ygnacio MARTIN & Maria Encarnacion BLEA; gp/ Salvador QUINTANA & Maria Soledad LUCERO.

TRUJILLO, Josef
bap 23 Mch 1816, ae 1 da; s/ Ant^{o} TRUJILLO & Manuela COCA; gp/ Pedro M(A)ESE & Rosalia SANDOVAL.

ALCON, Juan Domingo
bap *en el mismo dia, mes y año*, ae 4 da; s/ Juan Ant^{o} ALCON & Catarina BALLEJOS; gp/ Rafael ABILA & Mª Josefa DURAN.

BALDES, Pedro
bap 25 Mch 1816, ae 3 da; s/ Juan BALDES & Mª Soledad BEJIL; gp/ Fran^{co} PACHECO & Dolores BARELA.

PACHECO, Juana Maria
bap *en el mismo dia, mes y año*, ae 6 da; d/ Juan Pablo PACHECO & Man^{la} SAMORA; gp/ Juan LOVATO (only).

Frame 170
DURAN, Ana Maria
bap 26 Mch 1816, ae 5 da; d/ Ant^{o} DURAN & Rita LUCERO; gp/ Mariano FERNANDEZ & Cencion LUCERO.

GARCIA, Mª Rosa
bap *en el mismo dia, mes y año*, ae 6 da; d/ Juan GARCIA & Teodora CHAVEZ; gp/ Julian GARCIA & Mª ROMERO.

BALDONADO, Josef Benito
GARCIA, Josef Benito
bap 28 Mch 1816, ae 3 da; s/ Jose Man^{l} BALDONADO, single, & Clara GARCIA; gp/ Julian GARCIA & Mª ROMERO.

BEJIL, Juan Maria
bap *en el mismo dia, mes y año*, ae 2 da; s/ Amador BEJIL & Ygnacia QUINTANA; gp/ Carpio SALASAR & Lucia BEJIL.

CHAVEZ, Mª Ygnacia
bap *en el mismo dia, mes y año*, ae 3 da; d/ Juan CHAVEZ & Maria MONTOYA; gp/ Domingo DURAN & Getrudes DURAN.

BENABIDES, Jose Gregorio
bap 30 Mch 1816, ae 4 da; s/ Ant^{o} BENABIDES & Ant^{a} RIVERA; gp/ Rafeel RIVERA & Maria MONTOYA.

Frame 171
TAFOYA, Rafael
bap *en el mismo dia, mes y año*, ae 6 da; s/ Bartolo TAFOYA & Ant^{a} GONSALES; gp/ Ant^{o} Ramon MEDINA & Juana Teresa ESPINOSA.

LEAL, Josefa Alvina
bap *en el mismo dia, mes y año*, ae 7 da; d/ Rafael LEAL & Teresa BEJIL; gp/ Josef Man^{l} MESTAS (only).

MARTIN, Maria Encarnacion
bap 1 Apr 1816, ae 7 da; d/ Juan Maria MARTIN & Paula MARTIN; gp/ Juan del Carmen ROMERO & Maria Rosa MARTIN.

SANCHEZ, Ant^{o} Josef
bap 13 Apr 1816, ae 1 da; s/ Tomas SANCHEZ & Mª Rita LUCERO; gp/ Josef ROMERO & Mª de la Luz TRUJILLO.

MARTIN, Josef Dolores
bap 7 Apr 1816, ae 9 da; s/ Juan Felipe MARTIN & Manuela COCA; gp/ Josef Maria CORTEZ & Madalena BRITO.

MARTIN, Juan Ysidro
bap *en el mismo dia, mes y año*, ae 4 da; s/ Bentura MARTIN & Mª Rafela (sic) M(A)ESE; gp/ Rimundo CORDOVA & Mª Estefana GONSALES. (Frames 171-172)

Frame 172
ARCHULETA, Jose Dolores
bap *en el mismo dia, mes y año*, ae 5 da; s/ Clemente ARCHULETA & Paula ARMIJO; gp/ Agustin ROMERO & Mª Ylaria FERNANDEZ.

ARGUELLO, Mª Dolores
bap *en el mismo dia, mes y año*, ae 4 da; d/ Juan ARGUELLO & Clara SANDOVAL; gp/ Ant^{o} Aban TRUJILLO & Mª Man^{la} BUENO.

ROMERO, Josef
bap *en el mismo dia, mes y año*, ae 4 da; s/ Josef Ant^{o} ROMERO & Encarnacion CONCHA; gp/ Ju^{n} (n.s.) & Mª Ant^{a} (n.s.).

BEJIL, Mª Dolores
bap 8 Apr 1816, ae 4 da; d/ Fran^{co} BEJIL & Trinidad SALASAR; gp/ Fran^{co} BEJIL & Juan(a) Mª BEJIL.

AREYANO, Jose Ygnacio
bap *en el mismo dia, mes y año*, ae 3 da; s/ Ramon AREYANO & Anamaria ARMENTA; gp/ Ant^{o} ARMENTA & Ysavel SANCHEZ.

Frame 173
LALANDA, Mª Dolores
bap 9 Apr 1816, ae 3 da; d/ Bap^{ta} LALANDA & Polonia LUCERO; gp/ Josef Rafel (sic) LUCERO & Maria SANDOVAL.

ORTA, Juan Manuel
bap *en el mismo dia, mes y año*, ae 5 da; s/ Nicolas ORTA & Fran^{ca} MASCAREÑAS; gp/ Rafael CHAVEZ & Maria Ant^{a} MARTIN.

MARQUEZ, Aufemio (sic) Benito
bap *en el mismo dia, mes y año*, ae 3 da; s/ Mig^{l} MARQUEZ & Getrudes MONTOYA; gp/ Ant^{o} ARCHULETA & Felipa RAMIREZ.

RECILBA, Juan Bap^{ta}
bap 10 Apr 1816, ae 7 da; s/ Julian RECILBA & Rafaela ROMERO; gp/ Pablo SANCHEZ & Getrudes MARTIN.

MARTIN, Juana Mequela
bap *en el mismo dia, mes y año*, ae 2 da; d/ Felipe MARTIN & Miquela ROMERO; gp/ Juan del Carmen ROMERO & Mª Rosa MARTIN.

BEJIL, Mª de Jesus
bap *en el mismo dia, mes y año*, ae 3 da; d/ Pedro BEJIL & Josefa QUINTANA; gp/ Juan Christoval BEJIL & Biviana TORREZ. (Frames 173-174)

Frame 174
CRUZ, Jose Manuel
bap 12 Apr 1816, ae 4 da; s/ Fran^{co} CRUZ & Josefa MEDINA; gp/ Carpio SALASAR & Luisa BEJIL.

MARTIN, Josef Miguel
bap *en el mismo dia, mes y año*, ae 4 da; s/ Christoval MARTIN & Th(e)odora FRESQUIZ; gp/ Juan Nepumuseno CHAVEZ & Clara SANCHEZ.

ROMERO, Man^{l} de Jesus
bap 15 Apr 1816, ae 6 da; s/ Josef Maria ROMERO & Rafaela PINEDA; gp/ Juan Domingo FERNANDEZ & Dolores FERNANDEZ.

BUENO, Josef Benito
bap *en el mismo dia, mes y año*, ae 3 da; s/ Mateo BUENO & Josefa BEJIL; gp/ Acnador (sic) BEJIL & Ygnacia QUINTANA.

MONDRAGON, Mª Marta
bap *en el mismo dia, mes y año*, ae 6 da; d/ Christoval MONDRAGON & Mª Luisa ROMERO; gp/ Ant^{o} de la CRUZ & Dolores BIJIL.

Frame 175
BEJIL, Ant^{o} Josef
bap 18 Apr 1816, ae 3 da; s/ Juan Cristov^{l} BEJIL & Biviana TORAS; gp/ Faustin BEJIL & Mª de la Luz MARTIN.

SALASAR, Mª Serafina
bap 1 Aug 1816, ae 6 da; d/ Diego SALASAR & Mª SANDOVAL; gp/ Lonicio LARAÑAGA & Man^{la} DURAN.

LUJAN, Juan
bap 15 Aug 1816, ae 5 da; s/ Jose Ant^{o} LUJAN & Juana LOMA; gp/ Mª Teresa MIRAVAL & Juan Andres ROMERO.

PAIS, Mª Soledad
bap *en el mismo dia, mes y ano*, ae 5 da; d/ Mateo PAIS & Man^{la} BALDEZ; gp/ Yg^{o} MARTIN & Soledad JARAMILLO.

ROMERO, Fran^{ca}
bap *en el mismo dia, mes y ano*, ae 3 da; d/ Rafael ROM^{O} & Mª Mequela (sic) PADILLA; gp/ Maria Teresa GONSALES (only). (Frames 175-176)

Frame 176

ROMERO, M^a Yg^a
bap 20 Aug 1816, ae 4 da; d/ Felipe ROMERO & Mª TRUJILLO; gp/ Tomas SANCHEZ & Mª Rita LUCERO.

DURAN, Maria Dolores
bap *en el mismo dia, mes y ano*, ae 6 da; d/ Juan Fran^{co} DURAN & Rita BARGAS; gp/ Ant^o BUENO & Rosalia BALDES.

BEJIL, Maria del Refugio
bap *en el mismo dia, mes y ano*, ae 6 da; d/ Juan de Jesus BEJIL & Luisa SALASAR; gp/ Ramon SALASAR & Soledad BEJIL.

ARCHULETA, Jose Domingo
bap 30 Aug 1816, ae 4 da; s/ Ant^o ARCHULETA & Mª LEAL; gp/ Jacinto SILVA & Mª GUTIERRES.

ABILA, Lorenso
bap *en el mismo dia, mes y ano*, ae 6 da; s/ Rafael ABILA & Mª Josefa DURAN; gp/ Julian CHAVEZ & Man^{la} CORTES.

Frame 177

LUCERO, Josef Bartolome
bap 1 Sep 1816, ae 5 da; s/ Juan Ant^o LUCERO & Barvara CORDOVA; gp/ Feliz URIOSTE & Maria Polonia GUTIERRES.

MARTIN, Jose Ant^o
bap *en el mismo dia, mes y ano*, ae 2 da; s/ Jose Ant^o MARTIN & Gabriela BIJIL; gp/ Juan Ysidro FRESQUIZ & Rosa MARTIN.

GALLEGO, Luis de Alta Gracia
bap *en el mismo dia, mes y ano*, ae 1 da; s/ Pablo GALLEGO & Dolores MARTIN; gp/ Josef Pablo SANCHEZ & Getrudes MARTIN.

PAIS, Juan Bap^{ta}
CRUZ, Juan Bap^{ta}
bap 2 Sep 1816, ae 3 da; nat. s/ Juan Ant^o PAIS & Dolores CRUZ; gp/ Juan CHAVEZ & Clara SANCHEZ.

SUASO, Mª Lucia
bap 15 Dec 1816, ae 6 da; d/ Juan Ant^o SUASO & Mª CONCHA; gp/ Luis DELGADO & Bitoria DELGADO.

SANDOVAL, Juana Getrudes
bap *en el mismo dia, mes y ano*, ae 3 da; d/ Ygnacio SANDOVAL & Mª Guadalupe SANTISTEVAN; gm/ Maria SANCHEZ.

Frame 178

Año de 1817

GONSALEZ, Juan Manuel
bap 5 Jan 1817, ae 3 da; s/ Josef Ant^o GONSALEZ & Maria Ant^a ARAGON; gp/ Bernardo LUCERO & Tomasa MARTIN.

CASSILLAS, Josef Benito
bap 13 Jan 1817, ae 4 da; s/ Fernando CASSILLAS & Encarnacion LUJAN; gp/ Sevastian JARAMILLO & Soledad JARAMILLO.

SANDOVAL, Josef Maria
bap 18 Jan 1817, ae 2 da; s/ Felipe SANDOVAL & Polonia M(A)ESE; gp/ Tomas SANCHEZ & Maria Rita LUCERO.

GARCIA, Josef Candelaria
bap 2 Feb 1817, ae 4 da; s/ Bisente GARCIA & Juliana ROMERO; gp/ Mig^{l} GARCIA & Margarita LUCERO. ,

LUJAN, Maria Paula
bap *en el mismo dia, mes y año*, ae 7 da; d/ Juan Ant^{o} LUJAN & Barvara (n.s.); gm/ Maria Rosa ROMERO.

Frame 179
MARTIN, Maria de la Luz
bap 25 Feb 1817, ae 3 da; d/ Felipe MARTIN & Maria Gregoria SANCHEZ; gp/ Bentura BALDEZ & Paula BALDEZ.

GAVALDON, Maria Ysidora delos Dolores
bap 9 Mch 1817, ae 3 da; d/ Josef Man^{l} GAVALDON & Sicina (sic) MARTIN; gp/ Mariano JARAMILLO & Josefa LOVATO.

CORTES, Maria de la Luz
bap *en el mismo dia, mes y año*, ae 6 da; d/ Paulin CORTES & Consecion MARTIN; gp/ Juan Pablo de HERRERA & Ana Bentura DURAN.

PAIS, Juana Maria
bap 9 Apr 1817, ae 7 da; d/ Miguel PAIS & Soledad MAES; gp/ Man^{l} MARQUEZ & Man^{la} LUCERO.

TAFOYA, Jose Dolores
bap 10 Apr 1817, ae 6 da; s/ Ramon TAFOYA & Rosalia DURAN; gp/ Josef Fran^{co} BARELA & Dolores SANDOVAL.

Frame 180
BEJIL, Estefana
bap *en el mismo dia, mes y año*, ae 6 da; d/ Fran^{co} BEJIL & (n.n.) URTADA; gp/ Man^{l} FERNANDES & Maria Man^{la} FERNANDES.

GARCIA, Josef Benito
bap 28 Apr 1817, ae 3 da; s/ Juan Ant^{o} GARCIA & Dolores GAVALDON; gp/ Ant^{o} Josef SUAZO & Mª SUAZO.

BEJIL, Ant^{a} Teresa
bap 1 May 1817, ae 2 da; d/ Juan de Jesus BEJIL & Mª Rosa DURAN; gp/ Ramon PACHECO & Trenidad BEJIL.

DURAN, Maria Estipula
bap 4 May 1817, ae 7 da; d/ Juan Gabriel DURAN & Tomasa GARCIA; gp/ Josef Ant^{o} MARTIN & Barvara TRUJILLO.

BEJIL, Maria de la Luz
bap 8 May 1817, ae 2 da; d/ Rafael BEJIL & Elena LOVATO; gp/ Ant^{o} GOMES & Mª Rosa MARTIN.

Frame 181
SALASAR, Maria dela Luz
bap *en el mismo dia, mes y año*, ae 2 da; d/ Carpio SALASAR & Maria Luisa BEJIL; gp/ Salvador BEJIL & Maria BACA.

MONTOYA, Maria Manuela
bap 6 Jne 1817, ae 3 da; d/ Jose Ramon MONTOYA & Maria Lorenza CRUZ; gp/ Juan Yg^{o} ESPINOSA & Ant^{a} Yg^{a} GONZ^{S}.

MADRID, Juana Dominga
bap 8 Aug 1817, ae 5 da; d/ Pedro MADRID & Maria de la Luz MOYA; gp/ Juan LALANDA & Polonia LUCERO.

CASILLAS, Maria Eleuteri(a)
bap 24 Aug 1817, ae 6 da; d/ Christobal CASILLAS & Maria TAFOYA; gp/ Gregorio DURAN & Rosa URIOSTE.

SALASAR, Maria Dolores
bap *en el mismo dia, mes y año*, ae 3 da; d/ Mariano SALASAR & Fran^{ca} BENABIDES; gp/ Pablo BENABIDES & Maria SALASAR.

Frame 182
MONTOYA, Maria Dolores
bap *en el mismo dia, mes y año*, ae 6 da; d/ Rafael MONTOYA & Luciana CHAVEZ; gp/ J^{n} de Jesus (n.s.) & Salome ARCHULETA.

SANDOVAL, Juan Agustin
bap 27 Aug 1817, ae 2 da; s/ Pablo SANDOVAL & Maria COCA; gp/ Juan LOVATO & Ant^{a} LOVATO.

MEDINA, Josef Buenabentura
bap *en el mismo dia, mes y año*, ae 2 da; s/ Ysidro MEDINA & Maria CORDOVA; gp/ Felipe MARTIN & Mequela ROMERO.

ROMERO, Maria Fran^{ca}
bap *en el mismo dia, mes y año*, ae 3 da; d/ Juan de Jesus ROMERO & Candelaria QUINTANA; gp/ Manuel LUCERO & Andrella LAVADILLA.

MONDRAGON, Pedro Ant^{o}
bap 7 Sep 1817, ae 3 da; s/ Juan MONDRAGON & Fran^{ca} BEJIL; gp/ Rafael LEAL & Teresa BEJIL.

Frame 183
PADILLA, Maria Estefana
bap *en el mismo dia, mes y año*, ae 5 da; d/ Man^{l} PADILLA & Maria Ysavel SISNEROS; gp/ Josef Rafael ROM^{O} & Anamaria ORTIZ.

QUINTANA, Juana Maria
bap 8 Sep 1817, ae 5 da; d/ Salvador QUINTANA & Soledad LUCERO; gp/ Juan de Jesus AG(U)ILAR & Paula MARTIN.

ESPINOSA, Man^{l} Ant^{o}
bap *en el mismo dia, mes y año*, ae 5 da; s/ Juan de Jesus ESPINOSA & Maria MONTOYA; gp/ Bernardo MONTOYA & Mª MARTIN.

ROMERO, Ant^{a} Nicolasa
bap 17 Sep 1817, ae 7 da; d/ Jesus ROMERO & Ana Teresa BEJIL; gp/ Tomas DURAN & Ant^{a} BEJIL.

MARTIN, Juan de Jesus
bap 23 Sep 1817, ae 3 da; s/ Jesus MARTIN & Maria CHAVEZ; gp/ J^{n} de Jesus BEJIL & Lucia SALASAR.

Frame 184

BARELA, M^{a} dela Luz
bap 23 Sep 1817, ae 7 da; d/ Mig^{l} BARELA & Juana BARBERO (blot); gp/ Julian CHAVEZ & Man^{la} CORTEZ.

MEZ, Maria de Jesus
bap *en el mismo dia, mes y año*, ae 4 da; d/ Paulin MEZ & Maria GARCIA; gp/ Juan Ang^{l} GARCIA & Maria MARTIN.

NARANJO, Geronimo — Indian
bap 28 Sep 1817, ae 7 da; s/ Santiago NARANJO & Paula TUSA "who was the mother and *madrina* and deceived me (the priest), not by malice but through ignorance."

MEDINA, Maria Ygnacia
bap *en el mismo dia, mes y año*, ae 7 da; d/ Gregorio MEDINA & Maria Ysavel ROMERO; gp/ Pedro LUCERO & Mª FERNANDEZ.

Frame 185

BUENO, Mª Santana
bap 30 Sep 1817, ae 2 da; d/ Mateo BUENO & Josefa BEJIL; gp/ Agustin MARTIN & Candelaria CHAVEZ.

SANDOVAL, Josef Bisente
bap 5 Oct 1817, ae 6 da; s/ Fran^{co} SANDOVAL & Mª de Jesus (n.s.); gp/ Diego Ant^{o} MARTIN & Maria Rafaela de LUNA.

CORTEZ, Miguel
bap *en el mismo dia, mes y año*, ae 4 da; s/ Josef Maria CORTEZ & Maria BRITO; gp/ Mariano JARAMILLO & Josefa LOVATO.

CHAVEZ, Pedro
bap 17 Oct 1817, ae 3 da; s/ Juan Agustin CHAVEZ & Mª MEDINA; gp/ Josef Pablo MARTIN & Mª Josefa QUINTANA.

SALASAR, Polito
bap 18 Oct 1817, ae 4 da; s/ Pedro SALASAR & Mª HERRERA; gp/ Tomas ROMERO & Mª Ysidora MARTIN.

Frame 186

BARELA, Pedro Ant^{o}
bap 19 Oct 1817, ae 7 da; s/ Josef BARELA & Dolores SANDOVAL; gp/ Mig^{l} PAIZ & Soledad MEZ.

TRUJILLO, Maria Ygnacia
bap *en el mismo dia, mes y año*, ae 6 da; d/ Juan Mig^{l} TRUJILLO & Anamaria LUCERO; gp/ Josef Maria LUCERO & Mª Ygnacia ARCHULETA.

CHAVES, Fran^{ca}
bap *en el mismo dia, mes y año*, ae 4 da; d/ Juan Man^{l} CHAVES & Consecion ORTEGA; gp/ Bernardino MARTIN & Mª Man^{la} ARAGON.

SANDOVAL, Josef Rafael
bap 22 Oct 1817, ae 5 da; s/ Ramon SANDOVAL & Maria Ant^{a} TRUJILLO; gp/ Tomas LOVATO & Esmeregilda CASADOS.

MARTIN, Mª Petra
bap *en el mismo dia, mes y año*, ae 4 da; d/ Felipe MARTIN & Maria Mequela ROMERO; gp/ Bernardo MEZ & Mª Ygnes ARMIJO. (Frames 186-187)

Frame 187

FRESQUIS, Maria de Esquipulas
bap 24 Oct 1817, ae 2 da; d/ Juan FRESQUIS & Man^{la} DURAN; gp/ Ant^{o} GOMEZ & Rosa MARTIN.

LUCERO, Josef Fran^{co}
bap 5 Nov 1817, ae 4 da; s/ Man^{l} LUCERO & Andrea LAVADILLA; gp/ Juan Ant^{o} DURAN & Mª Rita LUCERO.

BEJIL, Maria Candelaria
*bap 4 Nov 1817, ae 3 da; d/ Juan BEJIL & Maria Josefa LOVATO; gp/ Jose de Jesus TAFOYA & Ygnacia QUINTANA.

LUCERO, Juan de Jesus
bap 10 Nov 1817, ae 3 da; s/ Pedro LUCERO & Maria FERNANDEZ; gp/ Ant^{o} TORRES & Maria FERNANDEZ.

Frame 188

AGUILAR, Maria Manuela
bap *en el mismo dia, mes y año*, ae 2 da; d/ Juan de Jesus AGUILAR & Juana Paula MARTIN; gp/ Josef Man^{l} MARTIN & Pascuala AGUILAR.

ARCHULETA, Maria Rosalia
bap *en el mismo dia, mes y año*, ae 5 da; d/ Juan ARCHULETA & Maria Getrudes MASCAREÑAS; gp/ Juan Ant^{o} SALASAR & Maria Rosa ARCHULETA.

GONSALES, Mª Teodora
bap 12 Nov 1817, ae 7 da; d/ Biterbo GONSALES & Pascuala SALASAR; gp/ Julian GARCIA & Josefa TRUJILLO.

ERRERA, Josef Benito
bap 16 Nov 1817, ae 8 da; s/ Nicolas de ERRERA & Fran^{ca} MASCAREÑAS; gf/ Josef Ramon GARCIA.

LUCERO, Maria Getrudes
bap *en el mismo dia, mes y año*, ae 4 da; d/ Ant^{o} Josef LUCERO & Mª Dolores BALDES; gp/ Juan de Dios ARMENTA & Maria del Carmen BALDES.

MARTIN, Diego Ant^{o}
bap 19 Nov 1817, ae 7 da; s/ Pedro MARTIN & Maria Man^{la} GONSALES; gp/ Juan Ant^{o} GONSALES & Maria GONSALES.

Frame 189

MARTIN (gp), Maria Dolores
bap 20 Nov 1817, ae 5 da; d/ unknown; gp/ Fran^{co} MARTIN & Josefa LEAL.

MARTIN, Josef Ant^{o}
bap 23 Nov 1817, ae 3 da; s/ Fran^{co} MARTIN & Maria SILVA; gp/ Miguel Ant^{o} SILVA & Maria SILVA.

SILVA, Jesus Maria
bap *en el mismo dia, mes y año*, ae 4 da; s/ Domingo SILVA & Maria MEDINA; gp/ Donicio BRITO & Maria CORTEZ.

BUENO, Josef Ant^{o}
bap 2 Dec 1817, ae 4 da; s/ Mateo BUENO & Josefa GONSALES; gp/ Juan Ygnacio ESPINOSA & Maria Ant^{a} GONSALES.

BALDES, Maria Dolores
bap *en el mismo dia, mes y año*, ae 4 da; d/ Juan BALDES & Maria Soledad BEJIL; gp/ Ant^{o} GALLEGO & Maria BEJIL.

CORTEZ, Andres
bap 3 Dec 1817, ae 2 da; s/ Josef Mig^{l} CORTEZ & Lugarda PADILLA; gp/ Tomas ARCHULETA (only).

Frame 190
MARTIN, Fran^{co} Ant^{o}
bap 7 Dec 1817, ae 4 da; s/ Ant^{o} MARTIN & Catalina SANDOVAL; gp/ Ant^{o} M^{a} M(A)ESE & M^{a} del Rosario MEDINA.

ROMERO, Ant^{o} Aban (Ant^{o} Abran in margin)
bap 7 Dec 1817, ae 3 da; s/ Tomas ROMERO & Ysidora MARTIN; gp/ Man^{l} BACA & Man^{la} CASADOS.

SAMORA, Josef Bentura
bap 18 Dec 1817, ae 4 da; s/ Pedro SAMORA & Rafaela CASILLAS; gp/ Josef MEDINA & Encarnacion MONTOYA.

AGUILAR, Maria Consecion
bap *en el mismo dia, mes y año*, ae 2 da; d/ Salvador AGUILAR & Maria Ant^{a} BALDES; gp/ Sipriano ESQUIBEL & Barvara QUINTANA.

SALASAR, Josef Nicolas
bap 22 Dec 1817, ae 6 da; s/ Diego SALASAR & Maria SANDOVAL; gp/ Josef Fran^{co} TRUJILLO & Maria Dolores MADRID.

Frame 191
LOVATO, Juan Ant^{o}
bap *en el mismo dia, mes y año*, ae 4 da; s/ Madalena LOVATO & (no father given); gp/ Juan Baptista CORTES & Maria MONTOYA.

ARMIJO, Josef Guadalupe
bap 24 Dec 1817, ae 6 da; s/ Santiago ARMIJO & Mª Rita SANCHEZ; gp/ Josef de Jesus (n.s.) & (A)namaria ROMERO.

ROMERO, Josef Guadalupe
bap *en el mismo dia, mes y año*, ae 2 da; s/ Juan Pedro ROMERO & Candelaria TRUJILLO; gp/ Josef Fran^{co} SANDOVAL & Tiodora ROMERO.

LUJAN, Juan Domingo Indian
bap *en el mismo dia, mes y año*, ae 8 da; s/ Man^{l} LUJAN & Fran^{ca} PRINSESA; gp/ Anamaria MUÑIS *del pueblo* (only).

LUJAN, Mª de Jesus
bap 25 Dec 1817, ae 3 da; d/ Josef LUJAN & M^{a} del Carmen (n.s.); gp/ Gervacio SALASAR & Mª SALASAR.

ARCHULETA, Mª Mequela
bap *en el mismo dia, mes y año*, ae 5 da; d/ Ant^{o} ARCHULETA & Mª AROLLOS; gp/ Mariano JARAMILLO & Josefa LOVATO. (Frames 191-192)

Frame 192
MONDRAGON, Lasaro Ant^{o}
bap 26 Dec 1817, ae 7 da; s/ Juan Josef MONDRAGON & Maria Antonia MONTOYA; gp/ Carpio CORDOVA & Mª Mequela GONSALES.

BALDES, Josef Alvino
bap *en el mismo dia, mes y año*, ae 7 da; s/ Felipe BALDES & Madalena GONSALEZ; gp/ Josef Maria LUCERO & M[a] Man[la] SANDOVAL.

LUCERO, Ant[o] Josef
bap 28 Dec 1817, ae 4 da; s/ Juan Josef LUCERO & Maria CHAVEZ; gp/ Jesus LUCERO & Rosalia BERNAL.

BEJIL, Josef Rafael
bap 29 Dec 1817, ae 3 da; s/ Ramon BEJIL & M[a] Barvara MARTIN; gp/ Fran[co] MARTIN & Maria SANCHEZ.

Año de 1818

ARELLANO, M[a] Dolores *V.*
bap 1 Jan 1818, ae 3 da; d/ Ricardo ARELLANO & Juliana BALERIO; gp/ Ant[o] Liaz (sic) ARMENTA & Ysavel SANCHEZ.

Frame 193
SOLANO, Juan Ygnacio *V.*
bap 4 Jan 1818, ae 3 da; s/ Jose SOLANO & Maria BARELA; gp/ Nerio DURAN & Ygnacia DURAN.

CRUZ, Maria Manuela *V.Q.*
bap *en el mismo dia, mes y año*, ae 4 da; d/ Josef CRUZ & Carmen ROMERO; gp/ Bisente GARCIA & Juliana ROMERO.

MARTIN, Juan Martin *V.Q.*
bap 6 Jan 1818, ae 1 da; s/ Diego MARTIN & Rafaela LUNA; gp/ Jose MIERA & Man[la] ROMERO.

SALASAR, Juan delos Relles *V.*
bap 7 Jan 1818, ae 3 da; s/ Gervacio SALASAR & Rosario COCA; gp/ Juan Nicolas MARTIN & Fran[ca] SALASAR.

ROMERO, Josef Manuel *V.*
bap 11 Jan 1818, ae 7 da; s/ Juan Domingo ROMERO & Juana LOMA; gm/ Teresa RUYBAL.

LUCERO, Buena Bentura *V.*
bap *en el mismo dia, mes y año*, ae 2 da; d/ Juan de Jesus LUCERO & Ygnacia ARAGON; gp/ Man[l] BALDES & Maria Catalina LOVATO. (Frames 193-194)

Frame 194
LUCERO, Maria Dolores *V.*
bap 15 Jan 1818, ae 3 da; d/ Juan Ant[o] LUCERO & Barvara CORDOVA; gp/ Cristoval MONDRAGON & Fran[ca] CORDOVA.

ROMERO, Maria Dolores de Jesus *V.Q.*
bap *en el mismo dia, mes y año*, ae 3 da; d/ Josef ROMERO & Biviana FERNANDES; gp/ Mariano MARTIN & Maria Dolores TORRES.

SANDOVAL, Maria Candelaria *V.*
bap 20 Jan 1818, ae 7 da; d/ Jesus SANDOVAL & Petrona LOVATO; gp/ Simon SAIS & Margarita LOVATO.

MARTIN, Juan de Jesus *V[o]*
bap *en el mismo dia, mes y año*, ae 2 da; s/ Felipe MARTIN & Maria TRUJILLO; gp/ Juan Ygnacio BEJIL & Paula QUINTANA.

PACHECO, Maria Juliana *V^{o}*
bap 21 Jan 1818, ae 4 da; d/ Fran^{co} PACHECO & Dolores BARELA; gp/ Tomas COCA & Lorensa SANDOVAL.

SILVA, Maria Ant^{a} *V^{o}*
bap 25 Jan 1818, ae 3 da; d/ Josef SILVA & Maria SAIS; gp/ Pablo GALLEGO & Maria MARTIN. (Frames 194-195)

Frame 195
MARTIN, Juan de Jesus *V.*
bap *en el mismo dia, mes y año*, ae 7 da; S/ Felipe MARTIN & Maria TRUJILLO; gp/ Ygnacio BEJIL & Juana QUINTANA.

GONSALEZ, Josef Benito
bap *en el mismo dia, mes y año*, ae 6 da; S/ Salvador GONSALEZ & Anamaria BEJIL; gp/ Josef LEAL & Guadalupe LEAL.

XIATA, Josef Manuel *P.*
bap *en el mismo dia, mes y año*, ae 8 da; S/ Juan Felipe XIATA & Vitoria TECOA; gm/ Rosalia (n.s.) *del pueblo*.

ROMERO, Josef Ant^{o} *P.Q.*
bap *en el mismo dia, mes y año*, ae 4 da; s/ Juan Domingo ROMERO & Luisa TECOA; gm/ Maria Rosa ROMERO.

LOMA, Juana Mequela *P^{o}*
bap *en el mismo dia, mes y año*, ae 8 da; d/ J^{n} de Jesus LOMA & Fran^{ca} PADILLA; gm/ Miquela CASILLAS.

(Look at Frames 408 and forward for more 1818 entries, below for Aug 1823).

(Note: Frames 196 for 7 Aug 1802 to Frame 351 for 26 Mch 1826 are burials).

Frame 352
Bautismos: Por falta de papel tomé de estas ojas pertenecientes a las partidas de los muertos "Baptisms: For lack of paper (I) took these pages that belong to burial entries" Fr. Manuel BELLIDO (also signing entries)

GALLEGO, Maria Guadalupe *Fernandes*
bap 7 Aug 1823, ae 5 yr; d/ *Nacion Caygua*, adopted d/ Pablo GALLEGO & Maria Dolores MARTIN; gp/ Pedro Bautista GALLEGO & Josefa CASAUS.

MARTIN, Jose Rafael *Fernandez*
bap 31 Jly 1823; s/ Juan Julian MARTIN & Maria Guadalupe BIJIL; ap/ Jose Ygnacio MARTIN & Ascencion BARELA; am/ Pedro BIJIL & Josefa QUINTANA; gp/ Bernardo DURAN & Feliciana BIJIL.

ROMERO, Antonia del Espiritu S^{to}
bap 31 Jly 1823; d/ Policarpio ROMERO & Maria Guadalupe DURAN; ap/ Juan del Carmen ROMERO & Maria Nazarena de LUNA; gp/ Antonio Jose QUINTANA & Maria Josefa BARELA.

GONZALEZ, Juan Jose *Ranchito*
bap 24 Aug 1823; nat. s/ Josefa GONZALEZ; gp/ Pablo BORREGO & Angela BELASQUEZ.

Frame 353
CORDOBA, Jose Rafael *Nacion Yuta*

bap 18 Aug 1823, ae 3 yr; s/ *Nacion Yuta*, adopted s/ Juan Felipe CORDOBA & Maria Jesus PINO who were the gp.

LOBATO (gp), Juan Cristobal *Nacion Americana*
bap *en el mismo dia*, ae about 40 yr; s/ (unknown); gp/ Juan Antonio LOBATO & Maria Ygnacia SANCHEZ.

SANDOBAL, Salvador Antonio *S^{n} Fernando*
bap 28 Aug 1823; s/ Antonio Jose SANDOBAL & Guadalupe VIGILA MONTES; ap/ Pablo SANDOBAL & Lugarda QUINTANA: am/ Julian VIGIL & Manuela FRESQUIS; gp/ Jose Benito TAFOLLA & Manuela de la Luz TAFOLLA.

PACHECO, Juan Luis *Rancho*
bap *en el mismo dia, mes y año*, ae 4 da; s/ Ramon PACHECO & Trinidad VIGIL: ap/ Antonio Jose PACHECO & Maria de la Luz SANDOBAL: am/ Juan de la Cruz VIGIL & Maria Clara FERNANDEZ; gp/ Jose Ramon SALAZAR & Maria Soledad VIGIL.

SALAZAR, Maria Guadalupe *S^{n} Fernando*
bap 27 Aug 1823; d/ Pedro SALAZAR & Maria Ursula de HERRERA: ap/ Juan Manuel SALAZAR & Maria Josefa DURAN: am/ Vicente HERRERA & Juana MONTOYA; gp/ Juan Fran^{co} LOBATO & Maria Guadalupe ROMERO.

Frame 354
HERRERA, Juan Bautista *Ranchito de S^{n} Fran^{co}*
bap *en el mismo dia, mes y año*; s/ Tomas de HERRERA & Fran^{ca} MASCAREÑA: ap/ Juan de HERRERA & Ysabel GARCIA: am/ Bautista MASCAREÑA & Maria Luisa MARTIN; gp/ Manuel PADILLA & Maria Meregilda VIJIL.

TRUXILLO, Jose de Jesus *Las Trampas de S^{n} Fran^{co}*
bap 31 Aug 1823; s/ Juan Ygnacio TRUXILLO & Maria Guliana (sic) MONTOYA; ap/ Raymundo TRUXILLO & Paula MARTIN; am/ Jose de Jesus MONTOYA & Rosa VIJIL; gp/ Fran^{co} ABILA & Josefa VIJIL.

GARCIA, Juan *Vecino*
bap 2 Sep 1823; s/ Estanislao GARCIA & Encarnacion BLEA: ap/ Simon GARCIA & Bibiana MARTINEZ; am/ Antonio BLEA & Barbara MONTOYA; gp/ Juan del Carmen SUASO & Dolores SUASO.

TRUXILLO, Jose Vicente *Vecino*
bap 2 Sep 1823; nat. s/ Maria Getrudis TRUXILLO; gp/ Miguel MARTIN & Maria Andrea MARTIN.

MARTIN, Maria Rosa *Arroyo Ondo*
bap 10 Sep 1823; d/ Antonio MARTIN & Catalina SANDOVAL: ap/ Eusebio MARTIN & Maria Antonia ARMIJO; am/ Culasa MESTAS & *su esposo* (n.n.); gp/ Manuel Antonio MONDRAGON & Maria Rosa ARELLANO. (As written)

Frame 355
MEDINA, Mariano de Jesus *Arroyo Ondo*
bap 12 Sep 1823; s/ Jose Encarnacion MEDINA & Maria de Jesus CORDOVA: ap/ Juan Pasqual MEDINA & Juana Teresa ESPINOSA: am/ Jose Antonio CORDOVA & Juana MARTIN; gp/ Juan Miguel TAFOLLA & Manuela Rafaela MARTIN.

GOMEZ, Maria Manuela *Pueblo*
bap 14 Sep 1823, ae 4 da; d/ Fran^{co} GOMEZ & Rosalia RIO; gp/ Jose Domingo SANCHEZ & Maria Manuela GOMEZ.

QUINTANA, Jose de Jesus *Arroyo Ondo*
bap 15 Sep 1823, ae 3 da; s/ Salvador QUINTANA & Soledad LUZERO; ap/ Juan QUINTANA & Balbaneda ROMERO; am/ Jesus LUZERO & Rosalia BERNAL; gp/ Jose Antonio TRUXILLO & Maria Fran^{ca} MARTIN.

MADRID, Jose Antonio *Vecino*
bap 16 Sep 1823; s/ Jose Maria MADRID & Maria de la Cruz CORDOVA; ap/ Ygnacio MADRID & Damiana MARTINEZ; am/ Antonio Jose CORDOVA & Cacilda AGUILAR; gp/ Juan MAES & Dolores SUAZO.

MONTOYA, Maria Rita *Los Ranchitos*
bap 16 Sep 1823, ae 2 da; d/ Antonio MONTOYA & Maria Paula GONZALEZ; ap/ Juan Antonio MONTOYA & Maria Dolores de AGUERO; am/ Antonio Segundo GONZALEZ & Maria Josefa BALDES; gp/ Jose Gregorio GONZALEZ & Maria Dolores BALDES. (Frames 355-356)

Frame 356
ARCHULETA, Jose Fran^{co} *S^{n} Fernando*
bap 20 Sep 1823, ae 3 da; s/ Jesus ARCHULETA & Juana Getrudis CASAUS; ap/ Pablo ARCHULETA & Barbara LOBATO; am/ Juan Antonio CASAUS & Catarina BACA; gp/ Jose Antonio SUASO & Maria Antonia GARCIA.

VIJIL, Ypolito *Ranchito*
bap 21 Sep 1823; s/ Cristobal VIJIL & Bibiana TORRES; ap/ Miguel VIJIL & Ana Maria LUNA; am/ Antonio TORRES & Qulasa (sic) SANDOVAL; gp/ Raymundo CORDOVA & Estefana GONZALEZ.

ARELLANO, Maria Juana *Arroyo Ondo*
bap *en el mismo dia, mes y año*; d/ Ricardo ARELLANO & Juliana VALERIO; ap/ Julian ARELLANO & Maria Luz TAPIA; am/ Julian VALERIO & Marta MARTIN; gp/ Antonio MARTIN & Maria Catalina SANDOVAL.

SALAZAR, Maria de la Luz *Vecina*
bap 23 Sep 1823, ae 4 da; d/ Diego SALAZAR & Cristerna SANDOVAL; ap/ Juan Manuel SALAZAR & Maria Josefa DURAN; am/ Alonso SANDOVAL & Maria Rita ROMERO; gp/ Tomas LUZERO & Maria Polonia Guillermo LUZERO.

Frame 357
OCANER, Ysabel *Nacion Francesa*
bap 23 Sep 1823, ae 4 yr; d/ Patricio OCANER & Nénsi (sic-n.s.); gp/ Jose GONZALEZ & Maria Teodora BACA.

LUT, Catarina *De la misma Nacion*
bap *en el mismo dia, mes y año*, ae 6 mo; d/ Fran^{co} LUT & Ysabel ESCOYENS; gp/ Fran^{co} GONZALEZ & Ygnacia GONZALEZ.

DURAN, Jose Fran^{co} *S^{n} Fernando*
bap 3 Oct 1823; s/ Domingo DURAN & Soledad LOBATO; ap/ Ygnacio DURAN & Maria Antonia SANCHEZ; am/ Salbador LOBATO & Candelaria CORDOVA; gp/ Pablo DURAN & Josefa TRUXILLO.

BALLE, Geronimo *Pueblo*
bap *en el mismo dia, mes y año*; s/ Antonio Jose BALLE & Juana ROMERA; gp/ Rosalia LOMA (only).

VASQUEZ, Juan Albino *Arroyo Ondo*
bap 9 Oct 1823, ae 8 da; s/ Juan Jose VASQUEZ & Maria Pasquala CORDOVA; ap/ Jose Antonio VASQUEZ & Maria Rosa ARELLANO; am/ Pablo CORDOVA & Antonia Margarita ROMERO; gp/ Manuel MONDRAGON & Maria Rosa ARELLANO.

Frame 358

MES, Fran^{co} *Vecino*
bap 13 Oct 1823; s/ Paulin MES & Maria Ygnacia BARELA; ap/ Domingo MES & Juana de HERRERA; am/ Juan Angel BARELA & Maria Manuela MARTIN; gp/ Fran^{co} Antonio CRUZ & Maria Polonia CRUZ.

SALAZAR, Salvador Nepomuceno *S^{n} Fernando*
bap 17 Oct 1823; s/ Gervacio SALAZAR & Maria del Rosario COCA; ap/ Juan Manuel SALAZAR & Josefa DURAN; am/ Jose Maria COCA & Juana BENABIDES; gp/ Jose Miguel LARAÑAGA & Maria de la Luz TRUJILLO.

ARELLANO, Jose Bentura *Arroyo Ondo*
bap 20 Oct 1823, ae 2 da; s/ Juan Domingo ARELLANO & Maria Rosa MEDINA; ap/ Juliali̲a̲ (sic) ARELLANO & Maria de la Luz TAPIA; am/ Cristobal MEDINA & Juana CORDOVA; gp/ Manuel MONDRAGON & Maria Rosa ARELLANO.

SANDOVAL, Jose Francisco *Terrardo*
bap 26 Oct 1823; s/ Ygnacio SANDOVAL & Maria Guadalupe SANTISTEBAN; ap/ Felipe SANDOBAL & Gregoria SENA; am/ Ysidro SANTISTEBAN & Juana MARTIN; gp/ Esteban SANCHEZ & Maria de la Luz BUENA.

Frame 359

MESTAS, Juan Luis Bertran *Rancho*
bap 26 Oct 1823; nat. s/ Juana Catarina MESTAS & unknown father; am/ Bernardo MESTAS & his wife (n.n.); gp/ Juan de la Cruz CORTES & Juana Antonia PADILLA.

CRUZ, Maria Rosa *Rancho*
bap 31 Oct 1823, ae 4 da; d/ Jose de la CRUZ & Maria del Carmen ROMERO; am/ Mariano ROMERO & Fran^{ca} ARMENTA; gp/ Jose Tomas FERNANDEZ & Maria Manuela FERNANDEZ.

RIO, Juan *Pueblo*
bap 2 Nov 1823, ae 1 yr; s/ Jose Antonio RIO & Dominga ROMERO; gm/ Maria CONCHA.

ROMERO, Buenabentura *Pueblo*
bap 3 Nov 1823; d/ Juan Miguel ROMERO & Maria Guadalupe DELGADO; ap/ Jose ROMERO & Rosalia LOMA; am/ Luis DELGADO & Josefa CUILO; gp/ Juan Antonio LOBATO & Maria Ygnacia SANCHEZ.

ESPINOSA, Jose Fran^{co} Nepumuceno Florencio *Fernandes*
bap 9 Nov 1823; s/ Felipe ESPINOSA & Josefa LUNA; ap/ Juan Antonio ESPINOSA & Teodora QUINTANA; am/ Rafael LUNA & Ana Maria TAFOLLA; gm/ Petra CORTES.

Frame 360

QUINTANA, Maria Bibiana *Arroyo Ondo*
bap *en el mismo dia, mes y año*; d/ Ramon QUINTANA & Maria de la Cruz ARCHULETA; gp/ Rafael MARTIN & Guadalupe LUZERO.

MARCO, Maria Antonia *Pueblo*
bap 14 Nov 1823; d/ Fran^{co} MARCO & Fran^{ca} CONCHA; gm/ Maria Antonia GOMEZ.

LUZERO, Maria Getrudis *Rancho*
bap 16 Nov 1823; d/ Manuel LUZERO & Maria Andrea LA BATIA; ap/ Juan Bernardo LUZERO & Tomasa ROMERO; am/ D^{n} Domingo LA BATIA & his wife (n.n.); gp/ Juan Antonio LUZERO & Maria Estefana ARAGON.

BORREGO, Clemente *Rancho*
bap 22 Nov 1823; s/ Juan Cristobal BORREGO & Santos TAFOLLA; ap/ Juan BORREGO & Dolores BERNAL; am/ Qulas (sic) TAFOLLA & Maria Ygnacia ROMERO; gp/ Jose Ramon SALUZAR (sic) & Maria Soledad VIJIL.

GONZALEZ, Juan Domingo *Rancho*
bap *en el mismo dia, mes y año*; s/ Jose Angel GONZALEZ & Josefa FERNANDEZ; ap/ Jose Santos GONZALES & Maria LISTON; am/ Mariano FERNANDEZ & his wife (n.n.); gp/ (blank space).

Frame 361
GONZALES, Jose *Rancho*
bap *en el mismo dia, mes y año*; s/ Cristobal GONZALES & Simona TRUXILLO; ap/ Diego GONZALEZ (sic) & Juana MONTAÑO; am/ Juan Antonio TRUXILLO & Juana Antonia BUENO; gp/ Fran[co] MARTIN & Maria Reyes FERNANDEZ.

MONTOYA, Maria Manuela *Rancho*
bap 30 Nov 1823; d/ Antonio MONTOYA & Dolores CRUZ; ap/ Manuel MONTOYA & Serafina ARCHULETA; am/ Alexos CRUZ & Guadalupe DURAN; gp/ Don Jose GRIÑE & Maria Manuela SANCHEZ.

GONZALEZ, Maria Rosa *Rancho*
bap *en el mismo dia, mes y año*; d/ Ygnacio GONZALEZ & Maria Josefa LALANDA; gf/ Felipe GONZALEZ.

FRESQUIS, Maria Andrea *Rancho*
bap *en el mismo dia, mes y año*; d/ Antonio FRESQU(I)S & Maria Reyes SANCHEZ; ap/ Antonio FRESQUIS & Maria Ygnacia CANO; am/ Diego SANCHEZ & Macdalena (sic) VIJIL; gp/ Manuel de Jesus FERNA(N)DEZ & Maria Ascension MARTIN.

VIJIL, Maria Josefa de Jesus *Rancho*
bap *en el mismo dia, mes y año*; d/ Fran[co] VIJIL & Candelaria SANTISTEBAN; ap/ Juan Ygnacio VIJIL & Maria Antonia ARAGON; am/ Feliciano SANTISTEBAN & Rafaela ESPINOSA; gp/ Juan de Jesus LUZERO & Maria Ygnacia ARAGON.

ROMERO, Juan de la Cruz *Rancho*
bap *en el mismo dia, mes y año*; d/ Maria Jesus ROMERO; gm/ Josefa CASAUS.

Frame 362
ROMERO, Maria de la Luz *S[n] Fern[do]*
bap 30 Nov 1823; d/ Juan Domingo ROMERO & Maria Ygnacia CHABES; ap/ Manuel ROMERO & Maria BARELA; am/ Jose Maria CHABES & Maria ORTEGA; gp/ Luis LLUBIS (sic) & Maria Ynes CHABES.

MARTIN, Juana Maria *Pueblo*
bap 3 Dec 1823; d/ Juan Jose MARTIN & Juana GOMEZ; gf/ Tomas MARTIN.

LUXAN, Juan Antonio *Pueblo*
bap *en el mismo dia, mes y año*; s/ Jose Manuel LUXAN & Ygnacia MARTIN; gp/ Juan SUASO & Dolores SUASO.

(Entry with no surname, a French child)

MEDINA, Maria Manuela *Rancho*
bap 7 Dec 1823; d/ Jesus MEDINA & Josefa MARTIN; ap/ Nepumuzeno MEDINA & Candelario VIJIL; am/ Gervasio MARTIN & Juana CORTES; gp/ Luis Manuel CHABES & Maria de la Luz QUINTANA.

SANCHEZ, Jose Fran^{co} *Rancho*
bap *en el mismo dia, mes y año*; s/ Felipe SANCHEZ & Juana Maria MARTIN; ap/ Juan Ygnacio SANCHEZ & Pasquala VIJIL; am/ Fran^{co} MARTIN & Maria Rosa ARMENTA; gp/ Jose Antonio GONZALEZ & Maria Concepcion URIOSTE.

Frame 363
TALACHE, Maria Catalina *Pueblo*
bap 16 Dec 1823; nat. d/ Anamaria TALACHE; gp/ Simon GARCIA & Bibiana MARTIN.

VIJIL, Maria Guadalupe S^{n} Fernando
bap 12 Dec 1823; d/ Dionisio VIJIL & Manuela TRUXILLO; gp/ Antonio Mariano de la CRUZ & Dolores VIJIL.

CHIRINO, Jose Teodoro S^{n} Fernando
*bap 2 Nov 1823; s/ Pedro CHIRINO & Rosalia SILVA; ap/ not given; am/ Santiago SILVA & Juana BENABIDES; gp/ Juan Manuel QUINTANA & Rosalia SANDOBAL.

GUTIERRES, Maria *Rancho*
bap 21 Dec 1823; d/ Fran^{co} GUTIERRES & Candelaria MARTIN; gp/ Andres MARTIN & Maria Antonia ORTIZ.

GUERRERO, Tomas Antonio *Pueblo*
bap 23 Dec 1823; s/ Juan Domingo GUERRERO & Maria Paula ROMERO; gf/ Rafael ROMERO.

PADILLA, Maria Dolores *Pueblo*
bap 23 Dec 1823; d/ Juan de Jesus PADILLA & Fran^{ca} Carmen (n.s.); gp/ Antonio VIJIL & Maria Simona MON(TO)YA. (Frames 363-364)

Frame 364
(*Año de 1824*)

MADRIL, Juan Manuel *Ranchito*
bap 1 Jan 1824; s/ Cristobal MADRIL & Maria Manuela PADILLA; ap/ Jose Juanico MADRIL & Prudencia (n.s.); am/ Pedro PADILLA & Lucia CHABES; gp/ Jose Miguel MARTIN & Maria Dolores MARTINEZ.

LUZERO, Maria del Refugio Arroyo Ondo
bap 4 Jan 1824; d/ Jose Maria LUZERO & Maria Ygnacia ARCHULETA; ap/ Cristobal LUZERO & Juana ARAGON; am/ Jose Antonio ARCHULETA & Maria Antonia CORDOVA; gp/ Jose Fran^{co} GONZALEZ & Maria Guadalupe ZISNEROS. (No mention of twins)

LUZERO, Juan de Jesus Arroyo Ondo
*bap 3 Jan 1824; s/ Jose Maria LUZERO & Maria Ygnacia ARCHULETA; ap/ Cristobal LUZERO & Manuela SANDOVAL; am/ Jose Antonio ARCHULETA & Maria Antonia CORDOVA; gp/ Juan GONZALEZ & Maria Getrudis ARCHULETA. (No mention of twins. Entry as written).

VALENCIA, Santiago S^{n} Fernando
bap 6 Jan 1824; s/ Pedro VALENCIA & Juana ARAGON; ap/ Antonio VALENCIA & Trinidad MES; gp/ Jose Antonio VALENCIA & Maria Rosa VALENCIA.

Frame 365
MARTIN, Maria Juana de los Reyes Sta Barbara
bap 6 Jan 1824; d/ Juan Ygnacio MARTIN & Maria Manuela MONTOYA; ap/ Eusebio MARTIN & Antonia ARMIJO; am/ Manuel MONTOYA & Maria Serafina ARCHULETA; gp/ Fran^{co} Antonio CORDOVA & Maria Guadalupe CORDOVA.

BARELA, Juan de los Reyes *Rancho*
bap *en el mismo dia, mes y año*; s/ Miguel BARELA & (blank space); gp/ Juan del Carmen SANDOVAL & Maria de Jesus MASCAREÑA.

LUXAN, Baltasar de los Reyes *Pueblo*
bap 11 Jan 1824; s/ Jose Manuel LUXAN & Maria ROMERO; gm/ Maria Antonia GARCIA.

MARTIN, Tomas de los Reyes *Pueblo*
bap *en el mismo dia, mes y año*; s/ Santiago MARTIN & Josefa RIO; gm/ Micaela CASILLAS.

MARTIN, Jose Fran^{co} S^{n} Fernando
bap 12 Jan 1824; s/ Manuel MARTIN & Isabel CORTES; ap/ Salvador MARTIN & Maria Balbaneda MONTOYA; am/ Jose Maria CORTES & Rafaela ROMERO; gp/ D^{n} Pablo LUZERO & Maria Paula LARAÑAGA.

ROMERO, Jose Fran^{co} S^{n} Fernando
bap 15 Jan 1824; s/ Manuel ROMERO & Maria del Carmen DURAN; ap/ Pasqual ROMERO & Barbara MARTIN; am/ Juan Nicolas DURAN & Getrudis QUINTANA; gp/ Fran^{co} MARTIN & Maria Encarnacion MARTIN. (Frames 365-366)

Frame 366
ARAGON, Juana Antonia de los Dolores
bap 15 Jan 1824; d/ Jose Antonio ARAGON & Maria Nicolasa QUINTANA; ap/ Antonio ARAGON & Maria Fran^{ca} VIJIL; am/ Juanico QUINTANA & Felipa MES; gp/ Antonio de Jesus GALLEGO & Petra de Jesus MARTIN.

DURAN, Jose Fran^{co} S^{n} Fernando
bap 24 Jan 1824; s/ Fran^{co} DURAN & Maria Josefa MARTIN; ap/ Ygnacio DURAN & Maria Antonia SANCHEZ; am/ Jose MARTIN & Maria Rita LUZERO; gp/ Bernardo LUZERO & Soledad LUZERO.

GARCIA, Maria Juliana Arroyo Ondo
bap *en el mismo dia, mes y año*; d/ Antonio Jose GARCIA & Guadalupe LUZERO; ap/ Juan Angel GARCIA & Maria Manuela MARTIN; am/ Tomas LUZERO & Candelaria MALDONADO; gp/ Nicardo (sic) ORELLANO & Juliana VALERIA.

VERNAL, Juan Antonio Fernandes
bap *en el mismo dia, mes y año*; s/ Pedro VERNAL & Maria Getrudis SUASO; am/ Miguel SUASO & Josefa PANDO; gp/ Miguel SUASO & Dolores SUASA.

Frame 367
MES, Jose Pablo S^{n} Fernando
bap 26 Jan 1824; s/ Miguel MES & Fran^{ca} MARTIN; ap/ Domingo MES & Juana Maria de HERRERA; am/ Juan MARTIN & Juliana VALLEJOS; gp/ Jose Rafael ROMERO & Ynes CHABES.

FERNANDEZ, Maria Paula *Rancho*
bap *en el mismo dia, mes y año*; d/ Francisco FERNANDEZ & Maria Antonia DURAN; ap/ Jose Mariano FERNANDEZ & Maria Asuncion LUZERO; am/ Ygnacio DURAN & Maria Antonia SANCHEZ; gp/ Feliz URIOSTE & Maria Carmen SANCHEZ.

CHABES, Maria Rafaela *Rancho*
bap *en el mismo dia, mes y año*; d/ Blas CHABES & Maria Dolores MARTIN; ap/ Juan Nepumuceno CHABES & Maria Clara SANCHEZ; am/ Ygnacio MARTIN & Paula SALAZAR; gp/ Manuel SANCHEZ & Nicolasa SANDOVAL.

BERNAL, Juan de Jesus Arroyo Ondo
bap 10 Feb 1824; s/ Felipe BERNAL & Maria Candelaria HERRERA; ap/ Vicente ESPINOSA (as written) & Juana ROMERO; am/ D[n] Jose HERRERA & Juana MONTOYA; gp/ Pablo Fran[co] CORDOVA & Antonia Margarita ROMERO.

LALANDA, Maria Felipa S[n] Fernando
*bap 8 Feb 1824; d/ Soledad LALANDA & unknown father; gp/ Pedro VALENCIA & Juana Maria LUZERO.

Frame 368
DURAN, Jose Doroteo Arroyo Seco
bap 10 Feb 1824; s/ Jose Fran[co] DURAN & Maria Teodora BARELA; ap/ Josefa ROMERO (only); am/ Juan Ysidro BARELA & Juanita MARTIN; gp/ Felipe de Jesus MONTOYA & Maria Manuela MONTOYA.

LOBATO, Maria Candelaria S[n] Fernando
bap 11 Feb 1824; d/ Juan LOBATO & Maria Guadalupe ROMERO; ap/ Tomas LOBATO & Candelaria GONZALEZ; am/ Jose ROMERO & Maria de la Luz TRUXILLO; gp/ Jose Antonio ALARID & Maria Rosa SANDOBAL.

MADRIL, Polonio S[n] Fernando
bap *en el mismo dia, mes y año*; s/ Antonio MADRIL & Maria Fran[ca] BUENA; ap/ Juan Antonio MADRIL & Luz MOYA; am/ Juan BUENO & Teodora BEYTA; gp/ Felipe ESPINOSA & Maria Josefa LUNA.

LEAL, Antonio Jose *Rancho*
bap *en el mismo dia, mes y año*; s/ Rafael LEAL & Teresa VIJIL; ap/ Juan Domingo LEAL & Beronica CORTES; am/ Dionisio VIJIL & Manuel DELGADO; gp/ Feliz URIOSTE & Maria del Carmen SANCHEZ.

FLOREZ, Jose Benigno Arroyo Ondo
bap 13 Feb 1824; s/ Martin FLOREZ & Encarnacion FERNANDEZ; ap/ Antonio FLOREZ (only); am/ Jose Miguel FERNANDEZ (only); gp/ Jose Fran[co] de HERRERA & Maria Juana GONZALEZ.

Frame 369
OCANER, Maria Juliana de Jesus *Nacion Franzesa*
bap 13 Feb 1824; d/ Patricio OCANER & Nens<u>i</u> (n.s.); gp/ Blas TRUXILLO & Maria Manuela SANCHEZ.

TRUXILLO, Maria Polonia S[n] Fernando
bap *en el mismo dia, mes y año*; d/ Luis TRUXILLO & Maria Getrudis SANCHEZ; ap/ Pablo TRUXILLO & Maria Teresa BARELA; am/ Miguel SANCHEZ & Maria Paula LOBATO; gp/ Antonio TRUXILLO & Maria Manuela COCA.

COCA, Jose Benito S[n] Fernando
bap 17 Feb 1824; s/ Jose Reyes COCA & Manuela SALAZAR; ap/ Jose Maria COCA & Juana B<u>E</u>NABIDES; am/ Hilario SALAZAR & Josefa MARTIN; gp/ Pedro Antonio DURAN & Maria de la Lus MONTOYA.

GRIJALBA, Romaldo Nepumuceno S[n] Fernando
bap 18 Feb 1824; s/ (unknown), left at the house of those who baptized him; adopted s/ Luziano GRIJALBA & Maria Rosa CORTES who were the gp.

GOMEZ, Juan Julian Arroyo Seco
bap 19 Feb 1824; s/ Antonio GOMEZ & Maria Rosa MARTIN; gp/ Nepumuceno CORTES & Maria de la Cruz MARTIN.

Frame 370

MONTOYA, Bentura *Rancho*
bap 22 Feb 1824; d/ Ramon MONTOYA & Maria Ygnacia TRUXILLO; ap/ Jose MONTOYA & Ygnacia BALDES; am/ Santiago TRUXILLO & Polonia ROMERO; gp/ Juan de Jesus VIJIL & Luisa SALAZAR.

ARCHULETA, Jose Marzelo Arroyo Ondo
bap *en el mismo dia, mes y año*; s/ Marcos ARCHULETA & Dolores SANCHEZ; ap/ Damian ARCHULETA & Juana Micaela (n.s.); am/ Miguel SANCHEZ & Paula LOBATO; gp/ Benito GALLEGO & Maria Micaela GARCIA.

GABALDON, Juan de Jesus S[n] Fernando
bap 23 Feb 1824; nat. s/ Maria Getrudis GABALDON; gp/ Benito LEAL & Anamaria GALLEGO.

ROMERO, Maria Margarita S[n] Fernando
bap 26 Feb 1824; d/ Juan Antonio ROMERO & Maria Luciana LOBATO; ap/ Juan del Carmen ROMERO & Nazarena LUNA; am/ Juan LOBATO & Margarita CHABES; gm/ Antonia Teodora LOBATO.

MONDRAGON, Maria Dolores *Rancho*
bap 2 Mch 1824; d/ Jose MONDRAGON & Lorenza DURAN; am/ Ygnacio DURAN & Maria Antonia SANCHEZ; gp/ Jose Rafael VIJIL & Maria Manuela BUENA.

Frame 371

CORDOVA, Ramon Domingo Arroyo Ondo
bap 4 Mch 1824; s/ Manuel CORDOVA & Maria Teodora MONDRAGON; ap/ Lorenzo CORDOVA & Maria Margarita MARTINEZ; am/ Mariano MONDRAGON & Maria Encarnacion ESPINOSA; gp/ Vicente MARTIN & Maria Anastacia LUZERO.

LUZERO, Maria Dolores S[n] Fernando
bap 10 Mch 1824; d/ Antonio LUZERO & Maria Rosa CORTES; ap/ Jesus LUZERO & Rosalia BERNAL; am/ Jose CORTES & Juana MONTOYA; gp/ Manuel BACA & Maria Manuela CASADO.

LOBATO, Antonio Jose S[n] Fernando
bap 4 Mch 1824; nat. s/ Madalena LOBATO & unknown father; gm/ Antonia Teodora LOBATO.

MONTOYA (gp), Maria Dolores Rancho
bap 11 Mch 1824; nat. d/ (unknown), (lines drawn through) Miguel MONTOYA & Maria Felipa RAMIRES; ap/ Jose Fran[co] MONTOYA & Maria Ygnacia BALDES; gp/ Juaquin MONTOYA & Maria Encarnacion FRESQUIS. (In margin note from priest): "*Me engañaron los padrinos* i.e., The godparents deceived me." (So it seems that parents and grandparents mentioned above should be deleted but they are in the record).

GOMEZ, Gregorio Antonio S[n] Fernando
bap 14 Mch 1824; s/ Juan GOMEZ & Maria Fran[ca] TRUXILLO; ap/ Nerio GOMEZ & Maria BALDES; am/ Blas TRUXILLO & Manuela SANCHEZ; gp/ D[n] Rafael LUNA & Ana Maria TAFOLLA.

DURAN, Maria Antonia Dolores *Rancho*
bap 10 Mch 1824; d/ (these names crossed through) Pablo DURAN & Maria Josefa TRUXILLO; gm/ Petra de Jesus PACHECO of el Rancho. (In margin note from priest): "*Me engañaron los padrinos* i.e., The godparents deceived me." (Although there was just a madrina. It seems that parents and grandparents mentioned above should be deleted but they are in the record).

Frame 372

LEAL, Jose Antonio *Rancho*
bap *en el mismo dia, mes y año*, s/ Manuel Jose LEAL & Mariana QUINTANA; ap/ Niquolas (sic) LEAL & Ambrosia MARTIN; am/ Simon QUINTANA & Maria TORRES; gp/ Nerio DURAN & Maria Manuela DURAN.

ROMERO, Maria Tomasa *Rancho*
bap 13 Mch 1824; d/ Anastasio ROMERO & Maria Romalda RIVALI; ap/ Mariano ROMERO & Fran^{ca} ARMENTA; am/ Juan Antonio RIVALI & Maria Juliana MAES; gp/ Jose Rafael PAIS & Margarita SILVA.

TAFOLLA, Pedro Patricio *Rancho*
bap 14 Mch 1824; s/ Romano TAFOLLA & Antonia Rosalia DURAN; ap/ Juan Domingo TAFOLLA & Dolores MES; am/ Manuel DURAN & Maria Geralda MASCAREÑA; gp/ Ventura DURAN & Maria de Jesus MARTIN.

VIJIL, Jose Tomas Rancho
bap *en el mismo dia, mes y año*; s/ Anastasio VIJIL & Maria de la Cruz QUINTANA; ap/ Juan de la Cruz VIJIL & Maria Clara FERNANDEZ; am/ Jose de la Cruz QUINTANA & Maria Micaela BALDES; gp/ Antonio VIJIL & Maria Simona MONTOYA.

MEDINA, Maria de la Luz Arroyo Ondo
bap 18 Mch 1824; d/ Jose Ysidro MEDINA & Maria Ysabel CORDOVA; ap/ Juan Pasqual MEDINA & Juana Teresa ESPINOSA; am/ Jose Antonio CORDOVA & Juana MARTIN; gp/ Jose de la Cruz MONDRAGON & Juana Josefa MEDINA.

VIJIL, Maria Josefa S^{n} Fernando
bap 21 Mch 1824; d/ Antonio VIJIL & Maria Manuela CHABES; ap/ Polo VIJIL & Maria de Jesus BALDES; gp/ Antonio Jose CORDOVA & Maria Rosa SANDOVAL.

Frame 373

BORREGO, Juana Maria *Ranchito*
bap *en el mismo dia, mes y año*; d/ Pablo BORREGO & Angela BELASQUEZ; ap/ Juan BORREGO & Manuela GARCIA; am/ Juan Jose VELASQUEZ (sic) & Maria Rosa TAPIA; gp/ Manuel MONDRAGON & Maria Rosa ARELLANO.

CORDOVA, Maria Petra Arroyo Seco
bap *en el mismo dia, mes y año*; d/ Serafino CORDOVA & Maria Candelaria MEDINA; ap/ Damaso CORDOVA & Maria Ysabel GONZALEZ; am/ Antonio MEDINA & Micaela VIJIL; gp/ Diego SANCHEZ & Maria Madalena MARTIN.

LUZERO, Juana Maria S^{n} Fernando *Nabajosa*
bap *en el mismo dia, mes y año*, ae 10 yr; d/ Navajos, adopted d/ D^{n} Pablo LUZERO & Maria Paula LA RAÑAGA; gp/ Cristobal Maria LA RAÑAGA & Ana Maria APODACA.

VIJIL, Maria de Jesus *Pueblo*
bap *en el mismo dia, mes y año*; d/ Julian VIJIL & Rafela ROMERO; gp/ Carpio TRUXILLO & Maria TRUXILLO.

GARCIA, Maria Rafaela (Maria Josefa in margin) Arroyo Ondo
*bap 18 Mch 1824, ae 8 da; d/ Antonio GARCIA & Maria Rita BACA; ap/ Juan Antonio GARCIA & Anamaria MOLINA; am/ Jose Antonio BACA & Maria Josefa VIJIL; gp/ Juan de Jesus TRUXILLO & Maria Catarina CORDOVA. (See bottom of next frame).

VARGAS, Jose Domingo *Rancho*
bap 23 Mch 1824; nat. s/ Maria VARGAS; gp/ Jose Mariano CORDOVA & Maria Josefa ESPINOSA. (Frames 373-374--repeated at end of Frame 374).

Frame 374
MARTIN, Antonio Jose *Nacion Yuta* Rancho
bap 28 Mch 1824, ae 7 yr; s/ *Nacion Yuta*, adopted s/ Bentura MARTIN; gf/ the same Bentura.

MARTIN, Maria Josefa *Nacion Opata adulta* Rancho
bap *en el mismo dia, mes y año*, ae 20 yr; *Nacion Opata*, adopted d/ Jose MARTIN; gf/ the same Jose.

ORTEGA, Felipe Santiago S[n] Fernando
bap 30 Mch 1824, ae 3 da; s/ Manuel ORTEGA & Maria de Gracia FRESQUIS; ap/ Nicolas ORTEGA & Maria del Carmen MARTIN; am/ Gregorio FRESQUIS & Maria Soledad PAIS; gp/ Felipe Santiago PADILLA & Maria Soledad MARTIN.

PAIS, Maria Encarnacion S[n] Fernando
bap *en el mismo dia, mes y año*, ae 3 da; d/ Miguel PAIS & Maria Soledad MES; ap/ Mateo PAIS & Maria Beronica MONTOYA; am/ Domingo MES & Juana Maria de HERRERA; gp/ Jose Faustin TAFOLLA & Maria Guadalupe ARMENTA.

GARCIA, Maria Josefa *Rancho*
*bap 22 Mch 1824; d/ Antonio GARCIA & Maria Rita BACA; ap/ Jua(n) Antonio GARCIA & Ana Maria MOLINA; am/ Jose Antonio BACA & Maria Josefa VIJIL; gp/ Juan de Jesus TRUXILLO & Maria Catarina CORDOVA.

VARGAS, Jose Domingo *Rancho*
bap *en el mismo dia, mes y año*, ae 3 da; nat. s/ Maria Rita VARGAS; gp/ Jose Mariano CORDOVA & Maria Josefa ESPINOSA. (See continuation from Frame 373 to 374).

Frame 375
MARTIN, Maria Encarnacion *Rancho*
bap 27 Mch 1824, ae 4 da; d/ Juan Antonio MARTIN & Maria Dolores DURAN; ap/ Felipe MARTIN & Maria TRUXILLO; am/ Pablo DURAN & Margarita SANCHES; gp/ Pablo DURAN & Maria Josefa TRUXILLO.

AGUILAR, Juana S[n] Fernando
bap 3 Apr 1824; d/ Salvador AGUILAR & Maria Fran[ca] CORTES; ap/ Antonio AGUILAR & Juana CORDOVA; am/ Cruz CORTES & Maria de la Luz MONTOYA; gp/ Jesus ARCHULETA & Juana Getrudis CASADOS.

GONZALEZ, Jose Dionisio *Rancho*
bap 8 Apr 1824, ae 2 da; s/ Ygnacio GONZALEZ & Josefa de LALANDA; ap/ D[n] Felipe GONZALEZ & Fran[ca] CHACON; am/ Bautista LALANDA & Maria Rita BEYTA; gp/ Raymundo CORDOVA & Maria Estefana GONZALEZ.

VIJIL, Maria Dolores Arroyo Seco
bap 10 Apr 1824; d/ Rafael VIJIL & Margarita BARELA; ap/ Juan VIJIL & Maria Juana TAFOLLA; am/ Juan Ysidro BARELA & Maria Juana MARTIN; gp/ Jose Victor SANCHEZ & Maria de los Dolores SANCHEZ.

COCA, Anastasio *Rancho*
bap 17 Apr 1824; s/ Tomas COCA & Lorenza SANDOVAL; ap/ Miguel COCA & Ana Maria ROMERO; am/ Matias SANDOVAL & Maria Ygnacia BUENA; gp/ Antonio TORRES & Maria Ysabel HERNANDEZ.

ARELLANO, Maria Antonia Arroyo Ondo
bap 18 Apr 1824; d/ Ramon ARELLANO & Anamaria ARMENTA; ap/ Julian ARELLANO (only); am/ Simon ARMENTA & Marta MARTIN; gp/ Antonio MARTIN & Maria Catalina SANDOVAL.

AGUILAR, Maria Manuela
bap *en el mismo dia, mes y año*; d/ Miguel AGUILAR & Guadalupe MADRIL; ap/ Lazaro AGUILAR & Concepcion PAIS; am/ Ygnacio MADRIL & Damiana MARTIN; gp/ Antonio SUASO & Benigna CORTES.

Frame 376
MARQUES, Juan Ygnacio *Rancho*
bap (folded faded); s/ Rafael MARQUES & Maria de la Crus ORTEGA; ap/ Alexandro MARQUEZ (sic) & Maria Micaela ATENSIO; am/ not given; gp/ Juan Miguel MARTINEZ & Maria de la Paz MARQUEZ.

CRESPIN, Juan *Rancho*
bap 27 Apr 1824; s/ Jose de la Ascencion CRESPIN & Maria Rosa MONTOYA; ap/ Jose CRESPIN & Maria Juana MADRIL; am/ Jose Rafael MONTOYA & Maria Luisa ROMERO; gp/ Fran^{co} Antonio ROMERO & Maria Soledad LUZERO.

BACA, Maria de la Cruz S^{n} Fernando
bap 1 May 1824; d/ Salvador BACA & Tomasa SILVA; ap/ Baltasar BACA & Anamaria (n.s.); gp/ Juan Nepumuceno de LUNA & Maria Candelaria BELARDE.

MONTOYA, Jose Fran^{co} S^{n} Fresnando
bap *en el mismo dia, mes y año*; s/ Manuel MONTOYA & Clara TAFOLLA; ap/ Tomas MONTOYA & Agueda MONTOYA; gp/ Tomas LOBATO & Meregilda CASADOS.

ROMERO, Maria Josefa S^{n} Fernando
bap *en el mismo dia, mes y año*; d/ Juan Pedro ROMERO & Candelaria TRUXILLO; ap/ Qulas ROMERO & not given; am/ Alexandro TRUXILLO & Manuela ARCHULETA; gp/ Antonio SUASO & Marcelina CASADOS.

BENABIDES, Maria de la Cruz *Rancho*
bap 3 May 1824; d/ Pablo BENABIDES & Rosa SALAZA(R); ap/ Juan BENABIDES & Getrudis ROMERO; am/ Fran^{co} SALAZAR & Santos CORDOVA; gp/ Jose Maria TRUXILLO & Maria Reyes MEDINA.

ORTIZ, Maria Manuela S^{n} Fernando
bap 7 May 1824, ae 4 da; d/ Antonio Jose ORTIZ & Maria Dolores LOBATO; ap/ Fran^{co} Jabier ORTIZ & Maria Fran^{ca} (n.s.); am/ (in worn part of page); gp/ Gregorio LUZERO & Maria Manuela M_. (Bottom of page worn). (Frames 376-377)

Frame 377
MARTIN, Maria Ygnacia *Rancho*
bap 8 May 1824, ae 5 da; d/ Andres MARTIN & Maria Ant^{a} ORTIS; ap/ D^{n} Pedro MARTIN & Ygnacia GARCIA; am/ D. Matias ORTIS (only); gp/ Faustin VIGIL & Maria de la Lus MARTIN.

AÑOQUEBIEN, Jose Rafael (Jose de la Cruz in margin) *Pueblo*
bap 8 May 1824; s/ Paulin AÑOQUEBIEN & Rosa SAMORA; ap/ *abuelo* not given & Ygnacia SAMORA; gp/ Jose Maria COCA & Teodora COCA.

SANDOVAL, Antonio Jose S^{n} Fernando
bap 10 May 1824, ae 4 da; s/ Manuel SANDOVAL & Benita MARTIN; ap/ Alonso

SANDOVAL & Rita ROMERO; am/ Juan MARTIN & Paula S^{a} GIL; gp/ Antonio SUASO & Benigna CORTES.

ROMERO, Jose de la Cruz *Pueblo*
bap 11 May 1824, ae 8 da; s/ Pablo ROMERO & Maria Dolores GONZALEZ; gp/ Diego Antonio BEYTA & Anamaria GONZALEZ.

VIJIL, Maria Soledad Rancho
bap 11 May 1824, ae 4 da; d/ Juan Ygnacio VIJIL & Maria Paula QUINTANA; gp/ Juan Felipe CORDOVA & Maria de Jesus FERNANDEZ.

MARTIN, Juan Antonio Rancho
bap 12 May 1824; s/ Santos MARTIN & Manuela ROMERO; ap/ Fran^{co} MARTIN & Barbara COCA; am/ Mariano ROMERO Fran^{ca} ARMENTA; gp/ Mariano JARAMILLO & Josefa LOBATO.

Frame 378
GARCIA, Jose Rafael Rancho
bap 16 May 1824, ae 4 da; s/ Miguel GARCIA & Margarita LUZERO; ap/ Jose GARCIA & Beatriz SANDOVAL; am/ Bernardo LUZERO & Maria Tomasa MARTIN; gp/ D^{n} Juan LOBATO & Maria Ygnacia SANCHEZ.

CORTES, Jose Fran^{co} Fernandez
bap *en el mismo dia, mes y año*, ae 4 da; s/ Bautista CORTES & Maria Antonia MON(TO)YA; ap/ Pedro CORTES & his wife, (n.n.); am/ Tomas MONTOYA & Agneda (n.s.); gp/ Jose Gabriel BEYTA & Serafina CORTES.

HURTADO, Maria de la Luz Rancho
bap 18 May 1824, ae 6 da; nat. d/ Juana HURTADO & unknown father; gp/ D^{n} Jose GRIÑE & Maria Manuela SANCHEZ.

MARTINEZ, Juana Maria Arroyo Seco
bap 19 May 1824, ae 4 da; d/ Felipe Antonio MARTINEZ & Maria Gregoria SANCHEZ; ap/ Manuel MARTIN (as written) & Ana Maria SALAZAR; am/ Juan Felipe MARTIN (as written) & Ygnacia VIJI(L); gp/ D^{n} Jose GONZALEZ & Maria Dorotea BACA.

CHABES, Juana Nepumucena Rancho
bap 20 May 1824, ae 3 da; d/ Juan Cristoval CHABES & Maria Dolores MONTOYA; ap/ Juan Pomuceno CHABES & Maria Clara SANCHEZ; am/ Manuel MONTOYA & Serafina (n.s.), his wife; gp/ Jose Manuel MARTIN & Maria Tomasa SANCHEZ.

MARTIN, Juan del Carmen Rancho
bap 27 May 1824, ae 5 da; s/ Fran^{co} MARTIN & Maria Ygnacia PINEDA; ap/ Jose MARTIN & Ysabel URI(OSTE); gp/ Pedro Nolasco LEAL & (Ma)riquita TAFOYA. (Frames 378-379) (Bottom of page folded and torn.)

Frame 379
GARCIA, Ant^{o} Jose Rancho
bap 27 May 1824, ae 3 da; s/ Pedro GARCIA & Rosa TRUGILLO; ap/ Jose GARCIA & Biatris SANDOVAL; am/ Reymundo TRUGIYO (as written) & Paula MARTIN; gp/ Juan Ygnacio SANCHES & Juan(a) SANCHES.

CHABES, Juan Jose S^{n} Fernando
bap 30 May 1824; s/ Maria Antonia CHABES & unknown father; gp/ Fran^{co} MES & Maria Ygnacia GABALDON.

ROMERO, Jose Rafael *Pueblo*
bap *en el mismo dia, mes y año;* s/ Juan Antonio ROMERO & Ascencion ORTIZ; gp/ Jose Rafael LUZERO & Maria Ygnacia ARAGON.

CORDOVA, Maria Antonia *Nacion Timpaniga*
bap 30 May 1824, ae 7 yr; d/ *Nacion Timpaniga*, adopted d/ Antonio Aban CORDOVA & Maria Juliana TORRES; gp/ Antonio Aban CORDOVA (only).

GONSALEZ, Fran^{ca} *Pueblo*
bap 3 Jne 1824, ae 4 da; d/ Jose Santos GONSALEZ & Maria Luz GOMEZ, *naturales del pueblo;* gm/ Fran^{ca} ORTIZ.

Frame 380
RIVERA, Jose Ramon S^{n} Fernando
bap 5 Jne 1824; s/ Tomas RIVERA & M^{a} del Carmen GONZALEZ; ap/ Jose Antonio RIVERA & Feliciana ORTIZ; am/ Segundo GONZALEZ & Maria Josefa BALDES; gp/ Jose Fran^{co} GONZALEZ & Maria de la Luz GONZALEZ.

PADILLA, Maria Manuela Rancho
bap *en el mismo dia, mes y año;* d/ Manuel PADILLA & Merejilda VIJIL; ap/ Pedro PADILLA & Lucia CHABES; am/ Marcelino VIJIL & Micaela MARTIN; gp/ Jose de Jesus GARCIA & Beatris SANDOVAL.

DURAN, Maria Cesilia Rancho
bap 10 Jne 1824; d/ Juan Nepumuceno DURAN & Maria de la Paz SANCHEZ; ap/ Manuel DURAN & Maria Geralda MASCAREÑA; am/ Felipe SANCHEZ & Anamaria MARTIN; gp/ Juan Antonio MARTIN & Maria Barbara ARAGON.

GARCIA, Maria Guadalupe S^{n} Fernando
bap 14 Jne 1824, ae 3 da; d/ Juan Antonio GARCIA & Dolores GABALDON; ap/ Juan de Dios GARCIA & Maria de la Luz FRESQUIS; am/ Feliz GABALDON & Maria Guadalupe TRUXILLO; gp/ Jose Ygnacio ALARID & Maria Dolores TRUXILLO.

CRUZ, Maria Petra Rancho
bap 11 Jne 1824; nat. d/ Antonia CRUZ & unknown father; gp/ Manuel TORRES & Rita SANCHEZ.

MARQUEZ, Pedro Antonio Rancho
bap *en el mismo dia, mes y año;* s/ Miguel MARQUEZ & Maria Getrudis MONTOYA; ap/ Lorenzo MARQUEZ & Simona LEAL; am/ Domingo MONTOYA & Maria GALLEGA; gp/ Jose Rafael LUZERO & Maria Gracia ARAGON.

Frame 381
MADRIL, Maria de la Luz
bap 13 Jne 1824; d/ Jose Migu(e)l MADRIL & Juana Maria SENA; ap/ Tomas MADRIL & Maria Antonia MONTOYA; am/ Jose Migu(e)l SENA & Maria Rafaela LUZERO; gp/ Juan Ygnacio CORTES & Maria Manuela CORTES.

MARTIN, Maria Antonia Ranchito
bap 17 Jne 1824; d/ Pablo MARTIN & Maria Soledad LUZERO; ap/ Antonio Jose MARTIN & Maria Rita BEYTA; am/ Juan de Jesus LUZERO & Ygnacia ARAGON; gp/ Jose Ramon ROMERO & Maria Rafaela VIJIL.

ARCHULETA, Maria Francisca Arroyo Ondo
bap 20 Jne 1824; d/ Honorato ARCHULETA & Dolores MESTAS; ap/ Damian ARCHULETA & Juana Micaela SALAZAR; am/ Jose MESTAS & Maria Barbara MARTIN; gp/ Jose Antonio TRUXILLO & Maria Francisca MARTIN.

MONTOYA, Maria del Carmen Arroyo Seco
bap 27 Jne 1824, ae 4 da; d/ Felipe MONTOYA & Maria Antonia SANDOVAL; ap/ Juan Domingo MONTOYA & Mariquita (n.s.); am/ Felipe SANDOVAL & Concepcion SANCHEZ; gp/ Pablo GALLEGO & Maria Dolores MARTIN.

MONTOYA, Maria Juana Rancho
bap 28 Jne 1824, ae 3 da; nat. d/ Maria Clara MONTOYA & unknown father; gm/ Luisa SANDOVAL.

Frame 382
LUZERO, Pedro Jose de Jesus Rancho
bap 29 Jne 1824, ae 5 da; s/ Jose Ygnacio LUZERO & Maria Estefana MARTINEZ; ap/ Juan LUZERO & Petrona BACA; am/ D^{n} Antonio Severino (MARTINEZ) & Maria del Carmen SANTISTEBAN; gp/ Antonio Jose MARTINEZ & Maria de la Luz MARTINEZ.

MEDINA, Salvador Marcial Arroyo Ondo
bap 4 Jly 1824; s/ Juan Bautista MEDINA & Maria Manuela MARTINEZ; ap/ Jose Antonio MEDINA & Juana Getrudis ROMERO; am/ Eusebio MARTINEZ & Maria Antonia TRUXILLO; gp/ Juan GONZALEZ & Maria Getrudis ARCHULETA.

NARANJO, Maria Concepcion *Pueblo*
bap 6 Jly 1824, ae 4 da; d/ Santiago NARANJO & Paula TUSA; gm/ Brijida ROMERO.

MONTOYA, Maria Lorenza S^{n} Fernando
bap 7 Jly 1824; d/ Juan Jose MONTOYA & Maria Candelaria ESQUIBEL; ap/ Bernardo MONTOYA & Maria Manuela MARTIN; am/ $Fran^{co}$ ESQUIBEL & Feliciana MARTIN; gp/ Juan de Dios MONTOYA & Rosalia MONTOYA.

GOMEZ, Santiago *Pueblo*
bap 23 Jly 1824, ae 5 da; s/ $Fran^{co}$ GOMEZ & Juana Maria ROMERO; gm/ Juana Pasquala ROMERO.

Frame 383
LUZERO, Jose *Pueblo*
bap 24 Jly 1824, ae 5 da; s/ Juan Domingo LUZERO & Rosa LASO; gm/ Soledad LUZERO.

MAES, Jose Lorenzo *Nacion* (illegible)
bap 10 Aug 1824, ae 3 yr; s/ adopted s/ Jose de Jesus MAES & Maria Josefa MAES; gp/ (not given).

BARELA, Maria de la Natividad Rancho
bap 17 Aug 1824, ae 2 da; d/ Jose Candelaria BARELA & Maria Concepcion SOLANO; ap/ Juan Antonio BARELA & Ygnacia BIGIL; am/ Juan Andres SOLANO & Maria Bibiana BALDES; gp/ Dionicio CORDOVA & Felipa LOBATO.

TAFOLLA, Maria Clara & Clara de Jesus Arroyo Seco
bap 17 Aug 1824; daughters/ Ypolito de Jesus TAFOLLA & Concepcion Mariana CHABES; ap/ Juan Paulin TAFOLLA & Maria Ysabel CORDOVA; am/ Antonio CHABES & Barbar(a) SANCHEZ; gp of Clara de Jesus/ D^{n} Felipe GONZALEZ (only); gp of Maria Clara/ Maria Manuela SALAZAR (only). (No mention of twins.)

(Note: Frames 384 to 407 are marriage entries for 15 Sep 1823 to 14 Oct 1825, with confirmations on Frame 403). Frame 408 (has baptismal records. Previous Jan 1818 begin on the last entry of Frame 192 and go to Frame 194. Note: At this point the extractions jump back to the year of 1818. The book was bound in this manner).

Frame 408
(Fr. Josef Benito PEREYRO signing entries)
SUAZO, Paula *Pueblo*
bap *en el mismo dia, mes y año*, ae 7 da; d/ Fran[co] SUAZO & Josefa OYENGUE; gm/ Micaela LUJAN *del pueblo*.

ARCHULETA, M[a] Ant[a] *Vec[a]*
bap *en el mismo dia, mes y año*, ae 8 da; d/ Man[l] ARCHULETA & Viviana GONSALEZ; gf/ Cristoval GONSALEZ.

URTADO, Maria Fran[ca] *V.*
bap *en el mismo dia, mes y año*, ae 2 da; d/ Man[l] URTADO & Getrudes BEJIL; gp/ Man[l] TORREZ & M[a] Rita SANCHEZ.

MARTIN, Josef Dolores *V[o]*
bap 26 Jan 1818, ae 8 da; s/ Juan Ant[o] MARTIN & Rosa BEJIL; gp/ Pablo DURAN & Margarita SANCHEZ.

ABILA, Jose Dolores *V.*
bap 30 Jan 1818, ae 3 da; s/ Rafael ABILA & M[a] Josefa DURAN; gp/ Rafael DURAN & Fran[ca] MARTIN.

Frame 409
PACENO, Juan Josef *V.*
bap 30 Jan 1818, ae 3 da; nat. s/ Josef Ant[o] PACENO & M[a] Reyes ESPINOSA; gp/ Juan Josef ROMERO & Teresa ROYBAL.

PACHECO, Juana Catalina
bap *en el mismo dia, mes y año*, ae 5 da; d/ Josef PACHECO & Veronica CRUZ; gp/ Juan Cristoval ROMERO & Margarita ARAGON.

ORTEGA, Ygnacia *V.*
bap 1 Feb 1818, ae 3 da; d/ Man[l] ORTEGA & Miquela BRITO; gp/ Julian TENORIO & Lorensa LOPEZ.

CHAVES, M[a] Candelaria *V[a]*
bap 4 Feb 1818, ae 3 da; *espuria* d/ Ynes CHAVES; gp/ Man[l] Ant[o] MARTIN & Maria MONTOYA.

CHAVES, Josef Ygnacio *V.*
bap *en el mismo dia, mes y año*, ae 3 da; s/ Blas CHAVES & Dolores MARTIN; gp/ Juan BEJIL & Viviana TORREZ.

MARTIN, José Ant[o] *V.*
bap 8 Feb 1818, ae 8 da; s/ Josef Pablo MARTIN & Getrudes BARGAS; gp/ Juan MARTIN & Yg[a] SISNEROS.

Frame 410
PADILLA, Rumaldo *V[o]*
bap *en el mismo dia, mes y año*, ae 2 da; s/ Bisente PADILLA & Ysidora MARTIN; gp/ Mateo LOVATO & Maria Rita LOVATO.

TAFOYA, Leonardo *V[o]*
bap *en el mismo dia, mes y año*, ae 2 da; s/ Man[l] TAFOYA & Rosa OLONA; gp/ Nerio SISNEROS & Teodora MARTIN.

MARQUEZ, Miguel Antonio V°
bap *en el mismo dia, mes y año*, ae 8 da; s/ Miguel MARQUEZ & Getrudes MONTOYA; gp/ Josef Ant° MARTIN & Maria LEAL.

SALAS, Maria Dolores V.
bap *en el mismo dia, mes y año*, ae 8 da; d/ Ant° SALAS & Maria SANCHEZ; gp/ Josef SANCHES (as written) & Juana LOPEZ.

TRUJILLO, Romualdo V.
bap 10 Feb 1818, ae 4 da; s/ Luis TRUJILLO & Maria SANCHEZ; gp/ Pedro SALASAR & Ursula ERRERA.

TRUJILLO, Mª Romualda
bap 10 Feb 1818, ae 4 da; d/ Pablo TRUJILLO & Feliciana ORTIZ; gp/ Pablo LUCERO & Paula LARRAÑADA.

Frame 411
PACHECO, Maria Polonia V.
bap 11 Feb 1818, ae 3 da; d/ Estevan PACHECO & Maria CASADOS; gp/ Ramon SANDOVAL & Maria TRUJILLO.

QUINTANA, Maria Dolores V.
bap *en el mismo dia, mes y año*, ae 3 da; d/ Ramon QUINTANA & Maria MARTIN; gm/ Mª Manuela SALASAR.

LEYBA, Jesus Maria V.
bap 15 Feb 1818, ae 7 da; s/ Bisente LEYBA & Encarnacion ESPINOSA; gp/ Josef Ant° GONSALEZ & Maria URIOSTE.

SANCHEZ, Mª Rosa V.
bap *en el mismo dia, mes y año*, ae 5 da; d/ Felipe SANCHEZ & Maria MARTIN; gp/ Juan Pablo DURAN & Soledad JARAMILLO.

CHAVEZ, Maria Viviana V.
bap *en el mismo dia, mes y año*, ae 4 da; d/ Juan CHAVEZ & Dolores MONTOYA; gp/ Juan CHAVEZ & Clara SANCHEZ.

Frame 412
FRESQUIZ, Catalina V.
bap *en el mismo dia, mes y año*, ae 4 da; d/ Ant° FRESQUIZ & Reyes SANCHEZ; gp/ Bernardo DURAN & Feliciana BEJIL.

BARELA, Josef Bisente V.
bap *en el mismo dia, mes y año*, ae 6 da; s/ Juan BARELA & Juliana TRUJILLO; gp/ Culas GARCIA & Josefa TRUJILLO.

TAFOYA, Mª Dolores V.
bap *en el mismo dia, mes y año*, ae 3 da; d/ Bartolo TAFOYA & Antª GONSALEZ; gp/ Romano TAFOYA & Rosalia DURAN.

GONSALES, Agustin P.
bap *en el mismo dia, mes y año*, ae 7 da; s/ Ant° GONSALES & Fran^{ca} RILLO; gm/ Mª PADILLA.

OÑENGUE, Jesus Maria V.
bap 22 Feb 1818, ae 7 da; s/ Diego OÑENGUE & Dolores ROMERO; gp/ (n.n.) FERNANDEZ & Josefa (n.s.).

BEJIL, Ugenio V°
bap *en el mismo dia, mes y año*, ae 5 da; s/ Ant° MONTES BEJIL & Ynes MARTIN; gp/ Juan CORDOVA & Margarita MARTIN.

Frame 413
LUJAN, Dominga P.
bap *en el mismo dia, mes y año*, ae 8 da; d/ Lorenso LUJAN & Soledad ROMERO; gm/ Juana SUAZO.

TAFOYA, Maria Marcelina V.
bap 26 Feb 1818, ae 6 da; d/ Josef TAFOYA & Fran^{ca} BERNAL; gf/ Josef Rafael ROMERO.

MESTAS, Josef Dolores V.
bap 1 Mch 1818, ae 5 da; s/ Asencio MESTAS & Juana JARAMILLO; gp/ Josef Gabriel MARTIN & Maria Luisa (n.s.).

TRUJILLO, Bentura (Buenaventura in margin) V.
bap *en el mismo dia, mes y año*, ae 3 da; d/ Josef Maria TRUJILLO & Reyes MEDINA; gp/ Bartolo TAFOYA & Maria Ant^{a} GONSALEZ.

PACHECO, Maria Getrudez V^{a}
bap *en el mismo dia, mes y año*, ae 6 da; d/ Ramon PACHECO & Trenidad BEJIL; gp/ Ramon BEJIL & Barvara MARTIN.

ARCHULETA, Mª Paula V.
bap *en el mismo dia, mes y año*, ae 3 da; d/ Marcos ARCHULETA & Dolores CHAVEZ; gp/ Fran^{co} Javriel (sic) LOVATO & Mª SANCHEZ.

Frame 414
BEJIL, Maria Teresa V^{a}
bap 3 Mch 1818, ae 3 da; d/ Rafael BEJIL & Maria SANDOVAL; gp/ Blas CHAVES & Maria MARTIN.

BERNAL, Pablo V.
bap 4 Mch 1818, ae 2 da; s/ Felipe BERNAL & Candelaria ERRERA; gp/ Jesus LUCERO & Rosalia BERNAL.

ROMERO, Maria Esquipulas (Maria de Jesus de Esquipulas in margin) V^{a}
bap 5 Mch 1818, ae 4 da; d/ Ant° ROMERO & Getrudis MONDRAGON; gp/ Pascual MONTOYA & Maria SANDOVAL.

TRUJILLO, Maria del Carmen V.
bap 7 Mch 1818, ae 4 da; d/ Fran^{co} TRUJILLO & Joaquina DURAN; gp/ Pedro LUCERO & Gregoria MEDINA.

(Bleed thru)

Frame 415
GONSALEZ, Juan Ramos V.
bap 5 Mch 1818, ae 5 da; s/ Jose Angel GONSALEZ & Josefa FERNANDEZ; gp/ Fran^{co} GONSALEZ & Ysavel BEJIL.

CASADOS, Juan Rafael V°
bap *en el mismo dia, mes y año*, ae 4 da; s/ Juan Ant° CASADOS & Gua(da)lupe GARCIA; gp/ Jose Gavriel MARTIN & Man^{la} CASADOS.

SUAZO, Maria Dolores *V.*
bap *en el mismo dia, mes y año*, ae 3 da; d/ Juan Ant° SUAZO & Juana GONSALEZ; gp/ Juan Domingo TAFOYA & Juana Getrudes CORDOVA.

GARCIA, Maria Dolores *V.*
bap *en el mismo dia, mes y año*, ae 4 da; d/ Pablo GARCIA & Juana SANCHEZ; gp/ Juan Ysidro BARELA & Juana MARTIN.

LUCERO, Maria Antonia *Pueblo*
bap *en el mismo dia, mes y año*, ae 5 da; d/ Lorenso LUCERO & Man[la] GAVILAN; gp/ Bernardo MONTOYA & Maria MARTIN *del pueblo*.

BALDES, Josef Francisco
bap 15 Mch 1818, ae 4 da; s/ Juan Man[l] BALDES & Maria Rosario MEDINA; gp/ Ant° BLEA & Maria MARTIN.

Frame 416
SALASAR, Josef Rafael *V.*
bap 26 Mch 1818, ae 7 da; s/ Ramon SALASAR & Soledad BEJIL; gp/ Juan Cristoval BEJIL & Viviana TORRES.

FRESQUIZ, Juan S[tos] *V.*
bap *en el mismo dia, mes y año*, ae 5 da; s/ Pedro FRESQUIZ & Josefa BRITO; gp/ Miguel LOVATO & Luciana LOVATO.

TORRES, Maria Josefa *V.*
bap *en el mismo dia, mes y año*, ae 4 da; d/ Ant° TORRES & Ysavel FERNANDES; gp/ Gregorio DURAN & Rosa URIOSTE.

MARTIN, Benita *V.*
bap 28 Mch 1818, ae 3 da; d/ Man[l] Gregorio MARTIN & Rafaela MEDINA; gp/ Josef Rafael LUCERO & Man[la] SANDOVAL.

MONTOYA, Miguel Ant° *V.*
bap *en el mismo dia, mes y año*, ae 3 da; s/ Ramon MONTOYA & Lorensa ORTIZ; gp/ Miguel MONTOYA & Maria RAMIRES.

Frame 417
ARCHULETA, Ermenegildo *V.*
bap 29 Mch 1818, ae 3 da; s/ Julian ARCHULETA & Manuela BARELA; gp/ Josef Ant° MARTIN & Barvara TRUJILLO.

MARTIN, Maria dela Encarnacion *V.*
bap *en el mismo dia, mes y año*, ae 4 da; d/ Ermenegildo MARTIN & Margarita RUIBAL; gp/ Juan de Jesus TRUJILLO & Juana BUENO.

ARELLANO, Maria Soledad *V.*
bap 30 Mch 1818, ae 3 da; d/ Ramon ARELLANO & Anamaria ARMENTA; gp/ Fran[co] QUINTANA & Balvaneda ROMERO.

MARQUEZ, Josef Ygnacio *V.*
bap *en el mismo dia, mes y año*, ae 4 da; s/ Man[l] MARQUEZ & M[a] LUCERO; gp/ Blas TRUJILLO & Manuela SANCHEZ.

BUENO, Pedro Nolasco V^o
bap 3 Apr 1818, ae 4 da; s/ Juan Ugenio BUENO & Teodora BEYTA; gp/ Nicolas SANDOVAL & Ygnacia BUENO.

Frame 418
COCA, Bentura (Buenabentura in margin in different ink & writing) V.
bap *en el mismo dia, mes y año*, ae 4 da; d/ Tomas COCA & Lorensa SANDOVAL; gp/ Pedro LUCERO & Luz FERNANDEZ.

MARTIN, Maria Paula P.
bap *en el mismo dia, mes y año*, ae 6 da; d/ Josef Ant^o MARTIN & Man^{la} (n.s.), *Yndios del pueblo*; gp/ Jose Ant^o MARTIN & Ygnacia SISNEROS.

GARCIA, Maria Paula V.
bap 9 Apr 1818, ae 3 da; d/ Juan Josef GARCIA & Teodora CHAVEZ; gp/ Juan CHAVEZ & Dolores MARTIN.

GARCIA, Man^1 Ant^o V^o
bap *en el mismo dia, mes y año*, ae 2 da; s/ Miguel GARCIA & Margarita LUCERO; gp/ Bernardo LUCERO & Tomasa MARTIN.

AVILA, Bisente V.
bap *en el mismo dia, mes y año*, ae 4 da; s/ Usevio AVILA & Mª PADILLA; gp/ Fran^{co} CORDOVA & Juana ROMERO.

LOVATO, Soledad (Maria Soledad in margin) V.
bap 14 Apr 1818, ae 3 da; d/ Fran^{co} LOVATO & Maria ARCHULETA; gp/ Candelario ARAGON & Getrudes GARCIA. (Frames 418-419)

Frame 419
RAEL, Manuel
bap 17 Apr 1818, ae 3 da; s/ Juan RAEL & Mª Dolores CORDOVA; gp/ Man^1 GARCIA & Trenidad QUINTANA.

MARTIN, Josef Francisco V^o
bap *en el mismo dia, mes y año*, ae 3 da; s/ Josef Fran^{co} MARTIN & Ysavel CORTES; gp/ Man^1 ARMIJO & Trenidad SANTISTEVAN.

TORRES, Manuel V.
bap *en el mismo dia, mes y año*, ae 4 da; *espurio* s/ Ysavel TORRES; gp/ Man^1 Ant^o (n.s.) & Maria MONTOYA.

BARELA, Anselma V.
bap 21 Apr 1818, ae 3 da; d/ Josef Candelario BARELA & Consecion SOLANO; gp/ Josef Man^1 LUJAN (only).

Frame 420
FLORES, Ricardo V.
bap 22 Apr 1818, ae 8 da; s/ Martin FLORES & Encarnacion GONSALEZ; gp/ Fran^{co} CHAVEZ & Lorensa CRUZ.

PAES, Jose Rafael V.
bap *en el mismo dia, mes y año*, ae 2 da; s/ Juan de Jesus PAES & Juana MARQUEZ; gp/ Pedro BUENO & Manuela ROMERO.

SAIS, Maria Ramona V.
bap 30 Apr 1818, ae 3 da; d/ Josef Man^1 SAIS & Maria MEDINA; gp/ Josef Maria SILVA & M^a del Carmen SAIS.

ROMERO, Juan dela Cruz *V.*
bap 3 May 1818, ae 3 da; s/ Santiago ROMERO & Josefa MARTIN; gm/ Rosa ROMERO.

ERRERA, Juan dela Cruz *V^{o}*
bap *en el mismo dia, mes y año*, ae 7 da; s/ Andres ERRERA & Juana MONDRAGON; gp/ Josef Pablo MARTIN & Josefa QUINTANA.

BEJIL (gp), Jose Antonio *V.*
bap 5 May 1818, ae 8 da; s/ Man^{l} (n.s.) & Rosa (n.s.); gp/ Ant^{o} BEJIL & Simona MONTOYA.

Frame 421
DURAN, Pedro Ygnacio *V^{o}*
bap 10 May 1818, ae 4 da; s/ Gregorio DURAN & Rosa URIOSTE; gp/ Ant^{o} TORRES & Ysavel FERNANDEZ.

SAMORA, Jesus Maria *V^{o}*
bap *en el mismo dia, mes y año*, ae 6 da; s/ Pablo SAMORA & Alvina ROMERO; gp/ Jesus Maria PEÑA & Maria Josefa BARELA.

CORTEZ, Josef dela Cruz *V^{o}*
bap *en el mismo dia, mes y año*, ae 6 da; s/ Man^{l} CORTEZ & Manuela ROMERO; gp/ Man^{l} MARTIN & Juana CORTEZ.

MIERA, Maria Catalina *V^{a}*
bap *en el mismo dia, mes y año*, ae 5 da; d/ Josef MIERA & Man^{la} ROMERO; gp/ Tomas LOVATO & Ermenegilda CASADOS.

Frame 422 (Fr. Theodoro ALCINA signing entries)
GAVALDON, Man^{l} Ant^{o} de Jesus *Vec^{o}*
bap 24 May 1818, ae 3 da; s/ Man^{l} GAVALDON & Maria Juana MARTIN; gp/ Jose Benito TRUXILLO & Maria Fran^{ca} TRUXILLO.

RIO, Maria Paubla de Jesus *Pueblo*
bap 26 May 1818; d/ Juan RIO & Madalena ROMERO; gp/ Bernardo CASILLAS & Maria Soledad HAGILA.

(Fr. Juan Bruno GONSALEZ signing entries)
ARMIJO, Maria Juana dela Trinidad Spanish
*bap 17 May 1818; d/ Antonio Eustaquio ARMIJO & Juana GARCIA; gp/ Jose Manuel VARELA & Maria Concepcion CHACONA *del Rio Colorado*.

BLEA, Jose Antonio Spanish
bap 17 May 1818; s/ Maria del Rosario BLEA & unknown father; gp/ Jose Antonio TAFOLLA & Fran^{ca} BERNAL, *vecinos dela plaza de S^{n} Fernando*.

MADRID, Ysidro dela Trinidad Spanish
bap 17 May 1818; s/ Christobal MADRID & Maria Manuela MARTIN; gp/ Juan Damian ARCHULETA & Maria Luisa GUTIERREZ *del Rio Colorado*.

(Fr. Josef de CASTRO signing entries)
ROMERO, Juan Antonio Indian
bap 4 Jne 1818, ae 7 da; s/ Christobal ROMERO & Paula LOMA; gm/ Maria Rosa ROMERO, *Yndios todos de este pueblo*.

DURAN, Maria Ygnacia Spanish
*bap 1 Jne 1818, ae 1 da; d/ Juan Antonio DURAN & Maria Rita LUCERO; gp/ Josef Fran^{co} DURAN & Antonia Getrudes SANCHEZ. (Frames 422-423)

Frame 423
MONDRAGON, Maria de Gracia
MANSANARES, Maria de Gracia Spanish
bap 4 Jne 1818, ae 5 da; nat. d/ Gervacio MONDRAG^{N} & Theresa MANZANARES; gp/ Bicente TRUGILLO & *su esposa*, Maria Dolores MADRID, *vecinos de S^{n} Fernando todos*.

BERNAL, Maria Fran^{ca} Spanish
*bap (not given) May 1818 by Fr. Jose Benito PEREYRO, dec; d/ Pedro BERNAL & Maria Getrudis SUAZO; gp/ Josef Pablo CHAVES & Maria Casimira CHAVEZ, *vecinod de S^{n} Fernando todos*. (Signed by above Fr. Josef de CASTRO).

31 May 1818 - Church visit - also appointment of Fr. Jose de CASTRO as pastor by (Fr.) D^{n} Juan Baptista LADRON del NIÑO GUEVARA.

MASCAREÑAS, Maria Desideria Spanish *del Rio Colorado todos*
PADILLA, Maria Desideria
bap 7 Jne 1818, ae 15 da; nat. d/ Juan Baptista MASCAREÑAS & Maria Dolores PADILLA; gp/ Antonio ARMIJO & Maria Josefa GARCIA.

Frames 424 to top of Frame 434
13 Jne 1818 the visit made by (Fr.) D^{n} Juan Baptista LADRON del NIÑO GUEVARA as visitor general and ecclesiastical governor for *Sor Marqués* Dr D^{n} Juan Fran^{co} de CASTAÑIZA, Bishop of Durango. (Signed) (Fr.) D. Juan Bautista GUEVARA, (&) Fran^{co} PERES SERRANO, *Not^{o}*

Frame 434
LOMA, Maria Fran^{ca} *Yndia*
bap 10 Jne 1818, ae 2 da; d/ Josef Ramos LOMA & Fran^{ca} ORTIZ; gp/ Juan Andres ROMERO & Maria Theresa ROYBAL, *vecinos del pueblo*.

RODRIGUEZ, Maria Antonia Spanish
bap 12 Jne 1818, ae 7 da; d/ Lorenzo RODRIGUEZ & Maria Josefa MARTIN; gp/ Antonio Candelaria ARAGON & Maria Barvara GUTIERREZ, *vecinos todos del Rio Colorado*.

BIGIL, Jose Antonio *Español*
bap 14 Jne 1818, ae 2 da; s/ Pedro BIGIL & Maria Josefa QUINTANA; gp/ Faustin BEGIL (sic) & Maria dela Luz MARTIN, *vecinos todos del Rancho*.

Frame 435
LUCERO, Juana Josefa *Española*
bap 14 Jne 1818, ae 4 da; d/ Jose Maria LUCERO & Ygnacia ARCHULETA, *vecinos de S^{n} Fernando*; gp/ Manuel PADILLA & Maria Ysabel ZISNEROS, *vecinos del Arroyo Hondo*.

GALLEGO, Jose Rafael *Español*
bap 16 Jne 1818, ae 3 da; s/ Jesus GALLEGO & Maria Micaela BIGIL; gp/ Jose Andres MARTIN & *su esposa*, Maria Antonia ORTIZ, *vecinos todos del Rancho*.

BIGIL, Juana Maria Spanish
bap 16 Jne 1818, ae 3 da; d/ Jose Amador BIGIL & Maria Ygnacia QUINTANA; gp/ Manuel LUCERO & Maria Andrea LAVADILLA, *vecinos todos del Rancho*.

CUMANCHITO, Juan Andres *Yndio*
bap 24 Jne 1818, ae 3 da; s/ Juan Antonio CUMANCHITO & Juana Josefa (n.s.), *naturales de este pueblo*; gp/ Anastasio AVILA & CHATARINA MARTIN, *vecinos del Arroyo Hondo*.

SANDOVAL, Juana Chatarina *Española*
bap 28 Jne 1818, ae 5 da; d/ Antonio Jose SANDOVAL & Maria de Guadalupe BIGIL; gp/ Jose Bentura SANDOVAL & Theodora ROMERO, *vecinos todos de S^{n} Fernando.*

MARTIN, Pedro Antonio *Español*
bap 28 Jne 1818, ae 3 da; s/ Jose Santos MARTIN & Maria Manuela ROMERO; gp/ Jose Manuel TORRES & Maria Rita SANCHEZ, *vecinos todos del Rancho.*

Frame 436
FERNANDEZ, Maria Dolores Spanish
bap 28 Jne 1818, ae 7 da; d/ Juan Domingo FERNANDEZ & Maria Fran^{ca} GARCIA; gp/ Pedro MARTIN & Maria delos Reyes PINO, *vecinos todos del Rancho.*

(Apparently no Jly or Sep entries)

(Fr. Andres CORREA signing entries)
BEJIL, Maria de Jesus Spanish
bap 24 Aug 1818, ae 3 da; d/ Rafael BEJIL & Maria dela Luz LUJAN; gp/ Pedro MARTIN & Maria delos Reyes PINO, *vecinos todos del Rancho.*

PADILLA, Jose Rafael Spanish
bap 8 Oct 1818, ae 6 da; s/ Man^{l} PADILLA & Meregilda BEJIL; gp/ Anastacio BEJIL & Mª Trinidad BEJIL, *vecinos todos del Rancho.*

CRUZ, Maria Barvara *Española*
bap 18 Oct 1818, ae 5 da; d/ Fran^{co} CRUZ & Mª Josefa MEDINA; gp/ Jose Mig^{l} ROMERO & M^{a} del Carmen ROMERO, *vecinos todos del Rancho.*

MARTIN, Man^{l} Ant^{o} Spanish
bap *en el mismo dia, mes y año,* ae 4 da; s/ Cristoval MARTIN & Teodora FRESQUIZ; gp/ Mª SANCHEZ (only), *vecinos todos del Rancho.*

Frame 437
BACA, Jose Dolores *Español*
bap *en d^{ho} dia mes y ano,* ae 3 da; s/ Lorenso BACA & Mª Guadalupe CORDOVA; gp/ Nerio SISNEROS & Teodora MARTIN, *vesinos del Arrollo Ondo.*

GARCIA, Juan Ant^{o} Spanish
bap 27 Oct 1818, ae 2 da; s/ Ant^{o} GARCIA & Rita ROMERO; gp/ Juan de Jesus PAIS & Juana TRUJILLO.

ROMERO, Man^{l} de Jesus Spanish
bap 4 Nov 1818, ae 2 da; s/ Jose Maria ROMERO & Rafaela PINEDA; gp/ Man^{l} de Jesus FERNANDES & Mª Man^{la} FERNANDES, *todos vesinos del Rancho.*

BEJIL, Mª Soledad *Española*
bap 12 Nov 1818, ae 3 da; d/ Juan Ygnacio BEJIL & Paula QUINTANA; gp/ Mariano JARAMILLO & Josefa LOVATO.

Frame 438
(Fr. Sebastian ALVAREZ signing entries)
CASILLAS, Jesus Maria Indian
bap 23 Nov 1818, ae 6 da; s/ Fernando CASILLAS & Micaela ROMERO; gf/ Juan Antonio DURAN [*vecino este, los otros Yndios de dicha mision*].

BASQUEZ, Maria Albina *Vec^{na}*
bap 24 Nov 1818, ae 3 da; d/ Juan Jose BASQUEZ & Juana CORDOVA; gp/ Diego

Ant° PACHECO & Maria de Jesus QUINTANA, [*todos vecinos de esta supra dha mision*].

SARBÉ, Ana Maria de Jesus *Vecina*
bap 25 Nov 1818, ae 3 da; d/ D^{n} José SARBÉ & D^{a} Maria Theodora LOVATO; gp/ Maria Joséfa VARELA (sic) & Lorenzo BACA, [*todos de esta vecindad*].

VIJIL, Maria del Refugio *Vecina*
bap 6 Dec 1818, ae 8 da; d/ Juan Christobal VIJIL & Bibiana TORRES; gp/ Antonio TORRES & Maria Ysabel FERNANDEZ, [*todos de esta vecindad*].

ERRERA, Maria de Jesus *Vecina*
bap 6 Dec 1818, ae 5 da; d/ José de ERRERA & Juana GONZALEZ; gp/ Fran^{co} Ant° GARCIA & Maria QUINTANA, [*todos de esta vecindad*].

LOVATO, Maria Dolores *Vec^{na}*
bap 10 Dec 1818, ae 3 da; d/ Tomas LOVATO & Maria CASAUS; gp/ José Gabriel MARTIN & Maria Luisa BACA, [*todos de esta vecindad*].

Frame 439
SALAZAR, Jose Maria Guadalupe *Vecino*
bap 14 Dec 1818, ae 3 da; s/ Juan Ant° SALAZAR & Rosa ARCHULETA; gp/ Jose Man^{l} MARTIN & Juana Maria MARTIN, [*todos de esta vecindad*].

VIJIL, Maria Guadalupe *Vec^{na}*
bap 15 Dec 1818, *nació ayer*; d/ Juan VIJIL & Maria de la Cruz LOPEZ; gp/ Juan Ant° ROMERO & Maria de Jesus BACA, [*todos de esta vecindad*].

MARTIN, Maria Rosa *Vec^{na}*
bap 21 Dec 1818, ae 5 da; d/ Francisco MARTIN & Maria SANCHEZ; gp/ José Mariano FERNANDEZ & Maria Asencion LUCERO, [*todos de esta vecindad*].

PADILLA, Juan de Dios *Vecino*
bap 24 Dec 1818, ae 2 da; s/ Fran^{co} PADILLA & Maria Micaela CHAVES; gp/ Salvador LOVATO & Maria Joséfa LOVATO, [*todos de esta vecindad*].

SANCHEZ, José Amador *Vec^{no}*
bap 24 Dec 1818, *nació ayer*; s/ José Julian SANCHEZ & Paula ARMIJO; gp/ José Amador VIJIL & Maria Ygnacia QUINTANA, [*todos de esta vecindad*].

ROMERO, Maria Dominga *Indian*
bap 27 Dec 1818, ae 8 da; d/ Pedro ROMERO & Manuela ORTIZ; gp/ Luiz DELGADO & Joséfa JUILA, [*todos Indios de d^{ha} mision*].

Año de 1819

LOVATO, Maria Manuela *Vecina*
bap 1 Jan 1819, ae 3 da; d/ Juan Christobal LOVATO & Maria Rosa GONZALEZ; gp/ José Pablo MARTIN & Maria Joséfa QUINTANA, [*todos de esta vecindad*].

Frame 440
ROMERO, Maria Reyes *India*
bap 6 Jan 1819, ae 3 da; d/ Fran^{co} ROMERO & Juana Maria SUAZO; gm/ Maria Rosa ROMERO, [*todos son Indios de d^{ha} mision*].

SANDOVAL, Maria de Gracia *Vecina*
LEAL, Maria de Gracia
bap 14 Jan 1819, ae 2 da; nat. d/ Mariano SANDOVAL, *vecino de Pecuries*, & Maria Dolores LEAL *de esta vecindad* both single; gp/ Pedro Ygnacio SANDOVAL *de esta Jurisdic^{on}* & Maria Natividad CHACHON *de (sic) la de Pecuries*.

GONZALEZ, Maria Paula *India*
bap 17 Jan 1819, ae 2 da; d/ Santiago GONZALEZ & Loreto ARCHULETA, *Yndios*; gp/ Diego Antonio ROMERO & Maria Manuela GARCIA, *vecinos*.

ROMERO, Maria del Rosario *India*
bap 23 Jan (sic) 1818, ae 7 da; d/ Santiago ROMERO & Maria Fran^{ca} PADILLA, *Indios de d^{hs} mision*; gp/ José Ramon GARCIA & Maria del Rosario APODACA, *vecinos*.

MARTIN, Maria Rafaela *Vec^{na}*
bap 31 Jan 1819, ae 4 da; d/ José Ant^{o} MARTIN & Maria VIJIL; gp/ Pablo DURAN & Maria Soledad XARAMILLO, [*todos de esta vecindad*].

LUCERO, Maria Paula *India*
bap 31 Jan 1819, ae 5 da; d/ Juan José LUCERO & Maria Rosa LUXAN; gm/ Maria Rosa ROMERO, [*todos de esta supradicha mis^{n}*].

Frame 441
SIBOLITO, Antonio Maria *Indio*
bap 31 Jan 1819, ae 5 da; s/ José Ant^{o} SIBOLITO & Maria Soledad LASO, *Indios de esta d^{ha} mision*; gp/ José Ant^{o} MAESE & Maria Man^{la} ROMERO *desta vecindad*.

ESPINOSA, Lorenzo *Indio*
bap 31 Jan 1819, ae 6 da; s/ José Ant^{o} ESPINOSA & Ana Maria PADILLA, *Indios de este pueblo*; gp/ Fran^{co} MAESE & Maria Yg^{a} GABALDON [*de esta vecindad*].

GONZALEZ, Juan Domingo *Vecino*
SALAZAR, Juan Domingo
bap 3 Feb 1819, ae 4 da; nat. s/ Ant^{o} GONZALEZ & Maria Ygnacia SALAZAR, *solteros*; gp/ Fran^{co} Andres TRUXILLO & Ana Joaquina DURAN, [todos de esta *vecindad*].

ROMERO, Pedro Nolazco *Vecino*
bap 3 Feb 1819, ae 3 da; s/ José ROMERO & Maria FERNANDEZ; gp/ Man^{l} FERNANDEZ & Maria M^{la} FERNANDEZ, [*todos de esta vecindad*].

CORTES, Maria Candelaria *Vecina*
bap 4 Feb 1819, ae 2 da; *bastarda* d/ Ysabel CORTÉS, *soltera*; gp/ José TAFOYA & Maria Fran^{ca} BERNAL, [*todos de esta vecindad*].

SANDOVAL, Felipe de Jesus *Vecino*
bap 19 Feb 1819, ae 15 da; s/ Felipe SANDOVAL & Apolonia MAESE; gp/ D^{n} Rafael ROMERO & D^{a} Ana Maria ORTIZ, [*todos de esta vecindad*].

CRUZ, Maria Dolores *Vecina*
bap 22 Feb 1819, ae 11 da; d/ Fran^{co} CRUZ & Maria Josefa MEDINA; gp/ Juan Nicolaz MONTOYA & Mª Gua^{pe} ESPINOSA, [*todos de esta vecindad*].

MARTIN, Maria Severina *Vecina*
bap 23 Feb 1819, ae 11 da; d/ Felipe MARTIN & Maria Micaela ROMERO; gp/ José Ant^{o} MAESE & Ana Maria ROMERO, [*todos de esta vecindad*].

Frame 442
GOMEZ, Maria Juana *Vecina*
bap 24 Feb 1819, ae 4 da; d/ Matheo GOMEZ & Silveria MARTIN, vecinos de la *mision de Abiquiu*; gp/ Man^{l} LUCERO & Andrea LABADIAS *de esta vecindad*.

LUIZ, Maria Lucia *India*
bap 28 Feb 1819, ae 7 da; d/ Juan Pedro LUIZ & Cicilia (n.s.); gm/ Ana Maria CORDOVA, [*todos Indios de d*[ha] *mision*].

PADILLA, Juan de Dios *Vecino*
bap 6 Mch 1819, ae 7 da; s/ Valentin PADILLA & Maria de Jesus JARAMILLO; gp/ Juan Mig[l] TRUXILLO & Maria MEDINA, [*todos de esta vecindad*].

SANDOVAL, José Fran[co] *Vecino*
bap 7 Mch 1819, ae 5 da; s/ Pablo SANDOVAL & Maria Dolores COCA; gp/ José TAFOYA & Francisca BERNAL, [*todos de esta vecindad*].

BORREGO, Juan de Dios *Vecino*
bap 7 Mch 1819, ae 3 da; s/ Pablo BORREGO & Angela BELASQUEZ; gp/ Feliciano SANTI ESTEVAN & Maria Rafaela TRUXILLO, [*todos de esta vecindad*].

VIJIL, Juan Bautista *Vecino*
bap 10 Mch 1819, ae 4 da; s/ Faustin VIJIL & Maria Joséfa MARTIN; gp/ Juan CHAVES & Maria Dolores MARTIN, [*todos de esta vecindad*].

CASILLAS, Maria Albina *Vecina*
bap 13 Mch 1819, ae 3 da; d/ Bartolomé CASILLAS & Maria Elena GONZALEZ; gp/ Ygnacio DURAN & Maria Ant[a] DURAN, *todos son de esta vecindad.*

VIJIL, José Mariano *Vecino*
bap 13 Mch 1819, ae 3 da; s/ Francisco VIJIL & Maria HURTADO; gp/ Juan Nepomuceno MEDINA & Maria VIJIL, *todos son de esta vecindad.*

Frame 443
LUCERO, Maria Barbara Gregoria *Vecina*
bap 15 Mch 1819, ae 3 da; d/ Mig[l] LUCERO & Maria Ramona GONZALEZ; gp/ Lorenso BACA & Maria Guadalupe CORDOVA, *todos son de esta vecindad.*

PACHECO, Maria Agapito *Vecina*
bap 16 Mch 1819, ae 3 da; d/ Diego PACHECO & Maria QUINTANA; gp/ José Man[l] MARTIN & Juana Maria MARTIN, *todos son vecinos agregados a esta supradicha mision.*

GONZALEZ, Maria de Jesus *Vecina*
bap 17 Mch 1819, ae 5 da; d/ Juan GONZALEZ & Gertrudis ARCHULETA; gp/ José Man[l] MEDINA & Antonia Teresa ARCHULETA, *todos son vecinos agregados a esta supradicha mision.*

LASO, Juan Esteban *Indio*
bap 23 Mch 1819, ae 5 da; s/ José LASO & Francisca (n.s.), *Indios de esta supradicha mis*[n]; gp/ Casimiro MARTIN & Maria Romualda MAESE *de esta vecindad.*

ROMERO, Paula *India*
bap 28 Mch 1819, ae 4 da; d/ Juan ROMERO & Maria Ant[a] (n.s.); gm/ Felipa ROMERO, *todos son Indios vecinos de esta supradicha mision.*

CONCHA, José Francisco *Yndio*
bap 28 Mch 1819, ae 9 da; s/ Juan Domingo CONCHA & Micaela ORTIZ, *Indios de esta dicha mision*; gp/ José PACHECO & Maria Dolores PACHECO *de esta vecindad.*

GALLEGO, Maria Francisca *Vecina*
bap 28 Mch 1819, ae 6 da; d/ Pedro GALLEGO & Lorenza ESPINOSA; gp/ Pablo CHAVES & Maria CHAVES.

ROMERO, Lazaro *Vecino*
bap 28 Mch 1819, ae 3 da; s/ Man^{l} ROMERO & Maria del Carmen DURAN; gp/ José MARTIN & Manuela COCA, *todos son de esta vecindad*.

ORTEGA, José Vicente *Vecino*
bap 28 Mch 1819, ae 3 da; s/ Man^{l} ORTEGA & Micaela BRITO; gp/ Juan de Jesus TRUXILLO & Maria Paula ORTEGA.

Frame 444
ROMERO, Maria Manuela *Vec^{na}*
bap 30 Mch 1819, ae 6 da; d/ Agustin ROMERO & Maria Ylaria FERNANDEZ; gp/ Ant^{o} VIJIL & Simona MONTOYA, *son vecinos agregados a esta supradicha mision*.

LOMA, Manuel *Yndio*
bap 4 Apr 1819, *nació ayer*; s/ Juan Domingo LOMA & Francisca ROMERO; gp/ Maria Teresa ROYBAL (sic) & Juan Andres ROMERO, *todos son Yndios de esta supradicha mision*.

MARTIN, José Vicente *Vecino*
bap 11 Apr 1819, ae 8 da; s/ Vuenav^{ra} MARTIN & Rafaela MAESE; gp/ Juan de Jesus LUCERO & Maria Ygnacia ARAGON, *todos son vecinos agregados a esta dha mision*.

LEAL, Maria Albina *Vec^{na}*
bap 11 Apr 1819, ae 8 da; d/ Man^{l} LEAL & Maria Dolores CONTRERAS; gp/ Juan Antonio ROMERO & Ylaria Bibiana ARCHULETA, [*todos de esta vecindad*].

SAMORA, José Maria *Yndio*
bap 11 Apr 1819, ae 9 da; s/ Fran^{co} SAMORA & Catarina PADILLA, *Indios de d^{ha} mision*; gp/ Bernardino MARTIN & Maria Dolores MARTIN *de esta vecindad*.

APODACA, José de Jesus *Vecino*
bap 12 Apr 1819, ae 3 da; s/ Ant^{o} José APODACA & Juana MARTIN; gp/ Fran^{co} PADILLA & Micaela CHAVES, *todos de esta vecindad*.

ARCHULETA, José Fran^{co} *Vecino*
bap 18 Apr 1819, ae 5 da; s/ Ant^{o} ARCHULETA & Catarina ARROYOS; gp/ Lorenzo CORDOVA & Mª Rafaela TRUXILLO, [*todos son de esta vecindad*].

MARQUEZ, Maria Dolores *Vecina*
bap 18 Apr 1819, ae 3 da; d/ Miguel MARQUEZ & Maria Gertrudis MONTOYA; gp/ Juan Christobal VIJIL & Antonia TORRES, [*todos son de esta vecindad*].

BACA, Maria Dolores de Jesus *Vecina*
bap 18 Apr 1819, ae 2 da; d/ Esteban BACA & Maria dela Luz VIJIL; gp/ Jose Buenav^{ra} SANDOVAL & Maria de Jesus MASCAREÑAS, [*todos son de esta vecindad*].

Frame 445
TAFOYA, Maria Dolores *Vecina*
bap 18 Apr 1819, ae 5 da; d/ Salvador TAFOYA & Juana MEDINA; gp/ Bartolomé MONDRAGON & Joséfa MEDINA, [*todos son de esta vecindad*].

VIJIL, Maria Dolores *Vec^{na}*
bap 18 Apr 1819, ae 4 da; d/ Fran^{co} VIJIL & Maria Candelaria PAES; gp/ Fran^{co}

MARTIN & Maria Ygnacia PINEDA, *todos son vecinos agregados a esta d^ha^ mision.*

VIJIL, Maria Reyes *Vecina*
bap 25 Apr 1819, *nació ayer;* d/ Juan de Jesus VIJIL & Luiza SALAZAR; gp/ José Maria MARTIN & Fran^ca^ TRUXILLO, *todos son de esta vecindad.*

VIJIL, Maria Paula *Vecina*
bap 29 Apr 1819, ae 4 da; d/ Ramon VIJIL & Barbara MARTIN; gp/ Juan Julian MARTIN & Asension VARELA, *todos son de esta vecindad.*

HURTADO, José Rafael *Vecino*
bap 1 May 1819, ae 3 da; s/ Miguel HURTADO & Mª LEYBA; gp/ Bartolomé MONDRAGON & Juana MEDINA, *todos son de esta vecindad.*

CASILLAS, Maria de la Luz *Vecina*
bap 3 May 1819, ae 2 da; d/ Christobal CASILLAS & Maria Luisa TAFOYA; gp/ Juan José DURAN & Juana MONTOYA, *todos son de esta vecindad.*

QUINTANA, Maria de la Cruz *Vecina*
bap 7 May 1819, ae 6 da; d/ Rafael QUINTANA & Maria de la Luz MONDRAGON; gp/ José Anastacio VIJIL & Maria de la Cruz QUINTANA, *todos de esta vecindad.*

MIERA, Maria Joséfa *Vecina*
bap 9 May 1819, ae 4 da; d/ José MIERA & Maria Man^la^ ROMERO; gp/ Martin LUNA & Maria Joséfa LUNA, *todos son de esta vecindad.*

ARCHULETA, José Tomas *Vecino*
bap 23 May 1819, ae 6 da; s/ Julian ARCHULETA & Maria Man^la^ VARELA; gp/ Tomas SANDOVAL & Mª Concepcion CHACON, *siendo vecinos de d^ha^ mision todos los referidos.*

Frame 446
SILVA, Maria Dominga *Vec^na^*
bap 30 May 1819, ae 8 da; nat. d/ Rosalia SILVA, *soltera;* gp/ Ramon MARRUJO & Mª Nieves SILVA.

AGUILAR, Maria Asension *Vecina*
bap 30 May 1819, ae 10 da; d/ Jesus AGUILAR & Juana Paula MARTIN; gp/ Juan LOVATO & Guadalupe ROMERO, [*todos de esta vecind^d^*].

SAMORA, José Manuel *Vecino*
bap 30 May 1819, ae 4 da; s/ Pedro SAMORA & Rafaela CASILLAS; gp/ Juan MONDRAGON & Ana Maria MONDRAGON, [*todos de esta vecindad*].

SUAZO, Maria Guadalupe *Yndia*
bap 30 May 1819, ae 4 da; d/ Paulin SUAZO & Rosa SUASO (sic); gm/ Micaela CASILLAS, [*todos son Indios de d^ha^ mision*].

TRUXILLO, Fernando Ant^o^ *Vecino*
bap 1 Jne 1819, *nació ayer;* s/ D^n^ Blas TRUXILLO & Dª Man^la^ SANCHEZ; gm/ Dª Ygnacia RIVERA, *todos son vecinos agregados a esta mis^n^.*

LUCERO, Ant^o^ José *Vecino*
bap 4 Jne 1819, ae 1 da; s/ José Ygnacio LUCERO & Estefana MARTIN; gp/ D^n^ Seferino MARTIN & Dª Maria SANTIESTEBAN, [*todos de esta vecindad*].

SANDOVAL, José Estanislao *Vecino*
*bap 16 May 1819, ae 10 da; s/ Franco SANDOVAL & Mariana TAFOYA; gp/ Esteban VACA & Maria de la Luz MARTIN, [*todos de esta vecindad*].

CHARVÉS, Maria Apolonia *Vec^{na}*
*bap 16 May 1819, ae 3 da; d/ José Man^{l} CHARVÉS & Dominga COCA; gp/ José Maria LUCERO & Mª Ygnacia ARCH^{TA}, *todos son de esta vecindad.*

GOMEZ, Juan Domingo *Vecino*
*bap 14 May 1819, ae 3 da; s/ Ant^{o} GOMEZ & Maria Rosa MARTIN; gp/ José Ant^{o} GONZALEZ & Maria URIOSTE, *todos vecinos de d^{ha} mision.*

Frame 447
SANCHEZ, Juana Maria *Vec^{na}*
bap 10 Jne 1819, *nació ayer;* d/ José SANCHEZ & Juana Maria LOPEZ; gp/ José Domingo SANCHEZ & Maria Gertrudis SANDOVAL, *todos son de esta vecindad.*

DURAN, Maria Basiia *Vec^{na}*
bap 21 Jne 1819, ae 7 da; d/ José DURAN & Maria Theodora VARELA; gp/ José Fran^{co} LUCERO & Maria Paula VARELA, [*todos de esta vecindad*].

LEAL, Maria Soledad *Vec^{na}*
bap 21 Jne 1819, ae 3 da; d/ Rafael LEAL & Teresa VIJIL; gp/ Dionisio VIJIL & Maria DELGADO, [*todos de esta vecindad*].

DURAN, Maria Margarita *Vec^{na}*
bap 23 Jne 1819, ae 6 da; d/ Juan Pablo DURAN & Maria Soledad JARAMILLO; gp/ D^{a} Rafael ROMERO & D^{a} Ana Mª ORTIZ, [*todos de esta vecindad*].

VIJIL, Juana Maria *Vecina*
bap 23 Jne 1819, ae 9 da; d/ Ant^{o} VIJIL & Simona MONTOYA; gp/ Juan de Jesus LUCERO & Mª Ygnacia ARAGON, [*todos de esta vecindad*].

ULIBARRI, Juana Maria *Vecina*
ARMIJO, Juana Maria
bap 23 Jne 1819, ae 7 da; nat. d/ Maria Joséfa ULIBARRI & Alfonso ARMIJO, *solteros;* gp/ Ant^{o} ARAGON & Maria de Jesus MADRID, *todos son de esta vecindad.*

PADILLA, Maria de los Reyes *Vecina*
MARTIN, Maria de los Reyes
bap 29 Jne 1819, ae 1 da; *espuria* d/ Salvador PADILLA, *casado,* & Ygnacia MARTIN, single; gp/ Ygnacio GONZALEZ & Maria Man^{la} SALAZAR, *todos los referidos son de esta vecindad.*

SANCHEZ, Maria Petra *Vecina*
bap 29 Jne 1819, ae 2 da; d/ Juan Nepomuceno SANCHEZ & Maria Leocadia GALLEGO, *vecinos de la mision de Picuries;* gp/ Ant^{o} LUCERO & Maria Dolores LUC^{O}, *feligreses.*

DURAN, Maria Soledad *Vecina*
bap 29 Jne 1819, ae 4 da; d/ Agustin DURAN & Rosalia SAMORA; gp/ Ygnacio MARTIN & Maria Barbara MARTIN, *todos son de esta feligresia.*

Frame 448
GOMEZ, Pedro *Indio*
bap 4 Jly 1819, ae 6 da; s/ Fran^{co} GOMEZ & Rosa RIO; gm/ Maria Apolonia CATUNÁ, [*todos Indios de esta supra dicha mision*].

MASCAREÑAS, Juana Maria *Vecina*
*bap 24 Jne 1819, ae 2 da; d/ Mig^{l} MASCAREÑAS & Maria Man^{la} BUENO; gp/ Maria Guadalupe GARCIA (sic) & José Gregorio CASAUS, *los referidos son de esta vecindad.*

ROMERO, José de Jesus *Vecino*
bap 6 Jly 1819, ae 3 da; s/ Policarpio ROMERO & Maria Gpe DURAN; gp/ Ramon SANDOVAL & Maria Ant^{a} TRUXILLO, *todos son de esta vecindad.*

TRUXILLO, Maria Estefana *Vec^{na}*
bap 7 Jly 1819, ae 3 da; d/ Juan de Jesus TRUXILLO & Maria Dolores MEDINA; gp/ Man^{l} Ant^{o} MONDRAGON & Maria Rosa ARELLANO, *todos son de esta vecindad.*

MEDINA, José Buenaventura *Vec^{na}*
bap 7 Jly 1819, ae 6 da; s/ José Ysidro MEDINA & Maria Ysabel CORDOVA; gp/ Juan Bautista MEDINA & Maria Man^{la} MARTIN, *todos son de esta vecindad.*

SALASAR, Maria Ysabel *Vec^{na}*
bap 11 Jly 1819, ae 4 da; d/ Diego SALASAR & Maria Cristerna SANDOV^{L}; gp/ Francisco VARGAS & Maria Ysidora MARTIN, [*el padrino es soldado de tierra afuera y los demas son de esta vecindad*].

DURAN, Pedro Ygnacio *Vec^{no}*
bap 18 Jly 1819, ae 1 da; s/ Domingo DURAN & Maria Soledad LOVATO; gp/ Mariano JARAMILLO & Maria Josefa LOVATO, [*todos de esta vecindad*].

ROMERO, Maria Ant^{a} *Vec^{na}*
SANCHEZ, Maria Ant^{a}
bap 19 Jly 1819, ae 8 da; *espuria* d/ Maria Pasq^{la} ROMERO, single, & Felipe SANCHEZ, married; gp/ José ARCHULETA & Maria Dolores MESTAS, *todos son de esta vecindad.*

VIJIL, Ant^{o} de Jesus *Vec^{no}*
bap 20 Jly 1819, ae 5 da; s/ Mathias VIJIL & Maria Man^{la} SALAZAR; gp/ Fran^{co} Xavier GARCIA & Maria APODACA, *siendo todos de esta Jurisdicion.*

LALANDA, Maria Soledad *Vec^{na}*
bap 20 Jly 1819, ae about 13 yr; d/ *India de Nacion gentil*, redeemed by the adoptive father, D^{n} Juan Bautista LALANDA *de esta vecindad*; gp/ Ant^{o} SALAZ & Juliana SANCHEZ, *vecinos de Abiqui(u).*

Frame 449
SANDOVAL, Juan Maria *Vec^{na}*
bap 21 Jly 1819, ae 4 da; s/ Ramon SANDOVAL & Maria Ant^{a} TRUXILLO; gp/ Juan LOVATO & Maria Guadalupe ROMERO, *todos son de esta feligresia.*

SANCHEZ, José Santiago *Vecino*
bap 25 Jly 1819, *nacido ayer*; s/ Esteban SANCHEZ & Maria de la Luz BUENO; gp/ Juan Ant^{o} LUCERO & Maria Barbara CORDOVA, *todos de esta vecindad.*

MONTOYA, Maria Salomé *Vec^{na}*
bap 29 Jly 1819, *nacida ayer*; d/ Felipe MONTOYA & Maria Ant^{a} SANCHES; gp/ Juan de Jesus MEDINA & Maria Salomé ARCHULETA, [*todos son de esta vecindad*].

(See Frame 450 for more Jly entries. Frames 451 & 452 have Jly 1820 entries).
VIJIL, Maria Margarita *Vecina*
TRUXILLO, Maria Margarita
bap 1 Aug 1819, ae 5 da; nat. d/ Marcos VIJIL & Simona TRUXILLO, *solteros;*

gp/ Juan Nicolas MONTOYA & Maria Guadalupe VALDES, [*todos son de esta vecindad*].

SANCHEZ, Juan de Dios *Vecino*
bap 2 Aug 1819, ae 6 da; s/ Cristobal SANCHEZ & Buenaventura PADILLA; gp/ Pablo CORDOVA & Ant^{a} Margarita ROMERO, [*todos son de esta vecindad*].

ARCHULETA, José Rafael *Vecino*
bap 22 Aug 1819, ae 3 da; s/ Jesus ARCHULETA & Gertrudis CASAUS; gp/ Julian GARCIA & Barbara LOVATO, [*el padrino es soldado de tierra afuera, los demas son esta vecind^{d}*.

ROMERO, Maria Encarnacion *Vecina*
bap 22 Aug 1819, ae 5 da; d/ Juan Pedro ROMERO & Maria Candelaria TRUXILLO *de esta vecindad*; gp/ Ant^{o} TRUXILLO & Maria Joséfa TAFOYA, *vecinos de la villa de la Cañada*.

MONTAÑO, José Bartolomé *Vecino*
bap 24 Aug 1819, ae 3 da; s/ Rafael MONTAÑO & Gertrudis TRUXILLO *de esta vecindad*; gf/ José RONQUILLOS, *vecino del Paso*.

SISNEROS, Rafael *Indio*
bap 24 Aug 1819, ae 5 da; s/ Juan Ant^{o} SISNEROS & Brigida ROMERO; gm/ Ana Maria PADILLA, [*todos son Ind^{s} de dicha mision*].

MARTIN, Juan de Jesus *Vecino*
bap 26 Aug 1819, *nacio antes de ayer*; s/ Juan de Jesus MARTIN & Maria Concepc^{on} VALDES; gp/ José Ramon SALAZAR & Maria Soledad VIJIL, [*todos son de esta vecindad*].

Frame 450
QUINTANA, Maria Luisa *Vecina*
bap 27 Aug 1819, ae 3 da; d/ Salvador Man^{l} QUINTANA & Maria Soledad LUCERO *de esta vecindad*; gp/ Jose Ant^{o} CARABAJAL, *soldado artillero de tierra afuera*, & Maria Dolores CRESPIN, *vecina de la villa de Sta Fe*.

MARQUEZ, Maria Rosa *India*
bap 29 Aug 1819, ae 3 da; d/ Juan Ant^{o} MARQUEZ & Maria Man^{la} ROMERO; gp/ Luiz DELGADO & Maria Joséfa JUILO, [*Indios de esta supradicha mis^{n}*.

ARMIJO, Maria Seferina *Vec^{na}*
bap 30 Aug 1819, ae 5 da; d/ Man^{l} ARMIJO & Maria Trinidad VIJIL; gp/ Felipe MARTIN & Maria Micaela ROMERO, [*todos son de esta vecindad*].

COCA, José Miguel *Vecino*
bap 5 Sep 1819, ae 5 da; s/ Tomas COCA & Lorenzo SANDOVAL; gp/ Diego ROMERO & Maria Man^{la} COCA, [*todos son de esta vecindad*].

COCA, Maria Rosa *Vecina*
bap 5 Sep 1819, ae 8 da; d/ Juan COCA & Maria de la Luz DURAN; gp/ Man^{l} HURTADO & Maria Gertrudis VIJIL, [*todos de esta vecindad*].

(See Frame 451 for Jly 1820 entries)
MARTIN, Juan Maria *Vec^{no}*
*bap 19 (sic) Jly 1819, *nació ayer*; s/ Felipe Anselmo MARTIN & Maria Gregoria SANCHEZ; gp/ Diego SANCHEZ & Magdalena MARTIN, [*todos son de esta vecindad*].

MADRID, José Agustin *Vecino*
bap 28 Aug 1819, ae 7 da; s/ Cristobal MADRID & Maria Man^{la} PADILLA; gp/ Juan Gab^{l} DURAN & Juana Tomasa GARCIA, [*todos son de esta Jurisdic^{on}*].

HERRERA, Maria Ludovina *Vec^{na}*
bap 29 Aug 1819, ae 5 da; d/ Julian de HERRERA & Fran^{ca} MASCAREÑAS; gp/ Pablo BORREGO & Angela VELASQUEZ, [*todos son de esta vecindad*].

ULIBARRI, José Santos (José de los Santos in margin) *Vec^{no}*
bap 7 Sep 1819, ae 23 da; nat. s/ Maria Romualda ULIBARRI; gp/ D^{n} José Rafael ROMERO & D^{a} Ana Maria ORTIZ, [*todos de esta vecindad*].

PADILLA, Maria Estefana *Mellisa vecina*
bap 8 Sep 1819, ae 4 da; twin d/ Salvador PADILLA & Joséfa MARTIN; gp/ Fran^{co} SANDOV^{L} & Maria Ygnacia CHAVES, [*todos de esta vecindad*].

PADILLA, Maria Joséfa *Geméla vec^{na}*
bap 8 Sep 1819, ae 4 da; twin d/ Salvador PADILLA & Joséfa MARTIN; gp/ Tomas LOVATO & Hermenegilda CASAUS, [*todos de esta Jurisdicion*].

(See frame 455 for rest of 1819 entries. See bottom of Frame 452 forward for Sep 1820 entries. See Frame 461 for beginning of 1820).

Frame 451 (Godparents are given before grandparents)

ROMERO, Maria Silveria Margarita *Vecina*
bap 24 Jne 1820, ae 4 da; d/ Tomás ROMERO & Maria Ysidora MARTIN; gp/ Andres MARTIN & Maria Ant^{a} ORTIZ, [*todos son de esta vecindad*]; ap/ Ant^{o} ROMERO & Maria Fran^{ca} RIVERA; am/ Man^{l} MARTIN & Dorothea ROMERO.

TRUXILLO, Maria Juana Paula *Vecina*
bap 29 Jne 1820, ae 4 da; d/ Marcos TRUXILLO & Maria Ygnacia MIERA; gp/ Ramon SANDOVAL & Maria Ant^{a} TRUXILLO, [*todos son de esta vecindad*]; ap/ Bartolomé TRUXILLO & Maria Paula MEDINA; am/ José MIERA & Man^{la} ROMERO.

FLORES, Juan Antonio *Vecino*
bap 6 July 1820, ae 4 da; s/ Martin FLORES & Maria Encarnac^{n} GONZALEZ; gp/ Man^{l} PADILLA & Ysabel SISNEROS, [*todos son de esta vecindad*]; the godparents did not know who were the grandparents of their godchild.

TORRES, José Tranquilino *Vecino*
bap 9 July 1820, ae 4 da; nat. s/ Maria Joséfa TORRES, single; gp/ Man^{l} JARAMILLO & Maria Fran^{ca} CABALLERO; am/ Diego TORRES & Maria Concepcion TRUXILLO.

CORTÉS, Jose de Jesus *Vecino*
bap 11 July 1820, ae 6 da; s/ Pablo CORTÉS & Maria Dolores PADILLA; gf/ Fran^{co} LOVATO, [*todos son de esta vecindad*]; ap/ José CORTÉS & Juana MONTOYA; am/ Pedro PADILLA & Lucia CHAVES.

MARTIN, José Rafael *Vecino*
bap 12 July 1820, ae 7 da; s/ José Fran^{co} MARTIN & Ysabel CORTÉS; gp/ José Fran^{co} DURAN & Theodora VARELA, [*todos son de esta vecindad*]; ap/ Joaquin MARTIN & Maria Candelaria CHAVES; am/ Cruz CORTÉS & Maria de la Luz MONTOYA.

DURAN, Juan Bautista *Vecino*
bap 23 July 1820, ae 4 da; s/ Juan Nepomuceno DURAN & Maria de la Luz SANCHEZ; gp/ Ygnacio DURAN and Lorenza DURAN, [*todos son de esta vecindad*];

ap/ Man^{l} DURAN & Geralda MASCAREÑAS; am/ Felipe SANCHEZ & Maria de la Luz MARTIN.

Frame 452

ORTEGA, Maria del Refugio Ygnacia *Vecina*
bap 23 July 1820, ae 3 da; d/ Man^{l} ORTEGA & Maria Micaela BRITO; gp/ *el Cabo de Artillenos* Fran^{co} GARCIA & Maria Benigna CORTÉS, [*todos a e<u>ss</u>epcion del militar, son de esta vecindad*]; "the godparents did not give the names of the grandparents of their godchild".

ARAGON, Maria de la Luz *Vecina*
bap 23 July 1820; nat. d/ Ana Maria ARAGON, single, *de esta vecindad*; gp/ D^{n} Jose Rafael ARAGON & D^{a} Ana (illegible) (n.s.) & parishioners Felipe SANDOVAL & Maria Ant^{a} SANDOVAL.

TRUXILLO, Maria Estefana de Jesus *Vecina*
bap 25 July 1820, b. yesterday; d/ Juan Ygnacio TRUXILLO & Juliana MONTOYA; gp/ José de Jesus MONTOYA & Maria Paula MARTIN; ap/ Raymundo TRUXILLO & Maria Paula MARTIN; am/ the same godparents.

DURAN, Juana Maria *Vecina*
bap 26 July 1820, ae 9 da; d/ Rafael DURAN & Maria Ant^{a} CHAVES; gp/ Man^{l} Ant^{o} MARTIN & Maria Man^{la} MONTOYA, [*todos son de esta vecindad*]; the godparents did not give the names of the grandparents of their godchild.

SILVA, Juana Maria Vecina
bap 30 July 1820, ae 4 da; d/ Jose Maria SILVA & Mª SAENS *de esta vecindad*; gp/ *el soldado de Santa Fé* Andres ORTEGA & his wife, Mª de la Luz XARAMILLO; *los padrinos no dieron razon de los abuelos de su ahijado.*

HURTADO, Maria Rosa *Vecina*
bap 3 Sept 1820, ae 4 da; d/ Miguel HURTADO & Maria Gertrudes VIJIL; gp/ José Ant^{o} MARTIN & Maria G^{pe} MARTIN, [*todos de esta vecindad*]; ap/ Mig^{l} HURTADO & Maria SANDOVAL; am/ Jose VIJIL & Petrona PACHECO.

LUCERO, Juan de Jesus *Vecino*
bap 5 Sept 1820; b. yesterday; s/ Mig^{l} LUCERO & Ramona VIJIL; gp/ Ant^{o} José CORDOVA & Maria Rosa SANDOVAL, [*todos son de esta vecindad*].

GONZALEZ, José Seferino *Vecino*
bap 8 Sept 1820, ae 5 da; s/ José Ant^{o} GONZALEZ & Maria Ant^{a} ARAGON; gp/ D. José Raf^{l} ROM^{o} & D. Ana Maria ORTIZ, [*todos son de esta vecindad*].

TRUXILLO, Juan Rafael *Vecino*
bap 8 Sept 1820, b. yesterday; s/ Esteban TRUXILLO & Mariana TAFOYA; gp/ Jose CHARVET & Antonia Theodora LOVATO, [*todos son de esta vecindad*]; *no dieron razon de los abuelos de este ynfante.*

Frame 453

LARRAÑAGA, José Regino de Jesus *Vecino*
bap 10 Sept 1820, ae 5 da; s/ Juan José LARRAÑAGA & Maria Manuela PACHECO; gp/ Juan Ant^{o} LUCERO & Maria Apolonia LU^{o}, [*todos son de esta vecindad*]; ap/ D. Christobal LARRAÑAGA & D^{a} Mª Gertrudis MESTAS; am/ José PACHECO & Maria Gertrudis TORRES.

RIO, José Ant^{o} *Indio*
bap 12 Sept 1820, ae 3 da; s/ José Ant^{o} RIO & Maria Gertrudis ROMERO; gp/ Geronimo ROMERO & Rosalia ROMERO, [*todos son Yndios de d^{ba} mision*].

MEDINA, Juan de Jesus *Vecino melliso*
bap 17 Sept 1820, ae 6 da; nat. twin s/ Gregoria MEDINA; gm/ Petrona PACHECO, [*todos de esta vecindad*].

MEDINA, Maria Gertrudis *Vecina mellisa*
bap 17 Sept 1820, ae 6 da; nat. twin d/ Gregoria MEDINA; gp/ Juan Antonio MARTIN & Maria Rosa VIGIL, [*todos de esta vecindad*].

MARQUES, Jesus Maria *Vecina*
bap 5 Oct 1820, ae 5 da; s/ Manuel MARQUES & Maria LUCERO; gp/ Jose Benito TRUXILLO & Thomasa GARCIA, [*todos de esta vecindad*].

LUCERO, Francisco Antonio *Vecino*
bap 8 Oct 1820, ae 4 da; s/ Pedro LUCERO & Maria dela Luz FERNANDEZ; gp/ Juan Cruz VIGIL & Clara FERNANDEZ, [*todos de esta vecindad*]; ap/ Nicolas LUCERO & Antonia MARTIN; am/ Antonio FERNANDIS (as written) & Barvarita ROMERO.

GONZALES, Jose Francisco *Vecino*
bap 22 Oct 1820, ae 10 da; s/ Don Jose GONZALES & Doña Dorotea BACA; gp/ Don Felipe GRIEGO & Rosalia BACA, [*todos de esta vecindad exceto el padrino es Alferes del Presidio nacional de Santa Fe*].

Frame 454
PACHECO, Maria dela Luz *Vecina*
bap 22 Oct 1820, ae 5 da; d/ Francisco PACHECO & Maria Dolores BARELA; gp/ Crus MARTIN & Maria de Jesus MARTIN, [*todos de esta vecindad*]; ap/ Juan Pedro PACHECO & Maria de la Luz MARTIN; am/ Miguel BARELA and Juana ROMERO.

MARTIN, Francisco Eduardo *Vecino*
bap 22 Oct 1820, ae 10 da; s/ Mariano MARTIN & Brigida TAFOYA; gp/ Don Felipe ROMERO & Catarina CORDOVA, [*todos de esta vecindad*]; ap/ Juan Felipe MARTIN & Ygnacia VIGIL; am/ Juan Domingo TAFOYA & Gertrudis CORDOVA.

ARCHULETA, Juan Cristoval *Vecino*
bap 22 Oct 1820, ae 2 da; s/ Norato ARCHULETA & Maria Dolores MESTAS; gp/ Dionicio CORDOVA & Felipa LOVATO, [*todos de esta vecindad*]; ap/ Damian ARCHULETA & Micaela MARTIN; am/ Jose MESTAS & Barvara MARTIN.

VALVERDE, Juan Nepomuseno *Vecino*
bap 22 Oct 1820, ae 5 da; nat. s/ Maria de Jesus VALVERDE, single *de esta vecindad*; gp/ Jose ESCAJEDA & Ygnes CHAVES.

PADILLA, Jose Miguel *Vecino*
bap 22 Oct 1820, ae 8 da; s/ Juan Antonio PADILLA & Maria Sencion ORTIZ; gp/ Baurito BARGAS & Maria FERNANDIS, [*todos de esta vecindad*].

Frame 455 (& forward for rest of 1819)
ARCHULETA, Maria Antonia *Vec^{na}*
*bap 9 Sep 1819, ae 5 da; d/ Man^{l} ARCHULETA & Maria Gertrudis TRUXILLO; gp/ Antonio VALENCIA & Maria Trinidad MAESE, [*todos son vecinos de esta Jurisdic^{on}*].

LUCERO, José Miguel *Vecino*
bap 9 Sep 1819, *nació ayer*; s/ Juan José LUCERO & Teresa SANCHEZ; gp/ José Dionisio LARRAÑAGA & Maria de la Luz TRUXILLO, [*todos de esta vecindad*].

MARTIN, Jesus Maria *Vec^{no}*
bap 12 Sep 1819, ae 5 da; s/ Francisco MARTIN & Maria Ygnacia ROYBAL; gp/ Diego ROMERO & Maria Man^{la} COCA, [*todos de esta vecindad*].

BUENO, José Rafael *Vecino*
bap 12 Sep 1819, ae 3 da; s/ Matheo BUENO & Joséfa VIJIL; gp/ Juan Ygnacio ESPINOSA & Ant^{a} GONZALEZ, [*todos de esta vecindad*].

CORDOVA, José Victor *Vecino*
bap 12 Sep 1819, ae 4 da; s/ Man^{l} CORDOVA & Maria Theodora MONDRAGON; gp/ Man^{l} Ant^{o} MONDRAGON & Maria Rosa ARELLANO, [*todos son de esta vecindad*].

ROMERO, José Natividad *Vecino*
bap 12 Sep 1819, ae 4 da; s/ D^{n} José Rafael ROMERO & Dª Ana Maria ORTIZ; gp/ Juan Antonio ABEYTA & Feliciana ORTIZ, [*vecinos de esta mision, ecepto el padrino que lo es de la villa de la Cañada*].

GARCIA, Jesus Maria Luciano *Vecino*
bap 18 Sep 1819, ae 3 da; s/ Vicente GARCIA & Juliana ROMERO; gp/ Julian GARCIA & Ana Maria CAMPOS, [*todos de esta jurisdic^{on}*].

ARGUELLO, Juan Felipe de Jesus Vecino
bap 19 Sep 1819, ae 10 da; s/ Jose Concepc^{on} ARGUELLO & Maria Ysidora MEDINA; gp/ Fran^{co} LOVATO & Maria Gertrudis PADILLA, [*todos de esta vecindad*].

Frame 456

LUCERO, José de Jesus *Vecino*
bap 19 Sep 1819, ae 5 da; s/ José Fran^{co} LUCERO & Maria Paula VARELA; gp/ Pablo CORDOVA & Antonia Margarita ROMERO, [*todos de esta vecindad*].

LUXAN, Maria de la Luz *India*
bap 21 Sep 1819, ae 8 da; d/ Juan José LUXAN & Maria Guadalupe PACHECO, *Indios de esta supradicha mision*; gp/ Juan Siriaco GARCIA & Maria Soledad MAESE, *vecinos de esta Jurisdic^{on}*.

TRUXILLO, José Lino *Vecino*
bap 24 Sep 1819, ae 1 da; s/ D^{n} Fran^{co} TRUXILLO & D^{a} Maria Gertrudis MARTIN *de la Jurisdic^{on} de Abiquiu*; gp/ D^{n} Seferino MARTIN & D^{a} Maria del Carmen SANTI ESTEBAN, *mis feligreses*.

FRESQUIS, Maria Micaela *Vec^{na} mellisa*
bap 29 Sep 1819, ae 7 da; twin d/ Ant^{o} FRESQUIS & Maria Reyes SANCHEZ; gp/ Juan DURAN & Maria Dolores MARTIN, [*todos de esta vecindad*].

FRESQUIS, Maria Joséfa *Vec^{na} geméla*
bap 29 Sep 1819, ae 7 da; twin d/ Ant^{o} FRESQUIS & Maria Reyes SANCHEZ; gp/ Juan DURAN & Maria Dolores MARTIN, [*todos de esta vecindad*].

ROMERO, Maria Josefa *India*
bap 29 Sep 1819, ae 5 da; d/ Juan Agustin ROMERO & Fran^{ca} GABILAN; gm/ Rafaela MIRABAL, [*todos Indios de este pueblo*].

DURAN, Maria Gertrudis *Vecina*
bap 3 Oct 1819, ae 3 da; d/ Gregorio DURAN & Maria Rosa URIOSTE; gp/ José Ramon SALAZAR & Maria Soledad VIJIL, [*todos son de esta Jurisdicion*].

DURAN, Maria Francisca *Vec^{na}*
bap 4 Oct 1819, *nació ayer*; d/ Juan de Jesus DURAN & Maria Man^{la} COCA; gp/ José Maria SANCHEZ & Theodora ROMERO, [*todos son de esta vecindad*].

ROMERO, Juana Maria *India*
bap 5 Oct 1819, ae 7 da; d/ Jose Rafael (n.s.) & Lucia ROMERO; gp/ Cruz MARTIN & Maria de Jesus MARTIN *de esta vecindad*.

TAFOYA, Maria de Jesus *Vecina*
bap 7 Oct 1819, ae 5 da; d/ Ant^{o} Roman TAFOYA & Ant^{a} Rosalia DURAN; gp/ Juan Pablo ERRERA & Ana DURAN, [*todos de esta vecindad*].

Frame 457

MEDINA, Maria Estefana *Vec^{na}*
bap 8 Oct 1819, ae 5 da; d/ José Manuel MEDINA & Ant^{a} MARTIN; gp/ Benito de Jesus SANDOVAL & Maria Petra LOVATO, [*todos de esta vecindad*].

VALDÉS, Ant^{o} José *Vecino*
bap 8 Oct 1819, ae 4 da; s/ Buenaventura VALDÉS & Catharina LOVATO; gp/ Juan Domingo TAFOYA & Gertrudis CORDOVA, [*todos de esta vecindad*].

MARTIN, José Fran^{co} *Vecino*
bap 9 Oct 1819, ae 5 da; s/ Fran^{co} Ant^{o} MARTIN & Maria Ygnacia PINEDA; gp/ José VIJIL & Rosalia MARTIN, [estos vecinos de Pecuries, aquellos de esta Jurisdicion].

PADILLA, Maria Francisca *Vecina*
bap 9 Oct 1819, ae 3 da; d/ Manuel PADILLA & Ysabel SISNEROS; gp/ Juan DURAN & Maria Dolores MARTIN, [*todos de esta vecindad*].

SUASO, Ana Maria *Vecina*
bap 16 Oct 1819, ae 4 da; d/ Mariano SUASO & Ana Maria CONCHA, *Indios de esta mision*; gp/ Juan de Jesus VIJIL & Rosa DURAN *de esta vecindad*.

VARELA, Juan Nepomuceno *Vecino*
bap 17 Oct 1819, ae 3 da; s/ Candelario VARELA & Maria Concep^{on} SOLANO; gp/ Pedro Ant^{o} LUCERO & Brijida MARTIN, *todos son de esta vecindad*.

ROMERO, José de Jesus *Vec^{no}*
LUNA, José de Jesus
bap 19 Oct 1819, ae 5 da; nat. s/ Felipe ROMERO, *soltero de la Jurisdicion de San Juan de los Caballeros*, & Maria Joséfa LUNA, *soltera de esta vecindad*; gp/ Juan Nepomuceno LUNA & Maria Candelaria VELARDE, *mis feligreses*.

ARCHULETA, Maria Fran^{ca} *Vec^{na}*
bap 19 Oct 1819, ae 8 da; d/ Julian ARCHULETA & Maria Man^{la} SALAZAR; gp/ Felipe SANCHEZ & Maria Luiza GUTIERREZ, [*todos de esta vecindad*].

CHAVES, Maria Theresa de Jesus *Vec^{na}*
bap 20 Oct 1819, ae 2 da; d/ Julian CHAVES & Man^{la} CORTÉS *de esta vecindad*; gm/ Maria Dolores ORTIZ *de la villa de Sta Fé*.

GONZALEZ, Juan de Jesus *Vecino*
bap 23 Oct 1819, ae 7 da; s/ José Biterbo GONZALEZ & Felipa ZALASAR; gp/ Tomas MARTIN & Rosalia LOMA, [*estos Indios de este pueblo, aquellos son vecinos*.

VACA, Juan Pedro *Vecino*
bap 23 Oct 1819, ae 4 da; s/ Lorenzo VACA & Maria G^{pe} CORDOVA; gp/ Ant^{o} MARTIN & Catharina SANDOVAL, [*todos son de esta vecindad*].

Frame 458
TRUXILLO, Jose An^{to} *Vecino*
bap 24 Oct 1819, ae 7 da; s/ Fran^{co} TRUXILLO & Maria An^{ta} TORRES, *genisaros del pueblo de Abiquiu*; gp/ Juan Buenav^{ra} MARTIN & Andrea MAESE *de esta vecindad.*

ORTIZ (patron), Maria Rafaela Rosalia *Vecina*
bap 30 Oct 1819 by the pastor of la Cañada Fr. D^{n} Juan Tomas TERRAZAS with permission, ae 5 da; d/ (unknown), placed in the house of Dª Maria Dolores ORTIZ, *vecina de Sta Fé y recidente en esta mision* who was the gm.

GALLEGO, Maria Rita *Vecina*
bap (31) Oct 1819, ae 8 da; d/ Pablo GALLEGO & Maria Dolores MARTIN; gp/ An^{to} LUCERO & Maria Dolores LUCERO, [*todos son de esta vecindad*].

CRUZ, Juan de Jesus *Vecino*
bap (31) Oct 1819, ae 8 da; s/ Domingo CRUZ & Maria Man^{la} MADRID; gp/ An^{to} LUCERO & Maria Dolores LUCERO, [*todos son de esta vecindad*].

ARMENTA, Juan Crisostomo *Vec^{no}*
bap (31) Oct 1819, ae 3 da; s/ Antonio ARM^{TA} & Ysabel SANCHEZ; gp/ Juan de Dios ARMENTA & Maria del Carmen VALDÉS, [*todos de esta vecindad*].

GARCIA, José Simon *Vecino*
bap (31) Oct 1819, ae 4 da; nat. s/ Clara GARCIA; gp/ An^{to} ROMERO & Ana Maria CAMPOS, [*todos de esta vecindad*].

SALAZAR, José Antonio *Vecino*
bap 1 Nov 1819, ae 10 da; s/ Mariano SALAZAR & Maria Fran^{ca} VENAVIDES; gp/ Juan de Jesus VIJIL & Rosa DURAN, [*todos son de esta vecindad*].

VIJIL, Maria Ramona *Vec^{na}*
bap 3 Nov 1819, ae 6 da; d/ Fran^{co} VIJIL & Maria Trinidad SALAZAR; gp/ Felipe Neri SISNEROS & Theodora MARTIN, [*todos son de esta vecindad*].

LUNA, José Benito *Vecino*
bap 5 Nov 1819, b. yesterday; s/ Mig^{l} LUNA & Juana VACA; gp/ Nicolaz TAFOYA & Maria Man^{la} MEDINA, [*todos son de esta vecindad*].

BUENO, Maria Dolores *Vec^{na}*
bap 7 Nov 1819, ae 4 da; nat. d/ Joséfa BUENO, single; gf/ Pedro MARTIN, [*todos son de esta vecindad*].

GONZALEZ, José Santos *Indio*
bap 7 Nov 1819, ae 7 da; s/ Jose Mig^{l} GONZALEZ & Ysabel TRUXILLO; gp/ Juan Domingo ROMERO & Lucia GABILAN, all Indians.

BENAVIDES, José Reyes *Vecino*
bap 7 Nov 1819, ae 4 da; s/ Pablo BENAVIDES & Rosa SALAZAR; gp/ José Man^{l} VENABIDES & Maria Gertrudis ROMERO, [*todos son de esta vecindad*].

Frame 459
GONZALEZ, Juana de Jesus *Vecina*
bap 11 Nov 1819, b. yesterday; d/ Juan GONZALEZ & Joséfa MESTAS; gp/ José de Jesus TRUXILLO & Maria G^{pe} TRUXILLO, [*todos de esta vecindad*].

LOVATO, José Francisco *Vec^{no}*
bap 15 Nov 1819, ae 3 da; s/ Fran^{co} LOVATO & Maria Gertrudis PADILLA; gp/ D^{n} Juan LOVATO & D^{a} Maria Ygnacia SANCHEZ, [*todos son de esta vecindad*].

MAESE, Maria Peregrina *Vecina*
bap 18 Nov 1819, ae 3 da; d/ Miguel MAESE & Fran^{ca} MARTIN; gp/ Felipe BERNAL & Maria Candelaria ERRERA, [*todos de esta vecindad*].

TAFOYA, Juan Ysidro *Vec^{no}*
bap 28 Nov 1819, ae 2 da; s/ Jesus TAFOYA & Lorenza QUINTANA; gp/ José Amador VIJIL & Ygnacia QUINT^{NA}, [*todos son de esta vecindad*].

SANDOVAL, Maria Natividad *Vecina*
bap 2 Dec 1819, ae 16 da; d/ José Ramos SANDOVAL & Maria Marta ORTEGA; gp/ Simon GONZALEZ & Maria An^{ta} SANDOVAL, [*todos de esta vecindad*].

ARMIJO, Juan Fran^{co} *Vec^{no}*
bap 2 Dec 1819, ae 4 da; d/ Santiago ARMIJO & Rita SANCHES *de esta vecindad*; gp/ *el soldado de S. Elzearia* Cosme RAMIRES, & *mi feligrés*, Maria Gregoria ARMIJO.

MADRID, José Guadalupe (José Maria G^{pe} in margin) *Vecino*
bap 10 Dec 1819, ae 5 da; s/ Ant^{o} MADRID & Maria Fran^{ca} BUENO; gp/ Juan José PACHO & Maria BUENO, [*todos son de esta vecindad*].

LUCERO, Maria de Jesus *Vecina*
bap 11 Dec 1819, ae 8 da; d/ Juan An^{to} LUCERO & Maria Barbara CORDOVA; gp/ Pedro An^{to} LUC^{O} & Maria Lorenza DURAN, [*todos son de esta vecindad*].

SALAZAR, Maria Guadalupe *Vecina*
bap 14 Dec 1819, ae 5 da; d/ Pedro SALAZAR & (blank space) *de esta vecindad*; gp/ *el soldado* Man^{l} RIVERA & his wife, Maria Peregrina PACH^{CO}.

ROMERO, José Buenaventura *Indio*
bap 17 Dec 1819, ae 13 da; s/ Juan Domingo ROMERO & Rosalia VARELA, *Indios de este pueblo*; gp/ *mis feligreses*, Juan de Jesus VIJIL & Rosa DURAN.

Frame 460
VARGAS, Miguel Ramos *Vecino*
bap 17 Dec 1819, ae 6 da; nat. s/ Maria Rita VARGAS; gp/ Nicolas MONTOYA & Maria Guadalupe ESPINOSA, [*todos son de esta vecindad*].

DURAN, Pedro Luiz *Vecino*
bap 17 Dec 1819, ae 6 da; s/ Juan José DURAN & Juana Fran^{ca} MONTOYA; gp/ José Ramon MEDINA & Maria Guadalupe ESPINOSA, [*todos son de esta vecindad*].

CRUZ, José Mariano *Vecino*
bap 19 Dec 1819, ae 3 da; s/ José CRUZ & Maria ROMERO; gp/ Man^{l} FERNANDEZ & Maria Asencion MARTIN, [*todos son de esta vecindad*].

PAES, Maria del Refugio *Vec^{na}*
bap 24 Dec 1819, ae 4 da; d/ Miguel PAES & Maria Soledad MAESE; gp/ José TAFOYA & Francisca BERNAL, [*todos son de esta vecindad*].

GOMEZ, Juan de Jesus *Indio*
bap 25 Dec 1819, ae 8 da; s/ Fran^{co} GOMEZ & Juana Maria ROMERO, *Indios de dicha mision*; gp/ Juan Esteban MARTIN & Maria Dolores MONTOYA, *vecinos de ella*.

LUCERO, Maria Tomasa *Vecina*
bap 27 Dec 1819, ae 5 da; d/ José Maria LUC^{O} & Maria Ygnacia ARCHULETA; gp/ Miguel LARRAÑAGA & Maria de la Luz TRUXILLO, [*todos son de esta vecindad*].

CORDOVA, Jesus Maria *Indio*
bap 26 Dec 1819, ae 5 da; s/ José CORDOVA & Maria Soledad LUC^{o}, *Indios de d^{ha} mision*; gp/ D^{n} Juan LOVATO & D^{a} Maria Ygnacia SANCHEZ, *vecinos de ella*.

SAMORA, Maria Magdalena *India*
bap 26 Dec 1819, ae 4 da; d/ Man^{l} SAMORA & Maria Rosa DELGADO, *Indios de esta d^{ha} mision*; gp/ Ant^{o} FRESQUIS & Maria Reyes SANCHEZ, *vecinos de ella*.

VALDÉS, Maria Francisca *Vec^{na}*
bap 26 Dec 1819, ae 6 da; d/ Juan Man^{l} VALDÉS & Maria del Rosario MEDINA; gp/ Antonio Tiburcio MEDINA & Maria Rosa MEDINA, [*todos son de esta vecindad*].

GONZALEZ, Maria Guadalupe *India*
bap 26 Dec 1819, ae 4 da; d/ Juan Domingo GONZALEZ & Rafaela CATUFÉ; gm/ Francisca ROMERO, [*todos son Indios de d^{ha} mision*].

Frame 461
GONZALEZ, Juana Gertrudis *India*
bap 26 Dec 1819, ae 9 da; d/ Fran^{co} GONZALEZ & Maria An^{ta} LUXAN; gm/ Maria SISNEROS, [*todos Indios de esta d^{ha} mision*].

ROMERO, Juan Domingo *Indio*
bap 26 Jan 1820, ae 5 da; s/ Juan Domingo ROMERO & Joséfa LOMA; gm/ Maria SUASO, *todos son Ind^{s} de esta d^{ha} mision*].

LOVATO, Juana Tomasa *Vecina*
bap 30 Dec 1819, ae 9 da; d/ José Maria LOVATO & Fabiana LUCERO; gp/ José Ant^{o} GONZALEZ & Maria Concepc^{on} URIOSTE, [*todos de esta vecindad*].

Bautismos
de Indios 027
de vecinos 136
Total 163

Año de 1820

VALDÉS, Jose Manuel *Vecino*
bap 1 Jan 1820, ae 8 da; s/ José Felipe VALDÉS & Magdalena GONZALEZ; gp/ *el Then^{te} D^{n}* Jose Antonio VALENZUELA & Maria Dolores ORTIZ, *recidentes en este Fuerte de S^{n} Fern^{do}*.

CASILLAS, Juan de Jesus *Vecino*
bap 5 Jan 1820, b. yesterday; s/ Cristobal CASILLAS & Luiza TAFOYA; gp/ An^{to} José TAFOYA & Ana Teresa BORREGO, [*todos son de esta vecindad*].

GOMEZ, Maria Manuela *India*
bap 5 Jan 1820, ae 2 da; d/ Fran^{co} GOMEZ & Juana Maria ROMERO; gm/ Juana ROMERO, *todos Indios de d^{ha} mision*].

TRUXILLO, Maria Reyes (Maria de los Reyes in margin) *Vec^{na}*
bap 7 Jan 1820, ae 3 da; d/ An^{to} TRUXILLO & Catarina SANDOVAL; gp/ José Man^{l} MEDINA & Ant^{a} MARTIN, [*todos de esta vecindad*].

LUXAN, José Santiago *Indio*
bap 8 Jan 1820, ae 7 da; s/ Fran^{co} LUXAN & Magdalena ROMERO; gp/ Maria Guadalupe ROMERO, [*todos son Indios de d^{ha} mision*].

Frame 462
PACHECO, José Luciano *Vecino*

bap 9 Jan 1820, ae 2 da; s/ Man^{l} Esteban PACHECO & Maria de Jesus CASAUS; gp/ Christobal LARRAÑAGA & Ana Maria APODACA, [*todos son de esta vecindad*].

GONZALEZ, Juan de Jesus *Indio*
bap 10 Jan 1820, ae 8 da; s/ Juan Ant^{o} GONZALEZ & Micaela MARTIN; gp/ Juan FRESQUIS & Francisca PADILLA, [*todos son Indios de d^{ha} mision*].

NARANJO, Maria Rafaela *Yndia*
bap 10 Jan 1820, ae 3 da; d/ Santiago NARANJO & Paula TUSA; gm/ Maria Rafaela MIRABAL, [*todos son Indios de esta mision*].

QUINTANA, Maria Dolores *Vecina*
bap 10 Jan 1820, ae 3 da; d/ Ramon QUINTANA & Maria de la Cruz MARTIN; gp/ Maria Balbaneda ROMERO & her son, Fran^{co} QUINTANA, [*todos son de esta vecindad*].

MEDINA, Juan de los Reyes *Vec^{no}*
bap 12 Jan 1820, ae 6 da; s/ Gregorio MEDINA & Ysabel ROMERO; gp/ Jose Ramon MEDINA & Ysidora TRUXILLO, [*todos de esta vecindad*].

ESPINOSA, Maria Juana de Jesus *Vecina*
bap 16 Jan 1820, ae 8 da; d/ Felipe ESPINOSA & Maria Candelaria ERRERA *de esta vecindad*; gp/ *el soldado* Juan ROMO & his wife, Maria Ygnacia SILVA.

VALDÉS, Maria Fran^{ca} *Vecina*
bap 21 Jan 1820, ae 6 da; d/ Ladislao VALDÉS & Maria Encarnac^{on} BLEA; gp/ Fran^{co} MAESE & Ygnacia GABALDON, [*todos de esta vecindad*].

SANDOVAL, Maria de Jesus *Vecina*
bap 28 Jan 1820, ae 7 da; d/ Fran^{co} SANDOVAL & Maria Ygnacia CHAVES; gp/ Benito SANDOVAL & Petrona LOVATO, [*todos son de esta vecindad*].

MARTIN, Maria del Pilar *Vecina*
bap 28 Jan 1820, ae 8 da; d/ Miguel MARTIN & Joséfa ARCHULETA; gp/ José An^{to} GALLEGO & Rosa MARTIN, [*todos son de esta vecindad*].

Frame 463
RAEL, José Candelario *Vec^{no}*
bap 4 Feb 1820, ae 3 da; s/ Juan Ygnacio RAEL & Maria Dolores CORDOVA; gp/ Ant^{o} MARTIN & Mª Catarina SANDOVAL, [*todos son de esta vecindad*].

GONZALEZ, José Dionisio *Indio*
*bap 6 Jan 1820, ae 10 da; s/ Ant^{o} GONZALEZ & Fran^{ca} RIO; gm/ Maria SISNEROS, [*todos son Yndios de esta d^{ha} mision*].

BERNAL, José Fran^{co} *Vecino*
bap 6 Feb 1820, ae 4 da; s/ Pedro BERNAL & Gertrudis SUASO; gp/ José Man^{l} SARBÉ & Dominga COCA, [*todos son de esta vecindad*].

CORTÉS, José Candelario (José Maria de la Candelaria in margin) *Vecino*
bap 6 Feb 1820, ae 5 da; s/ José Maria CORTÉS & Magdalena BRITO; gp/ Juan CORTÉS & Maria de la Cruz MARTIN, [*todos son de esta vecindad*].

VIJIL, Teresa de Jesus *Vecina*
bap 10 Feb 1820, ae 8 da; d/ Juan Ygnacio VIJIL & Maria Paula QUINT^{A}; gp/ Jose Ant^{o} GONZALEZ & Maria Concepc^{on} URIOSTE, [*todos son de esta vecindad*].

CORTÉS, Antonio Maria *Vecino*
bap 10 Feb 1820, ae 8 da; s/ Paulin CORTÉS & Maria Concepc^{on} MARTIN; gp/ Fran^{co} CORTÉS & Maria Ant^{a} CARRILLO, [*todos son de esta vecindad*].

ARELLANO, José Mariano *Vecino*
bap 13 Feb 1820, ae 3 da; s/ Juan Ricardo ARELLANO & Maria Juliana VALERIO; gp/ José Mariano ARMENTA & Maria ARM^{TA}, *todos son de esta vecindad*.

TRUXILLO, Maria Antonia *Vec^{na}*
ORTEGA, Maria Antonia
bap 13 Feb 1820, ae 8 da; nat. d/ *los viudos* Juan Mig^{l} TRUXILLO & Mª Concepc^{on} ORTEGA; gf/ Fran^{co} MAESE, *todos son de esta vecindad*.

TAFOYA, Juan Christobal Vecino
bap 15 Feb 1820, ae 3 da; s/ José TAFOYA & Fran^{ca} BERNAL *de esta vecindad*; gp/ *el Alferez D^{n}* Juan Christobal GARCIA & Rosalia VACA.

MAESE, Maria Benigna *Vecina*
bap 16 Feb 1820, ae 5 da; d/ Paulin MAESE & Ygnacia MARTIN; gp/ Fran^{co} LOVATO & his wife, Maria MONDRAGON, *todos son de esta Jurisdic^{on}*.

Frame 464
LARRAÑAGA, Maria Francisca *Vecina*
bap 19 Feb 1820, ae 2 da; d/ Dionisio LARRAÑAGA & Maria Rosario BLEA; gp/ Fran^{co} GUTIERREZ & Maria Man^{la} SALAZAR, *todos son de esta vecindad*.

FRESQUIS, Juan de Dios *Vecino*
bap 20 Feb 1820, ae 3 da; nat. s/ Maria de S. Juan FRESQUIS, *soltera*; gm/ Gregoria SANCHEZ, *todos son de esta vecindad*.

VARELA, José Mathias *Vecino*
bap 27 Feb 1820, ae 2 da; s/ Miguel VARELA & Mª Monserrate ROMERO; gp/ Rafael ROMERO & Romualda ROMERO, *todos son de esta vecindad*.

TAFOYA, Maria Ygnacia *Vecina*
bap 29 Feb 1820, ae 3 da; d/ Juan Bautista TAFOYA & Maria Ant^{a} GONZALEZ; gp/ Bernardo LUCERO & Mª Joséfa QUINT^{NA}, *todos son de esta Feligresia*.

CRUZ, Maria Dolores *Vecina*
bap 1 Mch 1820, ae 2 da; nat. d/ Maria Ant^{a} CRUZ, single; gp/ Juan Yg^{o} SANCH^{Z} & Mª Man^{la} SANCHEZ, *todos son de esta vecindad*.

RODRIGUEZ, Maria del Carmen *Vecina*
bap 1 Mch 1820, ae 4 da; d/ Lorenzo RODRIGUEZ & Joséfa MARTIN; gp/ Tomas CORDOVA & Mª de Jesus CORDOVA, [*todos son de esta vecindad*].

MONDRAGON, José Domingo *Vecino*
bap 2 Mch 1820, ae 3 da; s/ Bartolomé MONDRAGON & Joséfa MEDINA; gp/ Mª Ant^{a} MONTOYA (sic) & Man^{l} An^{to} MONDRAGON, [*todos de esta vecindad*].

BUENO, Pedro Nolasco *Vecino*
bap 4 Mch 1820, ae 3 da; s/ Juan Eugenio BUENO & Teodora VEITA; gp/ Man^{l} DURAN & Geralda MASCAREÑAS, [*todos son de esta vecindad*].

LUCERO, Maria Ant^{o} Gertrudes *Vecina*
bap 4 Mch 1820, ae 2 da; d/ Pedro LUCERO & Gertrudis DURAN; gp/ Juan Nepomuceno DURAN & Maria de la Luz SANCHEZ, [*todos de esta vecindad*].

SUASO, Maria Fran^{ca} *Yndia*
bap 5 Mch 1820, ae 15 da; d/ Fran^{co} SUASO & Joséfa MIRABAL, *Indios de d^{ha} mision; gp/ vecinos de esta* Luiz Maria CASILLAS & Fran^{ca} CASILLAS.

Frame 465
TAFOYA, Juan de Jesus *Vecino*
bap 11 Mch 1820, ae 5 da; s/ Man^{l} TAFOYA & Rosa OLÓNA; gm/ Joséfa VARELA, [*todos son de esta vecindad*].

(Entry with no surnames)

TRUXILLO, Maria Gregoria *Vec^{na}*
bap 16 Mch 1820, ae 4 da; d/ José Vic^{te} TRUXILLO & Maria Encarnac^{on} CORDOVA; gp/ Raymundo CORDOVA & Maria Juliana TORRES, [*todos son de esta vecindad*].

VIJIL, José Fran^{co} *Vecino*
bap 16 Mch 1820, b. yesterday; s/ Hermenegildo VIJIL & Joséfa MARTIN; gp/ Noverto SANDOVAL & Maria Fran^{ca} CASILLAS, [*todos son de esta vecindad*].

LUCERO, José Antonio *Vecino*
bap 19 Mch 1820, ae 9 da; s/ Bernardo LUCERO & Joséfa QUINTANA; gp/ Lorenzo CORDOVA & Mª Rafaela TRUXILLO, [*todos esta vecindad*].

CORTÉS, Maria Soledad *Vecina*
bap 19 Mch 1820, ae 3 da; d/ Bautista CORTÉS & Mª An^{ta} MONTOYA; gp/ Juan Ant^{o} ROMERO & Maria Rosa MARTIN, [*todos son de esta vecindad*].

REYNA, Juan *Yndio*
bap 27 Mch 1820, ae 4 da; s/ José Pablo REYNA & Micaela CASILLAS; gp/ Maria Ant^{a} ROM^{o}, [*todos son Yndios de d^{ha} mision*].

MIRABAL, Maria Bibiana *India*
bap 27 Mch 1820, ae 3 da; d/ Lorenzo MIRABAL & Maria Soledad DOMING^{z}; gm/ Mª Victoria DELGADO, all Indians of this mission.

LUXAN, Maria Joséfa *Yndia*
bap 27 Mch 1820, ae 5 da; d/ Juan Domingo LUXAN & Mª An^{ta} DURAN; gm/ Mª Asension LUNA, [*todos son Indios de d^{ha} mision*].

Frame 466
PACHECO, Maria Soledad *Yndia*
bap 27 Mch 1820, ae 4 da; d/ Pablo PACHECO & Man^{la} SAMORA; gm/ Maria Guadalupe PACHECO, [*todos son Yndios de esta dicha mision*].

LUCERO, Maria Ygnacia *India*
bap 27 Mch 1820, ae 15 da; d/ Lorenzo LUCERO & Mª Man^{la} AGUILA; gm/ Ygnacia RIO, [*todos son Indios de esta subredicha mision*].

ABILA, Maria Theodora *Vecina*
bap 2 Apr 1820, ae 3 da; d/ Anastacio ABILA & Maria Ygnacia LUCERO; gp/ Rafael SISNEROS & Mª Guadalupe SISNEROS, [*todos son vecinos quiza Españoles ágredados â dha mision*].

GARCIA, Maria Ant^{a} *Vecina*
bap 8 Apr 1820, ae 25 da; adopted d/ Mig^{l} GARCIA & Margarita LUCERO, who bought and rescued her from the Apacha Xicarilla Nation and were gp.

ROMERO, Maria Dolores *Vecina*
bap 8 Apr 1820, ae 2 da; d/ Josá Man^{l} ROMERO & Maria Rita SANCHEZ; gp/ Mariano MARTIN & Maria Brigida TAFOYA, [*todos son de esta vecindad*].

ARELLANO, José Julian *Vecino*
bap 9 Apr 1820, ae 4 da; s/ Ramon ARELLANO & Ana Maria ARMENTA; gp/ Man^{l} Ant^{o} MONDRAGON & Maria Rosa ARELLANO, [*todos son de esta vecindad*].

SANDOVAL, Jesus Maria *Vecino*
bap 9 Apr 1820, ae 3 da; s/ Benito de Jesus SANDOVAL & Petrona LOVATO; gp/ Tomas SANDOVAL & Mª Concep^{on} CHACÓN, [*todos son de esta vecindad*].

CHAVES, Maria Clara *Vecina*
bap 10 Apr 1820, ae 3 da; d/ Juan Christov^{l} CHAVES & Maria Dolores MONTOYA; gf/ Blas CHAVES, [*todos son de esta vecindad*].

LUCERO, José Gabriel *Vecino*
bap 10 Apr 1820, ae 3 da; s/ Man^{l} LUCERO & Maria Andrea LABADÍA *de esta vecindad*; gp/ Agustin LUCERO & Maria Gertrudis LABADÍA *de la jurisdicion de San Juan ó Rio Arriba*.

Frame 467
AGUILAR, Jesus Maria *Vec^{no}*
bap 10 Apr 1820, ae 8 da; nat. s/ Maria Ant^{a} AGUILAR, single; gp/ Andres MARTIN & Maria Ant^{a} ORTIZ, [*todos son de esta vecindad*].

SILVA, Maria Ludovina *Vecina*
bap 16 Apr 1820, ae 4 da; d/ José Maria SILVA & Maria Ant^{a} MONTOYA; gp/ Fran^{co} PADILLA & Maria Micaela CHAVES, [*todos son de esta vecindad*].

CORDOVA, Ant^{o} Abad
bap 17 Apr 1820, ae 3 da; s/ Raymundo CORDOVA & Estefania GONZALEZ; gp/ Juan Domingo TAFOYA & Maria Gertrudis CORDOVA, [*todos son de esta vecindad*].

LUCERO, Juan Miguel *Vecino*
bap 23 Apr 1820, b. yesterday; s/ D^{n} Pablo LUCERO & D^{a} Paula LARRAÑAGA; gp/ Miguel LARRAÑAGA & Maria de la Luz TRUXILLO, [*todos son de esta vecindad*].

VIJIL, Manuel Antonio *Vecino*
bap 23 Apr 1820, ae 3 da; s/ Anastasio VIJIL & Maria de la (Cruz) QUINT^{NA}; gp/ Mariano JARAMILLO & Maria Joséfa LOVATO, [*todos son de esta vecindad*].

VIJIL, Man^{l} Ant^{o} *Vecino*
bap 23 Apr 1820, ae 3 da; s/ Juan VIJIL & Joséfa LOVATO; gp/ José de Jesca MONTOYA & Maria Rosa VIJIL, [*todos son de esta vecindad*].

GARCIA, José Buenaventura *Vec^{no}*
bap 23 Apr 1820, ae 5 da; d/ Manuel GARCIA & Mª Trinidad QUINT^{NA}; gp/ Man^{l} PADILLA & Ysabel SISNEROS, [*todos son de esta vecindad*].

ROMERO, Miguel Antonio *Vec^{no}*
bap 23 Apr 1820, ae 6 da; s/ Vicente ROMERO & Maria CHAVES; gp/ Diego ROMERO & Manuela COCA, [*todos son de esta vecindad*].

GOMEZ, Maria Soledad *Vecina*
bap 25 Apr 1820, ae 5 da; d/ Juan GOMEZ & Maria Fran^{ca} TRUXILLO; gp/ Juan LUCERO & Maria Candelaria VEITA, [*todos son de esta vecindad*].

CASAUS, Maria Candelaria *Vecina*
bap 26 Apr 1820, ae 3 da; d/ Juan Ant^{o} CASAUS, dec., & Maria Guadalupe GARCIA; gp/ Fran^{co} SANDOV^{L} & Mariana TAFOYA, [*todos son de esta vecindad*].

TAFOYA, Maria Ramona *Vec^{na}*
bap 26 Apr 1820, ae 3 da; d/ Juan Domingo TAFOYA & Maria Gertrudis CORDOVA; gp/ Raymundo CORDOVA & Maria Micaela GONZALEZ, [*todos son de esta vecindad*].

Frame 468
SANDOVAL, Maria del Refugio Ygnacia *Vecina*
bap 28 Apr 1820, ae 3 da; d/ Ygnacio SANDOVAL & Maria Guadalupe SANTIESTEBAN; gp/ Fran^{co} GARCIA & Lorenza LOPES, [*todos son de esta vecindad*].

VARELA, Juan Fran^{co} *Vecino*
bap 28 Apr 1820, ae 4 da; s/ José VARELA & Maria SANDOVAL; gp/ Juan LOVATO & Maria Guadalupe ROMERO, [*todos son de esta vecindad*].

OYENGUE, Pedro *Yndio*
bap 29 Apr 1820, ae 1 mo; s/ José Miguel OYENGUE & Maria de la Luz ROMERO; gm/ Juana LUCERO, *todos son Yndios de dicha mision*].

GOMEZ, Maria de la Luz *India*
bap 29 Apr 1820, ae 4 da; d/ José GOMEZ & Joséfa ROMERO; gm/ Maria Soledad LUCERO, *todos son Indios de esta sobredicha mision*].

GARCIA, Juan An^{to} *Vecino*
bap 30 Apr 1820, ae 4 da; s/ José Ant^{o} GARCIA & Maria Reyes MARTIN; gp/ Pablo DURAN & Maria Josefa TRUXILLO, [*todos son de esta vecindad*].

FERNANDEZ, Juana Maria *Vecina*
bap 7 May 1820, ae 3 da; d/ Man^{l} FERNANDEZ & Maria Asension MARTIN; gp/ Francisco PINO & Marg^{ta} ROMERO, [*todos son de esta vecindad*].

DURAN, José Rafael *Vecino*
bap 28 May 1820, ae 4 da; s/ Bernardo DURAN & Maria Feliciana VIJIL; gp/ Mariano XARAMILLO & Maria Joséfa LOVATO, [todos son de esta Jurisdic^{on}].

CHAVES, Maria Gertrudis *Vec^{na}*
bap 28 May 1820, ae 15 da; d/ Blas CHAVES & Mª Dolores DURAN; gp/ Juan Christobal CHAVES & Mª Dolores MONTOYA, [*todos son de esta vecindad*].

TRUXILLO, Maria Ygnacia *Vecina*
bap 28 May 1820, ae 5 da; d/ Ant^{o} José TRUXILLO & Manuela COCA; gp/ Pedro MAESE & Maria Rosalia SANDOVAL, [*todos son de esta vecindad*].

SOLANO, Maria de Jesus *Vec^{na}*
bap 28 May 1820, ae 8 da; d/ Maximo SOLANO & Maria VARELA; gp/ José Ant^{o} ARAGON & Maria Barbara ARAGON, [*todos son de esta vecindad*].

Frame 469
CORDOVA, Maria Manuela *Vec^{na}*
bap 1 Jne 1820, ae 7 da; d/ Serafino CORDOVA & Maria Candelaria MEDINA; gp/ Lorenzo CORDOVA & Maria Rafaela TRUXILLO, [*todos son de esta vecindad*]; ap/ Damacio CORDOVA & Maria Ysabel GONZALEZ; am/ Ant^{o} José MEDINA & Micaela VIJIL.

VARELA, Maria Guadalupe *Vec^{na}*
bap 1 Jne 1820, ae 3 da; d/ Juan VARELA & Maria Juliana TRUXILLO; gp/ (sic) Juan Felipe CORDOVA & Maria FERN^{DZ}, [*todos son de esta vecindad*; ap/ Pablo VARELA & Magdalena LOPEZ; am/ Vic^{to} TRUXILLO & Maria Guadalupe CRUZ.

COCA, Juan Christobal *Vecino*
bap 4 Jne 1820, ae 4 da; s/ José Reyes COCA & Maria Man^{la} TRUXILLO; gp/ Pablo SANDOVAL & Maria Dolores COCA, [*todos son de esta vecindad*]; ap/ José Maria COCA & Juana VENABIDES; am/ Juan Christobal TRUXILLO & Maria Soledad ZALAZAR.

ARGUELLO, Maria Alberta *Vecina*
bap 7 Jne 1820, b. yesterday; d/ Fran^{co} ARGUELLO & Clara SANDOVAL; gp/ Rafael TAFOYA & Barbara MEDINA, [*todos de esta vecindad*]; grandparents not given.

ZALASAR, Ana Maria *Vecina*
bap 8 Jne 1820, ae 3 da; d/ Policarpio ZALASAR & Maria Luiza VIJIL; gp/ Juan de Jesus VIJIL & Luiza SALAZAR (sic), [*todos son de esta vecindad*; ap/ Juan Man^{l} SALAZAR & Maria Reyes MARTIN; am/ Salvador VIJIL & Maria Barbara VACA.

LOVATO, Maria Candelaria *Vecina*
bap 9 Jne 1820, ae 2 da; d/ Tomás LOVATO & Hermenegilda CASAUS; gp/ Pablo BUSTOS & Luiza BACA *de esta vecindad*; ap/ José Man^{l} LOVATO & Maria Ant^{o} ORTEGA; am/ Juan Ant^{o} CASAUS & Rosalia MARTIN.

SANCHEZ, José Quirino *Vecino*
bap 11 Jne 1820, ae 7 da; nat. s/ Juana SANCHEZ, single, *de esta vecindad*; gp/ the soldier Rafael LOPEZ & his wife, Juliana MESTAS.

SOLANO, Maria Ygnacia *Vecina*
bap 11 Jne 1820, ae 6 da; d/ Andres SOLÃNO & Serafina LEAL; gp/ José Ant^{o} GONZALEZ & Maria Barbara GONZALEZ, [*todos son de esta vecindad*]; ap/ Man^{l} SOLANO & Rosa DIMAS; am/ Man^{l} José LEAL & Ygnacia QUINTANA.

Frame 470
LARRAÑAGA, José Feliciano *Vecino*
bap 11 Jne 1820, ae 3 da; s/ Christobal LARRAÑAGA & Ana Maria APODACA; gp/ Tomas LUCERO & Maria de la Luz LUCERO, [*todos son de esta vecindad*]; ap/ D^{n} Christobal Maria LARRAÑAGA & D^{a} Maria Gertrudis MESTAS; am/ not given.

MARTIN, Manuel An^{to} *Vecino*
bap 15 Jne 1820, ae 5 da; s/ Fran^{co} MARTIN & Maria Nieves SILVA; gp/ Man^{l} Ant^{o} MARTIN & Maria Balvaneda MONTOYA, [*todos de esta vecindad*]; ap/ Juan Pablo MARTIN & Joséfa ESPINOSA; am/ Santiago SILVA & Juana VELASQUEZ.

ROMERO, José Man^{l} *Yndio*
bap 17 Jne 1820, ae 15 da; s/ Juan Domingo ROMERO & Maria Gua^{pe} SUAZO; gm/ Joaquina TAFOYA, *esta es vecina de esta Jurisdic^{on}, los demas son Yndios de d^{ha} mision.*

CONCHA, Maria Soledad *India*
bap 17 Jne 1820, ae 4 da; d/ Juan Domingo CONCHA & Micaela SUAZO; gp/ Luiz DELGADO & M(a)ria Joséfa JUILO, all Indians of this mission.

SALAZAR, Juan Christobal *Vecino*
bap 18 Jne 1820, ae 3 da; s/ Gervacio SALAZAR & Maria del Rosario COCA; gp/ Juan LUNA & Mª Candelaria VELARDE, [*todos son de esta vecindad*]; ap/ Juan Man^{l} SALASAR (sic) & Joséfa DURAN; am/ José Mª COCA & Juana BENAVIDES.

MEDINA, Fernando *Vecino*
bap 18 Jne 1820, ae 20 da; nat. s/ Paula MEDINA; gp/ (sic) Bernardo Joaquin MAESE & Maria Ynés ARMIJO, [*todos de esta vecindad*]; am/ Ygnacio MEDINA & Marg^{ta} CORDOVA.

MARTIN, Maria Man^{la} *Vecina*
bap 20 Jne 1820, ae 3 da; d/ Juan Ant^{o} MARTIN & Maria CHACON; gp/ Marcelo LOBATO & Maria Joséfa CHAVES, [*todos de esta vecindad*].

FERNANDEZ, Maria Manuela *Vecina*
bap 22 Jne 1820, ae 4 da; d/ José Mariano FERNANDEZ & Maria Asension LUC^{o}; gp/ Miguel GARCIA & Margarita LUCERO, [*todos son de esta vecindad*; ap/ Ant^{o} FERNANDEZ & M(ar)garita ROMERO; am/ José Mig^{l} LUCERO & Joséfa SALAZAR.

Frame 471
FERNANDIS, Juan Lorenzo *Vecino*
bap 5 Nov 1820, ae 3 da; s/ Francisco FERNANDIS & Antonia DURANA; gp/ Manuel LUCERO & Andrea LAVADIA, [*todos de esta vecindad*]; ap/ Jose Mariano FERNANDIS & Cencion LUCERO; am/ Ygnacio DURAN & Maria Antonia SANCHES.

CORDOVA, Salvador Manuel *Vecino*
bap 9 Nov 1820, ae 4 da; s/ Manuel CORDOVA & Maria Teodora MONDRAGON; gp/ Juan Cristoval MONDRAGON & Maria Francisca CORDOVA; ap/ Lorenso CORDOVA & Maria MARTIN; am/ Mariano MONDRAGON & Maria Encarnacion ESPINOSA.

MEDINA, Jose Julian *Vecino*
bap 9 Nov 1820, ae 6 da; s/ Manuel Gregorio MEDINA & Maria Rafaela MARTINA; gp/ Ygnacio ARMENTA & Maria Rosa ARMENTA, [*todos de esta vecindad*].

MEDINA, Maria Dolores *Vecina*
bap 12 Nov 1820, ae 3 da; d/ Jose Manuel MEDINA & Antonia Tereza MARTIN; gp/ Manuel Antonio MONDRAGON & Maria Rosa ARELLANO, [*todos de esta vecindad*]; ap/ Christoval MEDINA & Juana Josefa CORDOVA; am/ Gertrudis ARCHULETA (only).

VARELA, Maria Ramona *Vecina*
bap 14 Nov 1820, ae 3 da; d/ Jose Candelaria VARELA & Maria Concepcion SOLANO; gp/ Pedro Luiz MAES & Maria Rumalda MAES, [*todos de esta vecindad*]; ap/ Andres SOLANO (as written-only); am/ Felisiana (n.s.) (only).

Frame 472
MALINCHE, Maria Manuela *Yndia*
bap 15 Nov 1820, ae 2 da; d/ Juan de Jesus MALINCHE & Maria PADILLA; gp/ Juan Domingo MIRAVAL & Manuela ROMERO, *Yndios*.

TRUXILLO, Jose Martin Reyes *Vecino*
bap 19 Nov 1820, ae 9 da; s/ Luiz TRUXILLO & Maria Gertrudis SANCHEZ; gp/ Jose Maria TORRES & Josefa CHAVEZ, [*todos de esta vecindad*].

SANDOVAL, Manuel Antonio *Vecino*
bap 19 Nov 1820, ae 5 da; s/ Antonio Jose SANDOVAL & Maria Balvaneda (n.s.); gp/ Manuel Antonio MARTIN & Maria Balvaneda MONTOYA, [*todos de esta vecindad*].

AGUILAR, Jose Rafael *Vecino*
bap 3 Dec 1820, ae 8 da; s/ Salvador AGUILAR & Maria Antonio VALDEZ; gp/ Roque MARTIN & Gregoria ARMIJO, [*todos de esta vecindad*].

CONCHA, Juana *Yndia*
bap 8 Dec 1820, ae 1 da; d/ Juan Manuel CONCHA & Maria Dominga ROMERO; gp/ Maria MARTIN (only), [*Yndios de dicha mision*].

VIGIL, Maria Martina *Vecina*
bap 9 Dec 1820, ae 4 da; d/ Jose Francisco VIGIL & Maria HURTADO; gp/ Juan

Cristoval VIGIL & Antonia Biviana TORRES, [*todos de esta vecindad*]. (Frames 472-473)

Frame 473
CHAVEZ, Jose Guadalupe *Vecino*
bap 12 Dec 1820, ae 3 da; s/ Jose Manuel CHAVEZ & Dominga COCA; gp/ Margarita ESPINOSA (only), [*todos de esta vecindad*].

OYENGUE, Thomas *Yndio*
bap 16 Dec 1820, ae 5 da; s/ Diego OYENGUE & Maria Dolores ROMERO; gp/ Thomas MARTIN & Rosalia LUNA, [*todos Yndios de dicha mision*].

MONTOYA, Jose Guadalupe *Vecino*
bap 17 Dec 1820, ae 5 da; s/ Antonio MONTOYA & Maria Dolores (n.s.); gp/ Manuel TORRES & Maria Ygnacia DURAN, [*todos de esta vecindad*].

GUERRERO, Juan Domingo *Vecino*
bap 17 Dec 1820, ae 5 da; s/ Juan GUERRERO & Francisca ROMERO; gp/ Francisco ROMERO & Paula ROMERO, [*todos de esta vecindad*].

AGUILAR, Jose Maria Guadalupe *Vecino*
bap 19 Dec 1820, ae 6 da; s/ Maria Antonio AGUILAR, single; gp/ Antonio Jose ESQUIBEL & Barvara QUINTANA, [*todos de esta vecind*^{d}].

Frame 474
CORDOVA, Maria Eusebia *Vecina*
bap 20 Dec 1820, ae 5 da; d/ Don Lorenzo CORDOVA & Dª Maria Rafaela TRUXILLO; gp/ Don Thomas ROMERO & Luscia ROMERO, [*todos de esta vecindad*]; ap/ Don Antonio Aban CORDOVA & Dª Juliana TORRES; am/ Mariano TRUXILLO & Teodora BACA.

PACHECO, Manuel Antonio *Vecino*
bap 22 Dec 1820, ae 8 da; s/ Diego PACHECO & Maria de Jesus QUINTANA; gp/ Feliciano SANTI ESTEVAN & Rafaela TRUXILLO, [*todos de esta vecindad*].

PACHECO, Jose Miguel *Vecino*
bap 26 Dec 1820, ae 2 da; s/ Ramon PACHECO & Maria Trinidad VIGIL; gp/ Cruz VIGIL & Maria Clara FERNANDIS, [*todos de esta vecindad*]; ap/ Antonio PACHECO & Ygnacia SANDOVAL; am/ the godparents.

MARTIN, Maria Ygnacia *Vecina*
bap 26 Dec 1820, ae 5 da; d/ Juan Antonio MARTIN & Roza VIGIL; gp/ Juan Francisco GUTIERRES & Maria Candelaria MARTIN, [*todos de esta vecindad*]; ap/ Don Pedro MARTIN & Dª Maria Ygnacia GARCIA; am/ Jose VIGIL & Petrona PACHECO. (Frame 474-475)

Frame 475
ROMERO, Maria Manuela *Vecina*
bap 26 Dec 1820, ae 3 da; d/ Jose ROMERO & Maria Biviana FERNANDIS; gp/ Antonio GOMES & Maria Roza MARTIN, [*todos de esta vecindad*].

TORRES, Thomas *Vecino*
bap 26 Dec 1820, ae 5 da; s/ Antonio TORRES & Ysabel FERNANDIS; gp/ Pedro Antonio MARTIN & Maria Reyes PINO, [*todos de esta vecindad*]; ap/ Antonio TORRES & Nicolasa SANDOVAL; am/ Jose Maria FERNANDIS & Maria Sencion LUCERO.

CORTES, Maria Josefa *Vecina*
bap 26 Dec 1820, ae 8 da; d/ Manuel CORTES & Maria Manuela ROMERO; gp/ Manuel ROMERO & Anamaria ORTIZ, [*todos de esta vecindad*].

MONDRAGON, Juan Pasqual Ynosencio *Vecino*
bap 28 Dec 1820, b. yesterday; s/ Juan MONDRAGON & Maria Antonia MONTOYA; gp/ Domingo DURAN & Maria Soledad LOVATO, [*todos de esta vecindad*].

MONTOYA, Jose Maria Dolores *Vecino*
bap 30 Dec 1820, ae 3 da; s/ Juan Rafael MONTOYA & Maria Paula GARCIA; gp/ Barvara QUINTANA & Antonio Jose ESQUIBEL, [*todos de esta vecindad*]. (Frames 475-476)

Frame 476

Ano de 1821

TRUXILLO, Jose de Jesus *Yndio*
bap 1 Jan 1821, ae adult of about 9 yr; s/ *Yndios*, removed *de las naciones gentiles*, adopted s/ Blas TRUXILLO, *vecino de esta*; gp/ Francisco Xabier GARCIA & Maria del Rosario APODACA.

CRUZ, Maria Reyes *Vecina*
bap 6 Jan 1821, b. yesterday; d/ Jose CRUZ & Maria del Carmen ROMERO; gp/ Santos MARTIN & Manuela ROMERO, [*todos de esta vecindad*].

DURAN, Maria Reyes *Vecina*
bap 7 Jan 1821, ae 4 da; d/ Antonio DURAN & Maria Rita LUCERO; gp/ Domingo DURAN and Maria Soledad LOVATO, [*todos de esta vecindad*]; ap/ Ygnacio DURAN and Maria Antonia SANCHES; am/ Bernardo LUCERO & Thomasa MARTINES.

GONZALEZ, Thomas Antonio *Vecino*
TRUXILLO, Thomas Antonio
bap 8 Jan 1821, ae 8 da; nat. s/ Matias GONZALEZ & Maria Ygnacia TRUXILLO, *solteros*; gp/ D. Jose Rafael ROMERO & D[a] Anamaria ORTIZ.

Frame 477
SALAZAR, Juan Manuel *Vecino*
bap 8 Jan 1821, ae 8 da; s/ Ramon SALAZAR & Maria Soledad VIGIL; gp/ Juan Miguel MARQUEZ & Maria Gertrudis MONTOYA, [*todos de esta vecindad*].

SANCHES, Maria Rita *Vecina*
bap 9 Jan 1821, ae 2 da; d/ Felipe SANCHES & Juana Maria MARTIN; gp/ Jose Manuel ROMERO & Maria Rita SANCHES, [*todos de esta vecindad*]; ap/ Juan Ygnacio SANCHES & Pasquala VIGIL; am/ Francisco MARTIN & Roza ARMENTA.

MEDINA, Juan de Jesus Maria *Vecino*
bap 14 Jan 1821, b. yesterday; s/ Jesus MEDINA & Maria Josefa MARTIN; gp/ Juan Pablo DURAN & Maria Soledad JARAMILLO, [*todos de esta becindad*]; ap/ Juan Nepomuseno MEDINA & Maria Candelaria VIGIL; am/ Gervacio MARTIN & Juana CORTES.

HERRERA, Juan Antonio *Vecino*
bap 14 Jan 1821, ae 6 da; s/ Jose HERRERA & Juana GONZALES; gp/ Jose Antonio SUASO & Josefa CASADOS, [*todos de esta vecindad*]; ap/ Paulin de HERRERA & Maria del Carmen MADRID; am/ Juan GONZALES & Maria Antonia MARTIN.

Frame 478
FRESQUIS, Antonio de Jesus (Antonia de Jesus in margin) *Vecina*
bap 19 Jan 1821, ae 1 da; s/ Juan FRESQUIS & Maria DURAN; gp/ Juan Nicolas MONTOYA & Maria Guadalupe ESPINOSA, [*todos de esta vecindad*]; ap/ Antonio FRESQUIS (only); am/ Manuel DURAN & Geralda MASCAREÑA.

GARCIA, Jose Francisco *Vecino*
bap 19 Jan 1821, ae 4 da; s/ Juan Jose GARCIA & Maria Teodora CHAVEZ; gp/

Pablo DURAN & Maria Josefa TRUXILLO, [*todos de esta vecindad*]; ap/ Jose GARCIA & Beatric SANDOVAL; am/ Juan Nepomuseno CHAVEZ & Clara SANDOVAL.

VIGIL, Pedro Antonio *Vecino*
bap 19 Jan 1821, ae 4 da; s/ Rafael VIGIL & Juana SANDOVAL; gp/ Miguel ARCHULETA & Maria Santos TRUXILLO, [*todos de esta vecindad*]; ap/ Miguel VIGIL & Teresa ROMERO; am/ Juan SANDOVAL & Maria Teresa LOPEZ.

SANDOVAL, Maria del Refugio *Vecina*
bap 22 Jan 1821, ae 5 da; d/ Pablo SANDOVAL & Maria Dolores COCA; gp/ Jose TAFOYA & Joaquina TAFOYA; ap/ Felipe SANDOVAL & Gregoria SENA; am/ Jose Maria COCA & Juana VENAVIDES.

VIGIL, Juan Maria *Vecino*
bap 22 Jan 1821, ae 3 da; s/ Rafael VIGIL & Maria dela Luz LUJAN; gp/ Gregorio DURAN & Maria Roza URIOSTE, [*todos de esta vecindad*]; ap/ Juan Bautista VIGIL & Margarita MAESE & Juan LUJAN & Polonia AGUILAR. (Frames 478-479)

Frame 479
SANDOVAL, Juana Maria *Vecina*
bap 23 Jan 1821, ae 2 da; s/ Noverto SANDOVAL & Maria Francisca CASIAS; gp/ Ermenegildo TRUXILLO & Josefa TAFOYA; ap/ Felipe SANDOVAL & Gregoria SENA; am/ Bernardo CASIAS & Maria Dolores MADRID.

ROMERO, Maria Dolores *Vecina*
bap 23 Jan 1821, ae 7 da; *espuria* d/ Maria Biviana ROMERO, *soltera de esta vecindad*; gm/ Petrona PACHECO.

GONSALES, Maria Paula *Vecina*
bap 28 Jan 1821, ae 5 da; d/ Salvador GONSAL^{s} & Anamaria VIGIL; gp/ Manuel LEAL & Maria Dolores CONTRERAS, [*todos de esta vecindad*]; ap/ Jose Antonio GONSALES & Maria REYNA; am/ Santiago VIGIL & Maria Gertrudis TRUXILLO.

TRUXILLO, Maria Josefa *Vecina*
bap 30 Jan 1821, ae 3 da; d/ Pablo TRUXILLO & Feliciana ORTIZ, [*todos de esta vecindad*]; gp/ Juan Andres BERROTERASO & Maria Ygeves (sic) CHAVES; ap/ Bartolome TRUXILLO & Paula MEDINA; am/ Don Gaspar ORTIZ & D^{a} Francisca MARTIN.

VIGIL, Maria Ysavel *Vecina*
bap 31 Jan 1821, ae 8 da; *espuria* d/ Maria Antonia VIGIL; gp/ Juan Pasqual MEDINA & Juana Teresa ESPINOSA. (Frames 479-480)

Frame 480
MARTIN, Maria dela Luz *Vecina*
bap 2 Feb 1821, ae 12 da; d/ Salvador MARTIN & Maria Encarnacion SANDOVAL; gm/ Maria del Rosario APODACA, [*todos de esta vecindad*].

GONSALES, Maria Francisca *Vecina*
bap 2 Feb 1821, ae 6 da; d/ Juan GONSALES & Gertrudis ARCHULETA; gp/ Jose Francisco VIGIL & Maria Trenidad SALAZAR; ap/ Ygnacio GONSALES & Margarita BASQUEZ; am/ Jose Antonio ARCHULETA (only).

BASQUEZ, Pedro Nolasco *Vecino*
bap 4 Feb 1821, ae 5 da; s/ Juan Jose BASQUEZ & Pasquala CORDOVA; gp/ Elogio GONSALES & Maria Guadalupe SISNEROS, [*todos de esta vecindad*].

LA LANDA, Maria Guadalupe *Vecina*
bap 6 Feb 1821, ae 2 da; d/ Don Juan Bautista LA LANDA & Doña Polonia

LUCERO; gp/ Don Jose Gabriel MARTIN & Luicia BACA, [*todos de esta vecindad*]; am/ Christoval LUCERO & Manuela SANDOVAL.

MESTAS, Juan Andres *Vecino*
bap 14 Feb 1821, b. yesterday; *espurio* s/ Paula MESTAS, single, *de esta vecindad*; gp/ Juan Antonio MONTOYA & Maria Dolores AGUERO. (Frames 480-481)

Frame 481
MARTIN, Jose Visente *Vecino*
bap 18 Feb 1821, ae 3 da; *espurio* s/ Maria MARTIN, single, *de esta vecindad*; gp/ Margarita ESPINOSA & Jose Francisco OLONA; am/ Pablo MARTIN & Josefa MONDRAGON.

MARTIN, Maria Refugio *Vecina*
bap 18 Feb 1821, ae 5 da; d/ Felipe MARTIN & Maria Micaela ROMERO; gp/ Jose Francisco VIGIL & Maria Trinidad SALAZAR, [*todos de esta vecindad*]; ap/ Juaquin MARTIN & Dolores QUINTANA; am/ Manuel ROMERO & Maria Josefa BACA.

PACHECO, Buenaventura Claudio *Vecino*
bap 23 Feb 1821, ae 6 da; s/ Juan Antonio PACHECO & Francisca BUENA; gp/ Mariano XARAMILLO & Josefa LOVATO, [*todos de esta vecindad*]; ap/ Juan Antonio PACHECO & Josefa VIGIL; am/ Antonio BUENO & Francisca TAFOYA.

PACHECO, Jose Rafael *Vecino*
bap 25 Feb 1821, ae 6 da; s/ Juan Pedro PACHECO & Serafina MANSANAR^{s}; gp/ Pedro BUENO & Manuela ROMERO, [*todos de esta vecindad*]; ap/ Juan PACHECO & Francisca VALDES; am/ Antonio MANSANARES & Francisca TRUXILLO.

GARCIA, Jose de Jesus *Vecino*
bap 25 Feb 1821, ae 6 da; s/ Miguel GARCIA & Margarita LUCERO; gp/ Pedro Antonio LUCERO & Maria Luz FERNANDIS, [*todos de esta vecindad*]; ap/ Jose GARCIA & Beatris SANDOVAL; am/ Bernardo LUCERO & Thomasa MARTIN. (Frames 481-482)

Frame 482
DURAN, Pedro Antonio *Vecino*
bap 25 Feb 1821, ae 4 da; s/ Juan de Jesus DURAN & Manuela COCO; gp/ Pedro MAESE & Rosalia SANDOVAL, [*todos de esta vecindad*]; ap/ Juan Nicolas DURAN & Juana Antonia ROMERO; am/ Mateo COCO & Guadalupe TAFOYA.

ROMERO, Jose Rafael *Vecino*
bap 26 Feb 1821, ae 10 da; s/ Juan de Jesus ROMERO & Maria Candelaria QUINTANA; gp/ Don Juan LOVATO & Doña Ygnacia SANCHEZ, [*todos de esta vecindad*]; ap/ Antonio Domingo ROMERO & Maria COCA; am/ Juan QUINTANA & Balvaneda ROMERO.

VIGIL, Juan Matias *Vecino*
bap 27 Feb 1821, ae 4 da; s/ Faustin VIGIL & Maria Luz MARTIN; gp/ Juan Nepomuseno CHAVEZ & Clara SANCHEZ, [*todos de esta vecindad*]; ap/ Miguel VIGIL & Ana Maria BALLEJO; am/ Pedro MARTIN & Ygnacia GARCIA.

SANDOVAL, Maria del Carmen Romana *Vecina*
bap 4 Mch 1821, ae 4 da; d/ D. Felipe SANDOVAL & D^{a} Apolonia MEDINA; gp/ D. Felipe GRIEGO & Josefa MEDINA, [*todos de esta vecindad*].

ROMERO, Francisco *Yndio*
bap 6 Mch 1821, ae 10 da; s/ Jose Victor ROMERO & Maria GONSALES; gm/ Maria dela Lus ROMERO, [*todos Yndios de dicha mision*].

Frame 483
ROMERO, Jose Miguel *Yndio*
bap 6 Mch 1821, ae 6 da; s/ Juan Jose ROMERO & Maria ROMERO; gm/ Maria Albina ROMERO, [*todos Yndios de dicha mision*].

LOPEZ, Maria Juana Catarina (Maria Juana in margin) *Vecina*
bap 8 Mch 1821, ae 4 da; d/ Juan Ygnacio LOPEZ and Maria Josefa MUÑIZ; gp/ Thomas LALANDA (Origins, p. 365) & Maria Biviana PACHECO; ap/ Christoval LOPEZ & Teresa MARTIN; am/ Maria Gertrudis MUÑIZ (only).

PACHECO, Maria de Jesus *Vecina*
bap 11 Mch 1821, ae 3 da; *espuria* d/ Maria Dolores PACHECO, single, *de esta vecindad*; gp/ Buenaventura SANDOVAL & Maria MASCAREÑAS; am/ Jose Gregorio PACHECO & Maria Brijida TRUXILLO.

BORREGO, Maria Rosa *Vecina*
bap 11 Mch 1821, ae 7 da; d/ Pablo BORREGO & Maria Angela VELASQUEZ; gp/ Juan Antonio SANTI ESTEVAN & Maria Gertrudis MARTIN, [*todos de esta vecindad*]; am/ Juan Jose VELASQUEZ & Rosa Maria TAPIA.

VIGIL, Pedro *Vecino*
bap 22 Mch 1821, ae 3 da; s/ Juan Christoval VIGIL & Biviana TORRES; gp/ Jose Antonio GONZALES & Maria Antonia ARAGON, [*todos de esta vecindad*]; ap/ Miguel VIGIL & Ana Maria BALLEJOS; am/ Antonio TORRES & Nicolasa SANDOVAL. (Frames 483-484)

Frame 484
PAIS, Jose Gabriel *Vecino*
bap 23 Mch 1821, ae 11 da; s/ Juan de Jesus PAIS & Juana MARQUEZ; gp/ Francisco CORTES & Maria Rafaela MARTIN, [*todos de esta vecindad*].

MARTIN (patron), Jose Christoval *Vecino*
bap 25 Mch 1821, ae about 10 mo; *s/ Nacion Lluta*, purchased of his father by Juana MARTIN *de esta vecindad*; gp/ Jose MONTOYA & Ygnacia VALDES.

HERRERA, Pedro Antonio *Vecino*
bap 25 Mch 1821, ae 3 mo; s/ Nicolas de HERRERA & Francisca MASCAREÑAS; gp/ Balentin PADILLA & Maria de Jesus MADRID, [*todos de esta vecindad*].

CANO, Maria de la Luz *Vecina*
bap 1 Apr 1821, ae 4 da; d/ Francisco CANO & Maria Josefa MEDINA; gp/ Jose Antonio GONZALES & Maria URIOSTE, [*todos de esta vecindad*]; ap/ Vizente Cruz (CANO) & Dionicio BACA; am/ Jose MEDINA & Maria ESPINOZA.

Frame 485
VIGIL, Jose Visente *Vecino*
bap 8 Apr 1821, ae 4 da; s/ Amador VIGIL & Ygnacia QUINTANA; gp/ Mariano MARTIN & Brijida TAFOYA, [*todos de esta vecindad*]; ap/ Marselino VIGIL & Micaela MARTIN; am/ Juan QUINTANA & Felipa MAESA.

GARCIA, Jose Julio *Vecino*
bap 8 Apr 1821, ae 4 mo; *espurio* s/ Maria Dolores GARCIA, single, *de esta vecindad*; gp/ Maria Ygnes ARMIJO & Jose Antonio CRUZ.

VIGIL, Maria Dolores *Vecina*
bap 15 Apr 1821, ae 2 da; d/ Ramon VIGIL & Maria Barvara MARTIN; gp/ Manuel DURAN & Geralda MASCAREÑAS, [*todos de esta vecindad*]; ap/ Cruz VIGIL & Clara FERNANDIS; am/ Ygnacio MARTIN & Paula SALAZAR.

LUNA, Maria Francisca *Vecina*
TORRES, Maria Francisca
bap 29 Apr 1821, ae 6 da; nat. d/ Jose Antonio LUNA & Maria de los Reyes TORRES, *solteros de esta Jurisdicion*; gp/ Pedro Antonio MADRID & Maria Francisca BUENO, [*todos de esta vecindad*].

SANCHEZ, Maria Roza *Vecina*
bap 3 May 1821, ae 4 da; d/ Jose Antonio SANCHEZ & Juana LOPEZ; gp/ Antonio Jose MARTIN & Maria Ygnacia SISNEROS, [*todos de esta vecindad*].

Frame 486
URIOSTE, Maria Guadalupe *Vecina*
bap 3 May 1821, ae 3 da; d/ Juan URIOSTE & Maria VIGIL; gp/ Jose Rafael SANCHEZ & Maria Carmen SANCHEZ, [*todos de esta vecindad*].

CHAVES, Juan Ysidro *Ve^{no}*
bap 19 May 1821, ae 6 da; s/ Pablo CHAVES & Maria Dolores LEAL; gp/ Juan Ant^{o} MARTIN & Maria Encarnac^{on} MARTIN, [*todos de esta vecindad*].

GONZALEZ, Maria Dolores *Vecina*
ARCHULETA, Maria Dolores
bap 19 May 1821, ae 2 da; nat. d/ Matias GONZALEZ & Maria Man^{la} ARCHULETA; gp/ Mig^{l} GARCIA & Margarita LUCERO, [*de esta vecindad son todos*].

MARQUEZ, Juan Chrisostomo *Vec^{no}*
bap 22 May 1821/ ae 3 mo; s/ Ant^{o} MARQUEZ & Maria del Carmen ARAGON; gp/ Juan José ARAGON & Josefa GARCIA, [*todos son de esta vecindad*].

MONTOYA, Maria Estefana *Vec^{na}*
bap 23 May 1821, ae 4 da; d/ Rafael MONTOYA & Luciana MARTIN; gp/ Fran^{co} MAESE & Maria Dolores GONZALEZ, [*todos de esta vecindad*].

LEYBA, Maria Peregrina *Vec^{na}*
PACHECO, Maria Peregrina
bap 15 Jly 1821, ae 9 da; nat. d/ Ramon LEYBA, single, soldier, & Bibiana PACHECO, single *de esta vecindad*; gp/ Diego TORRES & Maria TRUXILLO.

MEDINA, Ant^{o} José *Vecino*
MARTIN, Ant^{o} José
bap 15 Jly 1821, ae 13 da; nat. s/ Nicolas MEDINA & Maria Trinidad MARTIN, *solteros de esta vecindad*; gp/ Felipe MONTOYA & Maria Ant^{a} SANDOVAL.

Frame 487
ROMERO, Juan Antonio *Vec^{o}*
LOVATO, Juan Antonio
bap 15 Jly 1821, ae 12 da; nat. s/ Juan ROMERO & Magdalena LOVATO; gp/ Juan Pedro ROMERO & Candelaria TRUXILLO, [*todos de esta vecindad*].

ESPINOSA, Maria del Carmen *Vec^{a}*
bap 21 Jly 1821, ae 5 da; nat. d/ Maria Encarnac^{on} ESPINOSA; gp/ José Cruz LEAL & Margarita LOVATO, [*todos de esta vecindad*].

ARMENTA, Maria Manuela *Vec^{a}*
bap 24 Jly 1821; d/ Atanacia ARMENTA, *soltera, de esta vecindad*; gm/ Maria del Carmen VALDÉS, *mi feligrés*.

TAFOYA, Maria Ysabel *Vecina*
bap 29 Jly 1821, ae 5 da; d/ Salvador TAFOYA & Juana MEDINA; gp/ Manuel LUCERO & Andrea LABAD^{A}, [*todos de esta vecindad*].

LOMA, Maria Soledad *Yndia*
bap 2 Aug 1821, ae 1 mo; d/ Ramon LOMA & Maria ORTIZ; gp/ Ygnacio ARMENTA & Maria Gertrudis MARTIN, [*todos son mis feligreses*].

SAMORA, Juan Lorenzo *Yndio*
bap 5 Aug 1821, ae 9 da; s/ Pablo SAMORA & Albina ROMERO, Indians of this mission; gp/ Juan Ciriaco GARCIA & Maria MAESE.

PADILLA, Maria Luiza *Vecina*
bap 5 Aug 1821, ae 8 da; d/ Man[l] PADILLA & Hermenegilda VIJIL; gp/ Felipe SANCHEZ & Maria Luisa GUTIERREZ, [*todos de esta vecindad*].

Frame 488
GONZALEZ, Maria Guadalupe *Vec[a]*
TRUXILLO, Maria Guadalupe
bap 12 Aug 1821, ae 7 da; nat. d/ Cristobal GONZALEZ & Maria Simona TRUXILLO, *solteros de esta vecindad*; gp/ Fran[co] PACHECO & Maria Dolores VARELA, *mis feligreses*.

VACA, Maria Rita *Vecina*
bap 12 Aug 1821, ae 2 da; d/ Fran[co] VACA & Maria Joaquina DURAN; gp/ Nicolaz SANDOVAL & Ygnacia BUENO, [*todos de esta vecindad*].

CHAVES, José Maria Guadalupe *Vecino*
*bap Jly 13 1821, ae 1 mo; nat. s/ Maria Ynés CHAVES, single; gp/ D[n] José Rafael ROMERO & D[a] Ana Maria ORTIZ, [*todos de esta vecindad*].

ARELLANO, Juan Nepomuceno *Vec[o]*
bap 7 Sept 1821, ae 12 da; s/ Juan Domingo ARELLANO & Maria Rosa MEDINA; gp/ José Maria LUCERO & Maria Ygnacia ARCHULETA, [*todos de esta vecindad*].

ROMERO, Maria Rosa *Vecina*
bap 8 Sept 1821, ae 14 da; d/ Man[l] ROMERO & Maria DURAN; gp/ Juan Baut[ta] MEDINA & Maria Man[la] MARTIN, [*todos son de esta vecindad*].

LOVATO, Antonio José *Vecino*
bap 8 Sept 1821, ae 22 da; s/ Fran[co] LOVATO & Gertrudis MONDRAGON; gp/ Ysidro SANDOVAL & Maria SANDOVAL, [*todos de esta vecindad*].

GOMEZ, Ygnacia *Yndia*
bap 14 Sept 1821, ae 25 da; d/ Fran[co] GOMEZ & Juana ROMERO; gm/ Lucia GABILÁN, [*todos son Indios de d[ha] mision*.

VARELA, Maria Rosa *Vecina*
bap 16 Sept 1821, ae 4 da; d/ Miguel VARELA & Maria ROM[o]; gp/ Juan de Jesus COCA & Maria DURAN, [*todos son de esta vecindad*].

Frame 489
ARCHULETA, Maria de Jesus *Vecina*
bap 16 Sept. 1821, ae 2 da; d/ Marcos ARCHULETA & Maria Dolores SANCHEZ; gp/ José Venancio CORDOVA & Maria de Jesus CORDOVA, [*todos son de esta vecindad*].

GONZALEZ, Pedro Ant[o] *Yndia*
bap 20 Sept 1821, ae 8 da; s/ Pedro GONZALEZ & Maria Soledad LASO, *Indios de esta sobredicha mision*; gp/ Simon GARCIA & Maria Encarnac[on] BLÉA, *vecinos*.

GUTIERRES, Maria del Refugio *Vecina*
bap 27 Sept 1821, ae 9 da; d/ Fran[co] GUTIERRES & Maria Candelaria MARTIN *de*

esta vecindad; gp/ José Feliz GARCIA & Juliana GARCIA, *vecinos de la ciudad de* Sta *Fé*.

FRESQUIS, José Fran^{co} *Vecino*
bap 8 Oct 1821, ae 7 da; s/ Juan Ant^{o} FRESQUIS & Maria Dolores GABALDÓN; gp/ José Benito TAFOYA & Joaquina TAFOYA, [*todos de esta vecindad*].

SANDOVAL, Maria del Refugio *Vecina*
TRUXILLO, Maria del Refugio
bap 8 Oct 1821, b. yesterday; nat. d/ Maria Ant^{a} SANDOVAL, single, and adopted by Hermenegildo TRUXILLO & Maria Josefa TAFOYA, who were the gp, *todos de esta vecindad*.

GARCIA, Maria Bibiana *Vecina*
bap 14 Oct 1821, ae 13 da; d/ Ladislao GARCIA & Maria Encarnac^{on} BLÉA; gp/ Ynés MARTIN & Ylario MONTES, [*todos son de esta vecindad*].

ARCHULETA, Maria del Refugio *Vec^{na}*
bap 14 Oct 1821, ae 1 da; d/ José de Jesus ARCHULETA & Maria Gertrudis CASAUS; gp/ D^{n} José SALAESES & Maria Luiza VACA, [*todos de esta vecindad* except for the padrino who is *Cabo-esquadra del Presidio de Santa Fe*]; ap/ Pablo ARCHULETA & Maria Barbara LOVATO; am/ Ant^{o} CASAUS & Catarina VACA.

GOMEZ, José Man^{l} *Vecino*
bap 19 Oct 1821, ae 9 da; s/ Juan GOMEZ & Maria Fran^{ca} TRUXILLO; gp/ D^{n} José GONZALEZ & D^{a} Dorothea VACA, [*todos de esta vecindad*]; am/ Blas TRUXILLO & Maria Manuela SANCHEZ.

Frame 490
LEAL, Maria Micaela *Vec^{a}*
bap 21 Oct 1821, ae 5 da; d/ Rafael LEAL & Teresa VIJIL; gp/ Pasqual MARTIN & Maria de la Luz MARTIN, [*todos son de esta vecindad*].

MARTIN, José Fran^{co} *Vec^{no}*
bap 28 Oct 1821, ae 4 da; s/ Juan Julian MARTIN & Maria Guadalupe VIJIL; gp/ José GONZALEZ & Gregoria MEDINA, [*todos son de esta vecindad*].

ROMERO, Juan Ant^{o} *Indio*
bap 1 Nov 1821, ae 12 da; s/ Juan Domingo ROMERO & Maria Rosa ROMERO; gm/ Brigida ROMERO, [*todos Yndios de esta supredicha mision*].

MARQUEZ, Jesus Maria *Vecina*
bap 2 Nov 1821, ae 4 da; s/ Miguel MARQUEZ & Maria Gertrudis MONTOYA; gp/ D^{n} Mariano XARAMILLO & D^{a} Maria Joséfa LOVATO, [*todos de esta vecindad*].

LUCERO, Maria Tomasa *Vecina*
bap 9 Nov 1821, ae 3 da; d/ Man^{l} LUCERO & Andrea LAVADIA [*de esta vecindad*]; gp/ *el Sargento, D^{n}* José Ant^{o} ALARÍ & Maria de la Luz TRUXILLO.

ROMERO, Maria Fran^{ca} *Yndia*
bap 13 Nov 1821, ae 20 da; d/ Rafael ROMERO & Juana Maria SUASO; gm/ Ygnacia SAMORA, [*todos son Yndios de esta sobredicha mision*].

ROMERO, Juan Ant^{o} *Indio*
bap 18 Nov 1821, ae 20 da; s/ Juan Miguel ROMERO & Fran^{ca} LOMA, Indians of this mission; gp/ Ygnacio GONZALEZ & Maria Joséfa LALANDA *de esta vecindad*.

LUXAN, Rosa Maria *Yndia*
bap 20 Nov 1821, ae 18 da; d/ José Man[l] LUXAN & Maria Ygnacia ROMERO, Indians of this mission; gp/ Mariano XARAMILLO & D[a] Ygnacia SANCH[z] *de esta vecindad.*

(See Frame 513 to middle of 514 for rest of Nov and Dec 1821)

Frame 491

Año de 1822

ESPINOSA, Maria Luiza *India*
bap 7 Jan 1822, ae 11 da; d/ José Ant[o] ESPINOSA & Maria PADILLA, Indians of this mission; gp/ Luiz CHAVEZ & Juliana AGUILAR *de esta vecindad.*

MEDINA, Maria Reyes *Vecina*
bap 9 Jan 1822, ae 3 da; d/ Ysidro MEDINA & Ysabel CORDOVA; gp/ Juan QUINTANA & Balbaneda ROMERO, [*todos son de esta vecindad*]; ap/ Juan Pasqual MEDINA & Teresa ESPINOSA; am/ José Ant[o] CORDOVA & Juana MARTIN.

AÑO NUEVO, Manuel Ant[o] *Yndio*
bap 12 Jan 1822, ae 4 da; s/ Paulin AÑO NUEVO & Maria Rosa SUASO, [*Yndios de esta sobredicha mision*]; gp/ Domingo DURAN & Maria Soledad LOVATO *de esta vecindad.*

LUXAN, Jose Ygnacio *Yndio*
bap 13 Jan 1822, ae 9 da; s/ Pedro LUXAN & Bibiana REYNA, *Indians of this mission*; gp/ Ygnacio MARTIN and Maria Asension VARELA *de esta vecindad.*

FERNANDEZ, Maria Asension *Vec[a]*
bap 13 Jan 1822, b. yesterday; d/ Fran[co] FERNANDEZ & Maria Ant[a] DURAN; gp/ Pedro Ant[o] LUCERO & Maria Gertrudis DURAN, [*todos de esta vecindad*]; ap/ José Mariano FERNANDEZ & Maria Asension LUCERO; am/ Ygnacio DURAN & Maria Ant[a] SANCHEZ.

DURAN, Jose Ramon *Vecino*
bap 19 Jan 1822, ae 3 da; s/ Juan Nepomuceno DURAN & Maria de la Luz SANCHEZ; gp/ Pablo VARGAS & Maria Ygnacia CORDOVA, [*todos de esta vecindad*; ap/ Man[l] DURAN & Geralda MASCAREÑAS; am/ Felipe SANCHEZ & Juana MARTIN.

Frame 492

GOMEZ, Maria Estefana *Vec[na]*
bap 22 Jan 1822, ae 2 da; d/ Antonio GOMEZ & Maria Rosa MARTIN; gp/ Juan Ygnacio SANCHEZ & Maria Manuela SANCHEZ, [*todos son de esta Jurisdic[on]*]; ap/ Juan Miguel GOMEZ & Maria ROMERO; am/ Ygnacio MARTIN & Paula SALAZAR.

ROMERO, José Pablo *Vecino*
bap 22 Jan 1822, ae 4 da; s/ Ant[o] Rafael ROMERO & Romualda RIVALÍ; gp/ D[n] Andres MARTIN & D[a] Maria Ant[a] ORTIZ, [*todos de esta vecindad*]; ap/ Mariano ROMERO & Fran[ca] ARMENTA; am/ Ant[o] RIVALÍ & Juliana MAESE.

CHARVET, Maria Guadalupe *Vecina*
bap 22 Jan 1822, ae 3 da; d/ *el Francés* José CHARVET & Theodora LOVATO; gp/ Ygnacio GONZALEZ & Joséfa LALANDA, [*todos son de esta Jurisdicion*]; am/ Tomas LOVATO & Maria Candelaria GONZALEZ.

VALENCIA, Maria Paula *Vecina*
LUCERO, Maria Paula
bap 25 Jan 1822, ae 3 da; nat. d/ single (parents) Ant[o] VALENCIA & Juana Maria LUCERO; gp/ José Maria LUCERO & Maria Ygnacia ARCHULETA, [*todos de esta vecindad*]; ap/ Pedro Ant[o] VALENCIA & Maria Trinidad MAESE; am/ Juan LUCERO & Juana ARAGON.

DURAN, Jesus Maria *Vecino*
bap 25 Jan 1822, b. yesterday; s/ Bernardo DURAN & Barbara VIJIL; gp/ Ygnacio GONZALEZ & Maria Joséfa LALANDA, [*todos son de esta vecindad*]; ap/ Man^{l} DURAN & Geralda MASCAREÑAS; am/ Cruz VIJIL & Clara FERNANDEZ.

RAEL, Maria Gertrudis *Vec^{na}*
bap 27 Jan 1822, ae 4 da; d/ Juan RAEL & Maria Dolores MARTIN; gp/ Juan Gabriel DURAN & Juana Tomasa GARCIA, [*todos de esta vecindad*].

ROMERO, Juan Domingo *Yndio*
bap 27 Jan 1822, ae 10 da; s/ Salvador ROMERO & Catarina ROMERO; gm/ Man^{la} ROMERO, [all Indians of this mission].

Frame 493
LUCAS, Maria Francisca *Yndia*
bap 27 Jan 1822, ae 3 da; d/ Juan Domingo LUCAS & Maria Gua^{pe} PACHECO, Indians of this mission; gp/ Jose Ant^{o} GONZALEZ & Maria URIOSTE *de esta vecindad*.

CORDOVA, José Antonio *Vecino*
bap 6 Feb 1822, ae 17 da; s/ Man^{l} CORDOVA & Maria Theodora MONDRAGON; gp/ Ant^{o} MARTIN & Maria Guadalupe CORDOVA, [*todos son de esta vecindad*]; ap/ Lorenzo CORDOVA & Margarita MARTIN; am/ Mariano MONDRAGON & Maria ESPINOZA.

TAFOYA, Maria Ygnacia *Vec^{na}*
bap 10 Feb 1822; b. yesterday; d/ Ramon TAFOYA & Rosalia DURAN; gp/ Jesus SALAZAR & Maria Luiza VEJIL, [*todos son de esta vecindad*]; ap/ Bartolomé TAFOYA & Maria Dolores MAESE; am/ Man^{l} DURAN & Geralda MASCAREÑAS.

VIJIL, Salvador Ant^{o} *Vecino*
bap 17 Feb 1822, ae 3 da; s/ José VIJIL & Margarita LOVATO; gp/ Ygnacio DURAN & Lorenza DURAN, [*todos son de esta Feligresia*; ap/ Rafael VIJIL & Lorenza LEAL; am/ Rafael LOVATO & Maria de la Luz ESPINOSA.

ZAMORA, Maria Eustaquia de Jesus *Yndia*
bap 27 Feb 1822, ae 6 da; d/ Juan Gabriel ZAMORA & Maria Asension LOMA, *Yndios de esta sobredicha mision*; gf/ José Gregorio MARTIN, *vecino del Embudo*.

MARTIN, Maria Joséfa *Yndia*
bap 28 Feb 1822, ae 7 da; d/ Juan José MARTIN & Juana GOMEZ; gm/ Maria Joséfa MIRABAL, [all are Indians of this mission].

QUINTANA, Jesus Maria Vec^{no}
MONTES, Jesus Maria
bap 28 Feb 1822, ae 2 da; nat. s/ Maria Manuela MONTES (sic) & Miguel QUINTANA, *solteros*; gf/ Juan Bautista MEDINA, [*todos de esta vecindad*].

Frame 494
VIJIL, Maria Cicilia *Vec^{na}*
bap 3 Mch 1822, ae 6 da; d/ Fran^{co} VIJIL & Maria Trinidad SALAZAR; gp/ Juan Pascual MARTIN & Maria Gertrudis MARTIN, [*todos de esta vecindad*].

CACHANA, Santiago *Indio*
bap 5 Mch 1822, ae 7 da; d/ Juan Andres CACHANA & Rafaela AYO; gm/ Juana LUCERO, all Indians of this mission.

NARANJO, Francisco *Indio*
bap 7 Mch 1822, ae 20 da; s/ Santiago NARANJO & Paula MOYA; gm/ Juana LUC^{O}, all Indians of this mission.

ZAMORA, Maria Paula *India*
bap 7 Mch 1822, ae 8 da; d/ Fran^{co} ZAMORA & Catarina PADILLA; gp/ Fran^{co} CHINAZO & Paula PADILLA, all Indians of this mission.

ROMERO, Maria Dolores *Vec^{na}*
bap 7 Mch 1822, ae 10 da; d/ Juan Pedro ROMERO & Maria Candelaria TRUXILLO; gp/ José SUASO & Joséfa CASAUS, [*todos son de esta vecindad*]; ap/ Nicolaz ROMERO & Gertrudis NIETO; am/ Alexandro TRUXILLO & Man^{la} ARCHULETA.

QUINTANA, Jose Tomas *Vecino*
bap 10 Mch 1822, ae 4 da; s/ José Candelario QUINTANA & Maria de la Cruz TRUXILLO; gp/ Ramon VIJIL & Maria Barbara MARTIN, [*todos son de esta vecindad*].

LUCERO, Maria Fran^{ca} Romana *Vecina*
bap 11 Mch 1822, ae 2 da; d/ José Maria LUC^{o} & Maria Ygnacia ARCHULETA *de esta vecindad*; gf/ D^{n} José SALAISES, *Cabo de Esquadra del Presidio de Santa Fé*.

Frame 495
ROMERO, Maria Rosa *Vecina*
bap 12 Mch 1822, ae 3 da; d/ José Man^{l} ROMERO & Maria Rita SANCHEZ; gp/ Man^{l} SANCHEZ & Nicolaza SANDOVAL, [*todos de esta vecindad*], who are also the am; ap/ Concepcion ROMERO & Maria Rosa QUINTANA.

DURAN, José Gregorio *Vec^{no}*
bap 15 Mch 1822, ae 3 da; s/ Domingo DURAN & Maria Soledad LOVATO; gp/ Fran^{co} MARTIN & Maria Ygnacia PINEDA, [*todos son de esta Juridic^{on}*]; ap/ Ygnacio DURAN & Maria Ant^{a} SANCHEZ; am/ Salvador LOVATO & Maria Candelaria CORDOVA.

LUCERO, Maria Dolores Gregoria *Vecina*
bap 17 Mch 1822, ae 5 da; d/ D^{n} Bernardo LUCERO & D^{a} Joséfa QUINTANA; gp/ D^{n} Ant^{o} LUCERO & D^{a} Maria Estefan<u>i</u>a ARAGON, [*todos son de esta vecindad*]; ap/ Man^{l} LUCERO & Manuela VALLEJOS; am/ Juan QUINTANA & Balbanera ROM^{o}.

LUXAN, Maria Joséfa *India*
bap 24 Mch 1822, ae 9 da; d/ Fran^{co} LUXAN & Magdalena LUCERO, Indians of this mission; gp/ Mariano JARAMILLO & Maria Joséfa LOVATO, *vecinos de esta*.

MEDINA, José Eusebio *Vec^{no}*
bap 24 Mch 1822, ae 6 da; s/ Juan MEDINA & Manuela MARTIN; gp/ Ant^{o} José CORDOVA & Maria Rosa SANDOVAL, [*todos son de esta vecindad*]; ap/ José Ant^{o} MEDINA & Juana Gertrudis ROMERO; am/ Eucebio MARTIN & Maria Ant^{a} ARMIJO.

ROMERO, José Francisco *Ind^{o}*
bap 24 Mch 1822, ae 10 da; s/ Rafael ROMERO & Lucia PADILLA, *Indios de dha mision*; gp/ Juan Ygnacio VIJIL & Juana Paula QUINTANA *de esta vecindad*.

Frame 496
FERNANDEZ, Maria de la Encarnacion *Vec^{na}*
bap 24 Mch 1822, ae 4 da; d/ Manuel FERNANDEZ & Maria Asension MARTIN; gp/ Juan CORDOVA & Maria de Jesus FERNANDEZ, [*todos de esta vecindad*]; ap/ Domingo FERNANDEZ & Maria Fran^{ca} GARCIA; am/ Ant^{o} MARTIN & Maria Reyes PINO.

CORTES, Maria Alvina *Vec^{na}*
bap 1 Apr 1822, ae 3 da; d/ Cruz CORTÉS & Juana PADILLA; gp/ D^{n} Juan LOVATO & D^{a} Maria Ygnacia SANCHEZ, [todos de esta vecindad].

CORTÉS, Maria Dolores Vec^{na}
bap 1 Apr 1822, ae 3 da; d/ Pablo CORTÉS & Maria Dolores PADILLA; gp/ Matheo

LOVATO & Maria Dolores LOVATO, [*todos de esta vecindad*]; ap/ José CORTÉS & Juana MONTOYA; am/ Pedro PADILLA & Lucia MARTIN.

QUINTANA, Fran^{co} Ant^{o} *Vecino*
bap 3 Apr 1822, ae 3 da; s/ Salvador QUINTANA & Maria Soledad LUCÉRO; gp/ Man^{l} GARCIA & Maria Trinidad QUINTANA, [*todos de esta Jurisdic^{on}*].

MADRID, Juana Rosalia *Vecina*
bap 9 Apr 1822, ae 1 da; d/ Ant^{o} MADRID & Fran^{ca} BUENO; gp/ José ZUASO & Maria Joséfa CASAUS, [*todos son de esta Jurisdic^{on}*; ap/ Pedro MADRID & Maria de la Luz MOYA; am/ Juan Eugenio BUENO & Theodora VEITIA.

VALDÉS, Juan Basilio *Vecino*
bap 21 Apr 1822, ae 8 da; s/ Fran^{co} VALDÉS & Maria Paula MAESE; gp/ D^{a} Paula LARRAÑAGA & D^{n} Ant^{o} LUCÉRO; ap/ Juan VALDÉS & Bibiana VACA; am/ Ant^{o} MAESE & Victoria SISNEROS.

Frame 497
CAYGUA, Maria Dolores *Yndia*
bap 21 Apr 1822, ae 10 da; d/ Santiago CAYGUA & Joséfa RIO; gm/ Maria Dolores ROMERO, [*todos son Indios de esta mision*].

BERNAL, Maria Soledad *Vecina*
bap 1 May 1822, ae 7 da; d/ Felipe BERNAL & Candelaria ERRERA; gp/ Jesus TRUXILLO & Maria del Refugio TRUXILLO, [*todos son de esta vecindad*].

VIJIL, Maria de la Cruz *Vecina*
bap 3 May 1822, b. yesterday; d/ Juan VIJIL & Joséfa LOVATO; gp/ Juan de Jesus VIJIL & Rosa DURAN, [*todos son de esta vecindad*]; ap/ Manuel VIJIL & Antonia ROMERO; am/ Salvador LOVATO & Maria Candelaria CORDOVA.

CHAVES, Juan Nepomuceno *Vec^{no}*
bap 5 May 1822, ae 3 da; s/ Blas CHAVES & Maria Dolores MARTIN; gp/ Man^{l} LUCÉRO & Barbara MARTIN, [*todos son de esta vecindad*]; ap/ Juan CHAVES & Clara SANCHEZ; am/ Ygnacio MARTIN & Maria Paula ZALAZAR.

ORTIZ, Maria Hylaria *Yndia*
bap 5 May 1822, ae 8 da; nat. d/ Fran^{ca} ORTIZ; gp/ Luiz DELGADO & Maria Joséfa JUILO, all Indians of this mission.

ARCHULETA, Maria de la Asension *Vec^{na}*
bap 24 May 1822, ae 8 da; d/ Manuel ARCHULETA & Bibiana GONZALEZ; gp/ Juan GONZALEZ & Joséfa MESTAS, [*todos son de esta vecindad*].

MARTIN, Maria Rita *Vec^{na}*
bap 27 May 1822, ae 5 da; d/ Buenaventura MARTIN & Rafaela MAESE; gp/ Santiago MARTIN & Maria de la Luz MARTIN, [*todos son de esta feligresia*; ap/ Ant^{o} José MARTIN & Man^{la} VEITIA; am/ Christobal MAESE & Juana Mª SANDOV^{L}.

Frame 498
LEAL, Maria Manuela *Vec^{a}*
bap 27 May 1822, b. yesterday; nat. d/ Juana Man^{la} LEAL; gm/ D^{a} Maria Ygnacia SANCHEZ, [*todos son de esta Feligresia*].

ARCHULETA, Juan de Jesus *Vec^{o}*
bap 30 May 1822, ae 3 da; s/ Julian ARCHULETA & Maria Man^{la} VARELA; gp/ José Miguel MARTIN & Maria Dolor^{s} MARTIN, [*todos son de esta vecindad*]; ap/ Damian ARCHULETA & Juana GONZALEZ.

LUCÉRO, Maria Ygnacia *Vecª*
bap 3 Jun 1822, ae 3 da; d/ Juan José LUCº & Maria Teresa SANCHEZ; gp/ Mariana MONTOYA & Juan Miguel ZUAZO, [*todos son de esta vecindad*.

CASILLAS, Juana Maria *Vecina*
bap 7 Jun 1822, ae 3 da; d/ Bartolome CASILLAS & Elena MARTIN; gp/ Domingo CHAVES & Maria Antª CHAVES, [*todos son de esta vecindad*].

DURAN, Lugarda *Vecina*
bap 21 Jun 1822, ae 6 da; d/ José Fran^{co} DURAN & Theodora VARELA, *de esta vecindad*; gp/ D^{n} Juan de Jesus ROMERO & Maria de la Cruz MARTIN.

SANDOVAL, Juana Antª *Vecina*
bap 23 Jun 1822, ae 4 da; d/ Fran^{co} SANDOVAL & Mariana TAFOYA; gp/ José ZUAZO & Joséfa CASAUS, [*todos de esta vecindad*]; ap/ Alonso SANDOVAL & Rita ROMERO; am/ Paulin TAFOYA & Ysabel CORDOVA.

TAFOYA, Maria de Gracia *Vecina*
bap 21 Jly 1822, ae 5 da; d/ Jesus TAFOYA & Lorenza QUINTANA; gp/ Felix URIOSTE & Maria URIOSTE, [*todos de esta vecindad*]; ap/ Salvador TAFOYA & Maria Ygnacia CANO; am/ Juan QUINTANA & Felipa MAESE.

CUERVITO, Maria Joséfa *Yndia*
bap 21 Jly 1822, ae 4 da; d/ Andres CUERVITO & Rosalia ZAMORA, Indians of this mission; gp/ José Pablo ARCHULETA & Barbara LOBATO, *vecinos*.

Frame 499
ROMERO, Ana Maria *Yndia*
bap 26 Jly 1822, ae 3 da; d/ Juan Domingo ROMERO & Luzia GABILAN, *Indios de esta sobredicha mision*; gp/ Jesus TRUXILLO & Maria del Refugio TRUXILLO *de esta vecindad*.

CORDOVA, Juan Roque Vecº
bap 18 Aug 1822, ae 3 da; s/ D. Policarpio CORDOVA & D. Micaela GONZALEZ; gp/ D. Raymundo CORDOVA & D. Estefan<u>i</u>a GONZALEZ, [*todos son de esta vecindad*]; ap/ D. Antº Abad CORDOVA & D. Juliana TORRES; am/ D^{n} Felipe GONZALEZ & D. Fran^{ca} CHACON.

VIJIL, Maria de Gracia *Vecª*
bap 21 Jly 1822, ae 9 da; d/ Juan de Jesus VIJIL & Rosa DURAN; gp/ Bern^{do} DURAN & Feliciana VIJIL, [*todos son de esta Feligresia*]; ap/ Tomas VIJIL & Antª Teresa MARTIN; am/ Man^{l} DURAN & Geralda MASCAREÑAS.

(Apparently no Sep entries)

CRESPIN, Juan de Jesus Vec^{no}
bap 1 Oct 1822, ae 4 da; s/ José CRESPIN & Maria Rosa MONTOYA; gp/ Nicolas SANDOVAL & Maria Ygnacia MARTIN, [*todos son de esta vecindad*].

MARTIN, Maria Rita *Vec^{na}*
bap 1 Oct 1822, ae 5 da; nat. d/ Maria Soled^{d} MARTIN, single, *vecina de Abiquiu*, who was left at the house of Christobal LARRAÑAGA & his wife, Ana Maria APODACA, who were gp.

ROMERO, José Miguel Vecº
bap 3 Oct 1822, ae 2 da; s/ José Antº ROMERO & Ana Maria ARRIETA; gp/ Mariano VARGAS & Nicomedes FERNANDEZ, [*todos son de esta vecindad*].

FLORES, José Maria *Vec^{o}*
bap 13 Oct 1822, ae 6 da; s/ Martin FLORES & Maria Encarnac^{on} GONZALEZ; gp/ Man^{l} Ant^{o} ARCHULETA & Pasquala ROMERO, [*todos son de esta vecind^{d}*].

Frame 500
LEAL, José Rafael *Vec^{no}*
bap 13 Oct 1822, ae 3 da; s/ Manuel LEAL & Maria Dolores CONTRERAS; gp/ Fran^{co} VIJIL & Cand^{a} PAES, [*todos de esta vecindad*]; ap/ Man^{l} José LEAL & Mariana MARTIN; am/ José CONTRERAS & Maria Encarnac^{on} (n.s.).

ROMERO, José Rafael Vec^{no}
bap 13 Oct 1822, ae 3 da; s/ Jesus ROMERO & Teresa VIJIL; gp/ Man^{l} TORRES & Maria Yg^{a} DURAN, [*todos son de esta vecindad*]; ap/ Mariano ROMERO & Fran^{ca} ARMENTA; am/ Carlos VIJIL & Juana SANCHEZ.

DURAN, Pedro Ygnacio *Vecino*
bap (sic) 3 Oct 1822, b. today; s/ Antonio DURAN & Maria Rita LUCERO; gp/ Ant^{o} TORRES & Maria Ysabel FERNANDEZ, [*todos de esta vecindad*]; ap/ Ygnacio DURAN & Ant^{a} SANCHEZ; am/ Bernardo LUCERO & Tomasa MARTIN.

GONZALEZ, José Miguel *Yndio*
bap 27 Oct 1822, ae 8 da; s/ Santiago GONZALEZ & Maria Loreto LUXAN, *Indios de esta supradicha mision*]; gp/ D^{n} Pablo LUC^{o} & D^{a} Paula LARRAÑAGA *de esta vecindad*.

SANDOVAL, Maria Luiza *Vecina*
bap 27 Oct 1822, ae 3 da; nat. d/ Maria Ant^{a} SANDOVAL, single; gp/ Nicolas TAFOYA & Manuela MEDINA, [*todos son de esta vecindad*].

ARMIJO, Andres *Vecino*
bap 9 Nov 1822, ae 5 da; s/ Man^{l} ARMIJO & Trinidad VIJIL; gp/ D^{n} José Maria MARTINEZ & D^{a} Maria de la Luz MARTINEZ, [*todos son de esta vecindad*].

BASQUEZ, Maria Ynés *Vecina*
bap 9 Nov 1822, ae 8 da; d/ Ant^{o} BASQUEZ & Rita ROMERO; gp/ Miguel MARQUEZ & Maria de la Luz MARQUEZ, [*todos son de esta vecindad*].

Frame 501
ZAMORA, José Manuel *Yndio*
bap 24 Nov 1822, ae 30 da; s/ Pablo ZAMORA & Albina ROMERO, *Indios de esta mision*; gp/ Y(s)idoro SANDOVAL & Maria Ant^{a} SANDOVAL *de esta vecindad*.

SARBÉ, Maria Ludovina *Vec^{na}*
bap 24 Nov 1822, ae 4 da; d. José Man^{l} SARBÉ & Dominga COCA; gp/ José Maria SANDOVAL & Maria SANDOVAL, [*todos son de esta vecindad*].

CORDOVA, José de Jesus *Vec^{o}*
bap 28 Nov 1822, ae 3 da; s/ D^{n} Raymundo CORDOVA & Dª Estefanía GONZALEZ; gp/ D^{n} Felipe GONZALEZ & Maria Joséfa LALANDA, [*todos son de esta vecindad*].

VIJIL, Ana Maria *Vec^{a}*
bap 1 Dec 1822, ae 3 da; d/ Jesus VIJIL & Maria Luiza ZALAZAR; gp/ Gabriel VEITIA & Serafina CORTÉS, [*todos son de esta vecindad*; ap/ Miguel VIJIL & Ana Maria VALLEJOS; am/ Juan Man^{l} SALAZAR (sic) & Maria QUINTANA.

TAFOYA, Maria de la Luz *Vecina*
bap 4 Dec 1822, ae 7 da; d/ Bartolomé TAFOYA & Maria Ant^{a} GONZALEZ; gp/ Geronimo GONZALEZ & Maria RODRIGUEZ, [*todos de esta vecindad*].

VARGAS, Pedro Antonio *Vecino*
bap 4 Dec 1822, ae 1 da; s/ Pablo VARGAS & Maria Ygnacia CORDOVA; gp/ D[n] Pedro MARTIN & Maria Reyes FERNANDEZ, [*todos son de esta vecindad*].

CASILLAS, Maria Dolores *Yndia*
bap 8 Dec 1822, ae 30 da; d/ Bernardo CASILLAS & Micaela ROMERO, Indians of this mission; gp/ Gregorio GONZALEZ & Maria Dolores VALDÉZ *de esta vecindad*.

MEDINA, Jose Man[l] *Vecino*
bap 8 Dec 1822, b. yesterday; s/ Jesus MEDINA & Joséfa MARTIN; gp/ Man[l] TORRES & Maria Ygnacia DURAN, [*todos son de esta vecindad*]; ap/ Juan Nepomuceno MEDINA & Candelaria VIJIL; am/ Gervacio MARTIN & Juana CORTÉS.

Frame 502
GONZALEZ, Maria Dolores *Vec[a]*
bap 12 Dec 1822, ae 6 da; d/ José Miguel GONZALEZ & Maria Ysabel VIJIL; gp/ D[n] Felipe GONZALEZ & D[a] Joséfa LALANDA, [*todos son de esta vecindad*].

DURAN, Maria Dolores *Vec[na]*
bap 13 Dec 1822, ae 4 da; d/ Buenabent[a] DURAN & Maria de Jesus MARTIN; gp/ José Man[l] ROMERO & Maria Rita SANCHEZ, [*todos son de esta vecindad*]; ap/ Man[l] DURAN & Geralda MASCAREÑAS; am/ Cruz MARTIN & Maria Dolores TORRES.

MONTOYA, Maria Guadalupe *Vec[a]*
bap 15 Dec 1822, ae 5 da; d/ Juan MONTOYA & Maria del Carmen ROMERO; gp/ Gabriel VEITIA & Maria Serafina CORTÉS, [*todos son de esta vecindad*].

ROMERO, Ant[o] José Indian
bap 15 Dec 1822, ae 6 da; s/ Juan Domingo ROMERO & Rosalia LUCERO, *Indios de dicha mision*; gp/ Fran[co] VIJIL & Maria Concepcion HURTADO *de esta vecindad*.

MIERA, Maria Albina *Vecina*
bap 18 Dec 1822, ae 2 da; d/ José MIERA & Manuela ROMERO; gp/ Juan LUNA & Maria Candelaria VELARDE, [*todos de esta vecindad*].

ROMERO, Jose Tomas *Vecino*
bap 21 Dec 1822, ae 3 da; s/ Vicente ROMERO & Maria Soledad CHAVES; gp/ José Maria TRUXILLO & Maria Reyes MEDINA, [*todos son de esta vecindad*]; ap/ Fran[co] ROMERO & Maria MANSANARES; am/ Domingo CHAVES & Maria Candelaria DURAN.

DURAN, Maria Soledad *Vecina*
bap 21 Dec 1822, ae 4 da; s/ Gregorio DURAN & Rosa URIOSTE; gp/ D[a] Maria Ygnacia SANCHEZ & Buenaventura LOVATO, [*todos son de esta vecindad*]; ap/ Ygnacio DURAN & Ant[a] SANCHEZ; am/ Fran[co] URIOSTE & Maria Rita MARTIN.

LUCERO, Maria Natividad *Vecina*
bap 25 Dec 1822, ae 4 da; d/ Pedro LUCERO & Maria Gertrudis DURAN; gp/ Man[l] FERNANDEZ & Maria Asension MARTIN, [*todos son de esta vecindad*].

Frame 503
MARTIN, José Tomas *Vec[o]*
bap 25 Dec 1822, ae 5 da; nat. s/ Ysidora MARTIN, wid., & a married man (n.n.); gp/ Juan Nicolaz VARELA & Apolonia CHAVES, [*todos son de esta vecindad*].

ROMERO, Maria Rosalia *Yndia*
bap 28 Dec 1822, ae 4 da; d/ Santi(a)go ROMERO & Fran^ca^ PADILLA, Indians of this mission; gf/ Pablo VARGAS, *vecino de esta.*

CONCHA, Juana Maria *Yndia*
bap 29 Dec 1822, ae 5 da; d/ Juan Manuel CONCHA & Dominga ROMERO; gp/ Juan Domingo GUERRERO & Paula ROMERO, all Indians of this mission.

De vecinos 66
De Yndios 21
87 bautismos se hizieron en el año de 1822.

Año de 1823

VARELA, Maria Manuela Antonia *Vecina*
bap 3 Jan 1823, ae 1 da; d/ Jose Candelaria VARELA & Maria Encarnac^on^ SOLÃNO; gp/ Mariano CRUZ & Veronica CRUZ, [*todos son de esta vecindad*].

ORTIZ, Antonio José Indian
bap 5 Jan 1823, ae 4 da; s/ Fran^co^ ORTIZ & Dominga ROMERO, Indians of this mission; gp/ Ramon MARTIN & Paula MARTIN *de esta vecindad.*

DURAN, Juan de los Reyes *Vec^o^*
bap 5 Jan 1823, ae 2 da; s/ Juan Pablo DURAN & Maria Soledad XARAMILLO; gp/ Juan Ant^o^ MARTIN & Maria Dolores DURAN, [*todos son de esta vecindad*].

VIJIL, Feliciana *Vecina*
bap 21 Jan 1823, ae 2 da; d/ Ramon VIJIL & Barbara MARTIN; gp/ Ant^o^ GARCIA & Maria Rita BACA, [*todos son de esta vecindad*].

Frame 504

SANDOVAL, Maria Paula *Vecina*
bap 24 Jan 1823, ae 2 da; d/ Pablo SANDOVAL & Maria Dolores COCA; gp/ Ysidora SANDOVAL & Maria Ant^a^ SANDOVAL, [*todos son de esta vecindad*]; ap/ D^n^ Felipe SANDOVAL & Gregoria SENA; am/ Jose Maria COCA & Juana VENABIDES.

SILVA, Maria Paula de los Reyes *Ve^a^*
bap 25 Jan 1823, ae 7 da; d/ Ciriaco SILVA & Maria Asension MEDINA; gp/ Ant^o^ José CORDOVA & Maria Rosa SANDOVAL, [*todos son de esta vecindad*].

MARTIN, Jesus Maria *Vec^o^*
bap 26 Jan 1823, ae 4 da; s/ D^n^ Andres MARTIN & D^a^ Maria Ant^a^ ORTIZ; gp/ D^n^ Tomas ROMERO & D^a^ Ysidora MARTIN, [*todos son de esta vecindad*]; ap/ D^n^ Pedro MARTIN & D^a^ Maria Ygnacia GARCIA; am/ D^n^ Mathias ORTIZ & D^a^ Maria Fran^ca^ VACA.

CHAVES, José Pablo *Vecino*
bap 26 Jan 1823, ae 2 da; s/ Ant^o^ CHAVES & Juana Maria BACA; gp/ Dionisio VIJIL & Manuela DELGADO, [*todos son de esta vecindad*]; ap/ Vicente CHAVES & Juana ARAGON; am/ José Ant^o^ BACA & Maria Joséfa VIJIL.

ESPINOSA, Jose Man^l^ Indian
bap 30 Jan 1823, ae 30 da; s/ José Rafael ESPINOSA & Maria Encarnac^on^ ZAMORA, Indians of this mission; gp/ Rafael SALAZ & Maria de Gracia GARCIA *de esta vecindad.*

SANDOVAL, Maria Candelaria *Vecina*
bap 2 Feb 1823, ae 4 da; d/ Nicolaz SANDOVAL & Maria Ygnacia MARTIN; gp/ Domingo DURAN & Maria Soledad LOVATO, [*todos son de esta vecindad*]; ap/ Mathias SANDOVAL & Ygnacia BUENO; am/ Ramon MARTIN & Paula MARTIN.

CORDOVA, Juan Antonio Indian
bap 2 Feb 1823, ae 15 da; s/ José CORDOVA & Maria Soledad LUCERO; gp/ José Ant° ZUAZO & Maria CONCHA, all Indians of this mission.

TRUXILLO, Adauto *Vecino*
bap 7 Feb 1823, ae 2 da; s/ Luiz TRUXILLO & Maria Gertrudis SANCHEZ; gp/ Ysidoro SANDOVAL & Maria Natividad SANDOVAL, [*todos son de esta vecindad*].

Frame 505
LUCERO, José Manuel Indian
bap 8 Feb 1823, ae 8 da; s/ Lorenzo LUCERO & Manuela GABILÁN, Indians of this mission; gp/ José Man[l] GABALDON & Maria Susana MARTIN, *vecinos de la misma*.

CORDOVA, José Maria Candelaria Vec°
bap 9 Feb 1823, ae 5 da; s/ Serafino CORDOVA & Maria Candelaria MEDINA; gp/ José SANCHEZ & Maria Soledad LOPEZ, [*todos son de esta vecindad*].

RAEL, Juana Maria *Vecina*
bap 12 Feb 1823, ae 3 da; d/ Juan RAEL & Maria Dolores CORDOVA; gp/ Fran[co] CHAVES & Lorenza CRUZ, [*todos son de esta vecindad*].

CASILLAS, Maria de la Luz *Vecina*
bap 16 Feb 1823, b. yesterday; d/ Cristobal CASILLAS & Luiza TAFOYA; gp/ Manuel TORRES & Ygnacia DURAN, [*todos son de esta vecindad*].

CORDOVA, Maria Soledad *Vecina*
bap 21 Feb 1823, ae 5 da; d/ nat. Maria Guadalupe CORDOVA, wid. *de esta vecindad*, & a married man (n.n.) *de la misma*; gp/ Juan Bautista MEDINA & Maria Man[la] MARTIN.

VIJIL, José Tomás *Vecino*
bap 23 Feb 1823, ae 8 da; s/ Fran[co] VIJIL & Maria Concepc[on] HURTADO; gp/ Fran[co] ARAGON & Maria Barbara ARAGON, [*todos son de esta vecindad*].

CORTÉS, Maria Dominga *Vecina*
bap 26 Feb 1823, ae 3 da; d/ Josá Maria CORTÉS & Maria BRITO; gp/ Jose Maria CHAVES & Ygnacia CHAVES, [*todos son de esta vecindad*].

Frame 506
MARTIN, Maria Leonarda *Vec[a]*
bap 2 Mch 1823; d/ Mariano MARTIN & Brigida TAFOYA; gp/ Pablo VARGAS & Ygnacia CORDOVA, [*todos son de esta vecindad*]; ap/ Juan Felipe MARTIN & Ygnacia VIJIL; am/ D[n] Juan Domingo TAFOYA & D[a] Maria Gertrudis CORDOVA.

MONTOYA, Maria de Jesus *Vecina*
bap 2 Mch 1823, ae 3 da; d/ Rafael MONTOYA & Luciana CHAVES; gp/ Hermenegildo TRUXILLO & Maria Josefa TAFOYA, [*todos son de esta vecindad*].

PACHECO, Maria del Carmen *Vecina*
bap 9 Mch 1823, ae 4 da; d/ Juan PACHECO & Fernanda BUENO; gp/ Juan Eugenio BUENO & Theodora VEITIA, [*todos son de esta vecindad*].

LARRAÑAGA, José Desiderio *Vec°*
bap 9 Mch 1823, ae 7 da; s/ D[n] Christobal LARRAÑAGA & D[a] Ana Maria APODACA; gf/ D[n] Ant° LUC°, [*todos son de esta vecindad*]; ap/ D[n] Christobal Maria de LARRAÑAGA & D[a] Maria Gertrudis MESTAS; am/ José APODACA & Gertrudis LUCERO.

ABILA, José Antonio *Vecino*
bap 9 Mch 1823, ae 6 da; s/ Anastasio ABILA & Maria Ygnacia LUCERO; gp/ José Ant^{o} MEDINA & Juana Gertrudis SANDOVAL, [*todos son mis Feligreses*].

MARTIN, Man^{l} de los Reyes Indian
bap 13 Mch 1823, ae 6 da; s/ José Ant^{o} MARTIN & Maria CONCHA *del pueblo*; gf/ Man^{l} MONDRAGON.

TRUXILLO, Juan Bautista *Vecino*
bap 17 Mch 1823, b. yesterday; s/ Juan TRUXILLO & Casilda QUINTANA; gp/ Buenabentura DURAN & Maria de Jesus MARTIN, [*todos son de esta vecindad*].

VIJIL, Maria de la Luz *Vecina*
bap 14 Mch 1823, ae 2 da; d/ Man^{l} VIJIL & Ygnacia QUINTANA; gp/ Man^{l} SANCHEZ & Nicolaza SANDOVAL, [*todos son de esta Feligresia*].

TAFOYA, José Maria de los Dolores *Vecino*
bap 23 Mch 1823, ae 4 da; s/ D^{n} Juan Domingo TAFOYA & D^{a} Maria Gertrudis CORDOVA; gp/ D^{n} Ant^{o} Abad CORDOVA & D^{a} Juliana TORRES, [*todos son de esta vecindad*].

TRUXILLO, José Miguel *Vecino*
bap 23 Mch 1823, ae 4 da; s/ Esteban TRUXILLO & Mariana TAFOYA; gp/ Jua(n) Fran^{co} LOVATO & Maria Guadalupe ROMERO, [*todos son de esta Feligresia*].

Frame 507
GUERRERO, Maria Paula *Yndia*
bap 23 Mch 1823, ae 7 da; d/ Juan de Jesus GUERRERO & Fran^{ca} PADILLA; gp/ Maria Paula LOMA, [*son naturales del pueblo*].

ZALASAR, Maria Dolores *Vecina*
bap 30 Mch 1823, ae 3 da; d/ Policarpio ZALASAR & Maria Luiza VIJIL; gp/ Lorenzo ARAGON & Joséfa VIJIL, [*todos son de esta vecindad*].

ZAMORA, Rosalia Indian
bap 30 Mch 1823, ae 5 da; d/ Juan Esteban ZAMORA & Maria ORTIZ; gm/ Rosalia ROMERO, [*todos son naturales del pueblo*].

LUNA, Juan Rafael *Vecino*
bap 1 Apr 1823, ae 4 da; s/ D^{n} Juan LUNA & D^{a} Maria Candelaria VEITIA; gp/ D^{n} Ant^{o} LUC^{o} & D^{a} Estefania ARAGON, [*todos son de esta vecindad*]; ap/ D^{n} Rafael LUNA & D^{a} Ana Maria TAFOYA; am/ D^{n} Joaq^{n} VEITIA & D^{a} Juana GARCIA.

TRUXILLO, Maria Ysidora *Vecina*
bap 6 Apr 1823, ae 4 da; d/ Ant^{o} TRUXILLO & Manuela COCA; gp/ Juan del Carmen ROMERO & Maria Rosa MARTIN, [*todos son de esta vecindad*]; ap/ Alexandro TRUXILLO & Maria Manuela ARCHULETA; am/ Manuel COCA & Rafaela MARTIN.

MEDINA, Ant^{o} José *Vecino*
bap 6 Apr 1823, ae 4 da; d/ Julian MEDINA & Maria Dolores VALDÉS; gp/ José Manuel SAENS & Trinidad MEDINA, [*todos son de esta vezindad*]; ap/ Ant^{o} MEDINA & Micaela VIJIL; am/ Fran^{co} VALDES (sic) & Fabiana HURTADO.

ZAMORA, Juan Ant^{o} Indian
bap 6 Apr 1823, ae 7 da; s/ Man^{l} ZAMORA & Fran^{ca} DELGADO, Indians of this mission; gp/ José ZUAZO & Joséfa CASAUS *de esta vecindad*.

LOBATO, José Tomas *Vecino*
bap 8 Apr 1823, ae 3 da; s/ Tomas LOBATO & Hermenegilda CASAUS; gp/ D^{n} Juan LOBATO & D^{a} Maria Ygnacia SANCHEZ, [*todos son de esta vezindad*].

ZUAZO, Maria Theodora Indian
bap 8 Apr 1823, ae 8 da; d/ Fran^{co} ZUAZO & Joséfa MIRABAL, *naturales de dicha mision*; gf/ D^{n} Christobal LARRAÑAGA *de esta vecindad*.

Frame 508
COCA, Maria Apolonia *Vecina*
bap 12 Apr 1823, ae 3 da; d/ Tomas COCA & Lorenza SANDOVAL; gp/ Santos MARTIN & Maria Manuela ROMERO, [*todos son de esta vecindad*].

DURAN, Maria Marcelina *Vec^{na}*
bap 26 Apr 1823, ae 11 da; d/ Bernardo DURAN & Feliciana VIJIL; gp/ Buenabentura MARTIN & Rosa VIJIL, [*todos son de esta vecindad*]; ap/ Man^{l} DURAN & Geralda MASCAREÑAS; am/ Cruz VIJIL & Clara FERNAND^{z}.

CORTÉS, Ant^{o} Maria Concepcion *Vecina*
bap 26 Apr 1823, ae 6 da; s/ Paulin CORTÉS & Maria Concep^{on} MARTIN; gp/ Santiago MARTIN & Juana CORTÉS, [*todos son de esta vecindad*]; ap/ Man^{l} CORTÉS & Maria Ant^{a} MARTIN; am/ Gervacio MARTIN & Juana CORTÉS.

SOLANO, Ant^{o} José Toribio *Vecino*
bap 26 Apr 1823, ae 11 da; s/ Maximo SOLÁNO & Maria ROMERO; gp/ Juana Maria LOBATO & Buenav^{ta} LOBATO, [*todos de esta vecindad*].

GONZALEZ, José Antonio *Vecino*
bap 27 Apr 1823, ae 12 da; s/ Biterbo GONZALEZ & Felipa ZALASAR; gp/ Ant^{o} DURAN & Maria Rita LUCERO, [*son todos de esta vecindad*].

ROMERO, Maria Rita *Vecina*
bap 27 Apr 1823, ae 2 da; d/ Juan de Jesus ROMERO & Maria Candelaria QUINTANA; gp/ José Man^{l} ROMERO & Maria Rita SANCHEZ, [*todos son de esta vecindad*]; ap/ Ant^{o} Domingo ROMERO & Maria COCA; am/ Juan QUINTANA & Balbanera ROMERO.

CRUZ, Maria Soledad *Vecina*
bap 4 May 1823, ae 3 da; d/ Fran^{co} CRUZ & Josefa MEDINA; gp/ Jose Maria TRUXILLO & Maria Reyes MEDINA, [*todos de esta vecindad*].

ROMERO, Jose de la Cruz *Vecino*
bap 6 May 1823, ae 6 da; s/ Jose ROMERO & Viviana FERNANDES; gp/ Fran^{co} GUTIERRES & Candelaria MARTINES, *todos de esta vecindad*; ap/ Consepcion ROMERO & Maria Rosa QUINTANA, both dec.; am/ Domingo FERNANDES & Fran^{ca} GARCIA.

Frame 509
ZALASAR, Maria Bibiana *Vec^{a}*
*bap 29 Apr 1823, ae 8 da; nat. d/ Maria Ygnacia ZALASAR; gp/ Juan Pasq^{l} MARTIN & Barbara ARAGON, [*todos son de esta vecindad*].

LOVATO, José Marcelino *Vec^{o}*
bap 8 May 1823, ae 12 da; nat. s/ Juana LOVATO; gp/ José Man^{l} ROMERO & Felipa LOBATO, [*todos son de esta vecindad*].

MARTIN, Juana Maria *Vecina*
bap 12 May 1823; ae 3 da; d/ Juan Ant^{o} MARTIN & Maria MADRID; gp/ José Fran^{co} GONZALEZ & Maria del Carmen GONZALEZ, [*todos son de esta feligresia*].

MARTIN, Juan de Jesus *Vecino*
bap 15 May 1823, ae 3 da; s/ Juan Ant^{o} MARTIN & Maria Dolores DURAN; gp/ Juan CORDOVA & Maria de Jesus FERNANDEZ, [*todos son de esta vecindad*]; ap/ Felipe MARTIN & Maria TRUXILLO; am/ Pablo DURAN & Margarita SANCHEZ.

VALDÉS, José Ladislao *Vec^{no}*
bap 16 May 1823, ae 9 da; s/ Fran^{co} VALDÉS & Paula MAES; gm/ Rafaela ARCHULETA, [*todos son de esta vecindad*].

LUXAN, Juan de Jesus Indio
bap 17 May 1823, ae 4 da; s/ Ant^{o} LUXAN & Bibiana REYNA, *naturales de dha mision;* gp/ Juan GOMEZ & Fran^{ca} TRUXILLO *de esta vecindad.*

QUINTANA, Maria Dolores *Vecino*
bap 1 May 1823, ae 3 da; d/ Rafael QUINTANA & Maria de la Luz MONDRAGON; gp/ Fran^{co} MARTIN & Maria Ygnacia PINEDA, [*todos son de esta feligresia*].

GONZALEZ, Maria Soledad *Vecina*
bap 19 May 1823, ae 3 da; nat. d/ Joséfa GONZALEZ, single; gm/ D^{a} Joséfa LOBATO, [*todos de esta vecindad*].

TRUXILLO, Maria de la Luz *Vec^{a}*
bap 22 May 1823, ae 6 da; nat. d/ Maria Ygnacia TRUXILLO; gp/ Rafael LOBATO & Maria de la Luz ESPINOSA, [*todos son mis feligreses*].

CORTÉS, Maria Reyes *Vec^{a}*
bap 22 May 1823, ae 7 da; d/ Pablo CORTÉS & Maria Dolores PADILLA; gp/ José Rafael LUCERO & Maria Joséfa LUCERO; ap/ José CORTÉS & Maria Ant^{a} MARTIN.

Frame 510
TRUXILLO, Pedro Regalado *Vec^{o}*
bap 25 May 1823, ae 5 da; s/ D^{n} Juan TRUXILLO and D^{a} Maria Catharina CORDOVA; gp/ D^{n} Raymundo CORDOVA & D^{a} Maria Estefania GONZALEZ, [*todos son de esta vecindad*]; ap/ Santiago TRUXILLO & Apolonia ROMERO; am/ D^{n} Ant^{o} Abad CORDOVA & D^{a} Juliana TORRES.

CORDOVA, José Manuel *Vecino*
bap 1 Jne 1823, ae 4 da; s/ D^{n} Lorenzo CORDOVA & D^{a} Rafaela TRUXILLO; gp/ D^{n} Severino MARTINEZ & D^{a} Maria del Carmen SANTIESTEBAN, [*todos de esta vecindad*]; ap/ D^{n} Ant^{o} Abad CORDOVA & D^{a} Juliana TORRES; am/ Bartolomé TRUXILLO & Maria Apolonia BACA.

ERRERA, Ana Maria *Vec^{a}*
bap 8 Jun 1823, ae 3 da; d/ Pedro de ERRERA & Maria Man^{la} MARTIN; gp/ Gregorio DURAN & Maria Rosa URIOSTE, [*todos son de esta vecindad*].

TAFOYA, Margarita *Vecina*
bap 8 Jun 1823, ae 3 da; d/ Salvador TAFOYA & Juana MEDINA *de esta vecindad;* gf/ Juan Agustin GUTIERREZ, *vecino de la Joya.*

MARTIN, Maria Dolores *Vecina*
bap 8 Jun 1823, ae 3 da; d/ Felipe MARTIN & Maria Micaela ROMERO; gp/ Juan Gabriel DURAN & Juana Tomasa GARCIA, [*todos son de esta feligresia*].

ARCHULETA, Maria Antonia *Vecina*
bap 11 Jun 1823, ae 5 da; d/ José Pablo ARCHULETA & Maria Guadalupe LEAL; gp/ Ant^{o} José SANDOVAL & Theodora ROMERO, [*todos son mis feligreses*].

MARTIN, Maria Dolores *Vecina*
bap 12 Jun 1823, ae 12 da; d/ Fran^{co} MARTIN & Maria SILVA; gm/ Margarita ESPINOSA, [*todos de esta vecindad*]; ap/ Juan Pablo MARTIN & Joséfa ESPINOSA; am/ Santiago SILVA & Maria Ant^{a} VELASQUES.

TAFOYA, Maria Ant^{a} *Vecina*
bap 12 Jne 1823, *nació ayer*; d/ José TAFOYA & Maria Ant^{a} SERDA; gp/ Fran^{co} ABILA & Joséfa VIJIL, [*todos son de esta vecindad*].

SILVA, Juan de Jesus *Vecino*
bap 15 Jun 1823, ae 4 da; s/ José Maria SILVA & Maria del Carmen SAENS; gm/ Dª Apolonia LUCERO, [*todos son de esta vecindad*].

MARTIN, Juana Maria *Vecina*
bap 16 Jun 1823, ae 4 da; nat. d/ Margarita MARTIN, single *de esta Jurisdic^{on}*; gp/ Pedro MAES & Maria Rosalia SANDOVAL, *mis feligreses*.

Frame 511
LOMA, Juana Indian
bap 17 Jun 1823, ae 10 da; d/ Juan Domingo LOMA & Juana Maria ROMERO, natives of this mission; gf/ parishioner Tomas LUC^{o}.

VIJIL, Juan Nepomuceno Vec^{o}
bap 24 Jun 1823, ae 6 da/ s/ Faustin VIJIL & Maria de la Luz MARTIN; gp/ Blas CHAVES & Mª Dolores MARTIN, [*todos son de esta vecindad*].

ROMERO, Maria Ygnacia *Vecina*
bap 24 Jun 1823, ae 12 da; d/ Juan Domingo ROMERO & Maria Ant^{a} LUXAN, Indians of this mission; gp/ Jose Pablo SANCHEZ & Maria del Carmen SANCHEZ *de esta vecindad*.

GONZALEZ, Juan Pedro *Vec^{o}*
bap 29 Jun 1823, ae 6 da; s/ Juan GONZALEZ & Gertrudis ARCHULETA; gp/ Balbanera ROMERO & Fran^{co} Ant^{o} QUINTANA, [*todos son de esta vecindad*].

LUCERO, Maria Dolores *Vecina*
bap 6 Jly 1823, ae 3 da; d/ Pedro LUCERO & Maria de la Luz FERNANDEZ; gp/ Fran^{co} FERNANDEZ & Maria Ant^{a} DURAN, [*todos son de esta vecindad*].

SANDOVAL, Juan José *Vecino*
bap 10 Jly 1823, ae 4 da; s/ Jesus SANDOVAL & Petra LOVATO; gp/ Ant^{a} Margarita ROMERO & Gregorio CORDOVA, [*todos son de esta vecindad*].

MEDINA, Maria Serafina *Vecina*
bap 13 Jly 1823, ae 7 da; s/ José Man^{l} MEDINA & Maria Ant^{a} MARTIN; gp/ Ant^{o} José CORDOVA & Maria Rosa SANDOVAL, [*todos de esta Feligresia*].

VIJIL, Juan de la Cruz *Vecino*
bap 13 Jly 1823, ae 4 da; s/ Ygnacio VIJIL & Paula QUINTANA; gp/ Man^{l} DURAN & Geralda MASCAREÑAS, [*todos de esta vecindad*]; ap/ Marcelino VIJIL & Micaela MARTIN; am/ Juan QUINTANA & Felipa MAES.

TENORIO, Buenabentura *Vecino*
bap 13 Jly 1823, b. yesterday; s/ Julian TENORIO & Lorenza LOPEZ; gp/ Maria de la Luz MARTIN & Lorenzo BACA, [*todos son de esta Jurisdic^{on}*].

Frame 512
VARELA, Maria Magdalena *Vec^{a}*
bap 13 Jly 1823, ae 6 da; d/ Juan VARELA & Juliana TRUXILLO; gm/ Magdalena

LO(PEZ), [*todos son de esta vecindad*]; ap/ Pablo VARELA & the godmother; am/ Vic^{te} TRUXILLO & Maria G^{pe} MARTIN.

(Fr. Manuel BELLIDO signing entries)
ROMERO, Pedro Antonio *Pueblo*
bap 15 Jly 1823; *s/* Pedro ROMERO & Maria Antonia MOYA; gm/ Juan(a) Maria MARTIN.

(Return to the usual form of listing the godparents at the end of the entry when grandparents are included).

LUZERO, Maria de la Cruz S^{n} Fernando
bap 17 Jly 1823; d/ Jose Fran^{co} LUZERO & Maria Juana MONTOYA; ap/ Jesus LUZERO & Rosalia BERNAL; am/ Jose Rafael MONTOYA & Maria Rita ROMERO; gp/ Jose Rafael ABILA & Maria de la Luz ABILA.

MARTIN, Juana Maria (illegible)
bap 27 Jly 1823; d/ Maria Dolores MARTIN (sic) & Jose Miguel MARTIN; ap/ Juaquin MARTIN & Candeleria CHABES; am/ Severino MARTIN & Maria de la Encarnacion SANTISTEBAN; gp/ Santiago MARTINEZ & Maria de la Luz MARTINEZ.

PACHECO, Santiago *Pueblo*
bap *en el mismo dia*; *s/* Pablo PACHECO & Manuela ZAMORA, *naturales del pueblo*; gp/ Juan Miguel MARQUEZ & Maria Getrudis MONTOYA.

SANDOBAL (gp), Jose Santana *Adulto del pueblo*
bap 27 Jly 1823; *s/ Nacion Apacha*; gp/ Felipe SANDOBAL & Polonia (n.s.), his wife.

(See middle of Frame 514 for rest of July 1823 but not rest of year)

Frame 513 (as filmed)
GOMEZ, Santiago Indian
ORTIZ, Santiago
bap 20 Nov 1821, ae 4 da; nat. *s/* Santiago GOMEZ, married, & Maria Manuela ORTIZ, widow, all Indians of this mission; gp/ Mariano XARAMILLO & Dª Maria Ygnacia SANCHEZ *de esta vecindad*.

JUILO, Maria Joséfa Indian
bap 19 Dec 1821, ae 9 da; d/ Tomas JUILO & Margarita SISLET; gm/ Maria Ant^{a} ARCHULETA, all Indians of this mission.

RIO, Maria Dominga Indian
bap 19 Dec 1821, ae 5 da; d/ Pedro Tomás RIO & Cicilia ROMERO; gm/ Maria Loreto ARCHULETA, all Indians of this mission.

CHAVES, Maria Tomasa *Vecina*
bap 23 Dec 1821, ae 2 da; d/ Loreto CHAVES & Gabriela ESPINOSA; gp/ Pedro BUENO & Manuela ROMERO, [*todos de esta vecindad*].

GARCIA, Maria Manuela *Vecina*
bap 30 Dec 1821, ae 4 da; d/ Ant^{o} José GARCIA & Maria Gua^{pe} CHAVES; gp/ Manuel Ant^{o} MONDRAGON & Maria Rosa ARELLANO, [*todos son de esta vecindad*].

RIBALI, Maria Pasquala *Vecina*
bap 30 Dec 1821, ae 4 da; nat. d/ Margarita RIBALÍ, single, *de esta Jurisdic^{on}*; gp/ Buenaventura LOVATO & Juana LOVATO.

Frame 514
MONTOYA, Hermenegildo *Vecino*
bap 31 Dec 1821, b. today; s/ Juan MONTOYA & Maria del Carmen ROMERO; gp/ Miguel GARCIA & Margarita LUCERO, *[todos son de esta Jurisdicion]*.

(Return to gp following parents)
MARTIN, Maria Ysabel *Vecina*
bap last (day) of Dec 1821, ae 4 da; d/ Fran^co^ MARTIN & Maria Ygnacia PINEDA; gp; José Ant^o^ GONZALEZ & Maria URIOSTE, [*todos de esta vecindad*]; ap/ Vicente MARTIN & Ysabel URIOSTE; am/ Jacinto PINEDA & Joséfa LEAL.

LIMISE, Maria French nation
bap 29 Jly 1823; d/ Luis LIMISE (Origins, p. 424) & Madalena (n.s.-blank space); gp/ Jose Antonio SUASO & Maria Josefa CASAOS. (No mention of twins.)

LIMISE, Felicita French nation
bap 29 Jly 1823; d/ Luis LIMISE & (blank space); gp/ Fran^co^ Esteba(n) TRUJILLO & Maria Antonia GARCIA. (No mention of twins.)

ROMERO, Pedro *Pueblo*
bap 3 Aug 1823; nat. s/ Josefa ROMERO & unknown father; gm/ Maria Rosa RIO.

BIJIL, Miguel Antonio S^n^ Fernaz^-^
bap 3 Aug 1823; s/ Jose de la Cruz BIJIL & Margarita LOBATO; gp/ Jose Fran^co^ BIJIL & Maria Candelaria SANTIESTEBAN.

Frame 515
PACHECO, Bernardo de Jesus
*bap 29 Aug 1824 (sic); s/ Diego Antonio PACHECO & Maria Jesus QUINTANA; ap/ Juan Antonio PACHECO & Lucia ARMIJO; am/ Jose de la Cruz QUINTANA & Maria Michaela BALDES; gp/ Jose Julian MEDINA & Maria Dolores BALDES.

(Fr. Antonio CACHO signing entries)
CORTES, Maria de la Luz S^n^ Fernando
bap 1 Sep 1824; d/ Jose Pablo CORTES & Maria Dolores PADILLA; ap/ Jose Antonio CORTES & Juana Getrudis MONTOYA; am/ Pedro PADILLA & Lucia CHAVES; gf/ Felipe ROMERO.

SALAZAR, Jose Ramon *Rancho*
bap 30 Aug 1824; s/ Ramon SALAZAR & Maria Soleda(d) VIGIL; ap/ Jose Manuel SALAZAR & Reyes MARTIN; am/ Miguel VIGIL & Ana Maria ARAGON; gp/ Fran^co^ MARTIN & Maria Ygnacia PINEDO.

CHAVES, Maria Guadalupe *Espuria S^n^ Fernando*
bap 4 Sep 1824; nat. d/ Maria Candelaria CHAVES & father unknown; am/ Jose CHAVES & Maria CANDELARIA; gp/ Juan Antonio GARCIA & Maria Dolores GAVALDON.

VIGIL, Maria Antonia *Rancho*
bap 17 Sep 1824, ae 13 da; d/ Rafael VIGIL & Juana Acacia SANDOVAL; ap/ Manuel VIGIL & Maria Antonia ROMERO; am/ Juan SANDOVAL & Antonia Teresa LOPEZ; gp/ Juan ARGUEO & Maria Clara SANDOVAL.

ROMERO, Maria Micaela (Illegible) *Seco*
bap 29 Sep 1824; d/ Juan de los Reyes ROMERO & Maria Manuela ROMERO; ap/

Marcelino ROMERO & Ana Maria MARTIN; am/ Jose Maria ROMERO & Maria Rafaela VARELA; gp/ Jose Ant° SANCHEZ & Maria Soledad LOPEZ.

GONZALEZ, Geronimo *Rancho*
bap 3 Oct 1824; s/ (torn)bo GONZALEZ & Felipa SALAZAR; ap/ Jose Ant° GONZALEZ & Maria Rey(es-torn-n.s.); (am-torn)/ Juana SALAZAR (only); gp/ Jose Maria de Jesus MARTINEZ & Maria Anton[a] (torn-MARTI)NEZ.

Frame 516
ROMERO, Juanas (sic) de los Angeles *Ranchito*
bap 4 Oct 1824; twin daughters/ Jose Ramon ROMERO & Maria Rafaela VIG[L]; gp/ (not given); twins died. (Juan de Jesus ROMERO in document but don't know why but might have baptised the twins because of necessity).

CHAVES, Maria Paula *Rancho*
bap 8 Oct 1824; d/ Loreto CHAVES & Gabriela ESPINOSA; ap/ Manuel CHAVES & Serafina SANCHEZ; am/ Vicente ESPINOSA & Maria de la Luz ROMERO; gp/ Manuel Gregorio DURAN & Maria Rosa URIOSTA.

GALLEGO, Fran[co] *Arroyo Hondo*
bap 9 Oct 1824; s/ Benito GALLEGO & Micaela GARCIA; ap/ Christoval GALLEGO & Bernarda TRUJILLO; am/ Juan Ang[l] GARCIA & Marta Manuela MARTINEZ; gp/ Ant° MARTINEZ & Patricia MARTINEZ.

CORDOVA, Juan Jose *Pueblo*
bap 10 Oct 1824; s/ Juan Domingo CORDOVA and Fran[ca] GONZALEZ; gp/ Juan Jose (n.s.) & Maria Teresa RUIVAL.

ARMENTA, Maria Ygnacia S[n] Fernando
bap 14 Oct 1824; nat. d/ Atanasia ARMENTA & unknown father; am/ Simon ARMENTA & Marta MARTIN; gp/ Antonio Elias ARM[TA] & Ysabel SANCHEZ.

TRUJILLO, Antonio Alexandro S[n] Fernando
bap 14 Oct 1824; s/ Estevan TRUJILLO & Mariana TAFOYA; ap/ Alexandro TRUJILLO & Manuela ARCHULETA; am/ Nicolas TAFOYA & Maria Manuela MEDINA; gp/ Jose Fran[co] GONZALEZ & Mar[a] Juaquina TAFOYA.

SANCHEZ, Maria Dolores S[n] Fernando
bap 16 Oct 1824; d/ Maria Rita (SANCHEZ) & unknown father; am/ Mariano SANCHEZ & (blank space); gp/ Jose PADILLA & Maria Fran[ca] CORTES.

TRUJILLO, Maria del Pilar S[n] Fernando
bap 17 Oct 1824; d/ Maria Ysabel TRUJILLO & unknown father; am/ Jose TRUJILLO & Maria Getrudis ALFONSO; gf/ Manuel Antonio MARTIN.

ROMERO, Antonio Jose
bap 24 Oct 1824; s/ Jose Mar[a] ROMERO & Rafaela PINEDA; ap/ Juan de Dios ROMERO & Maria Ant[a] LUJAN; am/ (torn) & Maria Manuela GONZA(LEZ-torn); gp/ (torn-Je)sus GALLEGO & Maria de Jesus GALLEGO. (Frames 516-517)

Frame 517
MONTES, Maria Rafaela *Rancho*
bap 27 Oct 1824; d/ Fran[co] MONTES & Juana Maria MONTOYA; ap/ Antonio MONTES & Ynes MARTINEZ; am/ Bernardo MONTOYA & Maria Ysabel SALAZAR; gp/ Jose Maria MARTINEZ & Maria Antonia MARTINEZ.

VIGIL, Juana Maria *Rancho*
bap 27 Oct 1824; d/ Ramon VIG[L] & Barbara MARTIN; ap/ Cruz VIGIL & Clara

MARTIN; am/ Ygnacio MARTIN & Maria Paula SALAZ^{R}; gp/ Andres MARTIN & Maria Antonia HORTIZ.

FREZQUEZ, Maria Juana *Arroyo Ondo*
bap 31 Oct 1824; d/ Juan Domingo FREZQUEZ & Maria de la Luz GALLEGO; ap/ Antonio FREZQUEZ Trinidad MARTIN; am/ Antonio GALLEGO & Maria Manuela RUIBAL; gp/ Juan Ygnacio MARTINEZ & Maria Manuela MONTOYA.

TRUJILLO, Antonio Jose *Rancho*
bap 31 Oct 1824; s/ Jesus TRUJILLO & Maria de Jesus MARTINEZ; ap/ Domingo TRUJILLO & Ana BORREGO; am/ Jose Guadalupe MARTIN (as written) & Rosalia LUCERO; gp/ Miguel GARCIA & Margarita LUCERO.

FERNANDEZ, Jose de Esquipula *Rancho*
bap 31 Oct 1824; s/ Manuel FERNANDEZ & Maria Ascension MARTIN; ap/ Juan Domingo FERNANDEZ & Fran^{ca} GARCIA; am/ Pedro MARTIN & Maria delos Reyes FERNANDEZ; gp/ Antonio GARCIA & Maria Rita VACA.

ROMERO, Juan Bentura *Pueblo*
bap 14 Nov 1824; s/ Juan Domingo ROMERO & Magdalena MARTIN; gm/ Maria Ylaria FERNANDEZ.

MEDINA, Maria Manuela *Rancho*
bap 15 Nov 1824; d/ Jesus MEDINA & Maria Josefa MARTIN; ap/ Juan Nepomuceno MEDINA & Maria Candelaria VIRGIL; am/ Gervasio MARTIN & Juana CORTES; gp/ Juan de Jesus URIOSTE & Maria Manuela VIGIL.

QUINTANA, Jesus Maria *Rancho*
bap 15 Nov 1824; s/ Gabriel QUINTANA & Mar(ia-torn) (torn-En)carnacion PACHECO; ap/ Gabrie(l) QUINTANA & Maria Antonia VIGIL; am/ Fran^{co} Pa(CHECO-torn) & Maria Luisa VIGIL; gp/ Juan Ygnacio SANCHEZ & Maria Nicolasa SA(torn).

Frame 518
ROMERO, Geronimo *Pueblo*
bap 20 Nov (1824-torn); s/ Tomas ROMERO & Juana (torn)ASO; gm/ Ygnacia MARTINA.

LUCERO, Maria Peregrina S^{n} Fernando
bap 21 Nov 1824; d/ Bernardo LUCERO & Josefa QUINTANA; ap/ Manuel LUCERO & Maria Manuela VALLEJO; am/ Juan QUINTANA & Maria Barbanera ROMERO; gp/ Cornelio VIGIL & Josefa LUCERO.

ROMERO, Maria Presentac^{n} *Pueblo*
bap 21 Nov 1824; d/ Santiago ROMERO & Maria Loreta del RIO; gp/ Juan GONZALEZ & Maria Getrudis ARCHULETA.

SANCHEZ, Juan de Jesus *Arroyo Ondo*
bap 21 Nov 1824; s/ Juan de Jesus SANCHEZ & Maria Leocadia (n.s.); ap/ Mig^{l} SANCHEZ & Josefa MARTIN; am/ Teresa GARCIA (only); gp/ Juan Jose LUCERO & Teresa SANCHEZ.

QUINTANA, Andres de Jesus *Arroyo Hondo*
bap 22 Nov 1824; s/ Salvador QUINTANA & Maria dela Luz GONZALEZ; ap/ Juan QUINTANA & Barbanera (sic) ROMERO; am/ Juan Antonio GONZALEZ & Maria Barbara VARELA; gp/ Martin FLORES & Maria Encarnacion GONZALEZ.

ESPINOSA, Maria Encarnacion *Pueblo*
bap 22 Nov 1824; d/ Rafael ESPINOSA & Maria Antonia ZAMORA; gf/ Bernardo MONTOYA.

BEITA, Jose Clemente *Ranchito*
bap 25 Nov 1824; s/ Diego BEITA & Ana Maria MARTIN; ap/ Andres BEITA & Barbara MARTIN; am/ Faustino MARTIN & Maria Manuela VALDES; gp/ Juan de Jesus LUCERO & Maria Ygnacia ARAGON. (See second below. No mention of twins).

MONDRAGON, Maria Catalina *Arroyo Hondo*
bap 27 Nov 1824; d/ Manuel MONDRAGON & Maria Rosa ARELLANO; ap/ Mariano MONDRAGON & Encarnacion ESPINOSA; am/ Julian ARELLANO & Juana (n.s.-blank space); gp/ Ventura SANDOVAL & Maria de Jesus MASCAREÑAS.

BEITA, Jose Clemente S^{n} Fernando
bap 4 Dec 1824; s/ Diego BEITA & Ana Maria MARTIN; ap/ Andres BEITA & Barbara MARTIN; am/ Faustino MARTIN & Maria Manuela VALDES; gp/ Juan de Jesus LUCERO & Maria Ygnacia ARAGON. (See second above. No mention of twins).

Frame 519
CARIER, Maria Barbara *Arroyo Hondo*
bap 5 Dec 1824; d/ Anastasio CARIER (Origins, p. 422) & Mar^{a} Guadalupe CORDOVA; ap/ Bautista CARIEL (as written) & Ynes (n.s.); am/ Lorenzo CORDOVA & Margarita MARTIN; gp/ Lorenzo CORDOVA & Guadalupe CORDOVA.

(Two entries with no surnames)

SAIZ, Jose Mig^{l} S^{n} Fernando
bap 10 Dec 1824; s/ Jose Manuel SAIZ & Trinidad MEDINA; ap/ Simon SAIZ & Margarita LOVATO; am/ Antonio MEDINA & Micaela BIGOYA; gp/ Jose Pablo GALLEGO & Maria Dolores MARTIN.

(Entry with no surnames)

CACHO (patron), Teresa *Navajosa*
bap 11 Dec 1824, ca 10 yr; d/ Navajos, ransomed by the RPF Antonio CACHO; gm/ (torn-Guada)lupe SANCHEZ.

TRUJILLO (patron), Maria Ynes *Navajosa*
bap 11 Dec 1824, ca 12 yr; d/ Navajos, ransomed by Blas TRUJILLO; gp/ (the above) & Maria Manuela SANCHEZ, his wife.

GONZALEZ, Antonia Rosalia *Vecina del Rancho*
bap 13 Dec 1824; d/ Jose Ygnacio GONZALEZ & Ysidora PACHECO; am/ Fran^{co} PACHECO & Luisa VIGIL; gp/ Roman TAFOYA & Rosalia DURAN.

PADILLA (gp), Fran^{co} and Fran^{ca} *Pueblo*
bap 16 Dec 1824; twin children/ Victor (n.s.) & Maria (n.s.); gm/ Fran^{ca} PADILLA.

ROMERO, Maria Guadalupe *Rancho*
bap 16 Dec 1824; d/ Vicente ROMERO & Soledad CHAVES; (ap-torn)/ Fran^{co} Estevan ROMERO & Dolores TRUJILLO; am/ Domingo CHAVES & Candelaria DURA(N); gp/ (torn-MAR)QUEZ & Maria de los Reyes SANCHEZ.

VAL(torn), Guadalupe Concepcion Pueblo
bap 17 Dec 1824; d/ Jose VAL(torn) & (torn); gp/ Fran^{co} LUJAN & Magdalena ROMERO.

Frame 520
CORDOVA, Maria Guadalupe *Vecina del Rancho*
bap 19 Dec 1824; d/ Lorenzo CORDOVA & Maria Rafaela TRUJILLO; ap/ Aban CORDOVA & Juliana TORRES; am/ Mariano TRUJILLO & Teresa BACA; gp/ Blas TRUJILLO & Maria Manuela SANCHEZ.

MARTIN, Antonia Dominga S^{n} Fernando
bap 25 Dec 1824; s/ Bentura MARTIN & Maria del Rosario HERRERA; ap/ Juan de los Reyes (MARTIN) & Maria Soledad LUCERO; am/ Jose HERRERA & Josefa REL; gp/ Mig^{l} LARRAÑAGA & Maria Cruz TRUJILLO.

SANDOVAL, Maria Juliana *Pueblo*
bap 25 Dec 1824; d/ Nicolas SANDOVAL & Ygnacia MARTIN; ap/ Matias SANDOVAL & Maria Ygnacia BUENA; am/ Ramon MARTIN & Paula MARTIN; gp/ Rafael TAFOYA & Barbara MEDINA.

GARCIA, Gregorio *Vecino*
bap 25 Dec 1824; s/ Ramon GARCIA & Ramona MONTOYA; ap/ Xavier GARCIA & Maria del Rosario APODACA; am/ Jose APODACA (sic) & Ygnacia CHRISPIN; gp/ Juan Gabriel DURAN & Juana Tomasa GARCIA.

CORTES, Jose Rafael (torn)
bap 25 Dec 1824; nat. s/ Ysabel CORTE(S) & father unknown; am/ Christoval CORTES & Fran^{ca} MONTOYA; gp/ Jose SUASO & Jose(fa) CASADO.

MARTIN, Jose Dolores (torn)
bap 26 Dec 1824; s/ Mariano MARTIN & Brigida TAFOYA; ap/ Juan Felipe MARTIN & Ygn^{a} VIGIL; am/ Juan Domingo TAFOYA & Getrudis CORDOVA; gp/ Fran^{co} ARAGON & Maria Barbara ARAG^{N}.

TRUJILLO, Demetrio Antonio
bap 29 Dec 1824; s/ Juan Bautista TRUJILLO & Casilda QUINTANA; ap/ Mig^{l} TRUJILLO & Rosa VIGIL; am/ Jose dela Cruz QUINTANA & Micaela VALDES; gf/ Luis CHAVES.

MARTIN, Maria Ysabel
bap 29 Dec 1824; d/ Santos MARTIN & Guad^{e} MANCHEGO; ap/ Juan Pablo MARTIN & Guad^{e} CHAVES; am/ (blank space); gp/ Ant^{o} Jos(e) OLONA & Marg^{a} ESPINOSA.

1825

ROMERO, Manuel Antonio
bap 3 Jan 1825; s/ Jose de la Merced ROMERO & Maria Josefa QUINTANA; ap/ Gabriel ROMERO & Rosalia TRUJILLO; am/ Greg^{o} QUINTANA & Concepcion VALDES; gp/ Jose Maria SANDOVAL & Maria dela Luz QUINTANA.

ESPALIN, Maria Soledad
bap 4 Jan 1825; d/ Jose (torn) ESPALIN (Origins, p. 414) & Maria VARELA; ap/ Jose ESPALIN & Maria Nieves ROBLES; am/ German VARELA & Ysi(dora-torn) (torn-JARA)MILLO, *todos del Paso del Norte*; gp/ Jose GONZALEZ & Dorotea BACA.

Frame 521
CONCHA, Santiago *Pueblo*
bap 9 Jan 1825; s/ Juan Manuel CONCHA & Dominga ROMERO; gm/ Fran^{ca} HORTI(Z).

TORRES, Santiago S^{n} Fernando
bap 9 Jan 1825; s/ Nicolas TORRES & Maria de la Luz MARTIN; ap/ Diego TORRES & Alberta VENABIDES; am/ Ant^{o} Jose MARTIN & Concepcion MARTIN; gp/ Jose MARTIN & Dolores MARTIN.

MEDINA, Juan de los Reyes *Arroyo Hondo*
bap 9 Jan 1825; s/ Manuel MEDINA & Maria Ant^{a} MARTIN; ap/ Juan Christoval MEDINA & Juana CORDOVA; am/ Bernardo MARTIN & Getrudis ARCHULETA; gp/ Fran^{co} MARTIN & Maria Encarnac^{n} MARTIN.

LUNA, Juan Luciano S^{n} Fernando
bap 9 Jan 1825; s/ Juan LUNA & Candelaria VELARDE; ap/ Rafael LUNA & Ana Maria TAFOYA; am/ Joaquin VELARDE & Juana GARCIA; gp/ Samuel CHAMBRES & Rosa GRIJALBA.

MASCAREÑAS, Maria Cecilia *Pueblo*
bap 12 Jan 1825; d/ Mig^{l} MASCAREÑAS & Maria Manuela (torn-BUE)NO; ap/ Bernardo MASCARENAS & Maria Juliana CORDOVA; am/ Ant^{o} BUENO & Maria Rosa(lia) (n.s.-torn); gp/ Jose Domingo DURAN & Maria Soledad LOVATO.

CRUZ, Maria Ylaria *Rancho*
bap 16 Jan 1825; d/ Mariano CRUZ & Vi(torn) (torn-COR)DOVA; ap/ Fran^{co} CRUZ & Franc^{ca} CORDOVA; am/ Andres CORDOVA & Mar^{a} D(torn) (torn-ARCHU)LETA; gp/ Ant^{o} de Jesus GALLEGO & Maria Micaela VIG^{L}.

ROMERO, Pedro Jose *Pueblo*
bap 16 Jan 1825; s/ Juan Domingo ROMERO & Maria Ygnacia (n.s.); gp/ Ypolito (torn).

VIGIL (patron), Maria Ant^{a} de la Luz *Nacion Yuta*
bap 19 Jan 1825, ae (torn) yr; d/ *Nacion Yuta*, rescued by Amadon VIG^{L}; gf/ Juan Domingo TAFOYA.

VALDES, Pedro Antonio *Ranchito*
bap 20 Jan 1825; s/ Bentura VALDES & (torn-n.n.) LOVATO; ap/ Pedro Antonio VALDES & Manuela GONZALEZ; am/ Antonio (LOVATO-torn) & (n.n.-torn) CHAVES; gp/ Pablo GALLEGO & Maria Dolores MARTIN.

VIGIL, Jose Pablo *Rancho*
bap 26 Jan 1825; s/ Jose Fran^{co} VIGIL & (torn); ap/ Juan Ygnacio VIGIL & Maria Ant^{a} ARAGON; am/ (torn) & (torn) TRUJILLO; gp/ Juan Christoval VIG^{L} & Anton^{a} Biviana TORRES.

Frame 522
(Entry without surnames)

SALAZAR, Juan Chrisostomo *Ran(cho)*
bap 30 Jan 1825; s/ Pedro SALAZAR & Maria del Carmen MEDINA; ap/ Asencio SALAZAR & Juana Rita MASCAREÑAS; am/ Joaquin MEDINA & Maria Fran^{ca} CHRISPIN; gp/ Joaquin MEDINA & Maria Fran^{ca} CHRISPIN.

LEDU, Antonio *Nac^{n} Panana*
bap 31 Jan 1825, barely 7 yr; s/ Antonio LEDU *de Nacion Francesa* & (not given) (Origins, p. 423); gp/ Mig^{l} ARCENON & Maria Rita SANCHEZ.

SANDOVAL, Maria Ypolita *Arroyo Hondo*
bap 1 Feb 1825; d/ Fran^{co} SANDOVAL & Maria Josefa ARCHULETA; ap/ Juan Domingo SANDOVAL & Marg^{a} (n.s.); am/ Julian ARCHULETA & Maria Manuela VARELA; gp/ Felipe SANCHEZ & Maria Lucia GUTIERREZ.

GARCIA, Maria de los Dolores (Torn)
bap 2 Feb 1825; d/ Xavier GARCIA & Maria Ysabel RUIBAL; ap/ Ramon GARCIA & Maria Teresa BACA; am/ Jose Ant^{o} RUIBAL & Maria Rosalia MAEZ; gp/ Juan Jose VAZQUEZ & Maria Pasquala CORDOVA.

SANCHEZ, Andrea (Torn)
bap 6 Feb 1825; s/ Jose Ant^{o} SANCHEZ & Juana Soledad LOPEZ; ap/ Joaquin SANCHEZ & Ant^{a} Rosa MARTIN; am/ Jose Antonio (LOPEZ) & Maria Ant^{a} ARMIJO; gp/ Juan Julian MARTIN & Maria Guadalupe VIGIL.

GONZALEZ, Hermeregilda (Torn)
bap 14 Feb 1825; d/ Salvador GONZALEZ & Ana Mar^{a} VIG^{L}; ap/ Jose Antonio GONZALEZ & Manuela del RIO; am/ Jose Ant^{o} VIG^{L} & Ana Mar^{a} MESTAS; gp/ Jose Ant^{o} MARTIN & Guad^{e} MARTIN.

VALLE, Jose Ant^{o}
bap 14 Feb 1825; s/ Jose VALLE & Juana ROMERO; gm/ Mar^{a} Ant^{a} MOYA.

DURAN, Juan Bernardo
bap 14 Feb 1825; s/ Bentura DURAN & Mar^{a} de Jesus MARTIN; ap/ Man^{l} DURAN & Geralda MASCAREÑAS; am/ Cruz MARTIN & Dolores TORRES; gp/ Bernardo DURAN & Feliciana VIG^{L}.

SANDOVAL, (torn)lina
bap 14 Feb 1825; d/ Ylario SANDOVAL & Maria Dolores RUIBAL; ap/ Miguel SANDOVAL & Ma(torn) (torn)AR; am/ Fran^{co} RUIBAL & Ana Maria CASADOS; gp/ Antonio Hermeregildo TRU(JILLO-torn) & (Ma)ria Josefa TAFOYA.

Frame 523

CORDOVA, Jose Candelario *Rancho*
MARTIN, Jose Candelario
bap 14 Feb 1825; nat. s/ Dionicio CORDOVA, married, & Maria Ysidora MARTIN, wid.; ap/ Gregorio CORDOVA & Maria LOVATO; am/ Geronimo MARTIN & Maria COCA; gp/ Lorenzo ARAGON & Barbara BACA.

(Fr. Buenaventura MURO signing entries.)

SANDOVAL, Mª Encarnac^{n} S^{n} Fern^{o}
bap 16 Feb 1825; d/ Pablo SANDOVAL & Dolores COCA; ap/ Felipe SANDOVAL & Teresa SENA; am/ Jose Mª COCA & Juana BENAVIDES; gp/ Ygn^{o} ALARID & Dolores TRUJILLO.

SANDOVAL, Juan de la Trinid^{d} S^{n} Fern^{o}
bap 18 Feb 1825; d/ Ant^{o} SANDOV^{L} & Guad^{e} VIGIL; ap/ Pablo SANDOVAL & Lugarda QUINTANA; am/ Julian VIGIL & Man^{a} FRESQUIS; gp/ Rafael LUNA & Ana Mª TAFOYA.

TAFOYA, José Rafael
bap 20 Feb 1825; s/ Bartolo TAFOYA & Ant^{a} GONZ^{z}; ap/ Domingo TAFOYA & Dolores MES; am/ Cayet^{o} GONZALES (sic) & Lorenza JORGE; gp/ Ant^{o} ARAG^{N} & Nicolasa QUINTANA.

CASILLAS, Jose Ventura *Rancho*
bap 20 Feb 1825; s/ Bartolomé CASILLAS & Elena GARCIA; gp/ Fran^{co} PACHECO & Dolores VARELA.

SILVA, Mª Romualda *Arroyo Hondo*
bap 20 Feb 1825; d/ Jose Mª SILVA & Mª Ant^{a} MONTOYA; ap/ Fran^{co} SILVA & Juana MARTINA; am/ Ant^{o} MONTOYA & Luisa SANDOVAL; gp/ Joaq^{n} MES & Ynes ARMIJO.

MERINO, J^{n} Lor^{zo} Severino *Trampas*
bap 21 Feb 1825; s/ Jose Concep^{n} MERINO & Mª Jesus CORDOVA; ap/ Pasq^{l} MERINO & Teresa ESPINOSA; am/ Ant^{o} CORDOVA & Juana MARTINA; gp/ Jose Mª TRUJILLO & Mª St^{os} REYES.

LUCERO, Mª Rufina *Rancho*
bap 21 Feb 1825; d/ Pedro LUCERO & Mª Luz FERNAND^{z}; gp/ Viz^{te} GARCIA & Juliana ROMERO.

Frame 524

RUIVAL, Mª Seferina *Rancho*
bap 22 Feb 1825; d/ Eleuterio RUIVAL & Mª Gracia ZUASO; ap/ Dom^{o} RUIV^{L} & Valentina FRESQUIS; am/ Ysidro ZUASO & Catarina VALDEZ; gp/ Juan HERRERA & Encarnac^{n} CORDOVA.

CORDOVA, Jose Ant^{o} *Arroyo Seco*
bap 27 Feb 1825; s/ Man^{l} CORDOVA & Mª MARTIN; ap/ Ant^{o} CORDOVA & Mª Ysabel (n.s.); am/ Ant^{o} MARTIN & Clara VARELA; gp/ Hypolito TAFOYA & Concepc^{n} CHAVES.

SANDOVAL, Jose Rafael S^{n} Fern^{o}
bap 27 Feb 1825; s/ Fran^{co} SANDOVAL & Mª Jesus VARELA; ap/ Felipe SANDOVAL & Greg^{a} SENA; am/ Mig^{l} VARELA & Juana ROMERO; gp/ Nepomuc^{o} LUNA & Candelaria VELARDE.

CORDOVA, Jose de Jesus *Rancho*
bap 27 Feb 1825; s/ Mariano CORDOVA & Josefa ESPINOSA; ap/ Man^{l} CORDOVA & Guad^{e} SERNA; am/ Viz^{te} ESPINOSA & Mª Luz TRUJILLO; gp/ Jesus COCA & Mª Luz DURAN.

VALLOS, Jose Ant^{o} *Pueblo*
bap 2 Mch 1825; s/ Ant^{o} Jose VALLOS & Pasquala ROMERO *del pueblo*; gp/ Jose Man^{l} ROMERO & Dolores GONZ^{z}.

MEDINA, Mª Guad^{e} S^{n} Fern^{o}
bap 3 Mch 1825; d/ Jose Ant^{o} MEDINA & Candelaria ZALASAR; ap/ Ant^{o} Jose MEDINA & Micaela VEGIL; am/ Gervacio ZALASAR & Rosalia COCA; gp/ Man^{l} SAIZ & Trinid^{d} MEDINA.

MURO, Jose Mig^{l} *Pueblo*
bap 6 Mch 1825, ae 3 yr; s/ *Nacion Navajo gentiles*, adopted s/ Fr. Buenav^{a} MURO who bought him; gp/ D. Lorenzo (torn-COR)DOVA & D^{a} Mª TAPIA.

Frame 525

VEGIL, Jose Fran^{co} *Rancho*
bap 7 Mch 1825; s/ Fran^{co} VEGIL & Juliana CONTRERAS; ap/ Julian VEGIL & Mar(ia) GARCIA; am/ Gerardo CONTRERAS & Encarna^{n} CHAVES; gp/ Man^{l} DURAN & Rosa URIOSTE.

ROMERO, Jose Santiago *Pueblo*
bap 7 Mch 1825; s/ Rafael ROM^{O} & Lucia PADILLA; ap/ Man^{l} ROMERO & Josefa ORTIZ; am/ Santiago PAD^{A} & Josefa (n.s.); gp/ Juan Carmen ZUASO & Mª Dolores ZUASO.

MARTIN, Juan Ant^{o} *Arroyo Seco*
bap 13 Mch 1825; s/ Man^{l} MARTIN & Dolores GONZ^{z}; ap/ Juan Jose MARTIN & Josefa MARTIN; am/ Ant^{o} GONZ^{z} & Bibiana (n.s.); gp/ Mig^{l} CORTES & Mª Crus MARTIN.

BRISOL, Jose Fran^{co} S^{n} Fern^{o}
bap 14 Mch 1825; s/ Bautista BRISOL (Origins, p. 409) & Manuela MONDRAG^{N}; ap/ Jose BRISOL & M^{a} (n.s.); am/ Jose MONDRAG^{N} & Dolores CASAUS; gp/ Juan Carmen (n.s.) & Dolores ZUASO.

ESPINOSA, Juana Mª *Rancho*
bap 16 Mch 1825; d/ Santiago ESPINOSA & Rosa LUCERO; ap/ Viz^{te} ESPINOSA & Luz ROMERO; am/ Pedro LUCERO & Mª Luz PINO; gp/ Jose Ant^{o} VARGAS & Mª Jesus PINO.

GARCIA, Mª Josefa *Rancho*
bap 16 Mch 1825; d/ Salv^{r} GARCIA & Lor^{za} CRUZ; ap/ Man^{l} GARCIA & Ant^{a} SANDOVAL; am/ Alexo CRUZ & Guad^{e} DURAN; gp/ Ramon DURAN & Margarita MEDINA.

ARCHULETA, Mª Ygnacia *Arroyo Hdo*
bap 16 Mch 1825; d/ Julian ARCHULETA & Man^{a} VARELA; ap/ Damian ARCHULETA & Micaela (n.s.); am/ not given; gp/ Fran^{co} GARCIA & Trinidad QUINT^{A}. (No mention of twins.)

ARCHULETA, Mª Juana *(Torn-Arr)oyo Hondo*
bap 16 Mch 1825; d/ Julian ARCHULETA & Mar^{a} VARELA; ap/ Damian ARCHULETA & Micaela MA(RTIN-torn); gp/ Fran^{co} QUINT^{A} & Luz QUINT^{A}. (No mention of twins.)

Frame 526
QUINTANA, Mª Agapita (torn-*Arro*)*yo Hdo.*
bap 16 Mch 1825; d/ Salvador QUINT^{A} & Soled^{d} LUCERO; ap/ Juan QUINT^{A} & Valbaneda ROMERO; am/ Jesus LUCERO & Rosalia BERNAL; gp/ Fran^{co} QUINT^{A} & Luz QUINT^{A}.

ARMIJO, Jose Greg^{o} S^{n} Fern^{o}
bap 17 Mch 1825; s/ Man^{l} ARMIJO & Trinid^{d} VEGIL; ap/ Jose ARMIJO & Luciana MARTIN; am/ Fran^{co} VEGIL & Fran^{ca} S^{N}TISTEVAN; gp/ Bern^{do} Joaq^{n} MAES & Ynes ARMIJO.

GONZALES, Jose Fran^{co} S^{n} Fern^{o}
bap 19 Mch 1825; s/ Navajos, adopted s/ D^{n} Jose GONZALES; gp/ Juan LUNA & Candelaria VELARDE.

VEGIL, Jose dela Cruz R^{cho}
bap 19 Mch 1825; s/ Fran^{co} VEGIL & Mª HURTADO; ap/ Mig^{l} VEGIL & Ana M^{a} (n.s.); am/ Juan HURTADO & Mariana ROMERO; gp/ Mariano (n.s.) & Ysabel FERN^{Z}.

TRUJILLO, Mª Luz R^{cho}
bap 20 Mch 1825; d/ Juan TRUJ^{O} & Catarina CORDOVA; ap/ S^{tiago} TRUJ^{O} & Polonia ROM^{O}; am/ Avan CORDOVA & Juliana TORRES; gp/ Faust^{o} VEGIL & Luz MART^{N}.

LUJAN, Juan Ant^{o} *Pueblo*
bap 20 Mch 1825; s/ Juan Ant^{o} LUJAN & Josefa ROMERO, Indians; gp/ Juan del Carmen ROMERO & Rosa MARTIN.

LUCERO, Mª Josefa *Rancho*
bap *en el mismo dia*; d/ Pedro LUCERO & Getrudis DURAN; ap/ Santiago LUCERO & Rosa AGUILAR; am/ Ygnacio (torn-DURAN) & Ant^{a} SANCHES, dec.; gp/ Mariano XARAMILLO & (torn-n.n.) LOVATO.

ROMERO, Ant° Domingo *Rancho*
bap 20 Mch 1825; s/ Juan de Jesus ROMERO & Candelaria QUINTANA; ap/ Ant° Domingo ROMERO & (torn n.n.) COCA; am/ Juan QUINTANA & Balvaneda ROMERO; gp/ Man^{l} TORES & Reyes DURAN.

(See Frame 536 for remainder of entries for March 1825 forward to beginning of Nov 1825).

Frame 527
BERNAL, Santiago
bap 14 (sic) Nov 1825; s/ Rafael BERNAL & Lucilla PADILLA; ap/ Juan M^{l} BERNAL & Josefa ROMERO; am/ Santiago PADILLA & Josefa ORTIZ; gp/ Jose SUASO & Josefa CASADOS.

LASO, Pablo
bap 14 Nov 1825; s/ (n.n.) LASO & Mª Ant^{a} LUJAN; ap/ Matias LASO & Rosa LUCERO; am/ Jose LUJAN & Rosa LUCERO; gp/ Jose Mª CORTES & Maria BRITO.

VEGIL, Jose Santiago *V*
bap 30 Nov 1825; s/ Ant° VEGIL & Simona MONTOYA; ap/ Julian VEGIL & Manuela GARCIA; am/ Felis MONTOYA & Rosa ROMERO; gp/ Juan LOVATO & Ygnacia SANCHES.

DURAN, Juana *Rancho*
bap 4 Dec 1825; d/ Gregorio DURAN & Rosa de los Reyes URIOSTE; ap/ Ygnacio DURAN & Ant^{a} Gertrudis SANCHES; am/ Fran^{co} URIOSTE & Rita MARTIN; gp/ Jose Ant° GONSALES & Maria Concepcion URIOSTE.

MARTIN, Mª Eduvige
bap 8 Dec 1825; d/ Ant° MARTIN & Catarina SANDOVAL; ap/ Eusebio MARTIN & Ant^{a} ARMIJO; am/ Fran^{co} SANDOVAL & Maria (n.s.); gp/ Juan Miguel TAFOYA & Patricia MARTIN.

MARTIN, Jose Hermenegildo
bap 12 Dec 1825; s/ Felip(e-torn) MARTIN & Micaela ROMERO; gp/ Cristoval TRUGILLO & (torn-Ni)eves ROMERO.

Frame 528
TORRES, Jose de Jesus
bap 15 Dec 1825; s/ Ant° TORRES & Ysabel FERNANDEZ; ap/ Ant° TORRES & Nicolasa SANDOVAL; am/ Marianao FERNANDES (sic) & Ascension LUCERO; gp/ Mariano FERNANDES (sic) & Clara FERN^{z}.

ESPINOSA (patron), Mª Guadalupe
bap 19 Dec 1825; d/ *Nacion Yuta*, bought for Mª Encarnacion ESPINOSA, who was gp together with her son, Jose Ant° MONDRAGON.

GONSALES, Mª Estefana
bap 25 Dec 1825; d/ Fran^{co} GONSALES & Mª Lus MARQUEZ; ap/ Jose GONSALES & Dorotea VACA; am/ Miguel MARQUES (sic) & M^{a} (n.s.); gp/ Ant° LUCERO & Estefana ARAGON.

REYNA, Manuela blank
bap 28 Dec 1825; d/ Juan Miguel REYNA & Guadalupe ROMERO; ap/ Jose REYNA & Rosalia LUJAN; am/ Juan Ant° ROMERO & Victoria DELGADO; gp/ Bernardino MARTIN & Manuela ARAGON.

Año de 1826

GONSALES, Jose Mª *Pueblo*

bap 4 Jan 1826; s/ Ant^{o} GONSALES & Micaela MARTIN; *abuelos* not given; gp/ Diego SANCHES & Magdalena MARTIN.

VIGIL, Jose M^{l} (S^{n}) Fer^{o}
bap 15 Jan 1826; s/ Ant^{o} VIGIL & Manuela CHAVES; gp/ (not given).

Frame 529
MARTIN, Juan Pablo S^{n} Fer^{o}
bap 20 Jan 1826; s/ Pablo MARTIN & Soledad LUCERO; ap/ Ant^{o} Jose MARTIN & Mª Rita BEITIA; am/ Juan de Jesus LUCERO & Ygnacia ARAGON; gp/ Juan TRUGILLO & Niebes ROMERO.

MARTIN, Ant^{o} Policarpio blank
bap same day; s/ Andres MARTIN & Mª Ant^{a} ORTIS; ap/ Pedro MARTIN & Ygnacia GARCIA; am/ Matias ORTIS & Fran^{ca} VACA; gp/ Jose Rafael ROMERO & Ana Maria ORTIS.

LUCERO, Jose del Carmen S^{n} Fer^{o}
bap 22 Jan 1826; s/ Ant^{o} Jose LUCERO & Dolores VALDES; ap/ Vicente LUCERO & Marta ATENCIO; am/ Juan Ant^{o} VALDES & Bibiana VACA; gp/ Ant^{o} MARTINEZ & Carmen VALDES.

TRUGILLO, Mª Pelegrina *Rancho*
bap same day; d/ Juan TRUGILLO & Casilda QUINTANA; ap/ Jose Miguel TRUGILLO & Rosa VEGIL; am/ Jose de la Cruz QUINTANA & Micaela VALDES; gp/ Jose Domingo DURAN & Soledad LOVATO.

CORTES, Jose Fran^{co} *Rancho*
bap 29 Jan 1826; s/ Jose M^{l} CORTES & Manuela SANCHES; ap/ Paulin CORTES & Concepcion MARTIN; am/ Felipe SAN(CHES-torn) & Ana Maria MARTIN; gp/ Candelario VEGIL & Ant^{a} DURAN.

Frame 530
CORTES, Juan M^{l} Arro(yo) Ho(n)do
bap 30 Jan 1826; s/ Pablo CORTES & Dolores PADILLA; ap/ Jose CORTES & Juana MONTOYA; am/ Pedro PADILLA & Lucilla CHAVES; gp/ Cristoval SANCHES & Bentura PADILLA.

RUBIDU, Mª Juana S^{n} Fer^{o}
ROMERO, Mª Juana
bap same day; nat. d/ Fran^{co} RUBIDU, the Frenchman, & Luisa ROMERO; am/ Tomas ROMERO & Ysidora MARTIN; gp/ Jose Ant^{o} SUASO & Josefa CASADOS.

BARELA, Maria Dolores *Ranchos*
bap 31 Jan 1826; d/ Jose Candelario BARELA & Concepcion SOLANO; ap/ Juan Ant^{o} BARELA & Ynacia VEGIL; am/ Andres SOLANO & Felisiana BALDES; gp/ Jesus GALLEGO & Ant^{a} VEGIL.

MOYA, Agustin *Pueblo*
bap *en el mismo dia*; s/ Ant^{o} MOYA & Magadalena ROMERO; ap/ Jose Ant^{o} MOYA & Josefa GABILAN; am/ Juan Domingo ROMERO & Mauricia MARTIN; gp/ Agustin DURAN & Lusiya SAMORA.

MIRABAL, Juan (torn-*(Pu)eblo*
bap *en dicho dia mes y año*; s/ Lorenso MIRABAL & Soledad REYNA; ap/ Salbador MIRABAL & Luciya ROMERO; am/ Domingo REYNA & Encarnacion GABILAN; gp/ Rosa LUJAN (only).

Frame 531

MONTES, Jose de Jesus *Rancho*
bap 4 Feb 1826; s/ Fran^{co} MONTES & Juana MONTOYA; ap/ Ant^{o} MONTES & Ynes MARTIN; am/ Bernardo MONTOYA (only); gp/ Jose PADILLA & Juana PADILLA.

SALASAR, Jose Bentura *Rancho*
bap 8 Feb 1826; s/ Carpio SALASAR & Luisa VEGIL; *abuelos* not given; gp/ Manuel LUCERO & Andrea LABADILLA.

ARELLANO, Mª de la Lus *Arr^{o} Hondo*
bap 10 Feb 1826; d/ Domingo ARELLANO & Rosa MEDINA; ap/ Julian ARELLANO (only); am/ Cristoval MEDINA & Juana CORDOVA; gp/ (not given).

MONTOYA, Ant^{o} Seferino *Rancho*
bap 15 Feb 1826; s/ Lorenso MONTOYA & Mª Josef(a-torn) LUCERO; ap/ Bernardo MONTOYA & Mª MARTIN; am/ Ju(an-torn) de Jesus LUCERO & Ygnacia ARAGON; gp/ Juan de Jesus LUCERO (only).

ANALLA, Josefa S^{n} Fer^{o}
bap 20 Feb 1826; d/ Rafael ANALLA & Mª GALLEGO; ap/ Jose ANALLA & Josefa ARAGON; am/ Luterio GALLEGO & Maria MARTIN; gp/ Ant^{o} VIGIL & Manuela CHAVES.

BASQUES, Jose Fran^{co} *Arr^{o} Hondo*
bap 24 Feb 1826; s/ (torn-n.n.) BASQUES & Pasquala ROMERO; ap/ Jose Ant^{o} (BASQUES-torn) & Rosa ARELLANO; am/ Pablo CORDOVA (sic) & Margarita (n.s.-torn); gp/ Nepomuceno CORTES & Cruz MARTIN.

Frame 532

VEGIL, Juan Jose
GONSALES, Juan Jose
bap 26 Feb 1826; nat. s/ Rafael VEGIL & Ana Teresa (GONSALES); ap/ M^{l} VEGIL (only); am/ Diego GONSALES (only); gp/ Ant^{o} BASQUES & Rita ROMERO.

CRUZ, Maria Fran^{ca}
bap 28 Feb 1826; d/ Mariano CRUZ & Bitoriana CORDOVA; ap/ Fran^{co} CRUZ & Fran^{ca} GONSALES; am/ Andres CORDOVA & Dolores VEGIL; gp/ Jose Mariano SOLANO & Magdalena VARELA.

(No March entries)

CRUZ, Jose Toribio
bap 4 Apr 1826; s/ Jose CRUZ & Carmen ROMERO; ap/ Vicente CRUZ & Rosa MARTIN; am/ M^{a}no ROMERO & Fran^{ca} ARMENTA; gp/ Juan de Jesus TRUGILLO & Mª BALERIO.

MARTIN, Mª de la Lus *Rancho*
bap 10 Apr 1826; d/ Ygnacio MARTIN & Dolores LOVATO; ap/ Juan Pablo MARTIN & Guadalupe CHAVES; am/ Rafael LOVATO & Lus ESPINOSA; gp/ Fran^{co} MARTIN & Ygnacia PINEDA.

MAES, Jose Encarnacion S^{n} Fer^{o}
bap 12 Apr 1826; s/ Paulin MAES & Ygnacia GARCIA; ap/ Domingo MAES & Juana Mª de HERRERA; am/ Juan Angel GARCIA & Manuela BARELA; gp/ Roque MARTIN & Gregoria ARMIJO.

Frame 533

PACHECO, Mª Hermenegilda (M^{a} in margin) *Rancho*
bap 20 Apr 1826; d/ Diego PACHECO & Gertrudis GONSALES; ap/ Fran^{co} PACHECO &

Luisa VEGIL; am/ Fer^{do} GONSALES & Dolores BERNAL; gp/ Jose de Jesus GARCIA & Beatris SANDOVAL.

PACHECO, Jose *Rancho*
bap 26 Apr 1826; s/ Jose PACHECO & Gertrudes GONSALES; ap/ Fran^{co} PACHECO & Fran^{ca} VEGIL; am/ Teresa GONSALES (only); gp/ Jose GARCIA & M^{a} (n.s.).

RAEL, Jose *Rancho*
bap 28 Apr 1826; s/ Ramon RAEL & Teresa VEGI(L-torn); ap/ Felipe RAEL & Manuela ROMERO; am/ Jua(n-torn) VEGIL & Josefa LOVATO; gp/ M^{l} GARCIA & Carmen RAEL.

(Entry with no surnames)

MARTIN, Jose Santiago *Rancho*
bap 4 May 1826; s/ (torn-n.n.) MARTIN & Ysabel MONTOYA; gp/ Faus(tin-torn) MARTIN & Paula GONSALES.

Frame 534
BARELA, Pedro Jose *Rancho*
bap 10 May 1826; s/ Miguel BARELA & Monserrate ROMERO; ap/ Cristoval BARELA & Juana Teresa MARTIN; am/ Mariano ROMERO & Fran^{ca} ARMENTA; gp/ Gregorio DURAN & Clara FERNANDES.

BALDES, Mª Petra
bap 15 May 1826; d/ father unknown & Gregoria BALDES; gp/ Bentu^{a} ROMERO & Rosario HERRERA.

PACHECO, Ant^{o} Jose *Rancho*
bap 20 May 1826; s/ Ramon PACHECO & Trenidad VEGIL; ap/ Ant^{o} Jose PACHECO & Ygnacia SANDOVAL; am/ Juan dela Cruz VEGIL & Clara FER^{z}; gp/ Juan Nepomuceno DURAN & Geralda MASCAREÑAS.

TAFOYA, Bernardo *Rancho*
bap 21 May 1826; s/ Ramon TAFOYA & Rosa DURAN; ap/ Juan TAFOYA & Dolores MAES; am/ M^{l} DURAN & Geralda MASCAREÑAS; gp/ Juan Fran^{co} MONTOYA & Josefa TRUGILLO.

(Rest of May on Frame 548 & forward)
Frame 535 (only entry on this frame & should have been filmed before Frame 534)
"Partidas de Bautismos desde 24 de Mayo de este Año de 1826"

Frame 536
GALLEGO, Mª Dolores S^{n} Fern^{o}
bap 21 Mch 1825; d/ Valentin GALLEGO & Juana MESTAS; gp/ Felipe Santiago PADILLA & Soledad MARTIN.

VARELA, Jose Dolores *Rancho*
bap 22 Mch 1825; s/ Juan VARELA & Juliana TRUGILLO; ap/ Ant^{o} VARELA & Magdal^{a} LOPES; am/ Vicente TRUGI^{o} & Guada^{e} (n.s.); gp/ Jose Mª TRUGILLO & Reyes MEDINA.

VEGIL, Jose Encarn^{n} *Rancho*
bap 29 Mch 1825; s/ Amador VEGIL & Micaela MARTIN; am/ Juanico QUINTANA (as written) & Felipa MAES; gp/ Juan Domingo TAFOYA & Juana Getrudis CORDOVA. (See Frame 485 for correct *abuelos*.)

HERRERA, Jose Encarn^{n} *Rancho*
bap 29 Mch 1825; s/ Cristoval de HERRERA & Mª LUCERO; ap/ Fran^{co} de HERRERA & Paula SALASAR; am/ Jesus LUCERO & Rosalia BERN^{L}; gp/ Juan GOMES & Getrudis ARCHULETA.

ROMERO, Ju^{n} Benito *Rancho*
bap 30 Mch 1825; s/ Rafael ROMERO & Ana Maria ORTIS; ap/ Miguel ROMERO & Man^{a} GARCIA; am/ Gaspar ORTIS & Fran^{ca} MARTIN; gp/ Juan Domingo TAFOYA & Getrudis CORDOVA. (Frames 536-537)

Frame 537
AGUILAR, Manuel Ant^{o} S^{n} Fern^{o}
bap on the same day; s/ Ant^{o} AG(U)ILAR & Juana CORDOVA; gp/ Felipe Santiago PADILLA & Soledad MARTIN.

SANCHES, Jose Damasio *Arroyo Seco*
bap *en dicho dia*; s/ Domingo SANCHES & Man^{a} GOMES; ap/ Mariano SANCHES & Rosa MARTIN; am/ Gaspar GOMES & Mª Biviana MES; gp/ Blas TRUGILLO & Mª TAPIA.

CHALLO, Mª Teodora *Pueblo*
bap same day; d/ Pedro CHALLO & Rosalia ROMERO, Indians; gp/ Pablo SANDOVAL & Mª Teodora COCA.

ROMERO, Mª Rosa *Rancho*
bap 31 Mch 1825; d/ Jose ROMERO & Fran^{ca} FERNANDES; ap/ Concecion ROMERO & Rosa QUINTANA; am/ Domingo FERNANDES & Fran^{ca} GARCIA; gp/ Jose Ant^{o} GARCIA & Mª Reyes MARTIN.

FRESQUES, Mª Paula *Rancho*
bap same day; d/ Ant^{o} FRESQUES & Mª Reyes SANCHES; ap/ Jose Ant^{o} FRESQUES & Ygnacia CANO; am/ Diego SANCHES & Madalena MARTIN; gp/ Ventura DURAN & Mª de Jesus MARTIN.

Frame 538
GOMES, Jose Santos *Rancho*
bap 3 April 1825; s/ Ant^{o} GOMES & Ygnacia ZALASAR; gp/ Juan Baut^{a} LEAL & Man^{a} LEAL.

SUR, Juan Nepomuceno S^{n} Fern^{o}
bap same day; s/ Fran^{co} SUR, *Frances* (Origins, p. 435) & Maria de Jesus MARTIN; gp/ Nepomuceno LOVATO & Mª Ygnacia LOVATO.

MEDINA (gp), Jose Fran^{co} *Pueblo*
bap 2 Apr 1825; s/ Jose Cristoval (n.s.) & Maria (n.s.), Indians; gp/ Julian MEDINA & Dolores VALDES.

LOMA, Mª de Jesus *Pueblo*
bap 7 Apr 1825; d/ Ramon LOMA & Fran^{ca} ORTIS *del pueblo*; gp/ Ventura SANDOVAL & Mª de Jesus MASCAREÑAS.

TAFOYA, Juana Mª *Rancho*
bap 8 Apr 1825; d/ Salvador TAFOYA & Juana MEDINA; ap/ Juan Domingo TAFOYA & Dolores MES; ap/ Juan de Jesus MEDINA & Candelaria PAIS; gp/ Faustin VIGIL & Mª de la Lus MARTIN. (Frames 538-539)

Frame 539
BUTIERRES, Jose Man^{l} (Jose Rafael in margin but see father) *Rancho*
bap 8 Apr 1825; s/ Jose Rafael BUTIERRES & Mª LOVATO; ap/ Miguel BUTIERRES

(only); am/ Salvador LOVATO & Mª CORDOVA; gp/ Juan Pablo DURAN & Soledad XARAMILLO.

RIBERA, Diego Antº — Sⁿ Fernº
bap same day; s/ Jose RIBERA & Mariana TORES; am/ Diego TORES & Concecion TRUGILLO; am (sic)/ Mª Antª (n.s.- only); gp/ "these same were padˢ".

ROMERO, Juan Miguel — *Rancho*
bap 10 Apr 1825; s/ Jose Antº ROMERO & Anamaria ARRIETA; ap/ Jose Concepcion ROMERO & Rosa QUINTANA; am/ Ramon ARRIETA & Dolores MES; gp/ Julian (n.s.) & Polonia LUCERO.

HERRERA, Mª Petra — *Rancho*
bap same day; d/ Pedro de HERRERA & Mª Manuela GARCIA; ap/ Pablo de HERRERA & Juana BENAVIDES; am/ Santiago MARTIN (sic-only); gp/ Jose OLONA & Margarita ESPINOSA.

VIGIL, Franᶜ Antº — Sⁿ Fernº
bap 10 Apr 1825; s/ Juan VIGIL & Madalena LUCERO; ap/ Gregorio VIGIL & Juana (n.s.); am/ Manuel ORTEGA (only); gp/ Mariano CRUZ & Dolores VIGIL.

Frame 540
ABILA, Juan Benito — *Arroyo Hondo*
bap 10 Apr 1825; s/ Anastacio ABILA & Ygnacia LUCERO; ap/ Pedro ABILA & Catarina MARTIN; am/ Vicente LUCERO & Marta (n.s.) who were the gp.

MONTOYA, Jose — *Rancho*
bap 29 Apr 1825; s/ Ygnacio MONTOYA & Mª TRUGILLO; gp/ Feliz URIOSTE & Carmen SANCHES.

MARTIN, Manuel — *Rancho*
bap 29 Apr 1825; s/ Jesus MARTIN & Concepcion CHAVES; gp/ Miguel MONTOYA & Felipa RAMIRIZ.

TAFOYA, Juan de Dios — Sⁿ Fernº
bap 29 Apr 1825; s/ Jose Faustin TAFOYA & Guadalupe ARMENTA; ap/ Nicolas TAFOYA & Mª Manuela MEDINA; am/ Cimon ARMENTA & Marta MARTIN; gp/ Antª Meregildo TRUGILLO & Mª Josefa TAFOYA.

ROMERO, Jose Francº — Sⁿ Fernº
bap 30 Apr 1825; s/ Juan Domingo ROMERO & Mª Ygnacia CHAVES; ap/ Manuel Jose ROMERO & Juana BARELA; am/ Jose Mª CHAVES & Mª ORTEGA; gp/ Juan Nepomuceno LOVATO & Mª Ygnacia LOVATO.

MADRIL, Jose Gregorio — Sⁿ Fernº
bap *el mismo dia*; s/ father unknown & Juana MADRIL; gp/ Pasqual ORTEGA & Miquela BRITO.

Frame 541
SANDOVAL, Jose Miguel — Sⁿ Fernº
bap 30 Apr 1825; nat. s/ Mª Antª SANDOVAL & unknown father; am/ Felipe SANDOVAL & Polonia MES; gp/ Antº LAMUR (Origins, p. 421, LAMORÉ LAMORÍ) & Ygnacia VACA.

MONTOYA, Jose — *Rancho*
bap 30 Apr 1825; s/ Ygnacio MONTOYA & Mª TRUGILLO; gp/ Feliz URIOSTE & Carmen SANCHES.

VIGIL, Mª Concep^{n} *Rancho*
bap 1 May 1825; d/ Jose VIGIL & Marg^{a} LOVATO; ap/ Rafael VEGIL (sic) & Lorensa LEAL; am/ Rafael LOVATO & Luz ESPINOSA; gp/ Ant^{o} OLONIA & Marg^{ta} ESPINOSA.

GUERRERO, Jose Rafael *Arroyo Hondo*
bap 2 May 1825; s/ Teodoro GUERRERO & Danislada MEDINA; ap/ Jose An^{to} GUERRERO & Dolores ESCOBEDO; am/ Eusebio MEDINA & Lugarda GALLEGO; gp/ Ma^{l} CORDOVA & Mª de Jesus MONDRAGON.

PADILLA, Mª Nicolasa *Rancho*
bap same day; d/ Balentin PADILLA & Mª de Jesus MADRIL; ap/ Juan PADILLA & Getrudis GARCIA; am/ Juanico MADRIL & Prudencia XARAMILLO; gp/ Nicolas de HERRERA & Fran^{ca} MASCAREÑAS.

SALAZAR (gp), Juan de la Cruz *Pueblo*
bap 5 May 1825; s/ Agustin (n.s.) & M^{a} (n.s.) *del pueblo*; gp/ Pedro SALAZAR & Ursula HERRERA, *vecinos*.

Frame 542
PANDO, Mª Ygnacia *Pueblo*
bap 6 May 1825; d/ Juan PANDO & Paula LUJAN; gp/ Agustin CRUS & Veronica CRUS.

URIOSTE, Mª de la Cruz *Rancho*
bap same day; d/ Juan URIOSTE & Mª VIGIL; ap/ Fran^{co} URIOSTE & Rosa MARTIN; am/ Juan Cruz VIGIL & Clara FERNANDES; gp/ Pablo MARTIN & Josefa QUINTANA.

MONTOYA, Mª de la Cruz *Rancho*
bap *en el mismo dia*; d/ Mateo MONTOYA & Josefa ROMERO; ap/ Man^{l} MONTOYA & Luisa SANDOVAL; am/ Jose Concep^{n} ROMERO & Rosa QUINTANA; gp/ Vitor MARTIN & Encarnacion MARTIN.

PADILLA, Domingo Ant^{o} *Rancho*
bap 8 May 1825; s/ Ant^{o} PADILLA & Mª Lus HORT^{z}; gp/ Jose ARAGON & Nicolasa QUINTANA.

CRUZ, Mª Guadalupe *Rancho*
bap same day; d/ Fran^{co} CRUZ & Josefa MEDINA; ap/ Vicente CRUZ & Rosa VACA; am/ Jose MEDINA & Guadalupe (n.s.); gp/ Juan Marcial HERRERA & Ana^{a} DURAN.

GONZALEZ, Mª Dolores S^{n} Fern^{o}
bap 2 Jne 1825; d/ Rafael GONZ^{z} & Man^{a} PANDO; gp/ Ant^{o} LUCERO & Dolores VALDES.

Frame 543
VIGIL, Jose Man^{l} *Rancho*
bap 5 Jne 1825; s/ Anastacio VIGIL & Mª Cruz QUINTANA; ap/ Juan Cruz VIGIL & Clara FERNANDES; am/ Jose Cruz QUINTANA & Miquela VALDES; gp/ Feliz ORIOSTE & Carmen SANCHES.

ROMERO, Mª Man^{la} *Pueblo*
bap 6 Jne 1825; d/ Santiago ROMERO & Fran^{ca} (n.s.) *del pueblo*; gp/ Jose Man^{l} SAIZ & Trenidad MEDINA.

LUCERO, Jose Man^{l} *Arroyo Seco*
bap same day; s/ Jose Fran^{co} LUCERO & Paula VARELA; ap/ Vicente LUCERO &

Marta ATENCIO; am/ Ysidro VARELA & Juana MARTIN; gp/ Juan de Jesus GOMES & Mª TRUGILLO.

ARMENTA, Mª Teodora — *S^n Fern^o*
bap 7 Jne 1825; d/ Ygnacio ARMENTA & Guadalupe MARTIN; ap/ Simon ARMENTA & Marta MARTIN; am/ Salvador MARTIN & Florentina SANDOVAL; gp/ Ramon ARELLANO & Ygnacio ARELLANO.

URTADO, Maria Dolores — *Rancho*
bap 12 Jne 1825; d/ Man^l URTADO & Getrudis VIGIL; ap/ Miguel HURTADO & Mª de Jesus SANDOVAL; am/ Jose VIGIL & Petrona ROXO; gp/ Fran^{co} ARAGON & Barbara ARAGON.

QUINTANA (gp), Jose Fran^{co} — S^n Fern^o
bap same day; s/ unknown; gp/ Juan Man^l QUINTANA & Dolores GABALDON.

GONZALES, Mª Ant^o — *Rancho*
bap 18 Jun 1825; d/ Ant^o GONZALES & Ysabel VIGIL; ap/ Ant^o GONZ(^{s}-blot) & Mª REYNA; am/ Stiago VIG^L & M^a (n.s.); gp/ Fran^{co} MARTIN & Ygnacia PINEDO.

Frame 544
MARTIN, Juana M^a — *Arroyo Hondo*
bap 24 Jun 1825; d/ Santi(a)go MARTIN & Dolores ARGUEYO; gp/ Tiburcio MEDINA & Juana Josefa ARCHULETA.

LOVATO, Mª Paula — S^n Fern^o
MARTIN, Mª Paula
bap 2 Jly 1825; nat. d/ Tomas LOVATO, married, & Mª de la Lus MARTIN; am/ Juan Felipe MARTIN & Ygnacia VIGIL; gp/ Diego SALAZAR & Cristerna SANDOVAL.

GONSALES, Jose Fran^{co} — *Rancho*
bap 2 Aug 1825; s/ Domingo GONSALES & Juana CHAVES; gp/ Jose Ant^o GARCIA & Mª Reyes MARTIN.

ZUAZO, Juan Domingo — S^n Fernan^o
bap 10 Aug 1825; s/ Ant^o ZUAZO & Benina CORTES; ap/ Miguel ZUAZO & Josefa VIA ALPANDO; am/ Jose Maria CORTES & Mª BRITO; gp/ Jose Ant^o ZUAZO & Mª Josefa CASADOS.

PACHECO, Jose M^a — *Rancho*
bap 20 Aug 1825; s/ Fran^{co} PACHECO & Mª Dolores BARELA; ap/ Juan Pedro PACHECO & Mª de la Lus MARTIN; am/ Miguel BARELA & Juana ROMERO; gp/ Jose Mariano XARAMILLO & Mª Josefa LOVATO.

VIGIL, Mª Marcelina — *Rancho*
bap 13 Sep 1825; d/ Faustin VIGIL & Mª Lus MARTIN; ap/ Miguel VIGIL & Anamaria ARAGON; am/ Pedro MARTIN & Mª Ygnacia GARCIA; gp/ Ramon VIGIL & Ba(r)vara MARTIN.

Frame 545
ROMERO, Mª Natividad — S^n Fern^o
bap 13 Sep 1829; d/ Hypolito ROMERO & Guadalupe DURAN; ap/ Juan Delcarmen (sic) ROMERO & Rosa MARTIN; am/ Nicolas DURAN & Ant^a (n.s.); gp/ Ant^o VIGIL & Man^a CHAVES.

VIGIL, Mª Buenav^a — *Rancho*
bap 13 Sep 1829; d/ Juan de Jesus VIGIL & Rosa DURAN; gp/ Jose Ant^o GONSALES & Concep^n URIOSTE.

VIGIL, Mª Marcelina *Rancho*
bap 16 Sep 1829; d/ Faustino VIGIL & Mª de la Lus MARTINES; ap/ Miguel VIGIL & Ana ARAGON; am/ Pedro MARTIN (sic) & Mª Ygnacia GARCIA; gp/ Ramon VIGIL & Barbara MARTIN.

ROMERO, Mª Jacinta *Rancho*
bap 18 Sep 1825; d/ Ramon ROMERO & Rafaela VEGIL; ap/ Miguel ROMERO & Manuela GARCIA; am/ Juan Ygnacio VEGIL & Jacinta ARAGON; gp/ Ant^{o} LUCERO & Estefana ARAGON.

MARTIN, Juan Ant^{o} blank
bap 25 Sep 1825; s/ Juan MARTIN & Juana LOMA; ap/ Juan Andres MARTIN & Lucia PAIS; am/ Mariano LOMA & Magdalena LUCERO; gp/ Jose Gabri(e)l MARTIN & Maria Ant^{a} GARCIA.

Frame 546
ESPINOSA, Mª Dolores
bap 25 Sep 1825; d/ Rafael ESPINOSA & Encarnacion SAMORA; ap/ Jose Ant^{o} ESPINOSA & Catarina ROMERO; am/ Santiago SAMORA & Rosa PRINCESA; gp/ Nicolas MADRID & Dolores BALLEJOS.

ROMERO, Juan Geronimo
bap 29 Sep 1825; s/ Juan Domingo ROMERO & Juana Mª CORDOVA; ap/ Juan MigueL ROMERO & Rosa LUJAN; am/ Juan CORDOVA & Ysabel PAIS; gp/ Gregorio QUINTANA (only).

ROMERO, Juan
bap 30 Sep 1825; s/ Juan Ant^{o} ROMERO & Juliana REYNA; ap/ Fran^{co} ROMERO & Juana NARANJO; am/ Juan Domingo REYNA & Encarnacion GABILAN; gp/ Ant^{o} LUJAN & Guadalupe PACHECO.

SARVE, Mª Altagracia
bap 5 Oct 1825; d/ Jose Mª SARVE & Dominga COCA; ap/ Jose SARVE (only); am/ Jose Mª COCA & Juana VENABIDES; gp/ Jose Gabriel MARTIN & Ant^{a} GARCIA.

MARTIN, Mª Refugia
bap 13 Oct 1825; d/ Hermenegildo MARTIN & Matiana CAMPOS; ap/ Felipe MARTIN & Ygnacia VEGIL; am/ (not given); gp/ Jose LOBATO & Ygnacia VACA who were the gp.

MARTIN, Mª Rufina
bap 15 Oct 1825; d/ Pablo MARTIN & Manuela TRUGILLO; ap/ Juan MARTIN & M^{a} (n.s.); am/ Visente TRUGILLO & Guad^{e} MARQUES; gp/ Mariano MARTIN & Brigida TAFOYA.

Frame 547
GONSALES, Jose de los S^{tos}
bap 20 Oct 1825; s/ Juan GONSALES & Gertrudis ARCHULETA; ap/ Ygnacio GONSALES & Margarita BARELA; am/ Ant^{o} ARCHULETA & Ant^{a} CORDOVA; gp/ Pedro GARCIA & Concepcion PADILLA.

LUCERO, Fran^{co} Ant^{o}
bap 30 Oct 1825; s/ Juan Ant^{o} LUCERO & Barbara CORDOBA; ap/ Santiago LUCERO & Rosa AGUILAR; am/ Manuel CORDOVA & Guadalupe SERDA; gp/ Felipe GONSALES & Manuela ZALAZAR.

CORDOVA, Mª Barbara
bap 4 Nov 1825; d/ Raymundo CORDOVA & Estefana GONSALES; ap/ Avan CORDOVA

& Juliana TORRES; am/ Felipe GONSALES & Fran[ca] CHACON; gp/ Mariana MARTIN & Brigida TAFOYA.

JARAMILLO, Cecilia
bap 5 Nov 1825; d/ Juan Felipe JARAMILLO & Ygnacia CORTES; gp/ Nicolas VARELA & Polonia CHAVES.

CORDOVA, M[a] Encarnacion
bap 6 Nov 1825; d/ Manuel CORDOVA & Teodora MONDRAGON; ap/ Lorenso CORDOVA & Margarita MARTIN; am/ Ant[o] MONDRAGON & Encarnacion ESPINOSA; gp/ Rafael ZALAS & Manuela MARTIN.

MARTIN, M[a] Micaela
bap 6 Nov 1825; d/ M[l] MARTIN & Fran[ca] MONTES; ap/ Mig[l] (MARTIN) & Dolores MARTIN; am/ Ant[o] MONTES & Ynes MARTIN; gp/ Jose M[a] MARTIN & Ant[a] MARTIN.

Frame 548
(Entries signed by Fr. Mariano Jose SANCH[z] VERGARA)
PADILLA, Juana Marcela
bap 24 May 1826, ae 4 da; d/ Baltasar PADILLA & M[a] dela Luz TRUXILLO; ap/ Santiago PADILLA & Juana Teresa LOVATO; am/ Pablo TRUXILLO & Feliciana ORTIZ; gp/ Pablo TRUXILLO & Feliciana ORTIZ, *vecinos del puesto de San Fernando en este partido*.

MONTES, Jose Cristoval
bap 24 May 1826, ae 4 da; nat. s/ Maria Manuela MONTES & unknown father; am/ Antonio MONTES & Ynes MARTIN, *vecinos delos Ranchitos*; gp/ Juan Bautista MEDINA & Maria Manuela MARTIN, *vecinos del Arroyo Hondo en este partido*.

MADRID, Maria Josefa — Los Ranchitos
bap 25 May 1826, ae 5 da; d/ Juan Cristoval MADRID & M[a] Manuela PADILLA; ap/ Juan MADRID & Prudenciana XARAMILLO; am/ Pedro PADILLA & Lucia CHAVES; gp/ Lorenso MONTOYA & Josefa LUCERO, *todos vecinos delos Ranchitos*.

SALASAR, M[a] Rufina
bap 25 May 1826, ae 3 da; d/ Gervacio SALASAR & M[a] del Rosario COCA; ap/ Jose Manuel SALASAR & Juana DURAN; am/ Jose Manuel COCA & Josefa BENAVIDES; gp/ Jose Trinidad BARCELO & Maria Dolores GRIEGO, *vecinos de San Fernando*.

Frame 549
LEDŰ, Pedro Celestino
bap 25 May 1826, ae 2 da; s/ Antonio LEDŰ, native of Canada, & Apolonia LUCERO; ap/ Antonio LEDŰ & Magdalena LUCIE (Origins, p. 423); am/ Cristoval LUCERO & Manuela SANDOVAL; gp/ Gerbacio NOLAN, *natural del Canada*, & Maria Rita GRIJALBA.

VIGIL, Juan de Jesus
bap 27 May 1826, ae 5 da; s/ Dionicio VIGIL & M[a] Manuela TRUXILLO; gp/ Juan de Jesus SANCHES & Maria Leocadia GALLEGO.

ROLE, Jose Manuel
bap 28 May 1826, ae 3 da; s/ Juan de Jesus ROLE, *natural del Canada*, & Maria Encarnacion MARTINES; ap/ Santiago ROLE & Maria Manuela MC COY; am/ Felipe MARTINES & Anna Maria TRUXILLO; gp/ Jose Mariano MARTINES & Maria Brijida TAFOLLA.

LUCERO, Juan Bautista
bap 30 May 1826, ae 4 da; s/ Juan Jose LUCERO & M[a] Teresa SANCHES; ap/ Greg[o]

LUCERO & Mariana SUAZO; am/ Jose Pablo SANCHES & Gertrudis BORREGO; gp/ Jose de Jesus MAESE & Juana Micaela PACHECO.

Frame 550
SANDOVAL, Antonio José
bap 1 Jne 1826, ae 5 da; s/ Diego SANDOVAL & Gertrudis GOMES; ap/ Juan de Dios SANDOVAL & Antonio MARTIN; am/ Antonio GOMES & Francisca ZANCHES; gp/ Manuel GARCIA & Trinidad QUINTANA.

VIGIL, Maria de Jesus
bap 5 Jne 1826, ae 2 da; d/ Antonio VIGIL & Maria dela Ascencion MARTIN; ap/ Juan de Jesus VIGIL & Rosa DURAN; am/ Cruz MARTINES (sic) & Maria Dolores TORRES; gp/ Hermenegildo MARTINES & Maria dela Asc<u>au</u>cion TRUXILLO.

COCA, José Benito
bap 6 Jne 1826, ae 3 da; s/ Tomas COCA & Lorens<u>o</u> SANDOVAL; ap/ Miguel COCA & Maria TALECHU; am/ Martin SANDOVAL & Ygnacia BUENO; gp/ Jose Candelario VIGIL & Maria Ygnacia DURAN.

ARCHULETA, Maria Feliciana
bap 17 Jne 1826, ae 4 da; d/ Antonio ARCHULETA & Juana LUCERO; ap/ Antonio ARCHULETA & Trinidad MAESE; am/ Juana LUCERO (only); gp/ Juan de Dios de LALANDA & Maria Antonia ABEITA.

LUJAN, Juan Antonio
bap 18 Jne 1826, ae 5 da; s/ Juan Domingo LUJAN & Maria Antonia BARELA; ap/ Geronimo LUJAN & Francisca ORTIZ; am/ not given; gp/ Maria Soledad GOMES (only). (Frames 550-551)

Frame 551
SALASAR, Maria Ygnacia
bap 25 Jne 1826, ae 3 da; d/ Jose Ygnacio SALASAR & Maria Dolores MONTOYA; ap/ Juan Cristoval SALASAR & Maria Margarita SAMORA; am/ Manuel Baltasar MONTOYA & Maria Rosalia ARMIJO; gp/ Juan Salvador MARTINES & Maria Manuela ROMERO.

SAMORA, Juana Maria
bap 25 Jne 1826, ae 8 da; d/ Pablo SAMORA & Albina ROMERO; ap/ Santiago SAMORA & Rosalia Josefa (n.s.); am/ Juan DOMINGO & Anna Maria ROMERO; gp/ Antonio TRUXILLO & Maria Manuela COCA.

CORDOVA, Jose de Jesus
bap 25 Jne 1826, ae 5 da; s/ Serafino CORDOVA & Maria Candelaria MEDINA; ap/ Damaso CORDOVA & Ysabel GONZALEZ; am/ Juan Antonio MEDINA & Micaela VIGIL; gp/ Jose Antonio SANCHES & Juana Sol(e)dad LOPEZ.

ROMERO (patron), Maria Silveria
bap 26 Jne 1826, ae 6 da; nat. d/ Maria Josefa (n.s.), Navajo Indian servant of Jose ROMERO; gp/ Jose Ramon ROMERO & Maria Rafaela VIGIL.

Frame 552
ROMERO, Juan Pablo
bap 29 Jne 1826, ae 4 da; s/ Manuel ROMERO & Carmen DURAN; ap/ Julian ROMERO & Barbara MARTIN; am/ Juan Nicolas DURAN & (blank space); gp/ Rafael TAFOYA & Maria Josefa BENAVIDES.

(An additional June 1826 entry in unfilmed entries {p. 303} as well as several July, August, September and October.)

DURAN, Juana Petra
bap 1 Jly 1826, ae 3 da; d/ Pedro Antonio DURAN & Maria Encarnacion MARTIN; ap/ Juan Nicolas DURAN & Maria Getrudis QUINTANA; am/ Manuel Gregorio MARTIN & Maria Rafaela MEDINA; gp/ Hermenegildo TRUXILLO & Maria Josefa TAFOYA.

COCA, Jose Vicente
bap 6 Jly 1826, ae 5 da; s/ Jose Reyes COCA & Maria Manuela ARELLENO; ap/ Jose Maria COCA & Juana BENAVIDES; am/ Ylario ARELLANO & Juana Maria MARTINES; gp/ Jose PADILLA & Serafina TRUXILLO.

HERRERA, German
bap 11 Jly 1826, ae 3 da; s/ Teodoro de HERRERA & Estanislada de MEDINA; gp/ Marcos SANCHES & Maria Paula SANCHEZ, *vecinos del Arroyo Seco*. (Frames 552-553)

Frame 553
CRUZ, Maria Navora
bap 16 Jly 1826, ae 6 da; d/ Felipe CRUZ & Maria Catalina GONZALES; ap/ Francisco Alexo CRUZ & Maria Guadalupe SANCHES; am/ Jose Miguel GONZALES & Maria Ysavel VIGIL; gp/ Maria Rosa VIGIL (only).

ARCHULETA, Maria del Carmen
bap 18 Jly 1826, ae 4 da; d/ Antonio Rafael ARCHULETA & Maria Clara SANDOVAL; ap/ Jose Balentin ARCHULETA & Maria Encarnacion GARCIA; am/ Gregorio SANDOVAL & Juana Teresa MESTAS; gp/ Buenaventura MARTIN (only), *vecinos dela plaza San Francisco en el Rancho*.

SANCHES, Jose Santiago
bap 30 Jly 1826, ae 5 da; s/ Felipe SANCHES & Juana Maria MARTINEZ; ap/ Juan Ygnacio SANCHEZ & Pascuala VIGIL; am/ Jose Francisco MARTINES (sic) & Mª Rosa ARMENTA; gp/ Juan Ant^o LOVATO & Mª Yg^a SANCHES, *v^s dela plasa del Rancho*. (No mention of twins.)

Frame 554
SANCHES, Juan Cristoval
bap 30 Jly 1826, ae 5 da; s/ Felipe SANCHES & Juana Mª MARTINES; ap/ Juan Yg^o SANCHES & Pascuala VIGIL; am/ Jose Francisco MARTINES & Mª Rosa ARMENTA; gp/ Juan Ant^o LOVATO & Mª Yg^a SANCHES, *vecinos del Rancho*. (No mention of twins.)

MARTINES, Juan de Jesus
bap 30 July 1826, ae 9 da; s/ Juan Ygnacio MARTINES & Maria Cacilda MARTINES; ap/ Jose Francisco MARTINES & Maria Tomasa SANCHES; am/ Juan Felipe MARTIN (sic) & Mª Concep^{on} TRUXILLO; gp/ Juan ROLES & Maria Encarnacion MARTINES, *vecinos del Rancho*.

(Blank half page; reverse side is also blank)

Frame 555
(Fr. An^{to} Jose MARTIN signing entries.)
ARELLANO, Juan Nepomuceno *Arroyo Ondo*
bap 15 Oct 1826, ae 9 da; s/ Ramon ARELLANO & Ana Maria ARMENTA, *vicinos del Arroyo Hondo*; ap/ Julian ARELLANO & Mª de la Lus TAPIA; am/ Simon ARMENTA & Maria MARTIN; gp/ Juan Nepomuceno ARELLANO (only), *vecinos del mismo lugar*.

CASILLAS, Jose Ventura *Rancho*
bap 15 Oct 1826, ae 5 da; s/ Bartolome CASILLAS & Maria Elena MARTIN, *vecinos de la plasa de S. Fran^{co} del Rancho*; ap/ Bernardo CASILLAS & Mª Ysabel

MADRIL; am/ Maria An^ta MARTIN (only); gp/ Ramon RAEL & Maria Teresa VIGIL, *vecinos de la misma plasa.*

GONSALES, Juan Ricardo *Rancho*
bap 15 Oct 1826, ae 4 da; s/ Joaquin GONSALES, *asi apellidado,* & Maria Guadalupe MARTIN, *apellidada asi, vecinos del Rancho;* ap/ Maria Luisa VIGIL father not legitimate; am/ Maria Josefa LEAL & father not legitimate; gp/ Vicente GARCIA & Maria Juliana ROMERO, *vecinos del mismo varrio de S. Fran^co del Rancho.*

MARTIN, Mª de la Luz *Pueblo*
bap 17 Oct 1826, ae 6 da; d/ Cecilia MARTIN & father unknown; am/ Juan Domingo MARTIN & Gertrudis ROMERO; gp/ Simon SUASO & Mª Ygnacia RIO, *todos naturales del pueblo de Taos.* (Frames 555-556)

Frame 556
VIGIL, Jose de Gracia *Rancho de S. Fran^co*
bap 19 Oct 1826, ae 5 da; s/ Fran^co VIGIL & Felipa PANDO, *vecinos del Rancho;* ap/ Pedro VIGIL & Guadalupe PATRON; am/ Calletano PANDO & Mª An^ta ARAGON; gp/ Juaquin Andres GARCIA & Mª Josefa TRUGILLO, *vecinos del Rancho.*

PADILLA, Jose Geronimo *Pueblo*
bap 21 Oct 1826, ae 7 da; s/ Santiago PADILLA & Maria Rosa ROMERO, *vecinos naturales del pueblo de Taos;* ap/ Santiago PADILLA & Maria Ant^a ORTIS; am/ Carmel ROMERO & Mª Josefa LUCERO; gp/ Fran^co SUASO & Mª Josefa MIRABAL. (Frames 556-557)

Frame 557
SANTANA, Jose Mª de Jesus *Pueblo*
bap 21 Oct 1826, ae 4 da; s/ Jose SANTANA & Mª Paula ORTIS, *vecinos naturales del pueblo de Taos;* ap/ unknown; am/ Fran^co ORTIZ (sic) & Lucia (n.s.) *del pueblo;* gp/ Meregirdo ARCHULETA & Mª Bartola LOPES, *vecinos de la plasa del San Fernando.*

GONSALES, Jose Santiago *Rancho*
bap 26 Oct 1826, ae 5 da; s/ Jose Miguel GONSALES & Maria Ysabel VIGIL, *vecinos de la plasa de S. Fran^co del Rancho;* ap/ Jose An^to GONSALES & Maria REYNA, both dec.; am/ Jose Santiago VIGIL & Mª Gertrudis CHAVES, also dec.; gp/ Ramon SALASAR & Maria Nicolasa SALASAR, *vecinos del mismo varrio de S. Fran^co.*

LOVATO, Manuel Ant^o San Fernando
bap 28 Oct 1826, ae 3 da; s/ Juan Fran^co LOVATO & Mª Rosa CORTES, *vecinos de la plasa de S. Fernandes;* ap/ Juan LOVATO & Margarita CHAVES, dec.; am/ Fran^co CORTES & Gregoria MEDINA; gp/ An^to MEDINA & Mª Candelaria VIGIL, *vecinos del Rancho.*

Frame 558
SALASAR, Jose Narsiso *Rancho*
bap 29 Oct 1826, ae 6 da; s/ Ramon SALASAR & Mª Soledad VIGIL, *vecinos del barrio de San Fran^co del Rancho;* ap/ Juan Manuel SALASAR, dec., & M^a de los Reyes MARTINES, dec.; am/ Miguel VIGIL & Ana Maria BALLEJOS; gp/ Jose Santiago MARTINES & Mª de la Lus LUCERO, *vecinos de San Fran^co del Ranchito.*

SUASO, Mª Guadalupe *Rancho*
bap 29 Oct 1826, ae 4 da; d/ Blas SUASO & Mª Ant^a MARTIN, *vecinos del barrio de S. Fran^co del Rancho;* ap/ Juan Jose SUASO & Nicolasa LOVATO; am/ Juaquin

MARTIN, dec., & Mª Josefa TRU(JE)QUES; gp/ Juan Miguel MARQUES & Mª Gertrudis MONTOYA, *vecinos del barrio de S. Franco del Rancho.*

DURAN, Maria Peregrina *Rancho*
bap 30 Oct 1826, ae 3 da; d/ Anto DURAN & Maria Rita LUCERO, *vecinos de la plasa de S. Franco*; ap/ Ygnacio DURÁN & Maria Antª SANCHES, dec.; am/ Bernardo LUCERO & Tomasa MARTIN, dec.; gp/ Juan Salvador (n.s.) & Maria Manuela ROMERO, *vecinos de la misma plasa del Rancho.*

SUASO, Mª Vicenta *San Franco del Rancho*
bap 2 Nov 1826, ae 5 da; d/ Juan Domingo SUASO & Juª Maria ARAGON, *vecinos de San Franco del Ranchito*; ap/ Jose SUASO & Nicolasa LOVATO; am/ (blank space) & Guadalupe VASQUES, dec.; gp/ Jose Luis SANDOVAL & Ana Maria MANCHEGO, *vecinos de la plasa de San Ferdo.* (Frames 558-559)

Frame 559
SANCHES, Mª Dolores *Arroyo Seco*
bap 5 Nov 1826, ae 5 da; d/ Miguel SANCHES & Soledad BACA, *vecinos de la Poblacion del Arroyo Seco*; ap/ Juaquin SANCHES, dec., & Anta Rosa MARTIN, dec.; am/ Anto BACA, dec., & Maria Gertrudis LOPES; gp/ Jose Anto SANCHES & Juana Soledad LOPES, *vecinos del Arroyo Seco.*

ROMERO, Ygnacio de Jesus (Ylario de Jesus in margin) S. Fernando
bap 5 Nov 1826, ae 4 da; s/ Juan Domingo ROMERO & Mª Ygnacia CHAVES, *vecinos de la plasa de San Fernando*; ap/ Manuel Jose ROMERO & Juana VARELA, dec.; am/ Jose Mª CHAVES & Mª ORTEGA, dftos.; gp/ Juan del Carmel ROMERO & Mª Rosa MARTIN, *vecinos de la plasa de San Fernando.*

ROMERO, Jose Santos *Pueblo*
bap 6 Nov 1826, ae 5 da; s/ Pablo ROMERO & Dolores GONSALES, *naturales de este pueblo*; ap/ Juan Anto ROMERO & Anamaria ROMERO; am/ Domingo GONSALES & Mª Anta LOMA, *naturales del mismo*; gp/ Jose Anto SUASO & Mª Josefa CASADOS, *vecinos de S. Ferdo.*

Frame 560
MASCAREÑAS, Mª Dolores *Rancho*
bap 16 Nov 1826, ae 4 da; d/ Miguel MASCAREÑAS & Mª Manuela BUENO, *vecinos del barrio de S. Franco del Rancho*; ap/ Vernardo MASCAREÑAS, dec., & Mª Juliana CORDOBA; am/ Anto BUENO & Mª Rosalia VALDES; gp/ Manuel BACA & Mª Rosalia VALDES, *vecinos el hombre del curato de Belen y la muger del Rancho.*

MARTIN, Jose Benito *Ranchito*
bap 17 Nov 1826, ae 5 da; s/ Casimiro MARTIN & Mª Antª SUASO, *vecinos de San Franco del Ranchito*; ap/ Ventura MARTIN & Mª Rafaela MARES; am/ Juan Jose SUASO & Mª Nicolasa LOVATO; gp/ Pedro Luis MAES & Mª Manuela ROMERO, *vecinos del Rancho.*

VARGAS, Jose Gregorio *Rancho*
bap 19 Nov 1826, ae 4 da; s/ Jose Roumaldo VARGAS & Juana Maria LOVATO; ap/ Marirelo VARGAS & Maria Nicomeda FERNANDES; am/ D. Juan Anto LOVATO & Mª Ygnacia SANCHES; gp/ Ventura LOVATO & Maria Josefa LOVATO, *todos vecinos del Rancho de s. Franco.*

Frame 561
MONTOLLA, Maria Estefana S. Fdo
bap 19 Nov 1826, ae 3 da; d/ Manuel MONTOLLA & Maria Clara TAFOLLA, *besinos de San Ferna(n)do*; ap/ Tomas MONTOYA & Maria Ageda ROMERO, both dec.; am/

Maria Antonia TAFOLLA (only); gp/ Jose Encarnacion MARTIN & Maria Ysabel CORTES, *vesinos de San Fernando*.

GONSALES, Maria del Carmel *Rancho*
bap 27 Nov 1826, ae 6 da; d/ Jose Ygnacio GONSALES & Maria Ysidora PACHECO, *vecinos del Varrio de San Fran^co del Rancho*; ap/ Fernando GONSALES & Maria de la Luz ROMERO; am/ Fran^co PACHECO, dec., & Maria Luisa VIGIL; gp/ Juan Nicolas FERNANDES & Mª Guadalupe MAES, *vecinos del mismo varrio de dich(o) Francisco*.

QUINTANA, Juana Maria *Arroyo Ondo*
bap 28 Nov 1826, ae 4 da; d/ Fran^co QUINTANA & Maria Josefa MAES, dec., *vecinos del Arroyo Ondo*; ap/ Juan QUINTANA & Balvuneda ROMERO; am/ Gabriel MAES & Maria Manuel(a) MESTAS; gp/ Rafael MARTIN & Guadalupe LUCERO, *vecinos del Arroyo Ondo*.

Frame 562
MARTIN, Feliciano de Jesus *Rancho*
bap 30 Nov 1826, ae 11 da; s/ Ysidora MARTIN & unknown father; am/ Geronimo MARTIN, dec., & Mª Varvara COSA, dec.; gp/ Jose Rafael ROMERO & Mamaria (sic) ORTIS, *todos vecinos del Rancho de S. Fran^co*.

CHACON, Mª de la Lus S^n Fernando
bap 5 Dec 1826, ae 4 da; d/ Jose Pablo CHACON & Mª Rafaela ARCHULETA, *vecinos de S Fernando*; ap/ Jose Mª CHAVES (sic) & Mª Gertrudis ORTEGA; am/ Jose Fran^co ARCHULETA & Maria Josefa SANDOVAL; gp/ Hermeregildo TRUGILLO & Mª Josefa TAFOYA, *vecinos de San Fernando*.

TRUGILLO, Juan Nicolas San Fernando
bap 5 Dec 1826, ae 3 da; s/ Luis TRUGILLO & Mª Gertrudes SANCHES, *vecinos de San Fernando*; ap/ Pablo TRUGILLO, dec. & Mª Teresa URTADO; am/ Miguel SANCHES & Mª Paula LOVATO; gp/ Juan ROLAN & Mª Encarnacion MARTIN, *vecinos de San Fran^co del Rancho*.

ROMERO, Antonio Jose San Fernando
bap 8 Dec 1826, ae 5 da; s/ Juan del Carmel ROMERO & Maria Madalena LOBATO, *vecinos de la plasa de San Fernando*; ap/ Jose ROMERO, dec., & Mª Josefa SANDOVAL; am/ Juan LOVATO (sic) & Margarita CHAVES; gp/ Mariano MARTIN & Maria Ysabel TRUGILLO.

MEDINA, Maria Guadalupe *S. Fernando*
bap 8 Dec 1826, ae 1 da; d/ Jose An^to MEDINA & Maria Candelaria SALASAR, *vecinos de la plasa de San Fernando*; ap/ An^to Jose MEDINA & Maria Miquela VIGIL; am/ Gregorio SALASAR & Mª Dolores COCA; gp/ Jose Benito TAFOYA & Mª de la Lus TAFOYA, *vecinos de S. Fernando*. (Frames 562-563)

Frame 563
DURAN, Maria Sisilia *Rancho*
bap 10 Dec 1826, ae 6 da; d/ Pedro Mauricio DURAN & Maria Varbara SANCHES, *vecinos del S. Fran^co del Rancho*; ap/ Manuel DURAN & Gerarda MASCAREÑAS; am/ Felipe SANCHES & Juana MARTINA; gp/ Vernardo DURAN & Feliciana VIGIL, *vecinos de S. Fran^co del Rancho*.

MAES, Jose Concepcion *Arroyo Ondo*
bap 10 Dec 1826, ae 5 da; s/ San Juan MAES & Maria Antonia ABILA, *vecinos del Arroya Ondo*; ap/ Luis CHAVES (sic) & Anamaria MARTIN; am/ Juan de Jesus ABILA & Mª Manuela SANCHES; gp/ Jose Concepcion MEDINA & Maria Ygnacia MEDINA, *vecinos del Arroyo Ondo*.

MARTIN, Jose Concepcion *Rancho*
bap 13 Dec 1826, ae 5 da; s/ Santos MARTIN & Maria Josefa GALBIS, *vecinos de San Fran[co] del Rancho*; ap/ Juan Pablo MARTIN & Guadalupe CHAVES; am/ Juan GALBIS & Manuela ESPINOSA; gp/ Mateo BUENO & Manuela ROMERO, *vecinos del Rancho*.

LUCERO, Maria de la Lus San Fernando
bap 13 Dec 1826, ae 3 da; d/ Vernardo LUCERO & M[a] Josefa QUINTANA, *vecinos de S. Fernando*; ap/ Manuel LUCERO & M[a] Manuela VALLEJOS; am/ Juan QUINTANA & Maria Valbaneda ROMERO, both dec.; gp/ Tomas SUAZO & Maria Polonia LUCERO, *vecinos de S. Fernando*.

SANDOVAL (patron), Jose Luciano (Juan Lucian in margin) San Fernando
bap 13 Dec 1826, ae 2 yr; s/ *Nacion Yuta*, redeemed by Jose Manuel SANDOVAL; gp/ Antonio LUCERO & Maria Estefana ARAGON, *vecinos de San Fernando*. (Frames 563-564)

Frame 564
LUCERO, Maria Guadalupe *Rancho*
bap 14 Dec 1826, ae 4 da; d/ Pedro LUCERO & M[a] Gertrudis DURAN, *vecinos del varrio de San Francisco del Rancho*; ap/ Santiago LUCERO & M[a] Rosa AG(U)ILAR; am/ Pedro Ygnacio DURAN & M[a] An[ta] SANCHES, both dec.; gp/ Jose MONDRAGON & Maria Lorensa DURAN, *vecinos del varrio de San Fran[co] del Rancho*.

MAES, M[a] Guadalupe S. Fernando
bap 14 Dec 1826, ae 4 da; d/ Juan MAES & Margarita MARTIN; ap/ Domingo MAES & Juana ESPINOSA, dec.; am/ Ramon MARTIN & Paubla MARTIN; gp/ Manuel SANDOVAL & Benita MARTIN, *vecinos de San Fernando*.

PACHECO; Pedro Ant[o] San Fernando
bap 15 Dec 1826, ae 5 da; s/ Manuel Estevan PACHECO & Maria de Jesus CASADOS, *vecinos de San Fernando*; ap/ Gregorio PACHECO & Brigida TRUGILLO; am/ Juan Ant[o] CASADOS & Rosalia MARTIN; gp/ Pedro MAES & Rosalia SANDOVAL, *vecinos de San Fernando*.

ROMERO, Juana Maria *Pueblo*
bap 15 Dec 1826, ae 6 da; d/ Juan An[to] ROMERO & Sencion ORTIS, *vecinos del pueblo*; ap/ Santiago ROMERO & Rosalia NARANJO; am/ Juan Andres ORTIS & Maquela (sic) GOMES; gp/ Juan Andres ROMERO & Paubla NARANJO, *naturales del pueblo*.

RIBERA, Maria Antonia *Plz. de la Purisima Concep[n]*
bap 15 Dec 1826, ae 5 da; ap/ Tomas RIBERA & Maria del Carmel GONSALES, *vecinos de la plasa de la Purisima Concepcio*; ap/ An[to] RIBERA, dec., & Maria Feliciana ORTIS; am/ Jose An[to] GONSALES & M[a] An[ta] MARTIN; gp/ Jose Yg[o] VALDES & M[a] Manuela SANCHEZ, *vecinos de S Fern[do]*.

GONSALES, Maria Lorensa *Rancho*
bap 21 Dec 1826, ae 4 da; nat. d/ Josefa GONSALES & unknown father, *vecina de San Fran[co] del Rancho*; am/ Juan Calletano GONSALES & Lorensa RODRIGES; gp/ An[to] Jose OLONIA & M[a] Margarita ESPINOSA, *vecinos de San Fran[co] del Rancho*. (Frames 564-565)

Frame 565
SALASAR, Maria Concepcion *Rancho*
bap 21 Dec 1826, ae 4 da; d/ Cristoval SALASAR & Barbara VALDES, *vecino(s) de San Fran[co] del Rancho*; ap/ Domingo SALASAR & Guadalupe GURULE; am/ Juan Bautista VALDES & Ana Maria ARCHULETA; gp/ Juan Bautista TRUGILLO & Maria Casilda QUINTANA, *vecinos de San Fran[co] del Rancho*.

MARTINES, Maria Concepcion *San Fran^{co} Ranchito*
bap 23 Dec 1826, ae 10 da; d/ Ventura MARTINES & Maria Rafaela MAES; ap/ *el incognito* & Maria Manuela ROMERO; am/ Cristobal MAES, dec., & Juana Maria SANDOVAL; gp/ Jose Maria LUCERO, *vecino de la Jurisdicion de S. Juan*, & Maria Soledad (n.s.) *de la plasa de S. Fernando*.

ATENCIO, Juan de Jesus *Arroyo Ondo*
bap 24 Dec 1826, ae 7 da; s/ Juan Ant^{o} ATENCIO & M^{a} B(e)atris GARCIA, *vecinos del Arroyo Ondo*; ap/ Juan Ygnacio ATENCIO & Maria Manuela ARCHULETA; am/ Patricio GARCIA & Maria Ygnacia SANDOVAL, dec.; gp/ Tomas SANDOVAL & Mª Concepcion CHACON, *vecinos del Arroyo Ondo*.

Frame 566
VALDES, Maria Natividad *Rancho*
bap 24 Dec 1826, ae 8 da; d/ Eusebio VALDES & Mª Manuela MARTIN, *vecinos del varrio de San Fran^{co} del Rancho*; ap/ Fran^{co} VALDES & Mª Luciana NARANJO, dec.; am/ Jose MARTIN, dec., & Anamaria MARTINES (sic); gp/ Pedro TAFOYA & Mª Juliana TAFOYA, *vecinos del varrio de S. Fran^{co} del Rancho*.

MONTOYA, Jose Tomas S Fern^{do}
bap 24 Dec 1826, ae 4 da; s/ Juan Manuel MONTOYA & Maria Dolores SEDILLO, *vecinos de S. Fernando*; ap/ Jose MONTOYA & Mª Gertrudis (n.s.-blank space); am/ Simon SEDILLO, dec., & Gertrudis MORA; gp/ Amable AMADOR & Mª Marcelina CASADOS, *vecinos de San Fernando*.

PINO, Maria Pascuala *Rancho*
bap 27 Dec 1826, ae 3 da; d/ Jose An^{to} PINO & Teodora MARTIN, *vecinos del varrio de S. Fran^{co} del Rancho*; ap/ Jose PINO & Mª GABALDON; am/ An^{to} MARTIN & Catarina TAFOYA; gp/ Pedro Ygnacio ESPINOSA & Maria Encarnacion ESPINOSA, *vecinos todos del Rancho*.

CORTES, Maria de la Lus S. Fern^{do}
bap 27 Dec 1826, ae 5 da; d/ Jose Maria CORTES & Mª Rita BRITO, *vecinos de S. Fernando*; ap/ Pedro CORTES & Teodora MARTIN; am/ Fran^{co} BRITO & Margarita ROMERO; gp/ Nicolas TAFOYA & Mª Manuela MEDINA, *vecinos de San Fernando*. (No mention of twins.)

Frame 567
CORTES, Maria Guadalupe San Fernando
bap 27 Dec 1826, ae 5 da; d/ Jose Maria CORTES & Maria Rita BRITO, *vecinos de S. Fernando*; ap/ Pedro CORTES & Teodora MARTIN; am/ Fran^{co} BRITO & Margarita ROMERO; gp/ Nicolas TAFOYA & Maria Manuela MEDINA, *vecinos de San Fernando*. (No mention of twins.)

VALDES, Juan de Dios
bap 28 Dec 1826, ae 2 da; s/ Ventura VALDES & Juana Catarina LOVATO, *vecinos de la plasa de la Purisima Concepcion*; ap/ Pedro An^{to} VALDES & Manuela GONSALES, both dec.; am/ Maria CHAVES (sic) & Antonio LOVATO, dec.; gp/ Juan de Jesus LUCERO & Maria Ygnacia ARAGON, *vecinos de la plasa de S. Fran^{co} del Ranchito*.

GONSALES, Maria Dolores *Arroyo Ondo*
bap 31 Dec 1826, ae 6 da; d/ Ologio GONSALES & Maria Guadalupe SISNEROS, *vecinos del Arroyo Ondo*; ap/ Juan GONSALES & Maria An^{ta} MARTINES, dec.; am/ Nerio SISNERO(S), dec., & Teodora MARTIN; gp/ Carlos SANTISTEVAN & Maria de la Lus LUCERO, *vecinos del Ranchito de S. Fran^{co}*.

NEW MEXICO BAPTISMS
CATHOLIC CHURCHES in TAOS
VOLUME I
19 June 1701 - 31 December 1826

ARCHIVES of the ARCHDIOCESE of SANTA FE
LOOSE DOCUMENTS
RECORDS NOT MICROFILMED YET
1826, 1827, 1834, 1835

1834-1835 Baptisms from San Lorenso de Picuris priest Antonio Jose MARTINEZ, incomplete, one loose page.

BARRERA, Juan Andres
bap 18 (torn) 1834, ae 14 da; s/ Juan Jose BARRERA & (torn-n.n.) MUÑIZ, *v^{s} de Sta Barbara*; ap/ Felipe BARRERAS (sic) & (torn)la GARBISO; am/ Juan Andres MUÑIZ & Mª Josefa VI(torn); gp/ Domingo MUÑIZ & Mª de Jesus ESPI(NOSA-torn) (del-torn) mismo lugar.

BAROS, Juan Andres
bap 25 (torn) 1835, ae 25 da, b. 19 (torn) 1834; s/ Ra(torn BAROS) & Mª Candelaria MESTAS; ap/ Matias BAROS & Maria (n.s.-torn); am/ Miguel MESTAS & Anna Mª ORTIZ, *v^{s} de la Cañada, recidentes de Picuries*; gp/ Juan Ysidro VIGIL & M^{a} (torn-MO)NTOYA, *v^{s} de S^{n} Juan Nepomoseno del Yano*.

MESTAS, Juan Vicente
bap 25 May (183)5 from the Picuries micion, bap 20 Dec 1834, ae 8 da; s/ Vicente MESTAS & (torn-n.n.) BAZQUEZ; ap/ Aparicio MESTAS & Pascuala GONZA(LES-torn); am/ (torn)^{to} & Biviana MESTAS, *v^{s} de las Trampas*; gp/ (torn).

MUÑIS, Jose Andres
bap (torn) 1835, ae 12 da; s/ (torn-n.n. MUÑIS) & Mª Gracia MEDINA, *vecinos de Sta B(torn)*; ap/ (torn-n.n.) MUÑIS & Mª Josefa PANDO; am/ An^{to} MED(INA-torn) & (torn-n.n.) GARCIA; gp/ Encarnacion TRUGILLO & (torn-n.n.) RAMIRES, *vesinos del mismo lugar*.

LOPES, Mª Soledad
bap (torn) Jne 183(5), ae (torn); d/ Sisig LOPES & M^{a} D(torn SUG-torn), *(ve)sinos de Sta Barbara*; ap/ (torn) & Rosalia GONSALES; am/ San Juan SUG(torn) & (torn-n.n.) MARTIN; gp/ Felipe (n.s.-torn) (end of record.)

1826 Baptisms from San Geronimo de Taos priest (Fr.) Antonio Jose MARTINEZ, pp 5-16 sewn together.
Page 5
GONZALEZ, Maria Apolinaria — S. Fran^{co} del Rancho
bap 23 Jne 1826, ae 12 da; d/ Viterbo GONZALEZ & Felipa SALAZAR, *vecinos de San Francisco del Rancho*; ap/ Domingo GONZALEZ & Maria RIOS; am/ Juana SALAZAR; gp/ D^{n} Santiago MARTINEZ & D^{a} Maria de la Luz LUCERO, *vecinos de la plaza de S. Fran^{co} del Rancho*.

VIGIL, Juan de Jesus — S. Fran^{co} del Rancho
bap 23 Jly 1826, ae 4 da; nat. s/ Maria Soledad VIGIL & *padre no conocido, vecina de S. Fran^{co} del Rancho*; am/ Cristobal VIGIL & Ana Maria MONTOYA; gp/ Jose Manuel ORTEGA & Maria Manuela ROMERO, *vecinos de la misma plaza de S. Fran^{co}*.

ARCHULETA, Jose Nazario Arroyo Ondo
bap 1 Aug 1826, ae 5 da; s/ Diego ARCHULETA & Maria Luz QUINTANA, *vecinos del Arroyo Ondo*; ap/ José Antonio ARCHULETA & Maria Antonia MEDINA; am/ Juan QUINTANA & Balvaneda ROMERO; gp/ Jose Rafael SISNEROS & Maria de Jesus ESPINOSA, *vecinos del Arroyo Ondo*.

SANCHES, Fran^{co} Estevan Plaza de la Purisima Concepcion
bap 4 Aug 1826, ae 2 da; s/ An^{to} SANCHES & Mª Viviana MAES, *vecinos de la plasa de la Purisima Concepcion*; ap/ Miguel SANCHES & Maria Rosa RUIVAL; am/ An^{to} MAES & Victoria SISNEROS; gp/ Juan de Jesus GOMES & Mª Francisca TRUGILLO.

Rest of page 5 and all of page 6-11 is visitation of S. VICENTE. (Fr.) 1826 Aug 7 NOTE: visitation of (Fr.) Agustin Francisco S. VICENTE. Other signator: Teodosio YNURTANDES

Baptisms cont'd
Page 11 (Fr. Mariano Jose SANCHES VERGARA signing entries).
MONTOLLA, Jesus Maria Ranchito
bap 8 Aug 1826, ae 4 da; s/ Juan Jose MONTOLLA & Maria Candelaria ESQUIBELA; ap/ Bernardo MONTOLLA & Maria Manuela MARTINES; am/ Jose ESQUIBEL & Feliciana MARTINES; gp/ Jose Antonio SANCHES & Maria Juliana TRUJILLO, all *ciudadanos de los Ranchitos*.

BLANCHARD, Antonio Domingo San Fernando
bap 10 Aug 1826, ae 7 da; s/ Antonio BLANCHARD & Juana Gertrudis TRUJILLO, *cuidadanos en la plasa de San Fernando*; ap/ Juan BLANCHARD & Susana la MONDE, *franceces del Canada*; am/ Juan Vincencia TRUJILLO & Margarita GONSALES, *ciudadanos dela Cañada*; gm/ Maria Agueda de Jesus FERNANDES, *residente en la plasa de San Fernando*.

(Fr. Jose MARTINES signing entries).
SANDOBAL, Maria Lucaria (Maria Luisa in margin) La Sienegia
bap 15 Aug 1826, ae 5 da; d/ Pomuseno SANDOBAL & Maria Tomasa JARAMILLO, *vecinos de la Sieneguilla*; ap/ Maria Concepcion SANCHES & *padre no conosido*; am/ Juan Manuel JARAMILLO & Maria Juliana MADRIL; gp/ Valentin PADILLA & Maria de Jesus MADRIL, *vecinos de San Fran^{co} del Ranchito*.

GOMES, Juan Antonio Martin Natural del pueblo
bap 15 Aug 1826, ae 5 da; s/ Juan Jose Manuel GOMES & Dominga REIGNA; ap/ Manuel GABILAN (sic) & Guadalupe MARTIN; am/ Jose REYNA (sic) & Maria Antonia ABILA, all *vecinos y naturales del pueblo*; gp/ Juan Bautista CORTES & Maria Josefa CORTES, *vecinos de San Fernando*.

Page 12
GABALDON, Maria Dolores Arroyo Ondo
bap 19 Aug 1826, ae 4 da; d/ Jose Manuel GABALDON & Maria Susana MARTIN, *vecinos del Arroyo Ondo*; ap/ Felis GABALDON & Maria Dolores AGUERO; am/ Manuel Ramos MARTIN & Maria Manuela SANDOBAL; gp/ An^{to} MARTIN & Maria Catarina SANDOBAL, *vecinos del Arroyo Ondo*.

NARANJO, Jose Agustin Natural de este pueblo
bap 27 Aug 1826, ae 7 da; s/ Santiago NARANJO & Paula MOYA, *naturales deste pueblo de Taos*; ap/ Juan Manuel NARANJO & Mª Catarina ROMERO; am/ Juan An^{to} MOYA & Lucia LUCERO; gp/ An^{to} MARTIN & Fran^{ca} RIO, *naturales recidentes deste pueblo*.

MARTINES, Jose Antonio San Fernando
bap 26 Aug 1826, ae 3 da; s/ Fran^{co} MARTINES & Maria de las Nieves SILVA,

vecinos de San Fernando; ap/ Juan Pablo MARTINES & Mª Josefa ESPINOSA; am/ Santiago SILVA & Juana VELASQUES; gp/ Juan Manuel LOVATO & Maria Ygnacia LOVATO, *vecinos de San Fernando*.

DURAN, Maria Josefa San Fernando
bap 27 Aug 1826, ae 5 da; d/ Juan Cristobal DURAN & Maria Encarnacion CHAVES, *vecinos de la jurisdiccion de la Cañada & residentes occidentales en San Fernando*; ap/ Juan DURAN & Mª Ascencion MEDINA; am/ Antonio CHAVES & Mª Varbara SANCHES; gp/ Anto Esmeregildo TRUGILLO & Maria Josefa TAFOLLA, *vecinos de San Fernando*.

Page 13
MEDINA, Maria Candelaria Ranchito
*bap 27 Aug 1827 (sic), ae 3 da; d/ Jesus MEDINA & Maria Josefa MARTIN, *vecinos de la (written over) del Ranchito*; ap/ Juan MEDINA & Candelaria VIGILA; am/ Gervacio MARTIN & Juana CORTES, *vecinos de la plasa de San Franco del Rancho*; gp/ Juan Bautista TRUGILLO & Casilda QUINTANA, *vecinos de San Franco*.

MAES, Maria Juana Agustina San Franco del Rancho
bap 4 Sep 1826, ae 8 da; d/ Jose Carlos MAES & Hermenegilda APODACA, *vecinos del Rancho*; ap/ Antº MAES & Miquela LUCERO; am/ Baltasar APODACA & Mª Magdalena SAIS; gp/ Bartolo MONDRAGON & Juana Josefa MEDINA, *vecinos de la plasa de Sn Franco del Rancho*.

TAFOLLA, Maria Ygnacia San Franco del Rancho
bap 8 Sep 1826, ae 7 da; d/ Jesus TAFOLLA & Maria Manuela ESPINOSA, *vecinos dela plasa de San Franco del Rancho*; ap/ Salvador TAFOYA & Maria Ygnacia CANÓ; am/ Antonio Jose ESPINOSA & Anna Maria CORDOBA; gp/ Antonio FRESQUIS & Maria de los Reyes SANCHES, *vecinos del la dhª plasa del Rancho*.

LÉ, Franco Anto Luis (Jose Franco Luis in margin) Adulto, extrang.
bap 9 Sep 1826, ae 19 yr; s/ Juan LÉ & Maria CARGUEL, *originario from the United States del Norte America*, belongs to *la secta Presbiteriana*; gp/ Dn Franco SANDOBAL & Mariana TAFOLLA, *ciudadanos de la plasa de S. Fernando*.

DURAN, Jesus Maria Rancho
bap 10 Sep 1826, ae 3 da; s/ Domingo DURAN & Maria Soledad LOVATO, *vecinos del Rancho, plasa de S. Franco*; ap/ Pedro Ygnacio DURAN & Maria Anta SANCHES; am/ Salvador LOVATO & Maria Candelaria CORDOBA; gp/ Pedro CONOLE (Origins, p. 412) & Maria de los Reyes DURAN, *vecinos de la misma plasa de S Franco*.

BERNAL, Jose Concepcion S. Ferndo
bap (blank) Sep 1826, ae 5 da; s/ Pedro BERNAL & Maria Gertrudis SUASO, *vecinos de San Fernando*; ap/ (blank space); am/ Miguel SUASO & Mª Josefa VIALPANDO; gp/ Manuel SUASO & Juana Teresa SANDOVAL, *vecinos de San Fernando*. An ojo sign next to it.

Page 14
ROMERO, Jose de la Crus Rancho de S. Franco
bap 16 Sep 1826, ae 4 da; s/ Antonio ROMERO & Maria Roumalda RUIBALIS, *vecinos del Ranchito de S. Franco*; ap/ Mariano ROMERO & Maria Franca ARMENTA; am/ (blank space); gp/ Jose Miguel MARTIN & Maria Dolores MARTINES (sic), *vecino del Ranchito de S. Franco*. An ojo sign (next to it but the connection the previous ojo is doubtful).

CAMPBELL, Jose Ricardo Extrangero
bap 16 Sep 1826, ae 27 yr; s/ Juan CAMPBELL (Origins, p. 409) & Rebeca (n.s.), originally from the United States *del Norte America*; gp/ Dn Pablo DURAN & Mª de Jesus VALDES, *ciudadanos de S. Ferndo*.

MADRIL, Jose Fran^{co} San Fernando
bap 16 Sep 1826, ae 2 da; s/ Miguel MADRIL & Juana Maria CENA, *vecinos de S. Fernando*; ap/ Tomas MADRIL & Mª Victoria GARCIA; am/ Miguel CENA & Maria Rafaela LUCERO; gp/ Juan MADRIL & Mª An^{ta} MARTIN, *vecinos de S. Fernando.*

PACHECO, Maria Dolores Rancho
bap 17 Sep 1826, ae 5 da; d/ Fran^{co} PACHECO & Maria Dolores VARELA; ap/ Juan Pedro PACHECO & Maria de la Luz MARTIN; am/ Miguel BARELA (sic) & Juana ROMERO; gp/ Juan Simon SALASAR & Juana SALASAR, *todos los dh^{o} son vecinos de San Fran^{co} del Rancho.*

TRUGILLO, Jose Dolores S. Fernando
bap 17 Sep 1826, ae 3 da; s/ An^{to} Jose TRUGILLO & Mª Manuela COCA, *vecinos de la plasa de San Fern^{do}*; ap/ Jose An^{to} Alejandro TRUGILLO & Maria Fran^{ca} ARCHULETA; am/ Jose Manuel COCA & Maria Rafaela MARTIN; gp/ Juan Felipe CORDOBA & Maria de Jesus FERNANDES, *vecinos del varrio de San Fran^{co} del Rancho.*

SALASAR, Juan An^{to} Arroyo Ondo
bap 19 Sep 1826, ae 7 da; s/ Maria Manuela SALASAR, *vecina dela poblacion del Arroyo Ondo*; am/ Juan Manuel SALASAR & Maria de los Reyes MARTINES, *dif^{s}*; gp/ Juan An^{to} SALASAR & Juana Maria SALASAR, *vecinos dela plasa de S Fran^{co} del Rancho.* (Pages 14-15)

Page 15
FRESQUIS, Maria Gertrudis San Fernando
bap 19 Sep 1826, ae 7 da; d/ Juan An^{to} FRESQUIS & Maria Dolores GABALDON, *vecinos de Sn (sic) Fernando*; ap/ Anna Maria FRESQUIS (only); am/ Jose Manuel GABALDON & Maria Guadalupe TRUGILLO; gp/ Juan de Jesus AGUILAR & Mª Juliana AGUILAR, *vecinos de San Fernando.*

GARCIA, Jose Maria de los Dolores Arroyo Hondo
bap 20 Sep 1826, ae 5 da; s/ An^{to} Jose GARCIA & Guadalupe CHAVES, *vecinos del Arroyo Ondo*; ap/ Juan Angel GARCIA & Maria Manuela MARTINES; am/ Candelaria BALDONADO & *padre no conocido*; gp/ Jose Benino MAES & Maria de Jesus GARCIA, *vecinos del Arroyo Ondo.*

TRUGILLO, Estefana Arroyo Hondo
bap 21 Sep 1826, ae 7 da; d/ Fran^{co} TRUGILLO & Mª de la Lus ABILA, *vecinos del Arroyo Hondo*; ap/ Alejandro TRUGILLO & Manuela ARCHULETA; am/ Rafael ABILA & Mª An^{ta} GALLEGO; gp/ Pablo CORDOVA & An^{ta} Margarita (n.s.), *vecinos del Arroyo Hondo.*

TRUGILLO, Maria Tomasa San Fernando
bap 24 Sep 1826, ae 8 da; d/ Juan de Jesus TRUGILLO & Maria de Jesus VALERIO, *vecinos dela plasa de San Fran^{co} del Rancho*; ap/ Damasio TRUGILLO & Leonicia JORUPA, both dec; am/ Fran^{co} VALERIO & Rosalia MARTINES; gp/ Felipe VALERIO & Rosalia MARTINES, *vecinos del Potrero perteniciente a la jurisdicion de la Cañada.*

CORTES, Jose Julian San Fernando
bap 27 Sep 1826, ae 7 da; s/ Fran^{co} CORTES & Mª Atanacia ARMENTA, *vecinos de San Fernando*; ap/ Jose An^{to} CORTES & Mª Juana MONTOYA, *difuntos*; am/ Simon ARMENTA & Maria MARTINES; gp/ Juan Ygnacio CORTES & Mª Teresa CHAVES, *vecinos de la plasa de S^{n} Fenando.*

Page 16
VIGIL, Jose Miguel San Fran^{co} del Rancho
bap 1 Oct 1826, ae 5 da; s/ Juan Bautista VIGIL & Juana Maria CACILLAS, *vecino de S. Fran^{co} del Rancho*; ap/ Pedro VIGIL & Maria Josefa QUINTANA; am/ Cristobal

CACILLAS & Maria Luisa TAFOLLA; gp/ Juan de Jesus ROMO & Anamaria CANDELARIA, *vecinos de S. Fran^{co} del Rancho.*

LOPES, Jose Geronimo San Francisco del Rancho
bap 1 Oct 1826, ae 2 da; s/ Manuel LOPES & Simona MARTIN, *vecinos de San Fran^{co} del Rancho*; ap/ Vernardo LOPES & Ysabel ANAYA; am/ Pedro MARTIN & Dolores SAIS; gp/ Ysidro de la HORA, *vecino de Sta Fe*, & Maria Lorensa LOPES, *vecina de S. Fernando.*

ROMERO, Maria Dominga Pueblo
bap 1 Oct 1826, ae 10 da; d/ Mª Guadalupe ROMERO, *vecina natural del pueblo* & *padre no conosido*; am/ Juan Domingo ROMERO & Anamaria SAPATA; gp/ Jose An^{to} BARELA & Maria Fran^{ca} CORDOBA, *vecinos de la plasa de S. Fernando.*

ARCHULETA, Maria Geronima Plasa de la Purisima Concep^{n}
bap 4 Oct 1826, ae 5 da; d/ Jesus ARCHULETA & Maria Gertrudis CASADOS, *vecinos de la plasa de la Purisima Concepcion*; ap/ Jose Pablo ARCHULETA & Maria Barbara LOVATO; am/ Juan An^{to} CASADOS & Catarina BACA, *difuntos*; gp/ the same Jose Pablo ARCHULETA & Maria Barbara LOVATO, *vecinos dela plasa de la Purisima Concepcion.*

GONSALES, Maria Paula Pueblo
bap 8 Oct 1826, ae 5 da; d/ An^{to} GONSALES & Ygnacia GOMES, *naturales de este pueblo de Taos*; ap/ An^{to} GONSALES & Mª ROMERO; am/ Jose GOMES & Ygnacia MARTIN; gp/ Juan An^{to} (n.s.) & Secilia MARTIN, all *naturales de dho pueblo.*

ARCHULETA, Manuel Estevan Arroyo Hondo
bap 8 Oct 1826, ae 7 da; s/ Novato ARCHULETA & Dolores MESTAS, *vecinos del Arroyo Hondo*; ap/ Damian ARCHULETA & Juana Miquela SALASAR; am/ Jose MESTAS & Barbara MARTIN; gp/ An^{to} Tiburcio MEDINA & Juana ARCHULETA, *vecinos del mismo lugar.*

TORRES, Jose Fran^{co} Arroyo Ondo
bap 8 Oct 1826, ae 8 da; s/ Martin TORRES & Mª Encarnacion GONSALES, *vecinos del Arroyo Hondo*; ap/ Domingo FLORES (sic) & Mª Encarnacion RIBERA; am/ Juan An^{to} GONSALES & Mª Barbara FERNANDES; gp/ Julian LUCERO & Mª Polonia LUCERO, *vecinos de S^{n} Fer^{do}.*

INDEX of BAPTISMS

It is important to look for alternate spellings of both surnames and given names. Names may appear more than one time on a page. Many names were abbreviated in the original records. They have been spelled out in this index. For the most part, prepositions have not been included in this index, but if they were present in the original record, they will be found in the manuscript.

ARCHULETA (continued)
Jose Vicente 100
Josef Santos 195
Juan Bautista 147
Juan Cristoval 164, 241
Juan Jesus 161, 265
Juan Jose 157
Juan Ysidro 176
Juana Gertrudis 156
Juana Guadalupe 149
Juana Maria 116
Julian 196
Manuel Estevan 307
Maria Antonia 223, 241, 273
Maria Asension 265
Maria Barbara 161
Maria Carmen 296
Maria Crus 180
Maria Dolores 180, 259
Maria Feliciana 295
Maria Francisca 221, 243
Maria Geromina 307
Maria Jesus 260
Maria Josefa 137
Maria Juana 284
Maria Juliana 119
Maria Luisa 148
Maria Luz 119
Maria Manuela 101
Maria Mequela 206
Maria Paula 190, 225
Maria Refugio 261
Maria Rosalia 205
Maria Soledad 101
Maria Tomasa 118
Maria Ygnacia 165, 284
Mariano 126
Miguel Antonio 131
Pedro 183
ARELLANO
Jose Bentura 211
Jose Julian 250
Jose Mariano 248
Juan Nepomuceno 260, 296
Juan Rafael 97
Maria Antonia 219
Maria Dolores 207
Maria Juana 210
Maria Lus 287
Maria Soledad 226
Maria Ygnacia 154
AREYANO
Jose Ygnacio 199
ARGUELLO
Jose Cruz 91
Jose Manuel 72
Jose Pablo 107
Juan Felipe Jesus 242
Juan Jesus 105
ARGUELLO (continued)
Maria Alberta 252
Maria Dolores 199
Maria Soledad 180
ARMARAN
Maria 13
ARMENTA
Anna Josefa Jacoba 116
Juan Crisostomo 244
Juan Ygnacio 88
Maria Augustina 97
Maria Guadalupe Ventura 140
Maria Josefa Rita Atanasia 124
Maria Manuela 259
Maria Teodora 292
Maria Ygnacia 277
Maria Ygnasia 82
Mariano 107
Nicolas Antonio 37
ARMENTIA
Maria Guadalupe 148
ARMIJO
Ana Maria 84
Andres 267
Antonio Jose Jesus 72
Jose Cipriano 76
Jose Gregorio 284
Jose Tomas 117
Josef Guadalupe 206
Josef Ygnacio 33
Juan Angel 191
Juan Francisco 245
Juana Maria 236
Juliana 166
Maria Antonia 83
Maria Dolores 157, 177
Maria Josefa 83
Maria Juana Trinidad 228
Maria Paula 163
Maria Seferina 238
Maria Ysabel 173
Miguel Antonio 147
ARMOSA
Anttonia 19
ASPECTIA
Gertrudis Rosalia 16
Maria Geronima 16
ATÁ
Juan 14
ATENCIO
Jose Francisco Maria 67
Juan Jesus 301
ATENSIO
Maria Candelaria 86
Maria Ursula 75
ATOMA
Juana 6
ATOQUE
Juana 9

BEJIL (continued)
Maria Encarnacion 173
Maria Gracia 192
Maria Jesus 200, 230
Maria Josefa 170
Maria Luz 202
Maria Manuela 190
Maria Rafela Jesus 187
Maria Refugio 197, 201
Maria Rosa 185
Maria Soledad 230
Maria Teresa 225
Maria Trinidad 183
Maria Ygnacia 179
Pablo Jose 175
Salvador Jesus 172
Ugenio 225
BELMONTE
Maria Dolores 171
BENABIDES
See VENAVIDES
Jose Gregorio 199
Maria Cruz 219
BENABIDEZ
Juan Gonsaga 177
BENAVIDES
See VENAVIDES
Antonio 160
Jose Francisco 158
Jose Pablo 40
Jose Reyes 244
Juan Jesus 40
Juan Nepomuceno 150
Manuela 29
BERNAL
See VERNAL
Bibiana 147
Jose Concepcion 305
Jose Francisco 247
Juan Jesus 215
Juana Maria 163
Maria Francisca 229
Maria Soledad 265
Pablo 225
Salvador 143
Santiago 285
BIGIL
See VIGIL
Jose Antonio 229
Juana Maria 229
BIJIL
See VIJIL, BEJIL
Miguel Antonio 276
BLANCHARD
Antonio Domingo 304
BLEA
Antonio Jose 87
Felipa Cayetana 133
Jose Antonio 228
BLEA (continued)
Jose Dionisio 141
Jose Teodosio 76
Josef 193
Josef Benito 173
Josefa Patricia 108
Juan Nepomuseno 182
Juan Pablo 68
Maria Casilda 63
Maria Jesus 123
Maria Encarnacion 69
Maria Guadalupe 118
Maria Luz 133
Maria Rafaela 31
Maria Serafina 189
Mariano Candelario Jesus 90
Miguel Cipriano 100
Ramon Antonio 77
BOCON
Maria Ana 41
Maria Anica 41
BORICA
Maria Tomasa Jesus 95
Micaela 117
BORIDA
Maria Manuela 86
BORREGO
Clemente 212
Juan de Dios 233
Juana Maria 188, 217
Maria Dorotea 181
Maria Reilles 194
Maria Rosa 258
BOYO
Paulin 48
BRISOL
Jose Francisco 284
BRITO
Francisco Dolores 57
Jose Dionicio 65
Jose Encarnacion 73
Jose Matias 114
Juan Nepomuseno 181
Maria Candelaria 197
Maria Concepcion 106
Maria Felipa 167
Maria Manuela 99
Maria Micaela 77
Rosa Mictica 50
Teodora 120
BRUNO
Maria Fernanda Isaac 66
BUENO
Andres Jesus 105
Antonio 132, 158
Antonio Jose 157
Jose Dionisio 144
Jose Rafael 101, 242
Jose Vicente 105, 137

BUENO (continued)
Josef Antonio 205
Josef Benito 200
Juan Antonio 123
Juana Josefa Serafina 72
Juana Paula 82
Maria Dolores 244
Maria Francisca 112
Maria Jesus 184
Maria Josefa 121
Maria Luz 118, 167
Maria Manuela 181
Maria Santana 204
Maria Ygnacia 141
Pedro Mateo 160
Pedro Nolasco 227, 248
Tomas 172
BUENO PANDO
Feliz Dolores 55
BUSTOS
Francisco 21
Josepha 20
Juan 20, 21
Maria 20, 21
Raphael 21
BUTIERRES
See GUTIERRES, GUTIERREZ
Jose Manuel 289
CAÃN
Francisca Dolores 55
CABIAM
Mariana Reyes 14
CABPUELA
Diego 11
CACHANA
Santiago 263
CACHO
Teresa 279
CAFLALA
Maria Anttonia 19
CAIAJE
Alonso 6
Yldefonso 6
CAIGUA
Diego Dolores 55
Gertrudes 87
Juan Domingo 102
CALA
Francisco 8
CALFIALU
Gregoria 23
CALO
Juan 13
CAMARGO
Jose Miguel 94
CAMPBELL
Jose Ricardo 305
CANBAY
Juan Antonio 47
CANNATE
Joachin 2
CANO
Maria Luz 258
CAÓ
Paulin Dolores 57
CAOS
Marcelina 139
CAPCHOLE
Micaela 10
CAPOALA
Micaela 8
CAPTESO
Anttonio 5
CAPULI
Joseph 12
CARIER
Maria Barbara 279
CASADO
Francisco 103
CASADOS
Josef Miguel 194
Juan Rafael 225
Juana Geronima 173
Juana Gertrudis 108
Maria Concepcion 121
Maria Dolores 192
CASAUS
Maria Candelaria 251
CASILLAS
Jesus Maria 230
Jose Ascencion 116
Jose Lino 156
Jose Ventura 282, 296
Juan Augustin 84
Juan Jesus 246
Juana Jesus 109
Juana Maria 266
Juana Paula 132
Luis 146
Luis Maria 85
Manuel 166
Maria Albina 233
Maria Dolores 268
Maria Eleuteria 203
Maria Francisca 92
Maria Guadalupe 182
Maria Josefa 130
Maria Luz 235, 270
Maria Manuela 130
Maria Rezurreccion 115
Maria Ygnacia 158
Micaela 92
Pedro Antonio 142
CASSILLAS
Josef Benito 201
CATHOTLE
Thomas 4

CATUFE
Maria Polonia 70
CATUGA
Maria Soledad 151
CATUGE
Juan 164
CATUJE
Juan de Dios Jose 28
CATUNE
Felipe 11
CAYGUA
Juan Antonio 133
Maria Dolores 265
CEQUE
Juan 23
CHABES
See CHAVES, CHAVEZ
Jesus Maria 178
Juan Jose 220
Juana Nepumucena 220
Maria Rafaela 214
CHACON
Fernando 84
Jose Martin 87
Maria Encarnacion 98
Maria Lus 299
CHAFALOTE
Jose Pablo 104
Juana 125
CHAGUA
Juan Jesus 45
CHALLO
Maria Teodora 289
CHAMA
Domingo 162
Maria Ascencion
CHANDAGO
Maria 3
CHARVÉS
See CHAVES
Maria Apolonia 236
CHARVET
Maria Guadalupe 262
CHAVES
See CHARVÉS
Eusevia Casimira 65
Francisca 204
Jose Antonio 149
Jose Benito 191
Jose Francisco 191
Jose Gabriel 123
Jose Miguel 155, 166
Jose Pablo 97, 269
Jose Maria Guadalupe 260
Josef Ygnacio 223
Juan Agustin 186
Juan Antonio 109
Juan Cristoval 68, 138
Juan Nepomuceno 265
CHAVES (continued)
Juan Ysidro 259
Luis Manuel Narsiso 43
Manuel Antonio 188
Manuel Dolores 56
Maria Antonia 128
Maria Apolonia 47
Maria Candelaria 156, 223
Maria Candelaria Dolores 51
Maria Clara 250
Maria Encarnacion 121, 164
Maria Gertrudis 144, 251
Maria Guadalupe 276
Maria Luz 38
Maria Micaela 94
Maria Paula 277
Maria Rafaela 108
Maria Rosa 160
Maria Serafina 190
Maria Soledad 61, 118, 176
Maria Teodora 79
Maria Theresa Jesus 243
Maria Tomasa 275
Maria Ygnacia 78
Mariano 177
Santiago 110
CHAVEZ
Antonio Nerio 89
Jose Guadalupe 254
Maria Serafina 198
Maria Viviana 224
Maria Ygnacia 198
Pedro 204
CHAYA
Ysidro 101
CHAYO
Jose 157
CHEABEA
Maria 18
CHELE
Augustina Cruz 17
CHENDA
Christina 5
CHEQUE
Lusia 11
CHIDE
Christoval 12
CHIECHO
Diego 10
CHIERCHAGU
Juana 3
CHIFAYO
Esteban 42
Maria 48
CHILMAGEL
Angelina 4
CHIMAYO
Juana Maria Dolores 56

CHINA
Maria Rosa 30
CHININI
Jose Santos 71
Juan Augustin 82
Lucia Geronima 44
CHINNAPO
Catalina 3
CHINO
Agustin 131
Francisco 94
Juan 80
Juana Dominga 88, 89
Santiago 73
CHIOO
Lusia 5
CHIQUITO
Juan Jesus 72
CHIRINO
Jose Teodoro 213
CHIRMAGER
Anttonio 9
CHIRMAQUEL
Rossa 1
CHIU
Antonia 8
CHIULO
Joseph 4
CHIUTLO
Anttonio 7
Diego 4
CHIUU
Rossa Maria 11
CHOLESE
Maria Josepha 18
CHOLUA
Maria Ascension 46
CHONGO
Josef Manuel 41
CHULA
Leonarda 89
Maria 101
CHULETA
See ARCHULETA
Josef Francisco Rafael 32
CHUPUNE
Joan 17
Lucia Monica 15
CISNEROS
See SISNEROS
Josef Rafael 35
Juan Domingo 33
Juana Bautista 80
Maria Guadalupe 144
CLAVES
Getrudes 30
COAGUACHORE
Anttonio 7
COAGUAQUEN
Margarita 5
COATOI
Juan 8
COCA
Anastasio 218
Andres 195
Antonio Espiritu Santo 40
Barbara Antonia 23
Bentura 227
Buenabentura 227
Cornelio 128
Diego Antonio 185
Jose Benito 215, 295
Jose Concepcion 154
Jose Francisco 161
Jose Miguel 238
Jose Rafael 39
Jose Reyes 68
Jose Vicente 296
Joseph Francisco 49
Juan Antonio 48
Juan Christobal 252
Juan Jesus 68
Maria 145
Maria Apolonia 272
Maria Dolores 77, 82, 137
Maria Dominga 100
Maria Juliana 181
Maria Manuela 60, 62, 90
Maria Rosa 238
Maria Rosa Dolores 57
Maria Rossario Dolores 58
Pasquala Rafaela 32
Pedro Ygnacio 192
Tomas 47
COCLA
Lusia 9
CONCHA
Francisca 124
Jose Francisco 233
Jose Miguel 186
Juan Manuel 82
Juana 253
Juana Maria 269
Lorenso 194
Maria Encarnacion Dolores 58
Maria Soledad 252
Santiago 280
Ysabel 74
CONDE
Juana Maria 152
CONTRERAS
Juan 188
Manuel Jesus 188
Maria Ysabel 102
CORDERO
Maria Anttonia 25

GARCIA (continued)
Josef Benito 174, 178, 198, 202
Josef Candelaria 202
Joseph 116
Juan 177, 209
Juan Antonio 230, 251
Juan Jesus 192
Juan Lorenzo 143
Juan Rafael 165
Juana Getrudes 194
Juana Maria 130
Manuel Antonio 227
Maria Antonia 249
Maria Bibiana 261
Maria Concepcion 74
Maria Dolores 104, 171, 226, 282
Maria Encarnacion 188
Maria Guadalupe 221
Maria Jesus 154, 161
Maria Josefa 217, 218, 284
Maria Josefa Luz 186
Maria Juliana 214
Maria Manuela 275
Maria Micaela 106
Maria Paula 227
Maria Rafaela 217
Maria Rosa 141, 198
Maria Sencion 193
Maria Tomasa 142
Miguel Antonio 97
Rafaela 38
Ysabel 170
GARDUÑO
Maria Dolores 183
GARZIA
Maria Rosario 35
GAVALDON
See GABALDON
Manuel Antonio Jesus 228
Maria Ysidora Dolores 202
GAVAN
Caietano 1
GAVILAN
Anna Maria 68
Francisca 91
Juan 1
Juan Jesus 45
Juan Reyes 113
Maria Manuela 73, 84, 95
Mariano 129
Ventura 123
GIELNUACHA
Micaela 45
GIGUACHAPO
Lusia 15
GIJOSA
Francisca Maria 19
GLUPE
Maria 15
GOMES
Jose Santos 289
Josef Santiago 173
Juan Antonio Martin 304
Juan Domingo 42
Juana 69
Manuel 194
Maria 40
Maria Ascension 39
Maria Juliana 45
Maria Paula 175
Maria Soledad 49
Micaela 41
Migel 61
Salvador 45
Ygnacia 187
GOMEZ
Alfonso 94
Ana Maria Dolores 59
Antonio 101, 185
Gregorio Antonio 216
Jose 87
Jose Antonio 91, 112
Jose Francisco 99
Jose Manuel 261
Jose Martin 104
Jose Miguel 185
Juan Antonio Rafael 33
Juan Domingo 236
Juan Francisco Dolores 50
Juan Jesus 245
Juan Julian 215
Juan Manuel 197
Juana 89
Maria Bartola 146
Maria Carmen 155
Maria Dominga 111
Maria Estefana 262
Maria Gertrudis 122
Maria Josefa 78
Maria Juana 232
Maria Luz 251
Maria Manuela 209, 246
Maria Micaela 35
Maria Rosa 33
Maria Rosario 75
Maria Soledad 99, 163, 250
Mariano 79
Nicolasa 20
Paula 188
Pedro 236
Santiago 144, 222, 275
Valentin Fransisco 27
Ygnacia 260
GONSALES
Agustin 224
Jose Andres Dolores 50
Jose Cruz 186
Jose Francisco 292

GONZALEZ (continued)
Pedro Antonio 260
Thomas Antonio 255
Tomas 128
Ygnacio Albino 90
GRIJALBA
Romaldo Nepumuceno 215
GUABLAPA
Yssavel 1
GUALAPABA
Michaela 1
GUALASI
Juan 9
GUALNACHA
Maria Michaela 17
GUARPAIS
Juana 12
GUECHAVA
Lusia 10
GUENA
Juan 1
GUERRERO
Jose Antonio 164
Jose Bernardo 151
Jose Candelaria 68
Jose Rafael 291
Juan Antonio 180
Juan Domingo 254
Juana Maria 141
Margarita 69
Maria Luz 119
Maria Paula 271
Maria Trinidad 119
Salvador 82
Tomas Antonio 213
GUIMAGEL
Pasquala 12
GUIONA
Diego 11
GUIPAT
Juana Catalina Dolores 53
GUIUJE
Ildelfonso 4
Maria 4
GUTIERRES
See BUTIERRES
Maria 213
Maria Refugio 260
GUTIERREZ
Getrudes 16
HANCHA
Juana 14
HAQUERMO
Lucia 12
HERRERA
See ERRERA
German 296
Jose Encarncion 289
Juan Antonio 255
HERRERA (continued)
Juan Bautista 209
Maria Guadalupe 174
Maria Ludovina 239
Maria Petra 290
Pedro Antonio 99, 258
Pedro Pablo 116
HIELO
Cristobal 2
HILO
Geronima 19
Geronimo Domingo 19
Maria Andrea 19
HOLGUIN
Jose Antonio 105
HURTADO
See URTADO
Jose Rafael 235
Maria Concepcion 76
Maria Guadalupe 35
Maria Luz 220
Maria Rosa 240
INACO
Fabiana 9
IQUI
Joseph 8
JABE
Vernardo 7
JAEPATO
Lusia 9
JARAMILLO
See XARAMILLO
Cecilia 294
JATUSE
Rosa 41
JIAGUIL
Santiago 45
JIAUPATLA
Ramon 14
JIGUACHAPO
Lusia 5
JIRON
Miguel Francisco 25
JUALACACHE
Maria Zapabepa 12
JUANAIO
Anttonio 3
JUANPONE
Raphael 13
JUEL
(n.n.) 62
JUENAPO
Juan 14
JUENAPU
Eusebio 11
JUENAYO
Maria 8
JUESPLA
Maria Michaela 19

LOVATO (continued)
Maria Manuela 231
Maria Paula 292
Maria Soledad 227
Soledad 227
LU(torn)
Cayetana 129
LUCA
Ana Rafaela 33
Jose Antonio Dolores 54
Juana 164
LUCAS
Francisca 86
Maria Francisca 263
LUCERO
See LUSERO, LUZERO
Antonio Jose 235
Antonio Josef 207
Buena Bentura 207
Domingo 79, 165
Felipe 135
Francisca Petra 65
Francisco Antonio 241, 293
Francisco Dolores 56
Geronimo 123
Jesus Maria 178
Jose Antonio 249
Jose Benito 171
Jose Bernardo Dolores 53
Jose Carmen 286
Jose Gabriel 250
Jose Jesus 242
Jose Julian 191
Jose Manuel 123, 148, 270, 291
Jose Miguel 241
Jose Pablo 110
Jose Pablo Dolores 57
Josef Bartolome 201
Josef Francisco 205
Josef Julian 179
Josef Miguel 180
Juan Antonio 36
Juan Bautista 122, 294
Juan Domingo 36
Juan Jesus 205, 240
Juan Miguel 250
Juana Josefa 229
Juana Maria 135
Lorenzo 166
Manuel Gregorio 130
Maria Antonia 144, 226
Maria Antonia Gertrudes 248
Maria Ascencion 42
Maria Barbara Gregoria 233
Maria Candelaria 184
Maria Dolores 207, 274
Maria Dolores Gregoria 264
Maria Francisca Romana 264
Maria Gertrudis 150
LUCERO (continued)
Maria Getrudes 205
Maria Guadalupe 169, 300
Maria Jesus 245
Maria Josefa 108, 133, 284
Maria Lus 300
Maria Luz 168, 176
Maria Margarita 79
Maria Micaela Dolores 59
Maria Natividad 268
Maria Paula 232, 262
Maria Peregrina 278
Maria Polonia 164
Maria Rosa 142
Maria Rufina 283
Maria Soledad 148, 149, 180, 196
Maria Tomasa 245, 261
Maria Ygnacia 249, 266
Pablo Baltasar Dolores 51
Pedro Antonio 184
Pedro Anttonio 159
Pedro Regalado 192
Tomas 136
Vernardo 189
LUIZ
Maria Lucia 233
LUJAN
See LUXAN
Antonio 74
Barbara 75
Cayetana 21
Dominga 225
Domingo Lorenzo 66
Esteban Dolores 57
Jose Antonio 75
Jose Antonio Dolores 55
Jose Bernardo 44, 73
Jose Francisco 44
Jose Fransisco 28
Josefa 38
Joseph 24
Juan 22, 200
Juan Antonio 284, 295
Juan Domingo 38, 183, 206
Juan Mata 27
Juan Miguel 73
Juana Maria 72
Juana Maria Dolores 56
Manuel Antonio 29
Manuel Ciriaco 36
Manuel Fransisco 28
Manuela 48
Maria 22, 38
Maria Antonia 71
Maria Catalina Dolores 59
Maria Concepcion Dolores 51
Maria Dolores 37
Maria Francisca 41
Maria Jesus 206

LUJAN (continued)
Maria Josefa 186
Maria Martina 64
Maria Narcisa 67
Maria Paula 28, 202
Rafael 40
Santiago 184
Santiago Dolores 55
Tiofilo Eginio 64
LUNA
Antonio Martin 143
Jose Antonio 155
Jose Benito 244
Jose Francisco 120
Jose Jesus 243
Jose Miguel 145
Jose Rafael 158
Juan Luciano 281
Juan Rafael 271
Maria Casimira 144
Maria Dolores 173
Maria Francisca 259
Maria Josefa Jesus 114
Maria Lorenza 93
Maria Luz 145
Maria Paula Bentura 184
LURENI
Domingo 8
LURTE
Magdalena 2
LUSERO
See LUCERO, LUZERO
Jose Rafael 150
Juana 74
Manuel 68
Maria Catarina 83
Maria Cecilia 64
Maria Concepcion 60
Maria Paula Dolores 120
Santiago 71
Soledad 69
LUSLI
Miguel 22
LUT
Catarina 210
LUXAN
See LUJAN
Ana Maria 124
Anacleta Rafaela 32
Andres 93
Antonia 130
Baltasar Reyes 214
Catarina 102
Domingo 114, 165
Francisca 113
Francisco 147, 166
Geronimo 94, 111, 122, 147
Jose 94, 140
Jose Manuel 107, 160

LUXAN (continued)
Jose Mariano 155
Jose Rafael 141
Jose Santiago 246
Jose Vicente 105
Jose Ygnacio 262
Josef Antonio Rafael 31
Juan Andres 127
Juan Antonio 98, 141, 212
Juan Domingo 163
Juan Gaspar 106
Juan Jesus 273
Juan Lorenzo 146
Juan Manuel 140
Juana 19, 61, 102
Juana Manuela 93
Juana Maria 85
Lorenzo 126, 148
Lucia 104
Maria 16, 128
Maria Dolores 135
Maria Dominga 87
Maria Encarnacion 125, 162
Maria Guadalupe 83
Maria Hipolita 88, 89
Maria Josefa 95, 249, 264
Maria Luz 242
Maria Magdalena 90
Maria Martina 112
Maria Rafaela 30
Maria Rosa 111
Mariano 103, 148
Rosa Maria 262
Santiago 134
Maria Soledad 91
LUXANA
Lucia Catharina 15
LUZERO
See LUCERO, LUSERO
Jose 222
Jose Rafael 98
Juan Jesus 213
Juan Manuel 92, 100
Juana Maria 217
Lorenzo 89
Maria Cruz 275
Maria Dolores 216
Maria Getrudis 211
Maria Refugio 213
Matiana Rita 77
Pedro Jose Jesus 222
M(torn)TIA
Juan Rafael 97
MADRID
(n.n.) 153
Jose Agustin 239
Jose Antonio 132, 144, 210
Jose Encarnacion 166
Jose Guadalupe 245

MADRID (continued)
Jose Maria Guadalupe 245
Jose Pablo 156
Josefa 108
Juan Antonio 135
Juan Bartolome 42
Juan Jesus 93
Juana Dominga 203
Juana Rosalia 265
Maria Angela 131
Maria Francisca 166
Maria Josefa 294
Maria Lorenza 105
Maria Luisa 161
Maria Monica 167
Maria Paula 149
Maria Rosalia 78
Maria Soledad 126
Maria Ygnacia 121
Santiago Antonio 110
Santiago Jose 110
Tomas 152
Ysidro Trinidad 228
MADRIL
Estevan 172
Jose Francisco 306
Jose Gregorio 290
Josef Benito 177
Juan Cristoval 174
Juan Manuel 213
Maria Dolores 178, 179
Maria Luz 221
Polonio 215
MAES
See MES, MEZ
Jose Lorenzo 222
Manuel Antonio 171
Maria Juana Agustina 305
Jose Concepcion 299
Jose Encarnacion 287
Maria Guadalupe 300
Maria Serafina 192
MAESE
Francisco 121
Juan Jose 153
Juliana 166
Maria Benigna 248
Maria Peregrina 245
Pedro 115
MALDONADO
See BALDONADO
Jose Miguel 184
MALINCHE
Francisco 86
Jose Francisco 128
Maria Manuela 253
Maria Ygnacia 47
MANSANARES
Jose Gregorio 29
MANSANARES (continued)
Maria Gracia 229
MAQUER
Juana 1
MAQUERO
Francisco 4
Juana 10, 15
MAQUI
Antonio 12
MARCO
Maria Antonia 211
MARQUES
Jesus Maria 241
Josef Benito 173
Juan Miguel 43
Juan Ygnacio 219
MARQUEZ
Aufemio Benito 200
Epifiano 186
Francisco 106
Jesus Maria 261
Jose Tomas 156
Josef Ygnacio 226
Juan Chrisostomo 259
Juan Domingo 88
Maria Antonia 131
Maria Dolores 234
Maria Fransisca 28
Maria Luz 139
Maria Rosa 102, 238
Maria Soledad 151
Miguel Antonio 224
Pedro Antonio 221
Santiago 189
MARTIN
Agustin 168
Ana Maria 132, 140
Ana Teresa 135
Angela 129
Antonia Dominga 280
Antonia Margarita 78
Antonia Rosa 121
Antonio Dionisio 120
Antonio Dolores Concepcion 51
Antonio Jose 83, 218, 259
Antonio Policarpio 286
Atanasia 153
Barbara 117
Barvara 193
Benita 226
Bisente 193
Catalina 42
Catarina Dolores 174
Cosme Damian 63
Diego Antonio 205
Diego Antonio Dolores 53
Dolores 187
Feliciano Jesus 299

MARTIN (continued)
Felipe Jesus 122
Francisca 105
Francisco 92, 125, 131
Francisco Antonio 206
Francisco Eduardo 241
Francisco Santos Dolores 54
Geronimo 169
Gregorio 132
Jesus Maria 242, 269
Jose 133, 137, 162
Jose Antonio 133, 153, 201, 223
Jose Benito 298
Jose Candelario 282
Jose Christoval 258
Jose Concepcion 300
Jose Cruz 99
Jose Dolores 280
Jose Francisco 69, 135, 144, 214, 243, 261
Jose Gabriel 127, 165
Jose Hermenegildo 285
Jose Inosencio Ermeregildo 64
Jose Manuel 85, 142, 160
Jose Mariano 85
Jose Miguel 107, 143
Jose Pablo 61, 118
Jose Rafael 152, 208, 239
Jose Santiago 119, 127, 288
Jose Santos 98
Jose Tomas 268
Jose Vicente 234
Jose Victor 139
Jose Visente 257
Jose Ygnacio 29, 147, 151
Josef Antonio 205
Josef Benito 170-172, 174, 176, 181
Josef Cruz 34
Josef Dolores 199, 223
Josef Encarnacion 173
Josef Felipe 172, 176
Josef Francisco 227
Josef Francisco Rafael 34
Josef Miguel 200
Josefa 118
Josefa Dolores 172
Josefa Rosario 172
Juan 133
Juan Agustin 48, 160, 168
Juan Antonio 115, 134, 143, 167, 168, 220, 283, 293
Juan Bautista 181
Juan Bentura 187
Juan Carmen 159, 220
Juan Christoval 49
Juan Domingo 139, 154, 179
Juan Domingo Dolores 55
Juan Francisco 182

MARTIN (continued)
Juan Jesus 62, 159, 203, 207, 208, 238, 273
Juan Jose Rosario 172
Juan Josef Rafael 31
Juan Maria 238
Juan Martin 207
Juan Nepumuseno 189
Juan Pablo 286
Juan Pasqual 138
Juan Rafael 39
Juan Reyes 183
Juan Tomas 120
Juan Ygnacio 82, 113, 118
Juan Ygnacio Jesus 105
Juan Ysidro 199
Juana 47, 119
Juana Maria 212, 272, 274, 275, 292
Juana Matiana 77
Juana Mequela 200
Juana Paula 88
Juana Rafaela 39
Juana Rafela 184
Julian 149
Magdalena 70
Manuel 43, 86, 107, 290
Manuel Antonio 230, 252
Manuel Gregorio 98, 181
Manuel Jose 106
Manuel Reyes 130, 271
Maria 151, 153, 166
Maria Andrea 30
Maria Antonia 94, 138, 221
Maria Ascencion 122
Maria Benita 170
Maria Casilda 158
Maria Catalina 73
Maria Claudia 170
Maria Crus 179
Maria Cruz 92
Maria Dolores 38, 51, 88, 108, 150, 169, 177, 198, 205, 273, 274
Maria Eduvige 285
Maria Encarnacion 72, 140, 144, 185, 199, 218, 226
Maria Francisca 109
Maria Guadalupe 156, 161
Maria Jesus 125
Maria Josefa 40, 150, 165, 218, 263
Maria Josefa Dolores 59
Maria Josefa Encarnacion 77
Maria Josefa Jesus 39
Maria Josefa Rafaela 34
Maria Juana Reyes 213
Maria Juliana 155
Maria Leonarda 270

MARTIN (continued)
Maria Lus 287
Maria Luz 114, 202, 256, 297
Maria Manuela 69, 100, 102, 122, 253
Maria Manuela Dolores 53, 59
Maria Marta 91
Maria Martina 87
Maria Marusia 63
Maria Matilde 60
Maria Micaela 109, 136, 294
Maria Olaya 107
Maria Paula 152, 227, 292
Maria Paula Luz 114
Maria Petra 204
Maria Pilar 247
Maria Polonia 143
Maria Rafaela 31, 232
Maria Ramona 131
Maria Refugia 293
Maria Refugio 257
Maria Resurrecion 125
Maria Reyes 61, 236
Maria Rita 265, 266
Maria Rosa 50, 71, 146, 161, 209, 231
Maria Rufina 293
Maria Serafina 154
Maria Severina 232
Maria Silveria 107
Maria Soledad 109
Maria Trinidad 119
Maria Ygnacia 102, 116, 150, 187, 194, 219, 254
Maria Ygnacia Concepcion 112
Maria Ysabel 276, 280
Maria Ysidora 69
Maria Ysidora Dolores 79
Matias 135
Miguel Angel Dolores 54
Nicolasa 187
Norverto 168
Pablo 132
Pablo Antonio 45
Pedro Antonio 168, 230
Policarpio 173
Santiago 143
Sebastiana Guadalupe 27
Tomas 142, 152
Tomas Jose 84
Tomas Reyes 214
Ygnacia 162
MARTINES
Jose Antonio 304
Juan Jesus 296
Maria Bibiana 92
Maria Concepcion 301
MARTINEZ
Dario Tomasa 67
MARTINEZ (continued)
Jose Santiago 127
Juan Antonio 93
Juana 132
Juana Maria 220
Manuel Dolores Jesus 56
Maria Ascencion 145
Maria Candelaria 97
Maria Rosa 123
MASCAREÑAS
Juana Maria 237
Manuel Antonio 145
Maria Cecilia 281
Maria Desideria 229
Maria Dolores 298
Maria Servula 64
MASSA
Rufina Rafaela 32
MATEO
Antonio 69
MEDINA
Antonio Domingo 155
Antonio Jesus 76, 91
Antonio Jose 259, 271
Fernando 252
Francisco Antonio 86
Jose Buenaventura 237
Jose Eusebio 264
Jose Francisco 289
Jose Julian 253
Jose Manuel 268
Jose Maria 124
Josef Buenabentura 203
Juan 141
Juan Antonio 187
Juan Jesus 241
Juan Jesus Maria 255
Juan Reyes 247, 281
Juana Jesus 157
Maria 128
Maria Candelaria 305
Maria Carmen 127
Maria Dolores 177, 253
Maria Estefana 243
Maria Felipa 167
Maria Gertrudis 241
Maria Guadalupe 197, 283, 299
Maria Jesus 144
Maria Luz 217
Maria Manuela 141, 163, 168, 212, 278
Maria Paula 98
Maria Petra Ysidora 66
Maria Reyes 262
Maria Rosa 166
Maria Rosa Bibiana 100
Maria Serafina 274
Maria Ygnacia 204
Mariano Jesus 209

MEDINA (continued)
Marta 182
Petra Ysidora 66
Ramon 110
Salvador Marcial 222
MERINO
Juan Lorenzo Severino 283
MES
See MAES, MEZ
Francisco 211
Jose Pablo 214
Maria Bibiana 60
MESTAS
Josef Dolores 225
Juan Andres 257
Juan Luis Bertran 211
Juan Vicente 303
Maria Manuela 131, 190
Maria Pascuala 187
MEZ
See MAES, MES
Maria Jesus 204
MIER
Ysabel 135
MIERA
Francisca Xavier 154
Francisco 139
Jose Clemente Bernardo 76
Jose Francisco 120
Maria Albina 268
Maria Catalina 228
Maria Gabriela 91
Maria Guadalupe 112
Maria Josefa 235
Maria Micaela 178
Vicente Higino 130
Ygnacia Atanasia 115
MIRABAL
Barbara 34
Jose Manuel 41
Josef Rafael 31
Juan 286
Juana Dominga 90
Maria Bibiana 249
Maria Manuela 73, 93
Maria Micaela 70
Maria Rosa 49
Maria Santos 41
MIRABALL
Juan Domingo 115
Maria Alvina 150
Maria Clara 99
Maria Jesus 118
Maria Dolores 136
Maria Luz 131
MIRAVAL
Jose Antonio 46
Juan Carmen 81
Maria Josefa 29
MIRAVAL (continued)
Miguel 42
Ygnacio Mariano 36
MIRAVALL
Santiago 108
MO
Stephania 10
MOIGE
Juana Magdalena 20
MOLINA
Maria Dolores 191
MONDRAGON
Anttonio Jose 61
Carlos 170
Geronimo 129
Jesus Maria 182
Jose 137
Jose Domingo 248
Jose Manuel 185
Jose Ubaldo 80
Josef Antonio 176
Juan 122
Juan Antonio 121
Juan Gabriel 120
Juan Manuel 111
Juan Pasqual Ynosencio 255
Juan Reyes 171, 190
Juan Xav 120
Juana 94
Juana Pasquala 163
Lasaro Antonio 206
Manuel Antonio Dolores 54
Maria Catalina 279
Maria Dolores 141, 216
Maria Francisca 117
Maria Gracia 229
Maria Manuela 147, 154
Maria Marta 200
Maria Paula 193
Maria Rosa 169
Maria Teodora Alvina 101
Maria Ygnacia 143, 156
Miguel Vicente 107
Pedro Antonio 203
Santiago 152
Servulo Albino 67
MONTAÑO
Jose Bartolome 238
MONTE
Felipe 139
Hilario 113
Maria Francisca 149
MONTES
See VIGIL
Jesus Maria 263
Jose Cristoval 294
Jose Jesus 287
Maria Juliana 131
Maria Rafaela 277

MONTOLLA
Jesus Maria 304
Maria Estefana 298
MONTOYA
Antonio Seferino 287
Bentura 216
Eusebio 156
Hermenegildo 276
Jesus Maria 196
Jose 137, 290
Jose Antonio 75, 85
Jose Encarncion 108
Jose Francisco 219
Jose Guadalupe 254
Jose Maria Dolores 255
Jose Rafael 97, 122, 130
Jose Tomas 301
Jose Victoriano 98
Juan Antonio 70
Juan Cristobal 166
Juan Cristoval 80
Juan Domingo 191
Juana 90
Juana Pasquala 90
Maria Anttonia 62
Maria Carmen 222
Maria Cruz 291
Maria Dolores 194, 203, 216
Maria Elena 88
Maria Encarnacion 181
Maria Estefana 259
Maria Francisca 121
Maria Guadalupe 167, 268
Maria Hilaria 149
Maria Jesus 186, 270
Maria Juana 79, 99, 222
Maria Lorenza 222
Maria Luz 186
Maria Manuela 136, 203, 212
Maria Manuela Natividad 183
Maria Rita 210
Maria Rosa 114
Maria Salome 237
Maria Soledad 193
Maria Trinidad 69
Miguel Antonio 226
Ramon 125
Vicente 127
MORA
Juana 4
Margarita Rosalia 19
MOYA
Agustin 286
Cayetano Joseph 19
Francisca Maria 19
Juan 164
Maria Anttonia 16
Maria Dolores 98
Maria Soledad 151
MOYA (continued)
Michaela 15
Miguel Francisco 16
Pedro Anttonio 16
MUGUICUY
Lusia 11
MUÑES
Josef Antonio 174
MUÑIS
Jose Andres 303
MUÑIZ
Jose Rafael 154
Maria Ascencion 116
MUÑOS
Maria Soledad 140
MUQUELE
Barbara 14
MURO
Jose Miguel 283
NACHALE
Pablo Cruz 16
NACHO
Lucia Juipte 12
NACHOLA
Christobal 14
NACHULA
Ana Maria 18
Diego Lujan 17
NACHULE
Juan 16
NAPCO
Lusia 10
NAPO
Pasquala 23
NAPOO
Juana 6
NARACHE
Lucia 13
NARANJO
Francisco 263
Geronimo 204
Jacinto 86
Jose Agustin 304
Jose Antonio 37, 141
Jose Rafael 157
Juan Andres 43, 44
Maria Antonia 134
Maria Candelaria 27
Maria Concepcion 222
Maria Dolores 174
Maria Rafaela 31, 247
Micaela 108
NASBEQUEAN
Juana 2
NASTOE
Maria 4
NATURE
Pedro 6

PACHECO (continued)
Pedro Antonio 300
Rosa 85
Salvador 74
Santiago 275
PACHILPA
Juan 20
PACOAGUACHOL
Ana Maria 6
Juana Maria 6
PACTEE
Joseph 20
PADILLA
Agustin 167
Ana Maria 92
Antonio Domingo 119
Antonio Feliz 159
Domingo Antonio 291
Felipe Jesus 191
Francisca 72, 279
Francisco 41, 138, 279
Geronimo 111
Jose Antonio 148
Jose Benito 182
Jose Geronimo 297
Jose Miguel 241
Jose Rafael 230
Jose Ramon 111
Juan de Dios 231, 233
Juan Jesus 104
Juan Santos 184
Juana Marcela 294
Maria Catarina 81
Maria Desideria 229
Maria Dolores 185, 213
Maria Estefana 203, 239
Maria Francisca 89, 243
Maria Geronima 147
Maria Josefa 239
Maria Juliana 191
Maria Lucia 60
Maria Luiza 260
Maria Manuela 221
Maria Nicolasa 291
Maria Polonia 168
Maria Reyes 236
Maria Viviana Candelaria Dolores 51
Pedro 138
Rumaldo 223
PAES
See PAIS, PAYS
Jose Rafael 227
Juan Ramos 73
Maria Refugio 245
PAEZ
Anastasio 151
Jose Miguel 138
Manuel Antonio 161
PAGUE
Lucia 3
PAIS
See PAYS, PAES, PAEZ
Angelina 42
Jose Francisco 191
Jose Gabriel 258
Juan 50
Juan Baptista 201
Juana Maria 202
Maria Encarnacion 218
Maria Luz 182
Maria Paula 197
Maria Soledad 200
Ygnacio Antonio Dolores 57
PAMAC
Maria 13
PAMPAM
Juana 13
PANCOS
Juan 10
PANDO
See VILLALPANDO
Juan Andres 139
Juan Antonio 123, 182
Maria Antonia 156
Maria Ygnacia 291
PAPTOO
Phelipe 5
PAQUAAGUACHEN
Juan Anttonio 2
PAQUEELINO
Francisca Cruz 36
PAQUEMO
See PAAQUEMO, PACENO, PAQUERO
Lucia 1
PAQUEMOTLE
Nicolas 10
PAQUERO
Catalina 7
Lusia 7
PAQUIME
Maria Anttonia 19
PAQUIMUTLUI
Agustina 3
PARLUNA
Ygnacia 46
PASOAGUAQUEAN
Angelina 6
PASPICETA
Luis 2
PASQUA
Francisco 105
PATAA
Getrudis 9
PATAH
Cristtobal 2
PATO
Lusia 11

RIOS (continued)
Pedro Tomas 67
RIVERA
See RIBERA
Francisco 191
Jose Ramon 221
Manuel Rafael 33
RODARTE
Juan Bautista 109
RODRIGUEZ
Maria Antonia 229
Maria Carmen 248
Maria Guadalupe 83
ROLE
Jose Manuel 294
ROMERO
Ana Maria 82, 146, 266
Ana Maria Dolores 53
Andres 103
Antonia Espiritu Santo 208
Antonia Nicolasa 203
Antonia Rosa Dolores 57
Antonio 105
Antonio Aban 206
Antonio Abran 206
Antonio Domingo 92, 285
Antonio Jose 268, 277, 299
Antonio Josef 43
Antonio Rafael 109
Bacilio Antonio 28
Barbara 26, 161
Benigna Juliana 65
Benito 170
Bibiana 143
Buenabentura 211
Buenaventura Dolores 58
Cayetana 129
Clara Rosa 23
Diego 167, 175
Domingo 30
Estevan 183
Eusebio 112
Felipe Jesus 65
Francisca 129, 200
Francisca Dolores 50
Francisco 45, 97, 112, 118, 181, 195, 257
Francisco Antonio 74
Francisco Dolores 52
Geronimo 105, 119, 127, 134, 151, 172, 278
Gregorio Fransisco 27
Higinia Reyes 65
Jose 92, 148, 156, 157
Jose Antonio 71, 94, 104, 118, 120, 134, 139, 163, 197
Jose Antonio Jesus 40
Jose Ascencion 83
Jose Buenaventura 245
ROMERO (continued)
Jose Casimiro 165
Jose Crus 305
Jose Cruz 220, 272
Jose Francisco 74, 115, 214, 264, 290
Jose Jesus 158, 237, 243
Jose Joaquin 190
Jose Manuel 98, 123, 142, 252
Jose Maria 39
Jose Maria Tranquilino 66
Jose Miguel 43, 95, 258, 266
Jose Natividad 242
Jose Pablo 78, 110, 262
Jose Rafael 148, 221, 257, 267
Jose Santiago 28, 283
Jose Santos 298
Jose Tomas 268
Jose Vicente 81
Jose Vicente Cleto 94
Jose Victor 62
Jose Yanuario 63
Jose Ygnacio 80
Josef 34, 199
Josef Antonio 208
Josef Benito 175, 177
Josef Guadalupe 206
Josef Manuel 207
Josef Mariano 30, 40
Josef Rafael 34
Josef Rafel 179
Josef Tomas 197
Josefa 85, 136, 187
Josefa Rafaela 31, 32
Juan 40, 62, 171, 293
Juan Agustin 39
Juan Andres 140
Juan Andres Dolores 54, 59
Juan Antonio 78, 108, 117, 124, 130, 195, 228, 259, 261
Juan Antonio Dolores 59
Juan Antonio Rafael 33
Juan Benito 289
Juan Bentura 278
Juan Buenaventura Dolores 56
Juan Cruz 212, 228
Juan Carmen 104
Juan Domingo 39, 93, 163, 196, 246, 263
Juan Domingo Dolores 51
Juan Geronimo 293
Juan Jesus 48, 193
Juan Jose 74, 146
Juan Jose Dolores 52
Juan Manuel 40
Juan Martin Dolores 52
Juan Miguel 108, 290
Juan Pablo 49, 295
Juan Rafael 33

ROMERO (continued)
Ygnacia 109
Ygnacio Jesus 298
Ylario Jesus 298
Ysabel 40
ROMO
Pablo 39
ROYBAL
Juan Nepomuseno 149
RUBIDU
Maria Juana 286
RUIBAL
Pablo 68
RUIVAL
Maria Seferina 283
SAIS
Maria Ramona 227
Maria Rita 194
SAIZ
Jose Miguel 279
SALA
Juana 6
SALAS
Maria Dolores 224
SALASAR
See ZALASAR
Antonio Jesus 181
Jose Bentura 287
Jose Narsiso 297
Josef Francisco 195
Josef Nicolas 206
Josef Rafael 226
Juan Antonio 306
Juan Manuel 183
Juan Relles 207
Maria Concepcion 300
Maria Dolores 184, 203
Maria Gracia 170
Maria Guadalupe 176
Maria Luz 202
Maria Rufina 294
Maria Serafina 200
Maria Ygnacia 295
Maria Ysabel 237
Miguel 175
Nicolasa 170
Polito 204
Rafaela 194
Ygnacio 177
SALAZAR
See ZALAZAR
Jose Antonio 244
Jose Maria Guadalupe 231
Jose Ramon 276
Juan Chrisostomo 281
Juan Christobal 252
Juan Cruz 291
Juan Domingo 232
Juan Manuel 255
SALAZAR (continued)
Juana Gertrudis 168
Maria Candelaria 149
Maria Guadalupe 209, 245
Maria Luz 210
Maria Manuela 124
Maria Serafina 160
Salvador Nepomuceno 211
SAMORA
See ZAMORA
Dolores 182
Graviel Encarnacion 65
Jesus Maria 228
Jose Manuel 235
Jose Maria 234
Josef Bentura 206
Juan Lorenzo 260
Juana Maria 295
Maria Antonia 194
Maria Magdalena 246
Ylario 181
SAN JUAN
Catarina Dolores 37
Juan Domingo 37
SANBO
Jose Tomas 64
SANCHES
Francisco Estevan 304
Jose Damasio 289
Jose Estevan 71
Jose Magdaleno 66
Jose Santiago 296
Juan Cristoval 296
Maria Dolores 298
Maria Getrudes 70
Maria Juana Guadalupe Dolores 54
Maria Paula 170
Maria Rita 255
Maria Soledad 186
SANCHEZ
Andrea 282
Antonio Josef 199
Estevan Rafel 189
Felipe Santiago Dolores 55
Jose Amador 231
Jose Anttonio 63
Jose Francisco 118, 213
Jose Quirino 252
Jose Santiago 237
Jose Victor 114
Juan de Dios 238
Juan Jesus 278
Juan Pablo 130
Juan Ygnacio 134
Juana Catarina 123
Juana Maria 236
Marcos 151
Maria Antonia 237
Maria Barbara 161

SANCHEZ (continued)
Maria Concepcion Dolores 53
Maria Dolores 196, 277
Maria Gregoria 86
Maria Guertrudis Phelipa 63
Maria Luz 113, 152
Maria Manuela 141, 146
Maria Petra 236
Maria Reyes 101
Maria Rita 117
Maria Rosa 224
Maria Roza 259
Maria Ysabel 78
Pedro Antonio 196
Pedro Ygnacio 189
Ygnacio 138
SANDOBAL
Jose Santana 275
Manuela Balvina 28
Maria Biviana 191
Maria Lucaria 304
Maria Luisa 304
Salvador Antonio 209
SANDOVAL
(torn)lina 282
Andres 30
Antonio 143
Antonio Jose 219, 295
Diego Antonio 32
Dolores 191
Felipe Jesus 232
Jesus Maria 250
Jose Benito 185
Jose Bicente 188
Jose Estanislao 236
Jose Francisco 157, 211, 233
Jose Guadalupe 196
Jose Julian 155
Jose Luciano 300
Jose Mariano Jesus 114
Jose Miguel 100, 290
Jose Rafael 283
Josef Benito 174, 177
Josef Bisente 204
Josef Maria 202
Josef Rafael 204
Juan 134
Juan Agustin 203
Juan Antonio 139
Juan Jose 274
Juan Lucian 300
Juan Maria 237
Juan Trinidad 282
Juana Antonia 266
Juana Chatarina 230
Juana Gertrudis 128, 168
Juana Getrudes 201
Juana Maria 256
Juana Teresa 170
SANDOVAL (continued)
Manuel Antonio 253
Manuel Esquipulas 193
Marcos 124
Maria Antonia 83
Maria Ascencion 158
Maria Candelaria 207, 269
Maria Carmen Romana 257
Maria Encarnacion 282
Maria Gracia 231
Maria Jesus 247
Maria Josefa 157
Maria Juliana 280
Maria Lorenza 75
Maria Luiza 267
Maria Margarita 117
Maria Natividad 245
Maria Paula 269
Maria Refugio 256, 261
Maria Refugio Ygnacia 251
Maria Rita 127
Maria Serafina 69
Maria Soledad 174
Maria Ypolita 281
Nicholas 87
Nicolas Ascencion 87
Teodora 147
SANTANA
Jose Maria Jesus 297
SANTISTEVAN
Juan Jesus 184
SAPATA
See ZAPATA
Antonia 22
SARBÉ
Ana Maria Jesus 231
Maria Ludovina 267
SARVE
Maria Altagracia 293
SASANTIA
Maria Rosa 43
SERNA
See ZERNA
Joachin 36
Manuela 106
Maria 14
Maria Paula 110
SERRANO
Marcelo 61
SERRNA
Josef Antonio 38
Lugarda 42
SIBOLITO
Antonio Maria 232
SILBA
Maria Esquipula 187
Maria Nieves Dolores 59
SILVA
Geronimo 88

SILVA (continued)
Jacinta 75
Jesus Maria 205
Jose Jesus 110
Jose Pablo 197
Josef Rafael 197
Juan Antonio 78, 90
Juan Jesus 274
Juana Maria 240
Juana Martina 120
Juana Paula 102
Maria Antonia 208
Maria Dominga 235
Maria Ludovina 250
Maria Manuela 113
Maria Paula Reyes 269
Maria Romualda 282
Maria Rosalia 104
Maria Ursula 67
SISNEROS
See CISNEROS
Maria Carmen 169
Maria Josefa 176
Maria Micaela Ypolita 63
Rafael 238
SOASO
Maria Dolores 175
SOAZO
Martin 184
SOLANO
Antonio Jose Toribio 272
Juan Ygnacio 207
Maria Jesus 251
Maria Ygnacia 252
SUASO
See ZUASO, ZUAZO
Ana Maria 243
Francisco Enrriques 66
Juan 103
Maria Concepcion 87
Maria Dolores 180
Maria Francisca 249
Maria Gertrudis 88
Maria Guadalupe 297
Maria Lucia 201
Maria Rossa 62
Maria Vicenta 298
Santiago 50
SUAZO
Juan Jose Dolores 51
Maria Dolores 226
Maria Guadalupe 235
Paula 223
SUCUE
Juana 11
SUESO
Jose Martin 59
SUISPCHAL
Maria 14
SULE
Maria Margarita 41
SUR
Juan Nepomuceno 289
TAÂ
Roque 9
TACHIVE
Magdalena 22
TACOLI
Ynes 11
TACOLINA
Maria Rossa 13
TAFOLLA
Clara Jesus 222
Maria Clara 222
Maria Ygnacia 305
Miguel Mateo 66
Pedro Patricio 217
TAFOYA
Bernabel 169
Bernardo 288
Cipriano 122
Francisca 44
Jose Antonio 192
Jose Concepcion 109
Jose Dolores 202
Jose Gregorio 136
Jose Maria Dolores 271
Jose Miguel 71, 166
Jose Rafael 147, 282
Josef Casarias 196
Josef Pablo 196
Josefa Enrique 127
Juan 132
Juan Christobal 248
Juan de Dios 290
Juan Jesus 110, 249
Juan Ysidro 245
Juana Catarina 103
Juana Maria 289
Juana Paula 122
Leonardo 223
Manuel Antonio 158
Margarita 273
Maria 138
Maria Agustina 153
Maria Antonia 165, 274
Maria Carmen 181
Maria Cencion 196
Maria Dolores 179, 224, 234
Maria Gracia 266
Maria Jesus 81, 243
Maria Josefa 77
Maria Juana 171
Maria Luz 267
Maria Marcelina 225
Maria Rafaela 154
Maria Ramona 251
Maria Resurrecton 137

TAFOYA (continued)
Maria Soledad 172, 196
Maria Veronica 151
Maria Ygnacia 248, 263
Maria Ysabel 259
Miguel Antonio 107
Rafael 199
Salvador Raymundo 121
Severino 195
TAGUA
Lazaro 3
TALACHE
Maria Catalina 213
TANE
Geronima 47
Juan Jose 43
TAO
Sebastian 5
TAOÔ
Miguel 10
TAQUE
Matias 9
TAQUEO
Cristobal 6
TAU
Maria Josefa 50
TAYA
Diego 7
TAYALA
Josefa 42
TECOA
Alfonso 116
Evaristo Santos 67
Jose Antonio 166
Jose Anttonio 60
Juan Pablo 50
Lucia 44
Maria Manuela 82
TEGUA
Maria Rosa 15
TENORIO
Buenabentura 274
Felipe 133
Francisco 110
Jose Rafael 153
Jose Santiago 110
Juan Cristoval 148
Juana Josefa 175
Maria Jesus 120
Maria Teresa 94
Venancio 126
TENORIO de ALBA
Miguel 2
THENORIO
Isabel 20
THENORIO de ALVA
Marcial Tadeo 18
TIA
Juana Catarina 141
TIO
Juana 104
Manuel 98
TLACAT
Maria Rosa 14
TLEQUE
Ana 5
Jeronimo 8
TOASQUISSAN
Juan 4
TOCHOLA
Maria 6
TOPIA
Domingo 18
TOLIA
Juana 3
TOPE
Juana 12
TORJUIRI
Lusia 11
TORRES
Antonio Jose 126
Jose Francisco 307
Jose Jesus 285
Jose Manuel 130
Jose Tranquilino 239
Manuel 227
Maria Encarnacion 162
Maria Francisca 259
Maria Josefa 226
Maria Manuela 190
Mariana 146
Mariano Reyes 113
Micaela Dolores 37
Pedro 179
Santiago 281
Thomas 254
Vicente 137
TRUGILLO
Estefana 306
Jose Dolores 306
Juan Nicolas 299
Maria Cruz Antonia 67
Maria Pelegrina 286
Maria Tomasa 306
Micaela 29
TRUJILLO
Antonio Alexandro 277
Antonio Jose 278
Antonio Josef 182
Bentura 225
Bisente 195
Buenaventura 225
Demetrio Antonio 280
Josef 198
Juan Estevan 69
Juana Rafela 188
Maria Carmen 225
Maria Clara Elena 194

VALERIO
Maria Angela 131
VALLEGOS
Maria Dolores 148
VALLEJOS
Antonio Jose 145
Jose Cruz 150
Jose Rafael 117
Juan Bautista 159
Juana Gertrudis 145
Leonarda 131
Maria Josefa 167
VALLE
See BALLE
Jose Antonio 282
VALLOS
Jose Antonio 283
VALVERDE
Juan Nepomuseno 241
Pedro Antonio 138
VARELA
See BARELA
Gregorio Jesus 128
Jose Antonio 126
Jose Dolores 288
Jose Francisco 144
Jose Franco 154
Jose Gabriel 142
Jose Mathias 248
Juan Cristoval Cruz 73
Juan Francisco 251
Juan Nepomuceno 243
Manuel Antonio 139
Maria Cruz 103
Maria Dolores 92
Maria Faustina 123
Maria Guadalupe 251
Maria Josefa 116
Maria Magdalena 274
Maria Manuela Antonia 269
Maria Ramona 253
Maria Rosa 260
Matias 124
Pedro Antonio 113
Ramona Jesus 89
VARGAS
See BARGAS
Jose 104, 145
Jose Antonio 91
Jose Domingo 218
Jose Francisco 137
Jose Gregorio 298
Jose Pablo 81
Jose Ramon 84, 160
Jose Vicente 122
Julian 121
Maria Francisca 135
Maria Getrudes 73
Maria Rita 92
VARGAS (continued)
Miguel Ramos 245
Pedro Antonio 268
VARRIGON
Juana 5
VASQUEZ
See BASQUEZ, BASQUES
Juan Albino 210
VAZQUES
Maria Dolores 158
VEGIL
Antonia Teresa 136
Antonio 151
Antonio Jose Sevastian 68
Bernardo 154
Ermenegilda Sotera 65
Jose Cruz 284
Jose Domingo 153
Jose Encarncion 288
Jose Ermenegildo Dolores 57
Jose Francisco 44, 283
Jose Rafael 143
Jose Santiago 285
Josefa 162
Juan Carlos 140
Juan Cruz 145
Juan Jose 287
Juan Lorenzo 151
Juan Rafael 165
Juan Ramon Cruz 66
Maria 132
Maria Albina 162
Maria Bentura 78
Maria Bibiana Rosa 64
Maria Dolores 168
Maria Josefa 168
Maria Josefa Dolores 57
Maria Juana 143
Maria Luz 133, 137
Maria Manuela Dolores 54
Maria Micaela Dolores 56
Maria Paula 156
Maria Trinidad Dolores 59
Matias 159
Ysidora 158
VEJIL
See BEJIL
Antonio Jose 126
Feliciana 78
Jesus 185
Jose Atanasio 83
Jose Francisco 117
Jose Manuel 119
Jose Mariano 80
Jose Rafael 100
Jose Ramon 111
Juan Christoval 44
Juan Cristoval 95
Juana Maria 106

ZAMORA (continued)
Maria Dolores 185
Maria Eustaquia Jesus 263
Maria Paula 264
Maria Rosa 120
Maria Ygnacia 139
Rosalia 271
Santiago 48
Tomasa 86
ZAPATA
See SAPATA
Domingo 20
ZERNA
See SERNA
Maria 21
ZUASO
See SUASO, ZUAZO
Domingo 147, 167
Francisca 129
Francisco 138
Geronimo 160
Jose Maria 135
Josefa 137
Juan Carmen 146
Maria Dolores 160, 162
Mariano 126
Miguel 134
Paula 127
Rosa 115
ZUAZO
See SUASO, ZUASO
Juan Domingo 292
Maria Theodora 272

INDEX of PARENTS

It is important to look for alternate spellings of both surnames and given names. Names may appear more than one time on a page. Many names were abbreviated in the original records. They have been spelled out in this index. For the most part, prepositions have not been included in this index, but if they were present in the original record, they will be found in the manuscript.

ARCHULETA
Antonio 88, 101, 119, 131, 134, 148, 149, 157, 165, 169, 176, 180, 183, 201, 206, 234, 295
Antonio Casimiro 118
Antonio Jose 147, 161
Antonio Rafael 296
Clemente 199
Damian 161, 190
Diego 304
Francisco 163
Gertrudis 233, 256, 274, 293
Honorato 221
Jesus 210, 238, 307
Jose Antonio 52
Jose Jesus 261
Jose Pablo 273
Josefa 176, 185, 247
Juan 205
Juan Domingo 101
Julian 116, 133, 137, 164, 195, 226, 235, 243, 265, 284
Loreta 183
Loreto 232
Luisa 122, 140, 165
Manuel 223, 241, 265
Manuel Gregorio 119
Marcos 156, 196, 216, 225, 260
Maria 140, 170, 227
Maria Antonia 185
Maria Cruz 211
Maria Encarnacion 141, 154, 179
Maria Gertrudis 92
Maria Josefa 281
Maria Luisa 130, 154
Maria Manuela 259
Maria Rafaela 299
Maria Ygnacia 213, 245, 264
Norato 241
Novato 307
Pablo 85, 90, 100, 126, 180
Rita 143, 161
Rosa 231
Serafina 186
Ygnacia 229
ARELLANO
Domingo 287
Juan Domingo 211, 260
Juan Ricardo 248
Maria Manuela 296
Maria Rosa 279
Rafaela 97
Ramon 154, 219, 226, 250, 296
Ricardo 207, 210
AREYANO
Ramon 199
ARGUELLO
Ana 83
Francisco 105, 252
ARGUELLO (continued)
Jose Concepcion 242
Juan 180, 199
Maria Concepcion 158
Ysidro 72, 91, 107
ARGUEYO
Dolores 292
ARMARAN
Juan 13
ARMENTA
Ana Maria 171, 250, 296
Anamaria 199, 219, 226
Antonio 244
Atanacia 259
Atanasia 277
Francisca 40, 44, 52, 57, 83, 109
Francisco 152
Guadalupe 290
Maria Atanacia 306
Maria Francisca 66, 93
Simon 82, 88, 97, 107, 116, 124, 140
Ygnacio 292
ARMENTIA
Ana Maria 154
ARMIJO
Alfonso 236
Andres 177
Antonio 163
Antonio Eustaquio 147, 228
Gregoria 109, 143, 189
Jose 72, 83
Josefa 84, 173
Juan Miguel 33
Manuel 238, 267, 284
Manuela 122
Maria Gregoria 100
Maria Josefa 84
Maria Ynes 166
Paula 199, 231
Santiago 117, 157, 191, 206, 245
Ynes 76, 83, 103
ARMOSA
Francisco 19
AROLLOS
Maria 206
ARORRO
Maria Catalina 180
ARRIETA
Ana Maria 266
Anamaria 290
ARROLLO
Catarina 157
ARROYO
See ARORRO
Catarina 169, 148
ARROYOS
Catarina 234

ATÁ
See ATTA
Salvador 14
ATENCIO
Bicente 67
Juan Antonio 301
ATENSIO
Marta 150
Vicente 86, 99
Visente 75
ATOMA
Lasaro 6
ATOQUE
Lasaro 9
ATTA
See ATÁ
Salbador 5
AVILA
See ABILA
Rafael 146, 160
Santiago 167
Usevio 227
AYO
Rafaela 263
AZA
Diego 13
Juan 12
BACA
See VACA
Bibiana 131, 142
Biviana 162, 191
Catarina 108, 121, 139
Dorotea 90, 103, 126, 140, 159, 197, 241
Esteban 124, 140, 151, 168, 234
Estevan 173
Jose Pablo 105
Juana 144
Juana Maria 269
Lorenso 230
Manuel 111, 125, 134, 145, 153, 164
Maria Rita 217, 218
Micaela 84, 98
Salvador 151, 166, 175, 188, 219
Soledad 298
BALDES
See VALDES
Anamaria 188
Bentura 189
Felipe 207
Francisco 188
Gregoria 288
Juan 142, 192, 198, 206
Juan Manuel 226
Maria 191
Maria Antonia 206
Maria Dolores 205
Maria Jesus 175, 179
BALDEZ
See VALDEZ
Manuela 200
Maria 171, 179, 196
Maria Antonia 198
Rosalia 184
BALDONADO
See MALDONADO
Jose Manuel 198
BALERIO
See VALERIO
Juliana 180, 207
BALLE
See VALLE
Antonio Jose 210
BALLEJOS
See VALLEJOS, VALLEGOS
Ana Maria 75
Catarina 198
Maria Gertrudis 102
BAPAONA
Santiago 65
BARBERO
Juana 204
BARELA
See VARELA
Dolores 208
Jose 182
Jose Candelaria 222
Jose Candelario 286
Jose Manuel 190
Josef 197, 204
Josef Candelario 227
Juan 178, 189, 224
Juana 101, 187
Manuel 29
Manuela 226
Margarita 218
Maria 181, 207
Maria Antonia 295
Maria Dolores 174, 241, 292
Maria Manuela 195
Maria Paula 179, 192
Maria Teodora 215
Maria Ygnacia 211
Miguel 155, 172, 191, 204, 214, 288
Ramona 170
Ynasia 192
BARGAS
See VARGAS
Estevan 72, 107
Getrudes 223
Marcelo 67
Rita 201
BARJAS
Maurilo 173
BAROS
Ra(torn) 303

BARRERA
Juan Jose 303
BASQUES
(torn) 287
BASQUEZ
See VASQUEZ, VAZQUES
Antonio 192, 267
Juan Jose 230, 256
BAZQUEZ
See VAZQUES
(n.n.) 303
BEEPAI
Diego 13
BEITA
See VEITA
Diego 279
BEITIA
See VEITIA, BEYTIA, VEITA, BEYTA
Jose Ygnacio 110, 133
Jose Ygnasio 120
Josefa 151
Juan Antonio 87
Rita 160
Simona 130
Teodora 112, 123, 137, 158
BEJIL
See VEJIL, VEGIL, MONTES, MONTES BEJIL
Amador 172, 198
Ana Maria 171
Ana Teresa 203
Anamaria 208
Antonio 192
Carlos 59
Dolores 180
Elena 182
Esmeregilda 191
Faustin 176
Francisca 203
Francisco 175, 190, 199, 202
Getrudes 223
Jabiela 172
Josef Francisco 169
Josefa 181, 200, 204
Juan 176, 185, 205
Juan Cristoval 173, 186, 200
Juan Jesus 201, 202
Juan Ygnacio 63, 230
Maria 175, 176, 183, 189, 190
Maria Antonia 88
Maria Getrudez 172
Maria Josefa 172
Maria Luisa 176, 202
Maria Soledad 198, 206
Matias 187, 197
Meregilda 230
Pasquala 63
Pedro 172, 200
Rafael 202, 225, 230
BEJIL (continued)
Rafel 170, 183
Ramon 179, 207
Rosa 223
Soledad 170, 181, 192, 194, 226
Teresa 199
Trenidad 195, 225
Xaviela 187
Ygnacio 179
Ysabel 195
Ysavel 179
BELASQUEZ
See VELASQUES, VELASQUEZ
Angela 217, 233
BELMONTE
Antonio 171
BENABIDES
Antonio 199
Francisca 203
Maria Alverta 176
Pablo 219
BENABIDEZ
Antonio Josef 177
BENAVIDES
See VENAVIDES
Alberta 114
Alverta 67
Dolores 150
Jose 160
Josefa 150, 153
Juan 40
Juana 49, 82, 100, 137, 161
Manuel 158
Mariana 76
Pablo 244
BENAVIDEZ
Francisca Ynez 41
BERNAL
See VERNAL
Jose 143, 147
Felipe 215, 225, 265
Francisca 196, 225, 248
Pedro 229, 247, 305
Rafael 285
BESSACHORE
Maria 4
BEYTA
Teodora 227
BEYTIA
See BEITIA, VEITIA, BEITA, VEITA
Rita 155
Teodora 144
BIGIL
See VIGIL
Jose Amador 229
Maria Guadalupe 230
Maria Micaela 229
Pedro 229

BIJIL
See VIJIL
Gabriela 201
Jose Cruz 276
Maria Guadalupe 208
BILLA
Juana 181
BLANCHARD
Antonio 304
BLEA
Antonio 69, 76, 87, 100, 108, 123, 133, 189
Encarnacion 184, 209
Joaquin 173, 193
Jose Joaquin 63, 68, 77, 90, 118
Josef Juaquin 31
Maria 153
Maria Encarnacion 198, 247, 261
Maria Lus 78
Maria Luz 93, 110
Maria Nasarena 133, 149
Maria Rosario 228, 248
Nasarena 167
BOCON
Santiago 41
BORICA
Jose Antonio 95, 117
BORIDA
Jose Antonio 86
BORREGO
Cristoval 181, 188
Juan Christoval 194
Juan Cristobal 212
Nateresa 196
Pablo 217, 233, 258
BOYO
Domingo 48
BRISOL
Bautista 284
BRITA
Madalena 182
Maria Magdalena 178
BRITO
Francisco 50, 57, 77, 99, 114, 181
Jose 106, 120
Josefa 226
Juan Francisco 65, 73
Magdalena 135, 148, 162, 247
Maria 204, 270
Maria Micaela 240
Maria Rita 301
Micaela 167, 234
Miquela 197, 223
BRUNO
Antonio 66
BUENA
Francisca 257
Maria Francisca 215
BUENO
Antonia 126, 143
Antonio 72, 82, 105, 118, 132, 141, 157, 184
Fernanda 183, 270
Francisca 265
Josefa 244
Juan 144
Juan Eugenio 123, 137, 158, 248
Juan Ugenio 227
Juana Antonia 157
Maria 174
Maria Francisca 245
Maria Luz 237
Maria Manuela 237, 281, 298
Maria Ygnacia 75, 114, 127, 143, 157, 185
Mateo 167, 172, 181, 200, 204, 205
Matheo 242
Pedro 101, 105, 112, 122, 160
Ygnacia 87, 100
BUENO PANDO
Antonio 55
BUSTOS
Margarita 189
Maria 174
BUTIERRES
See GUTIERRES
Jose Rafael 289
Juana Maria 173
BUTIERREZ
Maria 196
CAÀN
Bernarda 55
CABPUELA
Anttonio 11
CACHANA
Ana Maria 43
Juan Andres 263
CACHÊ
Maria Antonia 49
CACHO
Antonio 279
CACILLAS
See CASIAS, CASILLAS
Juana Maria 306
CAFLALA
Anttonio 19
CAGUI
Geronima 9
CAIAJE
Estevan 6
CAIGUA
Jose 87
Jose Manuel 55
Juan Domingo 102
CALA
Anttonio 8

CALFIALU
Antonio 23
CALO
Antonio 13
CAMAGER
Lucia 12
CAMARGO
Jose Maria 94
CAMNATE
Maria 10
CAMPBELL
Juan 305
CAMPOS
Matiana 293
CANA
Ignasia 62
CANBAY
Josefa 47
CANNABE
Maria 1
CANNATE
Maria 7
CANO
Francisco 258
Maria Ygnacia 42, 47
Ygnacia 34, 74
CAÓ
Jose Antonio 57
CAOS
Juan Antonio 139
CAPCHO
Angelina 5
Maria 10
CAPCHOLE
Maria 10
CAPOALA
Antonio 8
CAPSA
Angelina 12
CAPTESO
Juan 5
CAQUE
Geronima 1
CAQUI
Geronima 6, 15
CARGUEL
Maria 305
CARIER
Anastasio 279
CASADO
Francisco 103
CASADOS
Andrea 182
Dolores 147
Josefa 129
Juan Antonio 108, 121, 173, 194, 225
Manuela 111, 125, 134, 145, 153, 164
CASADOS (continued)
Maria 180, 187, 192, 193, 224
Maria Gertrudis 307
Maria Jesus 300
Maria Josefa 135, 146
CASAUS
Gertrudis 238
Hermenegilda 252, 272
Juan Antonio 251
Juana Getrudis 210
Maria 231
Maria Jesus 247
Maria Gertrudis 261
CASIAS
Maria Francisca 256
CASILLAS
See CACILLAS
Bartolo 182
Bartolome 142, 158, 233, 266, 282, 296
Bernardo 85, 92, 116, 130, 146, 156, 268
Christobal 203, 235
Cristobal 132, 246, 270
Cristoval 166
Fernando 230
Jose 92
Jose Lino 109, 115, 130
Maria Rafaela 139
Micaela 249
Rafaela 206, 235
Rafela 182
CASSILLAS
Fernando 201
CATAJE
Phelipa 75
CATHOTLE
Anttonio 4
CATUFE
Juan Domingo 70
Rafaela 246
CATUGA
Maria Rosa 152
CATUGE
Rosa 165
CATUJE
Domingo 28
Maria Rosa 101
CAYGUA
Domingo 133
Santiago 265
CENA
See SENA
Juana Maria 306
CENTENO
Josepha 72
Josefa 83
Maria Antonia 114, 142

CEQUE
Geronimo 23
CHABES
See CHAVES
Blas 214
Concepcion Mariana 222
Juan Cristoval 220
Luis 178
Maria Antonia 220
Maria Manuela 217
Maria Ygnacia 212
CHACON
Fernando 87, 98
Guadalupe 98
Jose Pablo 299
Maria 253
CHAFALOTE
Domingo 125
Jose Antonio 104
Maria Rosa 129
CHAGIO
Catharina 12
CHAGUA
Jose Antonio 45
CHALLO
Pedro 289
CHALO
Micaela 5
CHALPABAC
Lucia 22
CHAMA
Gertrudis 116, 162
CHANDAGO
Anttonio 3
CHARVÉS
Jose Manuel 236
CHARVET
Jose 262
CHATO
Micaela 9
CHAVACANO
Paula 102
CHAVES
See CHABES
(n.n.) 97
Ana Maria 51
Anne Maria 60
Antonio 269
Antonio Domingo 118
Blas 191, 223, 251, 265
Candelaria 105, 161
Concepcion 167, 290
Domingo 109, 128, 144, 155
Francisca 36
Gertrudis 159
Guadalupe 306
Jose Maria 65, 78, 110, 121, 138, 160
Josef Maria 176
CHAVES (continued)
Juan 108, 123
Juan Agustin 186
Juan Christoval 250
Juan Manuel 204
Juan Nepomoceno 68, 79, 94, 166
Juana 154, 292
Julian 164, 177, 188, 243
Loreto 275, 277
Lucia 138, 159, 167
Luciana 270
Luis 156, 190
Luis Manuel 43, 61
Lusiana 183
Luys 51
Manuel 56
Manuel Antonio 47
Manuela 286
Maria 100, 107, 250
Maria Antonia 240
Maria Candelaria 154, 276
Maria Encarnacion 188, 305
Maria Guadalupe 275
Maria Micaela 231
Maria Soledad 268
Maria Teodora 186
Maria Ygnacia 31, 68, 128, 139, 247, 290, 298
Maria Ynes 260
Pablo 259
Polonia 149, 165
Soledad 279
Ygnacia 63, 77
Ynes 223
CHAVEZ
Dolores 225
Jose Manuel 254
Juan 198, 224
Juan Agustin 204
Juan Nepumoceno 89
Julian 198
Luciana 193, 203
Maria 203, 207
Maria Teodora 255
Teodora 198, 227
CHAYA
Antonia 101
CHAYO
Cristoval 157, 168
Mariano 59
CHEACHA
Ana 1
CHEACHO
Maria 4
CHELE
Anttonio 17
CHENDA
Diego 5

CORTES (continued)
Mariano 89
Pablo 149, 167, 239, 264, 273, 286
Paulin 113, 128, 135, 157, 191, 202, 248, 272
Sarafina 109, 130
Veronica 60, 68, 82, 93, 111
Ygnacia 294
Ysabel 232, 239, 280
Ysavel 227
CORTEZ
Baptista 194
Cruz 81, 197
Josef Maria 204
Josef Miguel 206
Juan Bautista 169
Manuel 228
Maria Ysavel 194
CRESPIN
Jose 266
Jose Ascencion 219
CRUS
Antonio Casimiro 103
Josef Mariano 180
CRUTATA
Antonio 12
CRUZ
Alexo 84, 115, 132, 138, 163
Antonia 221
Dolores 201, 212
Domingo 244
Felipe 296
Francisco 188, 200, 230, 232, 272, 291
Jose 122, 130, 154, 211, 245, 255, 287
Josef 207
Josefa 86
Lorenza 284
Manuel 184
Maria 122, 130, 136
Maria Antonia 248
Maria Lorenza 203
Mariano 113, 125, 133, 147, 162, 281, 287
Mariano Antonio 100
Pedro 126
Veronica 223
CUALÒ
Ysabel 74
CUENPAER
Maria 36
CUERVITO
Andres 266
CUIELMAGUEL
Maria 9
CUINTLAQUGAN
Lusia 11
CUMANCHITO
Juan Antonio 229
CUNTCHE
Juana 14
CUYŨ
Santiago 46
CUYUCHULI
Micaela 46
CUYULCHULI
Micaela 50
CUYUSULI
Micaela 42
D(torn)
Maria 303
DEL NORTE
Antonio 165
DEL RIO
See DELRIO, RIO
Alonso 39
Antonio 59
Juan Antonio 40
Juan Domingo 38, 54
Lucia 38
Maria 90
Maria Antonia 51
Micaela 41, 54
Santiago 53
DEL RYO
See RIYO, RILLO
Santiago 58
Teodora 59
DELGADO
Francisca 271
Jose Antonio 44, 52
Jose Anttonio 60
Juan Luiz 61
Luis 35, 42, 49, 76, 89
Manuela 86
Maria Antonia 158
Maria Guadalupe 211
Maria Rosa 194, 246
Maria Victoria 125
Maria Vitoria 180
Paula 131
Victoria 133
DELRIO
See DEL RIO, RIO, RIYO, RILLO
Jose Francisco 46
DOMINGES
Juana 190
DOMINGO
Juan 28, 29, 34-36, 44-46, 48, 49, 60, 63, 67
DOMINGUES
Joseph 23
Manuelita 117
DOMINGUEZ
Diego 2
Maria Soledad 249

DON JUAN
  Lucia 45
DURAN
  Agustin 236
  Antonia Rosalia 217, 243
  Antonio 178, 198, 255, 267, 298
  Ascencion 112
  Bentura 282
  Bernardo 251, 263, 272
  Buenabentura 268
  Candelaria 109, 118, 128, 144, 155
  Carmen 295
  Dominga 99
  Domingo 210, 237, 264, 305
  Francisca 22, 94
  Francisco 38, 49, 52, 56, 73, 76, 214
  Fransisca 24
  Gertrudis 248
  Getrudis 284
  Gregorio 171, 228, 242, 268, 285
  Guadalupe 64, 84, 115, 132, 163, 292
  Joaquina 225
  Jose 46, 65, 236
  Jose Antonio 110, 126
  Jose Francisco 215, 266
  Jose Rafael 159
  Joseph 21
  Juan 58, 136, 158
  Juan Andres 108, 119, 192
  Juan Antonio 33, 64, 81, 92, 114, 119, 144, 157, 185, 228
  Juan Cristobal 305
  Juan Domingo 102
  Juan Francisco 201
  Juan Gabriel 202
  Juan Jesus 243, 257
  Juan Jose 245
  Juan Nepomuceno 62, 221, 239, 262
  Juan Nicolas 109, 118, 129, 140, 150, 166, 173
  Juan Pablo 236, 269
  Juan Ygnacio 68
  Juana 108, 180
  Juaquina 182, 195
  Lorenza 216
  Lucia 112
  Manuel 110, 127
  Manuela 68, 85, 162, 165, 205
  Marcos 91
  Maria 16, 18, 24, 25, 32, 38, 138, 154, 197, 255, 260
  Maria Antonia 214, 249, 262
  Maria Carmen 214, 234
  Maria Dolores 218, 251, 273
  Maria Gertrudis 237, 268, 300
DURAN (continued)
  Maria Guadalupe 208
  Maria Joaquina 260
  Maria Josefa 201, 223
  Maria Luz 238
  Maria Manuela 178
  Maria Rosa 169, 202
  Maria Rosalia 174, 192
  Micaela 135
  Miguel 150
  Nicolas 94, 101
  Pablo 74, 80, 98, 106, 115, 123, 131, 132, 136, 143, 149, 164, 175, 179, 196, 216
  Pablo Jesus 68
  Pedro Antonio 296
  Pedro Mauricio 299
  Pedro Ygnacio 103, 114
  Rafael 240
  Rafel 169
  Rosa 132, 266, 288, 292
  Rosalia 132, 147, 202, 263
  Salvador 91, 121, 133
  Soledad 115, 126, 133, 137, 145, 162
  Ygnacio 55, 61, 80, 91, 134, 153
DURAN y CHAVES
  Juan Nepomuseno 62
DURANA
  Antonia 253
EBALOLA
  Maria 1
ECOI
  Mariana 5
EELUCLI
  Diego 18
ELPIANCHORE
  Maria 3
EME
  Juna 7
EPATLOL
  Maria 5
EQUE
  Maria 14
EQUEI
  Maria 2
ERRERA
  See HERRERA
  Andres 228
  Candelaria 225, 265
  Jose 231
  Maria Candelaria 247
  Nicolas 205
  Paula 187
  Pedro 273
ESCOYENS
  Ysabel 210
ESPALIN
  Jose (torn) 280

ESPINOSA
  Encarnacion 80, 101, 111, 121, 193, 224
  Felipe 197, 211, 247
  Gabriela 275, 277
  Jose Antonio 111, 124, 159, 165, 232, 262
  Jose Anttonio 62
  Jose Eulogio 178
  Jose Rafael 269
  Josefa 88, 283
  Juan Antonio 129
  Juan Jesus 203
  Juan Ygnacio 183, 192
  Juana 157
  Juana Teresa 141
  Lorenza 234
  Lucia 65, 97
  Margarita 159
  Maria Encarnacion 54, 170, 259, 285
  Maria Josefa 114
  Maria Luz 122, 129, 143
  Maria Manuela 305
  Maria Reyes 223
  Rafael 279, 293
  Santiago 284
  Ygnacia 135, 148, 166
ESPINOSA VELASQUEZ
  Encarnacion 104
ESPINOSSA
  Josefa 62
ESPINOZA
  Encarnacion 61
ESQUIBEL
  Maria Candelaria 222
ESQUIBELA
  Maria Candelaria 304
ESQUIÑE
  Maria 65
EUQEDVEL
  Maria Josefa 65
EXARVE
  Josef 187
FAGILACELMEC
  Geronimo 43
FANFAN
  Francisco 17
FERNANDES
  See FRERNANDES
  Biviana 207
  Clara 66
  Francisca 289
  Jose Mariano 81
  Juan Domingo 174, 184
  Maria 91, 169
  Maria Lus 180
  Maria Reyes 92
  Maria Ysavel 179
FERNANDES (continued)
  Nicomeda 91, 173
  Viviana 272
  Ysavel 226
FERNANDEZ
  Antonio 51
  Clara 78, 83, 89, 158
  Domingo 130, 144
  Encarnacion 215
  Francisco 214, 262
  Jesus 195
  Jose Mariano 91, 104, 152, 253
  Josefa 212, 225
  Juan Domingo 161, 230
  Juan Jesus 139, 171
  Juan Jose 155
  Manuel 251, 264, 278
  Maria 73, 135, 142, 205, 232
  Maria Clara 54, 59
  Maria Luz 159, 241, 274, 283
  Maria Nicomedes 145
  Maria Reyes 99, 122
  Maria Ylaria 234
  Nicomeda 81, 104, 122, 137, 160
  Pedro 142, 178
  Ysabel 285
FERNANDIS
  Francisco 253
  Maria Biviana 254
  Ysabel 254
FERNANDO
  Juan Antonio 189
FIALUCHALMA
  Juan Domingo 47
FIASAY
  Maria Antonia 45
FLORA CHACHULE
  Ana 32
FLORES
  Martin 90, 115, 124, 125, 132, 159, 227, 239, 267
FLOREZ
  Martin 215
FRANFAEN
  Maria Josefa 31
FRERNANDES
  See FERNANDES
  Nicomeda 67
FRESQUES
  Antonio 289
  Barbara 30
FRESQUIS
  Antonio 42, 47, 53, 212, 242
  Blas 115
  Juan 162, 178, 205, 255
  Juan Antonio 261, 306
  Juan Lorenso 54
  Juan Ysidro 178
  Manuela 44, 49, 91, 113

GARCIA (continued)
Ramon 280
Salvador 284
Tomasa 138, 202
Toribio 171, 174
Vicente 242
Victoria 132
Xavier 282
Ygnacia 287
Yldefonso 188
GARDUÑO
Antonio Jose 183
GARSIA
See GARCIA
Fransisca 27
GARZIA
See GARCIA
Francisca 30
GAVALDON
See GABALDON
Antonia Ros. 110
Antonia Rosa 126
Dolores 202
Josef Manuel 202
Manuel 228
GAVAN
Felipe 1
GAVILAN
See GABILAN
Encarnacion 74
Jose 84, 95
Jose Antonio 68, 73, 129
Josefa 189
Juan Andres 45, 91, 113
Manuela 58, 226
Maria 48, 56, 74
Maria Antonia 123
Maria Luz 94
Pablo 1
GEAQUILPA
Juana 13
GELLA
Maria 13
GENACHULE
Lucia 12
GIELNUACHA
Francisco 45
GIGUACHAPO
Antonio 15
GLUPE
Diego 15
GOMA
Antonia 52
GOMES
Antonio 175, 289
Gertrudis 295
Jose Antonio 187
Juan 42, 45
Juan Antonio Juan 41
GOMES (continued)
Juan Anttonio 61
Juan Jose Manuel 304
Juana 68, 74, 194
Lucia 40, 75
Manuela 289
Manuela Manuela 29
Maria 38, 44, 49, 67
Maria Consecion 173
Pablo 39, 45
Pedro 69
Ygnacia 307
GOMEZ
Andres 20
Antonio 146, 155, 163, 185, 197, 215, 236, 262
Ascencion 153
Francisco 101, 112, 209, 222, 236, 245, 246, 260
Jose 87, 91, 99, 251
Jose Antonia 78
Josef 111
Juan 33, 75, 79, 94, 122, 216, 250, 261
Juan Antonio 188
Juana 38, 55, 82, 104, 263, 212
Juana Maria 33
Juliana 130
Lucia 36, 55, 59, 71, 85, 86
Maria 54
Maria Antonia 58
Maria Asencion 194
Maria Juana 57
Maria Luz 221
Maria Rosa 144
Matheo 232
Pablo 33, 35, 50, 59
Pedro 89, 185
Santiago 275
Tomaz 27
GONSALES
Ana Teresa 287
Antonia 199
Antonio 190, 224, 286, 307
Biterbo 205
Candelaria 190
Dolores 298
Domingo 292
Estefana 293
Francisco 285
Gertrudes 288
Gertrudis 287
Joaquin 297
Jose 46
Jose Antonio 50
Jose Miguel 56, 297
Jose Ygnacio 299
Jose Ynes 66
Josef Antonio 40

GONZALEZ (continued)
Rosalia 88, 103
Salvador 139, 282
Santiago 71, 109, 124, 125, 139, 232, 267
Viterbo 303
Ygnacia 112
Ygnacio 212, 218
Ysabel 110
GONZALEZ ROMERO
Teodora 119
GRIJALBA
Luziano 215
GUAGUACHENE
Maria 13
GUAGUACHORA
Maria 13
GUALASI
Magdalena 9
GUALASSE
Magdalena 2
GUALAX
Magdalena 5
GUALNACHA
Margarita 17
GUALNECHU
Cathalina 19
GUALPA
Antonia 6
GUARPA
Maria 12
GUARPAIS
Antonia 12
GUECHAVA
Stevan 10
GUENA
Anttonio 1
GUENACHULY
Zecilia 17
GUERRERO
Antonio Jose 82
Concepcion 107
Diego 180
Francisca 164
Francisco 119
Jose 68
Jose Antonio 151, 164
Juan 254
Juan Domingo 69, 213
Juan Jesus 271
Paula 85, 92, 119
Rosalia 156
Teodoro 291
GUILCHA
Maria 40
GUILLEN
Ana Maria 133
GUIMAGEL
Margarita 12
GUIONA
Lusia 11
GUIPAT
Santiago 53
GUIUJE
Estevan 4
GUTIERRES
See BUTIERRES, BUTIERREZ
Francisco 213, 260
Juana 183
HAQUERMO
Juan 12
HARRECHONE
Angelina 1
HERRERA
See ERRERA
Candelaria 197
Cristoval 289
Felipe 174
Jose 255
Jose Simon 99, 116
Josepha 18
Juana 50
Julian 239
Jusepa 23
Maria 204
Maria Candelaria 215
Maria Rosario 280
Maria Ursula 209
Nicolas 258
Pedro 290
Teodoro 296
Teresa 16, 19
Tomas 209
HIDALGO
See YDALGO
HIELO
Geronimo 2
HOLGUIN
See OLGUIN
Maria Gertrudis 105
HORTIZ
See ORTIZ
Maria Lus 291
HUAPAPA
Maria 3
HUIMOE
Lucia 12
HUIPATE
Magdalena 2
HURTADO
See URTADO
Josef Antonio 35
Juan 76
Juana 220
Manuela 159
Maria 169, 233, 253, 284
Maria Concepcion 270
Miguel 235, 240

LAVADIA
See LABADIA, BATIA
Andrea 261
LAVADILLA
Andrea 205
Andrella 189
Pablo 193
LAZARO
See LASARO
Josef Antonio 32
Santiago 37
LAZO
See LASO, LASSO
Francisco 113
Gertrudis 125
Jose Antonio 102
Marcos 89
Mathias 58
Matias 79
LÉ
Juan 305
LEAL
Alonzo 27
Domingo 68
Guadalupe 156
Josefa 79, 94, 106, 136
Juan Domingo 46, 52, 60, 82, 93, 101, 111
Juana Manuela 265
Lorenza 76
Manuel 53, 73, 234, 267
Manuel Jose 62, 88, 127, 134, 163, 217
Maria 201
Maria Dolores 160, 231, 259
Maria Guadalupe 145, 273
Maria Lorenza 119
Maria Monserrate 118, 131, 149, 165
Maria Simona 43, 47
Monserrate 183
Monsorrate 176
Rafael 199, 215, 236, 261
Rafel 189
Serafina 190, 252
Simona 56
LEDOUX
See LEDÚ
LEDÚ
Antonio 281, 294
LEIBA
Bisente 193
Dolores 142
Jose 149
Jose Antonio 123
Juana Paula 32
Maria Josefa 33
Maria Paula 28
LEIVA
Jose 46
LEYBA
Bisente 170, 224
Jose 56
Maria 235
Ramon 259
LEYVA
Jose 49, 65
LIMISE
Luis 276
LION
Jose Antonio 189
LIRA
Juan Lorenzo 111
LISTON
Jose 154
Juan Domingo 52
Juana 113, 139
Maria 57, 73, 81, 111, 128, 140
LISTONA
Maria 66
LLACA
Geronimo 1
LLUGE
Juan 17
LOAPAP
Francisca 4
LOBATO
See LOVATO
Antonia Teodora 167
Antonio 100, 104, 107, 151
Barbara 85, 90, 100, 126
Domingo 79, 93, 105, 167
Elena 111, 116, 140, 151
Francisco 108, 120, 131, 136, 141, 156, 160, 167
Jose 142, 157
Jose Domingo 138
Jose Manuel 131
Josefa 106, 136, 154
Juan 215
Juan Antonio 114, 137
Juan Jose 83, 116
Juana 161
Madalena 216
Magdalena 157
Margarita 276
Maria 72, 117
Maria Antonia 108, 117, 124, 136, 147, 152
Maria Dolores 219
Maria Luciana 216
Maria Luz 62
Maria Madalena 299
Paula 53, 63, 71, 111
Rafael 122, 129, 143, 159
Salvador 69, 80, 97
Soledad 210

LUCERO (continued)
Fabiana 246
Francisca 54, 86, 118
Francisco 192
Jose Antonio 56, 110
Jose Francisco 65, 242, 291
Jose Maria 229, 245, 264
Jose Ygnacio 235
Josef 179
Josefa 67, 106, 127, 137, 287
Juan 165, 166
Juan Antonio 36, 59, 123, 136, 178, 184, 201, 207, 245, 293
Juan Domingo 57, 130
Juan Francisco 51
Juan Jesus 133, 149, 168, 207
Juan Jose 232, 241, 266, 294
Juan Josef 207
Juana 295
Juana Maria 262
Lorenso 226
Lorenzo 249, 270
Madalena 290
Madelena 193
Magdalena 124, 264
Manuel 189, 205, 250, 261
Manuela 104
Margarita 170, 177, 191, 227, 249, 257
Maria 34, 37, 104, 185, 187, 226, 241, 289
Maria Asension 253
Maria Encarnacion 181
Maria Josefa 57, 287
Maria Polonia 183
Maria Rita 199, 228, 255, 267, 298
Maria Soledad 238, 246, 265, 270
Maria Ygnacia 249, 271
Miguel 171, 185, 233, 240
Miguela 65
Pablo 136, 142, 164, 176, 191, 250
Pedro 135, 142, 159, 180, 205, 241, 248, 268, 274, 283, 284, 300
Polonia 199, 256/257
Rita 150, 198
Rosa 284
Rosalia 268
Soledad 203, 284, 286
Vernardo 300
Vicente 150
Ygnacia 290
LUISGUANPA
Maria Rosa 47
LUIZ
Juan Pedro 233
LUJAN
See LUXAN
Antonio 48
Antonio Jose 55
Barbara 74
Encarnacion 201
Francisca 64, 70
Jose 38, 44, 184
Jose Antonio 66, 71, 73, 186, 200
Josef 41, 206
Josef Francisco 38
Josefa 27, 51, 72
Juan 27
Juan Antonio 28, 40, 44, 57, 64, 72, 75, 202, 284
Juan Domingo 51, 67, 73, 295
Juana 43, 57, 186
Juana Maria 28
Julian 28
Lorenso 225
Lucas 38
Lucia 187
Manuel 206
Maria 39
Maria Antonia 285
Maria Luz 230, 256
Maria Rafela 177
Maria Rosa 58, 75
Miguel 28
Paula 291
Santiago 36, 56, 59, 74
Vicente 29
Zecilia 38
LUJANA
Encarnacion 65
LUMBRE
Josepha 49
LUNA
Jose Antonio 259
Josefa 211
Juan 271, 281
Maria Josefa 243
Maria Rafaela 194
Maria Rafela 181
Miguel 144, 244
Nazarena 93
Rafael 114, 120, 143, 158
Rafaela 152, 207
Rafel 173, 184
LURENI
Diego 8
LURTE
Lucia 2
LUSERO
See LUCERO, LUZERO
Antonio 69
Anttonio 60
Ascencion 81

LUSERO (continued)
Asencion 91
Bernardo 68
Francisca 69
Jose Francisco 74
Josefa 71
Juan Antonio 64
Juan Domingo 71, 83, 123
Lucia 40
Luisa 38
Manuela 71
Pablo 120, 150
LUSLI
Diego 22
LUT
Francisco 210
LUXAN
See LUJAN
Agustina 168
Antonio 112, 147, 273
Encarnacion 95, 120
Francisca 69, 79, 98, 111, 115
Francisco 102, 135, 148, 166, 246, 264
Joan 19
Jose Antonio 91, 94, 122, 125, 130, 134, 140, 141, 155, 162
Jose Francisco 91, 106
Jose Manuel 212, 214, 262
Josef 30
Josefa 60, 81, 92, 104
Juan 16, 140, 160, 163
Juan Antonio 32, 85, 87-89, 94, 98, 102, 103, 114, 124, 127, 141, 147, 148
Juan Domingo 83, 90, 93, 95, 104, 105, 126, 146, 249
Juan Jose 242
Juana 125
Manuela 118, 159
Maria Antonia 246, 274
Maria Encarnacion 135
Maria Josefa 93
Maria Loreto 267
Maria Rosa 232
Micaela 117, 147
Pedro 262
Rafael 113
Rafaela 165
Salvador 111
Santhiago 61
Santiago 107, 111
Valentin 128
LUZERO
See LUCERO, LUSERO
Andrea 87
Antonio 89, 216
Bernardo 92
Guadalupe 214
LUZERO (continued)
Jose Francisco 275
Jose Maria 213
Jose Ygnacio 222
Josefa 93, 99
Juan Antonio 77
Juan Domingo 100, 222
Juan Jesus 98
Manuel 211
Margarita 220
Maria 28
Maria Nazarena 122
Maria Soledad 221
Pablo 217
Soledad 210
M(torn)TIA
Jose 97
MACUCHI
Juana Maria 45
MACULUM
Rosa 17
MADRID
Antonio 245, 265
Christobal 228
Cristobal 239
Cristoval 126, 135, 149, 166
Diego 121, 131
Diego Antonio 108
Dolores 85, 92, 116, 130, 142, 146
Horta 153
Jose Manuel 156, 161, 167
Jose Maria 210
Jose Pedro 166
Juan 105
Juan Cristoval 294
Maria 128, 272
Maria Dolores 112
Maria Manuela 244
Pedro 152, 203
Rafaela 158
Rosa 151
Salvador Horta 93, 110
Salvador Orta 78
Tomas 132
Ygnacio 144
Ysabel 28, 42
MADRIL
Antonio 215
Cristobal 213
Cristoval 174
Guadalupe 219
Jose Miguel 221
Josef Manuel 179
Juana 290
Maria Jesus 291
Maria Rosa 173
Miguel 306
Pedro 177

MARTIN (continued)
Cristoval 135, 153, 230
Cruz 159
Damiana 124, 144
Diego 151, 156, 170, 173, 181, 194, 207
Diego Antonio 152
Dolores 64, 115, 126, 134, 135, 148, 156, 164, 166, 191, 201, 223
Domingo 34, 40
Elena 266
Encarnacion 29, 69, 79
Ermenegildo 226
Estefana 235
Estevan 181, 185
Felipe 106, 125, 139, 158, 172, 187, 200, 202, 204, 207, 208, 232, 257, 273, 285
Felipe Anselmo 238
Feliz 112
Francisca 177, 190, 214, 245
Francisco 113, 118, 133, 143, 152, 172, 181, 183, 205, 220, 231, 242, 252, 274, 276
Francisco Antonio 243
Geronima 129
Geronimo 49, 54, 61, 69, 79, 107, 172
Geronimo Francisco 47
Gertrudis 144, 145
Gervacio 51, 119
Gervasio 60, 69, 77, 86
Getrudes 186
Graciana 55
Graciana Beatriz 32
Guadalupe 53, 58, 89, 98, 113, 127, 130, 141, 292
Hermenegildo 293
Jesus 203, 290
Jose 45, 50, 63, 78, 94, 116, 132, 135, 139, 143, 150, 159, 218
Jose Antonio 53, 55, 74, 107, 115, 117, 129, 138, 151, 154, 187, 201, 232, 271
Jose Francisco 125, 239
Jose Joaquin 105
Jose Manuel 149
Jose Miguel 43, 275
Jose Pablo 85, 102
Jose Roque 109
Jose Santos 230
Josef 34, 179
Josef Antonio 177, 227
Josef Francisco 227
Josef Pablo 223
Josefa 66, 98, 112, 128, 138, 143, 148, 152, 168, 191, 212,

MARTIN, Josefa (continued)
228, 239, 248, 249, 268
Josepha 68
Juan 132, 147, 153, 162, 165, 167, 174, 176, 293
Juan Antonio 218, 223, 253, 254, 272, 273
Juan Bautista 83, 168
Juan Candelario 121
Juan Candido 109, 140
Juan Carmen 107, 122
Juan Cruz 125
Juan Domingo 146
Juan Felipe 48, 59, 64, 85, 98, 187, 199
Juan Jesus 238
Juan Jose 114, 118, 142, 212, 263
Juan Julian 208, 261
Juan Maria 199
Juan Pablo 62, 69, 82, 88, 98, 135
Juan Phelipe 53, 73
Juan Ygnacio 213
Juan Ygnasio 61
Juana 71, 101, 113, 119, 123, 134, 142, 154, 167, 196, 234
Juana Agustina 54
Juana Dolores 113
Juana Maria 108, 161, 213, 255
Juana Paula 205, 235
Juana Rosa 88
Luciana 259
Lusia 145
Luz 95, 123, 140
Magdalena 78, 86, 101, 114, 127, 130, 151, 278
Manuel 63, 214, 283
Manuel Gregorio 118, 133, 140, 155, 187, 226
Manuel/Miguel 294
Manuela 97, 153, 264
Margarita 111, 274, 300
Maria 29, 44, 60, 74, 98, 108, 114, 116, 125, 149, 151, 152 176, 178, 191, 224, 257, 283
Maria Antonia 49, 55, 68, 69, 72, 88, 89, 102, 104, 108, 131, 146, 161, 179, 274, 281, 297
Maria Anttonia 61
Maria Ascencion 295
Maria Ascension 278
Maria Asension 251, 264
Maria Barbara 64, 72, 90
Maria Barvara 207, 258
Maria Candelaria 260
Maria Concepcion 113, 133, 157, 248, 272
Maria Cruz 192, 247

MARTIN (continued)
Maria Dolores 155, 157, 208, 214, 244, 263, 265, 275
Maria Elena 296
Maria Encarnacion 36, 88, 296
Maria Francisca 160
Maria Gertrudis 242
Maria Guadalupe 148, 297
Maria Jesus 268, 282, 289
Maria Josefa 184, 214, 229, 233, 255, 278, 305
Maria Juana 190, 228
Maria Lus 173, 292
Maria Luz 124, 151, 168, 257, 274, 281
Maria Magdalena 66, 108
Maria Manuela 106, 228, 273, 301
Maria Micaela 57
Maria Rafaela 133
Maria Reyes 177, 251
Maria Rosa 178, 215, 236, 262
Maria Soledad 266
Maria Susana 304
Maria Trinidad 259
Maria Ygnacia 126, 142, 178, 269
Maria Ysidora 165, 174, 239, 282
Mariano 241, 270, 280
Marta 82, 88, 97, 107, 116, 124
Matiana 172
Mauricia 144
Micaela 65, 84, 143, 247, 286, 288
Miguel 182, 247
Miguel/Manuel 294
Pablo 51, 54, 168, 170, 221, 286, 293
Patricia 137
Paula 69, 78, 102, 199
Pedro 122, 144, 150, 168, 169, 174, 176, 205
Rafaela 77, 90, 110, 116, 120, 126
Ramon 69, 91, 102
Roque 100, 143, 189
Rosalia 89
Salvador 34, 77, 107, 142, 173, 256
Salvador Manuel 88, 131, 162
Santiago 39, 214, 292
Santos 172, 188, 220, 280, 300
Serafina 135
Severino 127, 138
Sicina 202
Silveria 232
Simona 142, 307
Susana 183
Teodora 144, 176, 301
Teresa 73
Theodora 169

MARTIN (continued)
Tomas 87, 109, 143
Tomasa 79, 92, 108, 122, 135, 148
Varvara 169, 179
Ventura 120, 150
Victoria 56
Vuenaventura 234
Ygnacia 70, 212, 236, 248, 280
Ygnacio 51, 132, 184, 198, 287
Ygnasio 121, 122
Ygnes 171
Ynacio 42
Ynes 113, 131, 139, 149, 165, 225
Ysidora 145, 195, 206, 223, 268, 299

MARTIN LISTON
Maria Dominga 99

MARTINA
Maria 176
Maria Rafaela 253
Victoria 62

MARTINES
Antonia 63
Francisco 304
Juan Ygnacio 296
Juana Maria 296
Maria Cacilda 296
Maria Encarnacion 294
Maria Lus 293
Pedro 92
Petrona 75
Ventura 301

MARTINEZ
Catalina 51
Clara 93
Felipe 93
Felipe Antonio 220
Francisco 123
Gervacio 97
Jose Antonio 67
Jose Miguel 56
Juan Cruz 145
Juana Maria 141, 296
Maria Estefana 222
Maria Jesus 278
Maria Manuela 222
Marta 140

MASCAREÑA
Francisca 209

MASCAREÑAS
Bautista 145
Francisca 199, 205, 239, 258
Gerarda 110, 127
Juan Baptista 229
Maria Getrudes 205
Miguel 237, 281, 298
Nicolas 64

MASSA
Manuela 32
MATEO
Juan Domingo 69
MEDINA
Apolonia 257
Barbara 161
Cencion 187
Danislada 291
Estanislada 296
Felipe 163, 177
Gregoria 186, 241
Gregorio 128, 141, 155, 204, 247
Guadalupe 169
Jesus 212, 255, 268, 278, 305
Jose 167
Jose Antonio 283, 299
Jose Encarnacion 209
Jose Manuel 243, 253, 274
Jose Ygnasio 124
Jose Ysidro 217, 237
Josef Manuel 182
Josefa 200, 248, 272, 291
Juan 168, 264
Juan Bautista 222
Juan Cristoval 100
Juan Pasqual 141
Juan Ysidro 187
Juana 172, 234, 259, 273, 289
Julian 271
Manuel 281
Manuel Gregorio 253
Margarita 147
Maria 204, 205, 227
Maria Asension 269
Maria Candelaria 217, 251, 270, 295
Maria Carmen 281
Maria Dolores 237
Maria Gracia 303
Maria Gregoria 166
Maria Josefa 188, 230, 232, 258
Maria Rafela 187
Maria Rosa 211, 260
Maria Rosario 226, 246
Maria Ysidora 242
Nicolas 259
Pasqual 157
Paula 252
Rafaela 118, 133, 140, 155, 226
Reyes 225
Rosa 287
Rosalia 173, 193
Trinidad 279
Ygnacio 66, 76, 86, 98, 110, 127, 144
Ysidro 197, 203, 262
MEISLAC
Juana 22
MELENIA
Teresa 95
MELENUDO
Teresa 117
MERINO
Jose Concepcion 283
MES
See MEZ
Anttonio 60
Maria Soledad 218
Miguel 214
Paulin 211
MESTAS
Asencio 225
Dolores 221, 307
Jose Manuel 190
Josefa 131, 150, 163, 190, 244
Juan Cristobal 187
Juana 88, 119, 197, 288
Juana Catarina 211
Maria 143, 182
Maria Candelaria 303
Maria Dolores 241
Maria Ysabel 155
Paula 257
Rosa 116
Vicente 303
MEZ
See MES
Paulin 204
MIER
Juan 135
MIERA
Ana Maria 84, 94, 120
Jose 91, 115, 130, 139, 154, 235, 268
Josef 178, 228
Maria Ygnacia 239
MIRABAL
Domingo 73
Josefa 175, 249, 272
Juan Luis 90
Juana Maria 55
Juliana 28
Lorenso 286
Lorenzo 249
Maria 73
Maria Antonia 27, 34
Maria Juliana 32
Maria Rosa 41, 71
Rosa 31, 56
Tomasa 52, 70
Rafaela 78, 125
MIRABALL
Domingo 99
Juan Luis 118, 131, 136, 150
Maria 99, 145
Maria Rafaela 134
Rafaela 97, 161

MONTOYA (continued)
Maria Rosa 219, 266
Mariana 134
Martina 160
Mateo 291
Miguel 216
Rafael 114, 127, 167, 203, 259, 270
Rafel 80, 183, 193
Ramon 216, 226
Ramona 280
Simona 192, 236, 285
Thomas 62
Ygnacio 290
Ysabel 288
MORENO
Maria Antonia 39
MOYA
Antonio 286
Eusebio 152, 165
Eusevio 98
Juana 59
Luz 166
Maria 177
Maria Antonia 275
Maria Luz 203
Paula 263, 304
MOYA y ORTIZ
Maria Luz 152
MUGUICUY
Maria 11
MUÑES
Juan Antonio 174
MUÑIS
(n.n.) 303
Gertrudis 162
MUÑIZ
(n.n.) 303
Gertrudis 116
Juan Antonio 154
Maria Josefa 258
MUÑOS
Antonio 140
MUQUELE
Juan 1, 14
NACHALE
Geronimo 16
NACHO
Diego 12
NACHOLA
Juan 14
NACHULA
Juan 17, 18
NACHULE
Juan 16
NAPCO
Antonio 10
NAPO
Antonio 23
NAPOO
Antonio 6
NARANJO
Francisco 27, 141, 157, 174
Juan 31, 37
Juan Antonio 44
Juana Maria 110
Manuela 43, 75, 87, 99, 111
Maria 57, 65, 126
Maria Guadalupe 109, 121
Micaela 103
Santiago 86, 108, 134, 204, 222, 247, 263, 304
NASTOE
Juan 4
NATURE
Maria 6
NATURI
Lusia 9
NIETO
Guadalupe 163
NO SURNAME
Agustin 49, 291
Alonso 47
Ana 35
Ana Maria 44, 82, 179
Ana Maria Rosa 32
Andres 16
Angelina 20, 21, 24, 36
Antonia 21
Antonia Rosa 94
Antonio 18, 20, 21, 24, 48, 141
Anttonio 14
Augustin 19
Barbara 32, 37, 65
Barvara 202
Bernarda Princesa 44
Bernardo 170
Catarina 79, 117, 131, 182
Cathalina 17
Cezilia 19
Cicilia 233
Diego 18, 20, 25, 33
Domingo 21, 29, 47
Encarnacion 85, 170
Felipa 85, 94
Felipe 170
Francisca 20, 33, 39, 43, 64, 92, 101, 105, 181, 233, 291
Francisca Ascension 20
Francisca Carmen 213
Francisco 17, 21, 24, 34, 42, 44, 144, 197
Geronimo 19
Guadalupe 72, 79, 89, 105
Isabel 20, 21
Jeronimo 13
Joan 19
Joana 19

NO SURNAME (continued)
Rosalia 30, 189
Rossa 20, 21, 24
Salvador 15, 35
Sicilia 194
Soledad 182
Teodora 77, 91
Teresa 72, 76, 86
Theresa 21
Tomas 84
Tomasa 55
Victor 279
Ynes 19
Ysabel 15, 18, 42
NOCHEE
Pablo 13
NORI
Fernando 6
NORICHO
Juan 2
NURI
Fernando 9
OAQUER
Ana 1
OCANER
Patricio 210, 215
OCHOLA
Angelina 6
OCOI
Mariana 9
OCQUEZ
Ana 1
OCTOLA
Nicolas 3
OJAS AMARRADAS
Juana 100
OLGUIN
See HOLGUIN
OLA
Maria 9, 13
OLONA
Rosa 154, 223, 249
ONA
Anttonio 5
ONEA
Anttonio 9
OÑENGUE
Diego 224
Josefa 167
OPELEMOGUE
Lusia 10
OPELEMOHUE
Lucia 8
OQUELI
Ana 4
OQUIR
Ana 9
ORTA
Nicolas 199
ORTEGA
(n.n.) 110
Consecion 204
Juana 78
Manuel 63, 73, 81, 100, 112, 125, 136, 152, 164, 218, 223, 234, 240
Maria 97, 121, 138, 160, 176
Maria Concepcion 248
Maria Crus 219
Maria Luz 65
Maria Marta 245
Ygnacio 147
ORTIS
Ana Maria 52, 289
Feliciana 180
Francisca 289
Maria Antonia 41, 44, 219, 286
Maria Lucia 66
Maria Paula 297
Sencion 300
ORTIZ
See HORTIZ
Ana Maria 87, 130, 242
Anna Maria 60
Antonio Jose 84, 98, 219
Ascencion 221
Feliciana 224, 256
Felisisna 188
Francisca 229, 265
Francisco 109, 123, 140, 164, 178, 193, 269
Juan Andres 117, 146
Lorensa 226
Lucia 128
Luisa 32
Manuela 128, 193, 231
Maria 66, 260, 271
Maria Antonia 27, 30, 269
Maria Manuela 275
Maria Sencion 241
Maria Teodora 59
Micaela 233
OTOLA
Nicolas 6
OYENGUE
Diego 254
Jose Miguel 251
Josefa 223
PAAC
Ana 5
PAAQUEMO
Juan 4
PACENO
Josef Antonio 223
PACHECO
Antonio 74, 82
Bibiana 259
Concepcion 158

PACHECO (continued)
Diego 233, 254, 287
Diego Antonio 276
Dolores 143
Estevan 224
Francisco 208, 241, 292, 306
Gregorio 177
Guadalupe 164, 175
Jose 48, 288
Jose Ramon 165
Josef 223
Juan 17, 35, 46, 59, 75, 85, 270
Juan Antonio 127, 257
Juan Pablo 198
Juan Pedro 123, 257
Juana 50
Manuel Esteban 247
Manuel Estevan 300
Maria Dolores 159, 258
Maria Encarnacion 278
Maria Guadalupe 242, 263
Maria Manuela 240
Maria Ysidora 299
Miguel 90, 113
Pablo 249, 275
Ramon 195, 209, 225, 254, 288
Ysidora 279
PACHILPA
Antonio 20
PACHOGUE
Maria 10
PACOAGUACHOL
Diego 6
PACTEE
Geronimo 20
PADILLA
Ana Maria 232
Antonio 291
Balentin 291
Baltasar 294
Bisente 223
Buenaventura 238
Catarina 234, 264
Dolores 286
Francisca 208, 269, 271
Francisco 231
Guadalupe 147
Jose Antonio 41, 89
Juan Antonio 185, 241
Juan Jesus 213
Juana 163, 174, 184, 191, 197, 264
Julian 111, 119
Lucia 264, 283
Lucilla 285
Lugarda 167, 206
Manuel 191, 203, 221, 230, 243, 260
Maria 171, 227, 253, 262
PADILLA (continued)
Maria Consecion 193
Maria Dolores 192, 229, 239, 264, 273, 276
Maria Francisca 232
Maria Gertrudis 244
Maria Manuela 174, 213, 239, 294
Maria Mequela 200
Marta 147
Pedro 138, 159
Salvador 138, 148, 168, 184, 191, 236, 239
Santhiago 60
Santiago 51, 72, 81, 92, 104, 111, 297
Valentin 233
PADIYA
Dolores 188
PAÊ
Ana 10
PAEQUE
Maria 5
PAES
Domingo 73
Juan Jesus 227
Manuela 71
Maria Candelaria 234
Miguel 245
Ysabel 77
PAEZ
Concepcion 86, 99, 111, 125, 147
Juan 138
Juana 151, 164
Manuela 30
Maria Concepcion 137
Maria Ysabel 140, 146
Miguel 161
Nicolas 151
Ysabel 69
PAGMAJETA
Maria 41
PAGUE
Geronimo 3
PAIS
See PAYS
Josefa 52
Juan Antonio 57, 197, 201
Juan Jesus 258
Juan Domingo 50
Juan Domingo Juan 42
Juana 181
Manuela 39
Maria Juana 177
Mateo 200
Miguel 182, 191, 202, 218
PAMAC
Lucia 13
PAMAGUA
Lusia 8

PERNAUTE
Andres 3
PETA
Diego 7
PEUSILI
Maria 11
PEYEN
Maria 5
PHUONOTA
Antonio 18
PIA JUILE
Hissabel 3
PIACHAL
Francisca 14
PIACHELPO
Juana 13
PIACHOLE
Francisca 8
PIACHOLMO
Francisco 13
PIALOQUEGAN
Maria 5
PIALUCHONE
Salbador 18
PIANCHORI
Maria 2
PIANQUIPA
Maria 41
PIARLAPAPA
Francisca 47
PIASLU
Juan 16
PICURIES
Juan Cayetano 129
PIECHONE
Maria 10
PIEN
Geronimo 10
PIENCHORE
Lusia 7
PILNÁO
Rosalia 45
PILNAS
Rosalia 41
PILPAE
Francisca 7
PINEDA
Jacinto 76, 79, 106
Maria 35
Maria Ygnacia 220, 243, 276
Rafaela 102, 128, 148, 200, 230, 277
PINIDA
Jacinto 94
PINO
Antonio Fernandez 42, 45
Jose Antonio 301
Maria Jesus 209
Santiago 83
PISSI
Diego 5
PIUCHO
Maria 9
POAJE
Antonio 15
POAO
Anttonio 6, 9
POCA
Diego 9
POICHOLE
Maria 2
PONCHORE
Maria 11
POTUENTANO
Francisco 2
POYBO
Diego 8
PRACHALMO
Francisco 13
PRINCESA
Francisca 136
PRINSESA
Francisca 206
PUAEJE
Juan 4
PUALNACACHEL
Lorenso 5
PUANCHO
Fransisca 23
PUCHEQUI
Juan 8
PUENPATE
Juan 8
PUERNACHE
Lorenso 10
PUERPANA
Diego 11
PUETMALOY
Andres 6
PULULU
Maria Soledad 129
PUNTE
Jose Antonio 79
PUPA
Lucia 14
PUPAH THANO
Hernando 2
PUSE
Juan 2
PUSLAPAC
Josefa 39
QUAFUENTIELME
Santiago 46
QUANERA
Mariquita 45
QUANPAP
Ysabel 7

ROMERO
Agustin 234
Alberta 134
Albina 260, 267, 295
Alvina 228
Ana 34
Ana Maria 47
Anamaria 177, 178
Anastasio 217
Andres 18, 23, 78
Andres Juan 64
Angela 28, 53, 60, 69, 79, 89
Anna Maria 67
Antonia 48, 136
Antonica 67
Antonio 45, 52, 69, 78, 82, 88, 92, 94, 100, 103, 104, 108, 225, 305
Antonio Domingo 34, 40, 43, 48, 51, 153, 180, 196
Antonio Josef 175
Antonio Rafael 262
Anttonio 62
Baltasar 34
Balthasar 29
Balvaneda 167
Barbara 64, 102
Bentura 177, 185
Bitoria 177
Brigida 113, 129, 238
Brijida 90
Carmen 207, 287
Catarina 124, 165, 263
Catharina 62
Cayetana 34
Christobal 228
Christoval 195
Cicilia 275
Concepcion 54, 64, 72, 74, 83, 98, 107, 120, 134, 148, 165
Consecion 170, 175, 189
Cristoval 157, 168, 175
Diego 32, 37, 186, 195
Dolores 142, 155, 224
Dominga 211, 269, 280
Domingo 30, 37, 40, 43, 50, 64, 77, 117
Felipa 127
Felipe 179, 190, 201, 243
Francisca 38, 93, 104, 162, 192, 234, 254
Francisco 26, 70, 71, 74, 75, 85, 94, 107, 127, 129, 146, 147, 151, 231
Francisco Esteban 124, 134
Francisco Estevan 81, 101
Geronimo 52, 65, 72, 85, 89
Gertrudis 63, 64, 83, 100, 116, 132, 146

ROMERO (continued)
Getrudes 71
Getrudis 40
Guadalupe 71, 84, 92, 119, 131, 143, 152, 179, 193, 285
Hypolito 292
Jesus 203, 267
Josa Manuel 250
Jose 27, 38, 39, 44, 49, 54, 63, 76-78, 81, 106, 114, 118, 130, 149, 157, 160, 187, 232, 254, 272, 289
Jose Antonio 48, 59, 66, 71, 74, 92, 104, 105, 119, 139, 165, 266, 290
Jose Francisco 95, 122
Jose Jesus 163
Jose Manuel 146, 156, 264
Jose Maria 128, 148, 230, 277
Jose Merced 280
Jose Rafael 242
Jose Rafel 187
Jose Ramon 277
Jose Victor 257
Josef 30, 32-34, 38, 207
Josef Antonio 172, 181, 199
Josef Maria 200
Josefa 35, 43, 50, 52, 56, 57, 64, 67, 82, 87, 90, 101, 105, 109, 124, 126, 166, 251, 276, 284, 291
Josepha 70, 73, 75
Josesito 67
Juan 40, 54, 62, 66, 77, 78, 82, 86, 97, 109, 124, 125, 134, 161, 233, 259
Juan Agustin 242
Juan Andres 52, 190
Juan Antonio 39, 43, 52, 56, 58, 76, 103, 107, 180, 216, 221, 293, 300
Juan Carmel 299
Juan Christobal 34
Juan Domingo 28, 43, 57, 64, 65, 69, 70, 74, 78, 79, 82, 85, 95, 98, 101, 104, 115, 118, 120, 136, 140, 142, 145, 146, 158, 159, 164, 190, 195, 207, 208, 212, 245, 246, 252, 261, 266, 268, 274, 278, 281, 290, 293, 298
Juan Jesus 175, 183, 195, 197, 203, 257, 272, 285
Juan Jose 198, 258
Juan Miguel 92, 105, 118, 211, 261
Juan Pedro 206, 219, 238, 264
Juan Reyes 276
Juana 29, 36, 72, 81, 92, 103,

RUIBAL (continued)
Margarita 226
Maria Dolores 282
Maria Ysabel 282
Teresa 82
Tereza 62
RUIBALA
Micaela 35
RUIBALIS
See ULIBARRI
Maria Roumalda 305
RUIVAL
See RUIBAL
Eleuterio 283
Teresa 45
RUYBAL
Teresa 52
SAENS
Maria 240
Maria Carmen 274
SAIS
Jose Manuel 194
Josef Manuel 227
Maria 208
SAIZ
Jose Manuel 279
SALA
Estevan 6
SALAS
Antonio 224
SALASAR
See ZALASAR
Carpio 176, 202, 287
Cristoval 300
Diego 170, 175, 184, 200, 206, 237
Gervacio 177, 183, 195, 207, 294
Jose Ygnacio 295
Luisa 201
Manuela 197
Maria 175, 187
Maria Candelaria 299
Maria Manuela 306
Maria Soledad 194
Maria Trenidad 185
Mariano 203
Miquela 190
Pascuala 205
Pedro 204
Ramon 170, 181, 194, 226, 297
Trinidad 199
SALAZAR
See ZALAZAR
Diego 168, 210
Dolores 71
Felipa 277, 303
Francisco 124
Gervacio 211, 252
Gervasio 149, 160
SALAZAR (continued)
Juan Antonio 231
Juana Micaela 161
Lorenza 144, 168
Luiza 235
Manuel 149
Manuela 215
Maria Dolores 81, 101
Maria Manuela 237, 243
Maria Paula 132
Maria Trinidad 162, 244, 263
Maria Ygnacia 232
Mariano 244
Paula 121
Pedro 209, 245, 281
Ramon 255, 276
Rosa 219, 244
SAMORA
See ZAMORA
Encarnacion 293
Francisca 184
Francisco 194, 234
Manuel 246
Manuela 198, 249
Pablo 228, 260, 295
Pedro 182, 206, 235
Rosa 219
Rosalia 236
Santiago 65
Ylario 181
SAN AUGUSTIN
Soledad 157
SANBO
Juan Cristoval 64
SAN(CHES-torn)
Maria Antonia 55
SANCHES
Ana 57
Antonia 68
Antonio 304
Anttonia 61
Clara 166
Diego 66
Dolores 120
Domingo 289
Felipe 255, 296
Jose 70
Jose Pablo 186
Juana 44, 60, 64
Manuela 286
Margarita 68
Maria 172, 181
Maria Antonia 138, 237
Maria Clara 62, 68
Maria Gertrudes 299
Maria Getrudes 180
Maria Reyes 289
Maria Teresa 294
Maria Varbara 299

SAUSO (continued)
Maria Rosa 262
Mariano 243
Micaela 63, 56, 82
Miguel 88
Rosa 235
SUAZO
See SOASO, SOAZO, ZUAZO
Francisco 51, 223
Getrudes 69
Juan Antonio 226
Juana Maria 231
Luzia 28
Maria Getrudis 229
Maria Guadalupe 252
Micaela 70, 252
Michaela 53
Paulin 235
Soledad 104
SUCHIAPAKA
Maria 18
SUCUE
Diego 11
SUESO
Francisco 59
SUISPCHAL
Maria 14
SULE
Juan Thomas 41
SUR
Francisco 289
TAÂ
Josepha 9
TACHIVE
Gregorio 22
TACOLI
Domingo 11
TACOLINA
Francisco 13
TAFOLLA
Catalina 61
Clara 219
Graciana Beatris 66
Jesus 305
Juan Domingo 66
Maria Clara 298
Romano 217
Santos 212
Ypolito Jesus 222
TAFOYA
Ana Maria 114, 143, 158, 173, 184
Andrea 72, 84, 92, 120, 121, 135, 156
Antonio 132
Antonio Josef 196
Antonio Roman 147, 243
Bartolo 199, 224, 282
Bartolome 267
TAFOYA (continued)
Brigida 241, 270, 280
Clara 79, 138, 167, 196
Espirity Santo 181
Felipe 195
Graciana 72, 82
Guadalupe 62
Jesus 196, 245, 266
Jose 121, 136, 151, 153, 166, 248, 274
Jose Faustin 290
Jose Francisco 107
Jose Jesus 127
Josef 169, 196, 225
Juan Bautista 248
Juan Domingo 109, 122, 179, 251, 271
Juan Jesus 138
Juana 76, 93, 106, 171
Juana Catalina 43
Luiza 246, 270
Manuel 71, 77, 154, 223, 249
Maria 181, 203
Maria Antonia 107
Maria Josefa 261
Maria Luisa 132, 166, 235
Maria Resurreccion 134
Maria Resurrecion 124
Mariana 155, 174, 191, 236, 240, 266, 271, 277
Miguel 81, 103, 110
Nicolas 122, 137, 165
Ramon 171, 202, 263, 288
Romano 192
Salvador 158, 172, 196, 234, 259, 273, 289
Santos 194
Vartolo 181
TAGUA
Geronimo 3
TAHA
Josepha 13
TALACHE
Anamaria 213
TANE
Jose Antonio 47
Jose Manuel 43
TAO
Diego 5
TAOÔ
Diego 10
TAQUE
Diego 9
TAQUEO
Diego 6
TARPAUEQUE
Francisca 3
TAU
Juan Christoval 50

TAYA
Anttonio 7
TAYALA
Juan Domingo 42
TEAPU
Maria 19
TECOA
Dominga 70, 106, 120
Joaquin 116
Josefa 43, 52, 89
Juana 160
Lucia 101, 129, 149
Luisa 208
Maria Dominga 75
Maria Josepha 72
Miguel 44, 50, 60
Pablo 166
Toribio 67, 82
Vitoria 208
TEGUA
Antonio 15
TENORIO
Felipe 94, 110, 126
Francisco 148
Julian 110, 120, 133, 153, 175, 274
TEQUENA MAGUE
Maria 3
THOMAQUET
Juana 8
TIAPA
Maria 16
TIA
Juana 141
TIO
Jose Antonio 98, 104
Josefa 110
Maria 190
TLACAT
Xeronimo 14
TLEQUE
Geronimo 5, 8
TLUAPAP
Maria 8
TOCHOLA
Diego 6
TOI
Maria 12
TOICHAL
Maria 1
TOICHALA
Maria 7
TOIPA
Maria 18
TOLIA
Diego 3
TOLVACOI
Francisca 9
TOLVAQUEN
Francisca 5
TOMAQUEL
Juana 4
TONQUAM
Lusia 8
TOPE
Diego 12
TORAS
Biviana 200
TORES
Mariana 290
TORJUIRI
Joseph 11
TORRES
Antonio 179, 226, 254, 285
Bibiana 124, 210, 231
Biviana 173, 258
Diego 113, 130, 137, 146, 162, 190
Dolores 159
Maria Antonia 244
Maria Dolores 125, 145
Maria Josefa 239
Maria Juliana 221
Maria Reyes 259
Martin 307
Nicolas 281
Pedro 126
Ysavel 227
TORREZ
Biviana 186
TRUGILLO
Andres 67
Antonio Jose 306
Francisco 306
Juan 286
Juan Jesus 306
Juliana 288
Luis 299
Manuela 293
Maria 290
Rosa 220
Ylario 29
TRUJILLO
Andres 195
Antonia 180
Antonio 198
Blas 279
Brigida 177
Candelaria 206
Estevan 277
Francisco 182, 225
Jesus 278
Josef Maria 225
Josefa 196
Juan 195, 284
Juan Bautista 280
Juan Christoval 194

VIGIL
See MONTES VIGIL, VIGIL MONTES, BIGIL
Amador 258
Ana Maria 282
Anamaria 256
Anastacio 291
Antonio 286, 295
Dionicio 294
Faustin 257, 292
Faustino 293
Francisco 297
Getrudis 292
Guadalupe 282
Jose 291
Jose Francisco 253, 281
Juan 290
Juan Bautista 306
Juan Christoval 258
Juan Jesus 292
Maria 259, 291
Maria Antonia 256
Maria Micaela 159
Maria Rafaela 277
Maria Soledad 255, 276, 297, 303
Maria Trinidad 254
Maria Ysabel 297
Rafael 256, 276
Ramon 258, 277
Roza 254
Trinidad 209
Ysabel 292
VIGILA MONTES
Guadalupe 209
VIJIL
See BIJIL
Anastasio 217, 250
Antonio 217, 236
Barbara 263
Cristobal 210
Dionisio 86, 213
Faustin 233, 274
Feliciana 272
Francisco 212, 233, 234, 244, 263, 270
Hermenegilda 260
Hermenegildo 249
Jesus 267
Jose 263
Josefa 242
Juan 231, 250, 265
Juan Christobal 231
Juan Jesus 235, 266
Juan Ygnacio 220, 247
Julian 217
Manuel 271
Marcos 237
Maria 51, 232
Maria Feliciana 251
VIJIL (continued)
Maria Gertrudes 240
Maria Guadalupe 261
Maria Luiza 252, 271
Maria Luz 234
Maria Trinidad 238
Maria Ysabel 268
Mathias 237
Merejilda 221
Rafael 218
Ramon 235, 269
Ramona 240
Teresa 215, 236, 261, 267
Trinidad 267
Ygnacio 274
VILLALPANDO
See PANDO
Ambrosio 41
Rafael 117
VILLAPANDO
Antonio Severino 32
XARAMILLO
See JARAMILLO
Maria Antonia 70
Maria Soledad 269
Patricio 86
Prudencia 105
XIATA
Juan Felipe 208
XINNACHULA
Maria 14
YABATIT
Juana 14
YACHORE PACHORQUEAN
Maria 3
YAPATE
Juana 8
YAQUE
Sebastian 6
YARQUICHULE
Manuela 48
YDALGO
Gregoria 26
YPAPA
Jusepa 42
ZALASAR
See SALASAR
Candelaria 283
Felipa 243, 272
Maria Ygnacia 272
Policarpio 252, 271
Ygnacia 289
ZALAZAR
See SALAZAR
Francisco 85
Maria Luiza 267
ZAMORA
See SAMORA
Antonio 105

ZAMORA (continued)
Eusebio 120
Eusevio 86
Francisco 264
Guadalupe 72
Jose Francisco 42
Juan Esteban 271
Juan Gabriel 263
Juana 35
Manuel 271
Manuela 275
Maria Antonia 279
Maria Encarnacion 269
Pablo 185, 267
Pedro 139
Pedro Ygnacio 158
Rosalia 266
Santiago 91
ZAPATA
See SAPATA
Lucia 16
ZERNA
See SERNA, SERRNA
Manuela 56
ZISNEROS
See SISNEROS
Josefa 42
ZUASO
See SUASO
Antonio Jose 167
Francisco 138
Jose 129, 135, 146
Jose Antonio 137
Juan 126, 162
Juan Antonio 147
Juana Maria 122, 141, 157
Maria Gracia 283
Miguel 134, 160
Simon 115, 127, 160
ZUAZO
See SOASO, SUASO, SUAZO
Antonio 292
Francisco 272

INDEX of GODPARENTS, GRANDPARENTS, & OTHERS

It is important to look for alternate spellings of both surnames and given names. Names may appear more than one time on a page. Many names were abbreviated in the original records. They have been spelled out in this index. For the most part, prepositions have not been included in this index, but if they were present in the original record, they will be found in the manuscript.

ARAGON (continued)
Jose Rafael 240
Jose Vicente 115, 132, 157, 162
Josefa 287
Juan Jose 259
Juana 213, 262, 269
Juaquin 33
Lorenzo 271, 282
Manuela 128, 136, 150, 154, 156, 162, 285
Margarita 223
Maria 172
Maria Antonia 79, 103, 124, 126, 130, 131, 158, 186, 212, 258, 281, 297
Maria Barbara 221, 251, 270, 280
Maria Estefana 211, 300
Maria Estefania 264
Maria Gracia 221
Maria Jacinta 48, 56
Maria Jasinta 173
Maria Manuela 186, 193, 204
Maria Ygnacia 116, 119, 134, 142, 155, 180, 212, 221, 234, 236, 279, 301
Miguel 150
Miguel Antonio 154
Pascual 44, 69
Pasqual 50, 77, 82, 115
Pasqual Antonio 35
Vicente 168
Ygnacia 135, 136, 221, 286, 287
ARAOS
See AROS
Domingo, Fr. 15, 16, 20, 21
ARAOZ
Domingo, Fr. 23
ARCENON
Miguel 281
ARCHIBEQUE
Augustin 24
ARCHULETA
Ana Maria 300
Andres 12
Antonia 166
Antonia Teresa 233
Antonio 99, 113, 122, 163, 186, 200, 293, 295
Antonio Josef 192
Biviana 190
Cayetana 32
Damian 216, 221, 241, 265, 284, 307
Felipe 45
Gertrudis 253
Getrudis 281, 289
Jesus 218
Jose 197, 237
Jose Antonio 52, 88, 184, 213,
ARCHULETA, Jose Antonio (continued) 256, 304
Jose Balentin 296
Jose Francisco 299
Jose Norato 195
Jose Pablo 156, 198, 266, 307
Jose Ramon 146
Josef Pablo 169
Juan Antonio 128, 145
Juan Damian 228
Juan Manuel 126
Juana 307
Juana Josefa 292
Julian 144, 154, 161, 182, 281
Manuel 190
Manuel Antonio 267
Manuela 125, 197, 219, 264, 277, 306
Marcos 161, 177
Maria 153
Maria Antonia 275
Maria D(torn) 281
Maria Encarnacion 137
Maria Francisca 306
Maria Getrudis 213, 222, 278
Maria Loreto 275
Maria Manuela 195, 271, 301
Maria Rosa 205
Maria Salome 184, 237
Maria Serafina 213
Maria Ygnacia 204, 236, 260, 262
Meregirdo 297
Miguel 192, 256
Pablo 164, 210, 261
Rafaela 273
Salome 203
Serafina 212
Tomas 174, 206
Ylaria Bibiana 234
AREBALO
Lucas, Fr. 15, 19
ARELLANO
See ORELLANO
Juan Nepomuceno 296
Julialia 211
Julian 210, 219, 279, 287, 296
Maria Rosa 209-211, 217, 237, 242, 250, 253, 275
Ramon 164, 292
Rosa 287
Ygnacio 292
Ylario 296
ARGUELLO
Ana Maria 93
Anastacio 91
Anastasio 135
Jose 137
Jose Consecion 185
Josefa 120

BAJEMO
Manuela 45
BALDES
See VALDES
Felisiana 286
Jose Ygnacio 193
Manuel 207
Maria 216
Maria Bibiana 222
Maria Carmen 205
Maria Catalina 59
Maria Dolores 210, 276
Maria Encarnacion 184
Maria Jesus 217
Maria Josefa 193, 210, 221
Maria Micaela 217
Maria Michaela 276
Maria Paula 169, 179, 184
Maria Ygnacia 216
Pedro Antonio 184
Rosalia 201
Ygnacia 216
BALDESA
Maria Micaela 178
BALDEZ
See VALDEZ
Bentura 202
Maria 170
Paula 202
BALDONADO
See MALDONADO
Candelaria 306
BALERIO
See VALERIO
Maria 287
BALLEJO
See VALLEJO
Ana Maria 257
BALLEJOS
See VALLEJOS
Ana Maria 258, 297
Dolores 293
Juan Bautista 102
Juana 182
BARCELO
Jose Trinidad 294
BARELA
See VARELA
Ascencion 208
Cristoval 288
Dolores 198
Jose Antonio 307
Jose Francisco 185
Josef Francisco 202
Juan Angel 211
Juan Antonio 222, 286
Juan Miguel 64
Juan Ysidro 215, 218, 226
Juana 290
BARELA (continued)
Manuel 28
Manuela 287
Margarita 93, 103, 112, 293
Maria 182, 196, 212
Maria Josefa 208, 228
Maria Teresa 215
Miguel 241, 292, 306
Petrona 172
BARGAS
See VARGAS
Baurito 241
Juan Antonio 29, 39, 51
BAROS
Matias 303
BARRERAS
Felipe 303
BASQUES
See VASQUES
Antonio 172, 287
Jose Antonio 287
BASQUEZ
See VASQUEZ, VAZQUEZ
Margarita 256
BEGIL
See VEGUIL, VEGIL, MONTES BEGIL
Faustin 229
BEITA
See ABEITA, ABEYTA, VEITA, BEYTA
Andres 279
BEITIA
See VEITIA
Gertrudis 139
Jose Antonio 78
Jose Miguel 166
Jose Ygnacio 94
Josefa 149
Juan Antonio 107
Juan Ygnacio 77, 118
Maria 131
Maria Getrudis 51
Maria Rita 286
Rita 149
Teodora 77, 94
BEJIL
See VEJIL
Acnador 200
Ana Maria 172
Anastacio 230
Antonia 203
Antonio 228
Antonio Jose 183
Antonio Josef 174, 176
Cristoval 175
Cruz 61
Dolores 197
Faustin 169, 183, 197, 200
Feliciana 192, 224
Francisco 177, 199

BLEA (continued)
Maria Lus 92
Maria Luz 99
Nasarena 89, 141
BLEYA
Josef 170
BORREGO
Ana 278
Ana Teresa 246
Gertrudis 295
Juan 212, 217
Pablo 208, 239
BRISOL
Jose 284
BRITO
Donicio 205
Francisco 80, 301
Juan Francisco 80
Madalena 199
Magdalena 110, 156
Maria 285, 292
Maria Madalena 192
Maria Magdalena 130
Miquela 290
BROTONS
Francisco, Fr. 12, 14
BUENA
Juan Pedro 102
Maria Luz 211
Maria'Manuela 216
Maria Ygnacia 218, 280
BUENO
Ana Maria 191
Antonio 47, 70, 78, 201, 257, 281, 298
Anttonio 62
Juan 215
Juan Eugenio 265, 270
Juana 226
Juana Antonia 212
Maria 181, 245
Maria Francisca 259
Maria Manuela 199
Maria Rafaela 141
Maria Ygnasia 62
Mateo 168, 300
Pedro 126, 147, 227, 257, 275
Rafaela 101, 122, 123, 127, 130, 155, 165
Ygnacia 227, 260, 269, 295
BUSTOS
Francisco 20, 21
Josepha 20, 21
Juan 20
Pablo 252
BUTIERRES
See GUTIERRES
Maria 195
Maria Polonia 170, 175
BUTIERRES (continued)
Miguel 289
Polonia 173
BUTIERREZ
Maria Polonia 171
CABALLERO
Maria Francisca 239
CABIAM
Estevan 14
CACHO
Antonio, Fr. 276, 279
CACILLAS
See CASIAS, CASILLAS
Cristobal 306/307
CAJIOVE
Juana 12
CALA
Antonio 5
CALO
Catharina 5
CAMARGO
Anttonio, Fr. 4, 17, 26
CAMPAU
Josefa 46
CAMPOS
Ana Maria 242, 244
CANALS
Jayme, Fr. 84
CANATA
Catalina 6
CANDELARIA
Anamaria 307
Maria 276
CANDIDO
Jose 140
CANNATE
Maria 2
CANO
Maria Ygnacia 31, 46, 67, 109, 127, 212, 266, 305
Vizente Cruz 258
Ygnacia 109-111, 289
CAPCHOLE
Maria 5, 9, 10
CAPULI
Maria 12
CARABAJAL
Jose Antonio 238
CARIEL
Bautista 279
CARLOS
Pablo 27
CARRILLO
Maria Antonia 248
Miguel 2
CASADO
Josefa 280
Maria Manuela 216

CHAMBRES
Samuel 281
CHARVÈ
Jose 161, 164
CHARVET
Jose 240
CHASES
Maria 120
CHAVES
See CHABES, CLAVES
(n.n.) 281
Agustin 30, 38
Antonio 12, 305
Apolonia 268
Blas 225, 250, 274
Candelaria 103, 117, 127, 158, 160
Concepcion 283
Domingo 109, 136, 266, 268, 279
Encarnacion 283
Francisco 123, 166, 170, 174, 270
Guadalupe 280, 287, 300
Jose 276
Jose Maria 53, 86, 90, 131, 270, 290, 293, 298
Jose Pablo 299
Josef Julian 181
Josef Pablo 229
Juan 132, 137, 233, 265
Juan Christobal 251
Juan Nepomuceno 161
Juan Nepomuseno 67
Juana 81, 86
Juana Maria Candelaria 95
Julian 169, 188
Lucia 239, 276, 294
Lucilla 286
Luis 117, 127, 280, 299
Manuel 83, 115, 277
Manuel Jose 149
Manuela 287, 292
Margarita 297, 299
Maria 71, 111, 113, 115, 182, 189, 234, 301
Maria Antonia 266
Maria Candelaria 239
Maria Gertrudis 297
Maria Josefa 253
Maria Josepha 72, 75
Maria Micaela 250
Maria Miguela 186
Maria Teresa 306
Maria Ygeves 256
Maria Ygnacia 239
Micaela 234
Nepomuceno 86
Pablo 234
Pedro 12
Polonia 166, 294
CHAVES (continued)
Teodora 192
Vicente 269
Ygnacia 270
Ygnes 241
CHAVEZ
Agustin 27
Blas 196
Candelaria 91, 204
Domingo 195
Francisco 227
Josef Maria 193, 196
Josefa 253
Juan 201, 224, 227
Juan Manuel 197
Juan Nepomuseno 200, 256, 257
Julian 201, 204
Luiz 262
Maria Casimira 196, 229
Maria Josefa 169
Rafael 199
CHAYO
Maria 107
CHEABEA
Esteban 18
CHELMO
Francisco 20
CHIENE
Lusia 10
CHINA
Manuela 34
CHINAGO
Francisco 41
CHINAZO
Francisco 264
CHINO
Josef 30
CHINQUEPIENCHI
Maria 4
CHIU
Pablo 8
CHIUMAGUS
Lucia 13
CHIUPA
Maria 17
CHIUU
Pablo 11
CHRESPIN
See CRESPIN
Christoval 12
CHRISPIN
Maria Francisca 281
Ygnacia 280
CHUEQUEPIERCHOL
Maria 8
CHUÌPAFUÈ
Angelina 55
CHUIQUEPUENCHOLE
Maria 6

CHULA
Catarina 101, 105
CHUPUNE
Felipe 15
CISNEROS
See SISNEROS, ZISNEROS
Diego 140
Gregorio 86
Hermenegildo 102
Hermenejildo 124
Josefa 35, 36, 38
Manuel Antonio 178
Nerio 156
Polonio 83
Santiago 35
CLARAMONTE
Andres, Fr. 28
CLAVES
See CHAVES
Josef 30
COAGUACHORE
Maria 7, 8
COAGUAEQUEAM
Lusia 9
COAGUALHOLE
Maria 10
COAGUAQUEAM
Lusia 9
COCA
(n.n.) 285
Barbara 47, 63, 220
Dominga 247
Gertrudis 66, 77, 82, 99, 115, 148
Getrudes 73, 192
Getrudis 69
Jesus 283
Jose 105
Jose Manuel 294, 306
Jose Maria 47, 62, 124, 211, 215, 219, 252, 256, 269, 282, 293, 296
Juan Jesus 260
Manuel 47, 49, 51, 82, 271
Manuela 135, 234, 250
Maria 54, 102, 175, 257, 272, 282
Maria Antonia 29, 83
Maria Anttonia 62
Maria Dolores 252, 299
Maria Getrudes 33, 35
Maria Getrudis 44, 50
Maria Manuela 215, 238, 242, 295
Maria Rosario 173
Maria Teodora 289
Mateo 123, 133, 135
Miguel 23, 30, 48, 66, 73, 125, 218, 295
Rosalia 283
Teodora 219
COCA (continued)
Tomas 208
COCO
Mateo 257
COLORADO
Maria Rosa 103
Rosa 102
COMES
See GOMES
Lucia 64
COMPAÉ
Josefa 45
CONCHA
Maria 211, 270
CONEJO
Maria Concepcion 130
CONOLE
Pedro 305
CONTRERAS
Gerardo 283
Jose 267
Juan Cruz 133
Maria Dolores 256
CORDERO
Joseph 25
Juan Ray 7
CORDOBA
Anna Maria 305
Juan Felipe 209, 306
Maria Candelaria 305
Maria Francisca 307
Maria Juliana 298
CORDOVA
See GORDOVA
Aban 280
Ana Maria 233
Andres 281, 287
Antonia 293
Antonio 283
Antonio Abad 266, 271, 273
Antonio Aban 221, 254
Antonio Jose 210, 217, 240, 264, 269, 274
Avan 284, 293
Candelaria 210
Carpio 189, 206
Catarina 241
Damacio 251
Damaso 217, 295
Dionicio 222, 241
Encarnacion 283
Francisca 207, 281
Francisco 194, 227
Francisco Antonio 213
Gertrudis 241, 243
Getrudis 280, 289
Gregoria 134
Gregorio 274, 282
Guadalupe 194, 279

CORDOVA (continued)
Jose Antonio 209, 217, 262
Jose Mariano 218
Jose Venancio 260
Josefa 152
Juan 225, 264, 273, 293
Juan Felipe 181, 220, 251
Juan Lorenso 187
Juana 211, 218, 281, 287
Juana Getrudes 226
Juana Getrudis 288
Juana Josefa 253
Lorenso 184, 191, 253, 294
Lorenzo 154, 166, 216, 234, 249, 251, 263, 279, 283
Manuel 283, 291, 293
Margarita 87, 91, 106, 185, 252
Maria 84, 170, 171, 197, 290
Maria Antonia 213
Maria Barbara 142, 237
Maria Candelaria 264, 265
Maria Catarina 217, 218
Maria Francisca 253
Maria Gertrudis 250, 270
Maria Guadalupe 213, 233, 263
Maria Jesus 248, 260
Maria Juliana 281
Maria Pasquala 282
Maria Ygnacia 160, 262
Maria Ynes 30
Maria Ysabel 222
Mariana 76, 88, 89, 94, 110, 137, 162, 165, 166, 182
Pablo 210, 238, 242, 287, 306
Pablo Francisco 215
Raymundo 210, 218, 249, 251, 266, 273
Rimundo 199
Santos 219
Sevastian 36
Tomas 248
Ygnacia 270
Ysabel 266
CORREA
Andres, Fr. 230
CORTES
Benigna 219, 220
Beronica 215
Christoval 280
Cristoval 164
Cruz 80, 95, 120, 218, 239
Francisca 80, 83
Francisco 248, 258, 297
Jose 216, 239, 265, 273, 286
Jose Antonio 67, 81, 118, 121, 132, 276, 306
Jose Jose 111
Jose Maria 77, 107, 108, 130, 156, 192, 214, 285, 292
CORTES (continued)
Jose Pablo 148
Josef Antonio 177
Josefa Veronica 50
Juan 247
Juan Baptista 206
Juan Bautista 164, 304
Juan Cristoval 55, 72, 101, 121
Juan Cruz 68, 72, 93, 114, 211
Juan Ygnacio 221, 306
Juana 100, 116, 130, 212, 255, 268, 272, 278, 305
Manuel 51, 60, 69, 80, 126, 272
Manuela 160, 201
Maria 169, 181
Maria Antonia 100, 105
Maria Benigna 240
Maria Francisca 76, 277
Maria Josefa 304
Maria Manuela 221
Maria Serafina 268
Maria Veronica 44, 73
Maria Ysabel 299
Miguel 283
Nepomuceno 287
Nepumuceno 215
Paulin 85, 147, 286
Pedro 56, 220, 301
Petra 211
Rosalia 38
Serafina 112, 151, 220, 267
Veronica 160
CORTEZ
Cruz 83
Josef Maria 199
Juana 228
Manuela 204
Maria 205
COSA
Maria Varvara 299
COYO
Michaela 42
CRESPIN
See CHRESPIN, CHRISPIN
Jose 219
Maria Dolores 238
CRUS
Agustin 291
Veronica 291
CRUZ
Alexo 284
Alexos 212
Antonio 200
Antonio Mariano 197, 213
Baltasar 4
Esteban 16
Estevan 17
Francisco 3, 281, 287

GABALDON
See GAVALDON
Antonia Rosa 99
Anttonio, Fr. 25
Dolores 292
Felis 304
Feliz 221
Jose Manuel 270, 306
Maria 157, 301
Maria Ygnacia 220, 232
Ygnacia 247
GABILAN
See GAVILAN
Barbara 33
Encarnacion 286, 293
Josefa 286
Lucia 244, 260
Manuel 304
Pablo 20, 26
GALBIS
Juan 300
GALLEGA
Maria 221
GALLEGO
Anamaria 216
Antonio 206, 278
Antonio Jesus 165, 214, 281
Benito 216
Christoval 277
Gaspar 140
Jesus 177, 182, 277, 286
Jose Antonio 247
Jose Pablo 279
Lugarda 291
Luterio 287
Maria Antonia 168, 306
Maria Jesus 277
Maria Leocadia 294
Maria Luz 140
Pablo 208, 222, 281
Pedro Bautista 208
Tomas 169
GARBISO
(torn)la 303
GARCIA
(n.n.) 303
Alfonso 133
Ana Maria 179, 186
Anamaria 194
Antonia 73, 293
Antonio 269, 278
Bisente 174, 181, 195, 207
Culas 224
Francisca 171, 189, 272, 278, 289
Francisco 240, 251, 284
Francisco Antonio 231
Francisco Xabier 255
Francisco Xavier 187, 237
Gertrudis 143, 167
GARCIA (continued)
Getrudes 188, 227
Getrudis 291
Jose 87, 104, 131, 133, 140, 151, 164, 190, 220, 256, 257, 288
Jose Antonio 156, 289, 292
Jose Feliz 261
Jose Jesus 221, 288
Jose Maria 81
Jose Rafael 143
Jose Ramon 232
Josef Ramon 205
Josefa 259
Juan 119
Juan Angel 114, 116, 193, 204, 214, 277, 287, 306
Juan Antonio 148, 217, 218, 276
Juan Christobal 248
Juan Ciriaco 260
Juan Diego 64
Juan de Dios 221
Juan Jose 192
Juan Siriaco 242
Juana 129, 271, 281
Juana Getrudes 174, 179
Juana Tomasa 239, 263, 273, 280
Juaquin Andres 297
Julian 198, 205, 238, 242
Juliana 261
Manuel 192, 227, 265, 284, 295
Manuel/Miguel 288
Manuela 132, 217, 285, 289, 293
Maria 93, 98, 283
Maria Antonia 210, 214, 276, 293
Maria Encarnacion 296
Maria Francisca 142, 264
Maria Gracia 269
Maria Guadalupe 237
Maria Jesus 306
Maria Josefa 229
Maria Manuela 232
Maria Micaela 216
Maria Rosa 140
Maria Victoria 306
Maria Ygnacia 254, 269, 292, 293
Miguel 202, 249, 253, 259, 276, 278
Miguel/Manuel 288
Patricio 301
Pedro 179, 180, 186, 293
Ramon 194, 282
Simon 196, 209, 213, 260
Tanislado 193
Teresa 278
Thomasa 241
Tomasa 133, 174
Vicente 297
Vizente 283
Xabier 178

GARCIA (continued)
Xavier 280
Xaviera 81
Ygnacia 219, 257, 286
Ysabel 209
GARCIA JURADO
Ramon 14
GARZIA
Salvador 35
GAVALDON
See GABALDON
Maria Dolores 276
GAVILAN
See GABILAN
Andres 54, 90
Barbara 36
Juana Maria 114, 117
Manuela 39
Pablo 12
GEAQUERPA
Juana 15
GIJOSA
Francisca Anttonia 19
GOMES
See COMES
Antonio 202, 254, 295
Gaspar 289
Jose 307
Juan 289
Juan Jesus 292, 304
Juana 44, 49, 64
Juana Calista 47
Juliana 183
Lucia 44
Maquela 300
Maria 40, 42, 44, 45, 63, 64
Maria Soledad 295
GOMEZ
Antonio 197, 205
Francisca 108
Juan 27, 273
Juan Miguel 262
Juana 51, 59, 62, 98, 99
Maria 28, 31, 90, 127
Maria Antonia 211
Maria Ascencion 122, 137
Maria Gertrudis 27
Maria Getrudes 32
Maria Manuela 209
Maria Rosa 164
Maria Ygnacia 86
Nerio 216
Pablo 34, 58
Rosa 195
GONSALES
Antonio 307
Antonio Josef 175
Candelaria 174
Diego 287
GONSALES (continued)
Domingo 298
Elogio 256
Felipe 188, 293, 294
Fernando 288, 299
Francisca 287
Jose 285
Jose Antonio 186, 256, 285, 292, 297, 300
Josef 175
Josef Antonio 173, 181
Juan 177, 196, 301
Juan Antonio 205, 307
Juan Calletano 300
Juan Josef 175
Manuela 38, 195, 301
Margarita 304
Maria 176, 205
Maria Antonia 205
Maria Carmen 191
Maria Estefana 199
Maria Mequela 181, 189, 206
Maria Teresa 200
Paula 288
Rosalia 303
Salvador 184
Teresa 41, 288
Ygnacio 256, 293
GONSALEZ
Cristoval 223
Juan Bruno, Fr. 228
Francisco 225
Jose 72
Jose Antonio 192
Jose Biterbo 195
Josef Antonio 224
Juan 196
Maria Antonia 225
Micaela 102
Salvador 172
GONZALES
Antonia Ygnacia 203
Antonio 292
Cayetano 282
Diego 13
Jose 101
Jose Antonio 258
Jose Miguel 296
Jose Santos 212
Juan 255
Micaela 66
Pascuala 303
Sebastiana 101
GONZALEZ
Anamaria 220
Angela 156
Antonia 102, 242
Antonio 152, 166, 283
Antonio Segundo 210

JARAMILLO, Mariano (continued)
230, 237, 250, 264
Sevastian 201
Soledad 200, 201, 224
Ysidora 280
JATE
Francisco 7
JIMCHAR
Maria 6
JIRON
Maria Rosa 9
Miguel Enrriques 25
JOIPAP
Maria 7
JORGE
Lorenza 282
JORUPA
Leonicia 306
JORVAOCUI
Francisca 7
JUEPATU
Magdalena 19
JUESPLA
Teresa 19
JUILA
Josefa 231
JUILO
Jose 49, 74
Josef 30
Josefa 67, 72, 73, 82, 88, 89, 91, 126
Maria Carmen 74
Maria Josefa 69, 181, 190, 238, 252, 265
JUIPALUIA
Tomasa 5
JUIPATTOLCOI
Magdalena 9
JURE
Maria 2
JUSLI
Diego 22
LA RANAGA
See LARAÑAGA
Cristobal Maria 217
LA BATIA
Domingo 211
LABADIA
See LAVADIA
Andrea 259
Maria Gertrudis 250
LABADIAS
Andrea 232
LABADILLA
See LAVADILLA
Andrea 287
LADRON del NIÑO GUEVARA
Juan Baptista, Fr. 229
LAGO
Gabriel, Fr. 50
LALANDA
Bautista 149, 218
Josefa 262, 268
Juan 203
Juan Baptista 181
Juan Bautista 184, 190
Juan de Dios 295
Maria Josefa 261, 263, 267
Thomas 258
LAMUR
Antonio 290
LARAÑADA
Paula 180
LARAÑAGA
See LA RANAGA
Jose Miguel 211
Lonicio 200
Maria Paula 214
LARRAÑADA
Paula 169, 224
LARRAÑAGA
Christobal 240, 247, 266, 272
Christobal Maria 252, 270
Jose Dionisio 241
Maria Paula 194
Miguel 245, 250, 280
Paula 116, 125, 127, 131, 144, 150, 154, 155, 159, 179, 188, 265, 267
LASO
See LAZO
Gertrudis 130
Matias 285
LAVADIA
See LABADIA, LA BATIA
Andrea 253
LAVADILLA
See LABADILLA
Andrella 203
Maria Andrea 229
LAZO
See LASO
Maria Geronima 119
Mathio 60
LEAL
Benito 216
Domingo 160
Guadalupe 150, 208
Jose Cruz 259
Josef 208
Josefa 97, 101, 205, 276
Juan Augustin 28
Juan Bautista 289
Juan Domingo 44, 50, 101, 215
Juan Rafael 73
Juan Rafel 183
Juana 183

LOPES (continued)
Maria Bartola 297
Maria Gertrudis 298
Maria Lorensa 307
Vernardo 307
LOPEZ
Antonia Teresa 74, 276
Barbara 93
Christoval 258
Cristoval 135, 143, 151, 166, 167
Francisca 102
Jose Antonio 282
Jose Miguel 86, 93
Juana 224
Juana Soledad 295
Lorensa 223
Lorenza 129, 151
Magdalena 251, 274/275
Maria Antonia 132
Maria Magdalena 110
Maria Soledad 270, 277
Maria Teresa 256
Micaela 151
Miguel 119, 122
Rafael 252
Silvestre 86, 94, 98, 101
Tomas 107
LOPEZ GALLARDO
Pedro 25
LOPEZ TELLO
Joseph, Fr. 15, 16
LOVATO
See LOBATO
(n.n.) 284
Antonia 203
Antonia Theodora 240
Antonio 66, 281, 301
Antonio Jose 58
Antonio Josef 169
Barbara 238
Barvara 169
Buenaventura 268, 275
Felipa 241
Francisco 239, 242, 248
Francisco Javriel 225
Jose Antonio 58
Jose Manuel 252
Jose Rafael 65
Josefa 202, 204, 206, 230, 257, 288
Josefa Maria 65
Juan 174, 185, 186, 198, 203, 235, 237, 244, 246, 251, 257, 264, 285, 297, 299
Juan Antonio 237, 296, 298
Juan Domingo 58, 60
Juan Francisco 271
Juan Jose 49
Juan Joseph 58
LOVATO (continued)
Juan Manuel 305
Juan Nepomuceno 290
Juana 275
Juana Catarina 191
Juana Teresa 294
Lorenzo 58
Luciana 226
Manuel 65
Margarita 65, 173, 207, 259, 279
Maria 172, 282
Maria Barbara 261, 307
Maria Barvara 198
Maria Catalina 207
Maria Dolores 265
Maria Elena 172, 185
Maria Josefa 231, 237, 250, 251, 261, 264, 292, 298
Maria Madalena 198
Maria Nicolasa 298
Maria Paula 54, 55, 58, 299
Maria Petra 243
Maria Rita 223
Maria Soledad 255, 262, 269, 281
Maria Ygnacia 289, 290, 305
Mateo 223
Matheo 264/265
Miguel 226
Nepomuceno 289
Nicolasa 297, 298
Paula 54
Petrona 247
Rafael 263, 287, 291
Rafel 169
Salvador 231, 264, 265, 290, 305
Soledad 286
Tomas 174, 193, 204, 228, 239, 262
Ventura 298
LUCERO
See LUSERO, LUZERO
A(torn) 107
Agustin 250
Antonio 236, 244, 264, 265, 270, 271, 285, 291, 293, 300
Antonio Jose 184
Apolonia 274
Ascencion 107, 124, 135, 141
Ascension 285
Bernardo 113, 115, 120, 123, 133, 143, 144, 146, 155, 164, 201, 227, 248, 255, 257, 267, 298
Cencion 198, 253
Christoval 257
Cristoval 131, 132, 137, 138, 143-145, 149, 155, 294
Dolores 131, 145, 157, 168
Francisca 57, 58, 102, 122, 123, 129

LUCERO (continued)
Gertrudis 270
Gregorio 145, 148, 294/295
Guadalupe 66, 299
Jesus 207, 225, 284, 289
Jose Francisco 236
Jose Maria 236, 260, 262, 301
Jose Miguel 145, 253
Jose Rafael 273
Josef Maria 204, 207
Josef Rafael 226
Josef Rafel 174, 177, 199
Josefa 54, 55, 60, 115, 278, 294
Juan 136, 142, 180, 250, 262
Juan Antonio 35, 177, 180, 237, 240
Juan Jesus 116, 134, 135, 155, 234, 236, 279, 286, 287, 301
Juan Jose 278
Juan Manuel 189
Juana 251, 263, 295
Julian 124, 131, 155, 307
Lucia 52, 304
Magdalena 140, 293
Manuel 203, 229, 232, 253, 259, 264, 265, 278, 287, 300
Manuela 202
Margarita 190, 202, 249, 253, 259, 276, 278
Maria 173, 186, 189
Maria Apolonia 240
Maria Ascension 113
Maria Asencion 231
Maria Asension 262
Maria Carmen 180
Maria Dolores 60, 157, 174, 176, 177, 236, 244
Maria Dominga 189
Maria Josefa 189, 273, 297
Maria Lus 297, 301
Maria Luz 252, 303
Maria Nazarena 108
Maria Paula 177
Maria Polonia 190, 300, 307
Maria Rafaela 306
Maria Rita 124, 179, 183, 185, 201, 202, 205, 272
Maria Rosa 54
Maria Sencion 172, 254
Maria Soledad 196, 198, 251, 280
Martina 8
Micaela 56
Miquela 305
Nicolas 241
Pablo 117, 123, 127, 136, 144, 159, 169, 179, 188, 194, 224, 267
Pedro 133, 204, 225, 227, 284
Pedro Antonio 149, 243, 245, 257,

LUCERO, Pedro Antonio (continued) 262
Polonia 138, 144, 145, 148, 149, 171, 174, 181, 203, 290
Rafel 171
Rita 134, 162, 178
Rosa 285
Rosalia 278
Salvador 148
Santiago 137, 140, 166, 284, 293, 300
Soledad 192
Tomas 252, 274
Vicente 150, 153, 286, 290, 291
Ysabel 62

LUCIE
Magdalena 294

LUERAS
Diego Antonio 183

LUGAN
See LUJAN, LUXAN
Juana 23

LUJAN
See LUGAN, LUXAN
Ana 70
Antonio 21, 22, 293
Antonio Jose 44
Barbara 70, 74
Encarnacion 101
Francisca 188
Francisco 280
Francisco Antonio 74
Geronimo 295
Jose 285
Josef Manuel 227
Josefa 67
Joseph 24
Juan 9, 13, 17, 18, 256
Juan Antonio 180
Juan Baptista 194
Juan Domingo 183
Juan Ygnacio 187
Julian 55
Maria 37
Maria Antonia 56, 277
Maria Encarnacion 72
Maria Francisca 59
Maria Natividad 51
Micaela 223
Rafela 187
Rosa 286, 293
Rosalia 285
Vicente 49
Ysabel 36

LUJANA
Josefa 66
Maria 22

LUNA
Ana Maria 210

MARTIN, Andres (continued)
262, 278
Antonia 68, 133, 164, 241, 246, 294
Antonia Rosa 282, 298
Antonia Teresa 266
Antonio 66, 87, 114, 117, 146, 156, 174, 193, 194, 210, 219, 243, 247, 263, 264, 283, 295, 301, 304
Antonio Jose 162, 221, 259, 265, 281, 286
Antonio Jose, Fr. 296
Antonio Josef 196
Augustina 63, 81
Barbara 32, 42, 178, 214, 265, 279, 293, 295, 307
Bartolome 27, 30, 31, 33
Barvara 225, 241, 292
Bautista 121, 157
Benita 300
Bentura 218
Bernardino 136, 162, 186, 193, 204, 234, 285
Bernardo 281
Bibiana 213
Biviana 196
Brijida 243
Buenabentura 272
Buenaventura 296
Casimiro 233
Catalina 45
Catarina 88, 119, 125, 146, 182, 186, 290
Chatarina 229
Cisilia 189
Clara 277/278
Clemente 139
Concepcion 147, 281, 286
Crus 241
Cruz 139, 190, 243, 268, 282, 287
Damiana 219
Diego Antonio 148, 161, 164, 204
Dolores 227, 281, 294
Encarnacion 152, 291
Estefana 163
Estevan Rafel 189
Eucebio 264
Eusebio 209, 213, 285
Faustin 288
Faustino 279
Feliciana 222
Felipe 47, 51, 76, 78, 81-83, 87, 88, 107, 117, 122, 148, 149, 153 168, 175, 203, 218, 238, 273, 293
Felipe Santiago 125
Feliz 105
Filena 105

MARTIN (continued)
Francisca 140, 223, 256, 289
Francisco 137, 146, 205, 207, 212-214, 220, 234/235, 255, 264, 273, 276, 281, 287, 292
Geronimo 282, 299
Gertrudis 128, 151
Gervacio 116, 255, 268, 272, 305
Gervasio 100, 212, 278
Getrudes 200, 201
Graziana Beatriz 30
Guadalupe 60, 66, 282, 304
Hernando 18
Joaquin 91, 103, 239
Jos. Antonio 144
Jose 50-52, 59, 67, 101, 109, 115, 135, 150, 214, 218, 220, 234, 281, 301
Jose Andres 229
Jose Antonio 57, 67, 68, 70, 74, 77, 107, 115, 128, 141, 144, 191, 227, 240, 282
Jose Anttonio 62
Jose Encarnacion 299
Jose Gabriel 195, 231, 257, 293
Jose Gavriel 225
Jose Gregorio 263
Jose Guadalupe 278
Jose Joaquin 95
Jose Manuel 220, 231, 233
Jose Maria 235, 294
Jose Miguel 115, 213, 265, 305
Jose Norberto 139
Jose Pablo 231
Jose Ygnacio 208
Jose Ygnasio 106
Josef 30-36
Josef Andres 171
Josef Antonio 182, 202, 224, 226
Josef Francisco 173
Josef Gabriel 225
Josef Manuel 205
Josef Pablo 204, 228
Josef Rafel 169
Josefa 94, 115, 130, 139, 143, 144, 162, 215, 278, 283
Joseph 49
Juan 156, 193, 214, 220, 223, 293
Juan Andres 293
Juan Antonio 168, 176, 195, 221, 241, 259, 269
Juan Anttonio 28
Juan Baptista 31, 56
Juan Bautista 173
Juan Buenaventura 244
Juan Carmen 108
Juan Cristoval 69
Juan Crus 114
Juan Cruz 111, 126, 143

MARTIN (continued)
Juan de Dios 14
Juan Domingo 297
Juan Esteban 245
Juan Felipe 44, 47, 51, 66, 79, 191, 220, 241, 270, 280, 292, 296
Juan Jesus 98, 115, 130, 160, 162
Juan Jose 116, 283
Juan Julian 235, 282
Juan Miguel 30, 36
Juan Nicolas 207
Juan Pablo 59, 73, 252, 274, 280, 287, 300
Juan Pascual 263
Juan Pasqual 272
Juan Phelipe 54, 68
Juan Reyes 280
Juana 113, 128, 132, 173, 209, 211, 217, 226, 258, 262, 292
Juana Catalina 39
Juana Cathalina 33
Juana Getrudes 174
Juana Josefa 42, 152
Juana Maria 147, 160, 231, 233, 275
Juana Maria Gertrudis 28
Juana Paula 162
Juana Teresa 288
Juanita 215
Juaquin 257, 275, 297/298
Julian 178
Lucia 265
Luciana 284
Luz 159, 284
Madalena 289
Magdalena 69, 74, 94, 98, 105, 131, 142, 147, 238, 286
Manuel 184, 220, 228, 239
Manuel Antonio 223, 240, 252, 253, 277
Manuel Gregorio 127, 296
Manuel Ramos 304
Manuela 114, 125, 193, 294
Manuela Rafaela 209
Margarita 53, 59, 66, 69, 71, 74, 75, 78, 79, 84, 110, 116, 117, 121, 125, 138, 141, 159, 160, 165, 166, 183, 187, 191, 225, 263, 279, 294
Maria 83, 91, 104, 117, 126, 173, 176, 178, 183, 187, 191, 203, 204, 208, 225, 226, 253, 287, 296
Maria Andrea 209
Maria Antonia 51, 69, 80, 85, 87, 105, 119, 125, 126, 130, 137, 140, 151, 168, 199, 255, 272, 273, 297, 300, 306

MARTIN (continued)
Maria Anttonia 61
Maria Ascension 212
Maria Asencion 245
Maria Asension 268
Maria Augustina 78
Maria Barbara 221, 236, 264
Maria Candelaria 254
Maria Carmen 218
Maria Cecilia 176
Maria Crus 283
Maria Cruz 215, 247, 266
Maria Damiana 178
Maria Dolores 146, 154, 160, 171, 222, 233, 234, 242, 243, 265, 274, 279, 281
Maria Encarnacion 214, 259, 281, 299
Maria Francisca 210, 221
Maria Gertrudis 258, 260, 263
Maria Guadalupe 240, 275
Maria Jesus 217, 241, 243, 271, 289
Maria Josefa 100, 194
Maria Josepha 74
Maria Juana 218
Maria Luisa 209
Maria Lus 175, 219, 289, 292
Maria Luz 32, 72, 135, 138, 169, 183, 197, 200, 229, 236, 240, 241, 261, 265, 274, 306
Maria Madalena 217
Maria Magdalena 66
Maria Manuela 116, 138, 145, 211, 214, 222, 237, 260, 270, 294
Maria Paula 156, 240
Maria Rafaela 258, 306
Maria Reyes 252, 289, 292
Maria Rita 268
Maria Rosa 106, 125, 136, 141, 143, 148, 199, 200, 202, 249, 271, 298
Maria Roza 254
Maria Soledad 218
Maria Susana 270
Maria Tomasa 97, 220
Maria Ygnacia 68, 87, 103, 109, 114, 116, 133, 138, 139, 146, 156, 159, 164, 165, 167, 171, 175, 176, 191, 266
Maria Ysidora 140, 153, 204, 237
Mariana 267, 294
Mariano 207, 250, 258, 293, 299
Marta 86, 98, 101, 108, 111, 114, 116, 148, 163, 210, 219, 277, 290, 292
Mauricia 286
Micaela 221, 241, 258, 274, 284
Miguel 22, 43, 209, 294

MARTIN (continued)
Miguel San Juan 45
Nicolas 20, 182
Nicolasa 32
Pablo 257, 291
Pascuala 196
Pasqual 261
Patricia 123, 142, 285
Paubla 300
Paula 203, 209, 220, 269, 280
Pedro 103, 106, 109, 116, 121, 132, 134, 135, 139, 146, 158, 159, 168, 172, 173, 191, 219, 230, 244, 254, 257, 268, 269, 278, 286, 292, 293, 307
Pedro Antonio 254
Petra Jesus 214
Rafael 211, 299
Rafaela 82, 109, 118, 271
Ramon 269, 280, 300
Reyes 156, 276
Rita 285
Roque 114, 158, 176, 181, 182, 253, 287
Rosa 149, 164, 196, 201, 205, 247, 284, 287, 289, 291, 292
Rosalia 35, 37, 38, 52, 69, 71-73, 77, 78, 83, 85, 98, 105, 111, 112, 128, 134, 140, 145, 151, 168, 169, 194, 196, 243, 252, 300
Salvador 81, 214, 265, 292
Salvador Manuel 52, 73
Salvador Raymundo 31
Santiago 265, 272, 290
Santos 194, 255, 272
Secilia 307
Seferino 235, 242
Severino 131, 133, 151, 161, 166, 275
Soledad 288, 289
Teodora 156, 173, 189, 223, 230, 301
Teresa 258
Theodora 244
Thomas 254
Thomasa 257
Tomas 84, 212, 243, 267
Tomasa 86, 98, 100, 113, 115, 120, 123, 133, 143, 144, 146, 155, 164, 201, 227, 267, 298
Trinidad 278
Ventura 298
Vicente 216, 276
Vitor 291
Vizente 69
Ygnacia 85, 161, 179, 307
Ygnacio 200, 214, 236, 258, 262, 265, 278

MARTIN (continued)
Ynacia 91
Ynes 261, 287, 294
Ysidora 139, 180, 214, 269, 286
MARTIN BUENO
Francisco, Fr. 38, 42, 49
MARTIN LOVATO
Paubla 66
MARTINA
Juana 282, 283, 299
Lucia 65
Maria 79, 93
Maria Simona 36
Rosalia 29, 31
Ygnacia 278
MARTINES
Anamaria 301
Candelaria 272
Cruz 295
Feliciana 304
Felipe 294
Felix 11
Francisco 132
Hermenegildo 295
Jose Francisco 296
Jose Mariano 294
Jose Santiago 297
Jose, Fr. 304
Juan Pablo 305
Juan Salvador 295
Juana Maria 296
Maria 195, 306
Maria Antonia 77, 301
Maria Anttonia 60
Maria Dolores 305
Maria Encarnacion 296
Maria Manuela 304, 306
Maria Reyes 297, 306
Maria Ygnacia 64
Rosalia 306
Thomasa 255
MARTINEZ
Antonio 277, 286
Antonio Jose 222
Antonio Jose, Fr. 303
Antonio Severino 222
Bibiana 209
Cruz 97
Damiana 210
Diego, Fr. 63, 141, 148
Eusebio 222
Felipe Jesus 68
Feliz 14
Francisco 106, 153
Jose Francisco 93
Jose Julian 119
Jose Maria 267, 277
Jose Maria Jesus 277
Juan Miguel 219

MELENUDO
Teresa 112
MERINO
Pasqual 283
MES
Dolores 217, 282, 289, 290
Domingo 211, 214, 218
Felipa 214
Francisco 220
Joaquin 282
Maria Biviana 289
Polonia 290
Trinidad 213
MESA
Maria Polonia 174
MESTAS
Ana Maria 282
Aparicio 303
Bernardo 211
Biviana 303
Christoval Clemente 42
Clemente 41
Culasa 209
Francisco Xaviel 45
Gertrudis 141
Jose 221, 241, 307
Jose Ramon 60
Josef Manuel 199
Josefa 196, 265
Juana 196
Juana Teresa 296
Juaquin 116
Juliana 252
Maria 190
Maria Dolores 237
Maria Gertrudis 240, 252, 270
Maria Luz 58
Maria Manuela 299
Miguel 303
Ramon 52
MEZ
Bernardo 204
Soledad 204
MIERA
(torn) 83
Ana Maria 81, 82, 110, 113, 117
Anna Maria 76
Jose 76, 89, 94, 100, 111, 112, 121, 126, 149, 164, 165, 167, 175, 207, 239
Josef Antonio 170, 174, 175
Maria Ygnacia 167
Ygnacia 175
MINGUES
Juan, Fr. 11
MIRABAL
(n.n.) 93
Domingo 54
Jose 35, 36, 41, 88, 123
MIRABAL (continued)
Joseph 49
Juan 49-51
Juan Domingo 179
Juan Joseph, Fr. 24
Juan Luis 88, 162
Juana Maria 36, 52
Manuela 30, 65
Maria Antonia 31, 33
Maria Josefa 263, 297
Maria Rafaela 105, 247
Rafael 90
Rafaela 72, 92, 94, 242
Rosa 52
Rossa 61
Salbador 286
Tomasa 74
MIRABALL
(n.n.) 115
Domingo 128
Jose 107
Juan Luis 116, 125, 139
Rafaela 163
MIRANDA
Anttonio, Fr. 10
MIRAVAL
Jose 29, 37, 50, 81
Josef 40
Juan 43, 46
Juan Domingo 253
Manuela 41, 50
Maria Rosa 68
Maria Teresa 200
Rafaela 194
Rosa 48
MOLINA
Ana Maria 218
Anamaria 217
MONDE
Susana 304
MONDRAGON
Ana Maria 235
Antonia Josefa 73
Antonio 88, 89, 97, 119, 294
Antonio Jose 160
Bartolo 305
Bartolome 80, 92, 94, 111, 122, 137, 234, 235
Christoval 62
Cristoval 207
Gertrudes 137
Gertrudis 97, 120, 137
Jose 284, 300
Jose Antonio 73, 185, 285
Jose Cruz 217
Jose Manuel 53
Jose Mariano 50
Josefa 59, 147, 257
Juan 235

MUÑIS
(n.n.) 303
Anamaria 206
Gertrudis 162
Maria 142
MUÑIZ
Domingo 303
Encarnacion 82
Juan 116
Juan Andres 303
Maria Gertrudis 258
Miguel, Fr. 2, 4, 13, 15
MUÑOS JURADO
Diego, Fr. 29, 43, 93
MUÑOZ JURADO
Diego, Fr. 35
MURO
Buenaventura, Fr. 282, 283
NACAYA
Francisco 8
NANTORSE
Lusia 5
NAPO
Anttonio 5
NARACHE
Juana 3, 13, 14
NARACHES
Juana 4
NARANGO
Ana Maria 193
NARANJO
Juan Antonio 27
Juan Manuel 304
Juana 293
Lucia 40, 44, 133
Maria 72
Maria Luciana 301
Paubla 300
Rosalia 300
NAROCHE
Juana 7
NATOE
Diego 5
NIETO
Gertrudis 264
NO SURNAME
Agneda 220
Agustin 32
Ana 240
Ana Maria 15, 42, 284
Anamaria 219
Andres 142, 159
Anica 42, 46, 90
Antonia 292
Antonia Damasia 44
Antonia Margarita 306
Antonio 63, 150
Antonio Josef 183
Antonio Luis 18
NO SURNAME (continued)
Anttonia 16
Anttonio Jose 62
Augustin 113, 124, 135
Barbara 29
Bibiana 283
Concepcion 78, 92
Diego Anttonio 16
Dionisio 110
Elena 17
Esteban 140
Felipe 303
Felis 128, 132
Felisiana 253
Francisca 82, 83, 85, 181, 184, 195
Francisco 31, 34, 120, 166
Geronima 24
Geronimo 21, 22
Guadalupe 79, 85, 288, 291
Jose 134, 155
Jose Antonio 37, 105
Jose Domingo 173
Jose Gabriel 168
Jose Maria 141
Jose Miguel 37
Josef 32
Josef Antonio 29, 35
Josef Jesus 206
Josefa 35, 41, 50, 224, 283
Joseph Xavier 19
Josepha 49
Juan 2, 3, 12, 55, 59, 102, 199
Juan Alamo 15, 16
Juan Antonio 29-31, 79, 156, 307
Juan Carmen 284
Juan Christobal 34
Juan Jesus 203
Juan Jose 277
Juan Miguel 125
Juan Nepomuceno 55
Juan Policarpio 91
Juan Rafael 97
Juan Salvador 298
Juan Ygnacio 163
Juana 14, 16, 17, 20, 279, 290
Juana Maria 30
Juana Micaela 216
Juana Prudencia 127
Juana Rafaela 88
Julian 290
Lucia 19, 30, 42, 48, 59, 141, 297
Lucia Maria 22
Madalena 185, 186
Magdalena 24, 83
Manuel 21, 147
Manuel Antonio 227
Manuela 29, 30, 33, 38, 48, 148

NO SURNAME (continued)
Manuela Antonia 39
Manuela Francisca 32
Marcos 8
Margarita 60, 281, 287
Maria 15, 17, 18, 49, 171, 184, 198, 284, 285, 288, 292, 293, 303
Maria Agustina/Avelina 64
Maria Antonia 29, 33, 40, 53, 80, 173, 178, 192, 199, 290
Maria Avelina/Agustina 64
Maria Barbara 32
Maria Casimira 193
Maria Cecilia 37
Maria Claudia 170
Maria Damiana 188
Maria Encarnacion 79, 89, 170, 267
Maria Francisca 219
Maria Gertrudis 301
Maria Gracia 193
Maria Josefa 37, 79
Maria Luisa 225
Maria Luz 63
Maria Manuela 184
Maria Paula 78
Maria Rafaela 78
Maria Regina 93
Maria Reyes 277
Maria Rosa 46, 49, 63, 70, 82, 84
Maria Rosalia 281
Maria Soledad 64, 186, 301
Maria Ygnacia 79, 171, 185
Maria Ygnes 67
Maria Ysabel 283
Mariano 284
Mariquita 222
Marta 290
Martin 29
Martin Jose 37
Micaela 87, 284
Miguel 99
Miquela 181
Pasquel 128
Paulin 121, 140, 161
Pedro 135, 143
Pedro Leon 16
Polonia 275
Prudencia 213
Rafael 147
Rafel 176
Rafela 190
Ramon 143
Rosa 29, 34, 49
Rosalia 81, 208
Rosalia Josefa 295
Salvador 157, 168
Santiago 31

NO SURNAME (continued)
Serafina 220
Teodora 41
Teresa 11, 24, 105, 187, 193
Theresa 20
Tomasa 97, 99
Ventura 140
Ynes 279
Ypolito 281
Ysabel 94

NOLAN
Gerbacio 294

NORACHEI
Juana 2

OCONCHE
Juana 3

OJALA
Maria Angela 113

OLACA
Geronima 1

OLAETA
Jose, Fr. 27

OLGUIN
See HOLGUIN
Margarita 56

OLONA
Antonio Jose 280
Jose 290
Jose Francisco 257
Rosa 154

OLONIA
Antonio 291
Antonio Jose 300

ONTIBEROS
Josepha 21

OQUIR
Ana 10

ORELLANO
See ARELLANO
Nicardo 214

ORIOSTE
See HURIOSTE, URIOSTE
Feliz 291
Tomas 65

OROSCO
Josef Maximo 32

ORTEGA
See HORTEGA
Andres 240
Domingo 145
Jose Bivian, Fr. 93
Jose Francisco 147
Jose Manuel 303
Manuel 173, 290
Maria 90, 212, 290, 298
Maria Antonia 252
Maria Consecion 173
Maria Dolores 78
Maria Gertrudis 299

ORTEGA (continued)
Maria Paula 234
Nicolas 218
Pasqual 290
ORTIS
Ana Maria 286
Anamaria 177
Francisco 75
Gaspar 289
Jose 80
Jose Francisco 70
Juan Andres 300
Lucia 42, 53
Luisia 177
Mamaria 299
Maria Antonia 48, 297
Maria Feliciana 300
Maria Josefa 45
Matias 219, 286
Nicholas 7
Tomas 136
ORTIZ
See HORTIZ
Ana 123
Ana Maria 86, 179, 232, 236, 239, 240, 260
Anamaria 176, 196, 203, 254, 255
Anna Maria 303
Antonio Jose 84
Bernardo 88
Feliciana 221, 242, 294
Felisiana 190
Francisca 98, 221, 295
Francisco 297
Francisco Jabier 219
Gaspar 256
Gertrudis 148
Jose 85, 99
Josefa 283, 285
Juan Rafael 100
Lorenza 81
Lucia 58, 112, 141
Luisa 165
Maria Antonia 100, 213, 229, 239, 250, 262
Maria Dolores 243, 244, 246
Mathias 269
Miguel 84
Rosalia 37
Tomas 140, 143, 148, 150
Vicente 154
PACA
Juan 3
PACHA
Maria 4
PACHAR
Elena 10
PACHECO
Antonio 254
PACHECO (continued)
Antonio Jose 209, 288
Diego Antonio 230/231
Francisco 198, 260, 278, 279, 282, 287, 288, 299
Gregoria 186
Gregorio 300
Guadalupe 293
Jose 81, 84, 95, 184, 233, 240
Jose Gregorio 258
Jose Ramon 158, 162
Josef 172
Josef Antonio 197
Juan 13, 257
Juan Antonio 257, 276
Juan Jose 89
Juan Pablo 171
Juan Pedro 241, 292, 306
Juana Micaela 295
Manuel Estevan 186, 197
Maria Antonia 84, 89, 95
Maria Biviana 186, 258
Maria Dolores 136, 138, 233
Maria Francisca 171
Maria Guadalupe 249
Maria Peregrina 245
Maria Viviana 197
Petra Jesus 216
Petrona 71, 98, 99, 152, 240, 241, 254, 256
Ramon 160, 172, 178, 189, 202
Ysabel 43
PACHIRPAP
Elena 6
PACHO
Juan Jose 245
PACOAGAACHORE
Ana 8
PACUÁ
Jose 42
PADILLA
Ana Maria 238
Balentin 180, 258
Bentura 286
Concepcion 293
Felipe Santiago 218, 288, 289
Francisca 247, 279
Francisco 234, 250
Jose 277, 287, 296
Jose Antonio 51
Juan 291
Juana 287
Juana Antonia 211
Lugarda 156
Manuel 209, 229, 239, 250
Maria 224
Maria Antonia 88
Maria Encarnacion 147
Maria Gertrudis 242

PADILLA (continued)
Paula 264
Pedro 182, 213, 221, 239, 265, 276, 286, 294
Salvador 162, 194
Santiago 283, 285, 294, 297
Valentin 304
PAES
See PAEZ, PAIS
Candelaria 72, 79, 267
PAES HURTADO
See HURTADO
Juan 6
PAES URTADO
See URTADO
Juan 11
PAEZ
Candelaria 70, 75, 84, 87, 89, 95, 98, 110, 118
Juan Antonio 122
Juana 104, 125, 146
Maria Concepcion 95
Maria Ysabel 127
Mateo 135
PAHE
Ana 1
PAILA
Lucia 18
PAINACHEL
Maria 8
PAIS
See PAES, PAEZ
Candelaria 289
Concepcion 219
Jose Rafael 217
Juan Jesus 230
Lucia 293
Maria Soledad 218
Mateo 218
Miguel 183, 186
Ysabel 293
PAIZ
Miguel 204
PAJEMAC
Manuela 47
PALACIO
Jose, Fr. 36
PALACIOS
Jose, Fr. 42
PANDO
See VILLALPANDO, VIA ALPANDO, VIALPANDO
Calletano 297
Josefa 116, 214
Juana 56
Maria Josefa 303
Ysabel 39, 40
PÁPÂ
Maria 45
PAPAC
Maria 1
PAPAJUIA
Geronima 18
PAPAV
Maria 45
PAPPAÉ
Maria 41
PAQUEM
Teresa 5
PAQUEMOTTE
Diego 4
PAQUENIO
Maria 5
PATERO
Severo, Fr. 66
PATLEACOI
Juana 5, 9
PATRON
Guadalupe 297
PATTEAQUZ
Juana 4
PAYCHULE
Maria Martin 41
PEACHONE
Maria 15
PECHAQUE
Maria 1, 2
PECHOANA
Maria 1
PECHOGUE
Maria 4
PEDRASA
Maria Rosa 9
Maria Rossa 9
PEECHOO
Maria 5
PENPE
Francisco 10
PEÑA
Jesus Maria 228
Juan, Fr. 13
PERALTA
Pedro 8
PERES SERRANO
Francisco 229
PEREYRO
Jose Benito, Fr. 229
Josef Benito, Fr. 168, 223
Soledad 185
PIACHELA
Francisca 7
PIACHOLE
Francisca 8
PIAJUITLI
Ysabel 8
PIANAL
Magdalena 16

PICURIES
Juana Maria 93
PILNÃO
Rosalia 41
PINEDA
Jacinto 55, 111, 276
Juan 16, 22, 23, 25
Maria Ygnacia 235, 264, 273
Rafaela 136
Ygnacia 287
PINEDO
Maria Ygnacia 276
Ygnacia 292
PINO
Antonio 64
Anttonio 63
Francisco 251
Jose 301
Maria Jesus 209, 284
Maria Luz 284
Maria Reyes 230, 254, 264
PITORPAP
Chatalina 3
PIUCA
Maria 11
POBE
Ysabel 32, 34
PONSAY
Lucia 47
PORTIEZ
Nicomeda 132
PORTILLOZ
Nicomeda 132
PRADA
Jose, Fr. 41
PRINCESA
Rosa 293
QUABELA
Maria 1
QUAFIERO
Maria 12
QUALQUA
Catarina 11
QUATLAPAO
Catalina 6
QUAULLTA
Maria 10
QUAUTLA
Maria 3
QUEALA
Maria 2
QUERON
Jose 150
QUILO
Josefa 182
QUINTANA
Antonio Jose 208
Barvara 206, 254, 255
Candelaria 166
QUINTANA (continued)
Casilda 305
Dionisio 129, 142, 150, 154, 164, 165, 172
Dolores 257
Francisco 226, 247, 284
Francisco Antonio 274
Gabriel 278
Getrudis 214
Gregorio 280, 293
Jose Cruz 217, 276, 280, 286, 291
Josef Ramon 178
Josefa 142, 208, 228, 291
Juan 210, 257, 258, 262, 264, 266, 272, 274, 278, 284, 285, 299, 300, 304
Juan Cristoval 152
Juan Julian 113
Juan Lorenso 175
Juan Lorenzo 155
Juan Manuel 213, 292
Juana 208
Juana Paula 264
Juanico 214, 288
Lugarda 151, 152, 162, 174, 209, 282
Luz 284
Maria 231, 267
Maria Casilda 300
Maria Cruz 235
Maria Getrudis 296
Maria Jesus 231
Maria Josefa 62, 204, 231, 248, 306
Maria Luz 212, 280
Maria Manuela 150
Maria Rosa 61, 66, 82, 264, 272
Maria Trenidad 192
Maria Trinidad 265
Maria Ygnacia 171, 231
Mariana 149, 156, 188
Nicolasa 282, 291
Paula 196, 197, 207
Rosa 92, 150, 289-291
Salvador 177, 196, 198
Simon 151, 167, 169, 179, 184, 217
Teodora 211
Trenidad 227
Trinidad 284, 295
Ygnacia 147, 200, 205, 245, 252
QUIOJE
Estevan 14
QUIPATLOLEOI
Magdalena 8
QUIPAYO
Lusia 10
QUIPTOI
Lusia 7

QUIRCHONE
Lucia 13
QUIUNCHAL
Maria 11
RAEL
Carmen 288
Felipe 133, 288
Lasaro 171
Ramon 297
RAEL de AGUILAR
Alonso 9
RAMIRES
(n.n.) 303
Cosme 245
Felipa 128, 145
Maria 226
RAMIREZ
Felipa 200
RAMIRIZ
Felipa 290
RAMO
Pablo 113
RAMOS
Dolores 144
Jose 130
Manuel 90, 103
REDONDO
Francisco 31
Paula 138, 156
REINA
See REYNA
Cayetana 40
REL
Josefa 280
RENDON
Gabriel 146
Juan Gabriel 161
REYES
Damasia 35
Manuela 107
Maria 114
Maria Santos 283
REYNA
Antonio 22
Biviana 174
Domingo 286
Getrudes 71
Getrudis 52
Jose 285, 304
Juan Domingo 293
Maria 39, 124, 138, 256, 292, 297
Maria Antonia 93
Maria Josefa 59
Viviana 176
RIBERA
See RIVERA
Antonio 300
Maria Encarnacion 307
Rosalia 27
RIO
See DEL RIO
Francisca 304
Josefa 81
Juana 104, 115
Manuela 282
Maria 120
Maria Antonia 74, 138, 155, 297
Maria Rosa 276
Maria Ygnacia 297
Micaela 86, 155
Rafaela 117
Rosa 140
Rosalia 138
Ygnacia 125, 249
RIOS
Maria 303
Teodora 67
Ygnacio 99
RIVALI
Antonio 262
Juan Antonio 217
RIVERA
See RIBERA
Geronimo 30
Jose Antonio 221
Manuel 245
Maria Francisca 239
Maria Josefa 30, 32
Rafeel 199
Rita 163
Rosalia 32, 33
Ygnacia 235
ROBLES
Maria Nieves 280
RODRIGES
Lorensa 300
RODRIGUES
Barbara 90
Gertrudis 28
RODRIGUEZ
Antonio 131
Jose Miguel 93
Juana 27
Juaquina 33
Maria 267
ROIBAL
See RUIBAL, ROYBAL
Juana Maria 36
Teresa 105, 118, 154, 158, 160
ROJO
Petra Jesus 54, 64
ROLAN
Juan 299
ROLE
Santiago 294
ROLES
Juan 296

ROMERA
Maria Gertrudis 61
ROMERO
Agueda 78
Agustin 183, 199
Ana 34
Ana Maria 31, 35, 87, 98, 218, 232
Anamaria 206, 298
Angela 52, 61, 63, 73, 76
Angelina 42, 59
Anna Maria 295
Antonia 57, 75, 265
Antonia Getrudes 34
Antonia Margarita 210, 215, 238, 242, 274
Antonio 118, 120, 239, 244
Antonio Concepcion 58
Antonio Domingo 29, 54, 83, 102, 142, 257, 272, 285
Antonio Jose 76, 88-91, 95, 105, 111, 112, 120, 130
Antonio Josef 114
Anttonio Domingo 62
Apolonia 273
Balbaneda 210, 262
Balbanera 264, 272, 274
Baltasar 12, 31
Balvanada 155
Balvaneda 177, 226, 257, 285, 304
Balvuneda 299
Barbanera 278
Barbara 29, 33, 36, 40, 41, 59, 81, 88, 107, 117, 123, 163
Barvarita 241
Bentura 93, 288
Biviana 193
Brigida 261
Brijida 222
Carmel 297
Catalina 45, 48, 50, 63, 65, 67
Catarina 86, 87, 293
Cipriano 124
Concecion 289
Concepcion 61, 66, 82, 86, 107, 264, 272
Diego 2, 18, 20, 23, 238, 242, 250
Diego Antonio 232
Domingo 29, 31-33, 50
Dorothea 239
Felipa 118, 127, 143, 146, 157, 233
Felipe 241, 276
Francisca 85, 118, 180, 246
Francisco 55, 65, 180, 254, 268, 293
Francisco Antonio 219
ROMERO (continued)
Francisco Esteban 60, 119
Francisco Estevan 75, 279
Francisco, Fr. 26
Gabriel 280
Geronimo 240
Gertrudis 109, 162, 297
Getrudis 42, 46-48, 53, 219
Guadalupe 108, 235
Jose 42, 57, 153, 211, 215, 295, 299
Jose Antonio 100
Jose Concepcion 290, 291
Jose Manuel 183, 190, 255, 268, 272, 283
Jose Maria 70, 76, 136, 277
Jose Miguel 230
Jose Rafael 214, 239, 240, 255, 260, 286, 299
Jose Rafel 190
Jose Ramon 221, 295
Jose Tomas 95
Josef 175, 181, 194, 199
Josef Rafael 203, 225
Josef Rafel 176, 177, 179
Josefa 31, 38, 43, 50, 56, 59, 65, 77, 85-87, 100, 107, 135, 136, 139, 141, 215, 285
Juan 63, 65, 81, 142
Juan Andres 200, 229, 234, 300
Juan Antonio 75, 190, 231, 234, 249, 285, 298
Juan Augustin 108
Juan Baptista 43
Juan Carmel 298
Juan Carmen 149, 176, 191, 199, 200, 208, 216, 271, 284
Juan Cristoval 223
Juan de Dios 277
Juan Delcarmen 292
Juan Domingo 57, 64, 244, 286, 307
Juan Jesus 166, 170, 266, 277
Juan Josef 223
Juan Manuel 59
Juan Miguel 293
Juan Pedro 259
Juana 28, 46-49, 57, 64, 70, 76, 79, 86, 89, 90, 102, 106, 109, 113, 114, 177, 179, 215, 227, 241, 246, 283, 292, 306
Juana Antonia 257
Juana Gertrudis 264
Juana Getrudis 222
Juana Lucia 132
Juana Maria 55, 82, 101, 106
Juana Pasquala 222
Julian 41, 295
Juliana 91, 149, 174, 181, 195,

ROMERO, Juliana (continued)
207, 283, 297
Lazaro 134
Lorenzo 178
Lucia 60
Luciya 286
Luscia 254
Luz 284
Madalena 187
Magdalena 124, 280
Manuel 212, 254, 257, 283
Manuel Jose 290, 298
Manuela 35, 89, 94, 100, 102, 103, 111, 118, 121, 126, 133, 141, 144, 147, 149, 164, 165, 168, 170, 179, 182, 187, 194, 197, 207, 227, 239, 253, 255, 257, 263, 275, 288, 300
Marcelino 277
Margarita 30, 40, 43, 57, 61, 63, 64, 87, 128, 139, 251, 253, 301
Maria 29, 36, 37, 40, 43, 48-50, 54, 66, 67, 70, 71, 106, 112, 113, 123, 134, 145, 158, 193, 198, 262, 307
Maria Ageda 298
Maria Albina 258
Maria Antonia 43, 48, 51, 55, 56, 59, 63, 65, 77, 89, 124, 126, 134, 160, 193, 249, 276
Maria Balbaneda 247
Maria Balvaneda 175
Maria Barbanera 278
Maria Barbara 32, 46, 49, 50
Maria Carmen 230
Maria Catarina 304
Maria Clara 187
Maria Dolores 265
Maria Dorotella 174
Maria Gertrudis 244
Maria Getrudes 68, 75
Maria Getrudis 57
Maria Guadalupe 209, 237, 246, 251, 271
Maria Josefa 55, 65
Maria Juliana 297
Maria Luisa 219
Maria Lus 257
Maria Luz 100, 169, 192, 277, 299
Maria Manuela 95, 126, 174, 232, 272, 295, 298, 301, 303
Maria Matiana 46, 52
Maria Micaela 238
Maria Pascuala 190
Maria Phelipa 70
Maria Rita 210, 275
Maria Rosa 56, 94, 202, 208, 228, 231, 232
Maria Tomasa 101

ROMERO (continued)
Maria Valbaneda 300
Maria Ygnacia 129, 212
Mariana 284
Mariano 38, 40, 43, 67, 71, 85, 211, 217, 220, 262, 267, 287, 288, 305
Mariano Concepcion 29, 31, 49
Mariquita 56
Matiana 113, 124, 135, 143, 152, 168, 171, 176, 195
Mequela 203
Micaela 30, 33, 90, 91, 102, 115
Miguel 289, 293
Monica 28
Nicolas 177
Nicolasa 33, 55
Nicolaz 264
Niebes 286
Nieves 285
Pasqual 214
Pasquala 267
Paula 120, 121, 254, 269
Phelipa 68
Polonia 216, 284
Qulas 219
Rafael 127, 213, 232, 236, 248
Rafaela 104, 107, 108, 124, 214
Rafel 170
Ramon 189
Rita 173, 220, 266, 287
Romualda 248
Rosa 30, 228, 285
Rosalia 240, 271
Salvador 112
Santiago 31, 124, 300
Teodora 172, 188
Teresa 256
Theodora 230, 243, 273
Thomas 254
Tiodora 206
Tomas 139, 140, 153, 204, 269, 286
Tomasa 211
Valbaneda 284
Ventura 163
Ygnacia 137, 183, 185
Ysabel 135
ROMERO TALACHE
Jose 50
ROMO
Antonia 35
Juan 247
Juan Jesus 307
Nicolasa 170
RONQUILLOS
Jose 238
ROXO
Petra 94

ROXO (continued)
Petrona 83, 292
ROYBAL
See RUIBAL, ROIBAL
Juana Maria 150
Lucia 103
Maria Teresa 234
Maria Theresa 229
Teresa 149, 223
RUIBAL
See ROIBAL, ROYBAL
Barbara 155
Francisco 282
Fransisca 28
Jose Antonio 282
Lucia 61, 74
Maria Manuela 278
Teresa 183
RUIBALA
Micaela 30
RUIVAL
Domingo 283
Maria Rosa 304
Maria Teresa 277
RUYBAL
Teresa 55, 207
RYO
See DEL RYO
Maria Antonia 57
S. VICENTE
Agustin Francisco, Fr. 304
SA(torn)
Maria Nicolasa 278
SAENS
Jose Manuel 271
SAIS
Dolores 307
Jose Manuel 173
Maria Carmen 227
Maria Magdalena 305
Simon 207
SAIZ
Jose Manuel 291
Manuel 283
Simon 279
SALAESES
Jose 261
SALAISES
Jose 264
SALASAR
See ZALASAR
Carpio 198, 200
Domingo 300
Francisca 207
Gervacio 173, 175, 206
Gregorio 299
Jose Bernardo 47
Jose Manuel 294
Juan Antonio 205, 306
SALASAR (continued)
Juan Cristoval 295
Juan Manuel 252, 297, 306
Juan Simon 306
Juana 306
Juana Maria 306
Juana Miquela 307
Lucia 203
Luisa 185
Manuela 188
Maria 187, 203, 206
Maria Lorensa 173
Maria Manuela 224
Maria Nicolasa 297
Maria Trenidad 187
Mariano 170
Paula 289
Pedro 175, 224
Ramon 176, 184, 190, 201, 297
Rosa 182
SALAZ
See ZALAS
Antonio 237
Rafael 269
SALAZAR
See ZALAZAR
Ana Maria 220
Asencio 281
Diego 167, 292
Francisco 219
Hilario 215
Jesus 263
Jose Manuel 276
Jose Ramon 209, 238, 242
Josefa 253
Juan Manuel 209-211, 252, 267
Juana 277, 303
Juana Micaela 221
Lorenza 157
Luisa 216
Luiza 252
Maria Dolores 75
Maria Manuela 222, 236, 248
Maria Paula 278
Maria Trenidad 256
Maria Trinidad 257
Maria Ysabel 277
Paula 214, 258, 262
Pedro 164, 291
Ramon 162
Rosa 143, 166
SALUZAR
Jose Ramon 212
SAMORA
See ZAMORA
Lusiya 286
Maria Margarita 295
Santiago 293, 295
Ygnacia 219, 261

SANCHEZ (continued)
Mariano 277
Miguel 54, 55, 75, 85, 88, 215, 216, 278
Miguel Manuel 53
Miguel Mariano 53
Pablo 200
Pedro Ygnacio 27
Rita 221
Serafina 277
Teresa 278
Thoribio 3
Tomas 201, 202
Tomasa 106, 137, 153
Ygnacia 195, 257, 262
Ysabel 277
Ysavel 199, 207
SANCHEZ dela CRUZ
Juan, Fr. 20
SANCHEZ VERGARA
Mariano Jose, Fr. 294
SANDOBAL
Felipe 211, 275
Francisco 305
Juan Antonio 52, 55
Manuela 103
Maria Catarina 304
Maria Luz 209
Maria Manuela 304
Maria Rosa 215
Pablo 209
Rosalia 213
SANDOBALA
Maria Jesus 178
SANDOVAL
Alonso 210, 219/220, 266
Andrea 138
Antonia 284
Antonio 152
Antonio Jos. 122
Antonio Jose 273
Baltasar 169
Beatric 256
Beatris 143, 221, 257, 288
Beatriz 220
Benito 247
Benito Jesus 243
Biatris 220
Buenaventura 258
Catharina 243
Clara 256
Cristerna 292
Dolores 202
Felipe 222, 240, 256, 269, 282, 283, 290
Florentina 292
Francisca 111, 118
Francisco 72, 147, 239, 251, 285
Gregorio 134, 296
SANDOVAL (continued)
Jose Bentura 230
Jose Buenaventura 234
Jose Francisco 151, 162
Jose Luis 298
Jose Maria 267, 280
Jose Miguel 29
Jose Ramon 137
Josef Francisco 172, 206
Josef Ygnacio 196
Joseph 30
Juan 256, 276
Juan Antonio 74
Juan Carmen 214
Juan de Dios 295
Juan Domingo 281
Juana 82
Juana Acasia 108
Juana Gertrudis 271
Juana Maria 265, 301
Juana Teresa 305
Lorensa 208
Luisa 222, 282, 291
Manuel 111, 300
Manuel Antonio 105
Manuela 90, 132, 143, 184, 213, 226, 257, 294
Maria 159, 160, 170, 185, 197, 199, 225, 240, 260, 267
Maria Antonia 195, 240, 245, 259, 267, 269
Maria Catalina 210, 219
Maria Catarina 247
Maria Clara 276
Maria Dolores 148
Maria Francisca 101
Maria Gertrudis 236
Maria Jesus 292
Maria Josefa 299
Maria Manuela 137, 155, 184, 207
Maria Natividad 270
Maria Rosa 217, 240, 264, 269, 274
Maria Rosalia 251, 274
Maria Ygnacia 301
Martin 295
Mathias 269
Matias 141, 218, 280
Miguel 282
Nicolas 227, 266
Nicolasa 113, 114, 121, 125, 170, 172, 179, 186, 214, 254, 258, 285
Nicolaz 260
Nicolaza 264, 271
Noverto 249
Pablo 124, 252, 282, 289
Pedro Ygnacio 231
Qulasa 210

SANDOVAL (continued)
Ramon 224, 237, 239
Rosalia 198, 257, 300
Santiago 117
Tomas 165, 172, 179, 191, 235, 250, 301
Ventura 279, 289
Ygnacia 254, 288
Ylario 195
Ysidora 269
Ysidoro 267, 270
Ysidro 260
SANTI ESTEBAN
Maria Carmen 242
SANTI ESTEVAN
Feliciano 233, 254
Juan Antonio 258
SANTIESTEBAN
Maria 235
Maria Candelaria 276
Maria Carmen 273
SANTISTEBAN
Feliciano 212
Maria Carmen 131, 133, 151, 161, 162, 222
Maria Encarnacion 275
Ysidro 211
SANTISTEVAN
Carlos 301
Francisca 284
Guadalupe 196
Trenidad 227
SAPATA
See ZAPATA
Anamaria 307
SARBÉ
Jose Manuel 247
SARVE
Jose 293
SEDILLO
Simon 301
SEGURA
Jose Encarnacion 27
SENA
See CENA
Andres 32
Gregoria 211, 256, 269, 283
Jose Miguel 221
Juan Reyes 189
Maria Antonia 152, 158, 166, 169, 175
Teresa 282
SERDA
See CERDA
Guadalupe 293
SERNA
See CERNA, ZERNA
Christobal 14
Christoval 12, 14
SERNA (continued)
Guadalupe 283
Juan Antonio 179
Lugarda 92, 99
Micaela 92, 105, 144
SERRANO
Rafael 61, 62
SIANE
Lucia 1
SILBA
Santiago 59, 176
SILVA
Ascencion 134
Barbara 154
Francisco 282
Jacinto 201
Jose Maria 161
Josef Maria 227
Juan Cristoval 62
Margarita 217
Maria 205
Maria Ascencion 137
Maria Guertrudis 62
Maria Nieves 235
Maria Ygnacia 247
Miguel Antonio 205
Santiago 65, 69, 213, 252, 274, 305
Tomasa 182
Ursula 141
SISNEROS
See CISNEROS, ZISNEROS
Esmeregildo 66
Felipe Neri 244
Jose Rafael 304
Manuel Antonio 179
Maria 246, 247
Maria Guadalupe 184, 249, 256
Maria Ygnacia 259
Nerio 189, 223, 230, 301
Rafael 249
Rafel 184
Victoria 265, 304
Ygnacia 223, 227
Ysabel 239, 250
SISTÉ
Juan Thomas 41
SOAZA
Anamaria 178
Maria Soledad 174
SOBENES BARREDA
Gonsalo, Fr. 21
SOLANO
Andres 253, 286
Jose Mariano 287
Juan Andres 222
Manuel 252
SOPEÑA
Manuel, Fr. 18

SOUSA
Miguel, Fr. 14
SUAIT
Juana 20
SUASA
Dolores 214
SUASO
See ZUASO
Antonio 219, 220
Dolores 209, 212
Francisco 50, 55, 297
Jose 264, 280, 285, 298
Jose Antonio 106, 173, 210, 255, 276, 286, 298
Juan 212
Juan Carmen 209
Juan Jose 297, 298
Juana Maria 92
Manuel 305
Maria 246
Miguel 214, 305
Simon 297
SUAZO
See ZUAZO
Antonio Josef 202
Dolores 210
Jose Antonio 192
Josefa 51
Juana 225
Maria 202
Mariana 295
Tomas 300
SUG(torn)
San Juan 303
TACHOLE
Maria 22
TAFOLLA
Ana Maria 88, 211, 216
Bartolo 64
Bartolo Bartolo 63
Catarina 65
Jose Antonio 228
Jose Benito 209
Jose Faustin 218
Juan Domingo 217
Juan Miguel 209
Juan Paulin 222
Manuela Luz 209
Maria Antonia 299
Maria Brijida 294
Maria Josefa 305
Maria Juana 218
Maria Luisa 307
Mariana 305
Qulas 212
TAFOYA
Ana Maria 107, 108, 110-112, 124, 126, 145, 149, 154, 157, 158, 180, 271, 281, 282
TAFOYA (continued)
Antonio 108
Antonio Jose 72, 246
Anttonio 9
Bartolo 225
Bartolome 40, 42, 44, 45, 90, 263
Brigida 293, 294
Brijida 258
Catarina 301
Cristobal 17
Domingo 282
Francisca 257
Graciana 70, 78
Graciana Beatris 47
Guadalupe 257
Hypolito 283
Joaquina 252, 256, 261
Jose 109, 110, 155, 232, 233, 245, 256
Jose Benito 261, 299
Jose Francisco 93
Jose Jesus 127, 205
Jose Miguel 109
Josefa 256
Juan 288
Juan Domingo 71, 75, 82, 97, 109, 117, 124, 138, 181, 226, 241, 243, 250, 270, 280, 281, 288, 289
Juan Jose 77
Juan Miguel 285
Juana Catalina 46
Luisa 132
Manuel 92, 154
Maria 66, 146, 156, 174
Maria Antonia 139
Maria Brigida 250
Maria Clara 85, 146, 168
Maria Josefa 238, 261, 270, 282, 290, 296, 299
Maria Juaquina 277
Maria Juliana 301
Maria Lus 299
Maria Resurrecion 108, 119
Mariana 251
Mariquita 220
Miguel 114, 180, 187
Nicolas 267, 277, 290, 301
Nicolaz 244
Paulin 266
Pedro 301
Rafael 252, 280, 295
Roman 279
Romano 224
Salvador 266, 305
TAGLE
Joan, Fr. 18
TAGUEBAJUE
Josefa 46

VALENZUELA (continued)
Martin 13
VALERIA
Juliana 214
VALERIO
See BALERIO
Felipe 306
Francisco 306
Julian 210
Juliana 109, 126, 154
VALLEGOS
Manuela 124
VALLEJO
See BALLEJO
Anna Maria 75
Manuela 142
Maria Manuela 278
VALLEJOS
See BALLEJOS
Ana Maria 73, 83, 101, 106, 113, 131, 135, 144, 157, 167, 267
Catarina 166
Jose Miguel 150, 156
Juliana 214
Manuela 116, 117, 123, 131, 145, 150, 165, 167, 264
Maria Manuela 300
Rafael 154
VALVERDE
Juan Gabriel 137
VARELA
See BARELA, VERELA
Antonio 288
Antonio Jose 141
Asension 235
Clara 283
Cristoval 109
Dionisio 130
Dolores 282
Felipe 103, 109
German 280
Guadalupe 123, 166
Jose Manuel 228
Josefa 249
Juan Nicolas 166
Juan Nicolaz 268
Juan Ysidro 127, 128, 132, 141, 144, 152
Juana 298
Magdalena 287
Manuela 144, 161
Maria Asension 262
Maria Barbara 278
Maria Dolores 141, 149, 260
Maria Josefa 231
Maria Manuela 281
Maria Paula 236
Maria Rafaela 277
Miguel 114, 283
VARELA (continued)
Nicolas 294
Pablo 251, 275
Petrona 129, 142, 154, 164, 165
Rafael 110
Rafaela 109
Theodora 239
Ysidro 292
VARGAS
See BARGAS
Francisco 237
Jose Antonio 284
Juan Antonio 91
Mariano 266
Marirelo 298
Maurilo 132
Maurito 107
Pablo 262, 269, 270
VASQUES
See BASQUES
Guadalupe 298
Jose Mauricio 76
VASQUEZ
See BASQUEZ
Jose Antonio 210
VAZQUEZ
Juan Jose 282
VEASECUI
Juana 11
VEGIL
See BEGIL
Ana Maria 154
Antonia 286
Bautista 140, 145
Candelario 286
Carlos 57, 58, 63
Cayetana 135
Cruz 134, 148
Dionisio 138, 155
Dolores 287
Faustino 284
Francisca 167, 288
Francisco 138, 284
Jose 54, 64
Jose Bautista 134, 151
Jose Francisco 156, 158
Josefa 100, 159, 168
Joseph Bautista 134
Juan 156, 288
Juan Christobal 177
Juan Cruz 145, 152, 288
Juan Ramon 154
Juan Ygnacio 56, 123, 131, 158, 293
Julian 283, 285
Luisa 288
Manuel 63
Manuel/Miguel 287
Manuela 27, 154

VESEQUI
Juana 10
VI(torn)
Maria Josefa 303
VIA ALPANDO
See PANDO, VILLALPANDO
Josefa 292
VIALPANDO
Maria Josefa 305
VICTORINO
Anttonio, Fr. 10
VIGIL
See BIGIL, VIRGIL
Amadon 281
Antonio 287, 292
Cornelio 278
Cristobal 303
Cruz 254, 258, 277
Dolores 290
Faustin 159, 219, 289
Feliciana 282, 299
Gregorio 290
Jose 254, 292
Jose Antonio 282
Jose Candelario 295
Jose Francisco 256, 257
Jose Santiago 297
Josefa 257
Juan Bautista 256
Juan Christoval 253/254, 281
Juan Cristoval 253/254
Juan Cruz 209, 241, 291
Juan Jesus 295
Juan Ygnacio 281
Juan Ysidro 303
Julian 209, 282
Luisa 279
Manuel 276
Maria Antonia 278
Maria Candelaria 255, 297
Maria Guadalupe 282
Maria Luisa 278, 297, 299
Maria Manuela 278
Maria Micaela 281
Maria Miquela 299
Maria Rafaela 295
Maria Rosa 241, 296
Maria Soledad 209
Maria Teresa 297
Maria Trinidad 158
Maria Ysavel 296
Marselino 258
Micaela 295
Miguel 256-258, 276, 292, 293, 297
Pascuala 296
Pasquala 255
Pedro 297, 306
Ramon 292, 293
VIGIL (continued)
Rosa 280
Santiago 256, 292
Ygnacia 241, 280, 292
VIGILA
Candelaria 305
VIJIL
See BIJIL
Antonio 213, 217, 234
Candelaria 268
Candelario 212
Carlos 267
Cruz 263, 272
Dionisio 215, 236, 269
Dolores 213
Feliciana 266
Francisco 267, 268
Jose 240, 243
Jose Amador 231, 245
Jose Anastacio 235
Jose Rafael 216
Josefa 209, 271, 274
Juan 218
Juan Christobal 234
Juan Cruz 217
Juan Jesus 216, 243-245, 252, 265
Juan Ygnacio 95, 212, 264
Macdalena 212
Manuel 265
Marcelino 221, 274
Maria 233
Maria Francisca 214
Maria Gertrudis 238
Maria Josefa 217, 218, 269
Maria Meregilda 209
Maria Rafaela 221
Maria Rosa 250
Maria Soledad 212, 238, 242
Micaela 217, 251, 271
Miguel 210, 267
Pasquala 213
Polo 217
Rafael 263
Ramon 264
Rosa 209, 272
Salvador 252
Tomas 266
Ygnacia 220, 270
VILLALPANDO
See PANDO, VIA ALPANDO, VIALPANDO
Ambrosio 30, 33, 38
Cristina Catalina 25
Maria Josefa 106
Nicolasa 31
Ysabel 48
VILLANUEBA
Andres, Fr. 59

VIRGIL
See VIGIL
Maria Candelaria 278
XAN
Rafaela 97
XARAMILLO
See JARAMILLO
Jose Mariano 292
Juan 166
Lorenzo 100
Maria Luz 240
Maria Soledad 232
Mariano 251, 257, 261, 262, 275, 284
Prudencia 291
Prudenciana 294
Soledad 290
XATLA
Maria 15
XAVIER
Joseph 18, 19
XIMENEZ
Francisco, Fr. 4
YAONA
Martina 8
YGUALPA
Maria Rosa 45
YNURTANDES
Teodosio 304
ZALAS
See SALAZ
Rafael 294
ZALASAR
See SALASAR
Gervacio 283
ZALAZAR
See SALAZAR
Manuela 293
Maria Paula 265
Maria Soledad 252
ZAMORA
See SAMORA
Asencio 51, 54
Josefa 98, 110, 168
Juana 31, 38, 39, 48, 55, 77, 98, 110
Maria Antonia 57, 130
Pedro 151
Pedro Ygnacio 136
ZANCHES
See SANCHES
Francisca 295
ZAPATA
See SAPATA
Francisca 104
Joseph 19
Josepha 20
Maria 18
ZARTE
Francisco, Fr. 32
ZERNA
See CERNA, SERNA
Cristoval 21
ZISNEROS
See CISNEROS, SISNEROS
Hermeregildo 39
Josefa 39
Maria Guadalupe 213
Maria Ysabel 229
Santiago 34
ZUASO
See SUASO
Dolores 284
Jose 148, 157, 265
Juan Carmen 283
Juan Jose 136, 160
Maria Dolores 283
Maria Soledad 146, 147
Soledad 141, 147
Ysidro 283
ZUAZO
See SUAZO
Jose 266, 271
Jose Antonio 270, 292
Juan Miguel 266
Miguel 292

33730923R00257

Made in the USA
San Bernardino, CA
09 May 2016